GOD AND GRACE OF BODY

GOD AND GRACE OF BODY

Sacrament in Ordinary

DAVID BROWN

OXFORD
UNIVERSITY PRESS

OXFORD

UNIVERSITY PRESS

Great Clarendon Street, Oxford OX2 6DP

Oxford University Press is a department of the University of Oxford.
It furthers the University's objective of excellence in research, scholarship,
and education by publishing worldwide in

Oxford New York

Auckland Cape Town Dar es Salaam Hong Kong Karachi
Kuala Lumpur Madrid Melbourne Mexico City Nairobi
New Delhi Shanghai Taipei Toronto

With offices in

Argentina Austria Brazil Chile Czech Republic France Greece
Guatemala Hungary Italy Japan Poland Portugal Singapore
South Korea Switzerland Thailand Turkey Ukraine Vietnam

Oxford is a registered trade mark of Oxford University Press
in the UK and in certain other countries

Published in the United States
by Oxford University Press Inc., New York

© David Brown, 2007

The moral rights of the author have been asserted
Database right Oxford University Press (maker)

First published 2007

British Library Cataloguing-in-Publication Data

Data available

Library of Congress Cataloging-in-Publication Data

Data available

Typeset by SPI Publisher Services Ltd, Pondicherry, India
Printed in Great Britain
on acid-free paper by
Biddles Ltd, King's Lynn, Norfolk

ISBN 978-0-19-923182-9

1 3 5 7 9 10 8 6 4 2

Episcopis duobus:
alteri in gremio sedendo ad lectionem hortanti
alteri per ripas ducendo ad cogitationem incitanti

PREFACE

THIS is the second of three related volumes that deal with the question of religious experience through culture and the arts. *God and Enchantment of Place: Reclaiming Human Experience* appeared in 2004 (and in paperback in 2006). So it is good that this second volume has at last appeared. A third to follow shortly, *God and Mystery in Words: Experience through Metaphor and Drama*, completes the project.

Here it is important to record my debt to others in the writing of this present volume. A number of colleagues and friends have read specific chapters or sections, and their help has proved invaluable. In particular, a great debt of gratitude is due, among others, to Rosalind Brown, David Fuller, Matthew Guest, Charlotte Hardman, Anne Harrison, David Hunt, James Jirtle, Christopher Joby, Ann Loades, Robert MacSwain, and Corinne Saunders. The number of individuals who have encouraged me to widen my range of concerns is too broad to mention here. Suffice it to say that I much appreciate the interests that they shared, not least Ann Loades, who first encouraged me to overcome my prejudice against dance as an art form. She ensured that her vibrant enthusiasm eventually became my own. In addition to helpful comments on the manuscript, Chris Joby also undertook two key roles in securing permissions for visual and literary material, as well as helping with the index.

Last but not least, mention must be made of the two new companions who entered my life during this period. Having never had pets before, I was uncertain what impact acquiring a Burmese cat and a Cocker Spaniel dog might have on my life. To ensure proper respect, both were dignified by names of former bishops of Durham: Carilef and Tunstall. Brought up in Scotland, where ground elder (that pernicious enemy of the gardener) has been nicknamed bishop weed, I am all too conscious that the influence of bishops is by no means always welcome. Fortunately, the introductory Latin dedication indicates that my recent experience with these bishops at least has been quite otherwise.

David Brown
Durham University
Epiphany, 2007

CONTENTS

LIST OF PLATES

ACKNOWLEDGEMENTS

Although every effort has been made to trace and contact copyright holders before publication, the publishers will be pleased to rectify errors or omissions at the earliest opportunity, if notified of any.

Words from Bengali hymn © Dover Publications.

Words from 'Tirumantiram' by Tirumular © Oxford University Press.

Words from 'Tiruttonokkam' and 'Tiruccalal': Donald S. Lopez, Jr. (ed.), *Religions of India in Practice* © 1995 Princeton University Press. Reprinted by permission of Princeton University Press.

Lines from Mevlana Celaleddin Rumi and the Whirling Dervishes © T. S. Halman and M. And.

Words from *I Danced in the Morning* by Sydney Carter © Stainer and Bell.

Lyrics from Duke Ellington's 'David Danced' © G. Schirmer Inc.

Words from W. H. Auden's 'Thanksgiving for a Habitat' © Faber and Faber.

Words from '¡Ay, andar!' by Juan de Araujo from the CD *Moon, Sun and All Things:* Baroque Music from Latin America', Hyperion CDA67524 © Hyperion Records Ltd.

Lines from medieval Sufi poetry © HarperCollins.

Lines from Elizabeth Jennings' translation of Michelangelo sonnet © Carcanet Press.

Lines from R. S. Thomas' 'The Musicians' from *R. S. Thomas Collected Poems 1945–1990*, published by Phoenix Press, a division of The Orion Publishing Group.

Lyrics from 'Just Want to See His Face' © Jagger courtesy of EMI Music Publishing.

Lyrics from 'Nothing Fails' and 'X-Static Process' © Madonna.

Lyrics from 'The Ties that Bind', 'Drive All Night', 'Tunnel of Love', 'Cautious Man', 'Living Proof' and 'Into the Fire' © Springsteen.

Lyrics from 'Mothers of the Disappeared', 'Sunday Bloody Sunday', 'Yahweh' and 'Grace' © U2.

Words from 'The Mercy Seat', 'Into My Arms', 'Wife', 'God in the House' and 'Get Ready for Love! Praise Him!' © Nick Cave.

Words from 'Break On Through (to the Other Side)', 'Riders on the Storm', 'An American Prayer' and words from Jim Morrison's poetry and *Paris Journal* © Doors Music Company.

Lyrics from 'Stairway to Heaven' and 'Kashmir' © Led Zeppelin.

Lyrics from 'Horses', 'Easter', 'Privilege', 'Ghost Dance' © Patti Smith.

Lyrics from 'God is Love' and 'In My Life Today' © Lenny Kravitz.

Lyrics from *Jesus Christ Superstar* © Lloyd-Webber/Rice.

Lyrics from *Cats* © Lloyd-Webber.

Words from *Jerry Springer—The Opera* © Avalon.

Sadly, the charges at Sony Music Publishing were too high to justify inclusion of any of Bob Dylan's lyrics.

Introduction

THIS book is intended as a sequel to *God and Enchantment of Place: Reclaiming Human Experience*. Like its predecessor, it seeks to reclaim for religious experience great areas of human encounter with the divine that have been either marginalized in contemporary Christianity or almost wholly ignored. As much contemporary academic writing well illustrates, theology continues to see its main dialogue partner in a philosophy that identifies variants on the traditional arguments for the existence of God as the real heart of where the debate should lie.[1] I would not wish to challenge the intrinsic interest of such discussions, but it does seem to me that that is not what makes most of us religious believers or otherwise. Were such an Enlightenment model only confined to those with a strong interest in philosophy, that would be bad enough. But the position is considerably exacerbated by so much theology producing, as it were, a mirror image by way of reaction. The Christian revelation then becomes a self-contained entity that is seen as required to address and challenge the world's values rather than engage with them.

Inevitably, that previous paragraph grossly simplifies complex issues.[2] But rather than complicate the perspective with further qualifications here, let it stand, so that I can more accurately sketch where my own stance lies. It is that both sides are not just wrong, but seriously wrong. In effect, modern religion has become an optional extra, whereas through most of the history of religion it was seen as having a bearing on all aspects of life. God was not only

---

[1] Usually supplemented these days by one obvious argument against, the so-called 'problem of evil'. Since there is only a problem if it is thought that we have rights against God, even philosophy shows itself here to be conditioned like all else by historical context. The notion of rights against the Creator would have been unintelligible for much of human history.

[2] For more qualifications, see my *God and Enchantment of Place* (Oxford: Oxford University Press, 2004), 5–10.

the God of the biblical revelation and so concerned with prayer, morals and politics, he was also active in every aspect of his creation. Each detail of that world and the human understanding that goes with it was held—necessarily—to reflect some aspect of the divine nature. So, as I have sought to indicate over these two volumes and the third which follows it, God was found in every aspect of human experience. That was never seen as merely human aspiration or projection. God met the individual half way, as it were, in the very structuring of such experience. So it was no accident that, for example, some building styles spoke of God and others not, some garden designs could evoke a sense of divine presence and others not, and so on.[3] That helps explain why discussions about such matters in the past were so often animated. The architect's job was either to evoke or deepen the sense of a divine presence that was already there in relation to the world but needed to be made more explicit. Similarly, landscape artists never thought of themselves as simply recording the scene before them. The aim was to highlight those features that would draw the viewer more closely into an experience of God.[4]

Not that precisely the same features of the divine were always chosen. Inevitably, that raises the question of conflict. Sometimes competing features, despite their differences, could after all be seen as essentially complementary. More problematically, at other times the tensions appear more deep-seated. Baroque playfulness and its sense of drama, for instance, sit uneasily with a classical sense of order.[5] Again, Gothic transcendence must inevitably for the Christian border on the heretical unless balanced by some countervailing emphasis that stresses immanence.[6]

That might seem to require an immediate push towards criteria. I take a different view, not because I think the issue unimportant but because it seems to me that a more fundamental aim has to be achieved first: the need to take such experience seriously in the first place. So much contemporary Christian aesthetics pronounces from a position of prior certainties (allegedly built on secure biblical foundations) that it is little wonder that the outside

---

[3] For architecture, see ibid. 245–371; for gardens, 371–87.

[4] Ibid. 84–136.

[5] Ibid. 281–97.

[6] For my explanation for why Gothic art pursued quite a different direction from Gothic architecture, see ibid. 272–81.

world pays scant attention. There is preaching but no real engagement, no serious attempt to wrestle with whether God might not be also in what is encountered no less than in what is offered. Philosophers sometimes object to the woolliness of such a notion of experience, or even ridicule its very possibility. There is a category mistake involved, we are told. A God who transcends every human conception cannot possibly be encountered in this way.[7] That I do not for a moment believe. The fact that God in his totality cannot be experienced does not entail that the divine may not be experienced in part. In a similar way, the impossibility of grasping a great human mind hardly prevents some limited comprehension and experience of that intellect.[8]

So what this volume does is continue the work of its predecessor in demonstrating the range of such artistic and cultural experience that theology needs in my view once more to take seriously. While the main focus of *God and Enchantment of Place* was, as its title implies, on place, in this one the spotlight falls on the human body. So I consider how body might mediate experience of God. Part I focuses on some of the key ways in which body sometimes functions as a symbolic mediation for encounter with the divine, among them the body as beautiful, as sexual and as ugly, and in celebration such as dancing and feasting. Part II then turns to music. As a deliberate challenge to the reader, I try to indicate how God might be experienced through musical forms as varied as opera and jazz, Schubert and Led Zeppelin.

I have chosen to link music with the more earthed bodily expressions of Part I because it seems to me that it belies superficial appearance, in being at one and the same time ethereal and material. It thus forms a natural transition to Part III, where I want to insist on the reality of Christ's 'physicality' in the eucharist despite the ethereal character of that presence. This volume's sequel, *God and Mystery in Words*, will have more to say on how

[7] See e.g. B. Davies, *Introduction to the Philosophy of Religion* (Oxford: Oxford University Press, 1982), 64–76; *Thinking about God* (London: Geoffrey Chapman, 1985), 61–72 (more moderate); D. Turner, *The Darkness of God* (Cambridge: Cambridge University Press, 1995), e.g. 4.

[8] For that objection pursued in more detail and also the related criticism that to talk at all of religious experience is inevitably to downplay the presence of God in the everyday, see my essay 'Experience Skewed', in K. Vanhoozer and M. Warner (eds), *Transcending Boundaries in Philosophy and Theology* (London: Ashgate, 2007).

that is realized in the liturgy. But here I deliberately conclude the largely 'secular' discussion of the first two parts in this way, to emphasize that all the world should be seen as sacramental, as imbued through and through with divine presence.[9] It is for that reason that the book's subtitle adapts a famous phrase of the poet George Herbert in speaking of 'Sacrament in Ordinary'.[10] The activity of God is everywhere in the material world that is his creation, and not at all an isolated and occasional phenomenon. That is why it seems to me no accident that Christianity's central sacrament focuses on body and on a human body at that. It is no mere 'spiritual' presence that is on offer in the eucharist but one envisaged in definitely material terms. Earthly reality is present not just in the bread and wine but also through the whole humanity of Christ being once more made available, however transformed it has become through entering a new type of existence. That insight was central not just to Aquinas but equally also to Luther and Calvin.

In the process of referring to 'Sacrament in Ordinary', however, reasons for the choice of the book's primary title, *God and Grace of Body*, must not be forgotten. Thanks largely to St Paul 'grace' became a technical term in Christian theology, to be contrasted, like faith, with works. The stress, it is said, must be wholly on the divine initiative that saves fallen humanity. It is 'amazing grace', 'grace abounding'. While that stress is right and proper, expressions of grace got bogged down from Augustine onwards in a whole series of qualifications, characterized by such adjectives as 'effective', 'congruent' and 'prevenient'. These are not my concern here. What I intend to evoke in my title is the much wider sense of the term that links a number of Greek words and enables us to detect 'grace of body' as itself a divine gift.

The Greek term *charis* not only gives us *charismata*, the gifts of grace, but also *chara* (joy), *chaire* (hail or good day), and *eucharisteo* (thanks for *charis*). What links them is the idea of excess, of going beyond what might be expected. So *charis* is a favour rendered that could not be demanded or expected, and joy and thanks therefore the appropriate response. *Chaire* may seem the exception,

---

[9] This inclusive use of 'sacramental' was explored and defended in *God and Enchantment of Place*, 5–36, esp. 25–33.

[10] 'Heaven in Ordinary' is one of Herbert's descriptions of prayer in 'Prayer (1)': *George Herbert: Complete English Poems*, ed. J. Tobin (London: Penguin, 1991), 45–6, line 11.

but that is because I have provided the usual translation rather than what the phrase means literally: 'joy to you'. As such it is the usual conclusion of pagan Greek hymns to the gods. Luke also employs it as a pun in the angel Gabriel's address to Mary at the Annunciation. So far from being declared already 'full of grace' as in the Latin version of the Ave Maria, what the Greek actually says is more like 'Good day to you, God is being good to you.'[11]

None of this is to deny the existence of uses in both pagan writing and within the Bible itself unconnected with religion. For instance, Plato treats *chara* as equivalent to *hedone* and is therefore suspicious of it, in marked contrast, it must be said, to the Stoics, who tend to contrast joy and pleasure, identifying the former as one of life's legitimate aspirations.[12] But the element of excess does give us a clue to why such words do so often appear in religious contexts. There is a sense of being carried beyond the ordinary into the transcendent, being raised onto a quite different level. For the religious that should apply not just to the exuberance of dancing and feasting but also to each ordinary meal received. There is nothing special about particular individuals that entitles them to be fed while others go hungry.

But such excess also applies to the body itself. Just as the saying of grace before a meal can transform our sense of its significance, so graceful gestures can help us to read the body itself in new ways. So it comes as no surprise that the language of grace was once applied in the ancient world to the athlete, just as today the term is still commonly heard applied to the dancer. But even the relatively static body, when seen as beautiful and to be valued in its own right, can make a statement: that the universe is grounded in higher values than exploitation and lust. The names of the classical three Graces suggest a focus on celebration, and it is within such contexts that earlier artistic representation tends to be set.[13] Hesiod describes how 'from their glancing eyes flows a love that melts the limbs, and beautiful is their gaze from beneath their

---

[11] This translation was first suggested by Austin Farrer in a 1963 essay, 'Mary, Scripture and Tradition', available in A. Loades and R. McSwain (eds), *The Truth Seeking Heart: Austin Farrer and his Writings* (Norwich: Canterbury Press, 2006), 75.

[12] For a brief discussion, see R. Sorabji, *Emotion and Peace of Mind: From Stoic Agitation to Christian Temptation* (Oxford: Oxford University Press, 2000), 47–51.

[13] Their traditional names (from Hesiod onwards) are Aglaea (Splendour), Euphrosune (Gaiety) and Thalia (Feasting).

brows'.[14] It is intriguing to observe that only in later ancient history were they deprived of their clothes and their bodies now allowed in and of themselves to speak of proportion and harmony.[15] It was a theme taken up in much later art of the Christian era, and likewise in its poetry.[16] So it would be wrong to claim that that wider sense of grace was ever wholly lost. Nor is it a perception confined to the conventionally religious.

Henri Matisse in his negotiations with Fr Couturier over the decoration of the Vence Chapel shows himself fully alert to such issues, as is also clear, if less explicitly, in *The Dance*, his marvellous series of printings and murals of a dancing circle of girls.[17] In all of the various versions, the circle is incomplete, and deliberately so. An invitation is thereby extended to the viewer to join the graced circle as it strains against the edge of the frame, pulling or being pulled into the unknown beyond.

Strictly speaking, of course, Christian orthodoxy requires the latter. But, so far from decrying the former, we should welcome those human strainings, for, if nothing else, they at least represent the realization that there might be more to this world than what first meets the eye. It is not difficult for the Christian to find the Pauline sense of grace in a body wracked by the pain of crucifixion. But to leave matters there would be once more to separate theology and the world. We need also to discover a similar grace to what is illustrated by that work of Matisse, a dance that promises to take us beyond crucifixion into resurrection. It is a truth that is declared more profoundly, in my view, in the words of a pop song than in the writings of many an academic theologian:

> Grace, it's the name for a girl
> It's also a thought that changed the world...
> Grace she carries a world on her hips...
> No twirls or skips between her fingertips...
> Grace makes beauty out of ugly things.[18]

---

[14] Hesiod, *Theogony* 910–11 (my translation).
[15] For one such later type, see A. Steward, *Greek Sculpture* (New Haven, Conn.: Yale University Press, 1990), ii, no. 809.
[16] While in Botticelli they remain clothed, Canova presents the naked ideal.
[17] The front cover of this volume utilizes one such version, from 1910. The various changes Matisse made are discussed in Chapter 2.
[18] 'Grace', track 11 on U2's album *All That You Can't Leave Behind* (2000).

It is the reclamation of that wider sense of grace for the Church that I am seeking to achieve in this work, as I allow everything from ancient Roman religious uses of sexuality to twentieth-century 'secular' dance to help inform how we should understand God's generous offering of himself to human experience.

As with this volume's predecessor, there is no separate bibliography. Readers need, therefore, to be alerted to the fact that full bibliographical details are given in the first reference to a work within each chapter. Biblical quotations are from the Revised Standard Version, unless otherwise indicated.

Part I

Finding God in Bodies

I

Finding God in Bodies

In this first part I examine some of the ways in which bodies might open human beings up to the possibility of experiencing God or the divine through them.[1] Integral to our identity as embodied creatures is the fact that we communicate essentially through our bodies, in smiles and frowns, in violent gestures, in sexual concourse and in numerous other ways. Sometimes the individual is clearly in charge of what is being said through his or her body, but sometimes not. We are all aware of situations in which our bodies give us away, as it were. We avow one thing; but our bodily posture or the slight movement of the eye suggests another. The sideways glance, the sweaty palm, the twitch in the leg can all help to disclose a quite different underlying reality. If the success of a lie detector is premised on the assumption that the internal workings of the body are the best way of ascertaining the truth, there is no shortage of people who claim that careful attention to such gestures is no less indicative of the real situation. Yet that is to put matters altogether too negatively. The reassuring hug, the sympathetic smile, the confident walk can all be used to reinforce what we want to say, and are even sometimes sufficient on their own to make a point. The expressive character of the body is thus scarcely in doubt, nor indeed the way in which we augment this capacity in our desire to express ourselves better to others, for example through hair-styling, make-up and diet. But the very extent of such involvement with our bodies might seem to preclude a third party from speaking through them as well. So we need to consider carefully what space might be left for God.

[1] I sometimes substitute 'the divine' for God as a way of reminding readers that, while I would wish to attribute such experiences to the Christian God, the divinity so encountered is sometimes understood somewhat differently.

One way of making that space would be to say that bodies can at least sometimes point beyond themselves, that they are open to the possibility of transcendence. So, for example, sexual love points to a deeper, heavenly love, or a gentle human touch to the healing power of divine grace. In contemporary theology this is perhaps the most common way of introducing a sacramental understanding of body, and many valuable things have been said as a result. Nonetheless, to put matters that way still seems to me to make the divine presence altogether too extraneous to our world, as though it has always to be searched for, rather than being already there, deeply embedded in our world in virtue of the fact that God is the creator of all that is.

Certainly in the past, although there was an element of search, it was for the deepening of the awareness of what had already been perceived, not for its initiation. This is made wonderfully clear in one of the twentieth century's luckiest discoveries, the writings of the seventeenth-century poet and mystic, Thomas Traherne.

> Thou hast given me a body,
> Wherein the glory of thy power shineth,
> Wonderfully composed above the beasts,
> Within distinguished into useful parts,
> Beatified without with many ornaments.
> Limbs rarely poised,
>   And made for Heaven:
> Arteries filled
>   With celestial spirits:
> Veins, wherein blood floweth,
> Refreshing all my flesh,
>   Like rivers.
> Sinews fraught with the mystery
>   Of wonderful strength,
>   Stability,
>   Feeling.
>   .   .   .   .
> For God designs thy body, for His sake,
> A temple of the Deity to make.[2]

These few lines represent a recurring theme in Traherne's long work, *Thanksgivings for the Body*.

[2] 'Thanksgivings for the Body' in *Thomas Traherne: Selected Poems and Prose*, ed. A. Bradford (London: Penguin, 1991), 169–83, esp. lines 42–57, 462–3. The first rediscovery of his writings was published in 1903, the latest only in 1982.

However, in insisting upon a more intimate link it is not just to the mere fact of divine creation that Christianity can appeal, but also to the claims that lie at its very heart. God's pre-eminent form of communication is seen to lie in a particular human body and it is its interaction with other human bodies (including one's own) that constitutes humanity's way to salvation. Christ's suffering body demonstrated a new way towards identification with God. Risen and ascended, it now anticipates our own bodily destiny to live in close union with God. It is also that same body that is available to us in a special way in the Church's principal sacrament, to work the transformation of our bodies no less than of our souls. Now of course those subsequent bodies of Christ are not quite bodies in the same sense as the body he had during his ordinary earthly existence prior to the resurrection. Even the most conservative Christian must admit to some difference. Likewise, the body of the ascended Christ must be different again, in now sharing God's space—heaven—rather than ours. The risen Christ was able to pass through doors and to disappear from sight at will. Nonetheless, it is vital to assert continuities, for it is the totality of ourselves that is redeemed, not just some more spiritual aspects. So we may speak of something analogous to his earlier physical body, admittedly not now existing in our own space-time framework but still with the capacity to communicate in a way that retains significance for body and not just for the mind.[3]

That is to put the matter in explicitly Christian terms. The other major religions may explore the issues rather differently, but, as we shall see, they are no less insistent that the divine works in and through the material reality of the body, in what Christian theology would label sacramental action. So in what follows I want to take due cognizance of that fact and draw not just on Christianity or even only on the major contemporary religions but also on those of the past. The graced body is in fact a recurring theme across religions. The divine blesses us not just through our intellects but also by imparting something of itself to our bodies. It is, therefore, all the more regrettable that analysis of the experience of body has been so wholly conceded by theologians to other disciplines such as

---

[3] That is one reason why it is so important to many to have some visual image of Christ with which to engage. It is then no longer just telepathy between minds.

anthropology, history and sociology.[4] It is my hope that what follows will contribute in some small way to a reversal of that trend.

In the first chapter I pursue that theme through two aspects of body that are often said to be at the furthest remove from Christianity's own emphases: the body as beautiful and as sexual. The long history of Christianity's suspicion of sexuality and its numerous gruesome representations of the crucifixion might seem to confirm as much, and so make this a peculiarly odd place to begin for what purports to be a Christian analysis. Nonetheless, the choice is appropriate for at least three reasons. First, even if quite unsuited to Christianity, such claims to experience God through beautiful or sexual bodies are by no means inapplicable to all religion. Indeed, as soon as the net is extended more widely, it becomes obvious that there is no shortage of alternative religious perspectives where experience of the divine through such bodies is seen as integral. Secondly, such experience of God through body as beautiful or sexual is in many ways the easiest to comprehend, as indeed is indicated by the continued use even in today's highly secular culture of imagery connected with the divine for such bodies. Finally, and most importantly for me as a Christian, it is simply not true that Christianity need be wholly opposed to such experience. It needs to engage with such ideas, as it once did in the past and could do so again.

That is why I have singled out key moments of engagement from the earlier history of the Christian tradition. The ancient Greek understanding of beautiful bodies as graced by the divine was renewed at the Renaissance, just as the potentiality of sexuality as a religious metaphor was rediscovered in Baroque art. Indeed, I want to suggest that there is a desperate need for sexuality to be freed from the rather narrow range of associations it has come to acquire in the modern world. For much of human history it functioned as an important religious metaphor that spoke of the fruitfulness of relationships with the divine in intimate generosity and giving, and it could do so again. Christian Baroque art is

---

[4] For examples of such marginalization, intended or otherwise, see C. Classen (ed.), *The Book of Touch* (Oxford: Berg, 2005); S. Connor, *The Book of Skin* (London: Reaktion, 2004); C. Kosmeyer (ed.), *The Taste Cultural Reader* (Oxford: Berg, 2005).

unintelligible without such presuppositions, and in my view speaks all the more powerfully as a result.[5]

While Chapter 1 considers how human attractiveness might lead us into experience of the attraction of a creator who has put something of himself into his own creation, Chapter 2 in examining 'The Dancer's Leap' may seem to place too much stress on human initiative, in what might be depicted as merely human attempts to bridge the gap between that divine world and our own. But so far from considering the body a burden or hindrance to the possibility of such a relationship, worshippers found in dance a means for potentially transcending our own limitations. The lift from the ground that is so characteristic of this artistic medium suggested that the two worlds could not for ever be held apart. However, the fact that the initiative appears to lie with the dancers may lead some to object that any notion of grace is now lost: it is a human grasping at the divine rather than divine giving and patient human receiving. Historically, however, that is most certainly not how matters were seen. Dancers often waited for the gift of a divine trance before they began to move, while spectators remarked on the grace of any such performance. Even in the secular world of modern dance, there remains a sense of dependence on gift, since hard work alone is never sufficient in itself to achieve requisite standards of performance.

A quite different objection might be that this art form is in any case entirely marginal to religion. Certainly this is true of modern Christianity, though less true of some other religions, notably Hinduism. My reason for nonetheless placing the issue here and not with the rest of my discussion of music in the second part of the book is twofold. First, of all forms of music it is the one that most seeks total integration of body and mind and in a way, as I have just observed, that combines both divine gift and human pursuit, so essential in my view to any adequate understanding of grace. God is of course available everywhere. But it still takes some action on our part to make that presence sensible or visible. That is what dance is seeking to do. Secondly, dance provides an excellent example of what has been and continues to be in this volume one of my recurring themes, the sad divorce between

---

[5] The contributions of Bernini and Caravaggio will be examined at some length.

Christian theology and where experience of God is to be found. Encounter with God in such a context is now overwhelmingly pursued without reference to the Church or its theology.[6] But that does not mean that God has abandoned the medium. Dance's continuing engagement with the divine stands as a silent reprimand to the Church for so arbitrarily narrowing its own horizons. Such narrowing is no less evident in attitudes to food and drink, the subject of Chapter 3. Even otherwise devout Christians seldom now say grace before meals, and so fail to see their lives as particularly graced in this respect. This is all the more surprising in a world where everyone is aware of millions undernourished, with no obvious merit justifying the developed world being overfed while others go hungry. Christian theologians and preachers often mock the ancient pagan practices of drink libations and cereal and animal sacrifices as though they were merely cautionary activities to ward off possible jealousy or anger on the part of the gods. Although definitive evidence is lacking either way, I personally find it hard to doubt that basic attitudes of gratitude and gift were at their root in a way that much modern Christianity so conspicuously neglects. Certainly, that would explain a whole range of related activities discussed in this chapter, such as agricultural festivals, rules of hospitality and so on. But it is also my belief that much more has been lost. In particular, I draw attention to the various ways in which meals once communicated notions of interdependence, and so, through this social dimension, a dependence more widely in life as a whole on something greater than oneself or any other finite reality. Communal feasting is thus not necessarily a mark of self-indulgence. It can be a way of opening oneself up to others and thus, potentially at least, also to that greater Other who is God. But even those familiar Christian symbols of bread, water and wine, it seems to me, are often misunderstood. Their radical implications remain unnoted. So these too will be given detailed consideration.

Finally, I turn specifically to the more negative side of Christianity in a chapter entitled 'Ugly and Wasted'. As earlier chapters

---

[6] A more extreme example of such divorce, not pursued in that particular chapter although it might well have been, might be rave culture. See further R. Sylvan, *Trance Formation: The Spiritual and Religious Dimensions of Global Rave Culture* (London: Routledge, 2005). For a more secular perspective on the same phenomenon, see S. Reynolds, *Energy Flash* (London: Picador, 1998).

will have made clear, it is by no means my view that this is Christianity's sole emphasis. The modern secular mind is certainly wrong to take such attitudes as an invariable Christian norm. Such unqualified enthusiasm for the body as we find in Traherne is by no means rare within Christianity. At its inception the Gospels' insistence upon the Empty Tomb indicates the perceived indispensability of a body to the Risen Christ, however transformed that body might be. Equally, in hopes for the individual's own future salvation it was the resurrection of the body that was to be enshrined in the creeds and not the Greek immortality of the soul.[7] So, as we shall see, even in contexts where the body is apparently denied or demeaned by the faithful, it was intended, paradoxically, not as an ultimate rejection of its value but rather as a means to its greater glory. Indeed, that often continues to be the underlying rationale.

Even so, it cannot be denied that over its long history Christianity has often (perhaps more often than not) displayed deep suspicion of the body. Nor can the New Testament be allowed to escape such a critique, as though all the blame lay with the subsequent history of the Church. The later Church did not find it difficult to discover in New Testament texts support for celibacy as the higher ideal, and, whatever their deeper meaning, the contrasts in John and Paul of 'world' with 'flesh' easily lend themselves to a devaluation of material reality.[8] So the way forward is not to deny that history, but to consider how it might be possible to engage with it positively. What I shall suggest is that images of Christ's body wracked with pain or stories of ascetics pursuing related behaviour need to be set in their own intended wider context. Sometimes they were offered as answers to suffering or guilt (Christ, for example, seen as bearing our guilt or identifying with us in our suffering). Sometimes in the lives of the saints the primary motivation appears to have been as affective strategies of identification, conceived of as providing new resources for survival or flourishing rather than as necessarily debilitating. Paradoxical as it may seem, tears or fasting could be (and were) interpreted as divine gifts that empowered and transfigured. This does not necessarily legitimate

---

[7] While the Nicene Creed speaks of 'the resurrection of the dead', the Apostles' Creed asserts the matter twice over, as it were, in affirming 'the resurrection of the body'.

[8] For celibacy as the higher ideal, note Matt. 19.10–12; 1 Cor. 7.7–9.

such conduct, but it does help explain why ugly and wasted bodies might after all also provide a means of access to experience of the divine. The suffering God comes alongside individuals in their suffering. In imposing suffering on themselves, ascetics hoped to be graced with some of the divinity's own power.

As I turn now first to the question of experience of the divine as mediated through beauty and sexuality, one general observation about the conditioning of all such experience needs to be made. Unfortunately, it cannot be denied that on the whole the Christian tradition has given priority to male beauty, with female beauty understood more negatively as providing a source of sexual temptation to men. In a similar way, the affective value in identifying with Christ's suffering has been more commonly espoused by women than by men. Inevitably, despite my awareness of the bias behind such cultural conditioning, those cannot but have some impact on the choice of my examples, if I am not to be precluded from utilizing some of the most powerful and pertinent examples from art, story and history. Even so, the reader should not be misled. The experiential possibilities lie open on all counts to both sexes, and not just to one here and another there. I take up that point later, but it is worth asserting here at the outset.

I

Beautiful and Sexy

WHILE accurately reflecting its content, the title of this present chapter is deliberately ironic. The advertising industry judges, probably rightly, that these are the features that most human beings these days would like to possess: a body deemed both beautiful and sexy. Such perspectives may seem far removed from any positive religious concern. But occasional linguistic survivals such as 'she looks absolutely divine' suggest that some residual sense of the body pointing beyond itself may still survive even in such contexts. At all events it is that sense that I wish to explore here: how such bodies once opened up individuals to experience of the divine and might do so again. The application of each of the two terms across the centuries is explored in turn before a brief concluding section that bears more directly on our present situation.

While first reflections might suggest that the divine as a non-material reality would therefore communicate most effectively in ways that are less tied to the physical, so fundamental is bodily identity to what human beings are that no religion could possibly exclude a key role for body in mediating the divine. As a matter of fact, that is precisely what we find: the basic conviction across the world's religions that the divine, however different its own nature is, has expressed something of itself in giving us a bodily identity. Following the Christian tradition as I do, in what follows I shall explore this in terms of a grounding sacramental relationship. But to avoid any suggestion that such ideas are narrowly confined to Christianity, many of my examples will come from other religions. So, for instance, on issues of sexuality as sacramental I have sought to offer a sympathetic interpretation of attitudes among the ancient Romans. Again, to indicate how an apparently world-denying religion like Buddhism is no exception, I provide a detailed comparison between images of the Buddha and of Christ. None of this is done to dissolve the differences between the various religions, but is my way of insisting that God acts more widely and more generously than any particular religion's prejudices, and so they may appropriately learn from one another.

Modern culture often prides itself on having escaped earlier generations' psychological hang-ups in present-day attitudes to the body. While perhaps wanting to add a number of qualifications, many Christians also effectively add their own voice to such assumptions. I am much less convinced of human progress. As Part III will reveal, I believe that my fellow Christians operate with a far less material view of the eucharist than would have been true of major figures in Reformation times, whether Catholic or Protestant. Equally, in the modern age it is not true that attitudes to beauty and sexuality are now more subtle and nuanced. Indeed, in quite a number of ways they have become cruder and less perceptive, and in any case just as conditioned by cultural context as those of previous generations. Thus modern society has become so obsessed with questions of sexual activity that surprisingly little is now said or written about sexuality as a vehicle of attractiveness and meaning that can communicate without necessitating a specifically physical response. It is in that role as embedded metaphor that sexuality commonly functioned in the past in religion and in works of art alike but which the modern mind often seems incapable of comprehending except in much cruder categories. Equally, beauty in human bodies was once thought of as entailing so much more than simply physical attractiveness. Nowadays, however, beauty in the opposite sex is often reduced to availability and in one's own to power and self-containment.[1] What has been lost thereby is any real sense of a symbolic or mediating role, of how such beauty might be suggestive of a grace that is ultimately derived from elsewhere.

The Body Beautiful

On first reflection, it might seem that any august status for the body had already been ruled out for Christianity by its own deep Jewish

---

[1] Opinion surveys, for example, inform us that women like softer looks in men, whereas men themselves usually describe as handsome those of strong, muscular appearance.

roots. Although human beings were in the main seen as essentially psychosomatic unities (a single substance rather than the combination of two disparate elements, body and soul, as in the Greek tradition), we know that Jewish abhorrence of directly representing the divine extended even to the human figure.[2] Nothing was done to enhance bodily presence or any sense of its dignity, lest this be taken as an attempt to portray divinity, or, worse, ascribe divinity to human beings. Or at least that is the official or commonly held view. But, if we turn to the story of the creation of humanity in Genesis and the subsequent history of its exegesis, a rather different picture begins to emerge, and so some reason to question whether matters are after all quite that simple.

'So God created man in his own image, in the image of God he created him; male and female he created them' (Gen. 1.27). Like their patristic forebears, modern exegetes usually identify by way of explanation some appropriate shared spiritual characteristic such as reason, relationship or power.[3] But it has not gone unobserved that if the narrative is read at face value the most natural reading suggests something quite different: physical identity. The story would then have its origins not in the way it is more usually told but rather in the conviction that God passed on the splendour of his own corporeal identity.[4] Adam had been made 'perfect in physical beauty' because such also was the divine condition.[5] Whether universally assumed or not, such an interpretation would explain the willingness of some biblical authors to use physical imagery for God.[6] It would also account for why the later Kabbalistic tradition placed such a premium on the divine presence in sexual intercourse.

In the end mainstream Judaism did not follow that course, and in this I believe it to have been correct. Nonetheless, the existence of

---

[2] For increasing recognition of the presence within Judaism of alternatives to the psychosomatic account, see G. W. E. Nickelsburg, *Resurrection, Immortality and Eternal Life in Intertestamental Judaism* (New York: Oxford University Press, 1972); J. Barr, *The Garden of Eden and the Hope of Immortality* (London: SCM Press, 1992).

[3] For an historical survey of the more conventional approaches that includes Barth, see D. Cairns, *The Image of God in Man* (London: Collins, 1973).

[4] One major commentator who accepts that the image of God in human beings includes body is G. von Rad, *Genesis* (London: SCM Press, 1972 edn), 58–9.

[5] The inference drawn by Ezekiel: 28.12.

[6] e.g. Gen. 3.8; Exod. 33.23; Isa. 6.1; Ezek. 1.26; Amos 4.13; 9.1.

such an alternative tradition does indicate how, in marked contrast to the once-and-for-all incarnation of Christianity, the 'engenderment' of divine immanence could be presented as a constantly recurring theme for some elements of Judaism. For them 'this bodily form remains above all the bearer of signatures of the divine order'.[7] The notion of sacramental body is thus not as alien to Judaism as one might initially suppose. Acknowledging this fact might enable readers to look with more sympathy on the parallel Greek tradition that I am about to discuss, as also on the way in which the Buddhist tradition eventually adopted its own distinctive understanding of a divine grace to body. I shall examine these two approaches in turn before offering some reflections on what they might offer by way of response to, and critique of, the Christian tradition. Both are less apologetic in respect of their interest in beauty, while both also demonstrate a greater readiness to find beauty combined with openness and vulnerability rather than a self-contained innate strength.

The Greek Ideal

In seeking to place Greek idealization of the body in a religious context, it is important first to challenge the way in which Greek religion is so often portrayed as based on a rather crude anthropomorphism. Certainly, in its myths the gods are assigned all-too-human emotions and desires. The question remains, however, how literally these were understood.[8] But, leaving that issue aside, even if we confine ourselves to the question of the gods' bodies, a more complex picture emerges as soon as the matter is looked at in any detail. The bodies of the gods were in fact subject to such a wide range of exemptions from the normal behaviour of the physical that it becomes quite misleading to speak of a purely material characterization. So, for example, although the gods certainly sometimes partake in feasts, they have in fact no need for food

---

[7] For one example of such an argument, see C. Mopsik, 'The Body of Engenderment in the Hebrew Bible, the Rabbinic Tradition and the Kabbalah', in M. Feher (ed.), *Fragments for a History of the Body* (New York: Zone, 1989), i, 48–73, esp. 61, 67.

[8] For a defence of the value of such myths, see my *Tradition and Imagination* (Oxford: Oxford University Press, 1999), 171–207.

or drink (the fragrance from the sacrifice is enough).[9] Again, although their blood sometimes flows, it can never be subject to a haemorrhage and so they can never die. Likewise, although their bodies do appear on earth, it is important to observe that it is the gods who control to whom they appear. They can quickly hide themselves behind a mist. They are even capable of being present in more than one place at the same time.[10] So, although this is still far from full divinity, it does suggest diffused and competing divine attributes at work in our world rather than simply the human projection of a larger version of ourselves. One notes too that, instead of always acting in their own interest (though they do that as well), there is also a sharing from on high of what makes them divine. Such generosity is displayed in the *charis* or grace that the gods give to certain human bodies.[11] Such grace can come not only to athletes but also even to tired travellers when they have been refreshed by the divine presence.[12] So it is perhaps more like a rarefied form of physicality rather than just ordinary materiality. It is possible that this is also what the author of the Genesis passage had in mind.

Certainly, in considering the idealization of the human form in Greek sculpture, it is worth recalling that, as in the history of Christianity, there seems to have been some wrestling with the appropriateness or otherwise of giving anthropomorphic form to the gods. Such representation appears only to have emerged in the eighth century BC as a replacement for the earlier apotropaic forms that had once dominated Greek temples. Likewise, sculptures of Christ and the saints were long resisted, though by the later Middle Ages they were becoming increasingly lifelike, with even artificial aids sometimes built in, to simulate movement and so forth. The resistance in the Christian case is not hard to understand;

---

[9] The food and drink of the gods are described, respectively, as 'ambrosia' and 'nectar', but the stress is very much on their fragrance; they do not decay: e.g. *Odyssey* 4.445–6; *Iliad* 19.38–9.

[10] For these contrasts and some examples, see further J.-P. Vernant, 'Dim Body, Dazzling Body', in Feher (ed.), *Fragments*, i, 11–47.

[11] I discuss this issue in relation to the ancient Olympic games in *God and Enchantment of Place* (Oxford: Oxford University Press, 2004), 10–15.

[12] For the former, see e.g. *Homeric Hymn to Apollo* 1.151–3; for the latter, *Odyssey* 6.227–37, where Odysseus is transformed by Athene so that Nausicaa finds him 'glowing with beauty and graces' (237, my translation).

the worry was that too realistic a representation might be mistaken for the reality itself, and so idolatry be the inevitable result. In the ancient pagan world there may have been a not dissimilar concern, perhaps tempered by the fear that representation would be seen by the gods as the attempt to usurp a power that properly belonged to them alone. There are possible parallels with the biblical fear of uttering the divine name, as though even naming implied a claim to control.[13] If so, it is not hard to comprehend how much more so images might be thought of as usurping divine rights and prerogatives.

Nonetheless, such images came to be made, and on a massive scale. Phidias' statue of Athene in the Parthenon, for example, was 38 feet tall, with gold used for the drapery and ivory for exposed flesh. The scale of course was intended to suggest the more than merely human, as was also the case with the equally massive Zeus at Olympia. But their grandeur and grace were intended to mark more than just humanity writ large. Admittedly, less honourable motives did play a role. Phidias' statue helped highlight Athenian military prowess, just as later Byzantine Christs were used to reinforce the status of the emperor.[14] But it would be a mistake to think that this is all that is going on. Because of the deep involvement of the Greek gods with the natural order, the move-ment is really the other way, with 'the human body itself... seen to reflect the splendours of divinity'.[15] That is to say, although it has become a commonplace to describe such creations as amounting to no more than a projection of humanity idealized, the thought was really much more subtle than that. The divine was seen as active in our world. So that world (including our own bodies), it was believed, must reflect something of the gods' own world. That is no doubt why so many statues of ordinary but idealized human beings were made for religious contexts, the so-called *korai* and

[13] Initially, *Adonai* was used instead of the tetragrammaton YHWH. Later the vowels of the former were inserted into the latter, giving by the thirteenth century the familiar term, Jehovah.

[14] I am thinking here of the emperor-like Christs in Byzantine apses, but an equally pertinent example might be the colossal statue (over thirty feet high) which Constantine ordered of himself, parts of which still survive at Rome. Constantine was laying a claim to closeness to, if not identity with, divinity.

[15] S. T. Flynn, *The Body in Sculpture* (London: Weidenfeld and Nicolson, 1998), 27.

kouroi (maidens and youths) among them. The gods' handiwork was being made manifest.

Apart from one brief period in the nineteenth century it has also been such idealization that has dominated the history of sculpture. Rodin was horrified when he was accused of using plaster casts for his *Age of Bronze* (1866). Resistance to realism is also evident in the considerable shock experienced earlier when it was learnt that the Greeks had used polychrome to colour their statues, in order to make them more lifelike.[16] The English sculptor John Flaxman (d. 1826) insisted that it was the absence of colour that had left a legitimate space for the imagination. Jacques-Louis David, on the other hand, responded by including a coloured statue of the goddess Roma in one of his paintings (1789) and John Gibson by producing the statue of a fleshly *Tinted Venus* (1850), but the process never caught on.[17] One can see why. Sculpture would have ceased to be a serious rival to the life-size doll or to the camera, since all it would then have offered was a similar realistic portrayal. So it is hardly surprising that in the twentieth century sculpture moved, with few exceptions, even further away from realism, towards either the monumental (as in Henry Moore) or the semi-abstract or non-representational (as in Brancusi). Significantly, in the work of both sculptors religious themes and inspiration persisted.

Nonetheless, it is fascinating to consider why idealization lasted so long. It is to be found not only at obvious points influenced by the ancient world such as at the Renaissance or in Neo-Classicism, but also even in the Middle Ages. Comparisons were drawn between the outline plan of major churches and the body of Christ on the cross.[18] Again, the macrocosm/microcosm analogy was widely adopted, according to which the human body reflects the order and structure of the universe as a whole.[19] That said, perhaps we have part of the answer. The body spoke of its creator, and would do so still more clearly if idealized. Of course there was

[16] For the debate about colour, see ibid. 38–41, 103, 115–35.

[17] The latter is in the Walker Art Gallery, Liverpool.

[18] With the transepts representing Christ's extended arms. Somewhat surprisingly, Durandus, the best-known medieval authority, accepts the legitimacy of the circle as much as of the cross: *The Symbolism of Church and Church Ornaments*, ed. J. M. Neale and B. Webb (London: Gibblings, 1906 edn), 18.

[19] For a twelfth-century example from a manuscript of Hildegard of Bingen, see Flynn, *Body*, 44.

no sure-fire guarantee that such an intuition was correct, but the fact that the language of grace and of admiration bordering on adoration was common in this context shows that the move was perhaps inevitable. To many in the modern world such attitudes now seem strange. Yet, ironically, one major reason that people now find it difficult to think in such terms is precisely because of the strangeness of our own modern conventions. Under these admiration for another's body is immediately taken to betoken sexual interest, and so is regarded with suspicion, particularly where the same sex is involved.

But such suspicions Christians should resist, not least if they wish to be loyal to their own tradition. Of course there is much in that tradition that has been hostile to the body, and such aspects will need to be considered in due course. But there is equally another side that cannot be discounted, one that does not hesitate to find in the body beautiful a revelation of God. It is a claim that is to be found even among those that are better known for their asceticism. Take, for instance, Margery Kempe. When in one of her visions she sees the body of Christ lying before her, the description she offers is of 'the handsomest man that might ever be seen or imagined'.[20] Admittedly, this is only just before someone lacerates Jesus' breast with a dagger. So one reason for her choice of words may lie in the contrast. But that cannot be the whole explanation. Long before this the convention had become firmly established that Jesus as the incarnation of God must have had a beautiful body, even if we must wait until the Renaissance to find his naked body idealized as such in the Greek way. Look at almost any painting or sculpture of the first millennium, and you will see the process at work.

Buddha's Sensuous Body

Earlier I observed the way in which an earlier Greek aniconic tradition only gradually gave place to representations of deities in anthropomorphic terms. Not only is a similar gradualism to be found in Christianity,[21] this is still more true in Buddhism, where

---

[20] *The Book of Margery Kempe*, tr. B. A. Windeatt (Harmondsworth: Penguin, 1985), ch. 85, 249.

[21] Discussed in my *Tradition and Imagination*, 326–35.

it took a full five centuries for the first representations of the historical Buddha to appear. Even then, initially such statues were quite small.[22] Eventually, however, they surpassed in scale even the work of Phidias. The two Buddhas (dating from the sixth or seventh century AD) that were destroyed in 2000 in Afghanistan were more than a hundred feet high (one 180 feet, the other 120).

It is possible of course to argue that both Greek and Buddhist religion were wrong to move away from the aniconic. To me, however, such developments suggest a growing appreciation of the religious significance of body. In the case of Buddhism, this can be seen working itself out in the various ways in which the Buddha was portrayed. One recent study has drawn attention to comparable developments at different periods in the history of Buddhism and Christianity and also to some similar forms of representation.[23] While some parallels are obvious and convincing, at other times the author tends, in my view, to underestimate the differences and so overstate his case.[24] Even so, what is undoubtedly established is a similar movement towards using the body as a vehicle for suggesting divine presence.

If there is the same stress on the serenity of the face, strikingly different are the ways in which the rest of the body is treated. In common with eastern ideals of beauty, the Buddha's body is less obviously male. Indeed examples of Buddhas are not wanting where a female reading would be the more natural one.[25] Recessed genitals are used to emphasize chastity, a practice that runs counter to the Christian approach, where attention can even be drawn to

---

[22] These were images on gold and copper coins from the time of the Emperor Kanishka (first century AD). Prior to this, scenes from Buddha's life had appeared, but with Buddha himself represented by a royal umbrella, a footprint, an empty throne or some other such substitute.

[23] R. Elinor, *Buddha and Christ: Images of Wholeness* (Cambridge: Lutterworth, 2000). For comparable movements, see 145–57; for some examples of similar representations, 64, 68–9, 138, 166.

[24] He makes his desire for a common message clear in his conclusion (207), but sometimes this is bought at the price of forced parallels. So, for instance, in order to parallel the story of how Buddha's mother became pregnant, he speaks of how 'the Holy Spirit in the form of a white dove enters Mary's' ear' (40).

[25] For an excellent example from sixteenth-century Thailand, see ibid. 170. Elinor describes the Indian ideal of beauty as of 'a soft, rounded, lightly muscled physique' (56).

this part of the anatomy in order to stress masculinity.[26] The range of symbolic gestures employed by the Buddha is also considerably wider.[27] Recessed genitals contrast with the prominence of the hair knot or cranial protuberance, as also sometimes of nipples and navel, all of which have symbolic resonances.[28] The former was used to suggest surpassing intelligence and wisdom, the latter to indicate beauty of proportion.[29] Perhaps the difference between the two religions might be expressed as follows. Whereas the traditional western image of the beautiful Christ offers us a body that lays a calm but confident claim to power and authority, in the East Buddha is presented as at one and the same time serene and sensuous. While the open self-assurance of the latter is inviting, it is the former that more directly addresses us with a demand for obedience.

In making that tentative comparison (and of course there is no shortage of exceptions on both sides), my intention is not necessarily to arbitrate and declare one form better than another. Christian artists have clearly sometimes implicitly valued the Buddhist model over their own, and indeed occasionally resorted to specific imitation.[30] Here my concern is simply to ensure acknowledgement of the fact that the body is being used sacramentally in both cases, to suggest a more than human presence. One branch of Buddhism, the Theravada tradition, still shows some resistance to the whole process, refusing for example to countenance representations of the historical Buddha on stage or in film. Zen goes further in parodying such representations. Guatama is, for instance, portrayed as a lean and rather repulsive ascetic.[31]

[26] For an example of the former from the fifth century, see ibid. 161. For a brief discussion of the latter with references, see my *Tradition and Imagination*, 83–4.

[27] For a helpful survey of the complete range of gestures in Buddhism and Hinduism, see P. Kana-Devilee, *A Divine Gesture* (Amsterdam: Rijksmuseum, 1996).

[28] For an example of prominent nipples and navel, see Elinor, *Buddha and Christ*, 139. It is not always possible to distinguish between cranial protuberance and hair knot. For some examples, see Kana-Devilee, *A Divine Gesture*, 42, 43, 47.

[29] Even Augustine insists that male nipples must play an aesthetic role since they serve no practical function: *City of God*, bk 22, tr. H. Bettenson (Harmondsworth: Penguin, 1984), 1074.

[30] Both approaches can be illustrated from the works of Eric Gill, his *Deposition* of 1924 taking the former approach, his *Holy Face of Christ* of 1925 the latter. For illustrations, see J. Collins, *Eric Gill: The Sculpture* (London: Herbert Press, 1998), 50, 145, 147.

[31] Elinor, *Buddha and Christ*, 172.

Christianity of course exhibits similar tensions, now portraying Christ with beautiful body, now with it wracked by pain. Nor is that contrast the same as that between crucifixion and resurrection. Many a painting of the crucifixion (especially those dating from the Renaissance) has a beautiful Christ hanging on the cross. The point is that the body is being used to say more than what simply happened, in either case. The concern is to symbolize the significance of the life of a saviour, and thus of God mediated through that body. So even in the most agonized crucifixions it is rare not to see some countervailing sign, for example in calmness of expression or direction of gaze heavenwards. Indeed, without such qualifications, it is hard to see how the resultant pure negativity could say anything at all about God whatsoever. To express orthodox Christian belief, it must still be *God* in the hell of suffering, not just a hell of suffering. Otherwise Francis Bacon or any other artist hostile to Christianity could do the task just as well.

Secular Models and Human Vulnerability

A widely disseminated view of the history of attitudes to the body has it that Christianity suppressed the naked body, and that it is only in modern times that such freedom has been regained. Even if no account is taken of the Renaissance position, where the naked body is commonly used as a Christian symbol for the ideal, Adam and Eve naked in the Garden of Eden, Christ in his loincloth on the cross, and Mary Magdalene with breasts exposed all indicate a more complex reality. Nor are women presented as beautiful only when also shown as seductive. Apart from the face of the Virgin Mary, Eve's body as a beautiful naked whole is not uncommon even in medieval art. The cathedrals at Autun and Beauvais provide some fine examples.[32] Indeed, Vincent of Beauvais in his influential treatise on art decreed that all women must be shown as beautiful on the Day of Judgement since their condition, like those of men, had now been restored. To pursue such considerations further, however, would be to ignore deeper issues, about the extent to which any approach to the body is necessarily a social construction, with the modern view no less problematic in its own way. Perhaps

[32] For Autun, see G. Duby, X. Altet and S. Suduiraut (eds), *Sculpture* (Cologne: Taschen, 1989), ii, 41.

rather surprising to some, continuing suspicion of the body has been detected even among its most secular advocates.[33] It takes little to establish the culture-relative dependence of specific notions of beauty of body. Fat on women is an obvious instance. If Rubens' nudes often now appear to us overweight, that is because in the seventeenth century fat was seen as a sign of prosperity (and thus of health) and so was integrated into contemporary perceptions of what it was to be beautiful.[34] As such it parallels behaviour in a quite different cultural context, in some Melanesian islands where on puberty young girls are placed in special communal 'fattening houses'.[35] Numerous other examples could be offered. In ancient Egypt Queen Nefertiti's neck was artificially elongated in order to conform to the canons of the time.[36] Ironically, the Chinese cultivation of small feet through binding apparently originated as a way of reducing attractiveness (to the invading Tartars). Through time, however, it became for the native Chinese a symbol of beauty instead.

Like fat, a pale complexion was also once seen as a sign of prosperity and privilege. Yet, so far from indicating health, the methods employed to secure this were actually a way of slowly poisoning the woman concerned.[37] The modern equivalent of tanning is also now of course known to carry with it corresponding dangers, in cancer of the skin. Nor should the supporting role of clothes be forgotten, in men no less than women. The use of padded shoulders in military uniforms makes the point. What is less widely acknowledged is that adornment of the body by tattoos or lacerations often performs a similar function. What a westerner might read as nakedness is in fact to tribesmen accustomed to such practices more a matter of being appropriately robed.[38] Indeed, for

---

[33] This is the argument, among others, of M. Gill, *Image of the Body* (New York: Doubleday, 1989), esp. 327–428.

[34] Even his young wife, Hélène Fourment, is given sufficient loose flesh for her to have what would nowadays be seen as unbecoming knees: for this and other examples, see ibid. 266–70.

[35] So J. Robinson, *The Quest for Human Beauty* (New York: Norton, 1998), 21.

[36] Ibid. 72–4; for foot-binding, 75–6.

[37] In the use of ceruse the skin absorbed lead oxide, hydroxide and carbonate: so ibid. 149.

[38] e.g. ibid. 46.

a time this was the only form of ostentation available to the merchant class in Japan.[39] Japan is also different from other cultures in finding the clothed or partially clothed necessarily more alluring than the undressed.[40] The novelist Yukio Mishima saw himself as consciously rebelling against such an apparent lack of interest in the naked body. If across the course of the nineteenth and twentieth centuries there has been in the West progressive acceptance of the naked form, it remains highly contentious whether this has been accompanied by more tolerant and less sexist attitudes towards women, far less whether this is the source of the change. Some of the most famous paintings of the female nude from the nineteenth century seem to treat the woman concerned as pure object. Again, in the twentieth century a number of commentators have argued that many an artist treats the female form as, if anything, more manipulative and threatening than when Christianity was in the ascendant.[41] Picasso's attitude has been described as that of 'omnivorous predator', Balthus' one of 'erotic violence', Giacometti's the alienation of the brothel, Duchamp's 'the fetish of the machine' and Bonnard's 'the exoticism of the seraglio'.[42] That is precisely what makes the work of Cindy Sherman so challenging. The provocative gaze is now returned.[43]

In the case of men the rise of the physical fitness movement is of particular relevance.[44] The strongly muscled body presents a very special type of ideal that for most of its history has been concerned with creating a sense of invulnerability.[45] Indeed, some degree of continuity with ancient Greece is to be seen. The movement apes the internal strengths of gods and heroes such as Zeus or Hercules,

---

[39] Decorated kimonos were reserved for the nobility: ibid. 83.

[40] Possibly attributable to the universal practice of naked communal bathing: Gill, *Image*, 146.

[41] An obvious example is Manet's *Olympia*: discussed in Gill, *Image*, 300–4 and in W. Steiner, *The Trouble with Beauty* (London: Heinemann, 2001), 85–92.

[42] For the first three, see Gill, *Image*, 340 (cf. 346, 371), 375, 390–1; for the last two, Steiner, *Trouble*, 53, 158.

[43] For a good example (from 1982), see M. D. Alexander *et al.*, *Body Language* (New York: Museum of Modern Art, 1999), 45.

[44] For a history of its remarkable growth from the late nineteenth century onwards, particularly initially in Germany, see K. R. Dutton, *The Perfectible Body: The Western Ideal of Male Physical Development* (New York: Continuum, 1995), esp. 99–149, 199–227.

[45] Ibid. 291; Steiner, *Trouble*, 2.

using remarkably similar conventions.[46] So, for instance, sexuality is indicated indirectly rather than through focus on the genitals. Indeed, small briefs are the norm in modern contests, thus contrasting markedly with those worn by exotic dancers and strippers. Body hair too continues to be frowned upon.[47] It is almost as though the ideal sought is at the furthest remove possible from the merely animal. How much such a cult indicates masculine insecurities is a moot point. Even in distant cave paintings it is the women who were portrayed more closely to their natural condition (if sometimes with exaggerated breasts), while men seem to have felt the need to put on animal skins in order to simulate the beasts' power.[48]

All this may seem a long way from any religious concern, and indeed in some ways to run directly counter to it. Biblical injunctions against tampering with the appearance of the body, whether it be in hair, tattoo or more external ornamentation, are by no means uncommon.[49] Nonetheless, even secular writers note that part of what is involved in such pursuit of beauty is a search for self-transcendence.[50] That could be made to link in with the most influential theory of beauty of modern times, that of Kant. He drew a sharp distinction between the sublime and the beautiful: 'the beautiful . . . consists in limitation, whereas the sublime is to be found in an object even devoid of form, so far as it immediately involves, or else by its presence provokes, a representation of *limitlessness*, yet with a superadded thought of its totality'.[51] Thus described, the sublime more naturally suggests religion, and as such it is often identified with awe before the more overpowering aspects of divine creation as exemplified in paintings such as those of Caspar David Friedrich and the Hudson River School.[52] That may seem at a far remove from beautiful bodies, but no less a figure

[46] For Greek gods, see Dutton, *The Perfectible Body*, 43; for the modern contrast, 308–10.

[47] Ibid. 301–7. The practice also extends to the cinema. There has been only one hairy-chested Tarzan, and many actors in fact shave their chests (e.g. John Travolta).

[48] A contrast drawn by Gill, *Image*, 77.

[49] e.g. Lev. 19.27–8; Isa. 3.18–24.

[50] Dutton, *The Perfectible Body*, 291.

[51] *The Critique of Judgement*, ed. J. C. Meredith (Oxford: Clarendon Press, 1952), book 2, sects 23, 90.

[52] Discussed in my *God and Enchantment of Place*, 113–19.

than Winckelmann found in ancient Greek nudes a comparable evocation.

In theory Winckelmann reserved his greatest praise for 'sublime' bodies that were self-contained and awe-inspiring such as the Farnese Athena. Yet, when his writings are read a little more closely, one observes that it was precisely those statues that mixed the beautiful and the sublime that he held in most special regard.[53] Such a transitional character he detected as particularly evident in works such as the Venus de'Medici and the Apollo Belvedere.[54] In them vulnerability and accessibility were asserted and esteemed even as they were in the process of being transcended.[55] Yet it is that very quality of total independence and self-reliance in the sublime that so many modern writers continue to identify as most valuable in the pursuit of the beautiful: strength of form and the projection of internal self-confidence. One recent critique, however, has challenged whether this is not the wrong sort of transcendence, with such otherness bought at too high a cost, in a loss of other values such as mutuality and domesticity.[56] Mary Shelley's *Frankenstein* is presented as an early counter-attack, with Charlotte Brontë and George Eliot in their focus on plain women also encouraging readers of their own day to look elsewhere.[57] Whether there are similar trends in more recent writing and art-work seems to me more contentious.[58]

Certainly, a similar strain can be found in many of the paintings and drawings of Rembrandt. He seems concerned to force the viewer towards a truer appreciation of the actual realities of the human condition. The fat and folds he introduces have been replicated in the work of many a modern photographer.[59] As we

[53] For discussion of Athena with illustrations, see A. Potts, *Flesh and the Ideal: Winckelmann and the Origins of Art History* (New Haven, Conn.: Yale University Press, 1994), 132–6.

[54] Ibid. 118–23, 129–31.

[55] Although his analysis can sometimes be challenged, as with the Belvedere *Antinous*: ibid. 144–55, esp. 151–2.

[56] Steiner, *Trouble*, e.g. 209, 230.

[57] Ibid. 3–19, 25.

[58] Ibid. 191–240. Intriguingly, Rachel Whiteread is described as engaged in a work of 'magical transubstantiation': 234.

[59] With Rembrandt Bathsheba may have the degree of fat acceptable in his day, but Diana's folds are definitely realistic rather than alluring: Gill, *Image*, 275–9. For an un-selfconscious ninety-year-old posing naked, see W. A. Ewing, *The Century of the Body* (London: Thames and Hudson, 2000), 210–11.

all know, fortunes are still spent on denying that reality, in the attempt to improve appearances (now as much a feature of the lives of men as of women). While many are successful for a while in delaying the visible onset of age, the face of Michael Jackson well illustrates how badly wrong things can sometimes go.[60] Christians, it might be said, are called to ruthless honesty, in the face of such human folly and vanity. But there is, I think, something to be said on the other side.

Lack of attention to personal appearance can be as much a denial of the body given to us by God as costly attempts at self-improvement. More importantly, though, the question needs to be asked where in all of this any space for God might be found. Not only we ourselves but also even Christ will eventually be given one bodily form rather than another in our imaginations. That is to say, while some may at present hesitate about their own particular ideal and also that for Christ, most of us finally yield and conceive the ideal body under one particular form rather than another. So careful critiques of such representations surely cannot be avoided. In the case of Buddhism, for instance, pot-bellied Buddhas may be defended as a sign of prosperity, but it is hard not to see them as anything other than a corruption of religion into the narrowly material.[61] For some the more sensual Buddhas may suggest the same. Yet to my mind what they offer is an implicit and powerful critique of Christianity. Too often in the past and even today in theology no less than in art Christ has been portrayed as altogether too 'masculine', too self-contained. There is a grace and receptivity in such statues of Buddha that many an image of Christ lacks. Whether as Byzantine Pantocrator or as the Romanesque figure reigning on the cross, too often Christ emerges as more like Zeus than Apollo. Winckelman was onto something important when he reserved most praise for Greek statues that suggested both power and vulnerability, as in the Apollo Belvedere. To be human is to be vulnerable, as some of the greatest war photographs of our age all too poignantly illustrate.[62] But that very vulnerability can be transcended, not into a new self-

---

[60] For American statistics on male cosmetic surgery, see Dutton, *The Perfectible Body*, 184.

[61] Common in Chinese versions of the bodhisattva Maitreya: for an illustration, see ibid. 29.

[62] Although these are undoubtedly the most famous images of the twentieth century: Ewing, *Century*, 56, 92, 112, 142, 148.

contained being, as modern culture or ancient Greece so often desire, but rather into one living under the power and grace of God, as Christ did.

This is not necessarily to deny the validity of experiences based on more Zeus-like encounters. Surface conflict need not necessarily be ultimate. There are so many different aspects to the divine. It is simply to flag up an important caution. How the two types of experience might be integrated into a more overarching perspective is an issue to which I shall return at the end of this chapter.

Sexual Bodies

Our own age prides itself on the frankness with which it is able to discuss questions of sexuality. One might therefore have thought that it would be an age open to all the nuances of sexuality. In fact there is surprisingly little discussion of sexuality's various symbolic dimensions. So, for instance, pornography is largely discussed in terms of freedom of expression, scarcely at all with regard to the degree to which the forms of behaviour it popularizes appeal to an unhealthy male desire to dominate.[63] So symbols of power and control may be far more integral to its representation than many a viewer might care to admit. There are of course exceptions, but matters are complicated both by the difficulty of definition and the reluctance of feminist groups to find themselves in alliance with what they see as right-wing pressure groups.[64] Although attempts are sometimes made to speak of pornography in the ancient world and so of a continuing tradition, as I note below attitudes were so different that it is hard to make appropriate comparisons.[65] One obvious difference is that while in both ancient and modern worlds

[63] Illustrated by the apparent frequency of anal intercourse and of orgasm on the woman's face.

[64] The classic feminist case is Andrea Dworkin's *Pornography: Men Possessing Women* (New York: Putnam, 1981). How the two difficulties affected American legislation is outlined in L. O'Toole, *Pornocopia* (London: Serpent's Tail, 1998), 26–60.

[65] As in A. Richlin (ed.), *Pornography and Representation in Greece and Rome* (New York: Oxford University Press, 1992). Dworkin is rejected in favour of a more radical feminism in which such a wide definition of pornography is adopted (e.g. pp. xiv–xvii) that its application becomes questionable.

explicit imagery is easily available, in the ancient world it was part of the public sphere and not the private. Videos and the Internet mean that most modern consumers 'consume' or 'enjoy' on their own. Christianity may also have unwittingly contributed in creating a climate of the forbidden. At all events, it is remarkable how many porn stars have had a religious upbringing.[66] Some have even returned to the fold.[67] Again, to take a quite different example, although sex as an expression of love naturally continues to be a common theme, these days both believer and non-believer alike seem to find more comic than profound any suggestion of a transcendent dimension that includes the presence of God. A long-standing, earlier tradition has now largely fallen silent. It would be intriguing, for instance, to know how many contemporary Christians still think of the procreative act as acting 'on behalf of' (*pro*) God.

Still more problematic to the modern mind is any notion of sex as metaphor applying to situations other than those directly arising from the sexual act itself. An interesting test case of this is how the artists of Baroque Rome are now treated. Works by Bernini such as *The Ecstasy of St Teresa* are commonly treated as occasions for snide humour. The angel's arrow and Teresa's response are seen as essentially sexual, and that is all. Sexuality as a genuine metaphor for religious experience seems to pass by the majority of viewers, even most professional art critics. Again, take Caravaggio, working half a century earlier. His works are now most commonly read as early icons of gay liberation rather than the attempt of a creative spirituality to work towards new ways of symbolizing faith. What is worrying about such modern treatments is less the perhaps inevitable secular reading and more the characteristic Christian response, in the tendency of my fellow-believers to retreat before such criticism from the endorsement of such images. What I want to suggest here on the contrary is that it is only if Christianity

---

[66] This aspect is noted throughout in L. Ford, *A History of X* (Amherst, Mass.: Prometheus, 1999).

[67] True of both the principal stars of what is often seen as pornography's defining 'classic' (*Deep Throat*, 1972). Harry Reems is now a trustee of his local church. Linda Lovelace had even wanted to be a nun in her high-school days. The Rockland brothers, who were for a while major figures in gay pornography, were sons of missionaries. One at least has since returned to Christian practice.

recovers a more relaxed attitude to the use of sexuality as deep metaphor that it will be able to appreciate fully once more such great artistic achievements, and so the mediating sacramentality of sexuality.

Ironically, even at the beginning of the new millennium it seems to me that the modern world has still not fully escaped Victorian repression. The present climate remains obsessed with sex rather than able to fit it naturally among all the other human activities to which symbolic value is given and thus from which metaphors can easily be drawn. In a moment I shall illustrate what I have in mind by considering in detail some works by Bernini and Caravaggio. But first I want to indicate what a more natural and relaxed religious attitude might look like by considering two cultures quite different both from each other and from Christianity, Hinduism quite briefly and then, at rather more length, Roman practice.

Sexuality in Roman Religion

Before turning to Roman practice, I want first to look at Hinduism, a religion still vibrant in the modern world. I can do so quite briefly, as I have already said something on the subject in this volume's predecessor.[68] The highly charged erotic imagery of some northern temples often evokes western sniggers, precisely because the carvings are so totally without restraint.[69] It is not just love-making that they portray. They are frequently orgiastic as well. Although their actual origins are surrounded in mystery, such historical evidence as there is suggests that the images were never used to recommend such conduct to ordinary human beings. Rather, they were interpreted as a powerful symbol of the divine energy into which worshippers could tap if they were prepared to participate in that particular temple's worship. However, put that succinctly, something of central importance is omitted. This summary interpretation suggests entirely a pointing elsewhere, precisely the feature of so many Christian treatments of sexuality of which I complained at the beginning of this chapter. The images are in fact not simply symbolic of something else. They are also intended as in

---

[68] Brown, *Enchantment*, 352–9, esp. 357–8.
[69] The most famous are at Khajuraho.

some sense participatory, as the whole Tantric movement within Hinduism indicates.[70] Sexual activity in itself can be a way of drawing closer to the divine. Not that the Tantric movement is exclusively concerned with sexuality. There is also a mysticism about sound and sight. But sexuality is seen as one key way of coming to a deeper awareness of the immanence of the divine in all things, and for some versions erotic mysticism came to be the dominant form.[71]

Although the range of religious associations was in some ways narrower, the classical world offers an interesting parallel. And it is important to pursue it, not least because after a long period of neglect when Roman religion was not taken seriously, scholars are once more giving it the proper credit it is due. Nowadays among the general public only the brothel illustrations from Pompeii and suchlike tend to be well known. But, as in India, more often than not the aim of explicitly sexual art was in fact religious. One survey talks of the relationship between sexual imagery and religious belief being 'absolutely central' to the ancient world.[72] In particular, the author observes the degree to which sexual imagery permeated the temples and public festivals, not least because of concern with fertility, that crops and animals should give of their best, and humans also. If the most common votive or thank-offering is, somewhat surprisingly, a cast of feet, there is also no shortage of images of the penis that have been found.[73] Unlike the phallus used in fertility rites, these are not necessarily erect. Both forms alike point to a naturalness in how the divine relationship to sexuality was treated. Indeed, such practices were to survive in southern Italy in the form of votive offerings to the doctor saints, Cosmas and Damian, well into the twentieth century. In the eighteenth century Sir William Hamilton, British consul at Naples, had cited such behaviour to argue that Roman Catholicism was no more than a continuation

---

[70] Not by recommending orgiastic behaviour but rather through taking ordinary sexual practice and building on that towards the divine.

[71] As in the Vaisnava-Sahajiyas of Bengal and its related modern form, the Bauls.

[72] Catherine Johns, *Sex or Symbol? Erotic Images of Greece and Rome* (London: British Museum, 1982), 152.

[73] Ibid. 57–9. Feet were of course particularly important to the agricultural labourer.

of paganism, but as a prayer by sterile women or by the wives of impotent men the rite surely has a natural and inoffensive meaning, and indeed legitimacy.[74]

Another common variant in the ancient world was the use of an erect phallus as a way of warding off the evil eye. As such these appeared frequently as amulets or at the entrance of a house, sometimes in combination with *tintinnabula* or bells.[75] In response to those who find in such behaviour only pure superstition, one might respond by observing that it is very hard from the perspective of our own world to determine precisely where on a scale such practices should be placed compared to what continues to take place in our own day. Should we, for instance, think of the contemporary habit of crossing fingers for good luck (originally, though now no longer, the religious act of invoking the cross), or should we perhaps rather imagine the devout Christian who is found wearing a cross round her neck? Although the latter comparison may seem offensive, it is not intended to be so, not least because it may be nearer to the truth. The point is that both ancient phallic symbol and modern cross appeal to a wider framework of meaning, and in terms of both systems the primary symbolic reference becomes anything but superstitious. Indeed, it may be read as a natural desire to invoke divine protection. Thus, just as the devout Christian of today would not automatically think of violence as she puts on her cross in the morning, or modern Hindus of an actual penis as they anoint the *linga* during *puja*, so an ancient Greek or Roman seeing such phallic signs would not immediately conjure up images of sexual activity but rather think of the fruitfulness or prosperity that the gods' blessing can bring.

None of this is to deny the presence of explicit sexual imagery in what seem to be entirely secular contexts. Even here, however, we must be careful not to assume too easily that it would have been read as we might now be inclined to read it. Religious applications elsewhere may well have had an impact on the allegedly more

---

[74] For the discovery and its aftermath, see G. Carabelli, *In the Image of Priapus* (London: Duckworth, 1996). Hamilton's description of his discoveries at Isernia was entitled *An Account of the Remains of the Worship of Priapus* (1786). Certainly, no worship of the phallus was intended. For twentieth-century survivals, see Carabelli, *Image*, 16–18.

[75] For some examples, see Johns, *Sex or Symbol?*, illus. 13, 52, 54.

'secular' contexts. Even supposing this not to be so, the very frequency of religious imagery elsewhere must have meant that the 'secular' had less the feeling of the forbidden or naughty, and more of a matter-of-fact report of what actually took place. That might explain why, in contrast to modern pornography, the combination of explicit sex scenes and indicators of love is not uncommon. Representations of extreme actions are also often touched with humour rather than valued in their own right. Again, despite the reputation of the ancient world for violence, this element is almost entirely absent.[76] These details are interesting, not least because of the contrast with our own culture. Sexual imagery can appear in the most surprising of places, and for reasons quite different from contemporary motives for similar actions. So, for instance, to ward off the evil eye a visitor might find a love scene depicted above his head as he dined as a guest in his host's dining room, or again a huge black penis might suddenly appear to view on the mosaic floor of the house's bath.[77] If raising a goblet to your mouth or looking in a mirror produced similar depictions though for different reasons (delectation or amusement), as the mirror example illustrates, bias towards the adult male is far from as uniform as is commonly suggested.[78] Both women and youths are found taking the initiative in portrayals of the sexual act.[79] In any case, in reading the visual we need to guard against supposing that the most pleasing visual arrangement necessarily corresponded to what actually took place.[80]

It is not only modern believers that are found resisting the connection with religion in all of this. Rather surprisingly, one scholar who is happy to concede the origin of Greek nudity in

[76] For loving gazes, ibid. 123–7; for humour, 33, 90–6; for absence of violence, 113 (lesbianism and anal intercourse also almost never appear—101, 103, 133).

[77] J. R. Clarke, *Looking at Lovemaking: Constructions of Sexuality in Roman Art* (Berkeley: University of California Press, 1998), 120–36, 187–94.

[78] Ibid., 22–35.

[79] For a woman taking the lead role on a Metropolitan Museum glass dish, see ibid. 30–5; for a youth doing so on the Warren Cup, 85–6. For a woman taking the initiative on a mirror, see A. Stewart, *Art, Desire and the Body in Ancient Greece* (Cambridge: Cambridge University Press, 1997), 176–7.

[80] Used by Clarke to argue against Sir Kenneth Dover's theories of intercrural homosexual intercourse: *Lovemaking*, 20; by Stewart to argue against rear entry as the norm in heterosexual: *Art*, 159–61. Clarity of view and dignity of appearance pull the artists in other directions.

religious liminal festivals nonetheless wants to treat the famous *kouroi* statues as simply an expression of the dead's desire for immortality.[81] Since they lack individuality, I find such an account implausible. Body mediates the divine in Greek culture just as later in Roman culture we find Eros or Venus presiding over explicit acts of love.[82] If one starts from a belief in the divine as creative (the source of the world's fruitfulness), then not only does sexuality become a natural image for divinity at work, it also becomes less a subject of embarrassment in other contexts, as well as potentially more multivalent. Sex is viewed as potentially rich in meaning because the divine is seen as already present within it, reaching sacramentally beyond its immediate meaning. Even if now less willing to use such language, Christianity has of course long recognized this in the context of married love.

That insight, however, might be extended far more widely. How easy it might be to recover such wider symbolic resonances in the modern world, it is hard to say. Perhaps the reductionist pressures in the surrounding culture are just too strong. What we can say, however, is that paying careful attention to the practice of religion in very different contexts can undoubtedly alert us to a rich vein of alternative possibilities. God is not just at work within Christianity. Nonetheless, not dissimilar insights might be gained from the history of Christianity itself. Erotic imagery has had a long literary history. If Origen and Bernard can be dismissed as 'mere allegory', it is harder to give poets like Venantius Fortunatus and St John of the Cross similar short shrift. It is the visual, however, that has usually generated most opposition, and so it is to its inherent potential in the work of two key artistic figures that I now turn.[83]

Baroque Sensuality in Bernini

Although Christianity is often blamed for what survives of prudery in the modern world, apparently eighteenth-century Enlightenment

---

[81] For origins, see Stewart, *Art*, 28–33; for *kouroi*, 63–7.

[82] For an example of Eros blessing human love-making on a mirror, see Clarke, *Lovemaking*, 22–4.

[83] The material that follows on Bernini and Caravaggio was first presented in a lecture at the Gregorian University in Rome. I am grateful to those present who provided helpful comment and criticism.

attitudes also played their part.[84] As such they stand in marked contrast
to some conspicuous features of the previous century. I shall explore
these through the work of the sculptor Bernini before going still further
back in history to examine (at rather more length) the quite different
case of Caravaggio.

As Wittkower observes of Gian Lorenzo Bernini (1598–1680), 'it
was he more than any other artist who gave Rome its Baroque
character',[85] and this is what we find reflected in churches, foun-
tains, tombs, portrait busts and above all of course in St Peter's itself.
Most of this œuvre may seem to have little or nothing to do with
our chosen topic here, and that is largely so. But the baldacchino at
St Peter's may be used to indicate that Bernini's sculpture cannot be
narrowly compartmentalized. Although no body is present, even
here we find, I would suggest, the complete integration of the
language of body and spirit. Despite their weight and height, the
sensuous curves of the columns appear light and ethereal, a lightness
augmented by the fact that there is nothing above that they are
supporting. Of course, at one level the intention is to frame the
main altar, itself strategically placed above where St Peter's bones
are believed to lie. But to suggest that this is the primary impact of
the ensemble would be true only for those who place factual
knowledge above visual impression. Looking directly the length
of St Peter's, what above all confronts the eye is the way in which
those pillars frame the view beyond of St Peter's chair, thus greatly
adding to the existing upward thrust of that chair, generated by
its already raised position within its own sculpted complex.
Because nothing presses down on the pillars, the overall impression
becomes one of the whole ensemble being pulled upwards by
the descending dove of the Holy Spirit at the top and its
accompanying rays of light. The overall message is thus not simply
of the weight and majesty of the pope, a purely physical presence
as it were, but rather of that sacramental body being drawn
upwards to be in turn pulled downwards by those sinuous curves

---

[84] Johns notes an increasing stress in the late eighteenth century on 'delicacy'
and 'sensibility' that was to result in all such objects being locked up in an area of
the British Museum precluded from public access for almost two centuries: *Sex or
Symbol?*, 15. Contrast this with the notorious behaviour of members of the
contemporary Hell-Fire Club.

[85] R. Wittkower, *Bernini*, 3rd edn (London: Phaidon, 1981), 13.

once more into the liturgical performance of the mass under the guidance of the Spirit.[86] In achieving that effect, the light, sensuous curves of the pillars play no small part.

This is not to suggest that all Bernini's religious works have this dual quality of sensual body mediating elevated spirit. Far from it! In his translation of the story of the prophet Habbakuk being summoned to feed Daniel, for example, the body of Daniel is used to convey intense prayer and that of Habbakuk puzzlement and resistance, but in neither case would one wish to speak of sensuousness.[87] Even where the total complex was under Bernini's charge as at Sant'Andrea al Quirinale, the temptation is sometimes resisted. Although the statue above the picture of Andrew's martyrdom is used to point to the saint's eventual status in heaven (his body is already rising on a cloud), there is nothing to suggest a sensuous martyr either here or in the picture beneath. Of course, it could be argued that this is because painting and statue were commissioned under Bernini's direction rather than directly produced by him. Certainly, it is true that he could produce sensuous martyrs, as for example in his *St Sebastian*.[88] My suspicion is that he did not think it appropriate here, and for one obvious reason. The painting actually celebrated a lack of sensuousness, a lack of movement, in recording the legend of how Andrew refused to come down from the cross when given the chance to do so. He was immobilized so to speak, so strong was his determination to fulfil the divine will. Such commitment was the message the Jesuits wanted for this, their novices' church. That being so, to introduce curves, softness or suppleness of body would clearly have conflicted in the context with the necessary unambiguous expression of such an ideal of unyielding resolve.[89]

---

[86] The lightness of the columns is best seen in a colour photograph: ibid. 202. Unfortunately, this shot faces the wrong way to illustrate the framing of the whole complex, but for this in black and white, see ibid. 125.

[87] For illustrations, see ibid. 64–6. The statues are in the Chigi Chapel of Santa Maria del Popolo. The story is to be found at the conclusion of the Apocryphal additions to the Book of Daniel.

[88] For an illustration and commentary, see Plate 1 at the end of this book.

[89] For St Sebastian, see Wittkower, *Bernini*, 18; for a detailed account of the Sant'Andrea project, see G. Careri, *Bernini: Flights of Love, the Art of Devotion* (Chicago: University of Chicago Press, 1995), 87–101.

But elsewhere this was far from being so. Perhaps the easiest way of approaching the issue is by stages, and so to look at three projects that illustrate progressively greater degrees of engagement with the sensual and ultimately sexual body as a way of communicating spirituality. Bernini's first biographer described his ability to integrate sculpture, painting and architecture in a single ensemble as his *bel composto* technique.[90] A good example of this is the Fonseca Chapel in the church of San Lorenzo in Lucina. Here we have a bust of the individual looking heavenwards and being caught by the gaze of a cherub who draws his gaze into the painting beneath, which is a copy of an Annunciation by Guido Reni, Bernini's favourite contemporary painter. What is particularly interesting is the way in which an attractive black angel beneath parallels Mary's receptive pose. Fonseca, and thus viewers in general as they come to appreciate the dynamics of the interaction, are progressively drawn into a receptivity that is at one and the same time physical and spiritual, and that means a body which is shown to be yielding and pliant. Significantly, one commentator talks of the angel 'not communicating a piece of information but transmitting an attitude' and so 'the sacramental power of the mystery of the incarnation', with 'the sensibility of the body' as a result 'not opposed to the spirituality of the soul but rather its imaginary extension'.[91]

Much more pliant still is what is perhaps Bernini's most famous statue, *The Ecstasy of St Teresa*.[92] Here too there is an audience, as members of the Cornaro family in two opera-like boxes are made to discuss what is taking place below them. Teresa herself may have been unaware of the possible sexual connotations of the description she offers of her experience. However, it is certain that Bernini could have entertained no such doubts. In his early life he had had a mistress (the wife of one of his employees). Although his eventual marriage was to someone much younger and his social inferior, it does seem to have been happy, as well as fruitful—he fathered no fewer than eleven children.[93] On the other side it might be argued

[90] F. Baldinucci, *Vita di Bernini* (Milan: Edizioni di Milione, 1948; 1st publ. 1682).

[91] Careri, *Bernini*, 38, 42.

[92] In the Cornaro Chapel in Santa Maria della Vittoria, Rome.

[93] For his mistress, Constanza, and subsequent marriage, see H. Hibbard, *Bernini* (London: Penguin, 1965), 101–5, 114–15; for Teresa's own description, 137.

that by the time of this composition Bernini was very devout, attending mass each morning and returning again for vespers in the evening.[94] But one needs to recall that the piety encouraged by both the Jesuits and Oratorians of the time (the two orders with whom he was most intimately connected) demanded a lively and imaginative engagement with the narration of spiritual events. Although there is little from the time to suggest that the making explicit of the sexual analogy would have been acceptable, that is quite different from supposing that it might not be allowed to lie there implicitly, and so to be absorbed into the consciousness that way. Not only was there scriptural precedent in the way the Song of Songs was traditionally understood, but also numerous other paintings around, as we shall see, that worked on a similar level. Therefore, if one must concede that protests against nudity were common at the time, the surprise is that objections to sexual allusion are much less frequent. So perhaps we have to express matters differently for that culture than for our own post-Victorian and post-Freudian world. Sexual imagery could be used of mystical experience, provided it remained implicit. Presumably, the thought was that it remained a legitimate metaphor for the spiritual transformation that was occurring, because God created both alike.

Precisely because it is a little more extreme, Bernini's memorial portrayal of Ludovica Albertoni constitutes in some ways a more interesting test case.[95] For Whittkower she is in the agonies of death, but this is surely implausible since she did not die a martyr, or in some other out-of-the-ordinary circumstance.[96] In the painting above her recumbent figure Anne is receiving the Christ-child from Mary. So it is interesting to speculate whether there is not a similar, less literal reception taking place in the statue beneath. Ludovica lies on a bed in which the sheets are crumpled, and her clothes likewise, indeed in a manner that makes them gather in folds about her groin. Her face suggests both the pain and ecstasy of a transforming experience. That sexuality is being used once more as the relevant metaphor is suggested not only by the facts already indicated but also by a number of other, accompanying

[94] See Wittkower, *Bernini*, 196, for some other details.

[95] In the church of San Francesco a Ripa, Rome. For illustration and further commentary, see Plate 3 at the end of this book.

[96] Wittkower, *Bernini*, 58.

features. So, for instance, the emblem of the heart is repeated more
than once, while roses being scattered in the painting could be
taken, as indeed they often are, as a symbol of love or marriage.
One notes too the repeated use of pomegranates, sometimes
open, sometimes closed. It is hard not to detect at the very least
sensuous fruitfulness, if not something more sexually pertinent.[97]
My suggestion therefore would be that Bernini is indeed using
sexual metaphor here, but provided we understand it sacramentally
there is no need for any embarrassment on our part. Because we
know Bernini to have been devout, there can be no suggestion
of any attempt at reductionism or mockery. Indeed, quite the
opposite is suggested, that the sexual body is being treated seriously
as a sacramental sign of a potential for still greater and deeper
ecstasy, in which individuals can be united not just with one
another but also with the source of all that is, in God.

Caravaggio, Modern Projections and Earlier Values

Scholars note Bernini's indebtedness to Caravaggio. However,
readers may well doubt whether a similar approach can be applied
to the works of someone like Caravaggio, whose religious commitment is now so frequently called into question. Indeed, for many it
may seem that Bernini was in the end led down a false trail by
Caravaggio, and that is precisely why it is just as difficult to take
Bernini's sexual allusions seriously in our own day as those of
Caravaggio. But what I want to suggest instead is that the modern
tendency to secularize Caravaggio is entirely misconceived. His
works are still best understood within a religious framework, and
that is why Bernini is quite properly seen as one of his heirs.

Certainly, there is no shortage of contemporary writers who
want to place Michelangelo Merisi da Caravaggio (1573–1610) in
an entirely secular context. Indeed, one recent biography wants to
see nothing more than veneer in the apparently religious content of
so many of his works: Caravaggio's actual aim is the presentation
of a purely human reality without any of the customary supernatural props of the time and with all the dirt, violence and lust that
the actual world so often presents. Let me offer a few examples at

---

[97] I am heavily indebted at this point to Careri's acute observations: *Bernini*,
51–86, esp. 68–71.

random. Caravaggio's *Francis and the Angel* becomes 'an erotic take on saintly ecstasy': the saint 'sinking back between the angel's adolescent thighs' gives clue enough to its real, affective meaning. Again, *Rest on the Flight into Egypt* is an exercise in 'serene and gentle humour' inasmuch as only the donkey is 'looking really appreciative of the heavenly performer's music', while the performing angel himself is 'oblivious of the way the sight of his own pale adolescent nudity lit up the country stopover'. Finally, *The Call of Matthew* is described as 'purged of ... transcendental messages', with 'a sense of imminence, if not immanence' in the demand for action on the part of Matthew.[98] The tone of another recent study is set by the title of its opening chapter, 'The Artist as Outlaw', and its very first sentence: 'His life was sulphurous and his painting scandalous.' Throughout the assumption is that the rejections Caravaggio received were natural from anyone of religious sensibility: 'the Carmelites rejected the picture, needlessly to say'; 'the real patrons could hardly accept this'.[99] It is also the image that is portrayed in *Caravaggio* (1986), Derek Jarman's film of his life. Admittedly, some attempt is made to convey the passion in his painting (symbolized by the grinding and mixing of his materials) but where the main focus lies is in a wild and violent bisexual life, with the weight given to his homosexuality as in the director's own lifestyle. Significantly, religion again plays no part. Quotations from the Song of Songs are given purely secular application, while a crucifix offered by a Dominican friar to Caravaggio on his deathbed is violently thrown across the room.[100]

From the title of its opening chapter, 'Sexy Secrets', it might seem that yet another work on the artist is destined to move in exactly the same direction. But the author is soon suggesting that

[98] P. Robb, *M* (London: Bloomsbury, 2000), 77–8, 81–2, 124–5. The tone is maintained throughout. *The Martyrdom of Matthew* provides occasion to speak of 'thuggish nudes ... in a steam bath atmosphere' (134). With the *Rest on the Flight into Egypt*, Robb fails to consider that the joke might be at our expense rather than that of the Holy Family: the angel's nudity is covered for us because the viewer may find it problematic, whereas it is exposed to the Holy Family because we know that they will not.

[99] G. Lambert, *Caravaggio* (Cologne: Taschen, 2000), 7, 64, 75. The two paintings being referred to are *Death of the Virgin* and *Madonna dei Palafranieri*.

[100] In *Caravaggio* Jarman does at least hint that he is not offering a purely historical portrait, through his occasional references to more recent times, as in the use of typewriters.

'even the most languorous gay reader' will raise 'a virile shout'
against some of the common motives for attributing homosexuality
to Caravaggio, most notably in the 'limpness' of some of his painted
youths.[101] That of itself is scarcely sufficient counter-argument.
What is more surprising, given all the certainty with which the
issue seems currently to be treated, is the fact that there is really
very little firm evidence beyond the pictures themselves to
determine the matter either way. While it is incontestable that
Caravaggio led a violent and tempestuous life that included murder
and spells in prison, the occasional references to his homosexuality
are usually ambiguous or late or both. Such accounts were in any
case easily explicable in terms of the common calumnies of the
time, whereas there is no doubt that he frequented female
prostitutes and had affairs with them.[102] I say this not because
I would think any less of him as an artist if he were shown to
have been a practising homosexual. Rather, the point is that current
attempts to make him into a gay icon are not only thoroughly
unhistorical, they also prevent us from seeing that the body could
be read in a different way within his culture from our own, a
way that included religious belief. Homosexual acts at this time
in Rome in any case carried the death penalty and so Caravaggio
would have had to be relatively clandestine.[103] That argues against
explicit reference in his painting, while the fact that his patrons
were mostly religious (cardinals, religious orders and so forth)
must have meant that they perceived more than just the pretence
of religion in his works. That is why I find the suggestion from
the authors of 'Sexy Secrets' that the real clue to Caravaggio should
be sought elsewhere, in a general decentring of any privileged
position within the canvas, as no more satisfactory than the gay
explanation.[104]

None of this is to deny that some of Caravaggio's œuvre is
secular. So, although attempts have been made to impose religious

---

[101] L. Bersani and U. Dutoit, *Caravaggio's Secrets* (Cambridge, Mass.: MIT
Press, 1998), 9.

[102] For the evidence and its flimsy character, see C. Gilbert, *Caravaggio and his
Two Cardinals* (University Park, Penn.: Pennsylvania State University Press, 1995).

[103] This contrasts with an estimated 13,000 female prostitutes in a city of just
over 100,000 permanent inhabitants: H. Langdon, *Caravaggio: A Life* (London:
Chatto and Windus, 1998), 143–4.

[104] Bersani and Dutoit, *Caravaggio's Secrets*, esp. 73, 99.

(allegorical) meanings on such paintings as *Boy with Basket of Fruit*, *The Sick Bacchus*, *Boy Bitten by a Lizard* and so forth, I shall not seek to follow suit here. Nonetheless, it is worth recalling that the line between religious and secular was not nearly as fast or firm as most are inclined to draw it today. Certainly, Federico Borromeo, cousin and successor of the more famous and saintly Charles as Archbishop of Milan, not only acquired the artist's *Basket of Fruit* but also ascribed a religious meaning to it.[105] Indeed, Borromeo's acquisitions provide a useful lesson in never lightly assuming our own presumptions and perceptions to be also those of another age. To us Titian's *Penitent Magdalen* immediately suggests a mere excuse for the painting of a near-nude female. But that was not how Borromeo would have seen it (he owned a copy), nor indeed a very large number, perhaps even the majority, of his contemporaries. For the body was read symbolically as well as literally, as a vehicle both of potential glory and of possible downfall. If her voluptuous breasts represent an allusion to one key element in her presumed former trade, they also provided a way of carrying the viewer's initial, primarily erotic attraction onto a new and deeper plane, with the breasts now symbolic of the fruitfulness of the religious life.[106] Of course, things were changing to some degree. Not many years previously, the order had been given that the genitalia of Michelangelo's figures in the Sistine Chapel should be covered.[107] Yet one should not mistake that instruction for a general hostility to near-nudity, since this continues to remain a prominent feature in the sensuousness of much Baroque art.

The point can perhaps be pursued by asking what it was that led to the rejection of so many of Caravaggio's canvases. Modern commentators commonly point to hostility to sexual connotations, but this ought seriously to be questioned. Although we have no

---

[105] Langdon, *Caravaggio*, 116–19. All nature, even the most humble objects such as 'windfall apples and bruised pears', spoke of God.

[106] For Borromeo and some evidence of this kind of thinking, though the author doubts its power to persuade, see F. Mormando, 'Teaching the Faithful to Fly: Mary Magdalene and Peter in Baroque Italy', in F. Mormando (ed.), *Saints and Sinners: Caravaggio and the Baroque Image* (Boston: McMullen Museum of Art, 1999), 107–35, esp. 117. Note that the version now in Florence offers a more *déshabillé* Mary than that in Leningrad.

[107] The act was entrusted in the 1560s to his deathbed friend, Daniele da Volterra, earning him the nickname *Il Braghettone* (the breeches-maker).

definite evidence either way, other reasons do seem more plausible. Take, for instance, his two versions of *St Matthew and the Angel*. In the final version the boy angel is now in the sky instead of positioned close to Matthew and with his hand guiding Matthew's own. From this difference it might seem plausible to postulate worries about potential erotic implications in the earlier version, but in fact there is a much more obvious reason to hand: Matthew's bare feet would have been directly over the elevated host, projecting as they do out of the canvas.[108] Not only that, we know from the work of other painters that young angel and old man just as close to each other could be acceptable elsewhere.[109] Again, *The Death of the Virgin*, it is proposed, was rejected because Caravaggio chose as his model a local prostitute, while insufficient respect for Mary is indicated in the Virgin's feet being exposed and bare. Since, however, the commission was for the Discalced Carmelites, they could scarcely object to bare feet without undermining their own order. Again, in a city of a hundred thousand any resemblance to one far-from-prominent individual would surely in any case soon disappear from public consciousness. So much more likely as a cause for the rejection is the absence of any obvious connection with Mary's subsequent assumption, though the great red curtain in the background does seem to hint at a drama to come.[110] To my mind the only instance where sexually related considerations are likely to have played a role is in the rejection from St Peter's of the *Madonna dei palafrenieri*, in which Christ as a young child crushing a serpent appears naked. Since the work is throughout compatible with the theology of the time, it is hard to think of any other reason than this new sensitivity to total nudity.[111]

[108] For the two versions placed side by side, see J. Gash, *Caravaggio* (London: Jupiter, 1980), 66–7. Gash, wrongly in my view, emphasizes as the real motive the erotic content of the earlier version (destroyed in the bombardment of Berlin in 1945).

[109] As in Nicolas Régnier's painting with the same title from *c.* 1625: illustrated in Mormando (ed.), *Saints and Sinners*, pl. 14.

[110] Here at least Gash is more perceptive: *Caravaggio*, 104. Contrast Lambert, *Caravaggio*, 64. Even Robb concedes that 'not everyone thought that the supine figure looked like' the prostitute in question, while in any case 'where else could painters get their models?': *M*, 289–94.

[111] This is to disagree with some commentators, who think that the cardinals were afraid that Caravaggio had perhaps carried a papal bull of 1560 (which spoke of Mary's participatory role in our salvation) too far: e.g. H. Hibbard, *Caravaggio* (London: Thames and Hudson, 1983), 197–8.

Just as resistance to nudity is wrongly fused in the modern mind into a general objection to the body (I shall shortly provide further examples of contemporary acceptance of the sensual body), so advocacy of decorum is often misinterpreted as rejection of the presentation of the Christian story in very ordinary contexts. But it is one thing to object to feet dangling above the sacred host, quite another to criticize them for being bare or dirty as such. Some of course did, but even in such cases the argument should not necessarily be reduced to the supposition that the incarnation involved no such abasement. Rather, a different strategy of engagement with the Christian tradition was being envisaged, one in which viewers were to be drawn into an alternative and ideal world rather than made to face the fact that God identified with our world exactly as it is. So rather more is at stake when we compare Mary as aged nun in Caravaggio's *Entombment* with the Madonna of so many Renaissance artists such as Raphael or Michelangelo.[112] Although the founder of the Oratorians, St Philip Neri (d. 1595), was severely ill and already largely confined to his quarters by the time Caravaggio arrived in Rome, there can be little doubt that his whole approach to spirituality has had its influence on the artist, as would Jesuit advocacy of imaginative identification with the life of Christ.[113] Although Caravaggio's *Entombment* was accepted for the Oratorian church, the Chiesa Nuova, and it is only for purely historical reasons that the original is no longer there, it is worth observing that, however beautiful we judge that church now to be, its current artistic splendour speaks little of Neri's original ideals, which were precisely those of realism and a strong identification with Rome's poor.[114] Rather

[112] One writer does declare that 'the *Entombment* is as tragic as Michelangelo's Pietà'. While true, the effect is achieved quite differently. Mary's face is now worn and lined, unlike Michelangelo's virgin, who is as young as her son. For comment and illustration, see A. Moir, *Caravaggio* (London: Thames and Hudson, 1989 edn), 96–7.

[113] W. Friedlaender, *Caravaggio Studies* (Princeton: Princeton University Press, 1955), 123–30. In L. Ponnelle and L. Bordet, *St Philip Neri and the Roman Society of his Times* (London: Sheed and Ward, 1979 edn) one notes a number of points of potential relevance to Caravaggio: the earliest origins of the Oratory in a concern to care for the poor (107–11); the use of music, light and drama in the attempt to win over the ordinary populace (217–18, 224–6); Philip's physicality in his relations with others—'caresses' and 'blows' (135–8).

[114] The original was removed by the French invading army in 1797, and, when returned, placed in the Vatican Gallery, where it remains.

than the work of Pietro da Cortona and others, it is the dirty, barefooted pilgrims in Caravaggio's *Madonna of Loreto* that more adequately conforms to the saint's way of approaching issues, as does the shabby clothing of his two *Suppers at Emmaus*.[115]

Inevitably, such an attitude to human beings' more superficial features such as dirty feet and torn clothes carried with it further implications. The bodies themselves also became more everyday, as did divine interaction with them. This is often expressed in terms of the elimination of the supernatural. If by this is meant artificial props for identifying the divine (such as haloes), that is of course true. But of itself this scarcely entails a purely secular landscape. The signs are still there, only in a new, more ambiguous but ultimately more realistic form. I have already mentioned the great red curtain in Caravaggio's *Death of the Virgin*. This is a pattern repeated frequently elsewhere. So, for instance, an earlier version of the *Conversion of Saul* had Christ appearing in the sky supported by an angel. This was replaced by light alone producing its impact. Thereby not only did the scene become more biblical, it also presented the viewer with a less artificial scenario (even the rump of Paul's horse is illuminated).[116] Again, no angel is present to aid Mary Magdalene in her ecstasy but we are left in no doubt about the depth of her experience. A number of commentators choose to emphasize the darkness of the background as symptomatic of Caravaggio's feelings at this time, but more pertinent surely is the way in which bodily imagery perfectly captures an internal mood, not least the prominent ear, rather than the more traditional elevation of her body, being used to indicate her heavenly raptures.[117]

---

[115] The earlier version in London dates from 1601; the later (now in the Brera Gallery in Milan), from 1606. The poverty of the clothes in the latter is less pronounced, but the meal has become simpler (only bread and wine), with the tablecloth correspondingly more altar-like. For illustration, see Gash, *Caravaggio*, 81.

[116] More biblical, that is, if the versions in Acts are accepted and Paul in 1 Corinthians 15 is not taken to be laying claim to an actual physical appearance at this time.

[117] This *Magdalen in Ecstasy* of 1606 (in a Roman private collection) should be contrasted with his much earlier *Penitent Magdalen* of 1597 (in the Galleria Doria Pamphilj). Hibbard speaks of it expressing the artist's 'desperation' (*Caravaggio*, 211), Langdon of it being 'a stark image of exile, of anguish and guilt' (*Caravaggio*, 316), but I wonder if this is to deduce too much from the wider context of his life (he had recently killed a man). Gash offers what seems to me a more balanced estimate (*Caravaggio*, 106).

Likewise, in his *St Francis* the signs of the stigmata have been reduced to the minimum.[118] Obviously, some allusion had still to be made, in order to identify the reference. But, so far from sexuality taking over, as some have claimed, one observes that the groin area is made deliberately concave to preclude any such reading. What has happened is that it is now the reality of the internal experience that is being emphasized, with the body its appropriate vehicle and symbol, as in its obvious receptivity.[119]

This is not to say that a more aggressive sexuality does not obtrude elsewhere. The tautness of some of the male bodies in *The Martyrdom of Matthew* and in *The Taking of Christ* is undoubtedly being used to suggest alternative types of potential: violence versus commitment to the divine will. In the Matthew painting the near-naked men in the foreground are in fact preparing for baptism, while the individual at the centre of the action is launching the full force of his destructive energies against one of God's saints. Similarly, in the other painting Christ's arrest is presented as the moment for taking sides, for using one's potential one way or another, and so violence and drama are entirely appropriate in highlighting the choice.[120] Christ's hands are tensed in his firm resolve, while the dawn of recognition on Judas' face is obvious as he withdraws from his kiss, having just realized what he has done. That kiss was clearly on the mouth. However much it may surprise us now, that is precisely where in the past it would have been expected to be placed.[121] So it betokens no covert gay protest on Caravaggio's part. Indeed, among artists of the period there is no shortage of other, equally, and sometimes much more intimate, kisses.[122]

---

[118] Only the wound on the chest remains. Nothing is visible on the hands, and there is no heavenly vision. For illustration, see Moir, *Caravaggio*, 59.

[119] That is why in my view it succeeds better than Orazio Gentileschi's version, where the saint turns away from us into an angel's arms: illustrated in B. L. Brown, *The Genius of Rome: 1592–1623* (London: Royal Academy of Arts, 2001), 268. The painting is now in the Prado in Madrid.

[120] For illustration and further commentary, see Plate 4 at the end of this book.

[121] F. Mormando, 'Judas Iscariot and the Kiss of Betrayal', in Mormando (ed.), *Saints and Sinners*, 179–90, esp. 184–6. Even in the fifth century the poet Sedulius was making just such an assumption.

[122] Note, for instance, the treatment given by Lodovico Carracci in a painting of 1590: Mormando (ed.), *Saints and Sinners*, pl. 28, or that from an anonymous Flemish artist *c.* 1615, pl. 29.

However, I do not think that we should jump from this fact to the opposite extreme, and suppose that there is only ever sexual metaphor in Caravaggio. The relation between beauty and sexual attraction is complex and far from simple; sometimes the two go together and sometimes not. Fortunately, it is not relevant to our purposes here to explore why. What is relevant is to note that, just as the recognition of beauty in the body of another need not be taken to entail lust, so even sexual attraction should not always be assumed to imply the desire for this to be consummated in sexual intimacy. Sexual attractiveness is often a key element in drawing human beings closer to one another. Even where this is not unconscious or sublimated in some other way, it still will not necessarily follow that actual sexual activity must then move to the forefront of a person's consciousness. In our own day self-imposed censors are less firmly in control. That is why for some it is difficult to appreciate how much in the past sexual *frisson* and restraint could be held in creative tension. Something like this is what I suggest is being employed by Caravaggio (as indeed by many other artists). That would mean that there could be a sexual element in Judas' reaction to Jesus, without this automatically having to be read as entailing some kind of homosexual relationship or even unrequited gay love.

Of course, it is easier to concede such attraction in the case of obviously idealized bodies, for then it may be said that nothing sordid enters into the picture. That would explain why viewers experience less difficulty with the implicit sexual element in Rubens' muscular Christs, who seem so alive even in death. It also might make more acceptable the fashion that was becoming current at this time of portraying pastoral care in terms of an angel or St Irene attending the wounds of a St Sebastian who is both aesthetically charged and erotically beautiful.[123] The beauty of the body added to the sense of violation, and its sensuousness to the contrasting spiritual transformation (no longer the bareness of nakedness but the catching up into a new life).[124] But Caravaggio carried the process one stage further, with an erotic beauty much

---

[123] For a relevant example of Rubens' Christs, see Brown, *The Genius of Rome*, 200; for examples of this treatment of Sebastian by Baglione and Rubens, and a discussion of the introduction of this theme, 282–5. For a particularly sensuous example by Seiter, see Mormando (ed.), *Saints and Sinners*, pl. 18.

[124] As in the example from Margery Kempe mentioned earlier in the chapter.

nearer to the streets in some of his paintings. So we must face the issue of whether here, finally, he did overstep the mark, or whether it remains possible to defend his approach. His four to eight paintings of the young St John the Baptist are the obvious test cases, since there are large differences observable between at least some of them.[125]

Painting a young and beautiful Baptist had already become firmly established at the Renaissance. There is an especially fine example by Andrea del Sarto in which a muscular physique combines with gentle features and thoughtful gaze to suggest resolution for a difficult task.[126] Caravaggio's models are clearly more worldly. In one case it is difficult not to think of a rather sad street ruffian who has gone to seed, and so here I would suggest neither body nor mind make one think readily of God.[127] But in some of the other instances, even where the sexuality is quite explicit, there is more to be said on the other side. In a powerful variant from 1604–5 the body suggests an energy that it is difficult not to connect with sexuality, but this is balanced by the pose of the head and the dark, brooding eyes.[128] The net result is that one thinks at one and the same time of a deeply reflective mind and of a body ready to leap up at any instant. So I would suggest that in this case Caravaggio succeeds in conveying the vitality and depth of character that would have made John an enticing and attractive character, and in part this is achieved through the implied physical energy. In the only case where the boy is completely naked, commentators usually fight shy of any defence, and indeed it has been suggested that the work is merely a joke directed against the more famous

[125] How many depends partly on disputes about authenticity and partly on what is taken to indicate a significant difference and not just a minor variation in what is essentially a copy.

[126] For illustration and discussion, see A. Natali, *Andrea del Sarto* (New York: Abbeyville, 1999), 144, 148.

[127] The version in the Galleria Nazionale d'Arte Antica in Rome: illustrated in Gash, *Caravaggio*, 93. Much the same could also be said of the variant in the Galleria Borghese: illustrated in Bursani and Dutoit, *Caravaggio's Secrets*, 44. A version at the other extreme is the one in the museum of Toledo Cathedral, where there is innocence and an absence of sexuality but without any real feeling of depth: illustrated in Lambert, *Caravaggio*, 40.

[128] For black-and-white illustration and further commentary, see Plate 6 at the end of this book; for colour illustration, Brown, *Genius of Rome*, 299.

Michelangelo.[129] Certainly, there are clear elements of imitation, but that rather more is at stake and not just a joke or sex in the crudest sense is suggested by the vibrancy of the Baptist's pose. Moreover, the genital area is among the darkest in the painting. The viewer's line of vision is in fact taken up from the mullein (the saint's plant) at his feet through thighs, chest and head to the ram which the young lad is embracing, and so to the sacrifice of his cousin that he will foretell. The problem thus seems to me to lie not so much in the eroticism as in the fact that the work's religious import is conveyed through a dialogue between a not yet fully sexually awakened body and a mentally reflective ram. For that to work, a considerable effort of imagination is demanded, if the two are to interact in a way that will suggest the adult version of the boy combining both aspects as a true forerunner of Christ: that is, both energetic activity on behalf of God and perceptivity about Christ's future role.

This detailed discussion of Bernini and Caravaggio does, I think, have wider ramifications. Although our society is allegedly more open than previous generations on the subject of sexuality, it is in reality, it seems to me, still very much (in its reaction) a by-product of Victorian repression. The consequence is that it fails to engage adequately with the full breadth of the various ways in which sexuality can have an impact on us, and therefore reads narrowly paintings and sculptures that Christianity and religion generally ought really to reclaim as their own. Only then will the sensuous body once more speak of God no less than the safely but distantly beautiful.

Beauty and Sexuality in Today's World

Although attempting to draw some conclusions for today, most of my discussion of beauty and sexuality has had an historical focus. So here I want to add a few further remarks on possible implications for how the divine might be experienced in our own day.

---

[129] So Friedlaender, who talks of 'persiflage' and notes borrowings from an *ignudo* and from *The Sacrifice of Noah*, both in the Sistine Chapel. For an illustration, see Lambert, *Caravaggio*, 6.

Contemporary writers and preachers seldom encourage congregations to meditate on Renaissance or Romanesque depictions of the beauty of Christ. A crucifixion by Raphael would be quickly voted down in favour of the awfulness of Grünewald on grounds of greater realism. Comparable Byzantine presentations only survive on the pretext of some residual sense of mystery. I do find such judgements distinctly odd. It is almost as though modern Christians are incapable of any serious engagement with symbolism. Christ's body is beautiful on the cross not because there was any wish to deny the reality of Christ's suffering (indications are still there, for example in Raphael's case in blood dripping into chalices), but because there was a need to indicate how something more than ordinary human suffering was present. The beauty of Christ's body was there to suggest a human nature so intimately connected with the divine that it could triumph over suffering and death, and so open up a similar possibility for us also.

Of course it is not always with such an aim that Christ's body is rendered beautiful. Sometimes the point is power and self-sufficiency. As such it would seem to run counter to what is believed to have taken place in the incarnation, and so might seem singularly inappropriate in representing the human Christ. Even so, it could speak the truth, in drawing attention to the essential aseity of divinity, as source of all that is and not itself dependent on anything. Where it would go wrong is if such basic assumptions about divinity were then allowed to call into question the reality of the incarnation, or to provide an appropriate model for ourselves. That was one reason why I wanted to endorse the rather different types of representation of divinity seen in the beauty of an Apollo or a Buddha. Openness and accessibility need to be seen as attributes of divinity not just in the incarnation, but more widely. The danger is that when Christians' eyes are turned away from the historical reality, a God that refuses mutuality becomes once again the prevailing assumption.

Thus put, such observations are of course derived from, and based upon, Christian doctrine. But this is not the only way in which they might be supported. An experiential grounding might also be possible, in response to quite different artistic representations of divine beauty in human bodies, and the desire to complement one experience with the other rather than necessarily set them in opposition. Much the same might happen in contact with living human beings. Most of my examples have come from art, but those around us could also induct us into new ways of seeing the divine. Precisely because a beautiful woman is personal in obvious ways in which a beautiful landscape is not, sight of her might generate a fresh appreciation of the world more generally and thus also of the presumed source of such grace in God.

With sexuality one might actually start from the living being. Even with all the modern scientific aids to giving birth, parents still often experience the gift of a child as an awe-inspiring experience that reminds them of their essentially procreative role, acting on behalf of a greater than themselves. That used also to be the case in married relations more generally, as mutual love widened with the years to include a larger, extended family. Its very comprehensiveness helped to encourage a sense of a more all-encompassing love. Nowadays, however, heterosexual and homosexual relationships are alike more narrowly focused, and indeed one of the sad aspects of current disputes within the Church about the ethics of such relations is how the mutuality of a pair is presumed in itself of value without any further extension. Thereby is precluded the opening of the relation into an understanding of, or deeper grounding in, divine love.

More commonly expressed as a worry is the way in which in the main it was only male sexuality that was ever treated as a positive symbol. Female beauty was by contrast seen essentially as a problem, as a source of temptation from the Fall onwards. Some find the solution in new female representations, as in Edwina Sandys' *Christa*, which created such a storm of protest when it was first installed in the Anglican cathedral of St John the Divine in New York in 1983. But, as some female writers have also observed, so far from resolving the problem this may simply be to pose the same issues in a more acute form.[130] After all, the past history cannot be changed. Jesus was a man, and subsequent attitudes did turn out the way they did. Perhaps, though, matters are not quite so bad as they are sometimes presented. As soon as attention turns from the visual to the literary, there are much richer strains upon which to draw.[131] Again, even the visual tradition is not quite as wholly negative as is

[130] The conclusion of M. R. Miles, *Carnal Knowing: Female Nakedness and Religious Meaning in the Christian West* (London: Burns and Oates, 1992), 169–85, esp. 177–8.
[131] As Miles herself concedes: e.g. in her discussion of Hildegard of Bingen, *Carnal Knowing*, 99–105.

sometimes claimed. It is all too easy to detect misogyny every-where. Place Eve on God's left and she is made inferior to Adam, even if the serpent is situated on Adam's side, not Eve's.[132] Place her on a throne, and she becomes 'an enthroned temptress' threatening 'peasant Adam'. And so on. Moreover, however despised the female body may have been, it was never denied that it too had a glorious destiny in the resurrection of the dead.

Male as well as female artists were in fact capable of honouring the female body.[133] To present that body as sexually alluring as well as beautiful was not necessarily to dishonour it.[134] As I tried to indicate with Bernini's sculptures, female sexuality could be used within Christianity as a positive symbol. Equally, as some of the examples from Caravaggio indicate, the male sexual body could also be subject to similar treatment. So to my mind the real difficulty in trying to work towards a more balanced approach to representations of the sexes seems to me to lie not so much in past sexual attitudes as such as in the more deep-seated contrast between presumed forms of legitimate appropriation. While male nudity was given extensive metaphorical applications, apart from the regrettable imagery of the Fall this was not so with women. Instead, it was what they did with their bodies that counted, their caresses and their tears, if I can put it that briefly. The core was affective, and unfortu-nately inevitably, therefore, seen as secondary. While Christ, Peter and Paul modelled action, the two Marys (the Virgin and Mary Magdalene) were given an essentially responsive role. Certainly, it was assumed to be the right response for both male and female alike. But it was the male who was used to indicate the more primary position or act, to which the viewer or reader was then expected to respond. It is here that the more fundamental corrective is required, as will emerge more clearly in Chapter 4 when I turn to the body as 'ugly and wasted'. But, whether it is a matter of beauty

---

[132] My two examples come from P. H. Jolly, *Made in God's Image? Eve and Adam in the Genesis Mosaics at San Marco, Venice* (Berkeley: University of California Press, 1997), 54–5; 59 and 66.

[133] Female artists make a difference, but not necessarily as much as might have been expected. If Gentileschi offers heroic women, she can also provide ones naturally suited to the male gaze: M. D. Garland, *Artemisia Gentileschi* (Princeton: Princeton University Press, 1989), esp. 244–7 (on Cleopatra).

[134] K. Clark, *The Nude: A Study in Ideal Form* (Garden City, NY: Doubleday, 1956); *Feminine Beauty* (New York: Rizzoli, 1980).

and sexuality or forms of appropriation, men and women of our own day need to learn to transcend such limitations, and apply such insights indiscriminately across the sexes, rather than abandoning them altogether. Only that way will the cultural limitations of the past cease to act as a restraint on human experience. Instead of unnecessarily closing the door, physical beauty and sexuality may then once more open up ways towards experiencing the divine.

If that is still doubted, the way in which female sexuality is seen operating positively in dance, my next topic for discussion, may possibly lead readers to a change of mind.

2

The Dancer's Leap

To turn next to dance is not nearly as counter-intuitive as it might seem at first sight. In the previous chapter I examined the body functioning sacramentally in initiating experience of the divine. Two aspects were explored in some depth: the body as beautiful and the body as sexual. Each is capable of initiating or deepening experience of the divine. For the ancient world beauty was a sign of a divinely graced body. The gods had blessed humanity in this way with something of themselves and their own radiance. While it is just possible that the divine image in Genesis originally carried just such a meaning, it was only really in Renaissance art that Christianity once more came anywhere near to such a position, a view also to be found, as we observed, in Buddhism. Sexuality too could speak of the divine not just in the intimacy of sexual intercourse but also as a metaphor for fruitfulness and in the mere fact of attractiveness, men and women being thus drawn out of themselves. In dance it is precisely such attractive, graced beauty that dancers seek to present to us in their performance. It thus seems to me no accident that dance was once so central to worship. The complexity of movement that the dancer seeks to achieve, not least in lifts and leaps from the ground, hints at a world entered that is otherwise than our present flawed reality, and is thus symbolic of the possibility of a quite different form of joyful and ordered existence.

In making that claim I do not of course intend to imply that all dancing actually carries with it such a meaning or experience, only that it may under the right circumstances do so. Yet the remarkable thing is the actual degree to which, as we shall see, not only ancient traditions of dance have engaged with religious issues but also modern ballet and dance, and that despite virtually no encouragement from the churches. This is not to say that outside the Church such parallels remain entirely unobserved. Some will be mentioned later in this chapter. As a more general illustration, however, let me offer here the following on ballet class from an otherwise entirely secular work on the subject of dance:[1]

Sometimes when I look at my watch in the morning and notice that it is ten o'clock, I remember that at this particular hour in cities on every continent of the world a shared ritual is about to be enacted... This beautiful event has the quality of a secular liturgy, a celebration of the whole person, physical and spiritual. *Battements tendus, battements glissés, ronds de jambe à terre, grands battements, adage* and so on, an unquestioned devotion culminating in the joyful elevation of *grand allegro*.[2]

Although within contemporary Christianity there have been some attempts at revival, dance remains generally on the periphery of most Christians' consciousness, despite such inherent possibilities in the world of today. As with so many other areas of human life, religious belief and practice have set themselves apart. Indeed so much is this so that even those interested in the subject are seldom aware of how profound an association once existed between dance and religion generally. As I shall indicate in a moment, this quite different picture emerges not only from the continuing engagement that exists within several eastern religions but also from careful scrutiny of the Hebrew scriptures and of study of the situation in ancient Greece.

Occasional survivals in the history of Christianity could not prevent continuing accusations of potential licentiousness. The result has been the development of modern dance (including ballet) without any significant engagement by the Church or its theologians.[3] Nonetheless, such is the nature of this art form that choreographers and others have continued to wrestle with a potential religious dimension, and sometimes profoundly so. Religious experience through dance has thus in effect continued into the modern world

[1] The quotation is from D. H. Fraser, *Dancers* (Oxford: Phaidon, 1989), 22. I am grateful to Stephen Laird for drawing my attention to this work.

[2] *Allegro* is the third part of a traditional ballet class after the *adagio*, where the aim is to improve the liveliness of the dancers' performance and in particular their capacity to turn and leap at three levels: *terre à terre* (for very fast footwork), mid-level, and maximum height.

[3] An interesting exception in the late nineteenth century was Stewart Headlam, who defended the sacramentality of ballet (and of the music hall). For further details, see J. R. Orens, *Stewart Headlam's Radical Anglicanism: The Mass, the Masses, and the Music Hall* (Urbana, Ill.: University of Illinois Press, 2003).

but without the benefit of any creative interaction with Christianity. In what follows, therefore, my discussion proceeds by two stages. In the first half of the chapter I offer a largely historical examination of dance as it has functioned in various religiously sanctioned roles. Then, secondly, thereafter follows an exploration of how, despite its avowedly 'secular' context, the religious dimension does often still emerge in ballet and modern dance, though almost invariably without any hint of worship.

Dance and Worship

Here I want to begin with the Bible but then extend our discussion more widely, first to a western culture contemporary with the Hebrew scriptures, that of ancient Greece. Thereafter I shall turn to eastern religions, and explore some manifestations of continuing interest in Hinduism and Buddhism (Tibetan and Zen). Finally, I shall return to the western monotheisms, and note some survivals remaining in Islam and Judaism and to a lesser degree in Christianity also.

The Centrality of Dance for Ancient Greece and Israel

Undoubtedly the two most familiar references to dance in the Bible are the verse in the Old Testament that describes how 'David danced before the Lord with all his might' (2 Sam. 6.14) and that in the New which forms the culmination of the story of Salome's dance before her father, Herod Antipas: 'I want you to give me at once the head of John the Baptist on a platter' (Mark 6.25). In the latter case there is the drama of Herod trapped by his earlier promise; in the former, the contemptuous reaction of David's wife, Michal.[4] Both incidents associate dance with immodesty.[5] That is no doubt one reason why a suspicion of dance has periodically resurfaced within the Christian tradition; why too in both art and music Salome has come to encapsulate a dangerous

---

[4] Salome is not in fact named in the New Testament; this information comes from Josephus, *Antiquities* 18.136.

[5] Although strictly speaking David was not naked (he wore a linen 'ephod'), it must have been little more than a loincloth to justify Michal's rebuke that he was exposing himself: cf. 2 Sam. 6.20.

seductiveness in dance. Gustave Moreau (the teacher of Georges Rouault, often regarded as the greatest religious painter of the twentieth century) created a sensation in 1874 with his two paintings of the scene.[6] They helped inspire Oscar Wilde's play *Salome*, which in turn generated the still more controversial opera by Richard Strauss, first performed in 1905.[7] Dramatic tension in the opera is reinforced by the nature of the accompanying music. The composer set lyrical vocal melodies against a highly unusual chromatic and contrapuntal foundation. The erotic tension culminates in Salome's dance with its famous Dance of the Seven Veils, only to intensify further as an exhausted Herod orders his own daughter's death. His desire for her turns to disgust and rage when he sees Salome kiss the dead head's lips. She clearly prefers the dead prophet to the living king, and so he commands his soldiers to kill her.

Yet despite such apparent Christian hostility to dance, were one to examine the biblical witness as a whole, a quite different pattern would begin to emerge: no longer occasional, largely hostile reference but rather a sustained pattern of allusion that is often positive in its content. The problem is that nowadays not only do these other allusions to dance tend to be downplayed but also images of movement which resemble those of dance come to be treated as 'mere metaphors'. Take, for instance, these words from the Beatitudes: 'Blessed are you when men hate...and revile you... Rejoice in that day, and leap for joy, for behold, your reward is great in heaven' (Luke 6.22). The leap is in fact one of the main movements in dance, central to ballet as to many other forms of dancing. Sometimes, as we shall see, in the modern art form such leaps are used to indicate a transcendent dimension, and that is clearly also the case here. Thus, although dancing our way to heaven may initially appear to be a quite unbiblical image, once we start rummaging around, the verse from Luke is soon found to be by no means an isolated instance. Indeed, even as early as the

---

[6] For the two paintings and discussion, see G. Lacambre (ed.), *Gustave Moreau: Between Epic and Dream* (Chicago: Art Institute of Chicago, 1999), 164–71.

[7] In Germany the Kaiser allowed a performance only on condition that the star of Bethlehem was made to appear at the end (an odd requirement since Christ was already an adult by this time). In England no replica of the Baptist's head was allowed to appear and indeed his name had to be changed to the more indefinite 'the Prophet'.

following chapter we find Jesus comparing his own ministry to one of piping and dancing (Luke 7.32). A few chapters later, the return of the prodigal son is also seen as requiring a dance of celebration (15.23–25). But to find exactly the same Greek word as in Luke 6, with its mention of a 'leap for joy' (v. 23), we must return to Luke's infancy narrative, where the child within Elizabeth's womb is described as also leaping for joy, as it encounters Jesus for the first time (1.41, 44).[8] Birth and new birth are thus seen, as it were, as two sides of the same coin, both alike evoking imagery of the dance.

In the Hebrew scriptures language for dance is also used to describe such varied activities as the 'skipping' and 'gambolling' of animals, labour pains, and the fall of a warrior.[9] If the last two comparisons indicate the possible inclusion of painful events, and dancing in the context of mourning suggests this also, overwhelmingly the references are to joyful human celebrations: 'Thou hast turned my laments into dancing' (Ps. 30.11 NEB). One indicator of how frequently relationships with God were established through dance is in the range of vocabulary employed. One scholar detects at least ten different Hebrew words in use, with meanings that include the following: 'dance in a circle', 'turn about', 'skip', 'jump', 'whirl', 'pirouette', 'limp' and 'play'.[10] Although the derivation of the term 'Passover' from a limping dance is now widely discounted, the centrality of dance to Israel's rites of worship is not.[11] It suggests the transformation of experience that comes through close identification with, and vindication by, God. As Second Isaiah promises: 'Then shall the lame dance like a hart, and the tongue of the dumb sing for joy' (35.6).[12]

---

[8] In the Septuagint the Greek verb *skirtao* is also used of the skipping of sheep and other animals.

[9] For animals, see Ps. 29.6; Isa. 13.21; for labour pains, Isa. 21.3; for a warrior's fall, Ezek. 30.4.

[10] M. I. Gruber, 'Ten Dance-Derived Expressions in the Hebrew Bible', *Biblica* 62 (1981), 328–46.

[11] The derivation is rejected by Gruber (ibid. 340–1). A limping dance is attributed to the priests of Baal in 1 Kings 18.26. It is also the movement adopted to circumambulate the Kaaba by modern pilgrims at Mecca.

[12] I have substituted 'dance' for the more literal 'leap', to remind the reader that the word is the same as that used for a human leap in dance. Despite most translations favouring the former, the parallel with song in the second half of the verse surely suggests that song and dance should be more explicitly linked.

On quite a few occasions dancing and mourning are treated as opposites.[13] One commentator goes so far as to conclude: 'Worshippers drink the springs of divine life; their dance betokens the height of life, being the antithesis of the rolling of mourners in the valley of the death-shadow.'[14] Elsewhere, he talks of mourning as an 'anti-dance'. However, the actions of mourners did include crouching and rolling on the ground as well as breast-beating. So it is far from clear that such bodily movements should be classified as belonging to a wholly different category. Certainly, as we shall see in a moment, in other religions dancing was seen as essential to mourning, precisely as a way of transforming the purely negative connotations of what had just happened to a loved one. So it is not impossible that Jewish mourning rites also involved a positive role for dancing.[15] Such an inclusive contribution would chime well with the experience of the prophets. Although our only direct reference to prophets dancing is to those of Baal, it is probable that Yahweh's did likewise.[16] Ecstasy, song and dance form a natural alliance, but none need speak only of joy.

Rather than the male prophet, however, in the Hebrew Bible it is primarily women who are honoured for their dancing. The Shulammite woman, for example, is praised for the grace of her movements, as she weaves between her fellow-dancers; again, the men watch as the girls of Shiloh come out to dance in the vineyards.[17] The latter gives us an inkling of how harvest festivals might once have been celebrated. Less congenial to the modern imagination is the key role played by women in celebrating the ending of war. It is not so much how the women were employed as the fact that this was seen as an essentially religious activity. In ancient Israel, however, war was a sacred action, undertaken at the behest of the

[13] e.g. Eccles. 3.4: 'a time for mourning and a time for dancing'.

[14] J. H. Eaton, 'Dancing in the Old Testament', *Expository Times* 86 (1975), 136–40, esp. 139. For mourning as anti-dance, see 137. For the more detailed discussion upon which this article is dependent, see his pamphlet *Worship and Dance* (Birmingham: Institute for the Study of Worship and Religious Architecture, 1975).

[15] Given the lack of positive aspects to the afterlife in earlier Hebrew attitudes, the positive side in the dance would be more to do with changing the feelings of the mourners, partly through purgation of emotion, partly through recognition of what had been achieved by the dead person.

[16] So Eaton, 'Dancing', 138–9.

[17] S. of S. 6.13 (I assume the NEB translation to be the correct one); Judg. 21.21.

deity, and so victory too needed a sacred response.[18] The returning men were, therefore, welcomed back in a religious celebration led by the women. So, despite the more familiar version of the verse from Isaiah that runs, 'How beautiful on the mountains are the feet of him that bringeth good tidings, that publisheth peace' (52.7 AV), this should more accurately read: 'How beautiful are the dancing feet of the women who spread the good news of peace.' Since the participle is feminine, the image must in fact allude to the way in which women at home traditionally greeted returning warriors: dancing around them.[19] Archaeological evidence too supports the predominance of women in this role.[20] Quite a few small figurines have been found which indicate that, as they danced, the women beat drums, as well as singing.[21] Much later, in the time of Philo (d. AD 50), we know that one particular Jewish sect, the Thera-peutae, used what Miriam had done to legitimate a key role for their own participation in worship through singing and dancing.[22] Whether in earlier Israel such a role also implied an enhanced status for women is uncertain. The fact that such actions required preparation, were public, and also were performed in the presence of men has been used to argue that this was indeed so.[23] Certainly that is a possibility, but men of course also laid claims to similar abilities. When King David himself danced before the Ark, part of the reason may have been military.[24]

[18] Although that sacredness was interpreted in widely differing ways. For seven of these carefully distinguished, see S. Niditch, *War in the Hebrew Bible* (New York: Oxford University Press, 1993).

[19] Yet, surprisingly, this is resisted by most modern translations.

[20] For the evidence, see C. L. Meyers, 'Of Drums and Damsels: Women's Performance in Ancient Israel', *Biblical Archaeologist* 54 (1991), 16–27. She stresses that it was definitely drums that were used and not tambourines (i.e. there was no internal rattle or bell that helped to produce the sound). Men used cymbals (19).

[21] Key passages include the following: Miriam in Exod. 15.20–22; Jephthah's unnamed daughter in Judg. 11.34; women meeting David from the battlefield in 1 Sam. 18.6–7; Judith's own victory dance in Judith 15.12–13.

[22] For a discussion of the issue, see J. E. Taylor, *Jewish Women Philosophers of First Century Alexandria: Philo's 'Therapeutae' Reconsidered* (Oxford: Oxford University Press, 2003), 322–34.

[23] Meyers, 'Drums', 25.

[24] He is celebrating the fact that his possession of Jerusalem now seems secure. Note that the author implicitly blames Michal for criticizing David's dance; she is made barren (2 Sam. 6.23).

More pertinent is the key role exercised by male dancers in
Temple worship at Jerusalem. Psalm 150 enjoins: 'Praise him with
timbrel and dance'.[25] Here presumably all the dancers had to be
male, as the inner courts of the Temple were confined to men. This
seems confirmed by another of the Psalms: 'Let the sons of Zion
rejoice in their King! Let them praise his name with dancing'
(149.2–3). Here a round dance seems indicated of the type more
clearly alluded to in Psalm 118 (v. 27), where the worshippers bind
the horns of the altar with festal branches, as they circle round it.
Such a dance may remind the reader of a more famous instance
before the Golden Calf.[26] It is important to emphasize that, despite
the assertion of many scholars to the contrary, there is no evidence
whatsoever to suggest that orgiastic rites were involved. It may well
have been an orderly occasion. It was the idolatry that was seen as
wrong, not the dancing or 'playing'.[27] Given, therefore, the overwhelmingly positive character of references to dancing in scripture,
it is not at all implausible to suppose that dancing may even be
associated with God himself. Some find just such an allusion in
the passage in Proverbs that speaks of Wisdom 'playing in his
presence continually' (8.30 NEB).

Careful scrutiny of the text, I would suggest, transforms dancing
from a marginal activity to an essential element in our appropriation
of scripture. A not dissimilar witness is afforded by the ancient
world more generally. Archaeology, the decoding of ancient
sources, and so on have all disclosed a wide range of religious
applications in the ancient world that have reinforced scholarly
expectations of similar attitudes in ancient Israel. Although under
threat, such variety continues to this day on the continent of Africa.
Here dance is still employed in agricultural and initiatory rites,
as well as in contexts of war and as part of mating rituals.[28] If

[25] Ps. 150.4; cf. also Ps. 26.6–7 (round the altar) and 87.7.

[26] Exod. 32.1–6; immortalized in Poussin's famous painting of 1634, now in the
National Gallery in London.

[27] 'Play' is familiar from the AV translation (v. 6). It reflects the more neutral
meaning adopted by both the Septuagint and the Vulgate, in marked contrast to
the revelry of many a modern translation. For a rebuttal of the notion that orgiastic
activity was involved, see J. M. Sasson, 'The Worship of the Golden Calf', in H.
A. Hofner (ed.), *Orient and Occident: Essays Presented to Cyrus H. Gordon* (Neu-
kirchen-Vluyn: Neukirchener Verlag, 1973), 151–9.

[28] M. Huet, *The Dances of Africa* (New York: Abrams, 1996): for agricultural
rites, see 52, 57; for initiatory, 17, 170; for war, 33; for mating rituals, 29.

comedy and burlesque sometimes play a part, underlying all the various types is the profound African belief in the capacity of such ritual to bridge heaven and earth.[29] There is one difference. Rather than any jump heavenwards, it is movement through space that is used to underline the link between the two worlds. Presumably this is because of the closeness of the divine that African religion already presupposes. There is no distance to be transcended, only an already existing presence to be activated. Large masks that stretch upwards are frequently used to underline that new unity.[30] Although, as in ancient Israel, dance is used in the context of mourning, its purpose is not to suggest separation but to speed the deceased on into a new role in that other world.[31] So, again a more positive role is implied.

Ancient Greece in its funeral rites exhibited a more mixed response. Whereas the actions of the women suggested the disruption brought about by death, the men tended to engage in more orderly rituals.[32] Formal dances round the tomb, for example, were probably intended to purify the body but also perhaps to indicate resistance to the mortality and separation from the gods implied by the stillness of death.[33] In a similar way on other occasions, dancing round altars seems to have functioned as a means of renewing divine presence within such an environment.[34] As with ancient Israel, war was regarded as a sacred activity.[35] So here too there were various sorts of dances, including the so-called pyrrhic or weapon dance that was a boy's way of being initiated into manhood.[36] The nearest female equivalent sounds quite strange by comparison. The form of dancing involved was called 'playing the bear'.[37] The most likely explanation is that the prepubescent girl was identified with the bear and seen as needing 'taming' or ordering into her future role within society.[38]

---

[29] For comedy, see ibid. 91, 132; for the bridging of heaven and earth, 14, 75

[30] A three-metre-high Lorraine-like cross mask that swivels is used to make the point among the Dogon of Mali: ibid. 46; cf. 18, 154.

[31] Especially clear among the Kapsiki of Cameroon: ibid. 98.

[32] S. H. Lonsdale, *Dance and Ritual Play in Greek Religion* (Baltimore: Johns Hopkins University Press, 1993), 234–60, esp. 243, 247.

[33] Ibid. 252, 258–60.

[34] Ibid. 116.

[35] For the sacred oath associated with the carrying of weapons, see ibid. 164.

[36] Ibid. 137–68. The dance, however, was not exclusively confined to men: 9.

[37] Ibid. 169–205, esp. 171.

[38] Ibid. 180–6. Tamed bears were probably kept at the relevant shrine.

Such activities may all seem far removed from the interests of a philosopher like Plato. Yet Plato devotes extensive discussion to questions of dance in the principles of education that he advocates in his late work, the *Laws*.[39] It would be easy to dismiss such legislation as simply coercive, yet another means of exercising control over others.[40] But Plato appears to have had larger issues in mind, issues that reflect the greater significance given to dance within the culture of his own time. Dance was properly part of moral and religious education, and at root offered two key ways of cementing human society into the patterns of order determined by the divine: what might legitimately be summarized in the familiar contrast between the Apollonian and the Dionysiac. In the former an already existing order is made more perspicacious. Divine grace and harmony are copied by the dancers in a way that allows them also to appear god-like.[41] In Dionysiac or Bacchic ritual, by contrast, the role of the dance was actually to generate such order through direct encounter with the disruptive. Hephaestus lamed by his mother Hera, for example, once more gains his place among the gods; satyrs challenge but do not finally subvert the moral order.[42] One helpful analogy offered is the common response of a mother to her baby's crying.[43] Before tranquillity can return, it is not good enough for the mother to put the infant in a stiller, quieter place. Rather, she needs first to introduce yet more disruption (the familiar rocking movement).

In the midst of such detail the two key features in dance most valued by the Greeks should not be lost. First, there is the grace of movement that suggests order, intelligibility, beauty, and design, all of which Plato and his fellow Greeks would have naturally allied with the divine, or at least a major aspect of it. Secondly, there was the suggestion of possibilities for the world and its inhabitants to be otherwise than they are at any particular moment. Vase decorations of a little boy leaping into the air and of a man riding a dolphin say it all.[44]

[39] Books 2 and 7.

[40] *Laws* 657d scarcely suggests a repressive attitude, more delight in what is being done.

[41] Lonsdale, *Dance*, 44–75, esp. 66.

[42] Ibid. 76–110, esp. 83–8, 99–107.

[43] The example is Plato's: *Laws* 790d–e.

[44] For commentary on the rose decorations of the latter kind, see Lonsdale, *Dance*, 97–8; for the former illustrated, opposite p. 1.

Hinduism's Dancing God

In Greek religion the gods themselves dance, particularly Apollo and Dionysus. Earlier I alluded to the possibility that in the Old Testament dancing is associated also with the Hebrew God. That association continues into the modern world in at least one other major faith, Hinduism, most notably in the worship of the god Shiva. Because Buddhism arose out of Hinduism and continued to interact with it, there is also some influence on this faith as well. I shall look briefly at that influence, but I want to begin with Hinduism itself and the major role that Shiva plays.

Trying to generalize about Hinduism is notoriously difficult, since it exists at so many different levels. There are personal and local community gods, as well as those whom it is easy to place within a more widespread mythology.[45] Within that larger frame some commentators suggest that it is probably Shiva who has the edge in popularity over Vishnu, with Kali and the various other versions of the mother goddess not far behind.[46] Before turning to Shiva in his role as Lord of the Dance (Nataraja), however, it is vital that such worship be set in some wider context. Otherwise it would be all too easy for the prejudiced western reader to parody his dance as simply part of some debased eastern sexual cult.

This is because of the key role played by the *linga* or ithyphallic symbol in Shiva's worship. To understand sympathetically how such practices are to be understood, some recognition needs first to be given to the extent to which all Hindu worship is ritualistic. Typical in this respect are the *kolam*s and *yantra*s, intricate but temporary patterns laid out on floor or street.[47] Just as these are seen as an aid to worship, so patterns on or of the body repeat the same theme. Devotees of Shiva and Vishnu can easily be

---

[45] There are 630,000 villages in India, most of them with their own local deity. There are communal deities (*Gramadevata*), as well as household (*Kuladevata*) and personal (*Ishtadvevata*) gods. For an account of their various roles, see S. P. Huyler, *Meeting God: Elements of Hindu Devotion* (New Haven, Conn.: Yale University Press, 1999), 66–112.

[46] The most popular temple, though, belongs to Vishnu. In his temple at Tirumala in Andra Pradesh there is a staff of 16,000, with 20,000 free meals distributed each day: ibid. 153–4.

[47] For *kolam*s with illustrations, see ibid. 46, 52–3, 67, 88; for *yantra*s (more abstract and linear designs used to attract the energy of the deity), ibid. 204–5.

distinguished in this way. Three parallel horizontal lines on the brow (in ash, for example) are the sign of Shiva; two vertical ones of Vishnu.[48] Nor is it just Shiva's devotees who resort to the ritual of dance in order to increase devotion. In quite unrelated contexts it is possible to find a Hindu making his prayers in a pose that borrows from dance, or again dancing being used to induce mystical trances.[49] Yet of all the gods with whom one might potentially enter into a relationship in this way, Shiva is perhaps the most unexpected. Despite all the various myths associated with him and this particular image of him as Lord of the Dance, Shiva has undoubtedly come to function primarily in an aniconic way. While the evidence that the origins of the *linga* symbol were sexual is incontestable, and indeed seems confirmed by the way in which it is often complemented by the female *yoni*, equally clear is the fact that for most contemporary Hindus any literal sense to the image has now receded quite firmly into the background.[50] Nowhere does this emerge more strikingly than in the nature of the veneration that the *linga* receives. Adornment with oil, camphor, sandalwood, and flowers all seem far removed from any narrow sexual interest or commitment. Indeed, often the image is scarcely visible under the burden of its tributes. Stories of Shiva the ascetic also abound, while the *Linga Purana* speaks of the discovery of a *linga* that stretches to infinity and so represents the god as transcendent.[51]

Yet perhaps this is not altogether the right way to argue the case. Even on those occasions where the original meaning retains some role, this appears to be accepted without embarrassment: for example, when prayers to the *linga* are made for a successful pregnancy or to the *yoni* for fruitful crops.[52] Perhaps a parallel may

---

[48] D. Pattanaik, *Shiva: An Introduction* (Mumbai: Vakils, Feffer, and Simons, 1997), 102.

[49] For a dancer's pose in a prayer to the sun and in libations offered to the earth, see Huyler, *Meeting God*, 29.

[50] For some illustrations of *linga*s, see A. Mookerjee, *Ritual Art of India* (London: Thames and Hudson, 1985), 79–90. For one early story that makes the connection with sexuality explicit, see R. H. Davis, 'The Origin of *linga* Worship', in D. S. Lopez (ed.), *Religions of India in Practice* (Princeton: Princeton University Press, 1995), 637–48.

[51] Pattanaik is an excellent source for the various myths. For infinity and transcendence, see *Shiva*, 92, 117.

[52] For a painted prayer of a *yoni* on a house wall with vegetation growing out of it, see Mookerjee, *Ritual Art*, 62.

be drawn with reverence for Vishnu's feet, also sometimes represented on their own.[53] Just as in the one case it would be absurd to
posit a foot cult where the real motive is in fact to use the image
purely as a vehicle towards greater devotion, so here, even if a sexual
aspect is entertained, it seldom succumbs to narrowly erotic associations. Rather, it maintains an essentially innocent aim: sexuality
as a ready-to-hand metaphor for divine fruitfulness.[54] It is into this
way of thinking that dance as an image of divine creativity now
needs to be set.

Although the image of the dancing Shiva is found elsewhere, it is
especially popular in Tamil Nadu and above all in the temple at
Citamparam, where this image provides a particular focus for worship.[55] Those familiar with the Trimurti image in which Shiva
functions as the destroyer might be puzzled as to how he can here
operate as creator. His role as destroyer, however, is normally
glossed as getting rid of all that is corrupt and degenerate, so that
a new created order can then begin; 'he is thus the renewer, the
regenerator, the transformer'.[56] Another writer declares that what is
burnt is 'not merely the heavens and earth at the close of a world-
cycle, but also the fetters that bind each separate soul'. The opening
words of a Bengali hymn are quoted to good effect:

> Because Thou lovest the Burning-ground
> I have made a Burning-ground of my heart.[57]

Citamparam is one of the great temples of India, and its history
and present organization make for fascinating reading. It is now
the only remaining temple that has the dancing image of Shiva
in its central shrine. Although the forms of worship practised in
the temple have succumbed to various external pressures over

---

[53] Many temples only have the god's feet carved in stone. It is an obvious way
of pointing beyond the image to a more transcendent reality: Huyler, *Meeting God*,
150–1.

[54] Compare similar attitudes in ancient Rome, discussed in Chapter 1.

[55] For some other temples, see Pattanaik, *Shiva*, 112.

[56] In the three-headed Trimurti image, Brahma is identified as creator, Vishnu
as preserver and Shiva as destroyer. For this image, and the positive gloss, see ibid.
12, 120.

[57] Admittedly from a hymn to Kali, but Shiva is also described as dancing in
cemeteries and burial grounds. For the essay concerned, see A. K. Coomaraswamy,
The Dance of Śiva: Essays on Indian Art and Culture (New York: Dover, 1985), 56–66,
esp. 57, 61–2.

the centuries, its priesthood has been surprisingly resilient. State attempts at 'reform' were firmly resisted. Admittedly, later the temple was forced to yield to British colonial pressure for the abandonment of dance as a major element in its festivals. The size of the crowd was just too large to police.[58] Other changes have also occurred. Currently the image of the *linga* is now also present, as well as an image of the god Vishnu.[59] Even so, the 'high-church ritual' still climaxes in the worshipper's visit to the central shrine and thus in the sight of Shiva dancing, the kicking 'leg of grace', as it might be described.[60] While substitute images are used on the other days of the temple's major festival, great excitement is caused on the eighth when the actual dancing image of Shiva is processed outside the shrine. What particularly pleases the poor is the way in which the god is envisaged as actually joining the lower classes in their celebration. Various conventional distinctions are for the moment suspended.[61]

A key Hindu term for understanding all of this is *darshan*, which means roughly seeing and being seen by God, with the stress very much on the latter. Grace is, as it were, a visual rather than a verbal or intellectual experience. Its application to this particular temple's ritual would seem especially apposite, to judge by attitudes on the part of those granted sight of the image. The experience is one of encounter between the divine, graceful dancer and the graced believer. Indeed, for some the way in which the place's name has changed also reflects this sense of 'consciousness-space', of a transformed insight.[62] Many choose to focus on one particular leg in much the same way that, as I noted earlier, Vishnu's devotees might concentrate on that god's feet. Nevertheless, the image as a

[58] There is an endogamous community a thousand strong, of whom about two hundred serve as priests. Although the modern Tamil government has twice tried to break the Brahmin monopoly, on both occasions (in 1954 and in 1981) their attempts were defeated in the courts. For further details about the priesthood, see P. Younger, *The Home of Dancing Śivan* (New York: Oxford University Press, 1995), 13–45. Tamil adds an 'n' at the end of the god's name. For the role of the British colonial authorities, see 160.

[59] As a result of pressure from migrants from the north, Kali was expelled in the thirteenth century and Vishnu introduced in the sixteenth: ibid. 106, 111–12.

[60] Ibid. 33, 34.

[61] Ibid. 54–67, esp. 59–61.

[62] The meaning of Citamparam, in contrast to the earlier Cirrampalam or 'Little Hall'.

whole retains a clear and integrated meaning.[63] Shiva dances in the context of a ring of flames, symbol of his cosmic energy. Of his four hands, one holds a drum to vibrate the world into being, another a torch to destroy what is not appropriate, while a third is in a gesture of reassurance. Most pertinent of all, the fourth points to one of his two legs that is symbolically dancing release, while the other tramples on a demon.[64]

One of the best ways of appreciating the impact of that image and its associated rituals is through study of some of the poetry that has been generated as a result. During the third century AD the poet Tirumular observed:

> When one sees a tamarind the mouth waters,
> So it is with those who witness the dance.
> They shed tears of joy and melt with love,
> Blissful joy arises in their hearts.[65]

In what has been described as 'some of the most beautiful verses ever written' the ninth-century poet Manikkavacakar takes up similar themes. So close was Manikkavacakar's identification with Shiva under this form that he believed himself through these means to have experienced mystical union with his god. Again and again, foot or leg is used as a metaphor for the grace of the god's presence in transforming worshippers. The god's actions sacramentally reshape hearts and minds:[66]

> We quelled our pride and surrendered our minds,
> so play tonakkam, good ladies.
> As servants of the Southerner, the Lord worshipped in heaven,
> we'll turn our thoughts to his long feet.
> We'll receive the joyful Dancer's grace
> and enjoy supreme bliss.[67]

For the poet without the divine dance nothing at all would now be in existence:

---

[63] For an illustration of the 'leg of grace', see Younger, *Home*, 221.

[64] For further details and illustration, see ibid. 157 (illus. 122), 164.

[65] Quoted ibid. 193.

[66] For some other examples of focus on the leg or foot of the deity see ibid. 197, 199.

[67] Quoted in N. Cutler, 'Tamil Game Songs to Šiva' in Lopez (ed.), *Religions*, p. 156, no. 27.

> The Lord of the little hill at Tillai
> where cool fields flow with honey,
> this Lord performed a dance.
> Why is that, my dear?
> If he didn't dance
> this whole world would become a meal for Kali
> who wields a bloody spear.
> Don't you see?[68]

What is valued most is the profound spiritual transformation that can be effected by the dance:

> To me, untaught, most ignorant, the very lowest cur,
> In mighty grace he came, with heavenly beauty me to clothe.[69]

It is a matter of unbridled divine creative energy in which worshippers can also participate. Little wonder then that Ananda Coomoraswamy has gone so far as to declare that Shiva's dance is 'the clearest image of the activity of God of which any art or religion can boast'.[70]

If such poetry provides some indication of how a visual image might help found a personal relationship with the divine and deepen understanding of the creative process, elsewhere in India dance is used for a somewhat different purpose: to explore the particularities of life and how these should be received by ordinary men and women. Two extended examples will suffice, one from the south of India, the other from the far north. Although both are thus from the Indian subcontinent, it is important to note that the connection with religion remains equally strong among Hindus even where such dance techniques are transported to the West.[71]

It is in Kerala that the Kathakali dance-drama has its origins. Now quite familiar in the West, it was first documented in the seventeenth century, reached the height of its popularity in the late nineteenth century, and then declined, only to experience a revival once more in the 1920s.[72] British audiences were first introduced to

---

[68] Quoted in N. Cutler, p. 152, no. 10.

[69] Younger, *Home*, 198.

[70] *Dance of Śiva*, 56.

[71] Seen, for example, in the English Imperial Society of Teachers of Dancing (ISTD) dance examination videos, *Siksha Kathak* (2001) and *Siksha Bharatanatyam* (2001). Both begin with a prayer to Shiva. The ISTD is an international organization, well able to protect as well as to promote indigenous dance forms.

[72] P. B. Zarrilli, *Kathakali Dance-Drama* (London: Routledge, 2000), 17–30.

the form in 1939 through the work of the Indian dancer Ram Gopal and his company. More recently in 2002 a major success was achieved at the Edinburgh International Festival.[73] Currently, however, the dance form remains a highly contested area within India itself. While more secular variants have been attempted and these are supported by some, its roots are in fact deeply religious.[74] As many as five hundred plays survive, most of them drawing on the great Indian religious epic, the *Mahabharata*. That said, as with my other example from north India, it needs to be noted that the text is somewhat fluid. So, significantly different versions of the same story are found being utilized in the dramatic tradition.[75] Induction into the specifics of such drama and dance takes till about the age of forty. Only then can the actor/dancer claim to be fully trained.[76] Audiences too need to be aware of a wide range of conventions respecting the symbolism of particular movements, special dress codes, and so on.[77] An unusual feature is the special dye used to give the eyes greater luminosity.[78] Some elements in the training also borrow from the martial arts.[79] As anyone who has seen a performance will bear witness, grace and poise mark the movements of the actors. This is all the more remarkable given the stamina required. Although the pressures of modern life have curtailed proceedings, performances can still span several days and often last through the night.

It would be quite wrong to deduce from the professionalism of such performances that religion has in effect been reduced to a form of aesthetics. The dramas themselves really constitute worked

[73] Ram (1912–2003) heavily adapted the form, interspersing it with pieces of music in a variety of different styles. As reviewers noted, a major reason for the Edinburgh success was the decision not to play down the spiritual dimension; e.g. A. Macaulay in *Times Literary Supplement*, 6 Sept. 2002, 18–19.

[74] For modern secular versions, including a *King Lear* and a Marxist version, see Zarrilli, *Kathakali Dance-Drama*, 177–205.

[75] Zarrilli suggests we think of the kind of alterations made to Shakespeare at the Restoration and in eighteenth-century England: ibid. 40.

[76] Ibid. 66. Lines are sung twice, the second time more slowly to the accompaniment of hand gestures: 45, 47.

[77] For hand and facial gestures illustrated, see ibid., 74–8; for the symbolism of colours and beards, 53–5.

[78] Ibid. 57.

[79] Emphasized in P. B. Zarrilli's video *Introduction to Kathakali Dance-Drama* (2000), e.g. in the use of massage to make the body more supple.

examples of how divine action should be interpreted, and how the individual believer thus grows in grace. So, for example, one play tells of how Bhima, a hero of the epic and one of the Pandava brothers, is taught humility by the monkey god, Hanuman. Children apparently delight in the antics involved in the monkey's teasing mannerisms. It is a way of encouraging children to learn, without them even being aware that they are doing so.[80] Parents are also helped to come to terms with the loss of children in one story that parallels that of Abraham and Isaac, as in another where the children fail to survive but are protected by Vishnu in heaven. The fact that local children are used for these roles of course adds to the poignancy of the scene.[81] So such danced drama is scarcely just a form of entertainment or even simply a matter of praising the deity. It also helps to make religious devotion and practice part of the realities of ordinary life.

In the former northern kingdom of Garhwal, now India's newest state of Uttaranchal, the dancing has none of this southern sophistication. Nonetheless, here too it is possible to detect an understanding of divinity that has been worked out through dance and drama, as incidents from the *Mahabharata* are told in ways relevant to the people's current situation. So, for example, intimate personal relations are examined in a way that is currently not possible in normal family contexts, where a high degree of formality between father and son and so on is still expected.[82] Again, the complex relations between the two classes of brahmin and rajput are carefully renegotiated, while two figures from the drama, Draupadi and Kunti, are used to explore how women can find themselves simultaneously committed to goddesses as different as the wild Kali and the domestic Lakshmi.[83]

[80] In the play 'Flower of Good Fortune': Zarrilli, *Kathakali Dance-Drama*, 101–17, esp. 116–17.

[81] For the Abraham/Isaac story in 'King Rugmamgada's Law', see ibid. 158–74. For Vishnu's care of children in 'The Progeny of Krishna', see 135–58, esp. 136, 156–7.

[82] W. S. Sax, *Dancing the Self: Personhood and Performance in the Pandav Lila of Garhwal* (Oxford: Oxford University Press, 2002), 80–3.

[83] For brahmin and rajput and the different forms of hegemony involved, see ibid. 119–33; for Draupadi and Kunti, 134–56. The answer is that both are necessary to their identity and to the success of those for whom they are responsible.

Intriguingly, the local temple has fully committed itself to such tentative explorations. So it is itself exploring the proper direction of its own injunctions, whether towards continued rebellion against some of the major norms of Hindu culture or towards accommodation. Even the possibility of a different god being acknowledged by the temple authorities as the cult's true subject is currently under investigation.[84] The western anthropologist who lived with the people for some time as a way of exploring the significance of these rituals came eventually to the conclusion that it was impossible to separate God out from them. So his book treats the divine as a complex agent integral to any complete explanation.[85] Whether one follows him in that direction or not, he is surely right to resist the conclusion that dance is simply an epiphenomenon imposed on top of a more basic belief system. In effect, dance has in these circumstances become foundational to the community's understanding both of itself and of the divine that it believes underpins all of life.

More brief mention might be made of the rather different form of Hinduism and mediation of the divine to be found in Bali. There a key role is played by the *dalang*. The *dalang* may be scholar and performer, teacher and consecrated priest, poet, visionary and healer. He does not himself dance—his puppets do. The 'shadow theatre' performed in temples mediates the divine world whilst entertaining and instructing the audience, especially audiences of boys and men.[86]

Dance can also sometimes play a major role in Buddhism. So, given its own initial growth out of Hinduism and its continuing interaction with that religion, some examples are worth noting here. In a moment I shall look at what happens within Japanese Zen Buddhism, but first the more syncretistic Mahayana Buddhism of Tibet and Mongolia needs to be addressed. Tibet has two main types of dance, Achi Llamo and Cham. The former is thought to have originated in the fourteenth century with tales of the Buddha's birth.[87] Because female dancers were included, in the more distant

---

[84] Alcohol and meat are currently not forbidden: ibid. 190–1. For change, including the god's identity, see 193–9.

[85] Ibid. 158–61. Somewhat to my surprise, he seeks to draw support from the philosophy of Daniel Dennett.

[86] For the role of the *dalang* in Bali, see A. Hobart, *Dancing Shadows of Bali* (London: KPI, 1987).

[87] E. Pearlman, *Tibetan Sacred Dance* (Rochester, Vt: Inner Traditions, 2002), 114–15.

past such dance often had a rather seedy reputation. Now, however, it is proudly presented as a distinctive part of Tibetan culture, offering entertainment but also essentially moralistic danced tales for the edification of the laity.[88] By contrast, Cham is confined to the monasteries. Although it too has a story element, and influence from the earlier Bön religion is evident, the main objective has become the use of bodily movement to facilitate monastic meditation.[89] Deep musical sounds accompany very slow chanting that often makes it impossible for outsiders to identify the words but allows the monks themselves to meditate on their meaning.[90] All the time their bodies move in almost puppet fashion with perfect alignment between hands and knees.[91] Dances often take all day, made possible by the semi-trance-like state in which they are performed. Although such dances are seen as valuable in their own right (in offering praise or respect to the deities or individuals concerned), no less esteemed are the further consequences that are believed to flow from the dancing, in purgation of evil desires and in closer focus on the needs of others.[92]

Cham first entered Mongolia in 1811, other Buddhist influence earlier.[93] Prior to that time much dancing took the form of sympathetic magic, much like tribal dances the world over, where the attempt is made, for example, to dance rain into falling. However, the conversion of the country to Buddhism in the sixteenth century brought refinement to such understandings though, as in Tibet, not to the total neglect or abandonment of earlier religious forms. A shamanistic element survived, but with shamans now seen as called when they themselves were weak, to fight in others' battles against illness and evil.[94] The earlier dances were also incorporated into Buddhist festivals. So some of the exotic gear once worn for different

---

[88] For its disreputable past, see ibid. 112; for modern endorsement by the Dalai Lama, 165.

[89] For the influence of Bön, see ibid. 14; for recognition of Bön by the Dalai Lama as a legitimate Tibetan Buddhist school, 32.

[90] Ibid. 86–8.

[91] Ibid. 63–7. The curling inwards of the fingers as the knee moves up or down adds to the puppet-like appearance.

[92] Ibid. 57–60.

[93] The first Mongolian monastery to use Cham was at Urya: ibid. 46.

[94] An individual falling seriously ill was one of the principal signs employed in identifying someone called to this vocation: J. Vrieze, *The Dancing Demons of Mongolia* (London: Lund Humphries, 1999), 24.

purposes is now reinterpreted as symbolizing the Buddhist's own fight against hostile forces.[95] The beautiful depictions by the Mongolian patriarch and artist, Zanabazar (d. 1723), are perhaps easiest for us in the West to understand (with their use of gesture and repose to suggest transcendence).[96] However, even the apparently frightening figures of the traditional dance take on a quite different aspect, once we try to comprehend how they are in fact intended to function. They are meant to help believers fight against evil in their own lives.

All Japanese dance was by origin religious. This is reflected in a central creation myth. As the result of an insult the sun goddess had retreated to a cave. She could only be enticed out as the other gods and spirits danced before its mouth.[97] Although some performances continue to take place on occasion at temples, these now mostly occur on stage, such as in the splendid theatre at Kyoto.[98] Three traditional forms continue, Bugaku, Noh and Kabuki.[99] While there are romantic tales, such as a native version of *Swan Lake* or the story of the doomed love of a young woman for a monk, the dominant themes are those that reflect on the changing faces of nature.[100] For example, there is the challenging classical role of representing the gradual transformation of a quiet serving girl into a proud male lion, or again the use of a swaying bamboo to imply acceptance of constraints in life.[101] Although there is movement, it is the beautiful, elaborately embroidered costumes and the careful postures of the dancers that are most likely to imprint themselves on the memory. In effect, the tendency is towards 'a static position' and 'a final dramatic posture', especially in Kabuki.[102] Even the

---

[95] As in the Tsam festival. A dancer dressed as a deer (now reinterpreted as an earlier incarnation of Guatama Buddha) dialogues with a hunter to persuade him towards non-violence: ibid. 38–45, esp. 41; cf. 54–5. For more exclusively shamanistic costumes, see 18, 28.

[96] Ibid. 70–89, esp. 71, 81.

[97] H. Myers, 'Piercing the Mask of Japanese Dance Theater', in M. H. Nadel and M. R. Strauss, *The Dance Experience*, 2nd edn (Hightstown, NJ: Princeton Book Company, 2003), 39–54, esp. 39.

[98] Illustrated in M. Hata, *Tradition and Creativity in Japanese Dance* (Trumbull, Conn.: Weatherhill, 2001), 113.

[99] Noh is now the best known in the West, and much of it, though by no means all, is non-religious. Bugaku dates from the eighth century, Kabuki from the sixteenth.

[100] For the first two examples, see ibid. 14–17, 52.

[101] Ibid. 49–51, 89.

[102] Emphasized by Myers: 'Piercing the Mask', 46.

accompanying drums are extraordinarily elegant in their design.[103] This perhaps helps explain why Japan's most recent variant on its classical dance might in some ways almost be described as an anti-dance, or at any rate the very antithesis of the values represented in Japan's ancient forms.[104] Influenced by German Expressionism, Butoh uses Zen's free play of ideas to abolish all forms of repression.[105] Nudity and ugliness are, therefore, used to explore the dark side of life, but not with a view to endorsing it. Rather, with what has been described as a focus six inches below the floor, Butoh attempts to suggest a body earthed but ultimately subordinate to the transience of nature.[106] Every material value is rejected as a way of clearing a space in which life's fluidity and uncertainty is accepted as itself of spiritual value.[107] The danger of facile judgements is well indicated by the fact that one of Butoh's leading exponents, Kazuo Ohno, is in fact a devout Christian, who uses transvestite dances to call into question a range of social values.[108] My description thus far may suggest preoccupation only with moral and social issues. What, however, needs to be noted is that for Zen it is only through such transformed attitudes to nature that properly spiritual values can be realized.

Judaism and Islam More Engaged than Christianity

In a moment I shall turn to Christianity itself. The centrality of the incarnation to its belief system might have led readers to expect a similar endorsement of dance to that found in eastern religion. But matters did not turn out this way. What makes this all the more surprising is the presence of liturgical dance within the other

---

[103] For illustration, see Hata, *Tradition*, 20.

[104] The founder, Tatsumi Hijikata (d. 1986), first used the term 'dance of darkness' in 1961. It was his way of indicating his intention to exploit traditional social taboos and forbidden zones in Japanese society, as a means of advocating change: Myers, 'Piercing the Mask', 48.

[105] S. H. Fraleigh, *Dancing Darkness: Butoh, Zen and Japan* (Pittsburgh: University of Pittsburgh Press, 1999). For Expressionism, see 36, 68–70; for free play, 43.

[106] Ibid. 145, 173.

[107] Ibid. 203, 227, 239; Myers, 'Piercing the Mask', 50.

[108] For some further details, see B. S. Stein, 'Butoh: "Twenty Years Ago we were Crazy, Dirty, and Mad"', in A. Dils and A. C. Albright (eds), *Moving History/Dancing Cultures* (Middletown, Conn.: Wesleyan University Press, 2001), 376–83, esp. 376, 381.

two major western monotheistic religions, Judaism and Islam. Perhaps it was the very degree to which those two religions stressed the transcendence of God that produced such a powerful counterblast.

In the case of Judaism dance is particularly associated with the Hasidic movement. To this day dancing continues to occur during *Lekhah dodi*, the central hymn of the Kabbalat Shabbat service.[109] Some merely move to the rhythm in their seats. Quite a few, however, become so exuberant that their actions can seem to others present more like frivolous playtime than serious worship.[110] *Lekhah dodi* means 'Come, my friend', and alludes to the elaborate ritual developed by Kabbalists in sixteenth-century Safed (in upper Galilee) to welcome the divine Shekinah or presence.[111] Dressed in white garments, worshippers went out into the fields to welcome the Sabbath as Israel's bride, and danced her into the synagogue. Much earlier Maimonides had stressed the importance of dance to the celebration of the feast of Tabernacles, but it was really Ba'al Shem Tov (d. 1760), the founder of Hasidism, and one of his followers, Rabbi Nahman of Bratzlav (d. 1811), who made dance integral to this form of Judaism.[112] Meditating on what could be meant by the scriptural claim that at Sinai the people 'saw sounds', (Exod. 20.18), Tov suggested that what could be seen were expressions of joy.[113] Dance is one obvious such expression. Nahman, playing on two similar Hebrew words, *holah* (dance troupe) and *holeh* (sick person), develops this idea into the notion that dancing is one key way of making divinity present.[114] The dancer's

[109] It is now sung in all Jewish congregations, but those uninfluenced by Kabbalah mysticism will simply turn towards the synagogue door and bow.

[110] For the different reactions, see J. A. Summit, *The Lord's Song in a Strange Land: Music and Identity in Contemporary Jewish Worship* (New York: Oxford University Press, 2000), 49–51.

[111] Better known than the author of the hymn (Solomon Alkabetz) is Isaac Luria. Sabbath was identified with Shekinah, which for these purposes was treated as the female side of the divinity.

[112] For the wider importance of Maimonides (d. 1204) in connecting observation of the commandments with joy, see M. Fishbane, *The Exegetical Imagination: On Jewish Thought and Theology* (Cambridge, Mass.: Harvard University Press, 1998), 157–9.

[113] All hint of paradox is removed in the RSV translation: 'perceived the thunderings and lightnings'. For the commentary itself, see ibid. 173–4.

[114] Ibid. 173–84, esp. 176.

joy not only reflects the heavenly reality but also in embodying it transforms our world, including sickness.

In the case of Islam the whirling dervishes are known the world over. Supported by the wider Sufi mystic movement, the dances themselves probably owe much to earlier shamanistic versions performed in central Asia.[115] Although condemned by Sunni teaching authorities, the dervishes were not actively persecuted until the sixteenth century.[116] Kemal Ataturk banned them in post-Ottoman Turkey, but they continued underground, and have now made something of a comeback.[117] The great advocate for the role of dance in achieving mystical identity with God is the thirteenth-century poet Rumi.[118] A Persian born in what is now Afghanistan, he spent most of his life at Konya (Iconium), where he is buried.[119] Although he sometimes uses imagery of being caught up to heaven, more commonly he speaks of divine indwelling.[120] The 'rotating' dervish is someone drunk with God instead of wine:

> Like drunks we lie on the floor, wild with joy, in high heaven;
> No boys or belles with cups, no wine, no music for our trance.[121]

The rotation is like that of the heavens, but it brings a focus of divine illumination greater than was present even at Sinai.[122] As

---

[115] T. S. Halman and M. And, *Mevlana Celaleddin Rumi and the Whirling Dervishes* (Istanbul: Dost, 1983), 34, 54.

[116] L. M. J. Garnett, *The Dervishes of Turkey* (London: Octagon, 1990 edn), 182. This is still a useful book despite the Foreword's severe critique.

[117] They continued to exist elsewhere. An excellent CD and accompanying booklet is available of music from the Great Ummayad Mosque in Damascus: *Les Derviches tourneurs de Damas* (1999). An example of more recent Turkish tolerance is *The Music of Islam. Vol. 9: Mawlawiyah Music of the Whirling Dervishes*, a Celestial Harmonies CD recording of a ceremony from the Great Suleymaniye Mosque, Istanbul.

[118] 'Mevlana' is an honorific title meaning 'Lord' or 'Master'.

[119] Also known as Konia, on the south-west edge of Turkey's Anatolian plain. It became the capital of the Seljuk sultans of Rum. Because of those fleeing the advance of the Mongols, its greatest artistic period was during the reign of Ala eddin I (1219–36).

[120] 'The stairway of the whirling dance' is described as going beyond 'heaven's seventh sphere': quoted in Halman and And, *Mevlana Celaleddin Rumi*, 36.

[121] Quoted ibid. 32.

[122] For heavenly rotation, see Garnett, *Dervishes*, 126; cf. Milton, *Paradise Lost*, 5.620–2. For the comparison with Sinai, see Aflâkî, *Les Saints des Derviches tourneurs* (Paris: Sindbad, 1978), i, 176, 208.

one might expect from Islam, to achieve the effect no visual stimuli are deemed necessary.[123] Rather, what is required are *sema* and *zikr*, careful listening to the accompanying music and short invocations uttered in unison.[124] Although self-mutilation has occurred among some sects in the past, the mainstream has always avoided such asceticism.[125] Instead, it speaks of the ecstasy of being possessed by divine love, and in such an attitude it is often remarkably tolerant towards other religions, including Christianity.[126] Indeed, it has even been suggested that the circular form of their dance more naturally leads to tolerance than the sharp and angular cross.[127] Nor should it be seen as a purely individualistic quest. Rumi is strong on social critique. At a more basic level, the dancers in any case still need to be conscious of, and considerate towards, others if collisions between so many people all moving in a trance are to be avoided.[128]

To mention belly dancing in a discussion of religious dancing and its sacramentality might seem to some the height of perversity, but its common association with entertainment and doubtful morality belies its origins, and the attempts of some contemporary Muslim women to restore the dance to its earlier dignity. Its present low reputation apparently only dates from the nineteenth century. Earlier generations had built on practices that may well go back to Palaeolithic times.[129] Among other roles belly dancing was associated with other women helping one of their number who is pregnant to give birth more easily. Their own simulated movements were intended to induce a gentle birth. One Iraqi woman now living in Canada describes how that had also been her own experience while growing up as a child in Iraq. The dance

---

[123] Dances take place in halls where the only decoration is texts from the Qur'an and a *mirhab* for orientation towards Mecca: Garnett, *Dervishes*, 65.

[124] Halman and And, *Mevlana Celaleddin Rumi*, 58.

[125] For mutilation, see Garnett, *Dervishes*, 128, 131.

[126] Rumi declared that 'in all mosques, temples, churches I find one shrine alone': Halman and And, *Mevlana Celaleddin Rumi*, 46.

[127] So R. Wetzsteon, 'The Whirling Dervishes: An Emptiness Filled with Everything', in R. Copeland and M. Cohen (eds), *What is Dance?* (Oxford: Oxford University Press, 1983), 507–11, esp. 511.

[128] Halman and And, *Mevlana Celaleddin Rumi*, 40–1; Garnett, *Dervishes*, 147. The number of dancers varies between about 15 and 30.

[129] S. Helland, 'The Belly Dance: Ancient Ritual to Cabaret Performance', in Dils and Albright (eds), *Moving History*, 128–35.

was so used not only for pregnancy but also for puberty and other major events in her life.[130] Her argument is that associating the belly with spirituality empowers women.[131] Not only is the focus feminine and so aids release of inhibitions, but also the irregular, inconclusive beat of the music helps create a sense of eternity.[132]

Set against two such essentially transcendent religions, Christianity's low profile for dance is, therefore, all the more surprising. Admittedly, there are some exceptions. Shakers used the 'nineteen' references to dance in the Old Testament to argue that, 'as unity and harmony of exercise are emblematical of the *one spirit* by which the people of God are led, this unity and harmony of worship is beautiful and glorious'.[133] Their employment of ordinary country-dance tunes for this effect must once have seemed more startling than it does to us today.[134] Of greater potential impact for Christianity as a whole is perhaps the way in which altar boys at Seville continue to dance three times a year before its high altar, in their splendid costumes.[135] But elsewhere one must speak of attempted revivals rather than continuities.[136] Interest in dance during the medieval period was stronger than it is today, even if it took some odd forms. Among the most unusual was the ball game that took place each Easter in some French cathedrals.[137] Reformation suspicions were eventually to drive out what had once been seen as acceptable forms, whether religious or secular. Even apparently

---

[130] R.-F. Al-Rawi, *Belly Dancing* (London: Robinson, 2001), 22–3, 36, 188–90.

[131] Ibid. 86–7.

[132] Because of the absence of any obvious beginning or end: ibid. 110.

[133] Benjamin Youngs writing at the beginning of the nineteenth century: R. E. Whitson (ed.), *The Shakers: Two Centuries of Spiritual Reflection* (London: SPCK, 1983), 281, 282.

[134] Contrast the shock expressed in a 1785 account: ibid. 271.

[135] Known as *Los niños Seises*, the boys dress in blue and white damask silk for the feast of the Immaculate Conception, and in red and white for Corpus Christi and the beginning of Lent. They also wear elaborate feathered hats.

[136] Helpful histories include L. Backman, *Religious Dances in the Christian Church and in Popular Medicine* (London: George Allen and Unwin, 1952); J. G. Davies, *Liturgical Dance: An Historical, Theological, and Practical Handbook* (London, SCM, 1984).

[137] For a discussion, see my earlier volume *God and Enchantment of Place* (Oxford: Oxford University Press, 2004), 225–6.

harmless diversionary entertainment such as Morris dancing fell under suspicion.[138]

Perhaps the most tragic instance of such suspicions was how the 'vision quest' dances of native American tribes were treated by the Christian majority. The dances were employed as a means of finding guidance or answers to specific spiritual issues. Among Sioux Indians in Dakota the convention had grown up of wearing so-called 'ghost shirts' during such dancing. Their wearing was seen as preparatory to a forthcoming messianic age. While dancing with them on, visions of the age to come were expected, together with immunity from harm. So large were the numbers involved that such gatherings attracted the suspicions of the American government. Even so that hardly justified what happened in 1890, when it sent in almost half of its then army to suppress the movement. Approximately three hundred defenceless Indians were massacred (at Wounded Knee).[139] Even the bodies of the dead were shown no respect but stripped for souvenirs. It was only in 1999 that one such shirt taken from a dead body was finally returned to the tribal group concerned.[140] In the interim it had been sold to Glasgow Art Gallery after touring for a while in Buffalo Bill's Wild West Show. That return, it should be emphasized, was from the perspective of the Sioux less to do with righting wrongs or respecting alternative histories and much more a matter of the restoration of a sanctified presence. Their spirit world was now after all to achieve some effect in their lives in a restored and cherished dignity. The more 'advanced' Christian culture had at last been acknowledged to be in reality the more primitive. It saw in the dance and its associated symbols only difference and threat,

[138] Apparently worried by its lack of respect for the social order, Archbishop Grindal mounted an attack in 1571. Although dancing after church was defended by James I and Bishop John Cosin, the seventeenth century was to be marked by increasing hostility from church authorities: J. Forrest, *The History of Morris Dancing* (Toronto: University of Toronto Press, 1999), 186–214, esp. 191–3, 201, 204. Its pre-Christian origins, and the fact that it involves some cross-dressing, as well as the dancers' progress from pub to pub, made it vulnerable to criticism.

[139] The incident is made the culmination of Dee Brown's story of American mistreatment of its native population: *Bury My Heart at Wounded Knee: An Indian History of the American West* (London: Vintage, 1991 edn), esp. 415–45. Wovoka, the Pauite messiah, had enjoined: 'All Indians must dance; everywhere, keep on dancing' (416).

[140] S. Maddra, *Glasgow's Ghost Shirt* (Glasgow: Glasgow Museums, 1999), esp. 21–3.

whereas to the Indian it had always offered the transcending of
difference and the uniting of two worlds, the spiritual and the
earthly. Such unwillingness to learn from the colonized was by no
means unique. Even in India converts had a hard time persuading
their colonial leaders of the missionary potential of dance.[141]

In effect, within modern Christianity dance seems only to have
gained real acceptance in its role as metaphor. This is far from being
a new dimension. Although possibly intended literally, it seems
likely that the Gnostic author of the third-century apocryphal
Acts of John meant his description that way. The relevant incident
is set during the course of the disciples' last evening with Jesus.
They circle round him as he sings a hymn. Too long to quote
here, there are repeated references to dance, as in the following:
'Grace dances, "I will pipe. Dance, all of you."' The connection
with the Last Supper is also made clear: 'Now, if you follow my
dance, see yourself in me who am speaking... You who dance
consider what I do, for yours is this passion of man which I am to
suffer.'[142] In 1917 Gustav Holst set the passage to music as *The
Hymn of Jesus*. Memory of it in the interim, however, had not
been forgotten thanks to the popular medieval version 'Tomorrow
is my Dancing Day'.[143] Today the best-known variant is to be
found in Sydney Carter's popular hymn:

> I danced on a Friday when the sky turned black—
> It's hard to dance with the devil on your back.
> They buried my body and they thought I'd gone;
> But I am the dance and I still go on.
> *Dance, then, wherever you may be;*
> *I am the Lord of the Dance, said he*[.][144]

[141] Contrast initial Pietist acceptance with Anglican attempts to impose greater
conformity, complicated in part by the latter's laudable attack on caste distinctions:
D. D. Hudson, *Protestant Origins in India: Tamil Evangelical Christians* (Grand
Rapids: Eerdmans, 2000), 118–20, 129–35.

[142] W. Schneemelcher (ed.), *New Testament Apocrypha* (Cambridge: James
Clarke, 1992), ii, 181–4. For a discussion of the hymn in relation to other texts,
see the chapter 'Chorus and Charis' in J. Miller, *Measures of Wisdom: The Cosmic
Dance in Classical and Christian Antiquity* (Toronto: University of Toronto, 1986),
81–139.

[143] Text available in H. Keyte and A. Parrot (eds), *The Shorter New Oxford Book
of Carols* (Oxford: Oxford University Press, 1993), 226–7. The editors suggest that
it may originally have been part of a Cornish medieval drama.

[144] Verse 4 and part of the chorus of 'I danced in the morning when the world
was begun', one of the few modern hymns to make most hymnbooks, e.g. even

It is also as metaphor that dance is most likely to occur in contemporary theology. Creation and the Trinity are the two most favoured examples. Yet both applications are odd, especially the latter case, where there is no relation whatsoever to anything physical. Despite this, the language has become commonplace.[145] This is all the more surprising, as the meaning of *perichoresis* has in fact nothing to do with dance. It means 'reciprocity' and 'inter-penetration', whereas the Greek for 'to dance' has a short and not a long 'o'.[146] Even the application to creation is strange to this degree, in that what is not evaluated positively in its own right as inherently religious is nonetheless claimed to give meaning to what is. So it is not that modern uses of the metaphor are wrong or unilluminating, but that they seem to place the cart before the horse. Dance as metaphor can be exciting, but it ultimately under-mines itself, if it fails to follow through and offer some endorsement to its more literal counterpart.[147]

Of course dance does sometimes succeed in the contemporary church. In the case of my own cathedral of Durham a mass utilizing the music of Duke Ellington reached a magnificent conclusion with the distinguished tap-dancer Will Gaines leading the choirboys out down the aisle, dancing to the words:

> Harps and cymbals
> played out loud and clear.
> Chanting, singing
> trumpets ringing
> joy to every ear.
> David upped and danced.[148]

the conservative *New English Hymnal* (Norwich: Canterbury Press, 1986), no. 375. The tune, Simple Gifts, comes from the Shakers.

[145] As an example, note the casual introduction in D. B. Hart, *The Beauty of the Infinite* (Grand Rapids: Eerdmans, 2003), e.g. 161, 175.

[146] In the past I have been guilty of a similar fault, though at least there the fact that two unrelated words (*choreuo*, dance, and *choreo*, to go forth) are involved is fully acknowledged: D. Brown and A. Loades (eds), *The Sense of the Sacramental* (London: SPCK, 1995), 13. No allusions to dance are listed in G. W. H. Lampe (ed.), *A Patristic Greek Lexicon* (Oxford: Clarendon Press, 1961), s.v.

[147] For an example of application to modern understandings of creation, see G. Del Re, *The Cosmic Dance* (Philadelphia: Templeton Foundation Press, 2000); for one to life more generally, including creation, M. Mayne, *Learning to Dance* (London: Darton, Longman and Todd, 2001).

[148] Ellington's 'David Danced'. The mass, first performed in 1990 and again in 1993, is available on CD with the Stan Tracey Orchestra: *Duke: The Durham Connection* (1993).

But in most cases it fails to connect adequately, and one can see why. It has much to do with a lack of professionalism.[149] There is also little attempt to link with past modes of expression.

In the preceding survey that I have provided, dance showed itself capable of bearing a wide range of different meanings. Each variant, however, clearly gained its own special vitality through dependence on specific traditions of appropriate music and symbolism. Hand gestures are, for example, hugely important in Indian dance, posture more than movement in Japanese. Even the linking of heaven and earth can be expressed in quite different ways. The leap is by no means universal. The dervishes' trance requires no such lift from the ground. Nor indeed does African dance, where it is more a matter of movement through space that suggests communion with the spirit world rather than any lift upwards.[150] All of this requires patient observation and learning. Nor will it ever do simply to assume that Christians already have all the answers. Particularly sad is the automatic dismissal of all versions of Haitian voodoo. As a recent British tour indicated, it is possible to read even voodoo in a sympathetic and joyful way.[151]

In none of this am I suggesting that all points of conflict with Christianity can be avoided. Inevitably some approaches will express what Christianity has to offer better than others. All I am pleading for is the willingness to learn from others, to enter sympathetically into what is being said and claimed. A key inhibitor against a satisfactory approach to dance lies in my view in a general loss within the Church (Catholic no less than Protestant) of appreciation of how valuable

[149]   This is not to decry the valiant work done by groups such as Moving Visions Dance Theatre who tour some of the major English cathedrals each year, among them Durham. Their leader, Ross McKim, has done a doctorate on dance at Durham: 'The Production and Performance of Danced Pararituals as a Numinous Experience' (2000). See also R. McKim (ed.), *The Essential Inheritance of the London Contemporary Dance Theatre* (London: Dance Books, n.d.), which reprints vol. 6, no. 4 (Autumn 2001) of the international journal *Choreography and Dance*.

[150]   Here I agree with F. Y. Caulker, 'African Dance: Divine Motion', in Nadel and Strauss (eds), *The Dance Experience*, 17–28, esp. 19.

[151]   In the theatrical presentation *Vodou Nation* (2004). Like Brazilian Macumba it mixes Christianity with elements of native African religion (from Dahomey and Nigeria). Western focus on sensational attempts at manipulating the lives of others through magic needs to be set against a lively recognition of a single world uniting living and dead.

bodily expression, no less than mental, can be to worship.[152] The
Roman Catholic Church has removed much of its former ritual from
celebration of the liturgy, while it seems unaware of how significant
a role dance did occasionally play in its earlier traditions. Earlier
I quoted some examples from medieval Europe. In a South American
country like Bolivia lively responses continued much later. In an early
eighteenth-century composition dancers in the cathedral at La Plata
(now Sucre) were urged, 'Hey, come on, come on, come on! | play,
sing and dance!', as something like a jig was performed to the shaking
of tambourines and the kicking of heels.[153] Charismatic Protestant
Christianity may seem quite a different case, but despite all its dramatic hand and body gestures it is not clear that they speak of any real
interest in bodily expression as such. That may seem unfair, but there
is an extraordinary lack of variety in what the various gestures
are supposed to mean. They simply express a general sense of petition
or joy. The whole issue of the use of body in worship is one to which I
shall return in this volume's sequel.[154] In the meantime, I want to turn
now to an examination of the history of modern western dance
outside the confines of the Church. The surprise is how resilient
religious considerations are after all, despite an almost total absence
of encouragement from the Church itself.

Ballet, Modern Dance and Religion

Modern performance of dance, I suggested in my introduction to
this chapter, has remained engaged with religious issues despite
almost total indifference on the part of the Church and its theologians. In the past there might have been some excuse, in the charge
that society at large seemed in any case to regard professional dance

[152] Cf M. Kast, 'Can We Dance in Church?', *Image* 49 (2006), 24–9 on dance
and liturgy in the diverse cultures of the USA, and the necessity of recovering the
relationship between liturgy, dance, culture and life, even for 'Anglos'.

[153] The composition, '¡Ay, andar!', is by Juan de Araujo (1648–1712). There are
even some lines that run: 'Get dancing all you bunions! | For there's no excuse at
all. You'll be condemned to chilblains | if you try to dodge the dancing!' The
music is available as an Ex Cathedra choir recording on a Hyperion CD, *Moon,
Sun and All Things: Baroque Music from Latin America* (2005), track 16.

[154] *God and Mystery in Words* (Oxford: Oxford University Press, 2008), chs 5
and 7.

as an elitist and somewhat effeminate activity. But all that has
changed. The huge success of the Irish group Riverdance and of
Billy Elliot, film (2000) and musical (2005), have helped change
attitudes among men.[155] In the latter a determined teenager per-
suades a tough mining family of the virtues of ballet. His father's
initial refusal is met by irritated tapping of his toes that is quickly
transformed into dancing in the street. Significantly, when asked
why he wants to dance, the boy replies that it 'makes him feel like
a bird'.[156] So, not inappropriately, the closing sequence is of him
performing as a bird in Matthew Bourne's all-male version of *Swan
Lake*. No one film holds a comparable status for women in illustrat-
ing the potential for dance to help individuals transcend particular
circumstances, though twentieth-century dance forms have freed
women from the gendered images of nineteenth-century classical
dance.[157] The nearest American equivalent is perhaps Antonio
Banderas' *Take the Lead* (2006), in which he portrays the pioneering
work of Pierre Dulaine in New York schools. Convinced
that conventional ballroom dancing might encourage deprived
children towards greater respect for one another and for themselves, he gradually persuaded the school authorities to introduce
dance as part of the school curriculum. That way, children learnt
not only grace in movement but also manners and graced attitudes
towards one another.

If *Footloose* (like *Billy Elliot* both film and musical) failed to
interact directly with the religious significance of dance, it did at
least confront Christian objections to participation head on.[158]

---

[155] For the story of Riverdance's meteoric rise after their performance at the
1994 Eurovision Song Contest, see the video *Riverdance: A Journey* (1994). For an
example of Michael Flatley's choreography of 'hard-shoe' dancing, see *Riverdance:
Live from New York City* (1997). In a wider way *Saturday Night Fever* (1977), *Grease*
(1978) and *Strictly Ballroom* (1992) all helped.

[156] 'Like electricity' is another image used.

[157] Possible candidates would include *Flashdance* (1983) and *Save the Last Dance*
(2000). In the former a woman who is a welder by day and a 'modern' dancer by
night longs to join the Pittsburgh Ballet; in the latter a poor girl's ambition is to
train at the Julliard School in New York. *Dancing at Lughnasa* (1998) uses traditional dancing as an image of release for a family of Irish sisters, some of whom do
eventually leave home.

[158] *Footloose* (1984) is based on a true incident that happened in Elmore City,
Oklahoma. The pastor and city's opposition to dance is in part overcome by appeal
to biblical precedents.

However, to my mind the film of recent years that most powerfully expresses the transformative power of dance is undoubtedly *Dancer in the Dark* (2000). It is the story of a single mother going slowly blind whose only comfort in her dull machine job is to dream of herself dancing along to the largely industrial sounds that surround her. For reasons too complex to explain here she ends up on death row, sacrificing herself for her son. She gets through the trial by turning the members of the court into dancers. The film ends with a sympathetic female guard, at her request, tapping her to the place of execution. Quite a few other films also use imagery associated with dancing to explore spiritual issues. But only seldom is ballet specifically used. So it might be as well to begin our examination there, where for many people dance is at its most frivolous and superficial.

Ballet and Transcendence

Of all forms of dancing classical theatrical dance is the genre that is perhaps most often parodied. Its origins over the last five hundred years lay in royal courts and their accompanying theatres. It is perhaps, therefore, not surprising that until the twentieth century what prevailed was a view of it as entertainment at its most superficial. Plots with doomed love as the theme often appear absurdly sentimental. Others are more naturally suited to children, such as Delibes' *Coppélia*, Tchaikovsky's *Nutcracker* or Ravel's *L'Enfant et les sortilèges*.[159] Adults might argue that the quality of the music, the brilliance of the dancers and their dramatic performance, are quite enough. Choreographers, however, sometimes find even in these ballets a stimulus towards fresh thought, with some new twist introduced. So, for example, under Mark Morris' direction the *Nutcracker* of 1892 became *The Hard Nut* of 1991, a sustained questioning of gender roles.[160] Matthew Bourne's all-male cast and new choreography for *Swan Lake* (1996) also proved highly popular. More radical and more recent is Australian Dance Theatre's *Bird*

---

[159] The Ravel piece was originally intended as an opera; there is a fine performance by Netherlands Dans Theater on an ArtHaus DVD (1997) that also includes a Royal Ballet School performance of Prokofiev's *Peter and the Wolf*.

[160] The various transformations are briefly outlined in J. LaPointe-Crump, 'Of Dainty Gorillas and Macho Sylphs', in Nadel and Strauss, *The Dance Experience*, 159–72, esp. 163–4.

Brain (2005). Here thumping, raw disco rhythms are used to present a world of languid sexuality and humour in a context of frenetic energy.[161]

Yet even the most absurd of plots deserve some sympathy in their own right. In a highly perceptive essay one anthropologist warns that contrasting ballet with ethnic dance in other parts of the world is a great mistake.[162] It too is just as culturally specific. Although not applied to the earlier ballets in the repertoire, once that point is taken on board, some of those ballets must surely assume a quite different significance. Created at the height of the Romantic movement, ballets like *La Sylphide* (1832) or *Giselle* (1841), for instance, use supernatural spirits in effect to plead that not everything should be reduced to the rather narrow rationalism that was then so characteristic of certain elements in Europe's Enlightenment inheritance. In giving a space for the mystical they also gave room for religion. Nor is there any reason why they should not continue to exercise that role today. Ballet audiences are well aware of *Giselle*'s Act II setting in a forest, where as a sprite Giselle entices Albrecht to her cross-mounted grave, in order to protect him. The question both ballets pose is where the 'magic' of life, as it were, is to be found. In both the central male character learns too late that this should have been sought in a near rather than a distant reality. Matthew Bourne, in transposing *La Sylphide* to Glasgow's high-rise flats with their attendant *Trainspotting* problems, shows how easily such ballets can assume a contemporary relevance.[163]

So familiar are audiences nowadays with the performance of Romantic ballets that it is easy to forget how relatively recent such forms are. *La Sylphide* was created by Filippo Taglione for

---

[161] Its character as light entertainment should not be taken as indicative of this company's dance policy. In two other current productions, *Age of Beauty* deals with our fragile need of one another and *What God Has Wrought* with empathy towards various situations, including death.

[162] J. Kealiinohomoku, 'An Anthropologist looks at Ballet as a Form of Ethnic Dance', in Copeland and Cohen (eds), *What is Dance?*, 533–49. On the one hand, 'ethnic' dance is neither undeveloped nor lacking choreography; on the other, ballet's specifics included, at least until very recently, far from obvious conventions about the nature of female beauty (536, 538, 545).

[163] Bourne's version is called *Highland Fling*. Irvine Walsh's novel *Trainspotting* (which focuses on the drug youth culture of Edinburgh's outlying council estates) was made into a successful film in 1995.

his daughter Marie. It is often claimed, although this is uncertain, that she was the very first to dance in stiffened shoes so that she could take a pose on her toes.[164] The technique was intended to augment the sense of her as an ethereal, unattainable dream. This effect was supplemented by elaborate stage machinery that enabled her even to fly through the air. Théophile Gautier, the great French Romantic writer and critic, described Marie as pre-eminently 'a Christian dancer'. As such, he contrasted her with the other great dancer of the day, Fanny Essler, whom he saw as more suited to Giselle and her transformation between Act I and II from human to spirit.[165] Although Gautier's identification of the more ethereal as the more Christian reflects a sadly unearthed Christianity, the remark does at least indicate that theological issues were not being ignored in such developments.

Unfortunately, the later nineteenth century was to mark a real decline in the character of ballets in some of the major countries in western Europe that was not to be reversed until the arrival of Diaghilev's Ballets Russes in Paris in 1909. This was not entirely true of either the Danes or the Italians. But relatively few people saw the Danish company, while the Italians were perhaps better known for performance in the context of opera and music hall. Although Edgar Degas' paintings and sculptures may suggest a lively French scene, more detailed inspection proves otherwise. In fact what really interested him was not the art form as such but rather the way in which movement could be suggested simply by appropriate use of light and shade.[166] The absence of male dancers from Degas' work reflects the historical reality. They had become confined to minor supporting roles.[167] Therein lies an irony in that

---

[164] For the general context, see M. Fonteyn, *The Magic of Dance* (London: BBC Books, 1980), 201–41. Apparently, she was not the first (210). But the development of the stiffened 'point' to shoes was used in her case to great artistic effect, and certainly was an improvement on expecting female dancers to poise on their toes without support. Point shoes in the twenty-first century enable dancers to perform in ways inconceivable in the nineteenth.

[165] T. Gautier, 'Revival of "La Sylphide"', in Copeland and Cohen (eds), *What is Dance?*, 434–7, esp. 436.

[166] M. Clarke and C. Crisp, *Ballet in Art* (London: Ash and Grant, 1978), 73–87, esp. 73, 76. Although Degas did not die until 1917, most of his famous work was done long before 1910 (he was born in 1834).

[167] For further details, see R. Burt, 'The Trouble with the Male Dancer', in Dils and Albright (eds), *Moving History*, 44–55.

ballet had begun in court and theatre the other way round. Female
dancers were only introduced in the later seventeenth century.
Although well suited to the conventions of the French court, in
those early days both male and female costume was quite imprac-
tical in terms of facilitating movement.[168] Notoriously, Louis XIV
often made himself the star of such court ballets, with himself as
Apollo or the Sun King. Of course by the early nineteenth century
Paris and Copenhagen had moved things far on from there.[169] But
the Romantic ballet did present fresh problems in its turn.
The stress was now all on the star ballerina's lightness of being,
and so on a spiritual reality elsewhere. Indeed, the suspicion of male
weight and physicality seems to have run very deep.

Diaghilev and his new ballets changed all that. If the male was
now also encouraged to soar, it was in the context of endorsement
of a more earthly, if still spiritual, materialism. What was crucial
here was that Diaghilev could recruit from the best dancers
in Europe, including the Italians. Russian aristocrats had helped
to sustain Russian folk dance, and this was given theatrical
transformation in the companies on their great estates. The new
practice gave pride of place to men as well as to women. Many
of the works performed by the Ballets Russes did not draw
explicitly on classical technique, deliberately breaking with the
Romantic tradition. Although the best-known music from that
period is still Stravinsky's *Rite of Spring*, Stravinsky himself
eventually came to the view that this work actually functioned
better in its own right as music rather than as music for dance.[170]
Still, its portrayal of pagan ritual and sacrifice does at least indicate a
continuing engagement with religion. Recently, the Bolshoi's Andris
Liepa has attempted a stunning re-creation of three of Diaghilev's

---

[168] For some illustrations, see Clarke and Crisp, *Ballet in Art*, 28. Male dancers
wore a *tonnelet*, a wired skirt that was based on knights-at-arms' undergarments.

[169] Copenhagen is important because it is the revised version of *La Sylphide* by
August Bournonville that is performed today. In the era of Bournonville
(1805–1879), when men and women worked in the same class together, the
training produced a very different kind of female dancer from the conventional
'sylph'. It also ensured an unsurpassed sequence of great male dancers.

[170] The music is discussed in detail in Chapter 5. Nijinsky's attitude appears also
not to have helped: R. Buckle, *Diaghilev* (London: Hamish Hamilton, 1979),
246–7, but cf. 252.

original ballets.[171] If *Petrushka* continues the habit of bringing
dolls to life, at least the main figure is male, while the dance
of the Golden Slave is one of the most dynamic moments in
Scheherazade.[172] *Petrushka*, however, should not be seen as pure
entertainment. There can be little doubt that the choreographer
(Michael Fokine) also had a profoundly serious purpose. Petrushka
represents the downtrodden of the world. Although he is killed, his
spirit continues dancing on the rooftops. In other words, hope
remains.

A moral and spiritual purpose is also evident in Stravinsky's
Firebird. The story represents a straightforward fight between supernatural good and evil, in which human good triumphs only because
human generosity of spirit evokes a corresponding reaction in the
supernatural.[173] The evil Kaschey and his minions are danced to
death, as earlier Hilarion had been in *Giselle*. A variant on this
theme occurs with the first major film about ballet, Moira Shearer's
Red Shoes (1948), based on a Hans Christian Andersen fairytale, in
which a similar power is held to reside in the dancing shoes
themselves.[174] On this occasion it is good that is destroyed.[175]
Dance, the desire for transcendence, is thus displayed as a power
for both good and evil.

In moving straight from Romantic ballet to Diaghilev I have
hitherto ignored the source of the world's most famous ballets, late
nineteenth-century Russia. There an earlier tradition continued to
develop which in many places elsewhere had degenerated into a
shadow of itself. My reason for hitherto ignoring what was taking

---

[171] Available on DVD as *Return of the Firebird* (2002). Michael Fokine's original
choreography is followed. The settings are still those of Léon Bakst and others, but
updated to take account of the new possibilities that the film age brings. A less
dramatic 1996 version of *The Firebird* (along with *Les Noces*) is also available
(performed by the Royal Ballet). It is now back in the repertoire of the Birmingham Royal Ballet

[172] Strictly speaking Petrushka (the Russian Punch) is a puppet. The action
takes place at St Petersburg's Shrovetide Fair.

[173] The magic feather that saves Prince Ivan from Kaschey only comes into his
possession because he voluntarily yields the Firebird her freedom after having
captured her. Kaschey is also sometimes spelt Kastchei.

[174] Further details in P. Crowle, *Moira Shearer: Portrait of a Dancer* (London:
Faber and Faber, 1949), 56–61.

[175] Torn between love of dance and love of another human being, the heroine
commits suicide by throwing herself before a train.

place in Russia is because, marvellous though these were (and are) as spectacle, most of the new creations lacked religious content. Minkus' *La Bayadère* (1877) is an intriguing exception. Apart from the famous Kingdom of Shades dance, it had for long been dropped from the regular modern repertoire.[176] Now, however, it seems to be experiencing something of a revival.[177] Based as it is on a tale from Kathak temple dancing, it does offer rather more than a simple story of unfulfilled love.[178] The opium-induced dream that sees the dead Nikiya and her entourage (all in identical tutus) descend the staircase that leads from heaven to earth is an unforgettable image.[179]

Borrowings from other religions are by no means unknown. A rival to Diaghilev's company (the Ballets Suédois) produced a dance sequence that was based on the whirling dervishes.[180] Most interestingly, as recently as 2003 Birmingham Royal Ballet produced a triple bill that, as well as Stravinsky's *Apollo*, included David Bintley's *Sons of Horus* and Nahid Siddiqui's *Krishna*. Both can be seen in the context of Diaghilev's desire to bring another world of meaning to life on stage. Strange gods are taken seriously, with costumes and dance forms appropriate to the religious texts upon which such ballets draw. Bintley (b. 1957), who is also the director of Birmingham Royal Ballet, is among the most exciting of today's choreographers. His *'Still Life' at the Penguin Café* (to music by Simon Jeffes) is one of the great ballet successes of recent years. An image of the Ark is introduced into the final scene.[181] More

---

[176] According to H. Koegler (ed.), *Concise Oxford Dictionary of Ballet*, 2nd edn (Oxford: Oxford University Press, 1982), 48.

[177] There are two 1997 DVDs available (one a documentary) of Rudolf Nureyev performing with L'Opéra National de Paris. I also saw the St Petersburg Ballet version in 2005.

[178] It was based on a play by the Indian poet Kalidasa: S. Au, *Ballet and Modern Dance* (London: Thames and Hudson, 1988), 63–4.

[179] Not irrelevant to my theme is the apparent source of inspiration for that dance. It was derived from an illustration by Gustave Doré (following Botticelli) for Dante's *Divine Comedy*, of angels snaking their way to heaven.

[180] Premièred in 1920 to music by Glazunov. For further details, see B. Häger, *Ballets Suédois* (London: Thames and Hudson, 1990), 110–13, and G. Dorris, *The Royal Swedish Ballet, 1773–1998* (London: Dance Books, 1999), 131–45.

[181] Not that Bintley is consistently well disposed to religion. While in Act II of his *Hobson's Choice* (1989) he introduces a not unsympathetic dance sequence for the Salvation Army playing in the park, in a 'pop' version of *Carmina Burana* (1995) seminarians are portrayed in a far from flattering light.

pertinent here is the intention that lies behind his *Sons of Horus*. We are left in no doubt that what is expected of us is sympathetic engagement, not merely disinterested enjoyment of the re-creation a now long-dead past.[182] Spiritual values are expressed in the care shown by the four sons of the falcon god Horus for various parts of the body.[183] The ballet ends with the hieroglyph wall at the back of the stage being slowly raised to admit the dancers into the Field of Reeds that is the Egyptian heaven. The choreography is well matched by the composer Peter McGowan's music. His choice of minimalist music he describes as deliberately chosen to 'create a feeling of infinity'.[184] Such attempts to enter into another religion on its own terms are greatly to be commended, not least because so often some minimum common denominator is accepted instead. Despite the director Peter Brook's valiant efforts with the *Mahabharata*, that is often a criticism directed against his work in particular.[185]

Bintley has also choreographed a version of John Tavener's *The Protecting Veil*, an attempt by both composer and choreographer, as one commentator observes, 'to create a living icon in sound and movement symbolising the Mother of God and her veil sheltering Christianity'.[186] This was by no means the first attempt to represent more explicitly Christian themes in dance. In 1928, the centenary of the death of William Blake, Geoffrey Keynes (with the help of his cousin, the artist Gwendolen Raverat) brought together a nine-scene scenario based on Blake's etchings for the book of Job under the title *Job: A Masque for Dancing*. The artist's cousin, Ralph Vaughan Williams, wrote the score. First performed in 1930, it was followed the next year by the more familiar Ninette de Valois version. The title *Masque* was employed because the music used traditional dance forms. Although hardly a

---

[182] My interpretation is supported by Nicholas Dromgoole's accompanying programme notes.

[183] Lungs, liver, intestines and stomach are separately embalmed and kept in canopic jars carved in the image of the four sons.

[184] From the programme notes.

[185] e.g. Zarrilli, *Kathakali Dance-Drama*, 187.

[186] J. Taylor, 'Introduction', in J. Taylor (ed.), *Robert Heindel: An Exhibition of Paintings Inspired by David Bintley's Ballet to the Music of John Tavener* (London: The Gallery, Cork Street, 1999). Taylor observes how in some paintings Heindel has captured 'the fourth dimension of dance, and perhaps religion—soul'.

great success, other work on biblical themes followed, which were
more successful largely because greater attention was paid to the
limited possibilities of dramatic form.

While Stravinsky chose to explore his own professed faith indirectly through subtle alterations to classical myth, it was the same
choreographer who produced his *Apollo* who was also employed
on what is perhaps still the best-known balletic adaptation of a
biblical theme.[187] This was George Balanchine's production of
Prokofiev's *The Prodigal Son*.[188] Prokofiev's ballet music for
Romeo and Juliet and *Cinderella* is now better known.[189] *The Prodigal
Son*, however, does continue to enjoy periodic revivals, not least
because of Balanchine's original choreography.[190] First performed
in Paris in 1929, it also had scenery designed by the devout Roman
Catholic painter Georges Rouault. The music is firmly anti-
Romantic and is given a decidedly bombastic quality by what
are sometimes described as Prokofiev's 'motor rhythms'. Where
they aid understanding is through the force of contrast. So, for
instance, in the opening scene a dramatic difference is observable
between the dancing, high-spirited rhythms that represent the
prodigal's intended departure and the more lyrical melody which
accompanies the family at prayer and which the prodigal reluctantly
and briefly joins before going off on his own. Scenes of seduction
and drunkenness follow. Swift and disturbing clarinet phrases
then vividly introduce and paint the image of the young man
being stripped of all his possessions, and so render all the more
solemn the viola melody that follows, during which themes of
penitence and an awakening conscience are first encountered.[191]

---

[187] The myths of *Oedipus Rex* and *Persephone* were adapted to bring out
Christian issues of atonement. See further my discussion of Stravinsky in Chapter 5.

[188] I saw a production by Bordeaux Opera Ballet at the Edinburgh Festival in
2003. It is also available on the New York City Ballet DVD *Choreography by
Balanchine* (2004), and is in the repertoire of the Birmingham Royal Ballet.

[189] The various versions of *Romeo and Juliet* by different companies and choreographers necessarily include the involvement of a friar in the tale of the two
lovers, but usually little is made of the role.

[190] The rest of this paragraph follows closely the argument of an earlier essay of
mine in which Prokofiev's version is compared with those by Benjamin Britten,
Claude Debussy and Hugo Alfvén: 'Images of Redemption in Art and Music', in
S. T. Davis, D. Kendall and G. O'Collins (eds), *The Redemption* (Oxford: Oxford
University Press, 2004), 295–319, esp. 314–19.

[191] Contrast the episodes from Scene II entitled *Pillage* and *Réveil et remords*. In
both cases the melodic material is subsequently taken up by other instruments.

If the heavy tread of the son returning home is what one might expect from scripture, intriguingly it is his sisters who first act on his behalf and summon the father. A beautiful flute melody indicates the father's forgiveness and blessing, symbolized on stage by the father throwing his cloak over his son, who remains kneeling at his feet.[192] One reason for the ballet's initial success was the way in which the principal dancer, Serge Lifar, threw himself into the part, believing himself to be in his turn a prodigal son.[193] Balanchine was himself religiously inclined.[194] He it was who ensured that the temptations were more realistic than Prokofiev had at first intended. It may also be that the stress on corporate assistance in reconciliation (with the sisters' key role) reflected his Orthodox inheritance.[195]

Sir Frederick Ashton, who was awarded an OM (Order of Merit) for his services to ballet, is rightly still regarded as the greatest of English choreographers. He too was attracted to a religious vision of the world. He loved the ritual of the cathedral at Lima, where he spent his earliest years, and one of his earliest ballets was in fact *Four Saints in Three Acts*, the topic chosen, he claimed, because he was 'devout'.[196] Nowadays, Ashton is best known for ballets such as *La Fille mal gardée* (1960), *The Dream* (1964) and *A Month in the Country* (1976), none of which is religious.[197] During the Second World War, however, he went through a period of intense reflection when the Bible was apparently part of his daily reading. It was this period of his life that saw the creation of two ballets that are still performed today.

We need here to bear in mind the influence of what is now referred to as Central European Modern Dance, which stemmed from the work of Rudolph von Laban, Mary Wigman and Kurt

---

[192] As in a performance I saw by Birmingham Royal Ballet in 2001. The melody is in C major and so recalls the more positive aspects of the opening scene.

[193] Though a prodigal son in his case in relation to Diaghilev: B. Taper, *Balanchine* (Berkeley: University of California Press, 1984), 113–14.

[194] He spoke of himself as 'a servant of God': ibid. 314.

[195] Ibid. 111–12, 243–4. His Easter parties included performances by his cat of *jetés* and *tours en l'air*.

[196] J. Kavanagh, *Secret Muses: The Life of Frederick Ashton* (London: Faber and Faber, 1996), 21, 162–71, esp. 169–70. See also S. Jordan and A. Grau (eds), *Following Sir Fred's Steps: Ashton's Legacy* (London: Dance Books, 1996).

[197] *The Dream* (based on *A Midsummer Night's Dream*) was new; *Fille* was the latest and most popular version of a ballet two centuries old.

Jooss, and was a form of 'expressionism' in movement. Ashton was ever alert to dance forms alternative to those of the classical tradition, and one of his wartime ballets draws on expressionism. In *Dante Sonata* (1940) the music of Liszt is used to portray a battle between the Children of Light and the Children of Darkness, opposed in white and black costumes. Only the male Children of Light wear ballet shoes. There is a powerful solo for one of the female children. She tosses her head back and forth while she punches the air with her fists. The *pas de deux* for the lead dancers in the Children of Light also suggests search and struggle as both dancers make reaching and stretching shapes. All such gestures are set in deliberate contrast to the Children of Darkness, who move like animals along the ground, struggling and writhing, one on top of the other. If that suggests an unequal fight, in fact the leaders of both groups end up crucified. As the piano plays a delightful trill, a golden ray draws some of the good towards it, but even it is soon extinguished. Yet at least in the original version one small sign of hope is left. The ballet ends with a spotlight picking out the Beatrice figure.[198]

Ashton's *Symphonic Variations* (1946) sets a quite different mood. Like the Song of Songs, it uses erotic imagery as a metaphor for a higher love. Influenced at the time by the Carmelite mystics and by César Franck's own 'very religious' score, Ashton sought to portray an ascent 'towards pure gladness and life-giving light'.[199] While the various moments of stasis in the ballet had a practical purpose in allowing the lead dancers to recover their breath, there was also a more mystical purpose. Other dancers whirl round in a circle while the lead remains static in the middle, confidently expecting in quietude grace and peace from above.[200]

I have provided such details of key ballets that are still performed today to illustrate how the medium continues to provoke a religious sensibility and so the possibility of experience of the divine. However superficial they may initially appear, the stories

[198] For some discussion of the original version, see Kavanagh, *Secret Muses*, 257–9.

[199] Ibid. 313–16, esp. 313.

[200] Reflecting particularly St John of the Cross' stress on quiet waiting: e.g. *Ascent of Mount Carmel*, ii, 12–13, in K. Kavanagh and O. Rodriguez (eds), *Collected Works of St. John of the Cross* (Washington: ICS Publications, 1979), esp. 139–42.

open up the imagination to alternative possibilities. Some Christians, however, continue to be deeply suspicious of the medium, not least because of its supposedly gay ambience. Morality is not my concern here. But the issue well illustrates not only how much we are all subject to the specifics of cultural conditioning but also how grace and arrogance can all too easily arise from the same source.

Certainly, Ashton was notorious for a series of gay affairs, mainly with much younger men. Diaghilev's reputation was not dissimilar. The effect of AIDS on some dancers is also common knowledge, among them Rudolf Nureyev and Alvin Ailey (whose modern dance choreography is discussed later). Even in the very different world of 1937 'unnatural sex' was made integral to the plot of a series of popular ballet stories that was begun at this time.[201] Although prejudice on the matter still continues, with talk of the whole genre as effeminate, the occasional presence of gay people in this context probably tells us less about dance as such and more about how social attitudes on this matter stood in western society over the course of the twentieth century.[202] So long as people in general were hostile, like tended to attract like into what was seen as a refuge or place of haven, and in a context in which in any case, as with other performers in theatre, boundaries of all kinds are pushed to their limits and beyond, and thereafter the situation perpetuated itself. Certainly, in other cultures there is no necessary coincidence between dance and homosexuality, and nor is there in the West except in the minds of those unfamiliar with the actual world of dance. In fostering such prejudices, unsympathetic critics also forget the degree of strength required of the male dancer to perform his role adequately. That is well illustrated by the dance training incorporated into international performances and competitions by ice-dance skaters. Nor does the adjective 'effeminate' in any way reflect the steely strength and skill of the present-day female classical dancer or skater.

Morally and spiritually, much more interesting is a quite different issue that can be illustrated from a perceptive novel based on

---

[201] C. Brahms and S. J. Simon, *A Bullet in the Ballet* (repr. London: Hogarth Press, 1986), 40.

[202] For an exploration of the whole issue, see J. L. Hanna, *Dance, Sex and Gender* (Chicago: University of Chicago Press, 1988).

Nureyev's rise from obscurity to fame and apparent happiness, only to decline precipitately into poor performance on stage and promiscuity elsewhere. Early on, the boy is encouraged in his dancing by his teacher, who tells him that jumping is a way of 'hanging on to God's beard'.[203] That exuberant hope contrasts with his easy confidence later in life in accepting praise from dance critics who told him, 'you are a god when you dance'.[204] Such tension between perceived self-transcendence and a sense of being graced from elsewhere can also be illustrated from Ashton's own work. One reason he was attracted to Elgar for his *Enigma Variations* ballet (1968) was because he felt that, like the composer, he was no longer being appreciated enough in his declining years.[205] Ballet is relevant to religion precisely because it suggests the possibility of bridging the material divide that separates us from God. The danger, however, is that dancers then think everything is now up to them. The inevitable result is incomplete transcendence, or else reversion to an earlier condition. Ashton forgot his own reminder in *Symphonic Variations*, on the need to wait and receive. That is also perhaps why so many ballets end unhappily, not least those originally produced for court entertainment. They warn viewers that human ambition can destroy as well as create.

Modern Dance as a Search for Meaning

Although the term 'modern dance' was not coined until 1927,[206] its origins really lie further back at about the same time as Diaghilev was transforming ballet in Paris. Here the key figure is Isadora Duncan, who sought inspiration for a new approach to dance through visits to Greece and Egypt. The Greek trip even involved an Orthodox priest sacrificing a black cock in her new temple of dance, and the importing of a band of Greek boys into western Europe to demonstrate how things should be done.[207] One of her successors, Ruth St Denis, described Duncan as 'dancing God right in front of you'.[208] Although conventional religion was rejected,

---

[203] C. McCann, *Dancer* (London: Phoenix, 2003), 51.   [204] Ibid. 178.

[205] Kavanagh, *Secret Muses*, 503.   [206] Au, *Ballet*, 119.

[207] For the trip to Greece in 1903, see P. Kurth, *Isadora: A Sensational Life* (Boston: Little, Brown and Company, 2001), 109–16; for that to Egypt, 283.

[208] Quoted in J. H. Mazo, *Prime Movers: The Makers of Modern Dance in America* (London: A and C Black, 1977), 36.

two major influences on Duncan did ensure a continuing religious understanding of what she was attempting.[209] So strong was the attack of the German zoologist and philosopher Ernst Heinrich Haeckel (d. 1919) on the Church of his day that summaries of his thought often sound wholly anti-religious. But Duncan in common with many others drew from him a form of pantheism, and the religious dimension was reinforced by the underlying theory given to the kind of dancing she adopted from the writings of François Delsarte (d. 1871). Delsarte chose to base his entire system on the Trinity. Arguing that life reflected the Godhead's mutual interdependence, he found threes in everything and not only in music (rhythm, harmony and melody) and dance (ease, coordination and precision). Posture too was a matter of their right balance, with each of the three body zones (head, torso and lower limbs), for example, appropriately coordinated.[210] What characterized Duncan's dancing was simple gestures, soft curves and a focus on the solar plexus, all of which were designed to portray the body as free and vibrant. She threw away the 'corsetted' torso of the court costuming which had survived in ballet, and danced in bare feet—in contrast to the artificialities developed by Taglione and others.[211] In later life she became involved with Communism and with a rather severe preaching style. Her life was also to end tragically.[212] But she had succeeded in setting dance on a new course.

Inspired by the play of light through stained glass, one of Duncan's contemporaries, Loie Fuller, used light shining through her dress to suggest lightness of being.[213] More influential, Ruth St. Denis also

[209] For Haeckel, see Kurth, *Isadora*, 123–4; for Delsarte, 28–30.

[210] Helpfully outlined in J. Anderson, *Art Without Boundaries* (London: Dance Books, 1997), 13–15.

[211] Mazo, *Prime Movers*, 44, 44, 56. For an illustration, see 57. Ashton's *Five Brahms Waltzes in the Manner of Isadora Duncan* (1976) explores different aspects of her personality, and is Ashton's tribute to her importance for him, long anticipating that of Central European Modern Dance.

[212] For her unsuccessful inclusion of words in her dancing, see Kurth, *Isadora*, 330; for the founding of a school in Moscow, 415–17. Her neck was broken when her long scarf became entangled in the wheel of a car in which she was travelling (554).

[213] For the inspiration in her own words, see J. M. Brown, N. Mindlin and C. H. Woodford (eds), *The Vision of Modern Dance* (London: Dance Books, 1998), 11–19, esp. 13. For a general account, including an illustration of an ormulu lamp based on her performance, see Mazo, *Prime Movers*, 17–34, esp. 29.

wanted to suggest such lightness but by more conventional means. By background a Christian Scientist, it is probably true to say of her that religion ran more deeply in her veins than was the case with Duncan.[214] Given that sect's suspicion of matter, it was perhaps inevitable that dance was used rather paradoxically, to suggest the dissolution of the material into the divine.[215] A chance glimpse of an advert for Egyptian cigarettes led her to the symbolism of Isis. One of her earlier dances (*Rahda*) reflected another religion, Hinduism. Almost certainly, it was those earlier dancing traditions that drew her to dance with feet and midriff bare, with bells on her ankles, and a gold skirt swirling about her.[216] Despite such borrowings, she insisted that her aims were explicitly Christian: 'We are all Mary | Waiting to conceive | And bear the Christ Child.'[217] As if in confirmation, a dance group was formed with the specific aim of obtaining permission to dance in churches.[218] Eventually she married a Methodist divinity student, Ted Shawn, who pulled their joint performance in a more earthed direction. That is reflected in Shawn's own work on St Francis, *O Brother Sun and Sister Moon*, and also in his inclusion of dance in physical education at Springfield, the YMCA college where he taught. For some years the pair performed together under the name Denishawn. Although they remained good friends, they separated when they both fell in love with the same man, and Shawn felt it was no longer possible to deny his homosexuality.

With Martha Graham (d. 1991) we come to someone who is perhaps the pivotal figure for modern dance, with a formidable intelligence, and strong musical and theatrical sense. She developed a specific technique, with arms, legs and spine moving in concert under the control of the central torso.[219] She was so successful in this that Graham technique is now an essential component in all

---

[214] Although Duncan throughout her career had also included religious themes, among them a dance to Schubert's 'Ave Maria': Kurth, *Isadora*, 329.

[215] 'St. Denis exploits physical sensuality... in order to advocate that humanity emerge from beliefs in the reality of... the material world': K. L. La Mothe, 'Passionate Madonna: The Christian Turn of American Dancer Ruth St. Denis', *Journal of the American Academy of Religion* 66 (1998), 747–69; quotation from 756.

[216] For illustration, see Mazo, *Prime Movers*, 73.

[217] R. St. Denis, *Lotus Light* (Cambridge, Mass.: Riverside, 1932), 88. If this aim sounds unorthodox, recall similar images in the sermons of Luther.

[218] Named Her Rhythmic Choir: Au, *Ballet*, 95–6.

[219] Mazo, *Prime Movers*, 156. For illustration, see 155.

modern dance.[220] Her roots were Presbyterian, but more important as influences were her father's profession as a doctor and the family's Irish maid. The latter instilled in her a love of ritual; the former, the claim that 'movement never lies'.[221] Clearly there are elements of rebellion, not least in her dance manifesto *Heretic*, where angular movements are used to suggest oppressive social pressures. *Frontier* speaks by contrast of the potential for liberation. Yet a serious attempt to engage with religion is also suggested by quite a number of her dances.

Most negative is the use of extracts from Jonathan Edwards in *American Document* (1940) to speak of religious repression. An absolutely rigid upper body was contrasted with a pelvis rocking sensuously, to indicate the terrible tensions Edwards' dogmatic denouncements created.[222] More typical, however, is her classic work *Primitive Mysteries* (1931), which has three movements: 'Hymn to the Virgin', 'Crucifixus' and 'Hosannah'. Although such titles might be taken to indicate that the dance is orientated towards Mary and, as if in confirmation, 'Hosannah' is supposed to refer to the Assumption, the real focus is in fact on the rituals of native Americans, now converted Catholics.[223] The principal dancer (representing Mary) is first presented as a solitary, stationary figure in the midst of a group of moving women. As she interacts

[220] Whereas classical dance requires the elongation of the body ('pulling up') and a body of beautiful proportion, Graham technique requires movement to be initiated from the centre of the body in 'contraction' and 'release' and with much attention given to breathing in relation to the movements performed. Such movement can also be employed at the very height of jumps. Graham technique also does not require the training from a very young age required of the virtuoso classical dancer. The class, however, is as structured as a class in classical ballet, but it begins with dancers (bare-footed) in a stylized cross-legged position on the floor, requiring them to work at and engage the torso and the upper body. Then the dancers stand up (the equivalent of leaving work at the *barre* and moving into the centre in ballet) and repeat the movement with increasing elaboration, moving into the equivalent of *grand allegro*. Characteristic of Graham technique are 'spiralling' movements on and off the floor. Graham work has been immensely important in the West in getting adult beginners, especially young men, engaged with dance.

[221] J. L. Foulkes, *Modern Bodies: Dance and American Modernism* (Chapel Hill, NC: University of North Carolina Press, 2002), 30.

[222] Mazo, *Prime Movers*, 171.

[223] Mazo even offers a three-paragraph summary without alluding once to the Virgin Mary: ibid. 163–4. Contrast Au, *Ballet*, 121; Foulkes, *Modern Bodies*, 20.

with them, they begin to move more quickly. Eventually she comes to dance with them. So *Primitive Mysteries* is really more about the potentially positive effect of religious ritual. Like Ted Shawn's early native dances from which Graham drew her inspiration, however, there was no attempt to involve the native population itself.[224] *Appalachian Spring* (1944) is also worth noting. Here even the revivalist preacher is given a more positive aspect as a legitimate part of the creation of the original American dream. For a final example, we may note *Seraphic Dialogue* (1955), which tells the story of Joan of Arc, in a series of reflections and reactions to the course of her life. Set in a cathedral-like space, the saints of Joan's visions, Catherine, Margaret and the archangel Michael, form a mobile triptych, brilliant in costumes of purple, red and blue. Joan is revealed in turn by three different dancers as Maid, Warrior and Martyr, and finally as herself in the gold of a saint.

So far as the British scene is concerned, the Graham Company had a huge impact. Robin Howard saw them in London in 1954, and brought them to London and Edinburgh in 1963. His setting up of a trust to bring dancers from the Company to teach classes in her technique in London was to result in the London School of Contemporary Dance (from 1966 onwards a touring group), and then the London Contemporary Dance Theatre (LCDT) in 1969 with its own unique headquarters at The Place. By the time LCDT closed in the mid-1990s (having failed to find a successor to Robert Cohan as artistic director, choreographer and one of the great teachers of the last century) it had had a marked effect in education as well as in the theatre. One of the alumni of the Harehills School in Leeds was to be the founder of the Northern School of Contemporary Dance. From Harehills also came Darshan Singh Buller, who was instrumental in choreographing the impressive stage presentations for the Wheel of Life tour by Shaolin monks who sought to popularize Buddhist attitudes to movement and to kung fu in particular.[225] Graham's work also had a marked influence in Israel.[226]

[224] Foulkes, *Modern Bodies*, 136–8.
[225] For further details see my *God and Enchantment of Place*, 387–90.
[226] In the Batsheva Dance Company, founded in 1964, which made major strides under Ohad Naharin as artistic director, and became internationally appreciated for its programmes. The company had very rich resources on which to draw for some of its work, from a huge range of folk dance and song brought to Israel

The potential for the churches was most publicly demonstrated by the invitation to contribute a choreographed *Mass* for Liverpool Metropolitan Cathedral in its consecration year, in 1967.[227] Thirty-six dancers from all over the world, some of them from the new London School of Contemporary Dance, trained in both classical and contemporary technique, worked with Bill Harpe, who choreographed the dance in the great circle of liturgical space in the cathedral to Cavalli's *Messa Concertata*. It was not of course an act of worship, in the sense that no altar was used and there was no priest to celebrate the mass, but it was a most moving experience for those present, not least for the dancers, given the sheer novelty of such a unique invitation. The *Mass* was followed by a *Mass of Christ the King* for four dancers, with the music composed as *musique concrète*. Again those present were witnesses to an extraordinary venture, this time arranged by Pierre Henry, who had already had work performed in Paris churches (also one ballet, *Le Voyage*, based on the Tibetan Book of the Dead). With organ, Northern Sinfonia and the Welsh Choral Union giving voice to an abbreviation of the Ordinary of the mass, the Metropolitan Cathedral made possible a movement of re-engagement with dance which has unfortunately never been pursued either there or anywhere else since on that scale.

LCDT's repertoire included some remarkably moving items on Christian themes, among them Cohan's *Stabat Mater* (1975) for a group of women dancers to music by Vivaldi. Memorable too was Barry Moreland's *Kontakion* (1972) to Spanish Renaissance festival music, which was concerned with the life of Christ. The key dancer here as Christ was William Louther from the USA, the first African-American dancer to appear regularly with an English dance company, and a most moving interpreter of the role. A profoundly disturbing work in which Louther was never surpassed was his performance as Christ in Peter Maxwell Davies' *Vesalii Icones* from 1969 onwards. This remains a most demanding

from many countries, the horrors of the twentieth century, the dress of the 'Orthodox', and Israel's politics. Given twentieth-century costuming, the company has sometimes drawn the fire of the ultra-Orthodox.

[227] A possible American parallel might be Leonard Bernstein's *Mass: A Theatre Piece for Singers, Players and Dancers*, first performed at the Kennedy Center in Washington in 1971. However, despite the involvement of Alvin Ailey's company, the dance element was in fact far less integral to the performance.

music-theatre work (lasting forty minutes) for just one dancer, cello and instrumental ensemble, which includes amongst other 'instruments' a biscuit-tin full of broken glass and a manual typewriter. The traditional Stations of the Cross, the fourteen Vesalius drawings and the dancer's own body interrelate with three levels of music—plainsong, 'popular' music and Maxwell Davies' own music derived from the other two and fused together.[228] The fourteenth is entitled 'The Resurrection—Antichrist'. The work of composer and dancer unite in creating a foxtrotting 'Antichrist' who curses Christendom—the point being to provoke engagement with the problem of distinguishing the false from the true and the real.

Most recently, and as it were in succession to LCDT's ventures, Random Dance Company, choreographer Wayne MacGregor and John Tavener have all combined to produce *Amu*, Tavener's first score specifically for dance. It is full-length and requires an orchestra of fifty. Tavener himself was inspired by the work of two heart-imaging specialists who as a result of his own illness had conducted investigations on his own heart. Earlier Tavener had completed a score based on a Sufi love-poem about the search of the poet Majnun for his ideal love, Laila, and for union with God. The heart now becomes the symbol of humanity, as well as the life-centre of the human person. Heartbeats are marked every five beats of music by a drum, with the text sung by a group of seven singers in Arabic and using Arabic rhythms, and with images of the heart projected onto screens throughout the work. On stage, and on tour worldwide, the nine dancers and the production team create a moving vision of ascent to another realm of being. In Durham Cathedral, where the work was performed in 2006, over one hundred children from local schools were involved, who had worked with professional dancers for a year beforehand. The impact was quite extraordinary, with some participants and spectators describing the work as among the most profound spiritual experience of their lives. What was meant by such comments of

---

[228] See <www.maxopus.com/works> for the composer's own comments in more detail. Maxwell Davies also wrote a two-act ballet for Flemming Flindt's Circus Company, *Salome* (1978), which begins with the Roman occupation and ends with the execution and apotheosis of the Baptist. Louther transposed part of Eliot's *Murder in the Cathedral* into 1930s Louisiana in *Murder in the Town Hall*, using texts from Malcolm X and Martin Luther King, with himself in a non-dancing role as a Becket figure.

course varied widely, but certainly for some it was seen as opening up the possibility of a deeper relationship with God in which the contribution of other religions was at last taken seriously.

Quite different has been the black experience of dance. Usually furthest from the American dream have been descendants of those who came as slaves to the United States. A crucial breakthrough in classical dance for them was made by Arthur Mitchell, whose prodigious talent took him through the New York City High School of Performing Arts into the School of American Ballet and thence into the New York City Ballet. Founder of the Dance Theatre of Harlem, he has seen an explosion of theatrical talent emerging both from there and from other immensely talented individuals. One of the best known is Alvin Ailey (d. 1989), who spent his youth in racially segregated Texas, where he experienced some of the worst aspects of prejudice. His mother, for example, was raped by a white man when he was five.[229] Ailey's break came when he was offered a role in the film *Carmen Jones* (1954). Eventually he was to form his own dance company, which he racially integrated in 1963 after encountering racism in reverse (that is, with whites excluded). His choreography was to include quite a wide-ranging number of pieces, varying from *Hidden Rites* (1973), a hard-edged exploration of sexual encounters and mating, to *The Lark Ascending* of the previous year, a tribute to the Scottish countryside that employs the music of Vaughan Williams. Inevitably, black oppression was among the topics he tackled. *Cry* (1971 and dedicated to his mother) is a moving account of the black woman's experience, in which the dancer's scarf is used to indicate a number of contrasting themes. Initially, it functions as a totem to the gods of Africa, then becomes a swaddling cloth. Finally, it moves from being a cleaning rag to ending up as a sort of headdress that gives the woman her own particular dignity.[230]

One of his early religious explorations was in *Hermit Songs* (1961), which concludes with a floor-bound image of the cross. However, critics have sometimes complained that that particular sequence was more of an excuse for 'the theatrical revelation of his

---

[229] Foulkes, *Modern Bodies*, 179.

[230] Both this dance and *Revelations* are available on a 1986 American Dance Theatre DVD, *Alvin Ailey*.

torso' than primarily spiritual in content.[231] That cannot be said
of what undoubtedly will continue to be the piece for which he is
best remembered. In *Revelations* Negro spirituals are used to
explore mainly positive aspects of black religious culture in the
deep South. It went through various editions (1962, 1969, 1975),
with later versions not always an improvement on earlier ones. In
essence, though the order varied, the content remained constant.[232]
The sequence usually opens with 'I Been 'Buked', in which sor-
rowful pilgrims crouch with arms spread and palms and eyes facing
upwards.[233] If that suggests a somewhat obvious heavenly appeal,
the grouping of the dancers renders this all the more dynamic.
Their overall form constitutes a rising pyramid that could be
taken to suggest a bird of the Spirit that has, as it were, descended
on all of them. 'Fix Me, Jesus' is used for the central *pas de deux*,
in which a male dancer acts as guardian angel to a praying woman.
If again that suggests something conventional (in this case a
common dance position), it is transformed through hints that the
woman seems oblivious of such support, or rather is so trusting
that she has no need to be made aware of it. 'Wade in the Water'
accompanies a baptism in which rippling muscles on the dancers'
torsos are used to evoke the water, and they themselves build into
an ecstatic dance. In 'I Wanna Be Ready' two male dancers perform
an act of penitence. Bodies taut and tense alternate with controlled
breaths of acceptance and resignation. In that number several times
the bodies form the shape of a cross, suggestive of Christ's role in
mediating forgiveness. The final dances are set in a rural wooden
church, with now men, now women taking the lead in a dance that
includes several gestures of sexual advance. Secular and religious
ecstasy are thus made to unite in a powerful conclusion.

   Thus it is not just ballet that can speak of the divine. Modern
dance, far from seldom broaching the issue, can be repeatedly
encountered doing just that.

---

[231] T. F. DeFrantz, *Dancing Revelations: Alvin Ailey's Embodiment of African
American Culture* (Oxford: Oxford University Press, 2004), 48.

[232] For some evaluations, see ibid., 77–9, 89.

[233] As the dance order varies, I have followed that on the DVD. Judith Jamison,
Ailey's successor as artistic director of the company, followed the same order in the
performance I saw in Newcastle in 2005. Her own ballets include *Hymn* (1993),
her tribute to Ailey himself.

Form, Expression and the Reach of Transcendence

Readers may have been surprised that there has been little in what I have said thus far about general theories. The omission has been deliberate because it seems to me that all too often theologians move quickly to abstract reflections that bear little relation to the way the empirical reality is experienced. As I noted earlier, little is to be gained by talking of a dance within the Trinity unless ordinary human dance is itself taken seriously. My concern in any case has been with the actual phenomena of religious experience mediated through dance. As we have seen, this can take a wide variety of different forms, with its use on the whole better preserved in the major religions other than Christianity. In modern Europe and America it has been the apparently secular forms of ballet and modern dance that have made the greater contribution. How far that contribution will continue in the current situation is hard to estimate. Clearly, a contribution remains, in so far as many of the pieces I have discussed continue to be performed. Evaluating the aims and intentions of contemporary choreographers is a more difficult task. Although some of the creative ideas of David Bintley have already been noted, any wider discussion here would take me too far from my basic aim.[234] So, rather than attempting such a survey, by way of conclusion I want to offer some reflection on some more theoretical issues, particularly as these are reflected in the move of so much modern dancing away from expression to form as its primary *raison d'être*.

That move is especially associated with the work of the American choreographer Merce Cunningham. In his revolt against the expressionist approach of Graham, he attempted a purely formalist aesthetic.[235] The composer John Cage was enlisted to advise on how arbitrary sequences could best be generated. Whereas that may suggest cooperation between the arts, Cunningham was in fact hostile to that aim also. He wanted the shock of the new and unpredictable. Working at the same time as some of

---

[234] For a representative selection of their views, see Brown, Mindlin and Woodford (eds), *Vision*, 137–215.

[235] For a helpful discussion, see R. Copeland, 'Beyond Expressionism: Merce Cunningham's Critique of the "Natural"', in J. Ashead-Lansdale and J. Layson (eds), *Dance History*, 2nd edn (London: Routledge, 1994), 182–97.

America's greatest abstract painters, even here it was with Robert Rauschenberg and Jasper Johns that he sided rather than the better-known Jackson Pollock. Pollock for Cunningham was still too expressionist. Indeed, Pollock's admiration for native American sand painters demonstrates that his painting was less arbitrary than it might initially appear.

Few have gone quite so far as Cunningham. But there is no shortage of modern dance and ballet that relies on form alone as potentially attractive to its audience. Such form could of course contain a religious message in suggesting a larger design and pattern to our lives. However, on the whole it is expression that most analysts have chosen as the primary value in dance. One of the most influential has been Suzanne Langer. While conceding the extent of dance's religious origins, her contention is that these are no longer defensible, and so dance must be approached in a new way: 'The substance of such dance creation is the same Power that enchanted caves and forests, but today we invoke it with full knowledge of its illusory status, and with wholly artistic intent.'[236] That raises an interesting question, namely whether pretence can really exercise the same power as belief in a reality. To the non-believer dance can of course still hint at the possibility that things might be otherwise. But that hint would seem immeasurably weakened if there is no grounding belief that this openness is, potentially at least, without limit, and so able to carry us into a quite different world.

Havelock Ellis is now best known for his views on sex. In the past, however, he was a major influence on the appreciation of dance. His emphasis is quite different from that of Langer. For him dance needs to recover its earlier focus, and that way it might reinvigorate not only itself but also society more generally, including our attitude to work.[237] In that revolt against pure technique, the Church has played a role, most notably in the foundation of the Judson Dance Theater in 1962.[238] But for me the most powerful modern image of dance helping to give a meaning to the whole of

---

[236] S. K. Langer, *Feeling and Form* (New York: Charles Scribner's Sons, 1953); relevant extract available in Copeland and Cohen (eds), *What is Dance?*, 36–47, esp. 45.

[237] H. Ellis, *The Dance of Life* (London: Constable, 1923); relevant extract ibid. 478–96, esp. 491–2.

[238] The venue of some key New York dancers and choreographers was Judson Memorial Church. Al Carmines, one of its ministers, offered much inspiration and

life remains the film to which I alluded earlier, *Dancer in the Dark*. Although facing execution as a result of a chain of circumstances in no way her own fault, the blind woman around whom the plot revolves goes to her death dancing, just as she had used dancing to make bearable, and indeed overcome, the tedium of her factory job. For a very different example, consider one of the most unusual contexts in which dance has occurred in recent years, in the French film *Beau travail* (1999). The French legion acting as a single unit is conveyed by the director through not only their exercises but also even their fights and ironing taking a balletic form.

Christianity, I suggest, was once inspired by similar notions of a danced order to life. This can be seen in the seventeenth century by the readiness of a future pope to commission a painting that reflected precisely this idea. So let me draw the reader's attention to that painting, before turning finally to something quite different from the twentieth century that speaks more directly to our present situation and the possibilities of dance. The painting I have in mind is Nicholas Poussin's *Dance to the Music of Time*.[239] This dates from around 1640 and was commissioned by a certain Guilio Rospigliosi (to become much better known two decades later when he served briefly as Pope Clement IX, 1667–9).[240] Rospigliosi was devout and well educated. So almost certainly the symbolism behind the painting was his idea, although Poussin undoubtedly developed it, using both antique precedents and standard iconographical texts such as those of Cesare Ripa. It depicts a wheel of fortune with four dancing youngsters, each in due course giving place to another. The maiden who represents poverty is seen to give place to labour, labour then to prosperity, and finally prosperity in turn to pleasure. Pleasurable indulgence then once more yields to poverty. Only poverty is depicted as male, perhaps to suggest the effort needed to get beyond that state. Although labour is feminine, she is made sufficiently muscular to indicate that she is well up to her tasks. All this suggests a purely human perspective, as initially does Time at the bottom right, who sets everything in motion. Yet Time is not

support. That role is highlighted in the introduction to the 'New Rebels' section of Brown, Mindlin and Woodford (eds), *Vision*, 137.

[239] For illustration and further commentary, see Plate 7 at the end of this book.

[240] The work now hangs in the Wallace Collection, London. For coloured illustrations, its history and some discussion of the meaning, see R. Beresford, *A Dance to the Music of Time* (London: Wallace Collection, 1995).

left totally in control. There is a parallel dance in heaven, as Apollo's chariot makes its way across the sky. This suggests to me that Rospigliosi intended to imply divine endorsement for, and control over, what is happening below. So it looks as though what is being asserted is that there is a natural order to life here on earth that is a reflection of a deeper order in the heavens, ordained by God. That could of course be read in a very conservative way, as forbidding the possibility of change in the social order. But I doubt if that is the intention here. Rather, Poussin is proclaiming on behalf of his patron that our lives here can have a 'danced order' that as such participates in the very nature of God's own life and action. Not that God is poor or overindulgent, but that satisfaction in effort is part of a divinely ordained way of doing things.

By the time Matisse came in 1910 to paint a mural of a similar circular dance for the home of the Russian magnate Sergei Shchukin, such confidence had declined. The familiar preparatory painting is clearly intended as anti-Cubist in format, as the figures are linked through arabesque rather than by means of arbitrary Cubist overlaps.[241] The possibility of a religious meaning is at most hinted at, rather than made explicit. The figures press to the very edge of the canvas, while the circle seems to demand completion beyond itself since two of the dancers fail in their struggle to link hands. Such hints, however, were more fully developed in the early 1930s when a similar mural was commissioned this time for an American patron, Albert Barnes.[242] Here, not only is the tension in the earlier versions increased, with some of the dancers now collapsing in a bacchic frenzy, but there is also a more explicit suggestion of a striving for infinity. Their bodies are shown struggling with deliberation to push beyond the enclosed space.[243] Commenting

[241] Now in the Hermitage in St Petersburg. Illustrated on the front cover of this book and with commentary in J. Jacobus, *Matisse* (London: Thames and Hudson, 1983), 72–3.

[242] The first version of this work is now in the Musée Matisse at Nice. Barnes was a wealthy Pittsburgh collector who had just had a new home built in Philadelphia to house his extensive art collection. For current arguments about the future of the collection, see D. D'Arcy, 'Bye Bye Barnes', *Modern Painters*, Winter 2002, 32–5.

[243] Matisse miscalculated the sizes of the murals at Barnes' home and so had to paint two preparatory versions. For the relation between all these various works and illustrations of them, see G. Néret, *Henri Matisse* (Cologne: Taschen, 1999), 143–63. The reader's attention is also drawn to the front cover of the present work.

on the 1930s works, Matisse wrote that 'what was most important was to call forth a sense of measureless infinity in a confined space'.[244] Although Matisse was not himself a practising Christian, it would be wrong to infer from this an absence of all religious meaning. The words I have just quoted suggest that Matisse clearly detected the potential for dance to embody a cosmic meaning. Although at the time he probably interpreted this purely in terms of human striving, Matisse did at least leave room for a more sacramental understanding which speaks of a reaching out that is also matched by the divine at the same time coming towards us. In these murals and paintings the two worlds are after all allowed to meet, even if it is outside the architectural frame. Even in the 1910 works, as already noted, something had also been left for the viewer to complete, the circle of the dancers itself. The set of hands nearest to the viewer's vision are struggling to link with one another. Now, however, in the versions from the early 1930s completion is only realizable by a transcendent thrust from above or below.[245]

Not long before his death in 1954, Matisse observed of those same 1930s figures: 'I needed above all to give a feeling of immensity within a limited space. That is why I put in figures which are not always complete. About half of them are outside it . . . That is what I did in the chapel at Vence.'[246] The connection made with Vence is intriguing, as the Dominican Chapel of our Lady of the Rosary at Vence was Matisse's only religious commission. Matisse also regarded it as his greatest work.[247] There has been some dispute about whether Father Couturier was right to interpret Matisse's desire 'to create a spiritual space' as really the aim to convey some sense of infinity.[248] What cannot survive is any claim that Matisse's intention was in any way narrowly functional, for the detailed record of his correspondence and discussions of the work in progress provides fascinating revelations of the great care with

[244] Quoted in V. Essers, *Henri Matisse* (Cologne: Taschen, 1990), 69. The work had a number of false starts, and still exists in more than one version.

[245] While such a thrust is only visible to us in the bodies of the dancers below, in terms of completion fulfilment would equally be realized were there to be a comparable stretching out from above.

[246] Quoted in Néret, *Henri Matisse*, 147. The quotation comes from 1952.

[247] M. Billot (ed.), *The Vence Chapel: The Archive of a Creation* (Milan: Skira, 1999), 210: 'the crowning achievement of my life'.

[248] Ibid. 22–9, 354.

which Matisse approached the entire project. If there is no dancing in the most obvious sense of the word, movement and rhythm remain integral. So, for example, it is not just the lightness of the colours used in the stained glass that suggest an upward thrust but also the way in which their 'flames' or 'flowers' add to such an impact, as do the various figures on the walls: certainly the image of St Dominic cannot but draw the eye upwards.[249] Matisse observed that the practice of prayer itself requires a sense of movement.[250] If despite the presence of Stations of the Cross there is little to suggest the suffering aspect of religion, he was nonetheless clear that only Christ should be given a face, since all human impact must be through him.[251] Matisse's conviction that his attempt to convey 'liberation by joy and light' was ultimately wrought by a hand higher than his own also comes across powerfully.[252] Incomplete flowers and human figures can suggest the movement of transcendence to link with another world no less than physical bodies actually on the move.

Matisse's painting exhibits none of the confidence of Poussin's and so is clearly more suited to our own more sceptical age. Nonetheless, it does remain open to the possibility of otherness. That is important, as Matisse himself found in his own case, where atheism eventually yielded to a more receptive spirit. Not that stretching upwards towards infinity need be the only way of making such an acknowledgement. As I sought to illustrate earlier, different cultures and dance forms have exploited quite different ways of expressing the same idea. So, for example, the dervishes' circle is thought sufficient in itself to evoke the divine; African dance links two worlds by sweeping through the air rather than pushing upward; traditional Japanese dance tends towards stasis, poise and equilibrium, while its more modern form, Butoh, plays on the dissolution of all forms, without necessarily thereby being any less religious. What is common is only the power of movement itself

---

[249] He talks of 'creating a rhythm' and an 'upward thrust' with the patterns in the windows: ibid. 150. Of Dominic he speaks of the need to 'allow the eye to go up': 212.

[250] For 'perpetual motion' being implied in a place of prayer, see ibid. 133.

[251] For Christ alone 'projecting his personality on us', see ibid. 413.

[252] For liberation, with the 'weight of sin' mentioned, see ibid. 90; for his repeated claim that God is acting through him, e.g. 40, 71 ('It's always God who is holding my hand'), 303 ('God held my hand'), 379.

to express the capacity for change: change that refuses to be bounded by the world as it is and so offers another world, potentially that of the divine.

The tragedy for western Christendom is that modern performance of the liturgy is quite often less successful at conveying that sense of two worlds interacting than allegedly purely secular dance. Because for Christians there is a dogmatic belief that this must be so in the eucharist, much less time is expended in considering how to heighten the sense of this happening than is actually necessary in an earthbound world. By contrast, because ballet and modern dance make no such assumptions, the dream that matters might be otherwise is enacted in fresh and dynamic ways. Therein lies a terrible irony: the secular theatre sometimes conveys truth about God more effectively than the Christian Church. The performance of liturgy is a topic to which I shall return in this volume's sequel.[253] In the meantime, however, I want to move in a somewhat different direction, to the physical resources on which the body draws, to food and drink.

---

[253] *God and Mystery in Words*, chs 5 and 7.

3
Food and Drink

FOOD and drink continue to have numerous symbolic resonances in our own day, but these are often quite different from those that prevailed in earlier times. While not ignoring more modern connotations, recovering those earlier senses will help us to appreciate how widely food and drink did once function sacramentally, in opening up individuals to experiences of the divine in their lives. Sometimes this was in highly cultural-specific ways; at other times much less so. Looking at such dimensions will help reveal what Christianity has lost through modern neglect of those basic facts about food and drink in the way its central sacrament is now conceived. This remark is not intended to anticipate an argument for a literal return to a meal. Rather it laments the frequent neglect of any deep reflection on the symbolism associated with eating and drinking. For instance, the intimate connection with sacrifice is now no longer widely known, nor is there the same sense of thankfulness and corporate spirit that was once uniformly associated with eating and drinking. Even the radical implications of the imagery basic to the Christian faith in bread, wine and water often pass unnoticed by the modern Christian. So here I shall attempt to examine food and drink in all its variety, in particular the impact they had historically on people's perceptions. Such a discussion will expose the degree to which modern attitudes to food and drink necessarily—or only accidentally—preclude mediation of the divine through our experience of the various ways in which our bodies are sustained. The first part of the chapter is devoted to food while the second focuses on drinking, not just on water and wine but everything from beer to tea, for reasons that will become obvious in due course.

Meals and Food

Here I want to explore the symbolism particularly associated with food. Ironically, Ludwig Feuerbach, the famous nineteenth-century critic of Christianity, is now best known among the wider public for an unrelated comment in which he puns on his native German to indicate the importance of food: 'Der Mensch ist, was er isst' (Human beings are what they eat).[1] Anthropologists continue to debate how integral particular foods in fact are to human communal identity.[2] Less is written on their religious impact.[3] In due course I shall examine those aspects that proved most significant for Christianity, including the significance of bread. However, throughout I want to explore features that Christianity shares with other religious approaches to the world, in particular gratitude, change and interdependence. In my view it is no accident that the basic symbols of Christian worship did not arise *de novo* but built upon already existing widespread human experience of the divine as this was mediated through such basic activities. So shortly I shall examine how the symbolism of bread is intimately connected with change and transformation and how meals once fostered a sense of interdependence, all notions integral to the Christian faith. I shall begin, however, with the theme of gratitude and two related features prominent in the ancient world in a way that is scarcely conceivable now, but was once indispensable to how food was experienced.

Harvest, Hospitality and Gratitude

All of us of course continue, now and then, to offer hospitality to others. Equally harvests continue to be gathered in. The difference from the past is that with international trade making vegetables

---

[1] L. Feuerbach, in his 'Advertisement' for Moleschott's *Lehre der Nahrungsmittel* of 1850.

[2] For a helpful summary, see P. Scholliers' introductory essay in P. Scholliers (ed.), *Food, Drink and Identity* (New York: Berg, 2001), 3–22, esp. 7–12. In particular, Alan Warde's stress on their marginal role is contrasted with the quite different views of Lévi-Strauss and Mary Douglas.

[3] Discussion of sacrifice is the obvious exception. But here often the sacrificial content takes priority over all other religious aspects of the meal.

and flowers available throughout the year most city dwellers are only subliminally aware, if at all, of when harvests occur even in their own land. Again, with highly privatized lives hospitality is now less frequent than it once was, even towards more immediate family members. International tourism and its easily available hotels also ensure that we are never likely to be faced with the ancient problem of how to find shelter in an unfamiliar land. So we need to revisit such differences if we are fully to appreciate how these two key elements of the ancient world, harvest and hospitality, might once have been perceived, almost without forethought, as having a divine dimension.

So far as harvest is concerned, even in the city churches of our own day the autumn harvest thanksgiving service is often an occasion to which most of the congregation look forward with eager anticipation. Indeed, for many parishes it rivals Christmas and Easter in attendance figures. Yet, surprisingly, Harvest Festival is a relatively modern invention, for it was only in 1843 that the Revd R. S. Hawker instituted in his own parish of Morwenstow in Cornwall a modern equivalent of the more ancient forms that I shall note shortly.[4] So quickly did the idea catch on that within a decade numerous other parishes had followed suit, and today even city centre churches, literally miles from the nearest field, join in the general jamboree. No doubt there is an element of nostalgia and longing for a vanished world. More positively, however, the church building looking at its best prompts a spirit of joy. It encourages all present to recall how much they have to be grateful for in their lives, not least those summer days now past when the light of the sky above was bright, and walking in the countryside made them glad to be alive. In short, the festival speaks of life as gift, of something received but in no way particularly merited. Of course, it does not follow from this that there is a God to whom gratitude is due, but it is scarcely surprising if such occasions do in fact open up for some just such a possibility.

Yet, no matter how elaborate the modern Harvest Festival becomes, it can scarcely compete with what went on in ancient Israel, where there were no less than three such occasions each year.

---

[4] For a recent study of his rather eccentric life, see P. Hutton, *I Would Not Be Forgotten: The Life and Work of Robert Stephen Hawker* (Padstow: Tabb House, 2004).

In effect the three major events of the Jewish calendar, they were, very roughly, the nearest equivalents of the Christian festivals of Christmas, Easter and Pentecost. Their prominence is easily explained by the fact that ancient Israel was an agricultural and farming community. If initially the presence of three such festivals seems more puzzling, an explanation is not hard to find. The reason lies in the existence of three different harvest seasons. First came the barley harvest, then seven weeks later the wheat harvest and, last of all, the gathering in of the fruit. More was at stake, though, than simple acknowledgement of how important a successful harvest was to the people's livelihood or even the generosity of God in that provision. There was also, as will become clear when I examine how these institutions were linked with Israel's history, a desire to deepen the experience of thanksgiving and gratitude in various ways.

First, however, I want to emphasize that Israel was by no means unique in these more basic attitudes. Greece and Rome too had their agricultural festivals linked with various divinities, most notably Demeter in Greece and Ceres in Rome.[5] Gratitude and joy were also major themes here.[6] Likewise, as with ancient Israel, ways were sought of involving the divine in their more general eating and drinking. If the classical world's best-known text on food speaks of vulgar excess, the recent discovery of Menander's play *Bad-Tempered Man* indicates a different world, where sacrifice to the gods is integral to feasting and ordinary family meals.[7] Indeed, where meat-eating was concerned, this seems to have been the

[5] The most widespread festival of ancient Greece was the fertility festival of Thesmophoria, held in honour of Demeter (a corruption of Ge-meter and so 'mother earth'): S. Price, *Religions of the Ancient Greeks* (Cambridge: Cambridge University Press, 1999), 18–19, 98–100. For the move away from agricultural festivals in cosmopolitan Rome, see M. Beard, J. North and S. Price (eds), *Religions of Rome* (Cambridge: Cambridge University Press, 1998), 45–7.

[6] Other gods could also be involved. Pyanepsia was a feast of Apollo. Likewise, the Eleusinian mysteries of Demeter developed into something rather different. For an excellent description of both (surprisingly, in a detective novel), see M. Doody, *Mysteries of Eleusis* (London: Arrow, 2006), 38–41, 280–91, 419–86.

[7] For a discussion of the relevance of the play, see A. Dalby, *Siren Feasts: A History of Food and Gastronomy in Greece* (London: Routledge, 1996), 1–5. The obvious contrast is with Petronius' *Cena Trimalchionis*.

normal pattern among the Greeks.[8] Likewise, drinking symposia always included libations of wine to the gods.[9] As Xenophanes enjoins: 'Among us incense gives a holy scent... An altar in the middle is heaped with flowers... First the gods must be hymned by cheerful men in proper words and pure compositions. After libations, and prayers to be empowered to do right (these must come first), it is not wrong to drink as much as one can and still get home safely.'[10] Nor was Roman practice significantly different. At some point during a meal the household gods would be brought into the *triclinium* or dining room, to bless the festivities. The statues that represented them were ceremoniously placed on the table. The room also often had various other forms of symbolism present, to indicate the wider context within which the meal was being consumed. The ceiling might, for example, have a representation of the heavens, while Cerberus, the guardian of the underworld, would greet guests at the door on the mosaic floor.[11] So in seeking precedents for the practice of offering animal sacrifice at meals in medieval Byzantium or among contemporary Christians in Armenia there is no need to appeal to scripture alone.[12] The inherited attitudes of antiquity towards food as a gift of the gods also played its part, in making such expressions of gratefulness seem entirely natural.

It is also into such a context that the continuing practice of *puja* among Hindus should probably be set. The earliest form of offering to the gods had been in destruction through fire (known as

---

[8] Consumption of meat had in itself something of the nature of a celebration, as lentils, barley and wheat formed the staple Greek diet: so Dalby, *Siren Feasts*, 22–3. Various explanations have been offered as to why in general fish were not sacrificed (larger ones such as tuna apparently were): for some possibilities, see J. Davidson, *Courtesans and Fishcakes* (London: Fontana, 1997), 12; N. Purcell, 'Eating Fish: The Paradoxes of Seafood', in J. Wilkins, D. Harvey and M. Dobson (eds), *Food in Antiquity* (Exeter: University of Exeter Press, 1995), 150–61.

[9] Usually undiluted wine, unlike the shared mixed cup that followed. So far from involving less drunkenness, Spartan individual cups are thought to have offered more opportunities for deep drinking: so Davidson, *Courtesans and Fishcakes*, 36–69, esp. 45–6, 49–61.

[10] Quoted in Athenaeus, *Deipnosophists* 462c; translation from Dalby, *Siren Feasts*, 104.

[11] For further details and references, see R. Strong, *Feast* (London: Jonathan Cape, 2002), 30.

[12] For details and references, see Dalby, *Siren Feasts*, 208–9.

yanjna), but already in texts supplementary to the Vedas *puja* is being mentioned (*c.* 500 BC). With the rise of devotional cults at the beginning of the common era, this practice of setting before the god vegetable offerings and rice becomes the norm. The rituals of temple and home are quite similar. As well as token food, the image is also offered water and may even be bathed, either in whole or in part.[13] Thereby the links with hospitality are made manifest. The god is being treated as an honoured guest. Each Hindu home has a shrine, either in a separate room or in an alcove, where one person acting on behalf of the family performs the ritual before the symbolic presence of the deity.[14] At its conclusion the rest of the family then join in, offering prostrations and commonly also sipping the water with which the image has been bathed. In the case of some deities such as Vishnu the food that is now believed to have been graced by divine taste is also reverentially consumed. Despite objections, similar practices have also arisen in Buddhism. Admittedly, not all such behaviour is spiritually uplifting in those parts of the world where these two religions are in the ascendancy. In Nepal, for instance, flipping water off one's plate (as well as food offerings) seems intended as a way of appeasing the dead spirits that are believed to be near by.[15]

It would be grossly unfair, however, to characterize all such practices as exclusively cautionary, intended simply to ward off anger or resentment on the part of the gods. Motives were no doubt often mixed, but that is as likely to have applied within Judaism as beyond. The real advance made within the canon of scripture was not over this question but elsewhere. Each harvest thanksgiving came to be linked with a specific event in Israel's history. So opportunity for a deeper sense of gratitude was provided, one that could also generate a much stronger sense of dependence on divine grace. The barley harvest came to be associated with Passover and deliverance from slavery in Egypt; wheat with Pentecost and the giving of the Law; and the gathering in of the fruit with the festival of Booths and thus the time spent living

---

[13] Usually only the feet are bathed. In temples the image may even be formally placed in a bed overnight and then given a morning bath.

[14] For a more detailed account, see V. Voiels, *Hinduism: A New Approach* (London: Hodder and Stoughton, 1998), 63–5.

[15] C. E. Hardman, *Other Worlds: Notions of Self and Emotion among the Lohorung Rai* (Oxford: Berg, 2000), 41–58 (the chapter entitled 'The Ancestors are Angry').

in tents in the desert.[16] Certainly, all three were great occasions for joy. Passover, for instance, involved a sumptuous meal, a practice that continues among Jews to this day. Yet what is interestingly different from modern harvest festivals is that even so none were occasions of unmitigated joy.

Passover recalled a time of oppression and slavery in Egypt. So, as the farmers and labourers gathered the barley, their thoughts probably also turned to old wrongs and how God had righted them.[17] But much the same was true of the other two occasions as well. At the wheat harvest and thus the time of the festival of Weeks or Pentecost, people were expected to recall the giving of the Law and so to meditate on their obligations under that law. It is a connection that is continued in one reading often chosen for modern harvest festivals, Deut. 28.1–14. The most dramatic reminder of all, though, was at the gathering in of the fruit, at the festival of Booths. On this occasion the people were expected once more actually to take to living in tents for a week. This provided a powerful reminder of the food shortages and the oppression of the desert heat from which their ancestors had suffered and which only gradually gave way to better conditions as they approached the promised land.

Such linking of burdens and oppression on the one hand with the joy of harvest on the other, is, I think, no accident. It was not just an attempt to unite a nomadic people's history with the already existing agricultural traditions of the land they now occupied. It was also a way of ensuring through such practices that people learnt to have thankful hearts, even in contexts where obligations were being imposed on them, and suffering

---

[16] In the scriptures only the first connection is early. The third is post-exilic (cf. Lev. 23.42–43). The connection between Weeks and Sinai is no earlier than the Mishnah, although the Book of Jubilees experiments with an earlier variant, in the covenants between God and Noah and God and Abraham (6.17; 15.1). For further details, see R. Albertz, *History of Israelite Religion in the Old Testament Period* (London: SCM Press, 1994), i, 89–91; H. Ringgren, *Israelite Religion* (London: SPCK, 1966), 184–90.

[17] That at any rate was the intention of the biblical legislation. The multivalency of symbols no doubt meant that different elements were brought to the fore for different people, and for the same people at different times. For the condensation or density of symbols, see further V. W. Turner, *The Drums of Affliction: A Study of Religious Processes among the Ndembi of Zambia* (Oxford: Clarendon Press, 1968).

seemed the order of the day and the outcome far from certain. As the seventeenth-century poet Robert Herrick puts it:

> What God gives and what we take,
> 'Tis a gift for Christ his sake:
> Be the meale of Beanes and Pease,
> God be thank'd for those, and these:
> Have we flesh, or have we fish,
> All are fragments from His dish.[18]

Long after Jews had ceased to be primarily an agricultural community, their Passover celebrations continued to reflect that duality. If only a tiny minority continued with the sacrificial element, the roasted shankbone left to one side was still intended as a reminder of such invited divine participation.[19] Moreover, although the rounded unleavened character of the bread was given quite a wide variety of interpretations, the bread and wine seemed to continue to speak of both pain and joy in God.[20] The matzo's unleavened character at the very least recalled a departure in sorrow and haste, while the cup set aside for Elijah expressed expectations for a new age. Nor was any of this envisaged as simply a reminder of some dim and distant past event. Rather, that event was being made present once more in the life and experience of the community in the here and now.[21] It was the one period of the year when the Song of Songs was part of the liturgy.[22] If the choice of reading speaks of presence, joy and intimacy, it was also a joy that could be sustained in suffering. Only that way can sense can be made of the desire to break the normal rules through the use of tea or even leavened bread rather than forgo the experience of the festival in arduous or strained circumstances.[23]

---

[18] From his poem 'Graces for Children', in L. C. Martin (ed.), *The Poems of Robert Herrick* (London: Oxford University Press, 1965), 363.

[19] The practice continues among Samaritans and Falasha Jews: P. Goodman, *The Passover Anthology* (Philadelphia: Jewish Publication Society, 1961), 28, 36.

[20] For the variety of symbolic explanations for the round bread or matzo, see ibid. 135, 165; for the Elijah cup and hopes for his return, 43, 439.

[21] This is what one finds, for example, in the Mishnah and in Maimonides: ibid. 74–5, 174.

[22] Ibid. 274.

[23] Tea was used in Vilnius during World War I, leavened bread in Belsen: ibid. 383.

As quite a number of commentators have stressed,[24] bringing the past into the present is also integral to understanding the Christian eucharist. Some have sought to make the parallels still closer.[25] But here the basic point I want to emphasize is the way in which such festivals are about discovering gratitude to God in adversity no less than in joy. Perhaps nowhere in scripture is that demonstrated more effectively than in the extraordinary psalm with which the book of Habakkuk concludes:

> Though the fig tree do not blossom
> nor fruit be on the vines,
> the produce of the olive fail
> and the field yield no food,
> the flock be cut off from the fold
> and there be no herd in the stalls,
> yet I will rejoice in the Lord,
> I will joy in the God of my salvation. (Hab. 3.17–18)

It is not a sentiment that comes easily even to the most devout. Farmers who have lost everything might well feel only resentment in their hearts. But it does, I think, tell us something important about attitudes of gratitude and thankfulness. It is this: once individuals' hearts are opened to recognition of the fact that the material plenty they have is quite undeserved, it is but a short step to seeing that this holds equally when they have much less materially or in other ways. Indeed, gratitude might become all the more acutely felt, precisely because straitened circumstances now force just such a perception. Perhaps the face of Mother Teresa of Calcutta may be used by way of illustration. Its deeply etched lines are easily explained by the very hard life she had led, working among the poor and dying of Calcutta. But what her winning smile revealed was also a tremendous serenity that shone through whatever troubles she faced. She had learnt to see God's care for her and those around her in all the little details of life, and that made her untroubled and unafraid. For she knew that even where she appeared to have little she had in fact much: the love of her

---

[24] Most notably in J. Jeremias, *The Eucharistic Words of Jesus* (London: SCM Press, 1966), though that making present is seen as mediated through God's remembrance: 237–55.

[25] For a detailed attempt of this sort, see J. Stallings, *Rediscovering Passover* (San Jose, Calif.: Resource Publications, 1995 edn).

fellow-workers, the appreciation of those for whom she cared, all her basic needs provided, and above all the love and, if I may put it like this, the answering smile of God himself.

It is a similar reflection that John's Gospel offers in its treatment of the crowd's response to the miracle of the feeding of the five thousand (John 6.25–35). Christ's audience recall how their ancestors were once fed regularly with manna in the desert. So their hope becomes a world without famine, a world in which they would not need to earn their daily bread. But no, says Jesus, they are looking for satisfaction, for contentment, in the wrong place. Instead, he offers them the food of his own life, a life of toil and suffering but one in which the divine smile still shines through—in his care for the despised, in the humour of his parables, in his love of the companionship of shared meals. As Matthew puts it, 'The Son of man came eating and drinking, and they say, "Behold a glutton and a drunkard"' (11.19).

My argument here runs in the opposite direction from Charles Lamb's, who in his essay on 'Grace before Meat' finds the saying of grace natural only at the poor man's table: 'It is here that the grace becomes exceedingly graceful. The indigent man, who hardly knows whether he shall have a meal the next day or not, sits down to his fare with a present sense of the blessing which can be but feebly acted by the rich.'[26] Such a perspective seems to me unduly cynical. While it is perhaps true for some that only a period of want makes them appreciate plenty, it surely takes only a moment of reflection for most of us to acknowledge that there is nothing intrinsically in our worth that makes us more deserving of a life of ease than, say, the undernourished on the continent of Africa.

Yet it may seem that I too suffer from a not unrelated fault, in putting so much stress on contentment with little. Indeed, from that emphasis it would be easy to draw the conclusion that I think of the experience of thankfulness as inevitably leading to passivity and a lack of concern for change. Certainly, there will be contentment with what one has. But any further inference was fortunately blocked, at least in the ancient world, by the dynamic for change inherent in that most basic of all foods: bread. How precisely that dynamic works I shall consider in the next section.[27]

---

[26] In *Essays of Elia* (London: Macmillan, 1884), 130–7, esp. 131.
[27] Delayed to the next section because the symbolism of bread (and Jesus' miracle in particular) cannot be considered in isolation but needs to be set against a much wider history of how bread has functioned in human history.

In the meantime I turn to that other social feature of the ancient world that I said I would discuss at this stage, the importance of hospitality.

In order to understand its importance in the ancient world, it is essential to think ourselves back into a world without any proper police force or public transport, where travel was inherently dangerous and difficult. Little wonder, then, that in all ancient cultures hospitality was elevated into a sacred duty. Our word 'symbol' is in fact derived from a Greek word for a metal or pottery token.[28] The broken half created the expectation of food and shelter, wherever it could be matched with its other half, even if that other half was in the possession of a complete stranger. Similar attitudes are encountered within the Bible. Abraham, for example, has no doubts that it is his solemn duty to entertain the strangers whom he encounters under the oaks or terebinths at Mamre in Genesis 18. The reason why mention is so often made of that act of hospitality in subsequent Jewish literature is thus less because those visitors turned out to be angels and much more because of what their being angels represented: God's unique blessing on what Abraham was doing—showing hospitality to strangers. Within Christianity that is also often true, despite the fame of Andrei Rublev's quite different application in his icon of the Trinity.[29] It is into just such a context that the opening verse of the thirteenth chapter of Hebrews should therefore be set. The author is not urging his readers to a similar hospitality in the remote hope of a like encounter. Rather, it is because the nature of that unlikely encounter already indicated what a high value God placed on the act of being hospitable, even to strangers. It was a sacred duty.

That use of the language of 'sacred duty', however, is perhaps already to bring such actions into too modern a frame. It can suggest *individual* debts and obligations: particular persons *deciding* so to act rather than already being imbued with certain attitudes and patterns of behaviour. What needs to be recalled is that in many cultures, particularly the more ancient, the focus is much less on the individual and more on the collective or group-self.[30] In such a

---

[28] The Greek means literally to throw (*ballo*) together (*sun*), as are the two parts of the token, or two related realities in a modern symbol.

[29] As, for instance, in the famous mosaic at San Vitale in Ravenna: G. Bovini, *Ravenna* (Ravenna: Longo, 1991), illus. 19.

[30] Mauss' investigations of this (mentioned below) spanned not only ancient Europe but also Polynesia and North America.

society to want to be left alone is itself thought abnormal, even a sign of sickness. Much work has been done on such perceptions.[31] Indeed, I myself have suggested that they might help in providing some kind of analogy for the Trinity's interpersonal character.[32] In the writings of Marcel Mauss a strong contrast is drawn between how exchange in 'archaic' non-western societies was understood and how the matter is now conceived in the industrialized, capitalist West.[33] It is essentially about the bonding of groups rather than agreements between individuals. In this he was supported by Claude Lévi-Strauss, who pointed to the continuation of some aspects into more recent times.[34] In the south of France customers in cheap restaurants can be seen eating by themselves but giving their wine to their neighbours and receiving identical bottles in return. Such 'vestiges', he suggests, still assume the old notion of gift, with meals helping to achieve integration of the individual into the social whole. Although he does not say this, in the more distant past that would inevitably have also included the group's own relationship with the divine.

In the ancient world such hospitality was not permitted to be parsimonious or confined to food alone. The stranger was to be positively welcomed. Hot, dusty roads meant that the washing of a guest's feet must have come as an extraordinarily soothing and relaxing experience. In addition to this the face and hair were commonly anointed with oil. So, as the oil seeped into skin scorched with the heat of the sun, the stranger would feel refreshed and revitalized. Quite a number of New Testament incidents reflect precisely this form of behaviour. Readers will perhaps recall the host rebuked by Jesus for failing to wash his feet, unlike the penitent woman before him (Luke 7.44–7). Again, Jesus performs the same deed for his own disciples (John 13.1–11). Such assumptions

---

[31] e.g. B. Morris, *Anthropology of the Self: The Individual in Cultural Perspective* (London: Pluto, 1994); M. Fortes, *Oedipus and Job in West African Religion* (Cambridge: Cambridge University Press, 1983).

[32] D. Brown, 'Trinitarian Personhood and Individuality', in R. J. Feenstra and C. Plantinga (eds), *Trinity, Incarnation and Atonement* (Notre Dame, Ind.: University of Notre Dame Press, 1989), 46–78.

[33] M. Mauss, *The Gift: Forms and Functions of Exchange in Archaic Societies* (New York: W. W. Norton, 1967).

[34] C. Lévi-Strauss, *The Elementary Structures of Kinship* (Boston: Beacon Press, 1969), 58–60.

run deep throughout scripture. Indeed, they even form the premise on which Jesus urges the spread of the gospel. He sent out his disciples on their first mission with strict instructions to take nothing with them by way of provisions (Matt. 10.9). This cannot be explained as intended simply to test their faith, since expectations of hospitality are in fact mentioned in subsequent verses. So even the spread of the gospel was itself premissed on such antecedent assumptions about hospitality.

This second key feature of the ancient world was not unconnected with the first. As we saw, gratitude to God for his provision was integral to the ancient celebration of agricultural festivals. But hospitality was of course also about reciprocity, acknowledging dependence on another, even if on this occasion it was a human other. Yet matters can scarcely be left there. Not only does the importance attached to Abraham's encounter indicate divine involvement but also the exaltation of hospitality to a sacred duty far more widely than just within scripture.[35] Assumptions in Homer or among the pagans of Sodom indicate how widespread the phenomenon was in the ancient world.[36] Admittedly, many instances could be read as no more than a precautionary invocation of the gods, in order to secure more acceptable conduct. But there seems also to be acknowledged an element of transcendence in such openness to otherness. The sense of dependent gratitude is deepened in at least two ways. First, precisely because they are required to look to another's need, the individuals concerned are pulled out of themselves to perceive matters from the other's perspective. Secondly, because everything is done under the umbrella of a divinely sanctioned institution, the human and divine contributions are seen as existing in a single extended continuum. So gratitude to the divine becomes as natural as it is to feel indebted to one's fellow human being.

Perhaps that can also help explain why the range of hospitality is progressively extended across the biblical canon. In the Old Testament welcoming the poor had already been made basic to the

---

[35] I continue with the terminology of 'sacred duty' despite my earlier criticisms because I can think of no better term.

[36] For Sodom, see Gen. 19.1–11. Note that Lot appeals to shared assumptions about hospitality in v. 7. For Homeric references, including the importance of gifts as part of such hospitality, see O. Murray, *Early Greece* (London: Fontana, 1980), 50–2.

celebration of the Passover (Exod. 12. 43–49). To this day it is an integral part of Jewish celebrations of that feast. In a similar way most Christians would regard it as unthinkable to celebrate Christmas without making some attempt to welcome those who would otherwise be left alone into their own homes. Where the gospel is innovative is in suggesting inclusion of 'the lame, the crippled and the blind' (Luke 14.7–14). If such compassion now seems natural, it is salutary to recall that for most people in the ancient world, including those reared on the Hebrew scriptures, such individuals were seen as under a divine curse. Their sad condition was taken to demonstrate divine disapproval. Not only could no animal with such defects be offered to God, the Law in Leviticus explicitly states that the priesthood was likewise barred to men impaired in such ways (Lev. 21.18). Similarly, the book of Samuel informs us that anyone with such a handicap was to be precluded from entering the Temple (2 Sam. 5.8). Occasionally, a prophet appears to speak out against such practices, in talking of God saving the blind and the lame (e.g. Zeph. 3.19). But care is needed in interpreting such verses. It may be that all that is in mind is the eventual transformation of such unfortunate people, not God's full acceptance of them in the here and now, as they are. Certainly, there are injunctions against abusing the deformed, and King David is found showing 'the kindness of God' towards Saul's lame son.[37] But many of Jesus' contemporaries, including those belonging to the community at Qumran, continued the earlier prohibitions. Likewise, similar assumptions are to be found in the Targums (explanatory commentaries on the Hebrew sacred texts), and in the Mishnah.[38] Nor was the subsequent practice of the Church much different. The Epistle to the Hebrews' use of the same word ('without blemish') to describe Christ no doubt contributed.[39] While the positive side was seen in the desire to offer something perfect to God, the negative result was not only in unfortunate attitudes to handicap but also towards illegitimacy, which was likewise treated as a bar towards ordination.

---

[37] Lev. 19.14; Deut. 27.18; 2 Sam. 9.3.

[38] The Mishnah considerably expands the range of exclusions: H. Danby (ed.), *The Mishnah* (New York: Oxford University Press, 1933), 538–9 (Bekhoreth 7).

[39] Heb. 9.14 (*tamim* in Hebrew, *amomos* in Greek, *immaculatus* in Latin).

So in all probability Jesus is in fact being quite revolutionary at this point. The ritually polluted, those apparently condemned by God, are now to be made especially welcome at the tables of his followers. In trying to account for such an insight, it is tempting to put the matter in terms easily accessible to modern minds, and so speak simply of compassion. That may be right, but I doubt it. Although there is no way of knowing for certain, it seems to me much more likely that the general experience of hospitality played a key role. Openness to the other's perspective and gratitude to God for what is in no sense part of one's deserts, in a mind sufficiently sensitive to that way of thinking, could easily have pulled the logic further, into including all, irrespective of status, within such a compass. If in response it is suggested that I am making difficult an insight that is remarkably easy for a compassionate person, let me observe that even today many find such inclusiveness difficult. If the physically handicapped no longer encounter such problems, it is still the case that many a parish finds it difficult to include in its eucharistic meal one or more of the following: the ex-offender, the con-man, the Down's syndrome child, the mentally deranged, the gentleman of the streets, the drunk, the practising homosexual, the adulterer, the child molester, the asylum seeker, the person of little faith. Exchanging a handshake at the peace is the nearest modern equivalent to washing the strangers' feet and anointing their face with oil. Yet it is a gesture that many Christians still find trying or difficult in the case of some of those listed. But if the feast is Christ's and not the congregation's, it is surely not for us to judge or condemn.

If I am right about this and it was the experience of gratitude in harvest and hospitality that helped revolutionize the perceived extent of divine concern, then such experiences of thankfulness to God cannot be viewed as essentially conservative encounters. Nor was this the case in respect of a still more basic form of gratitude, in thankfulness for one's own everyday personal consumption. For the ancient world this focused on bread, for the obvious reason that bread was the staple diet of the ancient Mediterranean world. In that obvious fact what, however, is often ignored is the way in which bread is inherently open to symbolism and with that symbolism to a dynamic of change. Too often theologians write as though what matters in the central Christian sacrament is the symbolism of body and not also of the bread through which Christ's body is now mediated. What such an exclusive stress misses is the way in which Jesus in adopting that symbolism built upon experiences of the divine that were already widespread in the ancient world. It was those experiences that helped to give the new faith much of its power, and which modern Christianity therefore ignores to its own great loss.

Bread and the Dynamic for Social Change

Within some forms of Christianity it might well be argued that the use of bread has been so overlaid with additional elements of symbolism that its primary meaning is in constant danger of being lost. Certainly it is not easy to focus on the simplicity of the wafer when it is hidden in a monstrance, especially when the form and shape of the latter pulls one's reflections in a quite different direction. Christ as the sun and source of life has become the point, with the roundness of the wafer augmented by symbolic rays projecting from it.[40] Again, even when ordinary bread is used it has sometimes been subject to so many stamps or additional markings that it is these that the believer is led to contemplate and not the fact of bread as such.[41] Yet, as one can see from societies that have not lost touch with their agricultural roots, the associations of basic foods with religion and with experiences of thankfulness run deep. That is, for instance, what the Spanish found in the attitudes of the native peoples of Latin American to the corn they grew. Parallel attitudes to rice are to be found among the Chinese.[42] Occasionally, it is still possible to identify similar approaches within

[40] Christ as light of the world helps to facilitate identification of him with the sun (augmented in some languages by the play on 'sun'/'son'), though the sun's nurturing of the corn could also come to mind.

[41] In the Orthodox liturgy the faithful are given the *antidoron* (blessed but unconsecrated bread). Historically, this and similar bread has often had elaborate stamps placed on it, e.g. symbols of paradise, the cross and Jerusalem: G. Calavaris, *Bread and the Liturgy* (Madison, Wise.: University of Wisconsin Press, 1970), esp. 32, 36, 161. The consecrated bread is also treated to detailed symbolic divisions, e.g. to refer to Christ's dual nature or to the twelve apostles: for approaches within the Byzantine church, see 62–9; within the Coptic, 93.

[42] For Aztec and Inca practice, see M. Visser, *Much Depends on Dinner* (London: Penguin, 1989), 29–38. The Chinese emperor ploughed a sacred field just as in Inca practice, though in the latter case a special maize drink was also drunk and offered sacrificially: 34, 170.

contemporary groups. Algerian Muslims, for example, assign a religious significance to homemade bread that is totally denied to the more commonly purchased, industrially produced, French-style bread.[43] It would therefore be quite wrong to postulate that bread only has symbolic meaning within the context of specific religions. Of course, other distinctive factors sometimes enter in, as the Chinese experience illustrates. Yet even so the fact that rice and bread are both basic commodities means that much is shared in common.

Earlier I promised to return to the question of why such thankfulness seldom degenerated into pure passivity. I suggest that it had much to do with the basic underlying symbolism inherent in bread. To understand what made the difference, it is necessary to explore more carefully how the image actually works in cultures where bread still fulfils its role as basic, essential nutrition. Because the symbolism of it as life-giving is so obvious, the suggestion of a transition from one form of life to another was also a natural progression. This was sometimes aided by parallels drawn with sexual symbolism, as in the way in which the plough opens the earth's womb, in order to enable the corn to grow.[44] Another key feature of relevance is the frequency of bread shortages. This was particularly true of the ancient world. So, in seeking to understand that Gospel dialogue in John to which we referred earlier (John 6.25–35), it is important that the people's desire for bread should be set against, and in response to, precisely that phenomenon.[45]

Reading the history of the growth of civilization is almost like reading a history of bread shortages. As wealth generated progressively larger estates, it also repeatedly brought with it a worsening lot for the poor. In the classical world, for example, Italians with large holdings soon discovered that they could make more money by dispossessing the peasants in favour of sheep and cattle. So Rome soon found itself heavily reliant on imported grain, particularly

---

[43] W. Jansen, 'French Bread and Algerian wine', in Scholliers (ed.), *Food, Drink and Identity*, 195–218, esp. 200, 204–5. Such bread is often called '*aysh* ('life'), and is never cut, but always broken 'in the name of God'.

[44] For other such sexual analogies, see C. H. Heiser, *Seed to Civilisation* (Cambridge, Mass.: Harvard University Press, 1990 edn), 14–26.

[45] For the pattern of recurring economic crises, see Z. Safrai, *The Economy of Roman Palestine* (London: Routledge, 1994), esp. 457–8.

from Egypt, not least to feed the urban poor in Rome itself.[46] Under the Republic in the second century BC the Gracchi brothers tried to institute land reform, but both were assassinated for their pains. By the time of Christ perhaps a quarter of Rome's population of a million was on the dole, dependent on the largess of the emperor. To feed them, grain arrived at Rome's port of Ostia not only from Egypt but even from Judaea, required by law to send a quarter of its produce to the capital. To judge by the size of the ruins of priestly houses in Jerusalem, it looks as though Judaism was not doing any better than imperial Rome in securing fairness. So, against such a backdrop, whatever John meant, it is implausible to suppose that he interpreted Christ's message as a purely metaphorical one.

Equally, that was scarcely how it was usually heard in subsequent Christian history, where such shortages continued. In the fourteenth century, for example, the Jacquerie riots in France and the Peasants' Revolt in England were alike in large part motivated by bread shortages, as was the Peasants' War in Germany in the sixteenth century. Luther's savage response, no doubt in part motivated by fear of political instability, is well known: 'Because they are . . . setting themselves against the higher powers, wilfully and with violence, they have forfeited body and soul . . . Therefore, let everyone who can smite, slay and stab, secretly or openly, remembering that nothing can be more poisonous, hurtful or devilish than a rebel. It is just as when one must kill a mad dog; if you do not strike him, he will strike you, and a whole land with you.'[47] And 130,000 perished as a result. Yet there were Christians on the other side, Thomas Münster among them, just as in the Peasants' Revolt of 1381 in England the priest John Ball had played a major role.

Much of what Ball and Münster said and did as a result may have been naïve and misguided, but that hardly takes away from the essential rightness of their intuitions on this point. In the context of the Judaism of Jesus' day bread was in fact an obvious symbol of

---

[46] Much of the historical information that follows is conveniently summarized in H. E. Jacob, *Six Thousand Years of Bread: Its Holy and Unholy History* (New York: Lyons Press, 1997 edn; 1st publ. 1944). For Rome, see 75–89; for peasant revolts, 172–84.

[47] 'Against the Robbery and Murdering Hordes of Peasants, May 1525', in E. G. Rupp and B. Drewery (eds), *Martin Luther: Documents of Modern History* (London: Edward Arnold, 1970), 122.

change. The annual Passover feast highlighted that very fact, for it was at this time that unleavened bread was eaten in reminder of the haste of their ancestors' departure out of slavery in Egypt. It spoke of how a new world could emerge out of the oppression of the old. Yet, to derive such implications for change from the bread being used, it was scarcely necessary to be especially devout, nor even a Jew for that matter. The more basic grounding of the symbolism was available to all.[48] It was all a matter of the dramatic change in the constitution of the flour itself, as the bread was being made: a wonder accentuated by the fact that at the time no one understood quite why it happened. The ancient world was entirely without knowledge of the key role of bacteria. Indeed, probably because of this, the Romans even assigned a god (Fornax) to watch over the oven.

Equally, to an agricultural community the grain itself already spoke of transformation, so much so that medieval Christians were not averse to drawing out the parallel with the life of Christ himself. The process of sowing was begun deliberately on March the 25th, to correspond to the Annunciation to Mary that day (Lady Day).[49] It was a practice that was sometimes given additional justification by the fact that Bethlehem, the place where Christ was to be born, was itself taken to mean 'house of bread'.[50] If Robert Burns' poem about the personified John Barleycorn who comes to life once more is perhaps better known,[51] more specifically Christian examples are not wanting. The medieval poet Johann von Krolewiz, for instance, speaks of a Christ who 'was sowed, sprouted, stood in flower, grew, was mowed, bound like a sheaf, driven to the threshing floor, threshed, swept with a broom, ground, thrust into an oven, and left therein for three days, taken out, and finally eaten by men as bread'.[52] Less dramatic applications to the Christian believer found precedents in Augustine.[53]

[48] Again, as with my earlier comment on rice, under certain conditions. My later discussion of the role of the pig in northern Europe helps to make the point.

[49] Jacob, *Six Thousand Years of Bread*, 120.

[50] From *beth* as house and *lehem* as bread. For a later example of such an application, see Lancelot Andrewes' Nativity Sermon for Christmas Day, 1615: *The Sermons of Lancelot Andrewes*, ed. M. Dorman (Edinburgh: Pentland Press, 1992), i, ·57.

[51] *Poems and Songs of Robert Burns*, ed. J. Barke (Glasgow: Collins, 1955), 378.

[52] Jacob, *Six Thousand Years of Bread*, 58.

[53] As in one of his sermons: PL 46, 835.

But perhaps nowhere was such parallelism more explicit than in the festivities that took place each September at Eleusis in honour of the Greek goddess Demeter. Recalling the loss of her daughter, Persephone, to the underworld, the feast celebrated Persephone's annual return, like the grain harvest. Pilgrim processions walked slowly out from Athens to the site where new initiates were received. To this day it remains unclear what exactly happened, but the ritual may have been a very simple one. During the night initiates were exposed to some of the presumed terrors of the underworld. Next morning at dawn their first sight was of a young girl holding a fresh sheaf of corn.[54] So profound was the mystery's impact that even Roman emperors wanted to take part in the ceremony.[55] Undoubtedly, part of the explanation lay in the fact that not only was the annual return of the harvest being celebrated but also hope and new life amid the terrors of the old, including the possibility of a life beyond this one. When the distinguished Protestant Renaissance scholar Isaac Casaubon first read of these rites, he was shocked by the closeness of the parallel with Christianity. To my mind, though, such analogies in no way call into question the truth of Christianity. Rather, what they do is illustrate how deeply Jesus drew for his images on ordinary human experience. Far from natural religion and biblical revelation being necessarily in conflict, the latter can often effectively build upon the former.

Certainly there is much in the New Testament to suggest that Jesus' use of bread offered a not dissimilar message. There are numerous clues which indicate that this is precisely how John understood the miracle of the feeding of the five thousand (6.1–14), against which the dialogue about bread is set. Note for a start John's opening reference to Passover (v. 4). This is not in any of the other Gospels, although Mark does remark on how green the grass was (6.39). Given the nature of the Galilean climate this

---

[54] For a detailed discussion of the mysteries, see C. Kerényi, *Eleusis* (Princeton: Princeton University Press, 1967), 88–102. For how terror might possibly have preceded joy, see W. Burkert, *Ancient Mystery Cults* (Cambridge, Mass.: Harvard University Press, 1987), 92–5. For related associations in Roman religion, see B. S. Spaeth, *The Roman Goddess Ceres* (Austin, Tex.: University of Texas Press, 1996), 20–1.

[55] Beginning with the emperor Augustus himself: Kerényi, *Eleusis*, 100, 204 n. 72.

supports the view that the events in question must have taken place sometime in the spring, which is the time of Passover. Perhaps John knew that it was Passover time. More probably, however, given John's extensive use of symbolism elsewhere, the point of the reference is to set us immediately on one particular way of thinking: comparing what Jesus is now doing with what had happened to Moses and the people of Israel as they sought release from bondage in Egypt. The first Passover had of course made possible Israel's flight from Egypt. In the interim it initiated various trials in the desert. Among them was a hunger that was met by the divine response of manna dropping from heaven.[56] That had only offered a temporary respite, and here Jesus provides no more. Yet he does so in a way that points to something more permanent to come, as John makes clear later in the same chapter when Jesus is made to declare of himself: 'I am the bread of life' (v. 35).

In other words, we are being told, a greater than Moses is here. Indeed the crowd draws the same conclusion for itself, when at the end of the miracle they observe: 'this is indeed the prophet who is to come into the world' (v. 14) for talk of 'the prophet' was the traditional Jewish way of referring to Moses (cf. Deut. 18.15ff.). Were there any doubt, all is made clear twice later in this same chapter (vv. 31, 49), where similar comparisons are made. Further evidence comes from Mark's version of Jesus' walking on the water, the miracle that, as in John, follows the feeding of the five thousand. If in John (6.16–21) it appears to interrupt the sequence of events, Mark's version (6.45–52) provides an explanation.[57] Instead of Jesus merely walking towards the boat, Mark informs us that Jesus meant to 'pass by them' towards the other side of the lake, had they not called out. In other words, the waters were, so to speak, parting for Jesus to go safely across, just as once they had done at the Red Sea for the children of Israel under Moses.

In the Evangelists' understanding of the feeding miracle, allusions to the Passover deliverance are thus clear. A still greater liberator is now here. That said, the fact that Jesus' original reference to 'people' at the beginning of John 6.10 is specifically gendered in the next sentence of that verse as 'men' (cf. Matt. 14.21) could have

[56] Exod. 16.13–36; Num. 11.1–9.
[57] Here I follow the approach advocated in M. Hooker, *The Gospel According to St Mark* (London: A. and C. Black, 1991), 168–9.

a more interesting explanation than the usual one of sexual prejudice. All male devout Jews were expected to present themselves for Passover in Jerusalem, whereas here with 'Passover close at hand' they are allowed in effect to anticipate an alternative and greater rite, through sharing in a meal that foreshadows the significance of the Last Supper itself. If that seems far-fetched, think of the twelve baskets with which the story ends. Twelve is of course the typical Jewish round or perfect number. Yet it is surely strange that the gathering of the crumbs is even mentioned, for the bread would not in any case keep fresh. We are also centuries before the notion of litter louts, and the demand that we tidy up the countryside after us. So, more probably, the Evangelists are using the number to suggest that the feeding remains open and will not be perfected until others are drawn in, including later readers, who are now also invited to participate in this great feast of liberation and new life: the new Passover, the new feeding, the new Exodus into a promised land.

Images of feasting and of plenty in a new age are of course common in the Old Testament.[58] Here, though, there is a significant difference. The plenty emerges from very little. Not only that, it also emerges from the most common and ordinary. Indeed, while Mark speaks of ordinary bread and fish, John tells us that the bread was barley loaves, that is, bread not made from the usual wheat but the cheapest of the cheap, the food of the poor. The fish he also describes as dried little pieces (6.9): tinned sardines, as it were, rather than fresh salmon. In other words, it is not human efforts, we are being told, that will of themselves bring about change, but radically different attitudes, the kind of communal sharing and interdependency that only Christ can bring. As Thomas Aquinas, centuries later, was to put it in a eucharistic sermon: 'What the eye sees is small; yet what is therein contained is wonderful and excellent.'[59]

So gratitude for little emphatically did not entail acceptance of little without the possibility of change, however often this might be inculcated by those in positions of power and wealth. The specific history of Israel and Christ's teaching within that setting

[58] e.g. Isa. 25.6–8. It was sometimes associated with a renewed festival of Tabernacles or Booths: e.g. Zech. 14.16–19.
[59] From his 1264 sermon at Orvieto, celebrating the inauguration by Urban IV of the new feast of Corpus Christi: M. C. D'Arcy (ed.), *Thomas Aquinas: Selected Writings* (London: Dent, 1964 edn), 24–9, esp. 28.

ensured that this was not so. But so too did the basic, inherent, universal symbolism of bread, the transformation of the seed in the ground and the mysterious rising of the dough. Such talk of universals can, however, be misleading. Certainly, whether one thinks of ancient Egypt or of medieval western Europe, for the civilized Mediterranean world it was just such a universal, but that is not to say that bread functioned as such in all cultures. To focus the issue, let us imagine one small alteration to the Lord's Prayer: instead of 'give us this day our daily bread' it would say 'give us this day our daily pork'. 'Impossible', the reader may well respond, but not wholly so, I would suggest. The fact that the phrasing ended up one way rather than another is partly dependent at least on where and when Jesus was born and into what kind of community.

To explain. Were we to postulate the same date for his birth but instead a location somewhere in northern Europe beyond the frontiers of the Roman Empire, the result might well have been markedly different. It is important to recall that under such circumstances we move into a world without cultivated fields and so into a culture where bread was not part of the staple diet. Instead, the people lived off the fruits of the forest and the wild animals that roamed therein, and among them most common of all was the pig. So it is the pig and not bread that plays a key role in Celtic and Germanic mythology. Indeed, instead of the Bible's eternal bread of heaven it is everlasting pig that warriors are promised when they go to heaven, as in conversation in Snorri Sturluson's *Younger Edda*, in which each day a pig is boiled and by evening has become whole again—ever renewable pig![60] Even were we to confine ourselves to ancient Israel, a similar point could still be made. Thus, suppose for a moment that the incarnation had taken place centuries earlier, say at the time of the Exodus and the settlement of God's chosen people in the land he had promised them (usually dated to about 1200 BC). Certainly, there would then have been no mention of pig (an animal forbidden to Jews). But it by no means follows that bread would then have taken its place. Recall the repeated scriptural promise of 'a land flowing with milk and honey'. There is no mention here of bread, and for one obvious reason. It is as shepherds and not as farmers of arable land that the people will initially

[60] Ch. 38 (Gylfaginning). See also M. Montari, *The Culture of Food* (Oxford: Blackwell, 1994), 5–15, esp. 9.

live in their new homeland; hence their sustenance was to come from the milk of sheep and goats. Honey as a complement to milk is more puzzling. Almost certainly it does not mean the honey of cultivated bees, but rather that produced by their wild cousins, or perhaps not honey at all as we understand it, but rather the plentiful syrup that comes from the date palm. Anyway, the point seems to be that a luxury (honey) will be there to complement a basic need (milk). Milk would then have become the obvious food from which to draw appropriate images, not bread or pig.

No doubt, milk and pig might have generated a rich symbolism of their own. Indeed, one can see something of the former's possibilities in the way in which its imagery and use were extended to baptism.[61] Nonetheless, something would have been lost, in the inherent dynamism for change that bread contains. So the Christian may well feel impelled to the conviction that it is no accident that bread was the chosen image. Even so, historical contingencies entered at various other points. Over succeeding centuries the familiar petition, 'give us this day our daily bread', was to be plagued by the rarity in Greek of the word translated 'daily' (*epiousion*): it occurs only once elsewhere in the ancient literature that has come down to us.[62] Jerome in his Latin Vulgate translation insisted on a spiritualizing interpretation that spoke of the desire that God give us each day 'our heavenly bread': enough grace, that is, to keep us on the right road. Yet, given the roots from which the word is derived the more likely meaning is 'bread for the morrow'; in other words an oblique reference to this very miracle on which I have been focusing, to the promise of the great feast, as it were, that will usher in the new order and kingdom. If so, what the petitioner would be seeking is that he or she participates in the new life that Christ showed by anticipation to those five thousand and more all those centuries ago.

More Protestant Christians sometimes complain that any such revolutionary potential was destroyed when the meal element was

---

[61] If the common contention that the epistle is really a baptismal homily is true, I Pet. 2.2 would be an early reference of this kind. Milk and honey were administered as part of the baptismal rite in the early Church.

[62] So H. G. Liddell and R. Scott (eds), *Greek–English Lexicon* (Oxford: Clarendon Press, 1996 edn), s.v. Obviously with the advent of Christianity the word becomes more common, but still not greatly so: G. W. H. Lampe, *A Patristic Greek Lexicon* (Oxford: Clarendon Press, 1961), s.v.

abandoned within early Christianity. The wafer now replaced an earlier conviviality. That might have been so. But ironically the wafer too carries within it the symbolic dynamics for change. The first of August marks Lammas or 'loaf-mass', the day on which in medieval times newly baked loaves were offered at mass to celebrate the gathering in of the grain harvest. That might suggest a community united in celebration, but there was in fact a major contrast between the type of grain eaten by ordinary people and the type present in the eucharistic wafer. It was this contrast that guaranteed that the wafer continued to presage the possibility of change. For much of the history of Europe after the fall of the Roman Empire agricultural conditions were so bad that the growing of wheat had to be largely abandoned and replaced by an easier crop, rye, regarded by the Romans in fact as little more than a weed. The result was that for the great mass of Europe's population black rye bread replaced the white of wheat.[63] Indeed, at least one religious order chose to receive a daily ration of rye bread, precisely in order to remind themselves that they were 'Christ's beggars'.[64] Yet, when the people came to church, what they saw was a white wafer. The reason was that the Church insisted upon the best, but that best at the same time spoke to the ordinary people of how things might be otherwise, whatever their 'betters' thought.

Again, it was the same message that was associated with what is now the best-known presentation of Christ's agony on the cross, Matthias Grünewald's so-called Isenheim Altarpiece, now at Colmar in eastern France.[65] It was painted on the eve of the Reformation for a hospital of the Antonite order where patients were in acute pain, suffering from a disease known to the medieval world as St Anthony's fire. The picture would have been visible to patients from their sickbeds, and was intended to reassure them that

[63] Some, though, were even worse off. For many Scots oatcakes had to suffice. Oats cannot be used to produce raised bread. Hence Dr Johnson's famous dictionary entry: 'Oats, a grain which in England is generally given to horses, but in Scotland supports the people.' His comments are more moderate elsewhere: B. Allen (ed.), *Food: An Oxford Anthology* (Oxford: Oxford University Press, 1995), 65–6.

[64] The Carthusians: E. M. Thompson, *The Carthusian Order in England* (London: SPCK, 1930), 38.

[65] Particularly useful at exploring the medical context, although no mention is made of the white wafer, is A. Hayum, *The Isenheim Altarpiece: God's Medicine and the Painter's Vision* (Princeton: Princeton University Press, 1989).

Christ too was with them there in their pain. What is seldom appreciated is that both the source of their pain and its potential transformation were alike associated with bread. In the first place, the modern name for their illness is ergotism, a disease caused by fungus-infested rye, of which the Romans had knowledge but whose causes were unfortunately not rediscovered in modern Europe until the late sixteenth century. But if that side of bread was unknown to the patients, the other certainly was. The painting was on view precisely because their ward looked out on the chapel. Masses celebrated there using white bread spoke of the possibility of a different world, of their pain transformed.[66]

Bread is thus not a harmless or innocuous metaphor. It speaks both of physical hunger and of a social world transformed. So a eucharist that takes such imagery seriously is inherently a summons to hope and to change. The symbolic resonance of meals more generally ought also not to be discounted. I want, therefore, to end this part of the chapter on food by adding some more general remarks about meals and their symbolic significance: particularly the various ways in which past practice inculcated feelings of interdependency, and so also hinted at an even more fundamental dependency on divine grace.

Meals and Interdependence

Variations in papal practice may form a suitable opening illustration. Consider the following recipe: 'Take beaten eggs and as many oranges as you wish, squeeze, and mix the juice with the eggs and sugar. Then take olive oil and fat, heat in a frying pan, throw in the eggs and cook.' A simple recipe for an orange omelette, but intriguing for two reasons: first, it is recommended as an aphrodisiac; secondly, it comes from the first cookbook ever to survive in the history of the papacy. It is to be found in a collection of recipes recorded by Giovanni Bockenheym, the German-born cook of Pope Martin V.[67] Martin was the pope who reunited the medieval

---

[66] Sometimes, less commendably, the eating of white bread was even seen as a motive for becoming a monk. So Hubert of Romans, quoted in Montari, *The Culture of Food*, 51.

[67] Translated with Latin original in M. Rinaldi and M. Vicini, *Buon Appetito, Your Holiness* (London: Macmillan, 2000), 138. For the general attitudes of Bockenheym and Martin, see 129–34.

Church at the beginning of the fifteenth century after the Great Schism, when there had been two rival popes, one at Avignon in France and the other at Rome. Despite the recipe's description as an aphrodisiac, that particular pope was no profligate or glutton, however much this may have been true of others who have held his office before and since. A little over a century earlier, for example, his namesake Martin IV appears in Dante's *Divine Comedy* purging the sin of gluttony, in particular his love of eels from Bolsena and Varnaccia wine.[68] Contrast such behaviour with that of the great reforming pope Leo XIII, at the end of the nineteenth century. For him a simple lunch sufficed, served privately on a folding table and tray, with supper consisting merely of what was left over from earlier in the day.[69]

An odd assortment of facts, it may be thought, but these images are not quite as arbitrary as they may initially appear, for they tell us about rather more than just the predilections of particular popes. To begin with, the inclusion of an aphrodisiac menu in a papal kitchen register illustrates how seriously food was once taken as a spiritual issue. It mattered to your soul what you ate. So even an upright pope like Martin V needed to know what to avoid. As if in warning, the recipe describes itself not as an aphrodisiac but as something suitable for 'adulterers and panderers'. Again, the simplicity of Leo XIII's eating habits may well still appeal to us today. The irony, however, is that for most of human history such a practice would have been found deeply shocking, not because of what he ate but because he ate alone. Until relatively modern times eating was viewed as an essentially social activity.[70]

This was more than just a matter of convenience. It also spoke of interdependency. Eating together was seen in part as geared towards cultivating the right social attitudes. Just as saying grace at meals acknowledged thankfulness to God for a provision that was not entirely one's own, so sitting down with others indicated

---

[68] Dante, *Purgatorio* 24.21–3. A Frenchman from Tours, he is reputed to have died of the meal: 'dal Torso fu, e purga per digiuno | l'anguille di Bolsena e la vernaccia' (he is from Tours, and purges by fasting the eels of Bolsena and the Vernaccian).

[69] Rinaldi and Vicini, *Buon Appetito*, 316.

[70] This is not to deny that more informal eating might be solitary, as in Oxford's 'commons' or lunch: Allen (ed.), *Food*, 181–2.

mutual debts and obligations. As already indicated, the New Testament image of all sitting down to feast together was intended to
extend that sense, to include the marginalized. The contrast was
with feasts where others were excluded, whether because of fault or
impairment, or because the rich and powerful thought it enough to
let the poor rely on mere scraps from their lord's table. Either way,
the difference is considerable between what happened then and our
own modern TV dinners, under which even individual members of
the same family opt for separate meals rather than eating together as
a single unit.[71] The contrast, however, is even greater than this
initial comparison suggests.

The type of public lavatories provided in the ancient world and
sometimes later might help to make the point. Some indication is
provided by survivals from the forts on Hadrian's Wall, but perhaps
the best example comes from Lepcis Magna in North Africa, where
about a hundred seats were all placed next to one another.[72]
Occasionally, dual seats can still be seen in medieval British cas-
tles.[73] Less well known is the extent of sharing that went on prior to
that need to visit the loo. Look carefully at medieval paintings such
as Duccio's *Last Supper*, and interesting differences from today will
soon be noticed. Although there were at least thirteen people who
attended that meal, Duccio shows only three bowls, three knives
and four glasses.[74] In portraying matters thus, the artist was in no
way indulging in a clever ruse to avoid making the painting appear
otherwise too cluttered. Rather, he was actually reflecting the social
realities of the day. Forks were only introduced gradually from
Byzantium, first into fourteenth-century Florence and then slowly
elsewhere. Till then not only were knives shared but also glasses and
bowls, and sometimes even trenchers. Trenchers (thick bread functioning as plates) were sometimes shared when they acted as a sort

---

[71] An unforgettable image of such lonely eating is provided by Jack Lemmon
consuming his TV dinner straight from the foil in the 1960s film *The Apartment*.

[72] For illustration, see M. Wheeler, *Roman Art and Architecture* (London:
Thames and Hudson, 1964), 109.

[73] As in Doune Castle, near Stirling. At least their Roman equivalent at
Timgrad was adorned with dolphins: Wheeler, *Roman Art*, 49–50.

[74] Illustrated in C. Jannella, *Duccio di Buoninsegna* (Milan: Scala, 1991), 47.
Useful for comparison, although virtually without commentary, is the large
gathered collection of such paintings in J. Hasting (designer), *Last Supper* (London:
Phaidon, 2000).

of mess-plate. Because like most bread in earlier times they were usually round, it is very easy to draw from paintings the wrong conclusion, and suppose actual china to be represented.[75]

In the cinema it is not uncommon to find medieval meals portrayed as rather riotous and messy affairs. This is quite untrue to the facts. Precisely because of such sharing great care had to be exercised. Individuals often brought their own cutlery. Indeed, this may well be the likely origin of the silver spoon as a christening present.[76] It could be used again and again. But there were also numerous conventions that helped keep things tidy and clean. It was after all of no small moment how your neighbour behaved during a meal, when you were quite likely to be supping soup and so on from the same bowl or glass. Washing hands before meals was thus very far from being an empty or idle ritual. One medieval updating of an Aesop fable even has mice washing their paws before a meal.[77]

Such sharing can scarcely be put down to matters of economy, since it affected rich no less than poor. Rather, it was a way of expressing social solidarity and a sense of mutual interdependency. That is no doubt why Langland complains so bitterly in *Piers Plowman* about the removal of the rich from common dining with their servants in hall: 'Elying is the halle ... | There the lord ne the lady, liketh noughte to sytte.'[78] It may also be the explanation for why in the case of convents and monasteries such practices lasted very much longer, even deep into the twentieth century. One small example of this is a punishment common in convents until the 1960s, whereby the nun concerned was required to beg at table a little bit of food from each of her sisters' bowls.[79]

---

[75] M. P. Cosman, *Fabulous Feasts: Medieval Cookery and Ceremony* (New York: George Braziller, 1976), 35, 71.

[76] So A. Sim, *Food and Feast in Tudor England* (Stroud: Sutton, 1997), 3. Cosman suggests that the practice of extending the pinkie when holding a teacup may be a hangover from the need to keep certain fingers clean: *Fabulous Feasts*, 17.

[77] Quoted in B. A. Henisch, *Fast and Feast: Food in Medieval Society* (University Park, Penn.: Pennsylvania State University Press, 1976), 166. Intriguingly, because the mice were not deemed to be rational, they are excused from saying grace.

[78] 'There is something amiss with the hall, where the lord and lady do not care to sit': *Piers Plowman*, Text B, Passus 10, 94–5.

[79] P. Curran, *Grace Before Meals: Food Ritual and Body Discipline in Convent Culture* (Urbana, Ill.: University of Illinois Press, 1989), 17.

Not that all practices at meals in religious communities furthered such a communitarian sensibility. The emphasis Jerome had placed on the priority of spiritual 'bread' over physical inevitably encouraged a rather individual focus. In theory the aim was quite otherwise: complete subordination of the personality to the common good. But this was countered by a very individualistic view of salvation under which personal merit was acquired, often through dubious ways of subordinating body to soul.[80] Monks and nuns ate in silence in the attempt to focus their minds on what was being read to them, and not on what was being consumed. Indeed, not uncommonly the reading might consist of material on how to die well, particularly as this was reflected in the last moments of fellow-brothers or -sisters who had recently departed.[81] In addition, not only were elaborate signals invented to avoid any form of personalized contact, but also the tables were customarily so laid out that no one had a neighbour opposite whose eyes might accidentally be caught.

To the modern mind this must now inevitably seem an absurd over-subordination of body to spirit. Yet, despite their excessive individualism, such practices did at least give a moral context to what was being eaten. Today remoteness from the sources of our food can very easily allow us to ignore any larger issues raised by what we consume. Possible exploitation of workers in the Third World is thereby sidestepped, as also the moral issue of the use of intensive farming in our own land of a kind where the animals involved are reduced to mere products on a production line. What was regarded as a despised food at the beginning of the twentieth century (the hamburger) had by its end become a source of labour for almost four million workers in fast food restaurants worldwide.[82] Most were underpaid, but their conditions were not nearly as bad as the slaughterhouse process that went with such quick consumption.[83] A searing indictment is offered in the German novel *Blösch*, where the life of a cow of that name is followed to

---

[80] For an example, see ibid. 77.

[81] Ibid. 15–16.

[82] E. Schlosser, *Fast Food Nation* (London: Penguin, 2001): for changing attitudes to the hamburger, see 197–8; for numbers employed, 71.

[83] And largely true still today. For low wages, see Schlosser, 37, 73–4; for the appalling conditions for immigrant labour and the animals in American slaughterhouses, 169–90.

its bitter end. Even the traditionalist Swiss farmer with whom her story begins sees the writing on the wall: 'never mind if a cow has got an udder like a flabby bagpipe, with tits like thorns with warts on and all, who cares? Main thing is that she's got to give more milk than the competition.'[84]

It is a far cry from a world in which the kitchen could be described as 'a sort of culinary theatre where the daily ritual of the domestic *religio* was performed'.[85] It is so easy for the modern mind, even in those who are themselves devout, to suppose that all that is in contention in such attitudes is optional, dispensable additions such as the saying of grace before meals. The truth is quite otherwise. What is at stake is nothing short of a different way of experiencing the world. The point can be most easily highlighted by separate consideration of the two distinct phases of a meal: its preparation and its consumption.

With respect to the former, it is important to note how much meaning once attached to various forms of food has now been lost. Some pre-Christian associations continued.[86] Even as late as the Renaissance, astrology was an integral part of medicine. Theories continued to be developed about how the stars influenced the humours of the body, and so also about how those humours were in turn affected by what we ate.[87] In other cases new meanings arrived. If hot cross buns and Easter eggs still survive, it is salutary to recall how many other aspects are now lost.[88] Even the long association of fish and penitence is now gone, a true penitence in the days when most had to rely on the rock-hard dry fish known as stockfish.[89] Gone too is the linking of particular foods with

---

[84] B. Sterchi, *The Cow* (London: Faber and Faber, 1988), 36. The German original dates from 1983. There are occasional ironic contrasts with scriptural images: e.g. 96, 98.

[85] P. Camporesi, *The Magic Harvest: Food, Folklore and Society* (Oxford: Polity, 1998), 101.

[86] A point Camporesi is concerned to stress. A key element was providing an *imago mundi*, such as the moon shape of peasant bread: ibid. 13, 156–7.

[87] Sim, *Food and Feast in Tudor England*, 82.

[88] For example, even as late as the 1970s carling peas were still part of Northeast lore for the fifth Sunday of Lent: *Durham Town and County*, Spring 2003, 44–5.

[89] Henisch, *Fast and Feast*, 35; Sim, *Food and Feast in Tudor England*, 118. Partly in order to safeguard the fishing industry, such rules continued to be imposed in Elizabethan England: Strong, *Feast*, 143. Even among those fortunate enough to have access to fresh fish, throughout the Middle Ages such fare was generally held in low esteem: Montanari, *The Culture of Food*, 78–82.

particular characters.[90] Much is of course as irrecoverable as the way in which the time of meals was itself once a function of religious observance. The association of lunch with noon had come from the timing of the service of nones, while the tolling of bells for liturgical hours was still being used as late as the fourteenth century as a way of determining opening times for food markets.[91] Just as these disappeared, so too did the full range of associations that fish once had had. Others went simply because they were wrong, as with astrological associations for particular foods or the low esteem in which fruit and vegetables were held.[92]

Even so, much of value has, I think, been lost. Occasionally a profound dynamic is observable in the way in which those meanings were explored. Take what happened within Christianity to the lamb served at Passover. In the Gospels the future kingdom is presented as a great feast at which all will sit down together, and all have enough to eat (e.g. Matt. 8.11). As such it must have come as a hugely heartening image to Palestinian peasants who were more often than not on the breadline. Yet in the book of Revelation the focus is not on the food but on the Lamb as host, and one can see why. Lamb can all too easily suggest a weak and passive image, as in William Blake's familiar lines.[93] That is no doubt why the author of Revelation chose to give this particular lamb horns.[94] The feast will be under a Lamb with power, a Lamb that can make a difference. That ambiguity is then traceable through the rest of the history of Christianity. So, for example, by ancient tradition the pallium, given as a symbol of office to archbishops throughout

[90] As in Chaucer's *Canterbury Tales*: for an analysis, see Cosman, *Fabulous Feasts*, 103–5.

[91] Town clocks began to take over for markets from about 1379 onwards: ibid. 83. Another monastic example is the use of 'collation' to refer to a light snack (originally a monastic concession related to the reading of Cassian's *Collationes*): Henisch, *Fast and Feast*, 20–1, 32.

[92] Both were held in low esteem partly because of Galen's influence: Sim, *Food and Feast in Tudor England*, 73. Depending on how Dan. 1.12 is translated, it is possible that the Jews of the author's day already knew the high nutritional value of 'pulses': Heiser, *Seed to Civilisation*, 117–18.

[93] 'Little lamb I'll tell thee, | Little lamb I'll tell thee! | He is called by thy name, | For he calls himself a lamb: | He is meek and he is mild, | He became a little child.'

[94] The feast of the future kingdom is mentioned a number of times, e.g. Rev. 3.20; 19.7–9. The Lamb is portrayed with seven horns and seven eyes at 5.6, and elsewhere as bringing wrath and warfare: 6.16–17; 17.14.

the world, is still made from the wool of lambs dedicated on the feast of St Agnes at her church in Rome. The justification is a play on her name, *agnus* being the Greek for lamb. Had the presentation always spoken of gentle rule or humility that would have been welcome, but too often it was interpreted as a similar entitlement to power in the sense that the book of Revelation had first introduced.

As I have already conceded, most symbolic resonances for particular foods are now a lost cause. Despite surface appearances, more defensible may be the medieval tendency to equate the original primal sin with gluttony rather than lust.[95] It suggested that a reverence for all creation and a balance in its use was the only way properly to gain access to the divine Creator. Undiluted instrumentalism in our own attitude to what we need for sustenance, as with so many other aspects of life, is likely to be fundamentally deleterious to provision for the space and possibility to perceive our world differently. It is thus surely no accident that in that stress on gluttony it was food in its turn that was seen as reversing the Fall, in the eucharistic food that continues to be offered by Christ himself.[96]

Equally, the difference that forms of presentation made needs to be heeded. Manners were viewed as a distinctively human grace that set human beings apart from other animals and reflected the divine grace that they imitated. Against such a background it becomes much less surprising that Erasmus should devote his time to writing a book on the subject, or that an introduction to etiquette should treat the angel's address to Mary as foundational.[97] Of course there were also negative aspects, as, for instance, in the rigid hierarchy that so often went with earlier forms of eating, not only in seating arrangements but also in the different types of food served to different classes of individuals within the same room. Troubling too was the sustained borrowing of liturgical ritual that

[95] For discussion and references, see Cosman, *Fabulous Feasts*, 116–23. Artists, however, often sought to restore the connection with lust by making the apple as like a breast as possible: A. J. Grieco, *The Meal: Themes in Art* (London: Scala, 1991), 9.

[96] 'An undoing, by eating, of an evil deed caused by eating' is how Cosman puts it: *Fabulous Feasts*, 120.

[97] The relevant work of Erasmus is *De civilitate morum puerilium*. Sim refers us to a work which suggests that courtesy came to earth 'when Gabriel hailed our Lady by name': *Food and Feast in Tudor England*, 104.

was used to underpin the way in which royal meals were presented. Intended to surround monarchy with a sacrosanct awe, royal eating continued to be offered as public acts of ceremonial, even as late as the nineteenth century.[98] The canopy over the monarch's seat, the various processions and ritual washings and genuflections could not have failed to remind the viewer of the intended analogy.[99] Yet it would be wrong to suppose that all this amounted to was an attempt to bolster monarchy by allusions to religious practice. Also at stake was the monarch as representative of the nation, as embodying a particular way of doing things. It made a difference whether the king ate apart or interacted with family and courtiers, whether any of the food was distributed to the poor or not, and so on. Charlemagne, for instance, sought to emulate the monasteries by having readings at his table, while at the Renaissance Marsilio Ficino advocated music as a way of reminding banqueters of a heavenly harmony.[100] Such practices thus had at least the potential to embody a corporate ideal, and sometimes succeeded in doing so.

In one of his finer poems George Herbert celebrates the way in which all God's creatures are fed from God's bounty, even the fly:

> Thy cupboard serves the world: the meat is set,
> Where all may reach; no beast but knows his feed.
>
> .   .   .   .   .   .
>
> Nothing engend'red doth prevent his meat:
> Flies have their table spread, ere they appear.[101]

If this suggests a God concerned for the material needs of all the creatures he has made, we may use another Anglican poet to illustrate the image carried one stage further. Already in the Apocryphal book of Esdras (2 Esd. 6.52) its author had sought to build the future feast out of the two great terrifying sea monsters of the Bible, Behemoth and Leviathan. W. H. Auden builds on that

---

[98] As in the case of Charles X of France (1824–30), who allowed members of the public to walk past as he ate, flanked on each side by his wife and the dauphin: Strong, *Feast*, 277. For the different attitudes of Elizabeth and James, see 205–7; for Louis XIV's change of heart, 249–56.

[99] For how the ritual was performed at the court of the Dukes of Burgundy, see ibid. 91–3; for genuflection at the Hapsburg court, 203.

[100] For Charlemagne, see ibid. 65; for Ficino, 183–4.

[101] 'Providence', lines 49–50, 53–4: *George Herbert: The Complete English Poems*, ed. J. Tobin (London: Penguin, 1991 edn), 110.

thought, when, contrasting humanity with other animals, he observes:

> Only man,
> Supererogatory beast,
> Dame Kind's thoroughbred lunatic, can
> Do the honours of a feast,
>
> ......
>
> and, perhaps, Long Pig, will continue till Doomsday
> when at God's board,
> the saints chew pickled Leviathan.[102]

Auden's point is that fear itself will be overcome in that great feast. God has so made us that, unlike other animals, we eat not just to feed ourselves but also to celebrate, to draw ourselves closer to one another and to God, and all this will culminate in that final feast, when there will be no more suspicions, no more fears, but all united in God.

Esdras was still in a world of shared feeding implements. It is surely not without significance that the one area where that earlier sharing has survived into modern times is in the eucharist itself, in the shared chalice. Modelled as it is on a meal, the eucharist immediately reminds us that all life is a gift and comes by grace. We eat not by entitlement but by good fortune, and like every other meal it is a sacrament that has the potential to draw us closer to God. But it functions as such not in isolation but in the context of community. By placing others, both like and unlike ourselves, alongside us, we are drawn out of ourselves to see our world differently. The possibility of transcendence, an even more radical seeing of the other, is there, including a meeting with the absolutely Other in God himself. One element in making that possible is the reminder of equality and mutual interdependence given in the sharing of the chalice. Individual cups or the withdrawal of the cup altogether thus turn out to be issues of far from peripheral import.

The Language of Drinking

In this second part of the chapter I shall examine the symbolism of water and wine first before turning to more general questions about

---

[102] *Thanksgiving for a Habitat*, X, in *W.H. Auden: Selected Poems* (London: Feber and Faber, 1979), 271.

drink and the various other ways in which it is given symbolic significance. In the case of both water and wine, while not discounting traditional emphases, I want to draw attention to how closer examination of the multivalent character of their symbolism has the potential to enrich current understandings of the two major Christian sacraments. The final section will then consider the various ways in which both alcoholic and non-alcoholic stimulants (tea and coffee in particular) have in appropriate contexts also been seen as opening the human mind to wider perceptions of reality.[103]

Water's Power for the Future

Water may seem an inappropriate element to include in a discussion of drinking, when Christianity's principal public use is in the 'washing' of baptism. But it is precisely that primary image of washing that I wish to challenge here. The Bible has in fact a much richer vein of symbolism for water that such a sole application would suggest. So what I want to do here is explore how our understanding of both the Bible and the sacrament can be enriched by looking more widely. Within scripture three competing ideas have in fact operated, sometimes functioning as complementary, sometimes in opposition to one another. I shall end by focusing more narrowly on baptism, and suggest that, while water is not consumed in baptism, its meaning in that context is most appropriately drawn closer to the forward-looking character of the drinking image of living water. Too long has the Church looked backwards through its cleansing properties, and ignored that prospective reference.

It is in John 4 as part of an extensive exchange between Christ and the Woman of Samaria at the well that Jesus describes himself as 'living water'. As a result of the woman's desire for such water, her present marital status, or rather lack of it, becomes known. It may be that in presenting the dialogue in this way John is alluding to the cleansing power of water as well as its life-giving character. If so, it would be a rare example of drinking water being given the multivalent character that water has elsewhere, with its role not only in refreshment but also in cleansing and even in destruction.

---

[103] I mention 'drugs' only briefly, partly because they do not fall under the general heading of drinks and partly because here abuse seems more frequent than use.

Services of baptism commonly allude to all three roles. Here I am primarily concerned with water as drink. I do, however, want to suggest that the emphasis in baptism is wrong when its symbolism is pulled apart from the various uses of water elsewhere and made to focus exclusively on a cleansing action. There is no reason in principle why the drinking and washing function should not point in precisely the same direction. Modern motives for taking a shower are after all as frequently about refreshment before new tasks as they are about cleansing.

Intriguingly, in the following chapter of John the issue of living water once more returns but in a non-drinking context. There we are told (at 5.7) that the reason why the waters of the Pool of Bethesda have not hitherto healed the paralytic is because no sooner are they 'troubled' or 'stirred up' (depending on the translation used) than others run to anticipate him and he fails to get there in time.[104] Almost certainly what is meant by this unusual expression is that there was a spring beneath the pool. The 'troubled waters' were a sign of its renewed activity. As such the phrase picks up on a major theme in biblical writing, on how what we really need is living water, flowing water, not still or stagnant pools. A few chapters later, a blind man is told by Jesus to go and wash in the Pool of Siloam (9.7). At the Feast of Tabernacles water from this pool was actually symbolically offered within the Temple. It is not perhaps surprising in a country short of natural resources that 'living' or flowing water was treated with great respect. Indeed, the site of Jerusalem may well have been chosen precisely because of its closeness to Gihon, a spring that at irregular intervals throughout the day shot forth its refreshing waters. This was in fact the source that provided the Pool of Siloam with its own distinctive, refreshing water. It was this freshness that was celebrated at the Feast of Tabernacles. It was also this same renewal and joy to which the author of the book of Revelation alludes when he speaks of Christ as our 'water of life' (22.17).

That contrast between living and still or 'dead' water is, however, by no means the only one the Bible offers. There is also the more dramatic contrast between water that is refreshing and life-giving and that which threatens death, and so especially the

[104] The name of the pool is uncertain. Other manuscripts offer 'Bethsaida' and 'Bethzatha'. 'Troubled' is found in the AV and also elsewhere (e.g. RSV).

treacherous seas. Scholars are still divided about the extent to which there may have been other festivals associated with the Temple than those explicitly recorded in scripture.[105] One theory has it that the great laver or basin of water outside the Temple building[106] was there to remind worshippers of God holding back the waters of creation. Indeed, some of the psalms sung in Temple worship seem to hint at precisely this sort of festival, in that they would call to mind once more this threat overcome. So Psalm 93, for instance, celebrates God as Lord of creation but ends with this fascinating exchange: 'The floods have lifted up, O Lord, the floods have lifted up their voice, the floods lift up their roaring', and the response: 'Mightier than the thunders of many waters, mightier than the waves of the sea, the Lord on high is mighty' (vv. 3–4). So similarly in most baptism services not only does the life-giving power of water find mention but also its destructive capacities, as illustrated in the way in which the children of Israel were almost destroyed, had not God held back the waters as they crossed the Red Sea. Creativity and cost are thus linked not only in creation but also in each individual's life.

But competing with this threatening aspect there is also to be found in scripture a gentler image for water at the creation. This is in the notion of the four rivers associated with the earthly Paradise known as the Garden of Eden (Gen. 2.10–14). The identity of the first two rivers is somewhat uncertain, but of the latter two there can be no doubt. They are the Euphrates and the Tigris, even if some translations insist on leaving the latter in its quite different Hebrew name. The Euphrates is one of the great rivers of the world. Rising in the east of modern Turkey, it then flows through Syria before it finally reaches Iraq. The Tigris is not quite so impressive, but just south of modern Baghdad it joins the Euphrates in a single great stream that then carries on all the way down to Basra and the Persian Gulf. Quite a number of suggestions have been made for identifying the other two, including possibly the

---

[105] Contrast A. Weiser, *The Psalms* (London: SCM Press, 1962), 617–21 with J. W. Rogerson and J. W. McKay, *Psalms 51–100* (Cambridge: Cambridge University Press, 1977), 208–11. The existence of an Enthronement Festival under Babylonian influence that incorporated Psalm 93 is taken as virtually proven by Weiser, whereas Rogerson and McKay are more cautious.

[106] Exod. 30.17–18; 1 Kgs 7.23–6.

Nile and a river in modern Persia. All this would of course affect the
size of the garden. A big expanse between the rivers, and all the
then-known world would be encompassed within a single garden;
a very much smaller area sandwiched between the Tigris and the
Euphrates, and it proves quite compact, and easier to envisage as all
entrusted to the care of just these two persons.

We are not of course dealing with facts here. Nonetheless, the
central place given to such rivers tells us much. Any reader who
has been to Israel will know what a dry and unfruitful land it
really is. Galilee in the far north is fairly lush, but the rest of the
country is quite otherwise. There is the occasional stream or wadi
that dries up in the summer. Even the River Jordan is a great
disappointment. It is no large rolling river but merely a minor
country brook that certainly cannot stand comparison with any of
the major Scottish or English rivers. Yet water is absolutely essential
to agriculture. So it is hardly surprising that the Old Testament is
full of images of a very different Palestine, one in which there
would be water in abundance. Take the prophet Isaiah; that book
is full of dry land turning into rivers (e.g. Isa. 32.2; 35.6; 44.3). One
of the psalms even goes so far as to declare that 'there is a river
whose streams make glad the city of God' (46.4), though none such
is in existence at the moment. The prophet Ezekiel goes one
stage further, and envisages a great river flowing out of the Temple
itself, to water all the land. In chapter 47 it spreads out in four
directions, one river becoming four, just as in the passage from
Genesis referred to earlier. There is also much stress on the presence
of trees. Just as the Genesis passage includes trees other than the
symbolic ones of life and of good and evil (for example, fig trees at
3.7), so Ezekiel in his description of Eden (31.8ff.) expands the
Genesis description to include cedars, cypresses and plane trees.
While minimum maintenance (no hard bending) might be part
of the idea, undoubtedly more important is the notion of shade,
a rather important requisite in a hot climate.

Intriguingly, this focus on the spiritual significance of water was
one element in Judaism that was not only transposed to Islam but
greatly expanded as a result. Following repeated descriptions in the
Qur'an, gardens divided into four sections by water and known as
Paradise gardens were created, as a means of encouraging contemplation and offering some kind of anticipation of life with God in

heaven.[107] The Qur'an uses the image several times. On one occasion we are informed: 'Here is a parable of the garden which the righteous are promised: in it are rivers of water incorruptible; rivers of milk of which the taste never changes; rivers of wine, a joy to those who drink; and rivers of honey pure and clear.'[108] Even without knowing that Muslims are forbidden alcohol, the symbolic character of the description is quite clear. Milk and honey reflects the character of the promised land, while wine was to become a powerful metaphor in medieval Sufi poetry with its recurring theme of being drunk with God:

> O saki, when the days commence
> Of ruby roses, abstinence
> By none is charged; then pour me wine
> Like yonder rose incarnadine.[109]

Even the famous (or notorious) martyr Al-Hallaj goes to his death with talk of drink on his lips:

> My boon companion is not to be
> Accused of mean inequity.
> He made me drink like him the best.
>
> .   .   .   .   .   .
>
> Such is his fate, who drinks past reason
> With Draco in the summer season.[110]

Perhaps the image could be used so daringly precisely because all knew it was not intended literally. Even so, images of water, with God as spring or ocean, are more common.[111]

Such Islamic Sufic mysticism flourished under the Abbasid dynasty, who ruled from Baghdad over a great empire that lasted from 762 until 1258, when they were finally overthrown by a large

[107] For more detailed consideration of such paradise gardens, see my earlier volume, *God and Enchantment of Place: Reclaiming Human Experience* (Oxford: Oxford University Press, 2004), 373–5

[108] Sura 47.15: *The Holy Qur'an*, tr. A. Yusuf Ali (Leicester: Islamic Foundation, 1975), 1381–2.

[109] Words of the Persian mystical poet Sana'i (d. 1140); quoted in introduction to F. Al-Din Attar, *Muslim Saints and Mystics*, ed. A. J. Arberry (London: Arkana, 1966), 8.

[110] Attar, *Muslim Saints and Mystics*, 268. 'Notorious' because he claimed mystical identity with God.

[111] J. Fadiman and R. Frager, *Essential Sufism* (San Francisco: HarperCollins, 1999), 199, 201.

invading pagan army of Mongols or Moguls. At the time Baghdad was probably the largest city in the world, certainly very much larger than either London or Rome. It now looked as though Islam, and Sufism with it, had had its day. But it was not to be so. The conquered, though defeated physically, actually succeeded in spiritually vanquishing the conquerors, for in due course the Moguls themselves became Muslims. The result was that Sufism entered into its greatest period of influence, particularly in neighbouring Persia, and numerous Paradise gardens were laid out there by the conquerors.

To state the obvious, in a country like Britain, where water is in plentiful supply, water is unlikely to arouse any major symbolic resonances. In the Middle East, by contrast, the actions of water are often decisive for both good and ill and sometimes for good through ill. The experience it facilitates of the divine is likely also therefore to be significantly different. Ironically, precisely because in northern Europe there is so much of the commodity and usually so little needed, water is seldom experienced as a wondrous divine gift, even within farming communities. Matters are quite different, though, where water can make the difference between life and death, as was the case in the world of ancient Palestine and more generally in the Middle East.

If that relativizes water's impact between countries, the multivalency of the accompanying symbolism that has already been noted means that caution also needs to be exercised in determining the appropriate relative weight to be given to competing interpretations of how those different elements should be balanced out in the theology of baptism. Historically, the Church has found its clue most often in Paul, and so stressed baptism's cleansing role. But, as much modern writing on the subject notes, a quite different emphasis emerges if the starting point is Jesus' own baptism.[112] That suggests refreshment and new beginnings, marking as it does the inauguration of his ministry with the descent of the Spirit. The event thus looks forward rather than backwards. The Evangelists did not always find it easy to reconcile that fact with John the Baptist's own backward look to the forgiveness of sins.[113] But that

[112] Seen particularly among Roman Catholic liturgists who argue from Jesus as 'primordial sacrament': for example, K. Osborne, *The Christian Sacraments of Initiation* (New York: Paulist Press, 1987), esp. 79–81, 85–6.

[113] Seen particularly in Matthew's puzzling declaration that Jesus underwent the rite 'to fulfil all righteousness' (3.15).

becomes problematic only if we make such a retroactive reference a necessary element in all baptisms rather than simply its usual accompaniment. To suggest that newly born infants are polluted by sin, even 'original sin', is surely to make the child's condition predetermined by particular theological assumptions. Independent consideration of the child's status suggests a rather different assessment. Certainly, central to Paul's theology, like John the Baptist's, is a backward reference, in us dying with Christ. But to insist upon that reference even in the case of a newborn child is to forget the second half of Paul's declaration: that baptism is also about us rising with Christ.[114] Of course, one might talk of the burial being anticipatory in terms of the individual's future life. Once more, though, that is to try to force present experience into a predetermined pattern. For the child it is precisely the newly given resurrection life that makes that future burial with Christ a foreseen actuality. In other words, the movement is actually the other way round. It is because the child is now orientated towards the new life of the resurrection that crucifixion will subsequently also become part of his or her experience.

Certainly, burial with Christ is quite likely to be the first image upon which a new convert draws, where the sense of deliverance is still prominent in his or her mind. But for those who come to faith more gradually, including of course children, a more helpful image might well be another Pauline category, that of adoption.[115] As with the ordinary declarative act or legal papers in the secular case, the baptism only marks the beginning of a process, not an act absolute in itself. A story still remains to be told, of how the individual gradually grows into the death and resurrection of Christ, and, just as some adoptions are more successful than others (and frankly some fail), so much the same can be said about these divine stories: 'The Spirit is now there addressing the baptised through the community of faith, through parents and friends and in numerous other ways. But, sadly, as with adoption, the loving action does not always meet with an appropriate response, and the

---

[114] Rom. 6.1–11. For an excellent discussion of the issues, see the Durham University Ph.D. thesis by P. J. A. Robinson, 'Baptism in a Ritual Perspective' (1997).

[115] As in Rom. 8.15 and Gal. 4.6, where a Spirit of adoption enables us, along with Christ, to call God Abba or Father.

recalcitrance of the other party involved can make any further deepening of the relationship impossible.'[116]

Given the strength of resistance to such a forward-looking perspective, it comes as something of a surprise to discover how prominent that same forward-looking emphasis has been all along in the Church's treatment of Jesus' baptism within its liturgical calendar. It is treated as part of the Epiphany season, as one manifestation of his divine mission, to be set alongside the coming of the Magi or Wise Men and the miracle at Cana.[117] It is exactly this same emphasis that is to be found in Piero della Francesca's famous painting of Christ's baptism, now in the National Gallery in London.[118] Painted around 1460 for his native town of Sansepolcro, about ninety miles south-east of Florence, it is usually praised for its complex formal balances of triangles, circles and pentagons. More interesting to note here is the way in which such mathematical perfection is not sought at the expense of the liturgical tradition. Behind Christ in the distance and directly under another individual preparing for baptism are some men travelling along a road, all richly dressed in oriental clothes. Among indications of the object of their journey is one of them pointing heavenwards. There is thus no doubt that they are intended as an allusion to the Wise Men. Nor is the third epiphany discounted. Far from it, for the miracle at Cana is actually given a still more prominent place, though the casual observer of the painting might easily miss the allusion. On Christ's right and to the viewer's left are three angels in attendance. The fact that there are three and the various complementary proportions in the colour of their robes is no doubt intended to allude to the Trinity, but the wedding at Cana is there too. Two of the angels have clasped hands, one placing his hand on the shoulder of

[116] Doctrine Commission of the Church of England, *We Believe in the Holy Spirit* (London: Church House Publishing, 1991), 77. Although it was an agreed report, I was actually responsible for the chapter on sacraments. So the developed analogy with adoption (76–7) very much reflects my own views.

[117] The symbolism of baptismal fonts can also pull in different directions. If cruciform and tub point one way, womb and octagon suggest an alternative, more forward-looking reference. For further discussion of such issues, see R. Kuehn, *A Place for Baptism* (Chicago: Liturgy Training Publications, 1992).

[118] For an illustration and some exposition, see M. A. Lavin, *Piero della Francesca* (London: Thames and Hudson, 1992), 62–3. Obviously, Piero pays such attention to detail that a good large coloured illustration is a minimal requirement.

the other. This was the traditional form of marriage betrothal, each, as it were, taking possession of the other.[119]

Yet what makes this painting more than just a tissue of liturgical allusion, and also an impressive piece of theology in its own right, is the way in which biblical references to water, including Cana, are woven into its fabric to deepen the significance attaching to the painting's central theme: primarily Christ's baptism but also our own. Closer inspection of the Jordan waters reveals that the river has once more rolled back, thus repeating the opening of the book of Joshua and of course the earlier pattern with the Red Sea. Jesus' baptism will help effect our deliverance, we are being told, a message reinforced by the various wild plants flourishing on the river banks, such as buttercup, clover and convolvulus, all well known for their medicinal properties. Note too should be taken of the river stained red like wine in the background, where the Magi's robes are reflected in the river. There is more here, I think, than yet another allusion to what happened at Cana. A great walnut tree dominates the painting. In the fifteenth century viewers seeing this tree would have known that they were also being required to think of the death of Christ and of its significance for us. The walnut's hard outside wood was taken to speak of the harshness of the cross, its soft centre to allude to the result of that sacrifice, Christ's flesh now available to become life for all. It is likely to have been a piece of symbolism of which the painter was especially fond. 'Walnut' in Italian could easily be used to allude to the valley in which his own hometown of San Sepolchro (Holy Sepulchre) was situated, the Val de Nocea or Nut Valley: thus new life out of the tomb for his own townsfolk.

I have pursued these themes in Piero's painting for two reasons. First, they seem to indicate how in more clement regions the symbolism of water had to be supplemented, if biblical associations were to be truly naturalized. Secondly, focus on the believer's future is most likely to be what matters most, if understanding of the Christian's baptism is based on what happened in Christ's own. That is after all what emerges most clearly from the painting, even though it dates from a time when the Church held firmly to the conviction that unbaptized children were incapable of entering

---

[119] Though, as one might suspect of the times, primarily the husband of the wife.

heaven because of original sin. Intriguingly, that future reference parallels exactly how water was most commonly perceived symbolically when drunk, as in the declaration of Christ's with which this section began: 'whoever drinks of the water that I shall give him will never thirst; the water that I shall give him will become in him a spring of water welling up to eternal life' (John 4.14). As the painting illustrates, the cleansing power of water is not naturally the first thought that occurs. It is the power that water gives for the future which makes most sense of Christ's own baptism and of his effect on us, and thus of any attempt to apply that baptism to ourselves.

None of this is to deny the importance of water's cleansing role, only to insist on its subordination within that larger frame. In the chronology of Christ's life crucifixion precedes resurrection. But this is not necessarily so in the life of his followers. Just as Christ's own baptism and its glorious experience of sonship helped him to look forward to the culmination of his mission in crucifixion, so also sometimes it is only because of entering first into the new resurrection life that individual Christians are able eventually fully to appreciate the need for a crucifixion of much of their past.

Wine and the Divine Life

'Let us have wine and women, mirth and laughter | Sermons and soda water the day after.'[120] So wrote Lord Byron, thereby of course implicitly telling us as much about how sermons were viewed in his own day as about the long-standing connection between wine and celebration. Whatever later sermons may have had to say on the subject, wine and religion are certainly not opposed in the scriptures. One of the psalms informs us that it is wine 'that gladdeneth the heart of man' (Ps. 104.15).[121] Where that psalm would have been sung, before the Great Gate of Herod's Temple, there was in fact to be seen a huge, intricately carved, golden vine.[122] Wine was also regularly offered to God at the altars that stood in front of the Temple. Indeed, so indispensable was

---

[120] *Don Juan*, II, st. 178.
[121] Other positive references to wine include Gen. 27.28; Deut. 7.13; Eccles. 9.7; 10.19.
[122] So Josephus, *Jewish War* 5.210–11; *Antiquities* 15.395.

wine thought to be to the ritual of celebration that the Hebrew word for 'feast' or 'banquet' (*mishteh*) actually comes from the same root as the word for 'drink'. Admittedly, the occasional identification of religious fervour with drunkenness, as with Hannah in the Old and the apostles at Pentecost in the New,[123] might be taken to indicate an underlying suspicion but to me it suggests quite the reverse: that the joy which comes from religion was seen as closely allied to the exuberance that is characteristic of the wine drinker.

Nor does the New Testament do anything to undermine that positive estimate. However, it does so not simply through expansion of the same ideas but also through transforming them in the process. Here the Last Supper is of course crucial. What is clear is the way in which it blends into a new unity the wine and blood already associated with this time of year, at Passover: the escape from oppression symbolized in the doorposts marked with lamb's blood, and the joy expressed in the wine drunk in honour of that deliverance. The blood of Christ's impending sacrifice, it is suggested, will give Christians a similar, and indeed greater, joy. John's Gospel, however, does not leave matters there. The symbolism of wine is progressively enriched as his narrative advances.

Already in chapter 2, with the miracle of water turned into wine at Cana of Galilee, there is some anticipation of what is to come. The exaggerated character of the symbolism is sufficient to indicate that John is concerned with more than just telling a story. Note, for instance, the mention of 'six stone jars' of the type normally employed 'for the Jewish rites of purification' (v. 6). Cleansing rites require water, not wine, while six is one short of the perfect number seven. So it is hard to resist the conclusion that this is John's way of informing us that the imperfections of Judaism are now to be superseded by something better, indeed so much better that the difference is as great as that between water and wine. Yet not just wine but wine in abundance: in modern measurements the total amount produced is somewhere between 120 and 180 gallons, enough to generate hangovers in the guests for a week, far less a day. The overprovision is clearly deliberately absurd, in order to underline the boundless generosity of God: the new order will bring not merely an improved life but life in its richest

---

[123] 1 Sam. 1.13; Acts 2.13. Although both references are dismissive, they do suggest that one state could very easily be mistaken for the other.

abundance. It is therefore particularly sad that modern lectionaries often omit the introductory phrase 'on the third day'.[124] It is no incidental piece of chronology that was being recorded (and is now omitted). Rather, what is surely indicated is the qualitative difference that is now emerging with Christ, in the new resurrection life that he can offer.

That qualitative difference becomes even more marked in John 6. The relevant passage is best approached indirectly by looking first at Christ's description of himself as the fruitful vine in John 15.1–8. Here John builds on imagery from the Old Testament, particularly from Isaiah, where the two best-known passages occur. In chapter 5 Israel is compared to a vineyard that God owns but which has run wild: 'The vineyard of the Lord of hosts is the house of Israel, and the men of Judah are his pleasant planting; and he looked for justice, but behold bloodshed; for righteousness, but behold a cry!' (Isa. 5.7) Chapter 63 carries that element of judgement a stage further. God is now portrayed as operating a winepress that extracts the people's blood as a price for their sins. He is asked, 'Why is thy apparel red, and thy garments like his that treads the wine press?' And the answer is given: 'I have trodden the wine press alone, and from the peoples no one was with me; I trod them in my anger, and trampled them in my wrath; their lifeblood is sprinkled upon my garments' (Isa. 63.2–3). Such images find an answering chord in one of Jesus' parables that is to be found in all three synoptic Gospels. In the parable of the vineyard its owner sends various servants to collect the rent, only to learn later of their assassination. Finally he sends his own son, who then experiences a similar fate (Mark 12.1–9).

That parable shares two features with the images from Isaiah. Although a single vineyard, there is a plurality of vines; again, although acknowledged as the owner, God is seen as quite distinct and separate from the vineyard. In the passage from John 15, however, there is no longer a plurality of vines but a single vine: Christ himself, with his followers as the branches. Such a version is not wholly new to scripture. In the Old Testament a couple of

---

[124] As in the printed full-text lectionaries currently in use in the Church of England. A parallel example occurs in the text for the Transfiguration (Luke 9.28–36), where the phrase 'about eight days later' is omitted, although again it was probably intended to indicate the new order.

passing allusions had spoken of Israel as a single spreading vine (e.g. Ps. 80.8–9; Jer. 2.21). Even so, the image is undeveloped, whereas in John 15 interdependence is stressed: 'abide in me as I abide in you' (v. 4). But then note too the other side of the equation, this time without Old Testament precedent. God is no longer distinct from the vine. In Christ he has become one and the same thing. Scarcely any other conclusion can be drawn once sufficient account is taken of the various 'I am' sayings of this Gospel that precede Jesus' declaration here, 'I am the vine'. 'I am the good shepherd', 'I am the door' and so forth are all supposed to point us back to Exodus 3 and the great theophany at the burning bush that reveals God's name: 'I am that I am'. Were there any doubt about this, John removes it when he quotes Christ asserting a similar conclusion, 'Before Abraham was, I am' (8.58). Even imagery drawn from normal human relationships is found inadequate. Through the metaphor of the vine an intimacy so close is postulated that it is seen as deeper than friendship or love, deeper even than sexual union, perhaps precisely because it operates so often imperceptibly, almost unconsciously.

That is one way of understanding Christ's action in the eucharist, and it is to the eucharist that John is in all probability alluding earlier in chapter 6, for a natural way of reading the passage is as an account of how the Christian is now vouchsafed a part in the divine life itself. Occasionally in the Old Testament wine is identified as 'the blood of the grape' (e.g. Gen. 49.11; Deut. 32.14), but nowhere is the image reversed, and human blood actually identified with wine. Indeed, on the Old Covenant view of blood that would have been an impossibility, since blood was seen as the principle of life and as such belongs wholly and uniquely to God. This was why in sacrifice, though the carcass could be eaten, the blood had to be sprinkled on the altar as a sign that it really belonged to God (Lev. 17.10–12). Even in the words that institute the eucharist both Paul and Luke assume that Jesus spoke of 'the new covenant in my blood', thus avoiding any direct equation (1 Cor. 11.25; Luke 22.20). Matthew and Mark, however, take the contrary view (Matt. 26.28; Mark 14.24). Whoever is right, what cannot be doubted is that any such direct equation would have been hugely shocking to Jews of the time.[125] In effect, what appears to be a mere

[125] And indeed to Jews of today: H. Maccoby, *The Mythmaker* (London: Weidenfeld and Nicolson, 1986), 118.

human being usurps rights that belong uniquely and properly to God. Yet in John 6 there are no qualifications whatsoever. The equation is unhesitatingly made, without even the slightest hint of an equivocation. Christ declares: 'Except you drink... my blood, you have no life in you' (v. 53). The full implications of Christ's life are thus made startlingly and powerfully clear: the kind of life that was once uniquely a divine possession can now in future invade our own. Since his manner of expression is so different from our earliest tradition in Paul, it seems likely that John is developing, rather than simply reproducing, Jesus' teaching.[126] In the light of the resurrection the Church had now come to see Christ's deeper significance. His newly acknowledged status gave him the right to offer his disciples a share in the divine life.

The Old Testament images of wine as judgement were taken up in the book of Revelation. In chapter 14 the author foretells how 'the winepress was trodden... and for two hundred miles around blood flowed from the press to the height of the horses' bridles' (v. 20 NEB). The author depicts a real bloodbath. Through the centuries many a Christian has followed that precedent in envisaging a similar fate for all those who were seen as legitimately excluded from Christ's kingdom. John Steinbeck's novel *The Grapes of Wrath* and the Battle Hymn of the Republic remind us of the continuing application of such imagery in our day.

But not all left the winepress imagery as Revelation had presented it. Instead of Revelation's condemnation of others, from the fourteenth century onwards it became an image of Christ's love of us. If one result was some gruesome portrayals of Christ's suffering, a poet like George Herbert ensured that a more positive motive remained to the fore: 'Ev'n God himself being pressèd for my sake' (from 'Bunch of Grapes'). 'The Agony' perhaps expresses it best:

> Who knows not Love, let him assay
> And taste that juice, which, on the cross, a pike
> Did set again abroach; then let him say

---

[126] Even with that qualification, some New Testament scholars find it impossible to believe that any such identification could ever have been made in a Jewish context: see J. Fenton, 'Eating People' (together with R. Morgan's reply), *Theology* 94 (1991), 414–25.

If ever he did taste the like.
Love is that liquor sweet and most divine,
Which my God feels as blood, but I, as wine.[127]

Intriguingly, both Calvinism and Roman Catholicism have at times encouraged the use of white rather than red wine at eucharistic celebrations, in order to counter too literalistic an interpretation. Symbolism can of course degenerate into crude literalism. Nor need all references to the vine and wine within Christianity necessarily be eucharistic.[128] But what I suggest my brief survey indicates is that symbolism is in fact inherently creative in its capacity to enrich still further its own underlying metaphors.[129] Imaginative reflection has profoundly deepened an original simple metaphor in a direction that is entirely compatible with the thrust of the New Testament as a whole, but not at all its meaning when the image was first used. I say this both because our earliest texts of the Last Supper tell us a different story and because it is hard to envisage what the disciples at that particular moment would have made of any such claim. It was only in the light of the resurrection that John had sufficient confidence finally to draw this conclusion.

However the claim is understood, wine is now seen as the very life-blood of God, enabling us to live our lives in his. The eucharist thus provides an extraordinary foretaste of a greater and more profound heavenly reality. To the non-believer such developments might seem no more than strokes of poetic genius. For me much more is at stake. Such developments suggest that the early Church

---

[127] 'The Agony', 3rd stanza, in J. Tobin (ed.), *George Herbert: The Complete English Poems* (London: Penguin, 1991), 34. For 'Bunch of Grapes', see 119–20.

[128] In Dou's painting *Lecture de la Bible* a vine trailing through the window where the elderly couple are reading is almost certainly intended to recall Ps. 128.3 rather than anything to do with eucharistic devotion. For this and many other illuminating examples, see S. Bann, *The True Vine: On Visual Representation and the Western Tradition* (Cambridge: Cambridge University Press, 1989), esp. 53–5.

[129] In her treatment of medieval eucharistic devotion, Miri Rubin follows a similar line to John Fenton. It is the juxtaposition of the natural act of eating with cannibalism that gave the sacrament its power: *Corpus Christi: The Eucharist in Late Medieval Piety* (Cambridge: Cambridge University Press, 1991), 359–60. While no doubt some took this view, the claim inherent in Jesus' words as metaphor is surely startling enough.

was forced towards such distinctive metaphors because nothing less was adequate to their experience of the Risen Lord—no longer simply a powerful memory but divine reality itself in their midst.

From Beer to Tea: Stimulating Openness

In looking beyond water and wine, it might be thought that the relevance of drink to religion then becomes minimal, but this is far from being so. Even something as ordinary as tea and coffee once had religious, and indeed sacramental, significance, as we shall see. Although alcohol is also a drug, as mentioned earlier I deliberately exclude here hallucinogens, not because they are unimportant in the history of religion, but because their misuse is now on such a massive scale that they seem to require relegation to a quite distinct category, and with that separate treatment. All I shall do here, therefore, is briefly note their relevance to Hinduism and to shamanistic religious practice. In the Rig Vedas soma is conceived of as god, plant and juice all rolled into one. It is seen, as well as a way of gaining access to divine immortality, as making openness to experience of the divine more feasible.[130] The literature on shamanism is replete with examples of the use of not only alcohol and tobacco but also hallucinogens (from the leaves, stems, bark and sap of sacred plants) to aid access to ecstatic states and thus also to similar experience.[131] That may be the wrong way to reduce inhibitions, but that fact of course does nothing of itself to undermine the validity of any experiences so derived. The difficulty is in establishing validity where so much else is distorted, not least ordinary perceptions of the world. I shall return to soma in this volume's sequel.[132] But in the meantime I turn to a much more widespread human experience, in the effect of alcohol.

William James' comments are well worth noting:

The sway of alcohol over mankind is unquestionably due to its power to stimulate the mystical faculties of human nature, usually crushed to earth

---

[130] For further details, R. G. Wasson, *Soma: Divine Mushrooms of Immortality* (Cambridge, Mass.: Harcourt, 1971).

[131] An informative book is P. T. Furst, *Flesh of the Gods: The Ritual Use of Hallucinogens* (London: Allen and Unwin, 1972).

[132] *God and Mystery in Words*, ch. 3. The familiar hymn 'Dear Lord and Father of Mankind' was once part of a much longer poem, *Soma*, in which ritualistic religion is subjected to a sustained attack.

by the cold facts and dry criticisms of the sober hour. Sobriety diminishes, discriminates, and says no; drunkenness expands, unites and says yes. It is in fact the great exciter of the *Yes* function in man. It brings its votary from the chill periphery of things to the radiant core. . . . To the poor and the unlettered it stands in the place of symphony concerts and of literature.[133]

Of course, this is scarcely the norm. Indeed, despite his tone in this passage James does not hesitate to concede elsewhere the 'pathological' side to alcohol. Yet those more obviously religious aspects cannot be discounted.

At the same time it is important to set such experience within the wider framework of associated symbolism. Access to the possibility of experience of the divine is after all not simply self-determining but heavily dependent on wider assumptions, ideas and practices within society as a whole. Take, for example, the fact that beer rather than wine formed the usual pattern of consumption in England over many centuries. Although it is hard to determine its precise impact, it is unlikely that the fact that wine was absent from working-class Anglo-Saxon culture until quite recently did not have some influence on how the eucharist was perceived. It could have had an alienating effect, or it might have contributed to the 'exotic' character of the rite. The issue at least merits consideration. Certainly, the extent to which drink and the practices associated with it have in fact functioned across the centuries as forms of social exclusion or inclusion is quite extraordinary. Even today various 'rules' continue to attach to contemporary practice. Whether sherry or gin and tonic is served before 'supper' or 'dinner' already tells us much, as does whether care is exercised over providing white wine for fish and poultry, and red for heavier meats.[134] Again, port might be expected with the chocolates, but offering snuff would be seen as decidedly exotic, despite its tremendous capacity to clear the head and enable one almost to start

[133] W. James, *The Varieties of Religious Experience* (London: Fontana, 1960 edn), 373.
[134] Gin and tonic gradually replaced gin and orange after the Second World War, apparently thanks to the influence of those returning from imperial India (tonic contains quinine). Strict rules about particular wines only became possible once *service à la française* was replaced by *service à la russe*, in other words strictly consecutive courses: A. Barr, *Drink: A Social History* (London: Pimlico, 1998), 70–4.

anew. Snuff of course went because of its deleterious consequences for health, and that has also proved true for some forms of alcohol as well.

Given the lack of plentiful running water and adequate food supplies for much of human history, beer has functioned more often in the role of food and refreshment rather than as a mere adjunct to social drinking. However, as living conditions began to improve, so did the strength of the alcohol available.[135] The idea that such strong beverages—'spirits'—might be a way of access to the 'Spirit' was of course not new. One classic expression is to be found in Euripides' play *Bacchae*, where the ability of Dionysus (or Bacchus) to create or destroy through inebriation is fully acknowledged: a god 'to human beings most fearful and most kind'.[136] It was, however, a theme that was explored anew in the eighteenth century among a number of poets and writers. Robert Burns was in effect treated almost like an earlier equivalent of Jim Morrison of the Doors.[137] Like him he used stimulants to open up his powers of creativity.[138] That is of course not necessarily to suggest a religious dimension. There is a closer approximation in the attitudes of Charles Lamb and Samuel Taylor Coleridge. Coleridge, for example, speaks of Bacchus as 'representative of the energies of the Universe that work by passion and joy without apparent distinct consciousness', to generate 'something innate and divine'.[139] Both authors were in part responding to hints of the artificial nature of personal identity in writers such as Hume and Hartley. If Lamb was

---

[135] F. Braudel contrasts creation of such drinks in the sixteenth century with true popularization in the eighteenth: *Capitalism and Material Life* (New York: Harper and Row, 1973), 158, 170.

[136] *Bacchae* 860 (my translation). Although inebriation comes by other means in the play (particularly, dance), the point still holds, as the god in question is the god of wine. E. R. Dodds supports a similar duality in his survey of competing interpretations of the play: *Bacchae*, 2nd edn (Oxford: Clarendon Press, 1960), pp. xxxix–xlv; cf. also M. Detienne, *Dionysos at Large* (Cambridge: Mass.: Harvard University Press, 1989), 27–41.

[137] Morrison is discussed in Chapter 6, pp. 330–3.

[138] A. Taylor, *Bacchus in Romantic England* (New York: St Martin's Press, 1999), 37–8. Wordsworth reflected on this dimension of Burns for about twenty years: 42.

[139] Ibid., quoting an 1812 lecture: 120; cf. 112.

especially partial to gin, it was the now-banned drink of absinthe that generated similar reflections in nineteenth-century France.[140] Baudelaire was eventually to regret his addiction.[141] But he did detect in absinthe the power to expose his real self as two opposing streams, 'insistent flesh and searching spirit'. In this he was to influence both Rimbaud and Verlaine in their turn. Oscar Wilde expressed absinthe's power thus: 'After the first glass you see things as you wish they were. After the second you see things as they are not. Finally, you see things as they really are, and that is the most horrible thing in the world.'[142] Unfortunately, the heightened mental consciousness it afforded worked a quite different result in the body's digestive system, and that resulted in its eventual ban.

But mostly change in drinking habits has had little to do with questions of health, and everything to do with fashion, and not a little with manipulation by government and large financial concerns. Sherry before dinner and port afterwards are, for example, very modern ideas. Both were once served along with the main meal.[143] Again, gin may now be very much a middle-class drink, but go back three hundred years and it was the preferred tipple of the very poor.[144] The explanation lies in the fact that, when William of Orange came to the throne, he insisted on the abolition of all taxes on this Dutch drink.[145] The poor of London quickly found in it a means of drowning their sorrows amidst the dreadful housing conditions of the then rapidly expanding capital city. The result was gin shops that became the scandal of Europe. Such was the government's embarrassment that it eventually taxed them out of existence, even though many thought the earlier policy an excellent way of damping down any possibilities of rebellion

[140] For Lamb and gin, see ibid. 75. Charles Lamb thoroughly intoxicated at a famous celebrity dinner in 1817 is described in P. Hughes-Hallett, *The Immortal Dinner* (London: Penguin, 2001), 278–80. Absinthe was banned in France from 1915 onwards.

[141] Baudelaire's *Les Paradis artificiels* of 1860 was intended to represent this change of mind but was in fact widely misinterpreted: B. Conrad III, *Absinthe: History in a Bottle* (San Francisco: Chronicle, 1988), 16; cf. 25.

[142] Quoted without reference ibid. 37.

[143] Barr, *Drink*, 83–5. He also suggests that the 'sack' of Shakespeare's day was in fact sherry and not simply a dry wine: 79.

[144] For the history of gin, see P. Haydon, *Beer and Britannia* (Stroud: Sutton, 2001), 81–93, 163–80.

[145] As husband of Queen Mary in 1689.

among the lower classes. A century later, however, 'gin palaces' emerged as an attempt by the producers, as the name implies, to make the drink more socially acceptable.[146] Come the twentieth century, and there was further change, with gin now the favourite tipple of many a genteel lady and 'ladies' of a different kind—effeminate Anglo-Catholic clergy who came to be known for their 'gin, lace and bitchiness', to quote a familiar phrase.

To change the brew, not only is the popularity of lager new, so too is its invention. Indeed, ironically, if one wanted to taste the sort of beer that Englishmen characteristically once drank, it would be necessary to go well beyond most of the draughts currently on offer. Called porter, it was much stronger than any bitter now available in this country. By a strange quirk of colonialism, its nearest modern equivalent is to be found in Nigeria, where older traditions linger on.[147] Lager only began to come to prominence in the 1960s. It was in fact part of a powerful advertising campaign that sought the transformation of people's drinking habits, and in particular the enticement of women into bars. The city of Newcastle offers a powerful example of the extent of the resultant change.[148] From the 1850s its Scotswood Road had an armaments factory (Armstrong's) on one side and back-to-back houses on the other. At the end of each street stood a pub, 56 in all, and all were strictly men only, apart, that is, from the barmaid. When the factory closed and the old housing was demolished, the brewing companies sought ways of enticing in a more varied customer. So the focus now moved to larger city centre pubs with their lager culture. The bar was now no longer a further extension of one's locality. Rather, it was deliberately located elsewhere, and presented as a venue towards which one travelled in order to have 'a good time'. Some locals have of course survived, but they are a shadow of what was once meant by an English pub.

From such a brief history is easily seen the essential arbitrariness of modern conventions. There is much modern hype about the freedom modern society has brought compared with the tyrannies of the past. Instead of enhancing a sense of joy and celebration,

---

[146] Exterior and interior now looked good, but the clientele changed little.

[147] Even Guinness is served at double strength in Nigeria: N. Brownlee, *Alcohol* (London: Sanctuary, 2002), 68.

[148] For details see ibid. 13–16.

however, these modern drinking codes can be just as conformist. Backed by slick advertising, they may give the impression of decisions freely made but repeated patterns of behaviour tell a quite different story. There is also a deeper worry. The drinking places of the past, because they were mostly local and deprived of the possibility of loud music, once functioned as bastions of social support. The community could easily gather there, even if the negative side was often the exclusion of women or drink used to drown awareness of wretched social conditions. Such familiarity, however, did facilitate opportunities for individuals to open up to one another. Although this seldom explicitly included a divine Other, connections with the local church were easier to maintain in such tightly knit communities, and so at least the option was left open.

If this is still a long way from explicit religious experience, it is worth noting how easily one type of experience might merge into another within such gatherings. Plenty of examples of a natural transition are to found in other societies, if not in our own. So, for example, among the Masa beer is treated as 'the ambrosia of super-natural beings and ancestors', and accordingly offered regularly in libations with prayers.[149] In Vanuatu kava is used in contexts where contact with the dead is desired.[150] Again, among slaves taken from Africa to the West Indies squirting rum on a child's face was apparently used as a form of dedication to the tutelary deity, while gin was sprinkled on the deceased prior to burial.[151] Nor are explicitly Christian examples wanting. In the hospitality that greets a guest in the ancient land of Georgia alcohol plays the key role, as toasts are successively drunk over the course of a long evening. While some are concerned to reinforce family ties, others assume a more religious character: such toasts are intended to function more like a 'blessing' (*dalotsva*).[152] Nor should it be

[149] I. de Garine, 'Drinking in Northern Cameroon among the Masa and Muzey', in I. de Garine and V. de Garine (eds), *Drinking: Anthropological Approaches* (New York: Berghahn, 2001), 51–65, esp. 59.

[150] So Igor de Garine in his Introduction to *Drinking*, 7.

[151] F. H. Smith, 'Alcohol, Slavery and African Cultural Continuity in the British Caribbean', in de Garine and de Garine (eds), 212–24, esp. 215, 216.

[152] If mention of family and local heroes suggest the former, saints and the deceased imply the latter: '*Tamadoba*: Drinking Social Cohesion at the Georgian Table', in de Garine and de Garine (eds), 181–90, esp. 184–7.

forgotten that until the creation of alehouses in the England of the thirteenth century, the corporate drinking of beer appears to have been largely organized by the Church.[153]

This suggests some marked differences from the modern world. Even among Roman Catholics the temperance movement was to gain considerable dominance in church life.[154] The subsequent failure of prohibition in its turn generated a quite different set of attitudes. Even among once staunchly prohibitionist Methodists the ban on alcohol has become optional. Yet it is worth asking why there was such hostility in the first place. In earlier centuries opposition would not of course have been feasible, given the often lamentable state of the water available. Some motives for later opposition were undoubtedly good, in compassionate concern for the victims of abuse, particularly women and children, an abuse often intensified by situations of acute poverty. But there may have been less creditable factors at play, as alcohol came to be banned even from contained contexts, such as holy communion.[155] Although impossible to prove, there may have been an anxiety that not everything would then be assumed to proceed from grace, from divine action on the believer. Instead, the way in which alcohol can reduce inhibitions and make human beings more open to new experiences might raise the suspicion that, even if still from God, it was human action that really made the decisive difference, not a totally unmerited divine initiative. As such it would then be an illegitimate usurpation of the divine prerogative. But setting more favourable conditions for God to act is hardly the same as requiring him to do so.

Nonetheless, that may be one reason why John Wesley initially objected to the consumption of both tea and coffee: they were also artificial stimulants. Outside Christianity, however, one finds both given a sacred character. Indeed, in searching for equivalents to

---

[153] Haydon, *Beer and Britannia*, 5–6. Strictly speaking, the brew was more likely to have been ale or mead, since beer (i.e. ale with hops) only became common in the fifteenth century.

[154] Fr Theobald Matthew was hugely successful in nineteenth-century Ireland: Brownlee, *Alcohol*, 98; Haydon, *Beer and Britannia*, 207.

[155] It was even argued that all the positive references to wine in scripture were really to unfermented grapes: F. R. Lees and D. Burns, *The Temperance Bible Commentary* (London: no pub., 1868).

wine in other religions, it is tempting to identify non-alcoholic beverages as the nearest equivalent.[156] Thus, thanks to the sacred character of the cow in Hinduism, milk is often treated in a not dissimilar way to wine within Christianity. More especially, ghee or clarified butter plays an essential role in religious ritual in the anointing of images of the gods. Recently, controversy has been stirred in India by the claim that the cow has not always been so highly regarded as it is now. But, whether vegetarian or not at the earlier stages of its history, India does seem always to have had a reverential attitude to what the cow produced.[157] Again, coffee is given a spiritual role among the Sufis of Islam, especially among the dervishes as part of preparations for their famous dances. More familiar perhaps are the ritualized ceremonies associated with tea that have played a major part in Zen Buddhism over so many centuries.

In the case of coffee superficial connections with religion are easily made. Cappuccino, for instance, gets its name from the froth on top that was thought to resemble the pointed hoods of Capuchin friars. Mocha points to a more substantial connection: the Yemeni town of al-Makkha from which coffee was first imported from Africa. The use of coffee spread quickly through the Middle East, eventually reaching Europe in the seventeenth century. Its power as a stimulant was one reason why Islam debated whether, like alcohol, it should be banned.[158] Another was the way in which coffee houses became, as in Western Europe, meeting places for intrigue and sedition. Al-Makkha contains a major Sufi shrine.[159] It was the use of coffee by Sufis that contributed to the third element

---

[156] Although tea seems to have been deliberately cultivated within Zen Buddhism as a substitute for the role of sake (rice wine) in Japan's older religion of Shintoism: Visser, *Much Depends on Dinner*, 187–8.

[157] The book causing the stir is D. N. Jha, *The Myth of the Holy Cow* (London: Verso, 2002). His argument is not helped by his unnecessarily polemical tone. He talks of 'religious rigmarole' and opponents are labelled 'obscurant and fundamentalist': 17, 20. Yet even he concedes that the early practice of meat-eating was already accompanied by the rise of reverential attitudes towards the animal: e.g. 38, 41.

[158] Various bans were imposed in the sixteenth and seventeenth century, the former particularly in Arabia, the latter in Turkey.

[159] In Africa the beans were chewed. It is to al-Shadili, whose pilgrimage tomb is in a local mosque at Al-Makkha, that the first brewing is attributed, in *c.* 1200: S. L. Allen, *The Devil's Cup* (Edinburgh: Canongate, 2001), 39–50, esp. 46–8.

in Muslim hostility. Sufi mysticism with its use of dance and music seemed to call into question Islam's heavy stress on the clear and exclusive character of the Qur'an as the divine Word. To this day, although the Turkish authorities strictly control the whole ritual, the solemn drinking of coffee precedes dancing by the dervishes that results in mystical trances, as key verses from the Qur'an are recited.[160] The coffee is distributed by their leader from a shared pot, to the sound of religious chants accompanied on a flute. Normally, a red pot is used to symbolize participants' desire for mystic union with the divine. While a spiritual role for coffee is also found in a number of other contexts,[161] the Sufi use nicely illustrates the way in which stimulants might facilitate openness to the divine, even if prior dispositions might need to be there in the first place. Mormons may object, but that any harm results from such consumption is so far unproven.[162]

With tea the nature of the role is quite different. Zen is a religion that stresses the transitory and the mundane as a way of access to the ultimate nature of reality. To practitioners the West seems to offer only a cult of clutter, typified by homes crowded with objects and images.[163] Already a ninth-century classic was suggesting how the serving of tea might in itself be treated as an aesthetic and religious delight,[164] and this was pursued in Buddhist practice by offering tea before the statute of Bodhi-Dharma. Significantly, an early twentieth-century Japanese expert describes this process as itself a sacrament: 'the monks gathered before the image...and drank tea out of a single bowl with the profound formality of a sacrament'.[165] In any event, it was from this ceremonial context that there eventually developed the *tokonoma* or alcove of the

---

[160] Ibid. 100–3. Such religious use is not only paralleled for tea (see below) but also for chocolate. In the latter case Bishop Landa described its use as like a baptismal ceremony: S. D. and M. D Coe, *The True History of Chocolate* (London: Thames and Hudson, 1996), 17–104, esp. 62.

[161] Allen gives some other examples from Ethiopia and Bolivia: ibid. 25–8, 196–7.

[162] For the wider background to Mormon attitudes, see D. J. Davies, *An Introduction to Mormonism* (Cambridge: Cambridge University Press, 2003), 181–2.

[163] These are repeated themes in Okakura Kakuzo's *The Book of Tea* of 1906 (Tokyo: Tuttle, 2000 edn). For the absolute in the relative, see 43, 47–8; for the importance of the mundane, 52; for the need for a single focus, 66, 84.

[164] Lu Yu's *Classic of Tea* of 804. Even the boiling water is treated poetically with the insistence that it must be 'like fishes' eyes'.

[165] Okakura, The Book of Tea, 36.

Japanese home, where a simple display invites meditation.[166] The later tea ceremony, now bereft of images, was intended to evoke similar attitudes. A preliminary walk along a previously prepared garden path leads to a wooden tea-house where a minimum of accompanying items suggests transience but also value in the everyday.

As such the ceremony forms a dramatic contrast to the history of tea in the West. If coffee was one reason for the introduction of black slaves into the West Indies and Brazil, western imposition of the sale of opium on China was in part caused by the need to pay for the tea now being imported. Later in the nineteenth century tea production moved to Assam and Ceylon, but this was at great cost to the native populations. The present Tamil insurgency in modern Sri Lanka is a direct consequence of the importation of Tamil labourers to work on the tea plantations at this time.[167] Yet there was also a positive side. If genteel tea parties can conjure up middle-class values at their worst, as can debates about whether grace should be said on such occasions,[168] the other side was a slowing down of the pace of life that, as with Zen practice, encourages the valuing of small intimacies and pleasures. It may be no accident that Charles Rennie Mackintosh's famous tearooms in Glasgow introduced religious allusions. His wife, Margaret MacDonald, produced a fine set of murals based on Psalm 65.[169] God is to be found as much in the ordinary as in the extraordinary. The modern tea bag suggests a much more hurried pace for life in which God is less likely to find a place.[170] Against that trend, however, might be set the opening of specialist tea and coffee shops, and the offering of a variety of types of tea and coffee in the home.

[166] Ibid. 59, 66.

[167] For this more negative history, see R. Moxham, *Tea* (London: Robinson, 2003), 51–184. It is likely that several hundred thousand immigrant labourers lost their lives in tea plantations in northern India.

[168] Charles Lamb mocks two Methodist clergymen arguing over whether to say grace before a cup of tea in his essay 'Grace Before Meat': *Essays of Elia*, 136.

[169] Her stress is on vv. 9ff., with their emphasis on God's generous bounty; for illustration, see C. and P. Fiell, *Charles Rennie Mackintosh* (Cologne: Taschen, 1995), 120.

[170] Although tea bags were invented in 1908, their use in Britain grew only very slowly. In 1970 it was still only 10% whereas by 2000 it had reached 90%: Moxham, *Tea*, 201–3.

Cultures from the more distant past or else contemporary societies not too heavily influenced by western values are perhaps
now the most effective witnesses to the potential of mild stimulants
to initiate religious experience without threatening to distort mind
or intellect. By contrast, in our own hurried, competitive world
alcohol now seems primarily geared to relaxing sexual inhibitions
and tea merely to serve as a quick pick-me-up. Nonetheless, the
alternative potential remains, were our world ever to return to a
slower pace and to one in which other human beings and our
environment more generally were valued intrinsically for their
own sake.

Some Concluding Reflections

Changes in present living patterns, such as more dining out and
special meals, may help explain the current popularity of novels and
films that have food as their theme. Alternatively, the explanation
could possibly lie in the exact opposite aspect of the same phenomenon, namely the marked decline in the celebration of the ordinary,
in frequent meals together with family or friends. In a recent
influential book Robert Putnam has pointed to the way in which
this is part of a much wider social trend, the move away from those
features of society that sustain 'social capital', in reinforcing our
commitment to one another.[171] Certainly, whatever the explanation, food is now often treated as a powerful metaphor for deep
engagement, not least with issues of sensuality and love. Even
cannibalism is explored as part of this trend, as are psychological
uses of food.[172] Unfortunately, from a religious perspective there is
little to suggest much interest in investigating related sacramental

---

[171] R. D. Putnam, *Bowling Alone: The Collapse and Revival of American Community* (New York: Simon and Schuster, 2001), 93–115, esp. 101, 106, 115. For
similar patterns in participation in church activities, see 65–92; for possible causes,
283–4.

[172] In both Peter Greenaway's film *The Cook, the Thief, his Wife and her Lover* of
1989 and Jean-Pierre Jeunet's and Marco Caro's *Delicatessen* of 1990 cannibalism is
used to provide a dark, comic critique of contemporary society. The novelist Peter
Sheridan uses hilarious farce in order to explore the serious issue of child abuse and
the compulsive eating that sometimes functions as a means of dealing with it: *Big
Fat Love* (Dublin: Tivoli, 2003).

themes. Joanne Harris' highly successful *Chocolat* of 1999 continues a form of novel that Isabel Allende and Laura Esquivel had already made their own.[173] In Harris' book Vianne Rocher, a female mystic who makes chocolate for a living, is set against the local priest, Francis Reynaud, who is trying to ensure that his parishioners keep their Lenten fast.[174] Rocher is portrayed as a liberator of the locals in various ways, for example in one case from a cruel marriage and in another from a painful death.[175] In the latter case the fact that the key events take place on Good Friday and Easter Sunday leaves the reader in no doubt that it is alternative forms of redemption that are at stake, a liberating individualism as against what is seen as an arbitrary, self-denying and ultimately self-destructive authoritarianism.[176] Although the attack on the Church is justified, it is hard to find significant content in Harris' alternative, despite the depiction of Vianne as a sort of mystic (presumably intended to convey the idea that spiritual issues are not being ignored). Although in the course of enjoying the chocolate various personal dilemmas are resolved, there is no sense of the chocolate in itself opening up individuals to alternative spiritual horizons, as was the case, for example, in Aztec culture. Chocolate was seen as a gift of love from the god Quetzalcóatl, and was offered at sacrifices, in puberty rituals (where it was mixed with flowers) and at funerals. Indeed so prominent was its use in such religious contexts that in his classification of plants Linnaeus termed the cocoa plant *theobroma cacao* ('the gods' food'). It was also first to enter Christian culture through monastic use.[177] To this day during the Days of the Dead Festivities in late autumn Mexicans continue to place chocolate on home altars and on graves to welcome back the returning souls.[178]

[173] As in the former's novel *Aphrodite* and the latter's *Like Water for Chocolate*.

[174] In the film version the role of opponent is given instead to the local mayor. According to the director, this was done, not to dampen possible Catholic objections, but rather because otherwise the plot would have been too predictable (so Lasse Hallström in an interview on the 2000 DVD version).

[175] Joséphine in the former case, Armande in the latter.

[176] Nor is it surely an accident that there are 12 guests with inscribed name cards at the Good Friday feast: J. Harris, *Chocolat* (London: Doubleday, 1999), 293–4.

[177] Chocolate was first introduced into Aragon in the sixteenth century as a food and stimulant during periods of fasting. Still to be seen at the famous Trappist monastery at Poblet is its chocolate room with its own chimney.

[178] A recent Royal Academy exhibition celebrated the history of this practice; for further details, see *Royal Academy Magazine*, winter 2002, 63–7.

In Christian circles Karen Blixen's *Babette's Feast* is often seen as
the obvious contrast.[179] Both novel and film present an impressive
tale of how the joy of a single meal might be harnessed to transform
personal relationships. It tells the story of how a once-famous cook
living with a religious sect in nineteenth-century Norway per-
suades them to let her spend her lottery money on a superb meal.
Although the sect's members resolve not to yield to the sensuous
tastes, the meal gradually transforms all present, with various recon-
ciliations effected and so forth.[180] This time there is no doubt
about the spiritual dimensions to the plot. Yet one cannot help
wondering whether the religious content might not be too explicit
for contemporary culture. If Harris bypasses the wider potential of
the chocolate, the limitation in Blixen is that anterior Christian
belief could well be seen as necessary for the meal to push its
participants sufficiently in the right direction. Almost certainly
this was not Blixen's intention, but it does demonstrate how
Christian appropriation of the film has made it more difficult for
others to discover wider resonances in the way she tells the story.

   That is why admittedly lesser films such as *Leo the Pig Farmer* of
1992 and *Big Night* of 1996 might have more impact. In the latter a
financially ruinous great feast precipitates two brothers into discovery of their love for one another, not at the feast itself but as they
later share an ordinary omelette. In the former a comic narrative is
used to explore how the value of Jewish identity might be found by
first stepping beyond its food taboos.[181] Neither film explicitly
mentions God. But that is scarcely the point. Throughout this
chapter I have been trying to address the question of whether
food and drink might sometimes generate conditions that make
openness to experience of the divine more feasible. That is scarcely
likely for an Orthodox Jew unless he already regards food laws
on pork as integral to his own identity. Equally, unless one can find

---

[179] Karen Blixen (1885–1962) wrote mainly under the pseudonym Isak Dine-
sen. Her best-known work is the largely autobiographical *Out of Africa*, which has
also been made into a successful film.
[180] Two women who had slandered each other forgive each other; a brother
who had cheated on another confesses and is forgiven; and so on.
[181] Although neither has been made into a film, two novels that use food to
explore Hindu and Muslim attitudes respectively are Anita Desai's *Fasting, Feasting*
(London: Chatto and Windus, 1999) and Diana Abu-Jaber's *Crescent* (London:
Picador, 2003).

value in a simple shared meal, God is unlikely to become manifest in anything more elaborate.

The mistake is to suppose that only the most explicit forms of religion are of relevance. The same issue presents itself in modern art. Quite a number of negative images of food and drink have been produced that in effect offer a critique of modern social attitudes. Crass and arbitrary overindulgence is found displayed in Roy Lichtenstein's *Kitchen Stove* (1962).[182] By contrast, the desolation of the late-night coffee shop in Edward Hopper's *Nighthawks* of 1942 has become for many iconic of all that is wrong with contemporary society.[183] Other such images alert us to the possibility of how things might be otherwise. Think, for example, of Norman Rockwell's treatment of the Thanksgiving turkey in his *Freedom from Want* (1943).[184] The values of family, patriotism and religious gratitude are all implicit. That painting continues an earlier tradition. Rembrandt could paint so lovingly and so deliberately the hanging carcass of an ox that even for the most secular of viewers the crucifixion is likely to come to mind. Again, Zurburán paints fruit on a table in such a way that an altar may well suggest itself to the viewer, although there is no explicit religious symbolism in the work to force such a conclusion.[185] In making these observations I do not wish to deny that *Babette's Feast* approaches most clearly the Christian ideal of what should be mediated. But it is important to acknowledge that the implicit can be as effective as the explicit, and sometimes more so.

Similarly, it seems to me the wrong way round to start from scripture alone in imposing a particular meaning on sacrifice and what it might tell us about God. As I argued earlier in this chapter, the Bible in its symbolism often builds upon what was already part of human experience. Some kind of divine involvement has been integral to eating and drinking throughout history and across cultures. More often than not this has been given concrete expression in an associated offering to God as part of the process. Modern Christian analyses of sacrifice often divorce the notion from any meal element. But whether one takes the Passover sacrifice or that

---

[182] Illustrated in K. Bendiner, *Food in Painting: From the Renaissance to the Present* (London: Reaktion, 2004), 158–9, as is Hopper's painting (107–8).

[183] For illustration and commentary, see Plate 8 at the end of this book.

[184] Bendiner speaks of 'an act of national communion': *Food in Painting*, 71–2.

[185] For illustrations and comment, see ibid. 40–1, 54–6.

on the Day of Atonement as one's model, both alike involved a clear relation to food, even if in the latter case it was mainly by denial through fasting. So we need to see Christian understandings of Christ's death as continuing to relate to that wider context, however much such attitudes were modified in the process and given their own distinctive Christian slant.

However, rather than pursue directly that theme of sacrifice here, what I want to do next is to turn to how the body offered up in sacrifice is represented and understood, both as Christ on the cross and in sacrificial self-denying lives on the part of his followers. As such the body as 'ugly and wasted', the topic of the final chapter of this first part of the book, will provide a neat complement to its initial chapter. I began with the body as beautiful and sexy, but that scarcely remains the lot of any of us throughout our lives as a whole. I thus move from food and drink in plenty to food and drink denied.

4

Ugly and Wasted

FINALLY in this part of the book I want to focus on those aspects of Christian attitudes to the body that non-believers usually find most difficult. As a religion Christianity sometimes comes across as taking an almost perverted delight in suffering, whether it be of Christ or of his saints. To this day Christ himself is found portrayed on the great majority of crucifixes wracked with pain, while in the Lives of saints it is often the most repulsive features of their behaviour upon which most stress is laid. Asceticism often transformed what must once have been a beautiful body into one lacerated and thin. Saints even ate vomit and pus as part of what they saw as required of them in their devotion to Christ. There is no point in denying such a history. Instead, we need to face the issue head on, and ask whether any sense can be made of the exaltation of body as 'ugly and wasted'.

Some Christians might be tempted to reply that in such presentations of Christ at least only the truth is being spoken. But of course there are various ways of speaking the truth. To this day there is a reluctance to show on our television screens the worst aspects of human violence and brutality, not least because it is felt that this is to trivialize the awfulness of what happened and show insufficient respect for the dead. So Christianity might have followed a different course, and indeed did so for much of its history. If it took until the second millennium for the crucifixion in all its brutality to be portrayed, the fact that Raphael and Grünewald are contemporaries demonstrates how two competing perspectives continued to exist alongside one another even as the assertion of the glory of the painful body had achieved its greatest impact in Grünewald.[1] At one level what is thereby illustrated are the competing approaches of northern Gothic and

[1] Grünewald's work was discussed in Chapter 3.

Italian Renaissance. True, the Renaissance was inspired by Greek models rather than directly by the earlier Romanesque. But, as I tried to indicate in Chapter 1, it would be a mistake to suppose that purely pagan considerations dominated. Beauty of body was being used as a metaphor for divinity and for humanity's ultimate triumph over sin and death.

Equally, however, the ugliness of the pain so powerfully portrayed in northern Gothic should not be seen as simply a matter of realism. Nor will it do to twist language and speak of beauty after all in such pain. Rather, what needs to be addressed is the ultimate motivation in a desire to find in Christ a closer personal identification of the divine with our suffering, as also the possibility, in its contemplation and imitation, of a closer identification of ourselves with Christ as the one who can make possible a more intimate relation with God. Experiential considerations were thus to the fore. As noted earlier, Grünewald's painting allowed the patients in the hospital for which it was painted to experience Christ alongside them in their suffering. Readers and viewers alike, however, as they imaginatively filled out the bare bones of the Gospel story, were also able to reverse the process: to find themselves able imaginatively to draw alongside Christ in his suffering, and thus experience his forgiveness and his love. Again, the numerous ascetics who chose to imitate in their own lives Christ's own pain did not usually do so out of some perverted masochistic desire, but rather because they hoped thereby for a closer affective identification. If, quite wrongly, women were more frequently cast in this role than men, this does not mean that the whole tradition is now suspect. Rather, what it suggests to me is the need for us all, men as much as women if not more so, to see what we might learn from those past insights.

I will end this chapter with some consideration of where we might legitimately stand today on such issues. But most of the chapter will be concerned with a selective historical survey that seeks to interpret sympathetically some of the stranger aspects of Christian history. I begin by examining the types of changes that were made to the telling of the crucifixion story in order to make affective appropriation easier. It is not just the cross itself that becomes more gruesome. Additional extraneous features are also introduced to accentuate still further that horror, among them borrowings from contemporary instruments of torture such as the wheel. To presuppose perverse pleasure in such punishment would be totally to misread writers' and artists' intentions. The fundamental purpose of such innovations was to draw reader and viewer alike more closely into the significance of the drama that had occurred for their salvation. As such the overall purpose was essentially no different from the aims of the Gospel writers. Readers may choose to recoil from the methods. But, if so, they should at least first allow the strategies a proper hearing. That is why in the next section I attempt a comparison between one of the Gospels and the response of the fifteenth-century English mystic Margery Kempe in her own distinctive gift of tears. Thereafter, two more extreme types of reaction are explored: the asceticism of those, such as Catherine of Siena, who sought to live on virtually nothing; and the way in which the classical legend of the flaying of Marsyas was adapted to Christian ideals in normally quite restrained artists such as Michelangelo and Titian.

In pursuing this more sympathetic analysis, my intention is not after all to declare right and proper such extremes. Rather, it is to call into question blanket condemnations, as also to raise the question of whether the modern world is really necessarily any better in its approach. If all we ask of the Gospels is their factual basis or otherwise, distance between Christ and the believer is the almost inevitable result. Situate ourselves, however, within the narrative alongside one of the participants, and quite a different form of relationship then becomes possible. It is that experiential possibility that I want the reader to bear in mind throughout this chapter, and more especially as I begin with consideration of details introduced into the treatment of Christ's crucifixion that might seem initially only to intensify that sense of horror.

Affective Strategies for Engagement with Christ's Suffering

Let me begin with some basic remarks on representations of Christ's suffering. In portraying his path to the cross, the words of Isaiah have sometimes been appropriated: 'As one from whom men hide their faces'; 'he had no form or comeliness that we should look at him, and no beauty that we should desire him'.[2] Yet right from the beginning many a Christian has found it impossible to let this be

---

[2] Isa. 53.3, 2.

the last word. So, although in the first century Clement of Rome endorsed Isaiah, soon afterwards Origen was insisting that, though Christ's body was called 'ugly', it was not 'undistinguished'.[3] In a nutshell, the difficulty was that, if God is the source of all that is good and only of that which is good, it would seem odd to find in the event by which he wrought the salvation of humanity only ugliness and not also some beauty.

That is no doubt why in the history of Christian art artists generally have sought to include in their work, even when dealing with the suffering and death of Christ, hints of such beauty. Even in the most gruesome of paintings there is almost invariably some such pointer elsewhere, most commonly perhaps through allusions to the forthcoming resurrection. Not that the same strategies were employed through history. As a rough generalization, we may say that in the first millennium Christ is portrayed as reigning from the cross with the suffering only minimally indicated, if at all. So, for instance, his feet usually have a footrest and he often wears a full-length garment (the *colobium*) rather than a loincloth, both elements there to indicate his august dignity.[4] Although the loincloth is present in a fifth-century portrayal at Santa Sabina in Rome, even the arms of the cross are not immediately apparent, while the nails look more like a decorative feature than a real threat to Christ.[5] Indeed, so prevalent was such an approach in the West that in the discussions of 1054 that finalized the break between eastern and western Christendom, in marked contrast to later attitudes it is the West that we find expressing reservations about explicit portrayals of suffering, not the East.[6] However, by the end of the Middle Ages western images were common of the sort that now only produce revulsion among theologians of the East.[7] The West had now gone

[3] For Clement of Rome, see *Letter to the Corinthians* 16 (Christ came in self-abasement as Isaiah had foretold). Tertullian follows him: *On the Flesh of Christ* 9. For Origen, see *Contra Celsum* 6.75.

[4] The footrest (*suppedenaeum*) is paralleled elsewhere, in icons with saints and others elevated off the ground. The *colobium* was a sleeveless purple tunic that indicated royalty.

[5] Further information and illustrations available at <www.op.org/international/English/Curia/doors4.html>. As this web page explains, the doors were for long relegated to the twelfth century because it is extremely rare to find crucifixion imagery this early.

[6] In the objections of the papal delegate, Cardinal Humbert.

[7] As in the critique of Grünewald by M. Quenot, *The Icon: Window on the Kingdom* (London: Mowbray, 1992), 72–83, esp. 80.

well beyond copying the East, into far greater realism. Not that this was a uniform development. As already noted, restrained Renaissance imagery continued to contrast with the more violent tones of the Gothic art of northern Europe. If that suggests self-contained movements within particular areas of Christendom, Ireland illustrates how sentiments could move simultaneously in opposed directions. Sixteenth-century Ireland could produce both a Christ serene on the cross and one in the acutest agony. In a similar way the images of twentieth-century Ireland have varied between triumph and pain, with occasionally even the sensuousness of the Buddha's limbs also represented.[8]

Why western Christianity moved in the direction of more painful portrayals of the crucifixion I have already explored elsewhere.[9] Rather than repeat that wide causal analysis, I would like here to focus on only one key aspect, not least because it is so often misunderstood, and that is the whole question of engagement. Quite a few secular commentators have found in the awfulness with which the crucifixion came to be presented in the later Middle Ages evidence of an increasing preoccupation with issues of punishment and atonement.[10] So-called Doom Paintings indicate an element of truth to the claim. Anselm's satisfaction theory of the atonement is often held to point in the same direction. That seems to me a mistaken reading.[11] Strictly speaking, it is the death itself that for Anselm constitutes the act of compensation. It is only with Calvin that the focus moves to the suffering as itself part of what was required. What has gone wrong is the tendency to read Anselm's *Cur Deus Homo* in isolation. That work was intended as a strictly philosophical argument, with the actual historical person of Christ removed from consideration, *remoto Christo*, as it were. The actual effect of Christ's death on Anselm as a committed

---

[8] For the sixteenth-century contrast, with illustrations, see P. Harbison, *The Crucifixion in Irish Art* (Blackrock, Ireland: Columba Press, 2000), 48–9, 52–3. For twentieth-century triumph, see ibid. 94–5; for pain, 92–3; for sensuousness, 86–7.

[9] See my *Tradition and Imagination* (Oxford: Oxford University Press, 1999), 345–64, esp. 352–8.

[10] e.g. J. Delumeau, *Sin and Fear: The Emergence of a Western Guilt Culture 13th–18th Centuries* (New York: St Martin's Press, 1990).

[11] For the argument in more detail, see my 'Anselm on Atonement', in B. Davies and B. Leftow (eds), *The Cambridge Companion to Anselm* (Cambridge: Cambridge University Press, 2004), 279–302, esp. 293, 296–7.

believer is to be found in his much more accessible *Meditation on Human Redemption*, where it is clear that what matters to him is an affective response to the Saviour rather than any purely formal considerations.

That affective stress is also present in Bernard later in the twelfth century, where experience moves to the forefront of his thinking. However, it is really only in the following century with St Francis that the full impact on visual imagery becomes noticeable. The growing practice of elevating the host at the mass probably had some impact, in a desire for more conspicuous reminders of where the blood was shed, particularly in the associated iconography surrounding the altar.[12] More important, however, was the Franciscan desire to imitate Christ, and so for the more human aspects of his life to be clearly evident. This meant not only his suffering but also the various scenes associated with his passion. In order better to achieve that focus, in artistic representations some incidents are simplified. Judas' kiss of betrayal, for instance, is not always accompanied by Peter's violent act towards the servant of the high priest.[13] Again, Jesus is made to carry his own cross rather than allow this to be done by Simon of Cyrene. New artistic scenes are also introduced, such as the stripping of Christ and his ascent of the cross.[14] The symbolism of near-nakedness is used throughout, not least because that symbolism had also been a prominent feature in Francis' own life, though the metaphor is of course much older.[15] Jerome had even used it to define the essence of what it is to be a Christian: *nudus nudum Jesum sequi*.[16] The Old Testament is also ransacked to provide additional commentary. If sometimes the connections are so recondite as to be accessible only to a few (Calvary linked, for instance, to Elisha's being teased for his baldness), in other cases they add greatly to the poignancy of the

---

[12] The practice of elevation grew gradually through the thirteenth century.

[13] For evidence of moves toward the removal of Peter from this scene and of Simon of Cyrene carrying Jesus' cross, see A. Derbes, *Picturing the Passion in Late Medieval Italy* (Cambridge: Cambridge University Press, 1996), 35–71, esp. 39; 113–37, esp. 115.

[14] Ibid. 138–57.

[15] For nakedness as a Franciscan theme, see M. D. Lambert, *Franciscan Poverty* (London: SPCK, 1961), 61.

[16] 'Naked to follow a naked Christ': *Epistles* 52.5.

scene.[17] The drawing of parallels with the mocking of Job has long antecedents. The blindfolding of Jesus, however, may possibly have been utilized first in England.[18]

Such blindfolding is often found in the popular image of Christ as the Man of Sorrows. That image may be used to illustrate how even where the primary focus had moved to Christ's humanity his divinity was by no means forgotten. Signs were still planted to remind the viewer of the ultimate significance of such suffering. For example, sometimes Jesus' eyes were left open, despite the fact that the symbols on and immediately about him imply that he has just been taken down from the cross. Again, even where his eyes are closed, he is presented as though apparently standing self-supporting.[19] It is from this period that there comes the symbolic presentation known as the Arma Christi, a single image containing all the various instruments used to torture Christ. Picture books were also on offer where the wounds Jesus had received were reproduced in their alleged precise size, and offered for contemplation.[20]

Sometimes in images of the crucifixion or of the Man of Sorrows blood flowed directly into a chalice. It is a pattern that continued even into otherwise serene Renaissance images, such as the Raphael *Crucifixion*, now in the National Gallery in London. The eucharistic meaning is obvious. More dramatically, blood is occasionally to be found gushing directly onto one of the onlookers. Both Mary Magdalene and Joseph of Arimathea are depicted

---

[17] The link with Calvary depends on punning on the Latin form of the boys' address to Elisha as 'the bald one'—*calve* (2 Kgs 2.23): Derbes, *Picturing the Passion*, 155.

[18] So ibid. 102. The first appearance is in the *St Alban's Psalter* of 1120. For the mocking of Job, see Job 30.1–10.

[19] For two helpful discussions of the development of this image, see the articles by Bernhard Ridderbos and Michael Camille in A. A. MacDonald, H. N. B. Ridderbos and R. M. Schlusemann (eds), *The Broken Body* (Groningen: Egbert Forsten, 1998), 143–210. For examples of closed eyes but a self-supporting Christ, see ibid. 150, 161, 164, 165; for open eyes, 173, 184. The English title Man of Sorrows, unlike the German (*Vesperbild*), at least makes the allusion to Isaiah (53.3) clear.

[20] For Arma Christi and examples of precise measurements and their devotional use, see D. S. Areford, 'The Passion Measured', in MacDonald *et al.* (eds), *The Broken Body*, 211–38.

drinking blood in this way.[21] Again, the centurion (whom the tradition had come to call Longinus) is shown with Christ's blood touching one of his eyes and thereby curing his blindness.[22] Similar notions also occur in sermons and devotional literature. The medieval preacher John Mirk, for instance, describes how Christ's flowing blood could even lead to the conversion of some Jews: 'even' because of his anti-Semitism.[23] All this hardly suggests a hatred for the body. Indeed, the liturgical cycle actually encouraged a daily return to contemplation of the momentous sequence of events in due order. In fourteenth- and fifteenth-century Books of Hours, for example, it was recommended that the crucifixion should be recalled each day at sext, the entombment at compline, and the resurrection at matins.[24] The aim was not a masochistic wallowing in Christ's sufferings. Although the medieval Church thought terrible pains awaited the unrepentant after death, the more positive side was that there was no limit set to the possibility of forgiveness this side of death. So it is important to take seriously the repeated assertions in the literature of the time (alongside warnings of judgement) that the cross constituted a demonstration of divine love, the aim of which was to effect personal transformation.[25] Suffering alongside Christ was thus sought less as a way of atoning for one's own sins and more as a means of entering into that mission of Christ to the world. It is only then that Margery Kempe's belief becomes explicable, that her own crying and suffering will deliver thousands from purgatory. She sees herself not as imposing punishments on herself for former sins but rather as having the honoured role of acting as Christ's agent in the world.[26]

Crying is an issue to which I shall return in a moment. First, however, a little needs to be said about the legibility of Christ's body. In an extraordinary passage in James Joyce's *Finnegans Wake*

[21] In the Gorleston and Gough Psalter. Adam does so in the Taymouth Hours. For comment and illustrations, see E. M. Ross, *The Grief of God: Images of the Suffering Jesus in Late Medieval England* (New York: Oxford University Press, 1997), 50, figs 2.13, 2.15 and 2.16.

[22] Ibid. 51–2, figs 2.13, 217.

[23] J. Mirk, *Mirk's Festial: A Collection of Homilies* (London: Kegan Paul, 1905), 145–6.

[24] Ross, *The Grief of God*, 44, 115.

[25] A repeated theme in Ross: e.g. 1–9, 131–8. She talks of 'the somatization of divine love' (131).

[26] Ibid. 122–8.

Shem 'the Penman' covers his body with ink markings made in part from his own bodily fluids.[27] In effect, his body becomes a form of parchment or writing. Such a way of viewing the body, as something to be read, runs much deeper in modern culture than initial reflections might suggest. In the nineteenth century numerous attempts were in fact made to define the criminal body or head.[28] If that suggests a low evaluation of some bodies, on the other side might be mentioned first reactions to the discovery of spermatozoa.[29] There was great resistance to acceptance of the notion that some inferior sort of species like a worm might actually be operating inside male bodies. Linnaeus even sought to put them on the remote edge of his taxonomical system. Artists, depending on whether they have been realists or not, have sometimes strongly resisted representing the folds of skin that of course become more prominent on us all with age.[30] But such folds too can have a meaning, in suffering and in struggle, or in calm acceptance. Equally, this is true of stance, not least in the contrasting types of *contrapposto* employed by artists.[31] What I suggest was taking place during the late medieval period was real engagement with the sort of signals the actual physical body of Jesus might have conveyed, and which therefore in some sense still constitute his identity, however much that has been transformed in his post-resurrection state.

That is why the blood issuing from Christ's side was taken to be of more than incidental significance. It indicated whose that particular body was—both human like us but also with a power to transform viewers' lives. So that is why Christ's blood not only poured into chalices but also onto individuals and even in the form of a life-giving fountain.[32] Most such images of Christ's

[27] J. Joyce, *Finnegans Wake* (London: Faber and Faber, 1966), 185–6.

[28] For examples of phrenology extended more widely, see J. Elkins, *Pictures of the Body: Pain and Metamorphosis* (Stanford, Calif.: Stanford University Press, 1999), 76–85.

[29] Ibid. 226–31.

[30] Elkins contrasts Michelangelo and Grünewald in their attitude to skin: Ghiberti and Brunelleschi in their approach to *contrapposto*: ibid. 62–9; 84–92. (See next note.)

[31] The Italian term describes a twisted pose with, for example, hips and legs facing one way and chest and shoulders another. Michelangelo's virtuosity in such representations enthused many others.

[32] Sometimes so much blood flowed that the face was no longer visible: for an example, see MacDonald *et al.* (eds), *The Broken Body*, 2.

blood as a red-stained fountain of new life were to be destroyed at the Reformation. The notion, however, did survive as a powerful verbal metaphor in much Protestant poetry. Take, for instance, these lines from one of William Cowper's hymns:

> There is a fountain filled with blood,
> Drawn from Immanuel's veins;
> And sinners plunged beneath that flood
> Lose all their guilty stains.[33]

To the modern mind a taboo of good taste seems at the very least to have been broken. That, however, ignores the more positive side. It was a question of identification. The blood pouring freely was a sign not of some distant grace but of God in Christ coming right alongside us, totally one with us in our suffering. That is what first-millennium representations had failed to capture. In stressing the divinity and the victory of the humanity in the way they did, it remained a distant humanity rather than one with which we could directly engage.

That is also why, even with all these fresh variants in forms of expression, the new piety was still not content. In order to create a fully omnitemporal present reality, features from the culture of the artists' own day also found their way into depictions of the crucifixion. By the fourth century crucifixion as a form of punishment had disappeared. In its place had come hanging, and the wheel as an instrument of torture. While the form of Christ's own death is almost never changed, it is quite otherwise with the two thieves, by the medieval period commonly given the names of Dismas and Gestas.[34] Although the wheel seldom appears explicitly, by the later Middle Ages the bodies of the two thieves are often hideously distorted, in order to suggest that just such a punishment had happened to them previously.[35] The use of ropes and rods helped to make the allusion.[36] Punishments were of course still public at this time. So in effect the viewer was being invited to apply what was taking place in the picture's frame to their own day. In saying

---

[33] 'Praise for the Fountain Opened', no. 15 of the *Olney Hymns*: W. M. Rossetti (ed.), *The Poetical Works of William Cowper* (New York: Ward, Lock and Co., n.d.), 280.

[34] The names first appear in the fifth-century *Gospel of Nicodemus*.

[35] The history of this imagery is traced in detail in M. B. Merback, *The Thief, the Cross and the Wheel* (London: Reaktion, 1999), esp. 101–25.

[36] Ibid. 81, 96, 119–20.

this, it is important to note that according to medieval thinking, although punishment for the guilty could not be revoked, there was always the possibility of forgiveness. Confession and communion were both made readily available.[37] So the two thieves offered contrasting options in response to that possibility. What might be achieved thereby is well indicated by the cult of Dismas (the good thief) as an intercessor. He is portrayed in this capacity at Assisi, where he is given a beautiful resurrection body, unmarked by his ordeal.[38]

Cranach the Elder is a painter who before the Reformation immersed himself fully in this tradition.[39] In his later work, however, figures are made to group themselves round one thief or the other, in a way that indicates a major change in focus. For Cranach the point of the painting has now become essentially declarative, not one of engagement. Under Luther's influence, what is now seen to matter most is the issue of faith.[40] So the key demand was to indicate clearly which side the thief was on, not to engage imaginatively with what he himself might be going through in the process of crucifixion. In one late painting the contrast is even more marked. The centurion rides past.[41] His eyes, instead of being on the suffering figures, are directed to some words immediately in front of him that explain the events' meaning. Clearly, the viewer is now being treated by the painter rather like the reader of a text, where the main aim is to convey information, not the capacity to follow the details in one's imagination. It is important to note that major change in Christian sensibility.

The Gift of Tears

The Gospel writers were, I suggest, much nearer in approach to the medieval world than they were to the later Cranach. I want now to illustrate this by examining the way our earliest Gospel relates a

---

[37] Ibid. 142–50, esp. 148–9.

[38] Ibid. 223–4.

[39] For two examples from 1502 and 1503, see W. Schade, *Cranach: A Family of Master Painters* (New York: Putnam, 1980), illus. 3 and 5.

[40] For illustration of his 1538 *Crucifixion*, see ibid. illus. 104. The pattern is repeated in Cranach the Younger's work: Schade, *Cranach*, illus. 253, 254.

[41] Merback, *The Thief*, 287–8.

couple of incidents in the life of Jesus. What I want to suggest is that, despite initial appearances, Margery Kempe's notorious crying to excess can be seen in natural continuity with the methods of Mark and his more immediate successors. Thereafter, I shall explore changed attitudes to crying in our own day, and how that affects current religious experience.

Mark and Margery Kempe Compared

Despite the enormous amount of scholarly material on the Gospels, there remains surprisingly little on their strategies for encouraging their readers to engage with their text and its implications. But such techniques are evident everywhere, as one small extract from Mark may be used to exemplify. In Mark 5.21–43 the telling of one miracle story is placed within another in a way such that readers are encouraged to allow each incident to illumine the other. Such placement is unlikely to be solely for historical reasons, even if these were remembered. The result of the interruption to the narrative flow is greatly to add to the tension and drama inherent in the first story, of the ruler of the synagogue's appeal on behalf of his dying daughter. Readers are made to wait to hear what will eventually happen, while Mark relates the incident of the woman with a haemorrhage touching Jesus' garment.

This is but one example of Mark's considerable skill as a story-teller, concerned as he is to secure our maximum engagement with what is being recorded. His use of the present tense draws us into the presence of the observing crowd, almost despite ourselves. Again, a sense of expectancy is created by his repeated use of the Greek particle for 'immediately' (*euthus*), as also by the extraordinary, almost breathless, build-up of participles which he uses to describe the woman's condition (v. 26). Such strategies parallel the resources employed by artists to the same effect. Our involvement is secured.

The temptation is to suppose that there the parallel ends. These two miracles are about the overcoming of suffering created by taboos, it may be said, whereas devotional medieval practice simply brought with it new superstitions and fresh forms of suffering. Certainly, both woman and girl would have been seen in ancient Palestine as conveying ritual pollution. The woman with a haemorrhage was actually suffering from vaginal bleeding and so was ritually impure according the rules laid down in Leviticus (15.25–30). So equally was the young girl by the time Jesus encounters her, for by then she was dead and so subject to the same taboo. But Jesus' freedom is only part of the point. That something rather more is at stake is indicated by the fact that Mark uses as his word for 'heal' the word he uses elsewhere for 'save'. Again, his injunction to the girl to get up is actually the normal Greek word for 'rise', and so for resurrection.

The story as presented is really about how new life can be created for the reader in engagement with Christ as saviour. That there is more than one way of securing such engagement can be illustrated by one additional detail provided by Matthew. Jairus, we are told, has employed professional mourners to act on the family's behalf (cf. Matt. 9.23). That was common practice in the ancient world, but the detail is, I suspect, included not for historical reasons but to add poignancy to the scene. The ancient reader would have been immediately reminded of events in their own lives. The nearest modern equivalent is undertakers and funeral directors, but the contrast is greater than the similarity. The modern resource is employed to distance ourselves from the corpse, in order to limit displays of grief, whereas the ancient world's concern was to make such displays possible. Others releasing tears helped to release one's own. Engagement is, implicitly, being demanded of us all.

That is one reason why tears actually became a major theme in the history of Christianity. They were held to mark maximum involvement with the story of Jesus, not a standing apart. Yet there was also a difficulty, and that concerned the Virgin Mary. Certainly ordinary humanity must weep. But would the person who according to the orthodoxy of the time was closest to him, without sin, and knew perfectly his ultimate destiny also shed tears? Ambrose for one thought not.[42] Only John's Gospel has Mary at the foot of the cross, and there is no mention of her weeping. The result was a long history of conflicting views within the history of Christian spirituality about whether Mary would have cried then or not. Some, like Origen, argued that she must have. But for him this showed Mary's weakness, her lack of trust in the ultimate victory of her Son.[43] Others have her dry-eyed at the foot of the cross, with only

[42] *Letter* 63 (PL 16, 1271).   [43] *Homilies on Luke* 17.

the women in the distance weeping.[44] The work of the Flemish painter Gerard David may be used to illustrate the dispute. In a crucifixion now in the Metropolitan Museum in New York neither the Virgin Mary nor Mary Magdalene is weeping at the foot of the cross. Ten years or so later, in another painting by the same artist (also now in the same city), the Virgin Mary is still restrained, but Mary Magdalene is set apart to weep profusely.[45] The dispute rumbled on into the Counter-Reformation. Fortunately for the impact of the story (since many chose to enter it through Mary's role as a participating mother), common sense prevailed and on the whole her tears flowed. As well as uninhibited tears, there was also sometimes even laceration of the flesh: 'she tugged and tore with great torment, she broke her skin, bone, body and breast'.[46]

A good example of the resultant impact can be found in Margery Kempe. The negative side was that she wept so often that many of her contemporaries thought her mad. Indeed quite a few modern commentators join them in this judgement, and describe her as mentally unstable. But there was a positive side. In an age where clergy claimed a monopoly on how the Gospel should be interpreted, Margery was able to argue that she had an alternative source of authority: in effect she had been there, had been alongside Mary and so really knew from the inside, as it were, what it was all about.[47] The important point is, as we have seen, that the suffering appropriated through all those tears brings life and not death. For someone like Margery the woman's flow of blood in the Gospel story in effect now ceases, but in its place Jesus begins to bleed instead: a fountain of blood that brings life and not suffering or death. It is not that the suffering is valued in its own right but that it enables her to find forgiveness and release into

---

[44] Although all three synoptic Gospels mention the women observing from a distance, only Luke speaks of a 'smiting of breasts': Luke 23.48.

[45] For an illustration of the former (from 1495), see M. W. Ainsworth, *Gerard David* (New York: Metropolitan Museum, 1998), 123. The latter (from 1510) is part of the Frick Collection.

[46] From the fifteenth-century English lyric 'Filius Regis mortuus est'. For this and a contemporary extreme sculptured version, see K. Lochrie, *Margery Kempe and Translations of the Flesh* (Philadelphia: University of Pennsylvania Press, 1991), 182, 190.

[47] Ibid. 193, 196.

a compassion for the world that is Christ's own.[48] Hence the great stress in her book on Christ's divine love and on her own refusal to abandon the gift of tears, because of the 'merriment' it can bring in doing Christ's work in the world.[49]

Tears in the Modern Context

Nonetheless, the temptation remains in our own culture to mock at any potential value for such tears. It is too overblown, it will be said. A modern bishop of Norwich might well be less tolerant of having his sermon interrupted in this way.[50] But there is also something to be said on the other side. Over the long march of history contemporary culture is really quite untypical in its attitude to crying. Within scripture tears are frequently mentioned. Jacob, Saul, David and Peter all weep. Famously, the shortest verse in the Bible is 'Jesus wept.'[51] Even the Greeks expected men to cry and show other extremes of emotion, provided their source did not lie in cowardice or fear.[52] While the Renaissance reacted with hostility to how far matters had gone by the time of Margery, the seventeenth and eighteenth centuries exhibited a return to such attitudes in their cult of *sensibilité*.[53] Twentieth-century restraint could be defended as a response to Victorian sentimentality, a response typified perhaps in Oscar Wilde's recommendation that one should in fact laugh at the death of Dickens' Little Nell.[54] If film stars and public figures are now more commonly seen crying than would have been the

[48] For a helpful analysis, see E. Ross, 'She Wept and Cried', in U. Wiethaus (ed.), *Maps of Flesh and Light: The Religious Experience of Medieval Women Mystics* (New York: Syracuse University Press, 1993), 45–59, esp. 51.

[49] *The Book of Margery Kempe*, (London: Penguin, 1985), 1.77, (pp. 221–4).

[50] Ibid. 1.69 (p. 207).

[51] John 11.35. It is possible that some references in the Psalms ultimately derive from a liturgical lament of the Canaanite goddess Anat for Baal that brought him back to life: so T. Lutz, *Crying: The Natural and Cultural History of Tears* (New York: Norton, 1999), 33–4.

[52] Odysseus weeps quite a few times on his long road home, while in the *Iliad* Achilles and Priam alike tear their hair and cover themselves in dirt to demonstrate their grief.

[53] For hostile reactions from Alberti and Michelangelo, see J. Elkins, *Pictures and Tears* (New York: Routledge, 2004), 159–61.

[54] The heroine of Dickens' *The Old Curiosity Shop*. The novel was hugely popular at the time of its publication (1841). Wilde is quoted in Lutz, *Crying*, 54.

case half a century ago, the reasons all too often seem to mark less commendable expressions of self-pity or even the return once more of mere sentimentality.[55]

That is one reason why James Elkins' recent study is of particular value. He explores why it is that so few people in the modern world are reduced to tears before paintings. His researches led him to the conclusion that probably less than one per cent of his academic colleagues in the art world had ever had such an experience.[56] As he admits, even when it befell him,[57] it was not quite the real thing. In any case it was ruined for him once a more academic exploration of the painting in question followed. Rather than securing meditative engagement, conventional forms of art criticism create hindrances and obstacles to such deep personal involvement. Elkins thinks it quite wrong to suggest that film is a more natural medium for such effects, as though its commitment to the passage of time naturally aids such a process.[58] Paintings can equally tell a story and engage us. Even fresh tales can sometimes be generated, as the viewer explores possible meanings.[59] But most profound of all in evoking such a response in his view are those paintings that provoke a sense of divine presence or absence. Such an acknowledgement from him is made all the more remarkable by his own admission that he himself lacks religious convictions.[60] As he observes, religion is the great unmentioned in modern art criticism.[61] To quote one of his own examples, the distinguished art critic Michael Fried can even conclude an influential article with an allusion to grace but then refrain from any further comment.[62]

Elkins notes the way in which particular paintings and sculptures have played a decisive role in the lives of various saints. There was the painted crucifix that transformed the life of St Francis: so much so that thereafter 'he could never keep himself from weeping'.[63]

[55] For film stars, ibid. 189–92; for politicians, 230–3.
[56] Elkins, *Pictures and Tears*, 99.
[57] Before Bellini's *Ecstasy of St Francis*: ibid. 74–89.
[58] Ibid. 130–49.
[59] As in Diderot's treatment of Greuze's *Young Woman Weeping over her Dead Bird*: ibid. 108–29.
[60] For lack of religious allegiance, see ibid. 82. For divine absence, he takes Friedrich and Rothko as examples: ibid. 182–204.
[61] Ibid. 149.
[62] Ibid. 179.
[63] Thomas of Celano's words: ibid. 153.

Even more remarkable was the crucifix that helped produce stigmata in St Catherine of Siena in 1375, and Giotto's image of a boat
that appears to have caused paralysis in her limbs five years later.[64]
In the latter case the boat, tossed on the waves of the Sea of Galilee
and taken to represent the Church in trouble, overwhelmed her
with its own weight.[65] So far from rendering either saint incapable
of further action, however, such startling identification with imagery associated with the life of Christ actually empowered them
both. Yet to focus on such contentious extremes would be to
deflect attention away from a more central issue, the possibility of
an effect on the experience of the great majority of viewers rather
than just a tiny minority. Whether reading a text like Mark or
viewing a painter like Giotto, what the modern believer has lost is
the capacity to enter fully into the possibility of graced presence
through text or panel. A mental response is expected rather than
one that affects the body no less than the mind. Tears can carry one
into the story of salvation but also beyond into a relationship with
the divine.

This is to stand against a long tradition of Christian scholarship
that has praised the mystics of the *via negativa* and downplayed or
even parodied those more emotionally orientated such as Kempe.[66]
Such evaluations are in my view greatly mistaken. Of course there
were dangers in an approach like hers (but so too in the alternative,
in arrogant contempt for how most people of the time experienced
their faith[67]). Passivity might have been the result, but, as Kempe
herself indicates, this was far from being inevitable. So if the
Despenser Retable in her local cathedral of Norwich indicates a
bishop determined to argue from crucifixion to passivity as the
proper response to the Peasants' Revolt, even archbishops were
found yielding to Margery.[68] Indeed, it is important to realize that

[64] Ibid. 167–8. For more detail, see A. Curtayne, *Saint Catherine of Siena*
(Chumleigh, Devon: Augustine Publishing, 1980 edn), 83, 196–8. Curtayne
describes the crucifix as 'a strange conception . . . queer, unmoved'.
[65] For an illustration from a copy of the mosaic from Old St Peter's, see A.
M. von der Haegen, *Giotto* (Cologne: Könemann, 1998), 92.
[66] For examples of hostility from Evelyn Underhill, David Knowles and others,
see S. Beckwith, *Christ's Body: Identity, Culture and Society in Late Medieval Writings*
(London: Routledge, 1993), 15–17.
[67] A point insufficiently noted, but compare R. M. Gimello, 'Mysticism in its
Contexts', in S. Katz (ed.), *Mysticism and Religious Traditions* (Oxford: Oxford
University Press, 1983), 86 n. 1.
[68] Beckwith, *Christ's Body*, 23, 94.

her ideas were being worked out as contested concepts in a society
not wholly in agreement with itself. The Lollards, for instance,
offered quite a different perspective on many issues of the day. So,
to suggest that compared with great mystics, Kempe and others like
her worked in a framework of unthinking acceptance or pure
emotionalism is quite untrue.[69] They too had to work things
through. It is simply that this was pursued imaginatively rather
than in a purely verbal or abstract way. Their reflections were also
bodily orientated.

Fasting as a Power for Change

Frequent floods of tears may in the modern context seem distinctly
odd, but they are as nothing compared with the strangeness of the
extreme asceticism that characterized the lives of so many of the
Church's saints. Its extremes are one of the most difficult features of
late medieval piety for both contemporary Christian and non-
believer alike to comprehend. Once more, however, a different
evaluation becomes possible once such matters are examined more
closely. Fasting too was more than just a physical act.

Jesus and John the Baptist had both fasted. Nonetheless, Christ's
reputation is usually now taken to point in quite a different direction. The earlier biblical heritage, it is argued, had placed fasting
within strictly limited boundaries, largely for penitence and in
mourning rituals.[70] Nor did this change much in the earlier history
of the Church. Clement of Alexandria's comments are quite restrained, and this may also have been true of Origen, despite Eusebius' protestations to the contrary.[71] However, with Jerome and the
monastic tradition, it is clear that asceticism has become a major
strategy for control over the body as well as a means for securing
power over others (as in the image of 'the fasting hero').[72] Although

[69] Although Beckwith accepts some ambiguity, the central theme of his book is
that Kempe was consciously challenging some of the values of her society. See esp.
ibid. 112–17.

[70] For Christ contrasted with John the Baptist, see Matt. 11.18–19; for the
Jewish background, see V. E. Grimm, *From Feasting to Fasting: Attitudes to Food in
Late Antiquity* (London: Routledge, 1996), 14–33.

[71] Clement was less extreme than Philo: see ibid. 94–113, esp. 99; for Eusebius
distorting Origen's practice, see 152–3.

[72] For Jerome, see ibid. 157–79. He may even have been responsible for the
death of one young woman (Blaesilla): 170–1.

Jerome, Origen and Evagrius all identify fasting as a device for controlling sexual appetite, it is important to note that such an aim may well have been less central to most people's thinking at the time than their remarks may initially suggest.[73]

In a world of frequent food shortages bodily control might well be more readily located in control of hunger than, as is immediately assumed today, of sexual appetite. Indeed, for some fasting is seen as representing a return to Eden. That, it was assumed, had been a world without meat and wine.[74] So it is a repeated theme in the later eastern fathers that fasting can give individuals a foretaste of their future state by imparting something more like an angelic, paradisical body.[75] Sadly, while men are portrayed as achieving thereby a more graceful and youthful body, it is the ugliness of the female ascetic that is more often commended. The author of the Life of Pelagia, for instance, contrasts her pre-conversion beauty with her present state, in which even 'her pretty eyes had become hollow and cavernous' and 'the joints of her holy bones, all flesh-less, visible beneath her skin through emaciation'.[76]

Even so, it would be a mistake to think of the medieval extremes as constituting either an obsession with sex or a hatred of body. St Catherine of Siena is a good example to take. She is familiar to historians for the key role she played in trying to put an end to the fourteenth-century scandal known as the Babylonian Captivity of the Church, when the papacy resided at Avignon and were essentially puppets of the French king. Much of that influence in fact derived from the extreme austerity of her lifestyle. She lived on virtually nothing, supplemented by occasional bean-feasts that she

[73] Origen is the earliest known instance of the connection being made: *Contra Celsum* 5.49. For Evagrius' description of gluttony as 'the mother of lust', see *De vitiis* 2 (PG 79, 1141a–b).

[74] For fasting as a return to Eden, see T. M. Shaw, *The Burden of the Flesh: Fasting and Sexuality in Early Christianity* (Minneapolis: Fortress, 1998), 161–219. The absence of meat and wine was argued partly from the fact that nothing in Eden required labour (Gen. 3.17–19), while the eating of animals is only explicitly sanctioned after the Flood (Gen. 9.1–3).

[75] For Basil of Caesarea on Eden's diet, see *De ieuinio hominum* 1.3–5 (PG 31, 168a–169b). For Evagrius on lighter, angelic bodies, see Shaw, *Burden*, 198–205.

[76] S. P. Brock and S. A. Harvey, *Holy Women of the Syrian Orient* (Berkeley: University of California Press, 1987), 60. Contrast Athanasius' description of Antony in his Life of him: R. C. Gregg (ed.), *Athanasius* (London: SPCK, 1980), 42 (sect. 14).

not infrequently vomited up not long afterwards.[77] Like several other women of her time she also quite often deliberately spoilt such food as she did eat, either by diluting it with water or else by adding something unpleasant such as human pus.[78] Such a scenario may seem to proclaim her mad, or at the very least suffering from the medieval equivalent of what we now call anorexia or bulimia. That analysis has been accepted by some scholars who have considered the evidence over a great range of ascetics.[79] Others, however, have suggested that this is to confuse what are really consequences in the religious case with what must be seen as only symptoms where these illnesses are concerned.[80] Either way, such phenomena might well be taken to confirm the common suspicion about the Middle Ages, that it was really a period profoundly hostile to the body: salvation was seen essentially in terms of release into another immaterial world.

Such an analysis, however, sits oddly with a society for which the central moment of worship each week was the elevation of the host, the priest displaying to the people a piece of bread, something seen as intensely physical, mediating not just Christ's divinity but also his incarnate humanity as well. It is also the period during which marriage begins to be seen as more than just a social contract and so as something requiring sacramental celebration within a church building. It is perhaps therefore not surprising that some of those who have investigated the behaviour of such people in recent years have proposed a quite different explanation. This has essentially two elements. The first is the desire for total identification with Christ's suffering; the second, rebellion against the domestication of food, and so with it an alternative source for women of power and freedom.[81]

---

[77] In Raymond of Capua's biography 'ate nothing' is really equivalent to not eating normally: cf. C. W. Bynum, *Holy Fast and Holy Feast: The Religious Significance of Food to Medieval Women* (Berkeley: University of California Press, 1987), 83.

[78] Ibid. 172. Similarly, Francis mixed his food with water or ashes to spoil its taste: 95.

[79] See, for example, R. M. Bell, *Holy Anorexia* (Chicago: University of Chicago Press, 1985). As well as detailed analyses of Catherine (22–53) and Margaret of Cortona (92–102) among others, there are statistical tables (134–5, 146–7, 176–7) and an important 'Epilogue' from W. N. Davis supporting Bell's view.

[80] Bynum's view: *Holy Fast*, 194–207, esp. 205.

[81] These two motives are explored in Bynum: ibid. 189–244.

If the reception of the stigmata by St Francis on his own body is well known, less familiar is the fact that this phenomenon appears to have been far more conspicuous among women than among men.[82] It was of course part of the general late medieval desire to find salvation through total identification with Christ. He had suffered for others; so we too must suffer like him, and like him use that suffering to benefit others. If that meant fearless caring for those who were sick with the plague (so eating their pus), it also meant something much more difficult for us to understand, the deliberate buffeting of one's own body. Yet such self-imposed suffering was in no way regarded as a denial of the body. On the contrary, it was seen as a means of affirming its central importance. Christ's body through its suffering had brought new life to others. So the suffering bodies of his followers must also have a similar potential. Again, the rhythms of nature suggested that all life had to go through a winter of destruction and death before the summer harvest of new life could occur.[83] So, such women concluded, what they were doing was merely repeating the pattern established by God himself in his creation, as also in the life of Christ. The result was an extraordinarily rich battery of metaphors to describe this relationship, many of them erotic in character. Not only could one drink from Christ's wounds, the blood was also seen as like milk and Jesus himself as a mother.[84] Even a sensual kiss on the mouth might occur as an appropriate image for how close the relationship had now become.[85] As many of the women involved were married, sexual metaphors came naturally to mind.[86] Indeed, the marriage bed could itself be the occasion for thinking mystically.[87]

But there was also another motive. The preparation of food was seen at the time as an essentially female, domestic role, and with that went severe curtailment of religious and other opportunities for

[82] Even those that were consciously self-caused were seen as acceptable: ibid. 212.

[83] As in the images of the mystical mill and of stalks of wheat actually growing out of Christ's wounds: ibid. pls I, 1 and I, 4.

[84] Catherine places her mouth on Christ's wound: see ibid. 173. For milk seen at the time as a form of blood, 179.

[85] As in Hadewijch: see Bynum, *Holy Fast*, 155–6.

[86] Bell wisely protests against speaking of necrophilia in the case of Angela of Foligno just because she is so explicit about what she might like to do for Christ with her kisses: *Holy Anorexia*, 109.

[87] As with Kempe: *The Book of Margery Kempe*, 1.3 (p. 46) cf. 1.1 (p. 41).

women. To talk of living off the eucharistic bread (many of these
women were daily communicants) therefore offered an important
alternative perspective. Christ could be seen to speak directly to
them as they received the elements, and so bypass the usual male
controls of the home.[88] Significantly, their families and priests were
forced to treat such female ascetics with fresh respect, for such
fasting brought with it not only a new food but also a new freedom.
Vomiting at the mass might well be blamed on a deficient priest
rather than on defective behaviour on the part of the woman
communicant.[89] In Catherine's case seeing blood accompany the
wafer indicated a more intimate contact with the incarnate God
than that had by the celebrating priest himself. Herein, in numerous
details such as these, lay Catherine's confidence in upbraiding
Pope Gregory XI. She might still need food but for her the most
important food had now become in reality Christ's own body. So
the pope had better listen, when she urged him to act like 'a real
man'.[90] Not dissimilar motives were probably at work in mutually
agreed abstinence from sexual activity within marriage. The
women involved thereby acquired considerably wider possibilities
for action.[91] Nor, once more, will it do to speak of a horror of the
body and sex. Admittedly, some such marriages were unhappy, but
even here the changed circumstances could act as a catalyst for a
better relationship.[92]

In outlining such ideas my intention has not been to defend
such conduct. Undoubtedly, there was much unnecessary suffering.
Rather, my central point is this: giving up food in the medieval
period was actually a way of reinforcing the importance of the
body, not undermining it. An alternative body and an alternative
food were substituted as a way of indicating what Christianity
was really all about. Moreover, within such an instrumental view
that is combined with continued respect for the body as an end in

---

[88] After the freedom of childhood, Catherine found the controls of puberty
very constricting: Bynum, *Holy Fast*, 224.

[89] Ibid. 228–9; for blood with the wafer, see 232–3.

[90] 'I desire to see you a real man': K. Foster and M. J. Ronayne (eds),
I Catherine: Select Writings of Catherine of Siena (London: Collins, 1980), 123.

[91] As in the case of Margery Kempe. For a fascinating survey of the history of
the practice, see D. Elliott, *Spiritual Marriage: Sexual Abstinence in Medieval Wedlock*
(Princeton: Princeton University Press, 1993).

[92] As with Catherine of Genoa: ibid. 256–7.

its own right, there turns out to be after all some deep continuities with biblical perspectives. Part of the symbolism of John the Baptist feeding on honey in the desert is clearly its use in penitence in Isaiah (7.22) but honey's other association with future promise is probably there as well: in the oft-repeated phrase 'a land flowing with milk and honey' and perhaps even in its association with pleasure.[93] As Isaiah himself frequently asserts, the desert can indeed under God become a land of plenty (e.g. 35.1–10). A similar connection is made explicit in Jesus' own life. Not only does he fast like John in the wilderness, he also multiplies food for those listening to him, trapped far from home, in a place called literally a 'desert' (Mark 6.30). Although retained in the Authorized Version, sadly that meaning is lost in most modern translations. What has worried biblical scholars is that Bethsaida (the place of the miracle) was nowhere near a desert. But clearly what Mark is doing is playing fast and loose with geography in order to make his point. Under Christ the desert can indeed bloom. We reverse the Fall by fasting, by living a life of dependence on God; abundance is produced for others by learning restraint on ourselves. So, even if the image changes from blossoming desert to eucharistic body, an essential continuity remains: the enhancement of the material through its self-disciplining.

Moral Beauty and Flayed Skin

Although in presenting the suffering of Christ most artists continued to hint that however gruesome the suffering it did not have the last word, these hints were not always clear. An excess of suffering may obscure the point, or the reality of death appear altogether too unqualified.[94] That may be one reason why on turning to the Renaissance we find Michelangelo moving in a quite different direction. Although obviously this depended in part on his patrons, it seems significant that within his repertoire no major role was

---

[93] e.g. Prov. 24.13–14; S. of S. 4.11; 5.1.

[94] For the latter, note Holbein the Younger's *Body of the Dead Christ* of 1522, which so shocked Dostoevsky. For a helpful discussion of the painting and its implications, see J. Kristeva, 'Holbein's Dead Christ', in M. Feher (ed.), *Fragments for a History of the Human Body* (New York: Zone, 1989), i, 238–69.

given to the crucifixion or the extremes of Christ's sufferings. Instead, he sought through the moderate character of his allusions to ensure that there remained no doubt that life was also part of the meaning of what had taken place. So, for instance, in his *Entombment* in the National Gallery (London) he does not hesitate to base elements in his figure of Christ on a jolly figure of Bacchus that Mantegna had made. Again, in a later depiction of a related theme the accompanying figures, and indeed even Christ himself, seem almost to dance.[95] This is not to say that suffering played no part in his repertoire; far from it. His late Pietàs are among the most moving of his works, and famously in his Sistine *Last Judgement* he portrayed himself as the flayed Bartholomew. But there remains an insistence that beauty is somehow still present. I want to note here briefly first his insistence on moral beauty as ultimately capable of shining through physical ugliness, and then his controversial adaptation of the myth of Marsyas to his own condition.

Michelangelo on Transparent Moral Beauty

Michelangelo's approach to physical beauty and ugliness has been attacked from both sides. For some of his contemporaries his very moderation was a target of criticism. Giovanni Gilio, for example, writing in the year of Michelangelo's death, comments that 'it would be a stronger inducement to devotion to see Christ bloody and misshapen, than to see him beautiful and delicate'.[96] By contrast, one recent book on Michelangelo concludes with the following complaint against some of the artist's work: 'we can still wonder why the most meaningful body has to be a solitary body under strain and in pain'.[97] Michelangelo would, I think, have replied to both objectors that surface impressions are never enough; it is the role of the artist to draw us beyond them into a deeper comprehension of reality. Thus significantly, unlike Leonardo, he

---

[95] For a comparison of the *Entombment* with Mantegna's *Bacchanal*, see A. Nagel, *Michelangelo and the Reform of Art* (Cambridge: Cambridge University Press, 2000), 26, 88–91; for ancient and more recent uses of such an analogy, including Jerome, 94–7. For Nagel's own comparison with dance to describe Michelangelo's drawing of the *Lamentation* in the Albertina at Vienna, see 166–7.

[96] Quoted ibid. (158) from his treatise *Degli errori dei pittori* (1564).

[97] J. Hall, *Michelangelo and the Reinvention of the Human Body* (London: Chatto and Windus, 2005), 239. He opens with a sustained attack on the ice-like character of Michelangelo's Madonnas: 1–36, esp. 33.

shows no interest in copying or reflecting the natural world, and indeed this is one of his objections to the then popular Flemish art of the time.[98] Equally, though, the artist's role is not to surpass nature, for that would be to imply the hubris of attempting to outdo the creator.[99] Rather, the aim should be to find a beauty or tension in nature that points beyond itself and so bring that deeper beauty out of the material for the inspection and admiration of the viewer. Put like that, one can almost hear the influence of the Neo-Platonism of Pico della Mirandola and Marsilio Ficino from his youth. Equally important, though less well known, is the impact of Savonarola.[100]

We know that Michelangelo fell passionately in love quite a number of times in his life. His two most intense relationships, with Tommaso de'Cavalieri and Vittoria Colonna, were almost certainly never consummated.[101] Whether others had been when he was younger, scholars continue to disagree.[102] What we can say is that from his own perspective the most important thing was the way in which a particular person's body could reveal their underlying goodness and spiritual character. Certainly in his sonnet on the death of the young lad Cecchino Bracci, this is what he claims matters:

> Se l'un nell'altro amante si transforma,
> po' che sanz'essa l'arte non v'arriva,
> convien che per far lui ritragga voi.
>
> (You, his friend, must keep his image warm,
> And, if you fail, my art is called in doubt.
> I'll find his likeness in you alone.)[103]

[98] R. J. Clements, *Michelangelo's Theory of Art* (New York: Gramercy, 1961), 207–8.

[99] Dolce's proposed aim would thus have been rejected: 'non solo d'imitar, ma di superar la natura' (quoted ibid. 150).

[100] It is often forgotten that Savonarola was a cultured man as well as a religious zealot. Early biographers tell us that Michelangelo went to hear him often: ibid. 69.

[101] Evidence that might be used the other way is his presentation of what has been described as 'pornography' to Cavalieri. A counter-explanation is that this was intended to disgust his friend at the thought of sexual practice, but Hall finds such an account unconvincing: *Michelangelo*, 191–8.

[102] A major recent biography treats him as a celibate: G. Bull, *Michelangelo: A Biography* (London: Penguin, 1995), 241–4, 311, 351–2, 407.

[103] The poem marks his refusal to make a sculpture of the dead sixteen-year-old. Instead, he insists that it is in the moral spirit of his friends that his beauty will live on. A full text and more literal translation is in C. Ryan, *Michelangelo:*

Bracci may well have been handsome. What is fascinating, however, is the way in which Michelangelo makes similar claims for beauty in Colonna, although her age and the judgement of contemporaries were both ranged on the opposite side. The sonnets of Michelangelo repeatedly challenge such a negative view.[104] Perhaps the nearest modern parallel might be with those who talk of beauty in Mother Teresa of Calcutta's face. Although heavily lined, her face was seen to radiate an extraordinary depth of spirituality and love. Significantly, Colonna herself, when reflecting upon the hideousness of Christ's death, also speaks of a beauty that shines through: 'the ugliness of death' is made 'beautiful in this most beautiful face'.[105]

Similar attitudes are also to be found reflected in many of Michelangelo's art works as well. In his famous Medici monument, for example, he rejected an actual physical likeness in favour of the portrayal of character. Again, on the ceiling of the Sistine Chapel he shows no consistency in his presentation of Adam but instead makes body fit mood and action.[106] More attention to such features might afford the basis of a response to Sir Joshua Reynolds' objection that his love of *gigantismo* or magnitude sometimes actually veered over into the 'extremely ridiculous'.[107] The figures, it might be said, are sometimes deliberately distorted and made less than beautiful (women, for example, with male bodies) not to produce revulsion but in order that awe or a sense of *terribilità* might be evoked. Instead of confining their reflections to external beauty viewers should be drawn to reflect more deeply on what the figures represent. His use of grotesques may also be intended to serve a similar purpose.[108]

In any case what we observe is no easy identification of beauty in ugliness, but rather one towards which painter, portrayed and

---

The Poems (London: Dent, 1996), 170–1 (poem 193); a more poetic translation, the version quoted in the text, is by E. Jennings, in *The Sonnets of Michelangelo* (Manchester: Carcanet, 1988), 28.

[104] About forty poems are dedicated to her. For others not finding her beautiful, see *Michelangelo's Theory of Art*, 9–10, 154.

[105] Quoted in Nagel, *Michelangelo*, 181.

[106] Clements, *Michelangelo's Theory of Art*, 152, 155.

[107] Quoted ibid. 173.

[108] Bull, *Michelangelo*, 282–3; Clements, *Michelangelo's Theory of Art*, 214–16. The latter's stress on the desire to evoke awe rather than simple pleasure seems nearer to Michelangelo's intentions elsewhere.

viewer all need to struggle, in order to comprehend how moral beauty might win through, beyond apparent physical ugliness. That is why there is no real conflict with the opposition I expressed earlier at the beginning of the chapter against too quick a move towards speaking of beauty in the crucifixion. That should never be a simple or facile judgement. Otherwise, the reality of the distorting power of pain will remain underplayed.

Marsyas in Michelangelo and Titian

The most interesting case, however, is undoubtedly what Michelangelo does with his own image in the Sistine Chapel's *Last Judgement*. There, as already noted, he gives himself the flayed skin of the apostle Bartholomew. It is not a pretty sight, but it is a fascinating decision, not least because of the way in which the Renaissance treated the not unrelated figure of Marsyas. Almost certainly some allusion is intended here also.

In its literal version the story of Marsyas is the tale of a challenge from the foreign lute to Apollo's lyre and the resultant terrible punishment of a now vanquished pride. If across the centuries the curbing of pride is the most common lesson drawn from this myth, there were two further developments that pulled in almost opposite directions. At one extreme were those artists who looked at the matter entirely from Apollo's perspective. What they found in the deed was a celebration of the successful preservation of an adequate harmony to the world. Not surprisingly this was a reading that was greatly favoured by rulers, among them the emperor Augustus and the Renaissance papacy.[109] But Plato had also opened up an alternative possibility. A brief reference from Alcibiades in the *Symposium* had spoken of Socrates being as different in reality from his outward appearance as was Marsyas before and after his flaying.[110] It was a notion taken up by Pico della Mirandola and so firmly entered the stream of Renaissance Platonism.[111]

[109] For its use in an Augustan context, see E. Wyss, *The Myth of Apollo and Marsyas in the Art of the Italian Renaissance* (Newarks, Del.: University of Delaware Press, 1996), 29–30; for a papal context and Raphael's Stanza della Segnatura, 67–71.

[110] *Symposium* 215b. Contrast *Republic* 399c.

[111] 'If you looked within, you perceived something divine': quoted in Wyss, *The Myth of Apollo*, 63. Contrast Dante, whose Marsyas simply asks for Apollo's power on that occasion: *Paradiso* 1.19–27.

Apollo in effect had now become the agent of Marsyas' redemption, in securing the requisite transformation. Given the contrast that I have already noted Michelangelo making between inner and outer beauty, it is perhaps not surprising that this image of peeling back the skin appealed to him. In fact it recurs in a number of his writings.[112]

It was also to appeal to Titian late in his own life, as he struggled to make sense of his own sufferings and of those around him.[113] Significantly, however, Titian makes himself only an observer of the scene, whereas for Michelangelo he is himself Marsyas.[114] Some scholars have suggested that the version in the Sistine Chapel amounts to no more than an allusion to the troubles caused for Michelangelo by Aretino in his dispute with Michelangelo over his nudes.[115] What is perhaps the best-known reference to the myth in modern times offers a similar purely artistic interpretation. So impressed was Iris Murdoch by Titian's painting that she had her own portrait for the National Portrait Gallery in London painted with part of it quoted in the background. Her novel *The Black Prince* (1973) is often analysed as a literary version of the same theme: that artistic insight can come only through pain.[116]

But my own suspicion is that for Titian and Michelangelo alike something rather more was at stake. Titian's painting was a covert appeal that he might understand something of how the transformation of evil into good might be achieved. Against such a background the prominence given to water in his painting makes better sense. Pouring water over the victim was unlikely to do much to dull the pain, but what the symbol does hint at is an implicit appeal for purification. Whatever wrongs Marsyas has done, he could be healed. Michelangelo in effect makes a similar

---

[112] For some further references, see Wyss, *The Myth of Apollo*, 160 n. 15. In what is probably his last poem, Michelangelo addresses God: 'Signor mie car, tu sol che vesti e spogli' (My dear Lord, you who alone clothe and strip): Ryan, *Michelangelo: The Poems*, 242–3.

[113] For an illustration and discussion, see S. Biadene (ed.), *Titian* (New York: Prestel, 1990), 370–1. Cf. Wyss, *The Myth of Apollo*, 133–41.

[114] Titian portrays himself as Midas reflectively observing the scene. The painting is now in the archbishop's palace at Kromeriz in the Czech Republic.

[115] So Nagel, *Michelangelo*, 195–6.

[116] See *The Black Prince* (London: Vintage, 1998 edn), esp. 1, 350–1, 390–2. Her portrait is the work of Tom Phillips.

PLATES

Plate 1. Gian Lorenzo Bernini, *St Sebastian* (1615)

Himself the son of a sculptor, Bernini (1598–1680) was only a mere seventeen when he created his St Sebastian. At that age, inevitably it was more a matter of imitation than creative invention. The positioning of the legs indicates that one of Michelangelo's Pietàs probably made a contribution. So too, one might say, did the satiated Barberini Faun (the famous Hellenistic statue of a satyr sprawled in a drunken sleep), were it not for the fact that it was not rediscovered until some years later. Nonetheless, it was in works such as this that Cardinal Barberini observed the young sculptor's potential, and embarked on the process whereby as Urban VIII they could together help produce the largest number of sculptural commissions ever generated by the papacy.

Beyond the mere fact of his martyrdom little is known about the life of St Sebastian, but legend has it that he was initially punished by being shot with arrows. Surviving that ordeal through the care of St Irene, he was eventually flogged to death. Because the arrows were seen as leaving lacerations on the flesh not unlike the boils of the plague, in the late middle ages Sebastian, along with St Roch who had himself caught the plague, came to be one of the principal saints evoked in aid against such adversity. So paintings or sculptures of the assault under arrows were rather more than just a pretext for representations of a near naked-form. Also at stake was how the martyrdom could be presented in a way which indicated that neither it nor attack by the plague constituted a final victory for evil. Male beauty was employed as just such a symbol, and so the young Bernini was in fact doing nothing novel in representing the saint in such a way, though at a point beyond the assault where Irene might more commonly have been present as well. The difficulty from the religious perspective of the time was thus less to do with the beauty and sensuality of the body than with such contentment being shown on the face that the two arrows seem almost like optional, accidental accessories.

Plate 2. Jacob Jordaens' Last Supper (1654–5)

Jordaens (1593–1678) was a native of Antwerp who continued to assist Rubens with his paintings even after founding his own flourishing studio in the 1620s. After Rubens' death in 1640 he was widely acknowledged as the leading Flemish figure painter of his day. His canvases tend to be more 'earthy' than those of Rubens and he seems to have been especially fond of lively scenes of peasant merriment and conviviality. In 1655 he converted to Calvinism, and the result was much more subdued colours and topics. Indeed, this particular painting is often taken as evidence of the change (more obvious of course in a coloured reproduction).

Certainly, his earlier religious paintings can be very lively and colourful. His *Adoration of the Kings* (1646, now at Kassel), for instance, is extraordinarily rich in its gathered assembly. Not only are the black Balthasar and his entourage given a central place, a camel and horse are added to the customary ox and ass. Those features build on later elements in the Christian tradition that sought to ensure the continuing relevance of the scene. The need of all races for Christ was indicated by each king being seen to come from a different continent, while horses indicated a mode of transport more significant for Jordaens' viewers than the traditional camel. Similarly here, a dog is included (spaniels being especially popular in the seventeenth century), an impossibility at the Last Supper. This was not just a matter of the breed but because a quite different attitude to dogs prevailed in the Palestine of the time. They were seen essentially as scavengers, not as pets. So far from being affectionate, 'the little dogs' of Mark 7.27 (the Greek uses here the diminutive) is much more likely to be contemptuous. What the introduction of the animal does allow here is an intensification of the contrast with Judas. He dotes on the faithful hound even as he deceptively partakes of communion with the Lord whom he is about to betray. So even if now a Calvinist, Jordaens is continuing to enter creatively into a developing tradition which realizes that it cannot always speak in precisely the same way across time.

Plate 3. Gian Lorenzo Bernini, The Blessed Ludovica (1674)

While St Sebastian stems from Bernini's youth, this particular sculpture is the work of a man in his mid-seventies. It is thus intriguing to compare its use of sexual symbolism with its more famous counterpart, *The Ecstasy of St Teresa*, executed more than a couple of decades earlier (1645–52). Indeed, one cannot help wondering whether its relative obscurity has less to do with the qualities of the work and more with its location, situated as it is in a church off the main Roman tourist route at the far end of the Trastevere district.

The sculptured ensemble is in a rather dark side chapel but is itself lit by a concealed window (there appear once to have been two such windows). The result is a first encounter for the viewer under which Ludovica emerges unexpectedly in a great blaze of light. Such theatrical effects are of course common in Baroque but are as nothing compared with the drama of the sexual symbolism. Not only is her bed linen crumpled but the sheets are made to gather round her groin, she has one hand clasped on her breast, while her mouth is open and emitting what seems to be a sigh of ecstasy. To place such a piece immediately above an altar might seem to the modern mind to plumb the depths of blasphemy. But it is important to note the deliberate ambiguity in how the piece might be read. Ludovica Albertoni died of fever after a life of good works and piety. Her open mouth and twisted body might thus at one level be taken to indicate the results of the fever, with the bursting pomegranates behind her a sign of the immortality that was now hers. But the hints of sexual ecstasy could also speak metaphorically of the heightened, ecstatic spiritual state upon which she was now entered, a saint promised the intimacy of union with Christ in heaven. Indeed, the dual meaning is already inherent in those pomegranates. Originally associated with Venus as a symbol of fertility, the fruit's plethora of seeds was taken by Christianity to herald the abundance of new life that God could bring in the resurrection.

Plate 4. Caravaggio, *The Taking of Christ* (*c.*1602)

This is a painting that has only relatively recently been restored to the corpus of Caravaggio. Acquired as a work of Gerrit van Hornthorst in the eighteenth century by a Scotsman travelling in Italy, it eventually became the property of the Jesuits in Ireland. In the early 1990s it was finally recognized, and the Jesuits gave the painting to the National Gallery of Ireland on indefinite loan. Today, so widespread has the cult of Caravaggio as gay icon become that even the *Church Times* reviewer at the time of the discovery treated this painting in just such a way. Irrespective of Caravaggio's actual orientation, my quarrel with such an analysis is that it diverts attention away from how the artist intends bodies to function symbolically in paintings such as these.

The two figures on the margins of the canvas balance each other perfectly. On the right the young man (sometimes identified as a self-portrait) draws our attention inwards to the two central figures by moving his lantern in that direction, while the figure fleeing on the left helps to give greater weight to the Christ-figure despite the physical bulk of Judas and the two accompanying soldiers. The red robe being pulled from him also helps to frame the encounter. But note how he is not allowed to be nude despite the scriptural text (Mark 14.51–2) to which appeal might have been made, for this would have distracted from that central encounter. The way in which Judas is effectively enfolded in the armour of one of the soldiers adds to the sense that he has identified with a world of violence and brutality. That soldier's strong buttocks are thus there, not to provide a gay frisson, but to add to that sense of assault. Judas' challenge, however, is met not by a worldly confrontation with Judas' fixed stare but by Christ directing his eyes downwards towards his enfolded hands. These, placed at the very centre of the canvas, are locked firmly together, in what can be seen as an unbreakable commitment to his future destiny. The body as brute strength is thus not to be allowed the last word.

Plate 5. Donatello, *St Mary Magdalene* (*c*.1453–5)

Donatello (1386–1466) was a Florentine sculptor whose earlier works are clearly strongly indebted to classical antique models. Even his playful *David* (originally dating from 1409 butt reworked in 1416), which is so different from Michelangelo's version shows such influence not just in its nudity but also in its balanced distribution of weight. However, focus on beauty of form is so prominent (and in such a distinctly androgynous direction) that it is easy to lose any real sense of a great victory over the giant Goliath, whose head is at David's feet, or indeed of the downward gaze, which speaks of a gentle, introspective youth. So, despite its outstanding aesthetic qualities, the work cannot be pronounced a success in religious terms.

During the years 1443–53 Donatello spent a decade working away from Florence at Padua. Whether or not this was the cause of his change of perspective or not remains uncertain, but it is certainly the case that on his return he produced three great works that are quite different from his earlier style. There is a new dramatic and emotional intensity hitherto unparalleled in western sculpture. *John the Baptist* and *Judith and Holofernes* were cast in bronze. The finest of the three, however, *St Mary Magdalene*, was worked in wood. The polychrome statue dispenses with the usual indicator of the saint, her ointment jar, and in its place comes an intensification of her asceticism that for some will make them think only of death. Indeed, it is sometimes suggested that, as Donatello was himself ageing (he was now in his late sixties), the sculpture was actually intended as a *memento mori*. I do not believe it. Certainly Mary's skin is dried out and brittle, and her bones push through such little flesh as she has. But, unlike the earlier *David*, the deeper meaning lies close to the surface. Her straight back, praying hands and fixed, distant gaze all witness to the triumph of spirit over flesh, and her own fixed resolve about her ultimate destination.

Plate 6. Caravaggio, *Saint John the Baptist in the Wilderness* (1604–5)

By the time of Caravaggio numerous representations of John the Baptist as a young man already existed. Some were pretty, some sensual, and some succeeded in making a religious point. Caravaggio too experimented in the genre, producing no less than eight such depictions. Some are too intellectual, some too sensual. How far the latter were entirely Caravaggio's fault and how far a reflection on the nature of his model is a moot point. In this version, however, he does seem to me to have struck exactly the right balance, with sexual energy building on, and not fighting against, the religious dimensions of his subject.

What is conveyed by the portrayal is a youth bubbling over with energy. A reflective soul (indicated in the downcast eyes), he is nonetheless prepared to spring into action at any moment. He is, as it were, a young man in a hurry, which is precisely how the Baptist saw his mission. That sense of energy is conveyed in part by the angle of the body. The boy sits but only just, with his left buttock presumably already slightly raised from the seat and his right foot balanced on his toes. Parallel to his body and so also at a diagonal is the traditional staff of John's mission. An interesting detail is the way in which it is developed into the shape of a cross through being provided with a small upper beam. Thereby clear indication is given of John's role overall in the Christian dispensation. Inevitably these days attention is drawn to the sheep skin hanging under his thighs. Personally, I doubt a sexual reference, but even if there were, it would be compatible with the notion Caravaggio is trying to convey of a restless energy. The boy's tousled hair also suggests impatience, while the arc of light discloses a still developing body, good for a quick action like running rather than sustained physical heaving or effort. It is thus a body that throughout speaks of one eager to act as messenger of the Lord. It should, therefore, come as no surprise that, when the work was completed, a copy was ordered for the family chapel on Italy's western coast, where it still remains (at Cosciente in Liguria).

Plate 7. Nicholas Poussin, *Dance to the Music of Time* (1638)

This painting was commissioned by a future pope, Cardinal Giulio Rospigliosi (pope from 1667–9 as Clement IX), who was part of the circle of Pope Urban VIII. Rospigliosi had strong academic interests and even taught philosophy for a while at the University of Pisa. He also wrote classical allegorical plays, for some of which Bernini provided the staging.

In this painting Father Time sits on the right playing his lyre, while three young women and one young man dance to his music. We know from contemporary commentaries that the four dancers are supposed to represent poverty (the young man), labour (the woman immediately on his left), then wealth, then indulgence before she in turn hands on the baton, as it were, once more to poverty. The increasing brightness of the robes they wear indicates the transition in one direction, just as their corresponding progressive decline in muscular strength foreshadows the problems to come. In the foreground, two putti remind us of the passage of time. One blows bubbles, while the other holds an inverted hourglass.

That some more permanent message is intended is clearly indicated by the passage of Apollo's chariot across the skies. Apollo as the sun god is preceded by Aurora (dawn) and followed by female representations of the Hours. So we are clearly intended to think of there being an ordered or danced pattern to human existence that a higher power has decreed. We know from his letters that Poussin was attracted to Stoicism as a philosophy. So it would be easy to draw from the painting two common Stoic assumptions: the notion that the world operates on a series of cyclical returns and its fatalistic acceptance of the way things are. But it is also possible to read the painting more positively: as endorsing the legitimacy of the physical and moral effort required in order to bring about change, not just as a brute fact but as something ordained by the Christian God. Perhaps such ambiguity would have appealed to Poussin. What is not in doubt is his love of order and proportion, as represented by such dancing.

Plate 8. Edward Hopper, *Nighthawks* (1942)

The paintings of the American artist Edward Hopper (1882–1967) have come to epito-mize the sense of alienation that so often beset twentieth-century humanity. Already six feet tall at the age of twelve, Hopper seems to have felt himself quite early a lonely and isolated individual, which his parents' Baptist faith did little to assuage. His paintings repeatedly return to the theme of isolation. Sometimes this is conveyed through build-ings bereft of people, as in his two paintings of *Early Sunday Morning* (1926 and 1930) or his *House by the Railroad* (1925), in which a mansard-roofed Victorian house sits des-olately above an empty rail track. Originally the latter sketch seems to have been intended to speak of a lost past, whereas the use of a similar house in Alfred Hitchcock's film *Psycho* (1960) means that we are now more likely to think of the terrible things that, unsuspectingly, actually go on in the house.

However, the most evocative paintings are undoubtedly those populated by human beings who nonetheless fail totally to relate to one another, and among these *Nighthawks* is the most famous example. Although the couple on one side of the bar appear to have ordered something from the bartender, they look straight ahead rather than at one another, and their hands only tentatively stretch towards each other. Per-haps their assignation is quite recent. Meanwhile, the man on the opposite side of the bar completely ignores them, and they him. The street outside is quite empty, and the only thing visible in the shop opposite is its cash register. As Hopper's title, but also the unsmiling looks of the participants suggests, the atmosphere is threatening. Will a stranger suddenly appear to rob them, or is the aim of those already present like birds of prey, ready to see how they can take advantage of each other? The whole scene con-trasts so sadly with a now vanished age of cooperation and integration, with a world of communal eating and drinking.

prayer, that what will be disclosed from behind his own imperfect body will be a soul transformed through the rigours of a life disciplined by God.

Experience and Suffering in the Modern Context

Even if in later life he was fully prepared to satirize his own bodily pains, for a soul so sensitive to beauty it must have been particularly galling for Michelangelo that he suffered facial disfigurement early in life.[117] Yet, despite the growing asceticism of his later years, Michelangelo's attitude to pain and ugliness remained firmly under control. Both could be transcended, and in the process a new kind of beauty generated. The Middle Ages may not have expressed matters thus, but the sentiment was not dissimilar. Seldom were the extremes of fasting valued for their own sake.

Unfortunately, such restraint was not always observed in the later history of Christianity. Even as the extent of the suffering that was actually imposed declined, so a corresponding willingness to relish suffering for its own sake seems to have advanced. Not unconnected in nineteenth-century thought may have been a quite perverse mixing of sadism and religion. So, for example, it has been suggested that J. K. Huysmans' advocacy of Grünewald's Isenheim Altarpiece after his conversion may merely have continued his earlier fascination with sadistic behaviour.[118] Equally, the poet Paul Verlaine appears to have moved between extremes: 'je suis élu, je suis damné'.[119] Death too is sometimes brought into the equation. It is probably no accident that in a number of places Ovid juxtaposes the Latin words for love and for death, punning on the similarity of their Latin form.[120] Art too

---

[117] His nose was broken by a slightly older student, Pietro Torrigiano. The occasion was a fight they had in the Masaccio chapel in the church of the Carmine in Florence: Bull, *Michelangelo*, 15–16. For Michelangelo laughing at his own pains while painting the ceiling of the Sistine Chapel, see Ryan, *Michelangelo: The Poems*, 5.

[118] Thus E. Hanson, *Decadence and Catholicism* (Cambridge, Mass.: Harvard University Press, 1997), 108–68, esp. 109–10, 121, 138, 143–4.

[119] Ibid. 60–85.

[120] e.g. *Metamorphoses* 7.855: 'causam mihi mortis amorem'. Cf. 10.377. I owe these two references to Alan Griffin.

has oscillated between treating death as a seductive female and as a terrifying male reaper (or their opposites).[121] Those examples are not explicitly religious, but there is no shortage of cases where within a more explicitly Christian tradition sex and death have been brought into close alliance. There are numerous examples in the French Catholic Symbolists, as well as in Herder, Novalis and Eichendorff.[122] Nor are examples wanting from the medieval period. James of Milan, for example, puns on *vulnus/vulva*.[123]

I mention these associations to underline that it is in no way my intention to endorse every aspect of the earlier tradition. The unintended sadism of earlier generations was eventually used to justify its more explicit sexual variant. Even so, there was much that was valuable in that earlier tradition. In our desire to correct Christianity's long-standing suspicion of physical beauty and sexuality as means towards experience of God, it is important that the possibility of finding the divine also in the ugly and the wasted should not be entirely discounted. On the contrary, all human beings suffer pain at some point in their lives, even if this is for some only of a psychological kind, and so it is vital to have the resources to allow divine grace also to make itself felt under these circumstances as well. That will be made so much easier if older ways of reading scripture can once more be cultivated, with knowledge of the text and the 'facts' once more firmly subordinated to the experiential demand for a present intimacy with the events in question, a placing of readers inside the text as themselves participants. That way, lessons will be learnt for their own time of testing under suffering, and so the experience of Christ's love given from the cross renewed in a form more directly relevant to their present troubles.

In a world in which we all seek to disguise the ageing process and recoil from anything that lessens physical attractiveness, it is

---

[121] For a fascinating survey that looks at both art and literature, see K. S. Guthke, *The Gender of Death* (Cambridge: Cambridge University Press, 1999). The author denies that the issue is just a matter of language or specific culture. For a positive male figure in art, see 52; for a negative male figure, 102; for a positive female figure, 195; for a negative female figure, 153.

[122] For the connection in Herder, Novalis and Eichendorff, as against Lessing, see ibid. 138–44; for its use in nineteenth-century Catholic Symbolists, 196–208.

[123] In his *Stimulus amoris* (*vulnus* refers to Christ's wounds): W. Riehle, *The Middle English Mystics* (London: Routledge and Kegan Paul, 1981), 46.

salutary to recall that, while in its attitude to handicap at times religion too (including Christianity) has followed a similar course, an alternative tradition has also sometimes won through: one in which ugliness is taken as itself a sign of divine blessing and mediation, and not a curse. In many a 'primitive' religion it was the physically and mentally odd that were regarded as closest to the divine. Occasionally, that perspective continues into our own day.[124] It is important that it should. As Michelangelo saw despite his own love of physical beauty, there is a deeper beauty of the soul that can transform the most dreadful ugliness and the most horrible pain.

Of course it is not always easy to perceive that inner beauty. The smile of Mother Teresa is given only to a few who are in suffering or pain. But perseverance in the viewer can sometimes bring rewards out of all proportion to the effort required. Those who have seen the film *The Elephant Man* (1980) will perhaps recall this true story of a hideously deformed man and the treatment meted out to him in Victorian England.[125] To most he appeared a mere freak, to be exploited in circus acts. Even genteel 'Christian' folk seldom got beyond revulsion at his looks, but those who did discovered an open, generous creature of whom it could rightly be said that his love reflected that of the Creator himself.

That creature's deformity, however, was not self-imposed. So a better example would be Donatello's statue of Mary Magdalene.[126] Legend had it that after her conversion she combined a life of witness and preaching with severe austerities that were in marked contrast to her earlier life.[127] Part of the explanation for that tale may lie in further confusion. Just as in the western tradition she came wrongly to be identified with the penitent prostitute of Luke's Gospel, so also her identity merged with Mary of Egypt, who had endured a life of fasting in the desert.[128]

[124] As a token of good luck hunchbacks were still being employed at the cathedral at Amalfi in the mid-twentieth century, to distribute relics: N. Lewis, *Naples '44* (London: Eland, 1983), 139.

[125] Very unlike the director David Lynch's other films. John Hurt gives a superb performance as the disfigured John Merrick.

[126] Illustrated with further commentary in Plate 5 at the end of this book.

[127] I explore how the legend developed and its value in *Discipleship and Imagination* (Oxford: Oxford University Press, 2000), 31–61.

[128] The former was caused by inferring back from Luke 8.2 to 7.36–50. The fifth-century Mary of Egypt was an Alexandrian prostitute who was converted in Jerusalem and then spent 47 years in penitence in the desert.

Such confusions are, however, less important than what Donatello did with them. His sculpture is certainly of a haggard and emaciated body. But it is also a body that speaks of extraordinary inner strength and resolution. It is one that speaks not of self-destruction but of the triumph of the spirit in and through battle with adversity. The body was wasted, but not the soul.

Part II

Ethereal and Material

11

Ethereal and Material

SOME readers may be puzzled why the second part of the book is devoted to music. Compared with the presentation of body and the type of bodily activities discussed in Part I, they may detect what they see as a sharp decline, from the fullness of bodily commitment in the first part to a merely nominal association here. Such a view might seem to gain decisive support from those musicologists who identify the essence of a piece of music as lying in its score rather than in particular performances. That is not a view I share. Nor, where it is a matter of performance, do I subscribe to the idea that only parts of the body are involved (typically, hand or voice). Rather, although sometimes disguised perhaps to suggest a natural ease, performance at its best is virtually always a total commitment of the body. So, there is always the ethereal and the material working together, the apparently disembodied sound supported by total commitment in bodily movements and reactions.

The Welsh poet and priest R. S. Thomas captures beautifully that commitment, as he experienced it when observing at close quarters a performance by violinist Fritz Kreisler:

> A memory of Kreisler once:
> At some recital in this same city,
> The seats all taken, I found myself pushed
> On to the stage with a few others,
> So near that I could see the toil
> Of his face muscles, a pulse like a moth
> Fluttering under the fine skin
> And the indelible veins of his smooth brow.
>
> I could see, too, the twitching of the fingers,
> Caught temporarily in art's neurosis,
> As we sat there or warmly applauded

> This player who so beautifully suffered
> For each of us upon his instrument.[1]

So to make a sharp contrast, for example, between classical musicians and rock bands on the extent of bodily commitment would seem quite misguided. Occasionally indeed, the artificiality of hiding engagement is accepted by performers themselves. A good example is the work of the baroque ensemble Red Priest.[2] Named after Vivaldi with his shock of red hair, they deliberately seek maximum involvement and interaction with their audience, in look and gesture. Performing from memory ensures that as much attention can be given to appropriate bodily movements as to the notes themselves.

That engagement I pursue here across a great variety of music. Like music critics who support absolute music, for some Christians music has its own integrity and so has nothing to say to religion, irrespective of whether the music was intended for religious use or otherwise.[3] Others insist on certain formal qualities that can speak of Christian doctrine, for example the development from tension to resolution. In continuity with my general approach throughout this book, I have resisted the temptation to impose any obvious limits. So I range from Bach to Schoenberg, from Bob Dylan to Led Zeppelin, from *Don Giovanni* to *Jerry Springer—The Opera*. I am under no delusion that everything I discuss is of equal value. But I do want to resist the tendency of so many of my fellow-Christians to impose over-simplistic or narrowly specific criteria for what may or may not communicate the divine.

As one might expect, there is no shortage of novels and films about the uplifting character of music, and sometimes these can also draw us into a sense of God at work. While the transformation of a French reform school in *The Chorus* (2004) is moving but perhaps too predictable, *Story of a Weeping Camel* (2003) is quite magical in its effect. Set in the Gobi Desert, it describes how a mother camel is

---

[1] From 'The Musician', in R. S. Thomas, *Collected Poems 1945–1990* (London: Phoenix, 1993), 104.

[2] Seen also in the titles they have given to their live performances, e.g. 'Red Hot Baroque Show'.

[3] e.g. W. H. Ralston, 'Music and Belief—Two Questions', in R. A. Norris (ed.), *Lux in Lumine* (New York: Seabury, 1966), 144–57. Eduard Hanslick's advocacy of absolute music (music without any reference outside of itself) is discussed in Chapter 5.

reconciled to her albino child through music being played to her. The film ends with a violin lying on her back and sounding in the wind. For the religious the image might evoke a sense of the possibility of a larger and more inclusive reconciliation.

But it would be quite wrong to think that music's role in religious experience should only ever be uplifting. If God is to be found everywhere, then that presence should also be found in the more negative aspects of human life. Blues and jazz were in fact created in part as a response to the narrowing of perspective that constitutes gospel music as compared with its predecessor, the spiritual. Even to this day hymns fail to address the full range of emotions and issues that once characterized the psalms. Nor should the fact that sexuality bulks large as a theme in hard rock and in rap of itself preclude these media from also at times being used to say something about God and his presence there also. To say that they must necessarily fail would be rather like insisting that Bernard of Clairvaux's sermons and John of the Cross' poetry must have been corrupted merely because of their use of erotic imagery.[4] Even the Holocaust can be part of the religious meaning given to our world through music, as can the work of a man facing death from syphilis.[5] As these last examples (from Shostakovich and Schubert) illustrate, full and explicit Christian belief is scarcely a prerequisite for such mediation.

So I shall consider first instrumental music as this has been reflected within the classical tradition. Thereafter, I shall turn to various kinds of pop music before devoting a final chapter to other vocal forms that have sometimes (not without justification) seen themselves as a substitute for religion, among them blues, musicals and opera. As I indicate in this volume's sequel (through a comparison of the psalms and modern hymns), there has been a regrettable tendency to narrow down the range of experience that is allowed to be made explicit in worship.[6] Throughout I attempt to indicate

---

[4] Even though that imagery is largely drawn from a biblical book, the Song of Songs.

[5] Schubert's *Die Winterreise* is discussed in the next chapter. For a look at the Holocaust through Shostakovich's Piano Trio No. 2 in E minor, see A. Loades, 'On Music's Grace', in J. J. Lipner (ed.), *Truth, Religious Dialogue and Dynamic Orthodoxy* (London: SCM Press, 2005), 25–38, esp. 36–7.

[6] *God and Mystery in Words* (Oxford: Oxford University Press, 2008), ch. 3.

what features of the music help to communicate the presence of a God who is already there waiting to be experienced. The partial character of all such musical experience seems to me in no way to count against its veridical character. God could never in any case be experienced in his totality. So, inevitably, different aspects will be encountered through different types of musical performance. Of course, some may be deceptive, and lead to misperceptions of the divine. Devotees of classical music may well be inclined to denounce the vague transcendental leanings of some pop music as sheer self-indulgence or even simply drug-induced.[7] Certainly, they contrast markedly with more specific depictions such as divine order, awe or resurrection. But my own inclination is to insist that they should be treated seriously. If God is really our creator, then the urge to deepen contact with him is likely to permeate human creativity in whatever form it is found. I therefore plead for at least some initial sympathy on the part of readers for the range of work I am about to examine, even where such music lies far distant from their own natural preferences. In some cases this is no less true in my case, though in the interests of objectivity I have carefully refrained from indicating where my own particular preferences and prejudices lie.

Attention is devoted not only to specific examples, but also to theoretical foundations. That is where I shall begin in the chapter that now follows.

---

[7] In Chapter 5 I take Allan Bloom as representative of this sort of critic. For another, note Roger Scruton's chapter on 'Youfanasia' in his *Modern Culture* (London: Continuum, 2005 edn), 105–22.

5
Classical Music

WHILE all would concede that the earlier chapter on dance has an obvious relevance to the overall theme and title of this book (grace of body), music as such, it may be claimed, is at most of only marginal importance. Clearly without music in some form dancing is impossible, but it is the dancing, it will be said, that properly relates to the body, not the accompanying music. That is something intangible and of a quite different order. Such observations, however, can hardly withstand sustained reflection. As well as movement in the music itself, different tunes expect different types of bodily reaction. Irrespective of the precise nature of the music, both performer and listener can usually be seen physically entering into the movement and not just mentally. Head, hands or feet sway, while sweat may well appear on the brow as the heartbeat alters, and so on. That said, a different sort of objection may then arise. Whatever may be claimed about the power of dance to evoke an alternative, transcendent world, on its own music's sensuous power is to be feared, for it has the ability to drag us in precisely the opposite direction. That is why music needs to be controlled by interpretation, whether that be the ancient tradition of dance or the more lasting influence of words. Indeed, such subordination might seem entirely natural within the three main monotheistic religions, which see themselves as essentially religions of the word.

That demand has been a common one across their respective histories. So it might be thought easiest for our discussion of music in its own right also to begin there with musical accompaniments to texts, where fewer problems might be thought to arise. Mass settings and religious songs would then be our first focus. But that would be a mistake for at least two reasons. First, there is no agreement either across time or within our own contemporary situation about which particular types of settings of words are suited to facilitate access to experience of God, or for that matter what words themselves are most appropriate for such an aim. Indeed, some would argue that a less explicit vocabulary is sometimes more effective. So in the two chapters that follow this one I want to examine a much wider range of song than the reader might have expected. Consideration of more explicitly religious music will be deferred to this volume's sequel.[1]

Secondly, there seems little doubt that religious experience can in any case be generated through the power of music on its own without the help of words or any other type of accompaniment. Although Christian theologians have often in the past been suspicious of such claims, I do believe that they need to be taken seriously. Just because such experience does not always appear to accord well with the dictates of Christian orthodoxy, this is no reason for setting such claims aside. Apparent inconsistency in what is deduced from experience of instrumental music need not necessarily entail ultimate incompatibility. As with our experience of other human beings, terror and peace, for example, can come from the same source. Even where incompatibility does look more deep-seated, that experience should not be summarily dismissed. It would be the act of the coward not to explore further. That is why I want to consider here a wide range of potential examples, including work by composers on the fringes of faith. So, although I shall begin with the apparently safe case of Bach, it is my intention to explore much more widely, in particular in most detail across music of the nineteenth and twentieth centuries. Examples are in the main derived in this chapter from classical music, not because I want to privilege the instrumental in this form but to complement and balance the choice of pop music for consideration of song in the following chapter. Admittedly, classical music is now a serious interest only among a declining minority; even so it is a significant minority, and the quality of the music can scarcely be denied.[2]

Before turning to specifics, however, some attention to foundations is essential. So I shall begin with two more general but rather different types of foundation, first the question of biblical attitudes,

---

[1] *God and Mystery in Words: Experience through Metaphor and Drama* (Oxford: Oxford University Press, 2008), chs 3 and 6.

[2] In Britain engagement with classical music (measured by attendance at concerts and sales of CDs) is now well under 10 per cent and declining. But there are some more positive signs, such as the success of the radio station Classic FM and the use of classical music in film scores.

then more philosophical factors. As these two sections are quite long, those who prefer to work with specific examples might prefer to proceed straight to the second half of the chapter.

Foundations

Scripture: Support from an Ambiguous Witness

Those familiar with the many references in the psalms to the use of musical instruments may find the title of this section somewhat puzzling.[3] But it is important to recall that for much of history the interpretation of such verses was subject to the re-evaluation that characterized Christian approaches to the ceremonial and ritual aspects of the Hebrew scriptures in general. As with the ritual of sacrifice a new order was seen as inaugurated by the New Testament, and so more 'spiritual' understandings were offered. Nowadays, it might be possible to return to those passages for justification. But that strategy presents a number of difficulties. How much was purely instrumental is unclear, while there is little indication of what kind of rationale might have been given for the use of musical instruments in worship.[4] So here I shall adopt a rather different tactic. First, I shall note the sort of reservations that generated Christian resistance to instrumental music. Only thereafter shall I turn my attention to neglected features of the biblical witness that in fact strongly support a more positive approach, not least in the book of Chronicles. What makes these features of special importance is that they provide precisely the kind of theoretical justification in terms of religious experience that characterizes my approach in this book as a whole.

Consider first, then, the New Testament, where references are few and far between. Jesus, we are told, sang 'a hymn' with his disciples on Mount Olivet (Mark 14.26). Likewise, Paul enjoins his congregations to 'sing psalms and hymns and spiritual songs with thankfulness in your hearts to God' (Col. 3.16). While it is impossible to be certain,

---

[3] For allusions to the use of musical instruments in the psalms, see e.g. Ps. 43.4; 81.2–3; 150.3–5.

[4] Dancing in Temple worship (Ps. 149.3) might have been unaccompanied by words, but we do not know for certain.

the likelihood is that in such cases it was a matter of simple and probably unaccompanied singing.[5] Scarcity of resources would seem to argue in that direction, as would the novelty of new compositions.[6] The desire for purity of offering and contrast with Old Testament practices would also point the nascent community to the same conclusion. It seems a world impossibly remote from the singing of anthems and canticle settings to the accompaniment of an organ, let alone recitals of chamber music or orchestral performances. Of course, nothing is said as such to condemn these, but one might infer as much from some key passages in the Old Testament.

Take Daniel 3. Anyone who has ever heard that passage read in church could not possibly ever forget the emphatic repetition of the instruments, enumerated no less than four times within the same chapter: horn, pipe, lyre, trigon, harp and bagpipe (RSV) or, to give the list in more traditional language: cornet, flute, harp, sackbut, psaltery and dulcimer (AV). The point of such repetition is now seldom understood. So far from indicating appreciation, the intention was in fact to underline the corruption that music brings, in particular its association with pagan image-worship, in this case a golden statue of King Nebuchadnezzar.[7] Nor is this by any means an isolated instance. Lutes and drums were often associated with sexual excess.[8] Archaeology in the Holy Land has even thrown up instances of women portrayed apparently innocently playing the lyre, but men dancing naked nearby.[9] Prophetic denunciations of music are therefore by no means unknown. Examples are to be found in Amos (5.23–24; 6.5) and in Isaiah (5.11–12), where the nature of the reservations is remarkably similar to parallel attacks on the practice of sacrifice.[10]

---

[5] For a helpful discussion of what this might have involved, see W. A. Meeks, *The First Urban Christians* (New Haven, Conn.: Yale University Press, 1983), 144–6.

[6] New hymns such as Phil. 2.6–11 were probably kept free of association with music known to converts from other contexts. Gregory of Nyssa, however, argues that the mention of psalms does imply the use of instruments: *On the Psalms* 100.3.

[7] J. Braun, *Music in Ancient Israel/Palestine* (Grand Rapids: Eerdmans, 2002), 32–5.

[8] For lutes, see ibid. 83–5, 244–5; for drums, 29–30, 63. The latter were normally played by women, and were perhaps more like tambourines.

[9] Ibid. 73–5.

[10] e.g. Hos. 6.6; 1 Sam. 15.21–22.

In trying to understand such reservations, the early history of Christianity is of some help. In an implicit acknowledgement of music's power, writers expressed the worry that to allow music free sway would inevitably lead to corruption of the heart. Sometimes such objections were expressed in terms of idolatry (because of the common contexts in which music occurred).[11] More commonly, however, it was moral factors that were integral to such reservations. It ill becomes modern Christians, therefore, to give scant regard to Plato's condemnation of certain types of music in the *Republic* and elsewhere. Plato's worries were of the same fundamentally moral kind, though developed in a culture where 'music' exercised a more central role.[12]

It is important to recall that originally the Greek term *musike* would have included dance and poetry, that all lyric poetry was intended to be sung, and that Greek drama also included singing.[13] Whereas in earlier times there had been simple conventions about particular themes matching specific musical types, by Plato's day much more variety had become possible, and with it music was believed to have acquired dangerously seductive powers.[14] Resultant hostility to the flute well illustrates the point.[15] Yet Plato is in some ways less extreme than his Christian counterparts. He did at least allow certain types of music that involved both voice and instrument, whereas within some elements of Christianity no such concessions were made.[16] The Fathers again and again give allegorical interpretations of Old Testament references to instruments, insisting that what really matters is harmony of the soul.[17] Ironically, in seeing this as a reflection

[11] As, for instance, in Tertullian's worries about associations with drama, and so with Apollo, Minerva and so on: *De spectaculis* 10.8–9. This text is available, together with many others that illustrate the suspicion of instruments, in J. McKinnon (ed.), *Music in Early Christian Literature* (Cambridge: Cambridge University Press, 1987), 43.

[12] The key passages are *Republic* 397b–399d, 595–608; *Laws* 700a–701b, 812b–813a.

[13] Emphasized in G. Comotti, *Music in Greek and Roman Culture* (Baltimore: Johns Hopkins University Press, 1989), 1–34, esp. 3.

[14] Whereas Aeschylus kept to the 'nomes', with Euripides tragedy became more like 'melodrama with arias and duets': ibid. 33–4, esp. 34.

[15] Both Plato and Aristotle express anxiety about the variety of expression possible on the flute: Comotti, 70, 140–1. The Christian Epiphanius compares the instrument to a serpent: McKinnon, *Music in Early Christian Literature*, 78; cf. 84.

[16] Plato gives approval to the Dorian and Phrygian modes.

[17] As, for example, in Clement of Alexandria, where David is compared unfavourably with Christ: *Protrepticus* 1.5.3–7; McKinnon, *Music in Early Christian Literature*, 30.

of a wider harmony in the universe Greek ideas also had their impact.[18] Such allegorizing allowed for the possibility of eventually seeing instruments in sacramental terms.[19] Its more immediate consequence, however, was to set musical theory in the West in a very rationalist, analytic direction.[20]

The tendency to see instruments as either inherently wrong, or at best a concession to human weakness, was also strengthened by a further reflection. If the proper aim is mental or spiritual harmony and not appreciation of the music in its own right, would not God in any case want us to use our own natural abilities to further that end in our praise of him, and not artificial substitutes?[21] Although that was already a position adopted by an early precursor of the Reformation like Wyclif, such reflection gained added support during that period.[22] Although Calvin does at times speak well of music, he too was suspicious of its power. So it comes as no surprise that he banned all instrumental accompaniment from worship.[23] Islam had already done so nearly a millennium earlier. More surprisingly perhaps, such attitudes are also part of the history of Judaism. All other instruments apart from the ram's horn were eventually eliminated from worship, a practice that has survived to this day among the Samaritans.[24]

Nowadays it is widely assumed that music is inherently less exposed to the possibility of idolatry than either the visual or the verbal. Yet there are some grounds for conceding more legitimacy to ancient

[18] As in Origen's acceptance of the harmony of the spheres: *Contra Celsum* 8.67; McKinnon, *Music in Early Christian Literature*, 38.

[19] The sacramental possibility is noticed by McKinnon (ibid. 6). The point is that the instrument is effectively being treated as a pointer to something else.

[20] The latter is well illustrated in another edited collection by McKinnon: J. McKinnon (ed.), *Source Readings in Music History: The Early Christian Period and the Latin Middle Ages* (New York: Norton, 1998 edn); see especially the extracts from Boethius and the attack from Jacques of Liège (d. 1330) on the contemporary introduction of 'imperfect' time: 4–5, 7, 27–33, 159–68.

[21] For an example from St John Chrysostom that stresses 'no need for technique', see ibid. 16.

[22] For Wyclif's views, see *English Works of Wyclif*, ed. F. D. Matthew, Early English Text Society, orig. set. 74 (Woodbridge, Suffolk: Boydell and Brewer, 1988; 1st publ. 1880), 191–2.

[23] For a useful collection of his various incidental comments, see W. J. Bouwsma, *John Calvin: A Sixteenth-Century Portrait* (New York: Oxford University Press, 1988), 225.

[24] Braun, *Music in Ancient Israel*, 274–87.

suspicions than is usually conceded. Elsewhere I have indicated how thoroughly mistaken it is to suppose that word is inherently less liable to idolatry than the visual arts.[25] Here it is worth emphasizing that the temptation to place music above art is no less mistaken, despite the prevalence of such assumptions in the history of Christianity. Great painters and sculptors, I suggest, do not compel particular readings of their work but invite us to explore possibilities, whereas the composer surely often has no choice but to direct us along one path rather than another. As such the idolatry inherent in fixed meanings is much more likely to arise. As an example, consider the ending of Bach's *St John Passion*. In John's Gospel a delicate balance is struck between Christ's two concluding utterances, the human cry of 'I thirst' and the divine 'It is finished' (perhaps better translated as 'All is now accomplished'). When reading, one has time to stop and reflect, moving back and forth between the one verse and the other, but of course the music cannot do this. Bach had to lead us in one direction and not another. Intriguingly, his choice is to play down the triumph in 'It is finished.' We hear that phrase no less than three times before it is given a more confident note. This has led some (such as Karl Barth) to pronounce Bach's interpretation of John a failure, but what his strategy does allow us to do is absorb fully the death before we look to the triumph. Liturgically, of course that means that the music is particularly well suited to performance on Good Friday. Even so, there is no getting away from the fact that Bach is directing our emotions, not simply allowing them free sway. The space to explore is more likely to be found in the written version of the Gospels or in many a painting where divinity and humanity are set side by side on the cross and viewers left to themselves to decide as to how and when either is appropriated.[26]

I say this not to decry music. Sometimes the direction it leads is exactly the right one. Sometimes too alternatives are opened up, as for instance in rival interpretations of the same musical text. Again, in opera composers not uncommonly produce ensembles

---

[25] Brown, *God and Mystery in Words*, ch. 4.

[26] Techniques for indicating divinity are too numerous to mention here, but vary from the presence of angels to eyes looking heavenwards. For an unusual example, note Zurburán's *Crucifixion* of 1627, where one half of Christ's body is in darkness and the other in brilliant light; illustration in J. Brown, *Zurburán* (London: Thames and Hudson, 1991), 54–5.

for two or more voices whose sole theatrical purpose is to secure the simultaneous expression of opposing emotions and potential directions for the plot. All I intend by such observations is that there is no inevitability about the ranking of the three media and their degree of exposure to idolatry. A listener can be seduced by the sensuality of Wagner's *Tristan und Isolde* no less than Pygmalion's eyes were by the statue he created. Great poetry or powerful rhetoric can beguile no less than a Venus de Milo. Plato and those early Christian objectors did thus have a point, if not in my view a decisive one.

However, it is altogether too weak a defence to suggest that music is no worse at generating idolatry than any other medium. More needs to be said, and by that I do not just mean appeal to obvious practical considerations. Certainly, singing can be much easier when instrumental accompaniment is used to help ensure that the congregation remains in tune. Scripture, however, finds in music much more value than this. Take the following verse from Psalm 49: 'I will set my ear to catch the moral of the story and tell on the harp how I read the riddle' (v. 4 NEB). The psalm as a whole is concerned about the issue of why the wicked so often prosper, and the good do not. The riddle, the moral of the story, is discovered to lie in God's final vindication of the good in the next life:[27] God will deliver his soul 'from the power of Sheol', writes the psalmist (v. 15). However, it is not the truth or otherwise of that contention that concerns me here. Rather, what is of relevance is the exact sense behind the Hebrew of the verse in question. In the New English Bible translation as in many another, the harpist's accompaniment is presented as merely incidental to the solving of the problem. Contrast that interpretation with the nuance given to the words in the RSV: 'I will solve my riddle to the music of the lyre'. Here the music has ceased to be non-essential. The suggestion is that it actually helps in the search for meaning. Such an interpretation seems confirmed by Old Testament reflection on the matter elsewhere. It is precisely through music that God's word to humanity becomes known.

Both Samuel and Elisha, for example, prophesy under the influence of music (1 Sam. 10.5; 2 Kgs 3.15). Again, in the liturgy the shofar or ram's horn is clearly assigned what has been described as

---

[27] Or perhaps in delaying death, depending on the date of the psalm.

'transcendental powers', and that is no doubt why its use in worship was confined to priests.[28] Priests also wore bells on their garments. If that conjures up a primitive, apotropaic role, the practice does at least indicate the early emergence of the importance of sound in religious ritual.[29] No doubt, motives were mixed: some profound, some less so. The most basic motivation for the use of singing and instruments in worship may possibly have been no more than the desire to ensure that the divinity heard the worshipper's pleas.[30] Even so, the extent of that use cannot be denied. So, while the claim that Israel's musical liturgical traditions established Jerusalem as 'the cultural centre of the entire ancient Levant' can only be pronounced quite absurd in the light of the available archaeological evidence, there is certainly another story to be told than music only being reluctantly conceded a place in the community's religious life.[31]

A passing allusion in Genesis allowed Jubal in later Jewish and Christian tradition to be posited as an alternative to Apollo or Orpheus as inventor of music.[32] It should also not be forgotten that biblical precedent was found in Job for the legend of the harmony of the spheres, that primarily Greek notion of how the planets reflect, in the sound that they make as they move, the divine harmony implicit in all of creation.[33] At the creation we are told: 'the morning stars sang together, and all the sons of God shouted for joy' (Job 38.7). A creation that is balanced and ordered thus finds that harmony reflected in the song that comes from the heavens. Pythagoras need not after all be assigned the credit for such a reputed discovery. As interpretation of these two passages well illustrates, it was partly

---

[28] Braun, *Music in Ancient Israel*, 26–9, esp. 28: cf. also 11. Later in the main body of the text I have retained the conventional translation as 'trumpet', partly to remind readers of the fact that it is this instrument that is taken up once more in the book of Revelation.

[29] For the apotropaic character of this practice, see ibid. 25. The earliest form of instrument so far found in Palestine, the whirring stick or 'bullroarer', also had a cultic function: ibid. 54.

[30] So P. Gradenwitz in his recently reissued classic of 1949: *The Music of Israel: From the Biblical Era to Modern Times*, 2nd edn (Portland, Ore.: Amadeus Press, 1996), 83.

[31] Gradenwitz's estimate, based on always reading the Bible as historically accurate: ibid. 49.

[32] For Jubal, see Gen. 4.21 and Gradenwitz, *The Music of Israel*, 28–9. In much Christian literature, the name became Tubal.

[33] For the harmony of the spheres, see Gradenwitz, *The Music of Israel*, 111, and the next section of this chapter.

pressure from other cultures that helped generate such new readings
of scripture. The impetus for more practical developments may
also have come from outside. David's harp, for instance, was almost
certainly a lyre of a type common in the ancient world.[34] Likewise,
the superscription above some psalms may possibly indicate borrowings from folk tunes, possibly of native origin.[35] Even so, as can be
seen from the use to which the image of David as minstrel was
put, there was also a more positive Israelite tradition, upon which
further developments could then be seen as legitimately founded.

Perhaps the reason why this more positive aspect to biblical thinking is so seldom appreciated nowadays is because it is found most
prominently in a work little read in the contemporary Church, the
books of Chronicles. Certainly if we judge that work (probably
written in the fourth century BC) on purely historical criteria by
comparison with the earlier writings of the Deuteronomic school
in Samuel and Kings, it can only be pronounced chock-a-block
with inaccuracies and distortions.[36] Some emerged through
omission. For example, the author tries throughout to give a better
character to King David by omitting not only all reference to his
adultery with Bathsheba but also the various internal disputes within
David's family that so clouded the end of his reign. The result is
that not only does all the sex and violence go, Solomon is also made
to appear as David's inevitable and natural successor, whereas the
alternative account suggests that there was, to begin with at least, a
serious rival candidate in David's oldest surviving son. Adonijah was
supported both by Abiathar, the high priest, and by Joab, David's
chief commander (1 Chronicles 29; contrast 1 Kings 1). Were that not
bad enough, such omissions are compounded by specific alterations
of detail as well. To mention but one, whereas the second book of
Samuel implies that for the first seven years of David's reign
one of Saul's sons, Ishbaal, reigned in the north, Chronicles
explicitly states that David ruled over the whole nation from the
start (1 Chronicles 12; contrast 2 Samuel 2). Again, instead of David

---

[34] Gradenwitz, *The Music of Israel*, 111. The harp was in any case also a foreign
borrowing.

[35] Ibid. 70. He finds such borrowings a repeated pattern in both Judaism and
Christianity; for examples from fifteenth-century Christian Spain, see 117–18.

[36] I adopt here the most commonly suggested date of composition: see e.g.
S. Japhet, *I and II Chronicles* (London: SCM Press, 1993), 24.

at the end of his reign being bedridden and impotent, Chronicles portrays him still in full possession of his powers. He delivers a powerful address on the succession and on how the Temple should be constructed in his son's reign (1 Chronicles 28; contrast 1 Kings 1).

For the more literal-minded, inevitably, all this is acutely embarrassing. It is still not unusual to find commentaries that quietly ignore such conflicts. Some even speak of an author that 'had no need to distort the facts in order to get his message across'.[37] Such approaches seem to me wholly misguided, and ironically for precisely the same reason as makes me want to reject famous scholars who have mocked the book's worth. The great nineteenth-century German critic Julius Wellhausen, for instance, speaks derogatorily of a clear-cut historical figure being turned into what he derides as merely 'a holy picture, seen through a cloud of incense'.[38] Where scholar and popular writer are alike wrong is in both using the wrong standard of measure: serious academic history. Nowadays our ideal society is commonly set in the future as something to work towards, whereas earlier societies more commonly projected their ideal back into the past. If the Garden of Eden is perhaps the most obvious example, the author of Chronicles seems to be engaging in a not dissimilar exercise. The Jews of his day were a subject people living under Persian occupation. What the author therefore does is envisage how Israel might have lived and worshipped during the most perfect period of its distant past, the reigns of David and Solomon. Such facts as he does know are then viewed through this selective lens. So not only are the monarchs presented in a much better light than seems justified but also repeated stress is put on the fact that they never act on their own but only in consort with all the people. The building of the Temple is thus transformed from an individual, imperial act to a massive co-operative enterprise, with implications for the author's own day.

David is thus idealized, with Bathsheba, family disputes and decrepit old age all gone, not so much to idealize the monarchy (an irrelevance for the author's own time), but rather to encourage

---

[37] M. Wilcock, *The Message of Chronicles* (Leicester: Inter-Varsity Press, 1987), 14–17, esp. 16. He does, however, concede 'a tendency to exaggerate' (14).
[38] J. Wellhausen, *Prolegomena to the History of Israel* (Edinburgh: T. & T. Clark, 1885), 182.

whoever now leads among the people towards the highest standards of conduct, and in particular ones that would unite a potentially divided nation now existing under occupation. That is no doubt why, unlike with the earlier books of Kings, we hear almost no mention of the northern kingdom, which after Solomon's death had split off to become the separate nation of 'Israel', with only the small kingdom of Judah remaining in the south, loyal to Jerusalem and the Temple. That might suggest a small mind, but far from it. Unlike the almost contemporary writings of Ezra and Nehemiah, the author shows an amazing openness to non-Jews, welcoming them to share in Jewish worship, provided they can be seen to espouse similar ideals (2 Chron. 6.32–33). It is into such a context that the author's comments on music should be set.

Whereas in the earlier book of Kings it is the arrival of the Ark of the Covenant that marks the inauguration of God's presence in the Temple, here we are told that it is accompanied singing that fulfils this role (2 Chronicles 5), a task assigned to a specific group, the Levites.[39] A group of twelve take responsibility for the music at any one time, with them both singing and playing—nine on the lyre, two on the harp and one on cymbals.[40] Lest the singers think their task an entirely non-priestly one, however, the author quickly recalls them to their religious role by labelling them 'prophets': required, that is, to sing something that speaks God's word and message to the people who are present. It was a pattern that repeated itself twice daily in the dramatic Temple liturgy envisaged by the writer.[41] In common with the rest of the ancient world, sacrifice was conducted in the open air outside the Temple, with its inside reserved for a symbolic representation of the divinity. At the twice-daily offering, as well as at the major festivals, as everyone gathers outside the Temple building before the great sacrificial altar that was placed there, the author suggests the singers were given a privileged place on some steps leading down

---

[39] In her massive commentary Japhet appears to attach no significance to this fact: *I and II Chronicles*, 572–81. Here I follow the detailed argument to the contrary in J. W. Kleinig, *The Lord's Song: The Basis, Function and Significance of Choral Music in Chronicles* (Sheffield: JSOT Press, 1993), e.g. 164.

[40] Assuming the usual 24 divisions, the numbers can be inferred from 1 Chron. 25.7. The proportions between the instruments are those suggested by the Mishnah: M. Tunnicliffe, *Chronicles to Nehemiah* (Oxford: Bible Reading Fellowship, 1999), 73.

[41] And also in private offerings; so Kleinig, *The Lord's Song*, 21, 127.

from the outer courtyard into the inner area.[42] Worship then began by the priests making representative atonement for the sins of the people by symbolically sprinkling blood over the altar. Then two priests sounded their great trumpets (only the priests were allowed to play them), and the responding music from the Levites then began.[43] A pair of clashing cymbals appear to have marked each stanza or verse, while the singers themselves were accompanied by the two harps and nine lyres.[44] Meanwhile whole offerings were burnt upon the altar. It was as this happened and to the accompaniment of the music that all the people literally prostrated themselves in acknowledgement of the fact that God was now once more present in their midst. As the writer puts it, 'when all the children of Israel saw the fire come down and the glory of the Lord upon the temple, they bowed down with their faces to the earth' (2 Chron. 7.3).

How historically accurate any of this may be is, as I have already noted, a highly contentious issue. Hitherto I have spoken as though what I was comparing were two quite different things, popular sermon-like history in Chronicles and the more academic version in Samuel and Kings. For most of Christian history that is indeed how matters have been regarded. Archaeological investigations, however, are now beginning to suggest that those earlier histories too may have had a more complicated purpose than hitherto supposed. In 1993 there was great excitement among Hebrew Bible scholars when an ancient inscription was discovered at Tell Dan in northern Israel that could possibly be referring to King David.[45] But the court is still out, and the matter uncertain. If confirmed, its importance would lie in the fact that it would be our very first piece of archaeological evidence confirming the existence of King David, for at the moment there is none for the kings of Israel till almost two centuries later, in the eighth century. Indeed it now looks highly plausible that, though David almost

[42] For these steps, including a plan, see ibid. 71–3.

[43] For trumpets as the exclusive prerogative of the priests, see Japhet, *I and II Chronicles*, 927–8.

[44] For the role of cymbals, see Kleinig, *The Lord's Song*, 82. Kleinig notes the lack of archaeological evidence for harps in Palestine, but considers alternative translations rather than the surely more likely possibility of projection of the instrument back into Israelite worship (85).

[45] For some details, see J. Rogerson, *Chronicles of the Old Testament Kings* (London: Thames and Hudson, 1999), 8.

certainly did exist, he never did have the great empire that the Bible attributes to him. Instead the Bible represents the ambitions of a later age.[46]

If the historical choice between Kings and Chronicles is thus not quite so clear-cut as once supposed, the difference in theology at least remains clear. For the later author music was not simply an incidental or supplementary adjunct that helps beautify the proceedings. Nor was the objective merely to please the listeners or even to appease God, since, as we have seen, the confessional part of the service was kept quite separate.[47] Rather, it was there to aid a sense of presence, to help renew awareness of God in the people's midst. As the writer himself puts it, 'when the song was raised . . . the glory of the Lord filled the house of God' (2 Chron. 5.13–14). Music was thus in effect the means whereby God made his presence known to his people. It is perhaps not surprising, therefore, that the writer is insistent that the medium must have had a divine institution. 'The commandment was from the Lord through his prophets', we are told (2 Chron. 29.25): Gad and Nathan conveyed to King David what must be done.[48]

It is thus by divine decree that instrumental music helps to bring God near. Now God is of course by definition present everywhere. That is simply part of what we now understand by the term 'God': a universal presence. But it is one thing to make that claim, quite another to experience such a presence. Like the prophets uttering the divine word in ecstasy under the power of music, so the author of Chronicles envisages Temple worshippers discovering through music the very presence of God in their midst.

So, if on the one hand Plato's suspicions deserve a more sympathetic hearing because his position was one shared by the early Church, on the other hand (and more importantly) a deeper immersion in scripture suggests a more positive assessment of the role of instrumental music in making us aware of the divine presence and its action upon us.

---

[46] How far one should go down this path is a matter of some dispute. For an extreme but powerfully argued version of the case, see T. L. Thompson, *The Bible in History: How Writers Create a Past* (London: Jonathan Cape, 1999).

[47] Kleinig, *The Lord's Song*, 111–13.

[48] Gad is the prophet who rebuked David over the matter of the census: 2 Sam. 24.10–14.

Objectivity and Competing Traditions

Later in this chapter I offer for consideration some examples of religious experience made effective through the work of a range of composers from Bach onwards. In so doing my presupposition is that, as in the Temple's worship envisaged in Chronicles, so elsewhere music can help break down the barriers between the invisible world of the divine and our own. In other words, certain features of music help an already present God to be perceived. Clearly this is not true of all music, but there is a wide variety of possibilities. As in the relation between painter and viewer, a composer can help the listener through focus on certain features inherent in the music (such as order, transcendence, compassion or hope) to perceive external reality in general in a new way, and with that perception the ultimate ground for such ideas in God as ultimate reality itself.[49] To some that may seem mere delusion. Certainly, matters are often presented as though the choice were only between two extremes, either strong objectivist claims that it is widely held modern musical studies have undermined or else pure subjectivism. My own view is that it is possible to follow a middle course. By that I do not intend some version of postmodern pluralism whereby a positive religious role is seen as only legitimated in the light of Christian revelation but not otherwise subject to assessment. To my mind that is to retreat altogether too far from a God whose generous activity extends well beyond the Church. It is also to assume a purity for revelation in comparison with more worldly encounters that is simply not sustainable. Greater clarity on this matter is most easily achieved by exploring briefly some of the main possibilities.

I begin, therefore, with the strongly objectivist position, and some explanation of why it has come under strain. In the previous section I mentioned (almost in passing) the harmony of the spheres, the notion that human music reflects a harmony that characterizes the world as a whole, and which finds expression in the silent music made by the planets in their orbit.[50] It is often forgotten how powerfully that image once gripped the western imagination. Pythagoras is credited

---

[49] A point that is central to my conception of how the landscape artist can convey divine presence: see my *God and Enchantment of Place* (Oxford: Oxford University Press, 2004), ch. 3.

[50] Silent, it was believed, only because, being constant, there was no change to alert us to the sound.

with having found the simple mathematical relation for the octave
(a stretched string blocked at its midpoint and plucked will sound an
octave higher), and the further variants thereon. Their very simplicity (2 : 1, 3 : 2, 5 : 4 and so on) seemed to argue for a deep foundation
in reality.[51] So it is perhaps not surprising that such ideas predomi-
nated, including the picturesque one of its relation to the movement
of the planets, well into the nineteenth century. So natural was such
a belief to Shakespeare that it appears almost casually in one of
his plays:

> How sweet the moonlight sleeps upon this bank!
> Here will we sit, and let the sounds of music
> Creep in our ears: soft stillness and the night
> Become the touches of sweet harmony.
>
> . . .
>
> There's not the smallest orb which thou behold'st
> But in his motion like an angel sings
>
> . . .
>
> But, whilst this muddy vesture of decay
> Doth grossly close it in, we cannot hear it.[52]

It was in fact an assumption that passed easily from the classical world
to the Christian. Pythagoras' views were preserved by Aristotle, and
preserved for posterity especially through Cicero.[53] Cicero was well
known to Christian writers, but the position was also adopted in
Augustine and Boethius.[54] Nor was the idea by any means confined to
the pre-scientific world. Kepler in particular was an enthusiastic
exponent.[55] Rather than abandon the theory he adapted the newly
discovered elliptical course of the planets to produce new models of
mathematical harmonies.[56]

---

[51] 2 : 1 for the octave, 3 : 2 for the perfect fifth and 5 : 4 for the major third.

[52] *Merchant of Venice*, 5.1.54ff. (Lorenzo speaking).

[53] Cicero's *Scipio's Dream* (the most famous part of his *De republica* and often reproduced separately) was widely read throughout the medieval period. For the relevant
passages from Cicero and from Aristotle's *On the Heavens*, see J. James, *The Music of the
Spheres* (London: Abacus, 1995), 38–9, 63–4.

[54] Boethius' *De institutione musica* is more accessible than Augustine's *De musica*.
For a brief outline of the latter's position, see C. Harrison, *Beauty and Revelation in the
Thought of Saint Augustine* (Oxford: Clarendon Press, 1992), 28–31.

[55] Newton was another. Galileo's father wrote a treatise in defence of the
ancient view of music: James, *The Music of the Spheres*, 98, 164–5.

[56] In his *Harmony of the Universe* (bk 5) he 'solves' the problem by taking 'the
Master Geometer's' observation point as the sun: for further details, see James, *The
Music of the Spheres*, 140–58, esp. 151–2.

One recent survey blames Romanticism for the theory's collapse.[57] Structure and order were no longer the primary concern in music, and emotion replaced reason. That author portrays Schoenberg as part of an unsuccessful rearguard action, but there were in fact quite a number of twentieth-century musicologists and composers who sought to maintain the traditional view.[58] Not of course that this could be done any longer through maintaining literally the old-fashioned notion of the harmony of the spheres, but there was continuity to this extent, in the claim that the western diatonic tonal system represented a proper universal that reflected some deeper truth about the nature of the universe as such. Among those taking this view were Leonard Bernstein, Dereck Cooke, Paul Hindemith and Heinrich Schenker.[59] Commenting on Mozart's G Minor Symphony, the last named, for instance, observes that 'the superior force of truth . . . is at work mysteriously behind Mozart's consciousness, guiding his pen', a force that Schenker variously describes as Nature (with a capital N) and God.[60]

However, the position had been under strain for some time. Medieval music had found the Christian God in triple rhythms and the major triad.[61] Nonetheless the expressive potential that could be seen in the dissonant tritone (labelled the *diabolus in musica*) warned that tonality might not be quite the whole answer.[62] More substantial was the discovery that equal temperament could only be created artificially. The Pythagorean subdivisions of the octave were in practice not always compatible with each other or the octave, and produced irregular intervals between the semitones unless corrected.

---

[57] 'Blames' because James regrets what happened: ibid. 180–211.

[58] For Schoenberg, see ibid. 212–24.

[59] D. Cooke, *The Language of Music* (Oxford: Oxford University Press, 1959); L. Bernstein, *The Unanswered Question* (Cambridge, Mass.: Harvard University Press, 1976); P. Hindemith, *A Composer's World* (New York: Anchor, 1961). Hindemith even wrote an opera based on the life of Kepler, called *Die Harmonie der Welt*.

[60] H. Schenker, *The Masterwork in Music*, ed. W. Drabkin (Cambridge: Cambridge University Press, 1996), 59–96, esp. 60.

[61] C, E and G are the notes of the major triad in the key of C major, and the natural 'home' of a piece of music in that key (although, strictly speaking, tonality as we understand it did not develop properly until much later).

[62] The debate began *c*. 990 with Guido of Arezzo. A tritone is an interval of three whole tones (an augmented fourth or diminished fifth), such as C to F sharp or G flat. Britten uses tritones extensively in his *War Requiem* to intensify the uneasy relationship between Wilfred Owen's poems and the Ordinary of the Mass.

The fraction of error is sometimes known as 'the Pythagorean comma'. Its very complexity and irrationality seemed to speak against a perfect fit between music and an ordered divine creation.[63] Although known from about 1600, equal temperament was not generally applied to instruments until more than a century and a half later, but in the meantime of course it gave pause for thought. Added to this came the further difficulty that western music was now seen to be only one possible approach among many. Hindu music was found to use scales in which the octave is divided into intervals of less than a semitone, while much other non-western music confines itself to the more limited pentatonic scale.[64] A quite different form of critique has come from feminism, with the suggestion that western music is in fact male-biased in its very construction.[65] That claim can be supported by some of the terminology employed, but, as one recent female commentator observes, this has often more to do with particular social and cultural circumstances than with a more general scenario.[66] Even so, she finds modern western music still exhibiting a fundamental male bias.

Despite the extent of such opposing factors, one commentator still feels it legitimate to talk about what he calls 'near universals'.[67] His defence is too technical to enter into here. More plausibly, others have sought to build such claims on other types of cross-cultural comparison: among them infant aversion to dissonance and resultant similarities in the sort of music that makes an effective lullaby, and the apparent exclusive use of uneven divisions within any particular scale.[68] These are interesting claims, but I shall not

[63] The fraction is 531,441/524,288. For details of how this arises, see A. L. Blackwell, *The Sacred in Music* (Cambridge: Lutterworth, 1999), 155–6.

[64] There are 22 *sruti* or microtones to an Indian octave, and they are not all equidistant from each other. The pentatonic scale uses only five notes in the octave, for example only the black notes on the piano.

[65] e.g. S. McClary, *Feminine Endings: Music, Gender and Sexuality* (Minneapolis: University of Minnesota Press, 1991).

[66] L. Green, *Music, Gender, and Education* (Cambridge: Cambridge University Press, 1997). As an example of the former she mentions the labelling in the nineteenth century of the first theme of a sonata as 'masculine' and its second as 'feminine' (119). She later criticizes McClary's analysis of western music as necessarily built upon the male organism (e.g. 126).

[67] Blackwell, *The Sacred in Music*, 72, endorsing the views of D. P. McAllester. He treats the Pythagorean comma as a symbol of the need for the world's redemption from imperfection: 157–8.

[68] J. McDermott and M. Hauser, 'The Origins of Music: Innateness, Uniqueness, and Evolution', *Music Perception* 23 (2005), 29–59.

pursue them further here because it is not clear to me that they are strictly necessary in order to preserve the possibility of a divine role.

To see why, we need to turn to the other extreme and pure subjectivism. As well as listing some of the factors I have already mentioned, one recent introduction to music stresses the wide variety of approaches to performance, to acceptable styles and genres and to the reading of content.[69] From that survey the conclusion is drawn that music 'constructs rather than represents reality', offering 'ways of creating meaning rather than just representing it'.[70] Prescriptive judgements ought therefore to be abandoned.[71] But what such facts suggest to me is not the absence of all standards but rather that the appropriation of such standards can only be seen to work effectively within particular traditions. Part of the problem is that much modern musicology has sought to exalt instrumental music through establishing its independence in what has come to be known as 'absolute' music. This is music that allegedly has no further external referents but gives satisfaction purely in terms of its own form. There are now only internal criteria. So claims to objectivity become correspondingly more difficult, as what legitimates comparisons across different genres and approaches becomes less clear. However, all this is a very recent development. Even as late as Kant and Hegel instrumental music was still being evaluated in terms of its capacity to serve other ends.[72] Eduard Hanslick (1825-1904) was the great exponent of the alternative view, whom we shall meet once more later in this chapter, when discussing Bruckner. Romantic programmatic music was, he believed, music perverted.

If Wagner is the obvious example of someone who tried to integrate all the arts (with music once more subservient to a larger goal), and Brecht someone who refused such integration and set the arts against each other, what both these quite different artists well

[69] Hostile feminist readings of Beethoven or gay readings of Schubert are given as examples of how music can be approached very differently from the usual, more conventional canons of musicology: N. Cook, *Music: A Very Short Introduction* (Oxford: Oxford University Press, 1998), 108–15.

[70] Ibid. 76–7, 125–6.

[71] Ibid. 84.

[72] Both were suspicious of the value of music without words, since it then either lacks ideas, or else founders through its failure to serve any further ends such as military campaigns, dancing and so forth. For brief summaries and quotations, see C. Dahlhaus, *Esthetics of Music* (Cambridge: Cambridge University Press, 1982), 24–38, 46–51, esp. 30, 31, 47.

illustrate is the importance of a return to context.[73] Wagner (d. 1883) lived at a time when Germany was moving in general towards a more unitary ideal, whereas part of the motivation of Brecht (d. 1956) was a protest against nationalist and integrationist trends.[74] It is probably no accident that Schoenberg's challenge to tonality (in his use of dissonance and eventually serial composition) was emerging about the same time as Picasso's revolt in Cubism against the dominance of one perspective.[75] Equally, the modern love for relatively simple forms in religious music (as in the popularity of Gregorian chant or some of the compositions of Pärt and Tavener) may well tell us as much about the hectic character of modern life and our consequent reluctance to immerse ourselves deeply in anything whatsoever as it does about the nature of religion or music.[76] This is not to make a judgement on these composers' motives.[77] Simplicity could, for example, have been chosen to aid concentration. Nor is it to maintain that Pärt and Tavener on the one hand or Schoenberg on the other can therefore contribute nothing to our experience of God. To draw a parallel from the visual arts, both Poussin and Mondrian sought to say something about divine order in the cosmos but did so in quite different ways. To understand their paintings we need to immerse ourselves in those different ways and in the quite different assumptions of seventeenth- and twentieth-century viewers.[78] However, once that is done, their art can then draw us back into those wider claims, and allow us to experience what they themselves believed to lie behind that order.

Music exhibits a further complication in that there are rival candidates for what constitutes the 'work'. Whereas there is only one canvas, in the case of music there is both score and performance.

---

[73] Brecht wanted each art to undercut and alienate the other, so that what had grown customary and ordinary might strike listeners and viewers as strange and disturbing.

[74] I owe the contrast to Dahlhaus: *Esthetics of Music*, 64–9. The stress on context is my own.

[75] A work that takes seriously such parallels in the arts is D. Mitchell, *The Language of Modern Music* (London: Faber and Faber, 1993 edn), 63–94, esp. 85–6.

[76] This critique could of course be challenged, but for me the more interesting question is whether the popularity of such simplified music is not part of a wider cultural phenomenon, a general standing back in modern society from specific commitments.

[77] But for such a specific attack on Tavener and Pärt, for their failure to immerse themselves in the music of the Orthodox tradition, despite their claims to such an identity, see I. Hewett, *Music: Healing the Rift* (London: Continuum, 2003), 209–15.

[78] Something I offered in this volume's predecessor, *God and Enchantment of Place*, 84–152, esp. 106–8, 140–4.

Until relatively recently musicologists concentrated almost exclusively on the score, and this encouraged, and was encouraged by, the search for authentic performance. While that brought obvious gains, for instance in returning Bach to the Baroque era, it also has its limitations. Composers have often left behind more than one version of a work, and instructions on the score may not be as precise as was once supposed. Deciding the first issue is especially difficult in the case of someone like Bruckner, who was constantly revising his scores. But there is no shortage of other examples.[79] Again, despite his conviction that he is carefully following Beethoven's original intentions, it is possible that a conductor like Sir Roger Norrington in effect provides a less authentic performance, precisely because he ignores the openness to decisions of the moment that Beethoven had still left possible. If so, contrary to initial expectations, Wilhelm Furtwängler's more intuitive approach would then have actually captured Beethoven's intentions better. Certainly, it is an argument accepted by Daniel Barenboim, who praises Furtwängler for the way in which he operates 'a highly plastic process . . . which seems to be working itself out right then and there'.[80] So performance is all about 'becoming', not 'being', and the whole body must be involved as well as the mind, as conductor and players alike think themselves into the music.[81] Such potential lack of determinacy in the score is an issue to which I shall return.

The image of performers and audience entering imaginatively into a piece of music suggests to me that there are analogies to entering into a religious tradition. In forming an estimate, standing wholly apart in search of a more objective standard may actually distort what can be learned. Much can be missed unless judgement is temporarily suspended and a real creative engagement occurs. Certainly, my own evaluations of the other major religions have changed considerably in recent years as I have gone beyond amassing 'facts' into attempting to see things, as it were, from within. The result is not always discovery of further conflicts. Sometimes apparent deep incompatibility turns

---

[79] In the case of Chopin a piano piece in the author's own hand may differ significantly from three published versions (for France, England and Germany) and each of these differ in turn from each other, despite the fact that there is evidence that Chopin checked and endorsed all three. See further Cook, *Music*, 88–9.

[80] D. Barenboim and E. W. Said, *Parallels and Paradoxes: Explorations in Music and Society* (London: Bloomsbury, 2003), 22.

[81] Ibid. 21, 145.

out to be much more superficial than might otherwise have been envisaged.[82] The same can, I suggest, prove true in music, as sympathetic engagement with hugely different types of approach is allowed to yield what turn out after all to be similar experiences of the divine. Certainly, there is a remarkable unanimity among composers about how the action of God on them is experienced, despite the very different methods and compositional rules that they follow.[83] But those underlying similarities should only be allowed to surface once a prior deeper engagement has been made on the listener's part with those different techniques. Too often it is assumed that the music will simply operate in particular ways without any significant preparation on our part.[84] Haydn and Bruckner, for instance, were both devout Christians, but we shall gain little of the experience they sought to transmit, unless we work first at understanding their contrasting methodologies.[85]

If that remark applies to the complexities of the classical tradition in music, it is no less pertinent to the attempt explicitly to relate any one of the world's major religions and its own musical traditions. Take Islam. From the hostility to music of the Wahhabi movement in Saudi Arabia it would be all too easy to universalize this into a general Muslim position, whereas even Ayatollah Khomeini in Iran issued a *fatwa* that permitted most music as itself a reminder of God.[86] By this judgement the Ayatollah demonstrated that he stood in continuity with the more positive Persian tradition of the past. However, that

[82] On Abraham's sacrifice of his child, the three major monotheistic religions seem to agree neither on the child's age nor even his identity (Islam postulates Ishmael). But examining the story as three developing traditions discloses deeper underlying similarities. See my *Tradition and Imagination* (Oxford: Oxford University Press, 1999), 237–60.

[83] Well illustrated by a survey written by someone who is himself a composer: Jonathan Harvey, *Music and Inspiration* (London: Faber and Faber, 1999). The predominant feature is of the composer as medium or instrumental agent, as in an early quotation from Sibelius: ibid. 6.

[84] As in the long lists of recommendations for using music to instil various types of mood in a book like H. A. Lingerman, *The Healing Energies of Music*, 2nd edn (Wheaton, Ill.: Quest, 1995).

[85] Bruckner's piety is perhaps better known, but Haydn always prefaced any compositional work with prayer. For relevant quotations, see A. Storr, *Music and the Mind* (London: HarperCollins, 1992), 115–16.

[86] For further details, see S. H. Nasr, 'Islam and Music: The Legal and Spiritual Dimensions', in L. E. Sullivan (ed.), *Enchanting Powers: Music in the World's Religions* (Cambridge, Mass.: Harvard University Press, 1997), 219–35, esp. 224, 229–30.

tradition (which includes the Sufi movement) can also be used to illustrate the opposite danger, where the West neutralizes the distinctiveness of a particular tradition by in effect internationalizing it. A singer like Nusrat Fateh Ali Khan has been packaged in a way that ignores all the associated ritual practices.[87] With the potential for such misunderstandings the temptation is to suppose that uniqueness is best defended for one's own faith by refusing dialogue. That seems to me quite the wrong sort of response. As the incarnation so clearly demonstrates, God generously operates through the specificities of the various particular traditions within which human beings must function. So it behoves us ill to ignore attention to such detail.

That is why I want to resist the methodology of England's leading writer in the field despite the richness of the insights that he offers. Jeremy Begbie has done more than anyone else in England in recent years to re-establish connections between theology and music, but his approach is essentially illustrative rather than a learning exercise. That is to say, music is used to expound or develop biblical insights.[88] Ironically, his arguments would be considerably strengthened if he contended that the Bible was being weighed against how God is found to act elsewhere. But what is not allowed from his perspective is that God might reveal himself through music in ways that genuinely throw up challenges to the biblical picture.[89] A case in point is his attitude to the music of Messiaen and Tavener. Their stress on divine timelessness is criticized for having too negative a view of time and for failing to integrate sufficiently with a biblical christology that speaks of redeeming conflict within the temporal world.[90] My difficulty here is twofold. First, such music does genuinely aid what many have found to be an important side to their religious experience, and by no means solely as this has been mediated through music.

[87] P. V. Bohlman, 'World Musics and World Religions: Whose World?', in Sullivan (ed.), *Enchanting Powers*, 61–90, esp. 61–8.

[88] J. S. Begbie, *Theology, Music and Time* (Cambridge: Cambridge University Press, 2000). For two-natures Christology, see 24–6; for creation as continuous, 62–7; for the compatibility of imminent and delayed parousia, 118–23; for the demand for improvisation in Pauline theology, 255–69. All are illuminating. Detailed assessment, however, would require careful consideration of what is involved in comparing two such different areas of thought.

[89] The book ends with an emphatic rejection of natural theology: ibid. 274–8.

[90] Ibid. 140–1, 145, 150.

Secondly, apparent conflict with the biblical witness does not necessarily indicate deep incompatibility. There is in fact a long philosophical tradition within Christianity which insists that the timelessness of God and his engagement with a temporal world are both part of one and the same reality.

Begbie urges that care needs to be exercised because of the sinful world in which we live and the destructive ideologies that music can create. Here, however, our estimates of the authority of scripture diverge. For it seems to me that the Bible too, despite its indispensability to the Christian understanding, is replete with evidence of sinful, fallible individuals imposing their own perceptions as though they came from God.[91] So the ideal should be to allow all available sources of knowledge of God to interact, and not automatically to assume the absolute priority of one over all the others.

Against positions such as mine it is often objected that to allow natural religion such a large place is inevitably to exalt human reason in place of God, and to fail to wrestle seriously with the possible continuing relevance of scripture. It is neither. As my earlier discussion of the Bible on music indicates, it is by returning to neglected insights in the author of Chronicles that I believe a more exalted status for music can be justified: God's presence made manifest through music. The prophet Zephaniah went even further and spoke of God joining in our song when this happens: 'The Lord, your God, is in your midst... he will rejoice over you with gladness, he will renew you in his love... he will exult over you with loud singing, as on a day of festival' (3.17). That mystical image suggests that it is earlier Christian perceptions that went wrong when too narrow a focus was adopted from elsewhere in the canon, in an exclusive focus on order.[92] Rather, there is a great range of ways in which God's presence can be made known through music.

Such an understanding is, I believe, best captured by talking about the sacramental role of music. I am scarcely the first to do so. One recent writer on music adopts as a definition of the sacramental 'any

---

[91] Numerous examples are given in *Tradition and Imagination* and its sequel, *Discipleship and Imagination* (Oxford: Oxford University Press, 2000).

[92] An emphasis that is reflected in what is perhaps the most frequently quoted verse in patristic and medieval discussions of music, Wisd. 11.21: 'omnia in mensura, et numero, et pondere disposuisti' (you have assigned all things in measure, number and weight).

finite reality through which the divine is perceived to be disclosed and communicated, and through which our human response to the divine assumes some measure of shape, form and structure'.[93] Another proceeds more indirectly. Music is like a sacrament because it 'both creates and expresses a truth'.[94] Later he substitutes 'expresses and creates a mood', before finally settling on the declaration that 'a piece of music not only expresses what the composer is feeling, it is also a means of creating that feeling, that mood, in the listener. So music and sacraments convey a truth as well as stating it.'[95] That participatory stress is vital. Music is not simply an intellectual exercise, nor an experience confined to the composer alone. It is so designed that, as with the eucharist, the original experience can be re-enacted as God's presence in our midst once more made known. How that might work out in practice I now begin to consider by examining the works of some key composers in the classical tradition.[96]

Religious Experience in the Classical Tradition

In examining the work of specific composers I want to devote most attention to the nineteenth and twentieth centuries. That is partly because it is this music that has most shaped contemporary composition and listeners' expectations. But it is also because it was the nineteenth century that saw with the Romantic movement the growth of programmatic instrumental music and so more explicit discussion of the possibility of various types of religious experience through instrumental music. So far from welcoming such developments, however, many Christians view them as a further stage on the road to secularism. Music has become a human search for God rather than music graced by the Christian gospel. It is for this reason that the work of Johann Sebastian Bach (1685–1750) is often held up as the ideal, with even his contemporaries and immediate successors taken as already indicative of decline. It is a judgement offered by many a Catholic and Protestant theologian. So, for

---

[93] Blackwell, *The Sacred in Music*, 28.

[94] C. R. Campling, *The Food of Love: Reflections on Music and Faith* (London: SCM Press, 1997), 17.

[95] Ibid. 90, 124.

[96] Largely instrumental works, for the reasons indicated earlier.

example, to the American Lutheran Jaroslav Pelikan, Handel's *Messiah* is 'a concert piece whose theological content . . . need not get in the way of the performance'.[97] Again, the French Catholic Étienne Gilson remarks of the masses of Haydn and Mozart that 'such music is there for its own sake, and it does not speak to us of God, but of Haydn and Mozart'.[98] To my mind the wrong lessons are being drawn from Bach. So I want to examine some key aspects of his approach first, along with (more briefly) that of the equally devout Haydn (1732–1809). Thereafter the selection will include both the devout and those on the fringes of faith. The choice has been determined by the desire to illustrate the wide range of types of experience of the divine that can be generated by classical music.

Divine Order in Bach and Haydn

One irony in current Christian attitudes is that Bach's present prominence is in large part due to the very Romantic movement with which he is so often contrasted. Certainly, his name was by no means unknown before Mendelssohn. But it was Mendelssohn who initiated the long period during which Bach's works were treated in the Romantic manner, in additions to the music as well as treatment on a grander scale.[99] It was only slowly over the course of the twentieth century that his compositions were returned in performance to their simpler Baroque forms.[100] There has likewise been some oscillation in the treatment of his religious beliefs. Until modern times it was assumed that the cantatas were written gradually over the course of his 27 years at Leipzig. During the 1950s, however, it was discovered that the majority of his Leipzig cantatas were in fact written during the first two years of his appointment there (1723–5) and certainly all by 1727.[101] Because the rest of his

[97] J. Pelikan, *Bach among the Theologians* (Philadelphia: Fortress, 1986), 77–8.

[98] É. Gilson, *The Arts of the Beautiful* (New York: Scribners, 1965), 175. Gilson is equally disapproving of Bach's *Mass in B Minor* (though it was not written for liturgical use at a single celebration).

[99] Mendelssohn revived the *St Matthew Passion* with a performance in 1829. The following year saw the composition of his Fifth or 'Reformation' Symphony, whose fourth movement is an elaboration of Luther's 'Ein' feste Burg'. For further details, see Pelikan, *Bach*, 15.

[100] See further G. B. Stauffer, 'Changing Issues of Performance Practice', in J. Butt (ed.), *Cambridge Companion to Bach* (Cambridge: Cambridge University Press, 1997), 203–17, esp. 207, 213–14.

[101] He seems to have written about one a week throughout those two years.

time was now largely occupied with non-vocal compositions and included some disagreements with the church authorities, it was not long before some scholars were arguing that such phenomena marked a later sharp decline in religious belief.[102] However, discovery of the *Calov Bible Commentary* on an American farmstead pulled the evidence once more the other way.[103] There seems in fact no good reason to doubt the solidity of Bach's faith throughout his life. However, this is scarcely enough in itself to draw significant contrasts with Handel and Haydn, since they too exhibited a strong faith in God. And perhaps the same is true of Mozart also.[104]

Where Bach differed was in the great bulk of his compositions being at the service of his faith, in the worship of the Church. That can partly be put down to his luck in being born a Lutheran. Luther had bequested to the church that bears his name a strong commitment to a high doctrine of the use of music in church as a source of grace, placing it next to scripture in honour.[105] Among writers of Bach's own day that position was maintained by Andreas Werckmeister and Johann Kuhnau. Bach himself reflects similar ideas in his annotations to the *Calov Bible Commentary*, not least in his comments on the Chronicles passages that I discussed earlier in this chapter.[106] As he observes, 'in devotional music God is always

[102] For a brief outline of Friedrich Blume's resultant attack on Bach's piety and the contrast with Spitta's earlier, dominant view of a long process of writing (from 1723 to 1744), see C. R. Stapert, *My Only Comfort: Death, Deliverance, and Discipleship in the Music of Bach* (Grand Rapids: Eerdmans, 2000), 24–6.

[103] It had in fact been found in 1934, but its importance lay unrecognized in a seminary library until the late 1960s: Stapert, *My Only Comfort*, 9–11. Martin Neary also rejects Blume's in his introduction to R. Stokes (ed.), *J. S. Bach: The Complete Cantatas* (Ebrington, Glos.: Long Barn, 1999), p. xvi.

[104] Although this is more often contested in the case of Mozart, there seems little reason to doubt his faith. More contentious is the nature of his commitment to the specifics of Roman Catholic belief. Note, for instance, the range of private observations collected in F. Kerst, *Mozart: The Man and Artist Revealed in His Own Words* (New York: Dover, 1965), 95–9.

[105] In his 1538 treatise 'To the Admirers of Music'. He also sees it as a bulwark against idolatry because in his view audition cannot attempt to fix or circumscribe God in the way vision does. See further the Weimar edition of Luther's works, vol. 50, 348–74.

[106] For the views of Werckmeister and Kuhnau (Bach's predecessor at Leipzig), see the key chapter on 'The Lutheran "Metaphysical" Tradition' in E. Chafe, *Analysing Bach Cantatas* (New York: Oxford University Press, 2000), 23–41.

present with his grace'.[107] The Catholic mass did of course allow opportunities for composition but much less variety and innovation than was the case with the more freely structured character of Lutheran services. This was in part due to Luther's endorsement of the hymn, which meant that a greater range of music had by implication already been legitimated, including in effect the cantata (which achieved its first German form only about 1700).[108] Services began early, and although the sermon could last as long as an hour, a central position was given to music, with the cantata in effect acting as a commentary on the Gospel reading.[109] None of this is to deny that Bach was a Lutheran by conviction. In his only appointment to a Calvinist court he continued to attend the local Lutheran church.[110] My point rather is that the avenues of expression open to him went naturally down some tracks that were not so easily available to others.

Some, however, will insist that I am missing the point. Even within the structures of Lutheranism, it will be said, alternatives were available that he deliberately chose not to pursue, among them the attitudes of the Enlightenment and of Pietism: in other words rationalism and subjectivist emotionalism. It is therefore a very specific type of biblical commitment that is reflected in his music. This is something of which Pelikan makes much.[111] While it is true that Bach avoids the extremes in both movements, again there may have been an element of luck to this in that Leipzig's religion seems only to have moved in an Enlightenment direction after his death.[112] Indeed, one detailed study of the religious state of

[107] R. A. Leaver, *J. S. Bach and Scripture: Glosses from the Calov Bible Commentary* (St Louis: Concordia, 1985), 97. Bach describes 1 Chronicles 25 as 'das wahre Fundament aller gottfalliger Kirchen Musik' (the true foundation of all church music pleasing to God).

[108] For some statistics about Bach's own preoccupation with Luther's hymns, see P. Charru and C. Theobald, *L'Esprit créateur dans la pensée musicale de Jean-Sébastien Bach* (Sprimont, Belg.: Mardaga, 2002), 21–2.

[109] For the structure of services at Leipzig (with the main service beginning at 7 a.m.), see C. Wolff, *Johann Sebastian Bach: The Learned Musician* (Oxford: Oxford University Press, 2001), 256–9. Cf. also 160, 255.

[110] At Cöthen. See further ibid. 188, 191, 199.

[111] Pelikan, *Bach*, 29–55.

[112] Enlightenment figures at its university seem only to have had an impact on the practice of religion after Bach's death: G. Stiller, *Johann Sebastian Bach and Liturgical Life in Leipzig* (St Louis: Concordia, 1984), 31–3, 158.

the town during Bach's life demonstrates a vibrant commitment to traditional religion.[113] Communion attendance figures were high, and Catholic externals such as set readings, liturgical colours, chasubles and the sanctuary bell survived until well after Bach's death.[114]

Even so Bach can hardly have been entirely unaware of such movements. He had an extensive library, and included in its theological tomes were the writings of at least two Pietists.[115] If evidence for interest in the Enlightenment is less clear, it is thought quite likely that he would have possessed some of the works of his contemporary, the widely read pupil of Leibniz, Christian Wolff (d. 1754).[116] Nowadays we tend to value most the emotional elements in Bach's music that are such a prominent feature of Pietism. Astonishingly, Albert Schweitzer spoke of the irrelevance of the words. The texts 'are so insignificant that we need all the beauty of the music to make us forget them'.[117] But again and again it is the perfect match of music and words in Bach's music that draws our sympathies to the biblical story or a particular theological theme.[118] Detailed study of particular cantatas demonstrates the great care Bach took in suggesting, for example, divine creation of a beautiful soul, the way in which law and gospel are contrasted, or divine perfection set against human weakness in fulfilling God's commands.[119]

---

[113] The surviving sources are excellent: ibid. 35–6.

[114] For the contrast in communion figures before and after Bach's death, see ibid. 131–3, 164–5. For Catholic observance, see 64, 160–1.

[115] A. H. Francke and P. J. Spener: Stapert, *My Only Comfort*, 9.

[116] John Butt, 'A mind Unconscious that is Calculating?', in Butt (ed.), *Cambridge Companion to Bach*, 61. There are no philosophical volumes listed (apart from those on musical aesthetics), but Bach's biographer Christopher Wolff believes that his library is only partially recorded: *Johann Sebastian Bach*, 334–5.

[117] Quoted in Stapert, *My Only Comfort*, 6.

[118] For a good example of perfect integration, cf. the aria 'Wie zittern und wanken' in Cantata 105. 'Trembling and wavering' are indicated by a tremolo figure in the strings that proceeds at two different speeds.

[119] For the last two, see Chafe on Cantata 9 (*Analysing Bach Cantatas*, 7–10, 149–57) and Cantata 77 (183–219). In the latter, for example, Chafe detects a 'descent' pattern from major to minor, from sharp to flat, from major triad to minor: 219. For the first, see the exploration of 'Schmücke Dich' as cantata and chorale in Charru and Theobald, *L'Esprit Créateur*, 104–14.

Even situations where on first reflection the music seems incon-
gruous can turn out quite otherwise. Consider two examples from
the *St John Passion*. The first piece in a major key turns out to be a
surprisingly light-hearted setting for mention of the promise and
challenge of Christian discipleship. But, as it is followed by Peter's
denial, the music seems after all emotionally exactly right, in
suggesting how lightly as disciples we enter into what should
be our deepest commitments.[120] More central to the action, the
setting for what should be Christ's triumphant cry from the cross
(John 19.30) is often described as disappointing and contrasted
unfavourably with the drama created in the nearest equivalent in
his *St Matthew Passion*.[121] At the cry of dereliction in that work the
musical 'halo' round Christ that has been used throughout is
suddenly suspended.[122] Yet Bach is surely once more right.
A reader can halt to take in both the awfulness of Christ's death
and his triumph. The music, however, needs to give us space to do
so, and that is why Bach rightly forces a halt in death before
gradually building the Johannine cry into the triumph it really is
in the aria that follows.

There was also some sharing of Enlightenment values. As
I indicated earlier, there is a long-standing western tradition of
finding the divine within the harmony and proportions of music.
This was also a theme dear to the heart of Enlightenment, perhaps
in part because that theme so appealed to its mathematical and
scientific side. Leibniz, for example, illustrates his general theory
about the perfection of the created world from the way in which
dissonance in music, when ultimately resolved into consonance,
can generate a greater overall sense of harmony.[123] Here Bach
would have been in full agreement. It is important to note, however, that such conceptions go back much further through Luther
to the Church Fathers' sense of a divine harmony within the

---

[120] The piece is the soprano aria 'Ich folge dich' (no. 9) to a flute accompaniment. Peter's denial follows in nos 10 and 12.

[121] Earlier in this chapter I already used this same passage to illustrate a quite
different point.

[122] Elsewhere in this work it is only the words of Christ and not those of other
characters which are accompanied by strings.

[123] Quoted in Butt, 'A Mind Unconscious', 64. Charru and Theobald also think
Leibniz relevant, though they qualify this by introducing a mystic element: *L'Esprit
Créateur*, 52–4, 62.

universe as a whole.[124] The search for order, coherence and proportion were also part of the general musical ideal of the time, as can be seen from Bach's careful transcriptions of Vivaldi, whom Bach claimed 'taught him how to think musically'.[125] Such considerations may possibly explain why Bach so frequently revised his compositions. It was part of this 'quest for perfection', a perfection that would, so far as possible, reflect the divine perfection.[126] So it is perhaps not all that surprising that his most recent biographer closes a key chapter by observing that 'Bach's compositions, as the exceedingly careful musical elaborations that they are, may epitomise nothing less than the difficult task of finding for himself an argument for the existence of God—perhaps the ultimate goal of his musical science'.[127]

Such a comment will be anathema to all those who want everything Bach did to be the product of a simple faith that stands in sharp contrast to reason and natural religion. Among other indicators his attitude to musical 'parody' suggests quite otherwise.[128] Many a medieval mass setting is the product of just such a borrowing, of a song tune from a more secular context, and Bach proceeds similarly.[129] So, for example, the Christmas Cantata (no. 110) borrows from the French overture from his Fourth Orchestral Suite to set 'Let our mouth be full of laughter'. Again, the Christmas Oratorio utilizes music written to celebrate other, more human, royal birthdays.[130] Some want to make much of the fact that he never borrowed from the sacred to enhance secular compositions.[131] But I am not sure that

[124] Significantly, this is how one Swiss commentator on Bach chooses to open his discussion: J. Bouman, *Musik zur Ehre Gottes* (Basle: Brunnen, 2000), 11. Note that scientists like Kepler also maintained the view that music mirrored a wider harmony: Wolff, *Johann Sebastian Bach*, 7–8.

[125] Wolff, *Johann Sebastian Bach*, 170–2.

[126] Stressed in R. Stinson, *J. S. Bach's Great Eighteen Organ Chorales* (New York: Oxford University Press, 2001), 53.

[127] Wolff, *Johann Sebastian Bach*, 339.

[128] Here 'parody' merely has its technical music sense and has nothing to do with mocking an earlier application. The term was originally coined in the nineteenth century to identify the adaptation of the music of motet or chanson for the Ordinary of a mass, a procedure common in composers from Ockeghem to Palestrina.

[129] Such mass settings ended with Palestrina, but there are lots of examples from the late Middle Ages: e.g. Josquin's *Missa D'ung aultre amer*.

[130] For details, see R. A. Leaver, 'The Mature Vocal Works', in Butt (ed.), *Cambridge Companion to Bach*, 86–122, esp. 93, 96.

[131] Stapert, *My Only Comfort*, 40; Stiller, *Johann Sebastian Bach*, 225.

much can be made to hang on this fact, if for Bach all music was in fact seen as a reflection of the divine. As one commentator puts it, music was for him more discovery than invention.[132] So he was in a sense engaging in a natural theology of music, whatever he wrote. That is no doubt why he inscribed secular and sacred alike with 'Jesus help!' and 'To God alone be glory'.[133] Much, if not most, of the music thus 'discovered' was of course heavily overlaid with Christian belief. Yet in that it is surely not as vastly different from more conventional philosophy of religion as is commonly supposed. The God at the conclusion of the latter's arguments becomes quickly personalized in a way that is scarcely justified by those selfsame arguments.[134]

While Haydn and Mozart can be more securely placed within the context of the Enlightenment, it still makes good sense to see them as continuing the same general approach as we found in Bach despite the new focus on the concert hall. The strict symphonic structure continued to give listeners a sense of living in a divinely ordered world. Of course, one might protest that such confidence precludes key elements in the Christian faith, most notably the crucifixion. But it is one thing to talk of inherent limitations in such appeals to experienced order, quite another to deny its legitimacy altogether, and for that I can see no justification. In any case, neither Haydn nor Mozart showed such limitations. Even if their motivation had not been religious, there were good musical grounds for a broader approach. Order on its own can all too quickly become predictable and therefore boring. So, significantly, there was also a search for something else that anticipates the nineteenth century, the creation of the sublime in music, either through simple evocation of majestic power or else by contrast with something quite different.[135]

---

[132] Butt, 'A Mind Unconscious', 69. Not that music for Bach was ever a perfect reflection of the divine. Bach would have claimed only an approximation, in much the same way as Werckmeister finds in the impossibility of pure and perfect temperament an allegory for human imperfection: Chafe, *Analysing Bach Cantatas*, 24.

[133] J. J. (*Jesus iuva*); S. D. G. (*Soli deo gloria*): Butt, 'A Mind Unconscious', 52, 257 n. 26. Bach's practice, however, is not uniform. Equally, it should be noted that such ascriptions were also common among other contemporary composers.

[134] The impersonal God of Neo-Platonism or Hinduism might be just as fitting a conclusion for the cosmological and ontological arguments as the personal God of Christianity.

[135] Burke and Kant both write about the sublime, but it is only with one of Kant's followers, C. F. Michaelis, that one gets applications to music; so J. Webster, 'The

The effect can be seen in Haydn's oratorios and in some of his late symphonies. Think, for instance, of the opening of *The Creation* and the way in which through overture, recitative and chorus the listener's perceptions are turned from apparent chaos to the order generated by the creation of light, or again of the grandeur of the multipart chorus that concludes 'Spring' in the *Seasons*[136]. As an instrumental example the drum roll in Symphony No. 103 and the long, low-pitched notes in the slow passage that follow might be considered, not least because of the way in which it evokes a sense of awe and dread. The sublime is also there in the fugal coda to the final movement of Mozart's 'Jupiter' Symphony. Intriguingly, here too one finds overlap with the secular. The same type of contrasts that could produce sublimity might also be used to evoke humour.[137] One commentator on the Mozart passage finds a 'thunderbolt' from 'Jupiter himself'.[138] The symphony's nickname (not Mozart's own) of course justifies the comment, but used in our own day the application is perhaps deliberately intended to evoke the comic.[139] To my mind, however, the awe generated by such a sustained polyphonic conclusion emerging out of the seemingly simple classical starting point with which the symphony begins has all the necessary potential to draw the listeners' experience onto an altogether higher plane. The fact that this now happens in the concert hall rather than in church need not be seen as challenging that conclusion, nor was it so seen at the time. For the Romanticism that followed the Classical period the issue was how effectively this could be achieved. It is to such changes wrought to sensibility in the nineteenth century that I now turn.

Creation, Haydn's Late Vocal Music and the Musical Sublime', in E. Sisman (ed.), *Haydn and His World* (Princeton: Princeton University Press, 1997), 57–102, esp. 61–4.

[136] 'Ewiger, mächtiger, güttiger Gott' (no. 9).

[137] Webster gives as an example one of the late part-songs ('An die Frauen'), in which the beauty Daphne lacks is portrayed in music similar to 'The heavens are telling' in *The Creation*: 'The Creation', 78.

[138] E. Sisman, *Mozart: The Jupiter Symphony* (Cambridge: Cambridge University Press, 1993), 79. She offers a helpful general discussion of the sublime: 9–20.

[139] His contemporary, Johann Salomon, invented the nickname. In considering its significance one has to remember that in the eighteenth century 'Jupiter' was often a term for the Christian God and not simply a figure of myth or fun.

Beethoven and Schubert on Suffering

Over the course of the nineteenth century the order and harmony that is so integral to Classical music gradually yielded place to Romanticism. Partly because composers wanted to claim precedent in the work of such a major figure, until well into the twentieth century Beethoven was more often than not presented as falling on the Romantic half of the divide. That assumption was challenged by a number of historians in the earlier part of the twentieth century, and it is now more common to find him identified as essentially Classical in his approach.[140] There are factors pulling both ways. With Schubert, however, there has never been any doubt. Yet only a single year separates the two composers' deaths, and indeed they lie side by side in a Viennese churchyard.[141] So it will be interesting to compare how they approach a similar issue through their music. Beethoven suffered from the progressive advance of deafness; Schubert died young from syphilis. Both were religious, though not in the sense of Christian orthodoxy. Music was the vehicle they used, both to express and to explore the relevance of religious experience to their suffering. That more personal approach already puts the two of them more on the side of Romanticism. But where precisely Beethoven should be situated interests me here less than how in personal anguish the divine can be sought and found through music.

By 1800 Beethoven's decline into deafness could no longer be concealed.[142] Two years later he wrote a will, called the Heligenstadt Testament after the village in which it was composed. After declaring everything divided between his two brothers and speaking of only

---

[140] Most influential in bringing about the change were German and French scholars, particularly A. Schmitz, *Das romantische Beethovenbild* (Berlin: Dümmler, 1927) and J. Boyer, *Le 'Romantisme' de Beethoven* (Paris: Didier, 1938). The result can be seen in a standard introductory work such as S. Sadie and A. Latham, *The Cambridge Music Guide* (Cambridge: Cambridge University Press, 1985). Beethoven ends the chapter on 'The Classical Era' (261–80) and Schubert begins that on 'The Romantic Era' (281–99).

[141] Beethoven died in 1827, Schubert in 1828.

[142] Described in a letter of 1 June 1800 as already his condition for the two previous years: A. C. Kalischer (ed.), *Beethoven's Letters* (Dover: New York, 1972 edn). He speaks of himself 'at strife with nature and Creator': 17.

just having been saved from suicide, he nonetheless went on to affirm his continuing faith in God.[143] Further deterioration in his condition continued over the years, but it was not until 1816 that he needed an ear trumpet to hear and 1818 before he had to request for everything to be written down for him.[144] His music is often correspondingly demarcated according to these three stages of his life, with similar decisive changes detected in spirituality: an inaugural period that lasts till the first signs of his deafness in 1800, a middle period that culminates in the complete deafness of 1818, and a final period during which the only music he could hear was through his internal ear. As one writer puts it: 'in the first Beethoven saw the material world from the material standpoint; in the second he saw the material world from the spiritual standpoint; in the third he saw the spiritual world from the spiritual standpoint'.[145] If this is too sharp a contrast, there are undoubtedly changes to be observed. Certainly, it would be a mistake to find exact correspondences with his traumas over deafness, compounded as these were through lack of success in his emotional life. Nonetheless, it does seem true that in the middle period formal classical structures underwent significant modification, perhaps as a result of such unhappiness, and that this becomes more marked towards the end of his life.[146] Those alterations also went with an intensification of religious belief and expression.

For the Romantic Berlioz, Beethoven's Fifth Symphony of 1808 is the most justly celebrated of all his symphonies. Its first movement he describes as 'devoted to the expression of the disordered sentiments which pervade a great soul when a prey to despair'. As evidence he points to 'those chords in dialogue between wind and strings which come and go whilst gradually growing weaker, like the painful respiration of a dying man', only at last to give place to

---

[143] Ibid. 38–40.

[144] For progression and possible causes, see L. Lockwood, *Beethoven: The Music and the Life* (Norton: New York, 2003), 190–4. It is possible that his deafness was symptomatic of wider problems. The most recent theory argues from analysis of a surviving lock of Beethoven's hair that his death should be attributed to lead poisoning: R. Martin, *Beethoven's Hair* (London: Bloomsbury, 2000).

[145] M. M. Scott, *Beethoven* (London: Dent, 1934), 79.

[146] To his lack of success in relations with the opposite sex must be added the long struggle for control of his nephew, Karl, from 1815 onwards, out of which Beethoven does not emerge well: Lockwood, *Beethoven*, 355–8. In 1826 Karl attempted suicide.

'a phrase full of violence, in which the orchestra seems to rise
again reanimated by a spark of fury'. By contrast the Scherzo that
is the third movement is for him 'mysterious and sombre'.[147] But
that is not how the work ends. C minor becomes C major in a
gloriously triumphant sound, enhanced by a double bassoon, three
trombones, and a piccolo that announces 'darkness defeated by
light'.[148] Of course, much will depend on how the work is played.
Traditional performances allowed one to hear the triumph of good
over evil. As with the Third Symphony, however, modern performers are often embarrassed by the potential for bombast or what
is seen as the unduly heroic. As a consequence contemporary
conductors like Roger Norrington and John Eliot Gardiner
tend to perform at a speed that makes Beethoven's symphonies
more naturally classical in sound, whereas someone like Wilhelm
Furtwängler assumed that Beethoven would have authorized
flexibility of tempo and so would also have allowed a more mystical
feel to the music.[149] Certainly, Beethoven's contemporary, the
novelist and critic E. T. A. Hoffmann, found that for him the
Fifth Symphony 'unfolds Beethoven's romanticism more than any
of his other works and tears the listener irresistibly away into the
wonderful spiritual realm of the infinite'.[150]

Yet his more explicitly religious works of this time are much less
successful. The cantata *Christ on the Mount of Olives* (1803)[151] is
seldom performed these days, and one can see why. It is more like
melodrama than serious engagement with the Gospel narratives.
Although the introduction of a soprano Seraph might have added
to the sense of conflict for Christ, most of the devices employed

---

[147] H. Berlioz, *A Critical Study of Beethoven's Nine Symphonies* (Urbana, Ill.:
University of Illinois Press, 2000; 1st publ. 1862), 61, 62–3, 65.

[148] So Sadie and Latham, *The Cambridge Music Guide*, 270.

[149] Helpfully explored in C. Wilson, *Notes on Beethoven* (Edinburgh: Saint Andrew
Press, 2003), 31–6, 62–6. For the same issue applied to the Ninth, see N. Cook,
Beethoven: Symphony No. 9 (Cambridge: Cambridge University Press, 1993), 61–4.

[150] Hoffmann's review is translated in full in E. Forbes (ed.), *Beethoven Symphony
No. 5 in C Minor* (London: Chappell and Co., 1972), 150–63. If Edmund Burke can
be seen as an eighteenth-century anticipation, another contemporary who took the
same view was C. F. Michaelis: P. le Huray and J. Day, *Music and Aesthetics in the
Eighteenth and Nineteenth Centuries* (Cambridge: Cambridge University Press,
1981), 69–74, 286–92.

[151] The final version dates from 1811.

seem forced, such as when the demi-semiquaver is used to indicate fear.[152] The Mass in C Major is more convincing, and it is a fine touch to have the 'Dona nobis pacem' in the Agnus Dei at the end recapitulate the Kyries with which the work began. The mass does seem to have a more personal devotional quality lacking in the other work. Again, it was much praised by Hoffmann for its religious qualities.[153] Even so, it must not be supposed that such feelings equated with orthodox Catholicism. Some blame Beethoven's aloofness from conventional practice on the fact that he spent his earliest years in a corrupt ecclesiastical state.[154] Whether or not this is so, it is perhaps possible to detect a religious development that spans the three stages: from nominal belief through Enlightenment concern with nature to a more experientially based orientation which nonetheless continued to take seriously the Enlightenment's concern with other religions.

Although Beethoven's reference to a famous phrase of Kant's about 'the starry skies above me and the moral law within me' dates from 1820, a preoccupation with divine presence in nature is very much characteristic of his middle period. Heavily annotated is his copy of an 1811 work entitled *Reflections on the Works of God in Nature*, and he himself describes how inspiration for the second Razumovsky Quartet came to him while 'contemplating the starry sky and thinking of the music of the spheres'.[155] One might also note the extensive involvement of the composer with nature in the Sixth or 'Pastoral' Symphony. God is specifically introduced in the penultimate movement in a sketch note where Beethoven speaks of the need to thank God after the cessation of the storm.[156] Theologians often deride such religion. That seems to me a mistake. The stars were for the time a powerful symbol for transcendence, and that is no doubt why Beethoven was at ease in setting Schiller's poem to music in the finale of the Ninth

---

[152] At no. 8.

[153] Lockwood, *Beethoven*, 272–3.

[154] Scott, *Beethoven*, 13–14. Bonn was capital of the electorate and archdiocese of Cologne.

[155] M. Solomon, *Late Beethoven* (Berkeley: University of California Press, 2003), 52–7, esp. 54. It is the Adagio (the slow movement) of op. 59 that Beethoven has specifically in mind.

[156] Beethoven wrote 'Herr, wir danken Dir': Lockwood, *Beethoven*, 229.

Symphony where, significantly, God is once more located beyond the stars.[157] Yet such continued belief in transcendence in his later years also went with a strong sense of experiential immanence. In part this may have been due to the influence of the liberal Catholic theologian Johann Michael Salier, but also to his own wide reading in other religions. Hindu passages that spoke of divine omnipresence were noted down, and a framed copy of a pantheistic inscription to Isis was even placed on his desk.[158] The difference can be seen in three late works, his final symphony, the *Missa Solemnis* and the later quartets.

Particularly because of its final choral movement, the Ninth Symphony has found a home in a wide variety of contexts. Apart from use of part of the setting of Schiller's 'Ode to Joy' as the anthem for the European Union, it has also been played for Hitler's birthday and for the collapse of the Berlin Wall, for the infamous 1936 Olympic games no less than as the anthem for the two Germanies at those same games before the two states fully functioned as two separate entities.[159] Such diversity would seem to preclude any interpretation as final, but that is very far from conceding the absence of a religious meaning. When performed in certain ways, the music undoubtedly has the potential to convey a particular type of religious experience, what Romain Rolland characterized as the religious conviction of joy through suffering.[160] Here once more, many find Furtwängler best at suggesting this.[161] His freedom with metronome markings had already been anticipated in the nineteenth century by Wagner, who increasingly moved towards a religious interpretation. At the laying of the foundation stone at Bayreuth in 1872 Beethoven's Ninth was

---

[157] 'Such' ihn übern Sternenzelt! | Über Sternen muss er wohen' (Seek him beyond the curtain of the stars; he must dwell beyond them).

[158] Lockwood, *Beethoven*, 403–5; Solomon, *Late Beethoven*, 68–9, 173–8. After Beethoven's death, Salier was to become Bishop of Regensburg.

[159] E. Buch, *Beethoven's Ninth: A Political History* (Chicago: University of Chicago Press, 2003), 205, 209, 221, 260.

[160] R. Rolland, *Beethoven* (London: Kegan Paul, 1927; 1st publ. 1903), esp. 15, 42. For the French debate, see Buch, *Beethoven's Ninth*, 121, 169–70, 213–14.

[161] Called 'rapt, mystical religiosity' by Cook: *Beethoven: Symphony No. 9*, 64. Cook supports the conductor's freedom both on grounds of Beethoven's own practice and the presence of only occasional metronome markings in the composer's manuscript: 51, 64. The issue is complicated by the unreliability of the device in Beethoven's day and by uncertainty about how much of the subsequent music a particular indication was meant to control.

clearly treated as a precursor of Wagner's own *Parsifal*, as part of the 'ideal Divine Service' of which he had written two years earlier.[162] In trying to understand the music's power one might note the way in which the uncertainties of the first movement contrast with the crescendo of conviction that is at the heart of its choral finale.[163] The words move from a merely human brotherhood to a truly cosmic sense of unity. If the language is still of a god beyond the stars, it is also of a 'loving Father'. Admittedly, some have detected in elements of the accompanying music that message's own deconstruction. A case in point is the so-called 'Turkish music', where talk of the seraph standing with God is juxtaposed with 'absurd grunts' from bassoons and a bass drum.[164] But the intention is of course to contrast two realms, that of the seraph and the worm. The 'grunts' thus have a point, which is in any case a biblical one.[165]

In the same year as Beethoven completed the final version of his Ninth Symphony (1824), his *Missa Solemnis* was first performed in St Petersburg. Although it has sometimes been interpreted as having a Masonic text, it is really quite different from his earlier religious works despite its character as more oratorio than mass.[166] Composing for his friend the Archduke Rudolf's elevation as Archbishop of Olmütz, Beethoven clearly took great care to immerse himself in researching the precise meaning of the words and also the range of possibilities that the long history of such compositions opened up.[167] The result is a richly expressive and deeply moving work in which the music encourages the listener to hear in the words much more than dogma. Instead, there is a real

[162] Ibid. 51–2, 76–7.

[163] The 'uncertainties' lie in the key signature, which seems to vacillate between D minor and D major. For a discussion, see ibid. 30–1.

[164] Ibid. 103. For other possible examples, see ibid. 104, 107. In the Victorian period (and occasionally even today) English translations tended to be more explicitly Christian than the German warrants: e.g. G. Grove, *Beethoven and his Nine Symphonies* (London: Novello, 1896), 383.

[165] For man as worm, see e.g. Isa. 41.14; as grasshopper, Isa. 40.22.

[166] For a Masonic reading, see W. Mellers, *Beethoven and the Voice of God* (London: Faber and Faber, 1983), 295–300. In his last comments on the subject he describes the 'Incarnatus est' as 'Man made God': W. Mellers, *Celestial Music?* (Woodbridge, Suffolk: Boydell and Brewer, 2002), 118.

[167] Stressed in W. Drabkin, *Beethoven: Missa Solemnis* (Cambridge: Cambridge University Press, 1991), 4–5, 15, 20–1. As the work was too late for Archduke Rudolf's consecration, Beethoven had to re-advertise it as more like an oratorio, which it was in any case.

invitation to participate in the particular details of divine presence and action as they are enunciated. So, for example, in the Creed four distinct sections are identified through the repeated use of 'credo', with most focus inevitably given to Christ's life. That section opens with a flute's slow trill portraying the descent of the Spirit on Mary.[168] 'Sepultus', 'resurrexit' and 'ascendit' are also nicely integrated. The first and third are, as it were, at opposite extremes, while 'resurrexit' remains visionary with its suggestion of an observing choir of angels. Again, one might note the way in which trombones are used to evoke divine power, or a solo violin the presence of Christ on the altar.[169] But it is in the Agnus Dei that Beethoven becomes perhaps at his most personal. A long exchange of anxiety-laden pleas between male and female soloists appears to reach its climax and resolution in 'dona nobis pacem', only for that peace to be shattered by a drum roll evocative of the Napoleonic wars.[170] Yet peace is certainly the passage's final message as the last solitary drumbeat fades away. Beethoven inscribed his manuscript at this point with the words 'a prayer for inner and outer peace'.

In another work dedicated to Rudolf, the 'Hammerklavier' Sonata, some have also found religious overtones. The opening of the Adagio has been described as conjuring the approach to something sublime such as an altar, while the closing of the Allegro is taken to carry hints of a devout pilgrimage with its melodic echoes of a Bach-style chorale.[171] But it is to the late quartets that many now turn to find Beethoven's definitive view. In opus 132 one movement is given the title, 'Holy Song of Thanksgiving to God from one healed from sickness, in the Lydian mode'. There seems little doubt that this inscription was intended as a guide to the meaning of the whole. The revival of the ancient mode adds to its prayerful character.[172] More puzzling is opus 135, which has some strange written remarks on the manuscript. Its concluding comment probably alludes to the acceptance of purpose even in the

---

[168] The trill on the flute might have been intended to suggest a fluttering dove.

[169] Trombones occur at 'omnipotens' in the Gloria and at 'iudicare' in the Creed. The solo violin passage is in the Benedictus. Beethoven is of course not the first to use trombones in this way to evoke divine power.

[170] A shock that is augmented by a sudden, unexpected key change and by military-sounding trumpets.

[171] Solomon, *Late Beethoven*, 201, 203.

[172] Lockwood, *Beethoven*, 456–7, Solomon, *Late Beethoven*, 236–7.

face of suffering.[173] However, it is opus 130 that is to my mind the most profound.[174] It too was dedicated to Rudolf. In a striking departure from precedent, however, Beethoven marked the style of playing for its Cavatina in German as 'beklemmt', thereby indicating an almost physical 'sticky' oppressiveness to the movement's dark melancholy, which he admitted moved him to tears.[175] As finally published, the quartet now ends in a great celebratory rondo that recalls Haydn. While such a conclusion pleased his public, that was altogether too simple an answer for the composer, whose original thoughts were encapsulated in the Grosse Fuge that still survives. There we find numerous paths that appear to lead nowhere, only finally for all to come together in an unexpectedly coherent conclusion. Beethoven clearly abhorred easy answers. He struggled towards a conviction of divine grace in pain. That struggle, however, does not belittle its reality nor lessen the possibility that his music might provide access for his listeners to a similar experienced reality.

For Schubert Beethoven was one of his great heroes and indeed his hope was that he might be regarded as Beethoven's successor. In reality his talents were quite different. Schubert's range was altogether narrower, save in the field of song, where in retrospect he can now be seen as perhaps pre-eminent.[176] Like Beethoven, however, he did have to face the issue of suffering, and it is that aspect of his music that I want to explore here. Although the product of a devoutly religious home and one to which he returned on the first outbreak of his illness, he seems to have rebelled early, perhaps in part under the influence of his elder brother, Ignaz.[177] Even his first teenage mass setting omitted from the text of the Creed belief in the Church, and this was extended in later settings

---

[173] 'Es muss sein' (It must be) is easier to understand than 'Der schwer gefasste Entschluss' (the hard-won decision); for some options, see Lockwood, *Beethoven*, 481. Contrary to the way in which I have interpreted 'Es muss sein', some have even suggested that it was merely a matter of the need to pay some bill.

[174] Others might argue for op. 131.

[175] Solomon, *Late Beethoven*, 239.

[176] Schumann, Wolf and Strauss could all be said to build on his foundations.

[177] His father continued to write caring, if somewhat over-pious, letters to him throughout his life. Ignaz was a Mason and deist. In one recent study he is described as 'Ignatius der Unheilige' and contrasted with Franz's stress on 'die Unfassbarkeit und die Milde Gottes' (incomprehensibility and gentleness of God): V. Beci, *Franz Schubert: Fremd bin ich eingezogen* (Düsseldorf: Artemis und Winkler, 2003), 56–62.

to exclude resurrection of the dead.[178] Contempt for what he saw as superstition on the part of the clergy continued into adulthood.[179] Yet none of this should be mistaken for atheism or even agnosticism. Surprising as it may seem, some of these masses were performed in the churches of his own day. What must be reckoned with is the impact of the Enlightenment on at least some of the clergy. Immortality of the soul or more mystical notions of union were widely regarded as an acceptable substitute for what was seen as the crudely physical understanding of bodily resurrection.

A significant proportion of the songs Schubert wrote are in fact religious in theme. Some were specifically commissioned, many not. Nor did their Christian character or otherwise necessarily have anything to do with whether their source was in such a commission. Schubert seems to have especially liked Marian themes, though his 'Ave Maria' actually emerged out of the Romantic movement itself.[180] Its source lay in a series of songs derived from Sir Walter Scott's poem 'Lady of the Lake'. Romanticism no doubt is also behind a song of nostalgia for the lost immanence of the Greek gods.[181] Some want to treat his masses in similar vein.[182] But the common criticism that they are just jolly and lack any real depth is deeply unfair. If his innovations are not always successful, the later ones do at least try to engage with what might be described as the darker side of God: the awe as well as the reassurance.[183] A good example is the Mass in E Flat, written not long before his death.

---

[178] 'Genitum non factum' is also sometimes omitted, and even once 'ex Maria virgine'. For the Enlightenment context, see J. Reed, *Schubert* (Oxford: Oxford University Press, 1997 edn), 40; L. Black, *Franz Schubert: Music and Belief* (Woodbridge, Suffolk: Boydell and Brewer, 2003), 4–5, 41.

[179] His letter of 29 Oct. 1818 to his brother Ignaz is a good example. But contrast this with his prayer of 8 May 1823. Both are available in M. Korff, *Franz Schubert* (Munich: Deutscher Taschenbuch, 2003), 64, 110.

[180] He wrote five Salve Reginas. His famous 'Ave Maria' was originally part of the song cycle *Ellens Gesänge* (no. 3).

[181] His setting of Schiller's 'Die Götter Griechenlands'.

[182] Reflecting on the Mass in E Minor, one commentator observes that Schubert 'served the cause of the gods rather better than God': M. Rowlinson, *Schubert* (London: Everyman, 1997), 141.

[183] In the E flat Mass the return to the music of the 'incarnatus est' after the crucifixion is often criticized. Arguing against the legitimacy of such a return is Christianity's stress on historicity and thus on uniqueness. In favour, however, is the way this helps to underline the significance of Christ's presence in the mass.

The Romantic obsession with the inevitability of death as a way of helping to define the significance of life entailed that Schubert was already setting poems of this kind to music long before the onset of his illness in 1822.[184] However, there is a depth to what comes thereafter that is unmatched by his earlier writing, and which seems most readily explicable in terms of interaction between his musical gifts and the now more personalized character of that on which he was reflecting. So, although his 'Tragic' or Fourth Symphony dates from 1816, the Eighth or 'Unfinished' of 1823 is in quite a different league. Whereas its second movement is brightly optimistic, the first is dark and sombre but also very beautiful, which is no doubt why this work remains the most popular of all Schubert's instrumental music. A low-pitched, ominous opening leads into a rustle of strings over which can be heard oboe and clarinet playing in unison in B minor before the cellos introduce a D major melody. The music has a yearning or longing quality that makes the second movement seem the natural conclusion it was never intended to be. Of course, one could read the resolution in purely human terms, but the pressures that lead commentators to speak of 'cosmic despair' in the first movement[185] are precisely those that make the ear hear supernatural consolation in the second.

If that sounds as though Schubert might be proceeding along paths similar to Beethoven, his song cycle of the same year, *Die schöne Müllerin*, tells a quite different tale. It was adapted from a series of poems by the Prussian poet Wilhelm Müller (1794–1827). Müller's somewhat distant reflections are completely integrated into the composer's own consciousness in a way that gives them a real universality for the listener. In theory it is a simple story of the love of a young miller for the 'fair maid of the mill'. The miller's apparent success is, however, in fact challenged by a rival and so eventually yields to the realization that love is really only completely fulfilled in death.[186] That at any rate seems to be the message of the final song. But the cycle is about more than doomed innocence.

---

[184] Reed, *Schubert*, 53 with examples. Some recent writers have suggested a homosexual source for the infection, but there is no real evidence to substantiate this claim. For the argument, see M. Solomon, 'Franz Schubert and the Peacocks of Benvenuto Cellini', *Nineteenth-Century Music* 12 (1989), 193–206; L. Kramer, *Franz Schubert: Sexuality, Subjectivity, Song* (Cambridge: Cambridge University Press, 1998).

[185] The phrase is Reed's: *Schubert*, 89.

[186] Contrast 'Mein' with 'Trockne Blumen'.

There is also reflection on how far disillusion springs in any case from the way the world is and how much from our own lack of appropriate internal resources.[187]

Not that Schubert was cast into a mood of permanent sorrow as a result of his disease. Joyous music as well as late parties continued. His long 'Great' (C Major) Symphony of 1825 has been read in various ways. Certainly it is not sad, and quite a few have found in it a joyous celebration of divine presence in nature.[188] More relevant to our theme of response to suffering is his stark song cycle *Die Winterreise*. Here in effect it is the composer's own death that is being faced, as he sets to music another cycle of poems, once more written by Wilhelm Müller. Their nominal theme is an individual setting out on a journey, as he seeks to come to terms with rejection in love. Schubert, however, deepens their meaning, and makes the issue much more than just the typical Romantic exaggerated despair and longing for death. After a number of tempestuous and troubled songs, with the last three there seems a real attempt to face impending death. A song about courage in the absence of the gods leads into a mysterious vision of three suns,[189] with the final song then a bleak musical meditation on a lonely hurdy-gurdy player working on the edge of town. Not once is there any reference whatsoever to the Christian God or to heaven. Yet, despite some who wish to speak of a decline in faith or even atheism, there is rather more than just the mere acceptance of the inevitable.[190] It is more like an achieved, if somewhat bleak, serenity in the face of suffering and death. Of course, much will again depend on performance and interpretation. Dietrich Fischer-Dieskau, for example, paced the last song more slowly in later life than he did earlier in his career, and so succeeds in stressing that acceptance.[191] Again, Ian Bostridge speaks

---

[187] Jealousy of the hunter pulls in one direction, the associations of the colour green (in 'Die Liebe Farbe') in another.

[188] For some of the possibilities, see Black, *Franz Schubert*, 125–44.

[189] Based on the phenomenon known as parhelia, when two phantom suns are seen either side of the real one.

[190] Schubert's *Notebook* for 1824 indicates a sensitive man for whom faith is still central: Rowlinson, *Schubert*, 96. Black seems to me quite wrong to dismiss *Winterreise* as of no relevance save as indicative of a decline in belief: *Franz Schubert*, 191, 194.

[191] Contrast the Deutsche Grammophon 1979 recording (Barenboim accompanying) with the EMI 1955 one (with Gerald Moore).

of a 'religious aura', particularly in respect of the suns' song.[192] That would seem confirmed by the fact that about the same time Schubert was writing his last mass, which has a mystery and solemnity about it that the earlier ones lack.[193]

This is not to say that *Winterreise* is really Christianity in disguise. It is not. Where, though, it does address Christianity, it seems to me, is in the often too glib appeals of Christians to resurrection and life after death. Schubert seems to be saying that even where life is bleak and one feels thrown onto the edge of things like the hurdy-gurdy player, acceptance of one's destiny is important: perseverance whatever the future may bring. To look only to the promised marvellous coda to our lives for closer intimacy with God is to forget that this life too has had its value and its integrity, even if there is nothing beyond, and for that we should be accepting, even grateful. Thus, although the message is significantly different from Beethoven's, where the value of an afterlife is clearly affirmed, it is not simply a case of being forced to choose between the two. Both composers can speak of life graced through suffering. While Beethoven points to a resolution that may not occur till beyond the grave, Schubert stresses the value of what has already been received, however stark that may appear.

Searching for Meaning in Mahler and Bruckner

That learning how to bear suffering from the fringes of faith that Beethoven and Schubert so beautifully illustrate will be a debt that some Christians may be reluctant to concede. It is, however, a pattern of learning that, I believe, repeats itself once more in an interesting way in the later history of Romanticism. In trying to comprehend how experience of God might be facilitated through music the work of Anton Bruckner and Gustav Mahler provides an interesting point of comparison and contrast. Both are late nineteenth-century Romantic composers with a not dissimilar reception history. But whereas one (Bruckner) was a deeply devout and orthodox Roman Catholic, the other (Mahler), although received into the Catholic Church, stood much more on the margins of that faith, and indeed of any specific faith at all. That being so, it might be thought self-evident

[192] When interviewed in the BBC DVD version (2000).
[193] The Mass in E Flat, with its mysterious opening Kyrie, majestic Gloria, and dramatic symbolism in the Creed.

that Bruckner is the more obvious choice, if opportunities for religious experience are to present themselves. In the case of Beethoven and Schubert I have already suggested that matters are not necessarily that simple. Here I want to carry that observation a stage further by noting how, even when a composer of explicit faith is available, a more complicated dynamic may be more appropriate.

The increased esteem in which the two composers are now held a century after their deaths may be illustrated by successive editions of one standard work of reference. Percy Scholes' *Oxford Companion to Music* was first published in 1938 and was still being reprinted in the early 1980s. 1983, however, saw its replacement by the so-called *New Companion*, edited by Denis Arnold. Whereas in the former Mahler and Bruckner receive only brief mention, in the latter both are given extensive coverage, though Mahler more so than Bruckner.[194] Such differences not only reflect changes in the esteem with which the two composers had come to be regarded, but also, so far as their relative fortunes are concerned, the fact that Mahler is still thought of as the more obviously accessible of the two, as well as the more significant historically.[195]

Mahler (who died of a heart condition at the age of 51 in 1911) is undoubtedly much nearer to where most westerners now stand on the question of faith. A convert to Catholicism from Judaism for perhaps largely pragmatic reasons (it advanced his career in imperial Vienna), he was nonetheless profoundly religious.[196] As a child he was known for his capacity to sit quietly meditating for hours at a stretch.[197] While he sang in both Jewish and Christian places of worship, he felt himself an outsider: 'How I long once again to hear the sound of the organ and the peal of the bells. A breeze as of heavenly wings flows through me when I see the peasants in their finery at church. . . . Ah it is long since there was any altar left for me: only, mute and high, God's temple arches over me, the wide

[194] D. Arnold (ed.), *The New Oxford Companion to Music* (Oxford: Oxford University Press, 1983). Instead of a brief paragraph for each, Bruckner's entry now extends over two pages (277–8), and Mahler's over no fewer than four (1118–21).
[195] Bruckner was without significant influence on later composers, whereas the influence of Mahler can be seen in Schoenberg, Berg and Webern among others.
[196] He formally converted in 1897 just before his appointment as Conductor and Artistic Director of the Court Opera at Vienna.
[197] *Selected Letters of Gustav Mahler*, ed. K. Martner (London: Faber and Faber, 1979), 25–6.

sky. . . . Instead of chorales and hymns it is thunder that roars, and instead of candles it is light that flickers.'[198] If that suggests nature mysticism, Mahler, though never a dogmatist, was rather more of a searcher than these words would appear to imply, as his music clearly indicates.

Mahler talks of music enabling us 'to rise once again to Heaven' as we seek 'to reach God and his angels . . . on the soaring bridge of music that joins this world and the hereafter'.[199] Although he later abandoned the practice, for his earlier symphonies he actually offered specific programmatic accounts as guides to their meaning. What these suggest is that he saw their composition as an essential part of this search for a meaning to life. So, for example, for his Second Symphony, the so-called 'Resurrection' Symphony, no less than three slightly variant programmes exist. According to these the first movement was intended to depict life as a titanic struggle, the next three as more an interlude or dream, and thereafter resolution in the final movement through faith in the future.[200] Mahler's spirit was very much in flux and restless. There is considerable conflict and development within each of his symphonies. Also, with the appearance of each new symphony, the pendulum seems to swing just as decisively in the opposite direction. Two neighbouring symphonies will be found to evince equally strong expressions of, if not actually opposed, then not easily reconcilable, positions. Thus, for example, in contrast to the Second Symphony the First had been focused on a single hero engaged in Promethean conflict, whereas the Third is a sort of pantheistic meditation. As one of his early advocates, Bruno Walter, puts it, 'when he had won the answer for himself, the old question soon raised its unassuageable call of longing in him anew. He could not—such was his nature—hold fast to any achieved spiritual position.'[201]

While this places the stress on the purely human side of the equation, for Mahler that was by no means all there was. He firmly

---

[198] Ibid. 58. For Mahler's singing and playing for both faiths from an early age, see P. Franklin, *The Life of Mahler* (Cambridge: Cambridge University Press, 1997), 10–11, 20.

[199] Quoted in Franklin, *The Life of Mahler*, 88.

[200] The three accounts are given in full in D. Mitchell and A. Nicholson (eds), *The Mahler Companion* (Oxford: Oxford University Press, 1999), 123–5. Note how the final one ends: 'an almighty feeling of love illumines us with blessed knowing and being'.

[201] B. Walter, *Gustav Mahler* (New York: Greystone Press, 1941), 129.

believed that music could bring with it disclosure of the divine. Theodor Adorno uses the phrase *Durchbruck* ('breakthrough') as a key theme in his analysis of Mahler's music.[202] While that might suggest once more a purely human achievement, this was not so even for Adorno, who spoke of an 'Other' breaking in. But for Adorno it remained an Other of this world, whereas there is good reason to believe that Mahler's fellow-composer Arnold Schoenberg was nearer the truth in speaking of a 'mystic revelation' for Mahler that involved the transcendent.[203] Certainly, in a letter to his wife, Alma, describing his Eighth Symphony Mahler speaks of the 'intransitory behind all appearance . . . which draws us by its mystic force', while in the creation of the Second he even speaks of 'conceiving by the Holy Ghost'.[204] Particularly intriguing to observe is how one commentator in seeking to introduce Mahler's attitudes to his work resorts to Heidegger and his use of *Freundlichkeit* to translate *charis* (the Greek for grace). For Heidegger poetry is a matter of the 'appeal of the measure to the heart in such a way that the heart turns to give heed to the measure'; in other words composer and listener alike find themselves responding to a kindness, a grace, already given.[205] Yet Mahler is equally insistent that acceptance of such a dimension should not be taken to mean that his music can be tied down too specifically. Indeed, in rejecting his earlier programmatic approach, he draws a parallel with the inadequacy of all revealed religions, in their 'flattening and coarsening' of the divine, in pressing towards too much detail.[206]

Among the most frequently performed today of all Mahler's works is his *Das Lied von der Erde (Song of the Earth),* in which a series of oriental songs is used to express resignation before death. It is here that he comes closest to the ideas of a philosopher whom he greatly admired, those of Arthur Schopenhauer in *The World as Will and Representation.*[207] Happiness can only come through suppression of

---

[202] T. Adorno, *Mahler: A Musical Physiognomy* (Chicago: University of Chicago Press, 1992).

[203] Franklin, *The Life of Mahler,* 7, 135.

[204] First quotation in Mitchell and Nicholson (eds), *The Mahler Companion,* 5; second ibid. 88.

[205] Nicholson, in his 'Introduction', ibid. 4. The quotation comes from M. Heidegger, *Poetry, Language and Thought* (New York: Harper and Row, 1975), 229.

[206] Quoted in Mitchell and Nicholson (eds), *The Mahler Companion,* 95.

[207] Stressed in the opening page of S. E. Hefling, *Mahler: Das Lied von der Erde* (Cambridge: Cambridge University Press, 2000), 1.

the egoistic will, as this is achieved particularly in Buddhism and in some forms of aesthetic contemplation. Yet resignation is perhaps not quite the right word. As one detailed analysis of the work suggests, Mahler does much more than simply set the German translation of the Chinese texts to music. It is adapted, personalized, and given a specific context within eastern religious ritual through the use of specific instruments and scales.[208] The result is 'a luminous dissolution', 'an ecstatic acceptance of the radiant void, the promise of the continuity of the earth, which transcends mortality'.[209] The music helps to suggest this by the free structures that follow the rigours of the last march and the repeated final *ewig* ('eternal') that gradually fades into silence.[210] Not only was Benjamin Britten quite overwhelmed as a young man by the way in which the work ends, he also unhesitatingly draws on religious language to describe his own experience of the work. He talks of Mahler painting 'serenity literally supernatural . . . that final chord is printed on the atmosphere . . . At the moment I can do no more than bask in its Heavenly light.'[211]

Das Lied von der Erde, however, had been immediately preceded by his Eighth Symphony or *Symphony of a Thousand* (so called because of the number of performers required). There, as if to confirm his oscillating spirit, there is no such quiet resignation, but a powerful assertion of how all will be resolved positively. Human restless searching will find its completion in the overcoming of death, with all caught up into the purposes of the divine which is Love. Intriguingly, to advocate that message Mahler combines a medieval hymn dedicated to the Holy Spirit with a

---

[208] D. Mitchell, *Songs and Symphonies of Life and Death* (Woodbridge, Suffolk: Boydell Press, 1985), 355. The pentatonic scale without semitones is used. Although also found in western folk music, this is characteristic of much eastern music. Again, the arresting stroke on the tam-tam during the final song suggests eastern ritual. For the two figures in the final song personalized as a single reflection on the composer himself, see Mitchell, *Songs and Symphonies*, 431; Hefling, *Mohler*, 113–14 (where a comparison is drawn with the lovers in *Tristan und Isolde* dissolving into a single unity with one another).

[209] Mitchell, *Songs and Symphonies*, 346. Hefling is much more hesitant: 'a work of uncertainty, it stops at the moment of liminal transition, and ventures only an inkling of what is beyond' (*Mahler*, 80).

[210] For *ewig*, see Mitchell, *Songs and Symphonies*, 347; for the finale's contrast with the funeral march, 362. Mitchell talks of the march expressing death, and the free alternative 'liberation from death'.

[211] Quoted ibid. 339–40.

setting of the conclusion of the German language's most influential
poem, Goethe's *Faust*, in which the Protestant Goethe had used the
feminine and in particular the Virgin Mary as a symbol for the
divine. Some have found the combination 'an absurdity...both
theologically and poetically'; others, more charitably, have spoken
of the symphony as a matter of the two elements combining to
produce 'a celebration of God the creator and the creative spirit in
man'.[212] Certainly, there is a radiant confidence in the music,
particularly in Mahler's use of his celestial key of E, which sets it
firmly apart from the very different colours of *Das Lied von der
Erde*.[213] But, however put, we are still a long way from Christian
orthodoxy, Catholic or Protestant. It is joy without judgement, a
pattern that had already emerged in his earlier Resurrection
Symphony.[214] For some that may raise questions about whether
Mahler's music could ever conceivably convey experiences of the
Christian God. Before attempting an answer I want first to turn to
his more devout contemporary, Anton Bruckner.

If Mahler had some obvious signs of success during his short
life (he transformed the performance of opera in imperial Vienna),
and he was also to win some appreciation for his own compositions
relatively quickly, Bruckner had more of an uphill struggle. His
contemporary Hanslick constantly complained of his 'dream-
disturbed, cat's misery style', a disagreement that was intensified by
Hanslick's personal dislike of any music that went beyond a purely
formal approach.[215] Even in his religious music Bruckner won only
limited approval. If his treatment of the resurrection clause in the
creed is quite often the high point within his masses, only the Mass
in E Minor met the exacting standards of the Cecilian Movement,

---

[212] For the former, see John Williamson, 'The Eighth Symphony', in Mitchell
and Nicholson (eds), *The Mahler Companion*, 407–21, esp. 411; for the latter, Mitchell,
Songs and Symphonies, 574.

[213] Mitchell, *Songs and Symphonies*, 526, 576. Both E major and E minor are
employed, as in the Fourth Symphony's Adagio movement.

[214] Mitchell and Nicholson (eds), *The Mahler Companion*, 120–1.

[215] Hanslick's description in this case is of the Eighth Symphony: D. Watson,
Bruckner, 2nd edn (Oxford: Oxford University Press, 1996), 41. In his *Vom Musica-
lisch-Schönen* Hanslick saw beauty as a matter of the structure of sounds, having
nothing at all to do with events or ideas: P. Barford, *Bruckner's Symphonies* (London:
Ariel Music, 1986), 32.

which was at the time campaigning for unaccompanied mass settings.[216]

But there is also the greater difficulty in any case of Bruckner's intended message in his symphonies. If there are some obvious helpful recurring features, and quotations from his religious music help to focus the listener's attention, what has been called their 'vast cathedral space' militates against any easy comprehension.[217] In the first fifty bars of the opening of the Fifth Symphony, for instance, the architectural space is employed merely to generate a series of huge harmonic contradictions that must await future resolution.[218] Yet, all that complexity also seems to refuse complete resolution. Light eventually dominates over darkness but it does not exclude it. What we are offered is light in the midst of darkness, or, to quote an antiphon suggested by one commentator, 'in the midst of life we are in death'.[219] It has been suggested that such an approach may unconsciously reveal an element of profound doubt even within the apparent firmness of Bruckner's faith. More likely, it is simply Bruckner's attempt to reflect the way the world is.[220] Faith works within the contours of a world where not all is clear, and so faith and uncertainty sometimes go hand in hand and not always in opposition.[221]

That Bruckner intended his symphonies to draw others into an experience of God can hardly be challenged. This was especially

---

[216] For details of the conflict, see Watson, *Bruckner*, 90–3. It is also dicussed in my *God and Mystery in Words*, ch. 6.

[217] For the quotation, see Barford, *Bruckner's Symphonies*, 53. Recurring features include a quiet opening, pauses, and what has been called 'the Bruckner rhythm': Watson, *Bruckner*, 65, 67. The pauses may reflect his organ playing, and the way in which organists must sometimes wait, particularly after massive chords, until the echo in the church subsides: Barford, *Bruckner's Symphonies*, 9. Quotations from his masses are found in symphonies 0, 2, 3 and 9 and from his *Te Deum* in no. 7.

[218] Barford's example: see *Bruckner's Symphonies*, 45.

[219] D. B. Scott, 'Bruckner's Symphonies — A Reinterpretation: The Dialectic of Darkness and Light', in J. Williamson (ed.), *Cambridge Companion to Bruckner* (Cambridge: Cambridge University Press, 2004), 92–107, esp. 93.

[220] See Scott's analysis of the way in which there is no final victory for light in the Adagio of the Seventh Symphony: ibid. 106.

[221] That is why I disagree with Wilfrid Mellers' view that symphonic form is essentially 'geared not to faith but to strife', and so with his claim that Bruckner found himself caught between the certainty of the faith he espoused and the musical form within which he was expected to express himself: 'Mahler and the Great Tradition: Then and Now', in Mitchell and Nicholson (eds), *The Mahler Companion*, 566.

true of his Adagios. By the late nineteenth century there was already a strong tradition of seeing the potential of that particular type of movement for opening up the possibility of religious experience. Earlier in the century Kant's theories on the sublime had been applied to music, and Beethoven and Wagner were now being quoted as offering suitable examples.[222] In particular, there was the slow movement of Beethoven's Ninth Symphony and the Cavatina of his opus 130 String Quartet, while Wagner's advocates quoted his ideal of *unendliche Melodie*. It is here that Bruckner's general technique came precisely into its own, with structures that offer no definitive closure.[223]

That is not of course to say that only the Adagio was relevant. If the Seventh is perhaps the most accessible in understanding structure, it is the 'Apocalyptic' or Eighth that best reveals Bruckner's underlying religious motivation.[224] Listening to the third movement (the Adagio), one hears what must be reckoned among the greatest musical descriptions of the transcendent or sublime ever written. 'The all-loving Father of humanity is given to us in his entire, incalculable Grace', wrote the author of the programme notes for its first performance in 1892.[225] But, if that is Bruckner's response to threatening elements in the preceding movements, the final movement that follows by no means brings everything to a complete resolution, as Mahler's music might have done, with the negative quite dislodged. It is the calm of faith but with darkness and evil still present and acknowledged, a calm that is achieved by something other than a purely human struggle. The end 'blazes with calm', but emerges as its own 'unveiling' rather than as part of the music's syntax and progression, although it might have done.[226]

---

[222] For details of the theoretical background, see B. J. Korstvedt, *Bruckner: Symphony No. 8* (Cambridge: Cambridge University Press, 2000), 55–9.

[223] For a very helpful analysis, see M. Notley, 'Formal Process as Spiritual Progress: The Symphonic Slow Movements', in Williamson (ed.), *Cambridge Companion to Bruckner*, 190–204. The intention to evoke 'religious experience' (e.g. 190) is treated seriously.

[224] Unlike other nicknames quoted in the text, this is not a uniform usage. Nonetheless, it seems to me highly apposite.

[225] Less plausible is his analysis as a whole, or indeed Bruckner's own suggestions (an implausible analogy with *Tannhäuser* is drawn, probably in order to please the conductor): Korstvedt, *Bruckner: Symphony No. 8*, 49–51, esp. 50.

[226] Korstvedt's telling analysis: see ibid. 48–9. Bruckner uses a plagal cadence (from subdominant directly to tonic), avoiding a decisive perfect cadence (dominant

In making such comparisons with Mahler my point is certainly not that Bruckner was profoundly influenced by the other composer and develops his work further in the right direction. Bruckner was in fact much the older man (he had died in 1896 aged 72 when Mahler was still in his thirties). Indeed, in so far as note should be taken of any earlier composer, it is to the influence of Wagner that we should turn.[227] Nonetheless, it has been the experience of many that Bruckner is most easily approached through Mahler, that a love of Mahler's music helps with comprehension of Bruckner's work. That, I suggest, applies in two ways, particularly in our modern context. First, as noted earlier, although Mahler is usually more complex in form, harmony and orchestration and is also the more atonal of the two, precisely because of his influence on later composers he now sounds closer to us. Secondly, although it is totally unfair to present Bruckner as espousing in his music a simple, uncomplicated faith, Mahler certainly more accurately reflects the restlessness of modern religious belief. So even for committed Christians like myself access to Bruckner has come through growing appreciation of Mahler, and that despite the fact that it is Bruckner who more accurately expresses the Christian vision. Even some professional musicians have felt the same.[228]

In saying this I am of course conceding that religious experience through Bruckner's music must therefore come for many through prior exposure and acclimatization to a less orthodox context. That, however, is in fact a point that might be more generally applied, even to biblical revelation itself. Nowadays Christian preachers love to quote the later chapters of Isaiah with their magnificent descriptions of the universal God of all creation. Little thought is given to the pagan Cyrus, who is also assigned a divine role within the compass of that book's pages. What I want to suggest is that Cyrus may have been no less indispensable to the vision of Isaiah than is Mahler in helping

directly to tonic) or even an 'authentic' cadence (from subdominant to dominant and then tonic).

[227] He dedicated his Second Symphony to Wagner, and put Wagnerian quotations into the original version of the Third. But as Watson notes, the extent of this influence is often exaggerated: see *Bruckner*, 64–5.

[228] Stravinsky finds Mahler easily accessible and only reluctantly concedes the 'truly inspired' character of the Adagio of Bruckner's Ninth: I. Stravinsky and R. Craft, *Memories and Commentaries* (London: Faber and Faber, 2002), 57–8, 63.

those of us who are Christians towards a proper appreciation of Bruckner.

To expand. The first 39 chapters of the book of Isaiah record the activities of a prophet working in Judah in the eighth century BC. Beginning, however, with chapter 40 we find a ministry that is more naturally set in a quite different context, and so the prophet of this time is commonly referred to as Deutero- or Second Isaiah. His concern is to reassure the now exiled community that God has not abandoned them, and that his purposes for the nation will still find fulfilment through them in due course. He especially finds hope in the fact that their erstwhile conqueror, Babylon, has overstretched itself, and is in his view about to succumb to a new empire, that of the Persians under Cyrus, who is explicitly declared to have been 'anointed' by God for the work in question (44.28–45.1). Given the uncertain situation Second Isaiah displays great bravery in declaring to his fellow-Jews that, despite attempts by the Babylonian king, Nabonidus, to ward off the threat, Cyrus will nonetheless prevail, and bring them great benefit. Fortunately for the prophet events did turn out as he had predicted.

Cyrus' tolerance of other religions was in fact in marked contrast to how Nabonidus had behaved. Nabonidus had even replaced the state cult of Marduk with that of his own favoured god.[229] By contrast Cyrus not only restored to the Babylonians the previous status quo for their god Marduk but also gave freedom of religion to all the peoples over whom they had ruled, including the Jews.[230] The sad side of that tolerance, however, was that, while Second Isaiah welcomed it, he nonetheless appears to have thought of Cyrus as a mere passive instrument in the hands of his own God who would eventually allow the Jews to dominate over other cultures as vassals in their turn (e.g. 43.3–4, 45.25). Indeed, little sympathy is shown for the resultant sufferings of the Babylonians among whom he lived (ch. 47). Yet, ironically, Second Isaiah's great visions of God as universal creator may have been something that the prophet had subconsciously learned from the monotheistic Persians.[231] Certainly up to that time the Jews had characteristically

[229] By a strange quirk of language, actually called 'Sin'.

[230] For an excellent, accessible portrait of Cyrus, see T. Holland, *Persian Fire* (London: Abacus, 2005), 9–20.

[231] These days it is the dualistic character of Zoroastrianism that tends to be better known, with the world seen as a battleground between good and evil on the

failed to raise the question of whether their own God was unique rather than just one god among many but with a particular concern for their own nation. So, however powerful and inspiring Deutero-Isaiah's vision undoubtedly is, probably he owed far more to Cyrus than he would ever have been willing to concede.

The debt of Judaism, and thereafter of Christianity, to the 'pagan' (or Zoroastrian) Cyrus is thus in all likelihood far more extensive than is commonly acknowledged. In a similar way, then, it might be possible to speak of Mahler. Neither Cyrus nor Mahler was merely transitional, as though, once the new position was reached, any permanent significance could be dispensed with. Just as the breadth of Cyrus' tolerance reminds us of the limitations of Isaiah's vision despite Cyrus' faults in other directions, so Mahler's music remains great religious music, whatever the limitations of its doc-trinal content. Indeed that content may itself continue to challenge the contemporary Christian. So, for example, it would be easy to assert that there is nothing of divine grace in Mahler, with every-thing left to human striving. Yet, balancing Goethe in the Eighth Symphony, there is that preceding evocation of the Holy Spirit. So it is possible to hear in the work a transformation rather than simple acceptance of Goethe's intentions. Similarly, Cyrus' edict of tolera-tion had a breadth of vision that Judaism at the time lacked, and which failed even to find a proper echo in Isaiah himself. Religious experience is thus not about discovering everything about the divine at once, but rather the gradual unfolding of what remains essentially a mystery. So, particularly for those who feel themselves alienated from any larger reality, it is sometimes necessary to hear the warmth of divine acceptance that so characterizes Mahler's music before one is in a position to accept the awe and judgement that is so central to Bruckner's mediation of the divine. The final movement of Bruckner's last (uncompleted) symphony contains what is perhaps the greatest dissonant chord of the nineteenth century (a chord of ten consecutive semitones) before it launches into a quotation of the Kyrie from one of his earlier masses that is succeeded in its turn by a gentler message.[232] Judgement and grace have seldom been better juxtaposed. But to insist that Bruckner

---

supernatural as well as the natural plane. But its monotheistic credentials are also not in doubt. Ahura Mazda is sole creator of heaven and earth.

[232] All in the Adagio of his Ninth Symphony.

rather than Mahler is the only way to hear God would be to confuse
the whole truth with the capacity of us all to learn only by degrees.

Innovation and Tradition in Schoenberg and Stravinsky

Mahler, unlike Bruckner, survived into the twentieth century. That
century is often portrayed as antithetical to religion and also,
more generally, to whatever builds on the past. Certainly, in the
industrialized world there has been a marked decline in church
attendance. Some have seen the arts taking over at least some
of the roles once exercised by religion. However, in this volume's
predecessor and elsewhere I have sought to emphasize how much
the visual arts have continued to engage with religious issues, and
in this respect music seems to me no different.[233] Indeed, if we take
the two composers who are often treated as most representative
of trends in the twentieth century, Schoenberg and Stravinsky, it is
true of them both that religion played a large part in their approach
to composition. Nor is it the case that their innovations were seen
by either of them as operating within a vacuum. Rather, both
stressed the dynamic possibilities for originality within a developing
tradition. That provides, I believe, valuable added support to my
detailed arguments in some earlier work as to how Christianity
should view its own changing imaginative and doctrinal content, if
it is ever to find appropriate resources with which to speak afresh in
new contexts.[234]

Arnold Schoenberg (1874–1951) was the son of a freethinking
father and an Orthodox Jewish mother. Although he went through
a period of non-belief and also was a Lutheran, his formal reception
back into the Jewish faith reflects a commitment that in effect spans
almost all of his adult life.[235] Even in his Lutheran period his main
interest was in the Hebrew scriptures.[236] More marked was his move

---

[233] In my *God and Enchantment of Place*, 136–50, and 'The Incarnation in
Twentieth-Century Art', in S. T. Davis, D. Kendall and G. O'Collins (eds),
The Incarnation (Oxford: Oxford University Press, 2002), 332–72.

[234] *Tradition and Imagination; Discipleship and Imagination.*

[235] He was officially a Lutheran from 1898 till 1933. That his Lutheranism
was more about 'spiritual thirst' than specifically Christianity is stressed in
A. L. Ringer, *Arnold Schoenberg: The Composer as Jew* (Oxford: Clarendon Press,
1990), 7–8, 26.

[236] His most important earlier religious work, *Die Jacobsleiter (Jacob's Ladder)*,
dates from 1917.

from German nationalism to Zionism.[237] Before his expulsion from Nazi Germany he had spoken confidently of the 'hegemony of German music'. As an accomplished painter he had exhibited in 1911 with the group known as Der Blaue Reiter.[238] His music prior to this time was also deeply expressionist, exploring as it were the inner soul. That can be observed particularly in his huge choral work *Gurrelieder*, which culminates in tormented love transfigured through pantheist contemplation of nature.[239] It was also around this time that he wrote his *Harmonielehre*, in which he implicitly explored why he believed the traditional patterns of western music had reached near-exhaustion and so demanded a new approach.[240]

The strained harmonic language in Wagner's *Tristan und Isolde* is the most commonly quoted example of a nineteenth-century anticipation. More often than not when the first chord in the Prelude (the 'Tristan chord') recurs, it is used to lead the music into yet another key rather than confirm harmonic expectations. But there were many other instances along the way before Schoenberg's own complete abandonment of tonality. Traditionally, only chords based on a three-note triad were thought consonant and music moved within a single key signature towards eventual rest on the tonic (doh) and away from the dominant (sol). However, throughout the nineteenth century composers increasingly used dissonance in order to increase the desire for, and expectation of, consonance. The result was that in the twentieth century, even where tonality is preserved, players performing together (sometimes even on the same instrument) may be assigned two different key signatures, or a piece so modulates between major and minor that no choice is made in the

---

[237] Seen already in his 1926 play *Der biblische Weg*.

[238] The group included Klee, Kandinsky and Marc. Their aim was to give importance to the spiritual side of experience, which they felt had been unduly neglected by the Impressionists. Schoenberg remained friends with Kandinsky until they fell out with one another in 1922: A. Shawn, *Arnold Schoenberg's Journey* (Cambridge, Mass.: Harvard University Press, 2002), 175–6. For a discussion of Schoenberg's art, see 59–83.

[239] The way in which Waldemar eventually finds comfort for the loss of his beloved Tove. *Gurrelieder* was written in 1901 but not premièred until 1913.

[240] Only 'implicitly' because the great bulk of the work is concerned with the principles of harmony in their own right: *Theory of Harmony* (London: Faber and Faber, 1978; 1st German edn 1911). He was writing some of his early atonal works such as *Erwartung* about the same time.

work's title.[241] Schoenberg is thus simply carrying much further a process that was in some ways already quite far advanced.

Here two key works are *Erwartung* (1909) and *Pierrot Lunaire* (1912). The 'expectation' and 'waiting' present in the title of the former is conveyed by the absence of a clear beginning or ending. A shifting present is thus suggested, with no sense of possible sources from which focus might come. In the song cycle revolving round the pathetic, clownish figure of French pantomine, *Pierrot Lunaire* ('Moonstruck Pierrot'), such confusion is given a more personal and possibly blasphemous reference.[242] What is evoked is a surreal vision of a poet drunk on moonlight who seeks escape through clowning and elements of nostalgia and sentimentality. While the words (not Schoenberg's own) achieve this through the inversion of Christian symbolism, the music reinforces the effect through hovering round possible key centres while in fact dispensing with the security of tonality. That might be taken to imply that such an approach could only suggest negativities, but Schoenberg's development of the twelve-tone system in the 1920s ensured that this was far from being so.[243] Expectation and order were in effect reintroduced with a system of rules determining which notes in the chromatic scale should follow one another in any particular piece.[244]

Schoenberg's unfinished opera *Moses und Aron* (which is based on a single tone row) is concerned to emphasize the impossibility of conveying adequately the nature of 'the invisible and unimaginable God'.[245] That is quite different, though, from taking the work to imply the absence of experience of God. Limitations on conveying

---

[241] Such as Stravinsky's *Serenade in A* and his ballet *Petrushka*. In the latter case one clarinet plays in C major and another in F sharp minor. For a helpful, brief exposition of the issues mentioned in the text, see R. Kamien, *Music: An Appreciation*, 7th edn (Boston: McGraw Hill, 2000), 445–9.

[242] 'Rote Messe' could be read as a parody of Christianity, but seems intended rather as a sardonic underlining of Pierrot's mental chaos.

[243] The law-like character of the system may also have appealed to his Judaism: see Ringer, *Arnold Schoenberg*, 73. A Prague lecture on Mahler also demonstrated such affinities: ibid. 171–5.

[244] That is to say, all twelve notes in an octave (black and white on the piano keyboard) were to be used. Nothing determines their initial order. Thereafter, however, that order is maintained according to some pre-established principles.

[245] 'der unsichtbarer und unvorstellbarer Gott'. The difficulty in representing this musically was perhaps the reason why the opera was abandoned unfinished in 1932.

the full import of experience are not at all the same thing. Moses confines himself to ordinary speech, in order to underline such contrasts. Yet the certainty of Schoenberg's own vision is made clear at the only time Moses does turn to song. 'Purify your thought,' he urges; 'Set it free from earthly things.'[246] While Schoenberg's final work, *Modern Psalm*, offers anxious uncertainty and awe in equal measure, the short, twelve-tone *A Survivor from Warsaw* from a few years earlier ends on a powerfully optimistic note despite the tragic events it records.[247] Already in the opening account, as the narrator speaks of 'the old prayer they had neglected for so many years', a French horn intones the beginning of the melody that will return at the end, with the chorus singing in unison the Hebrew words for 'Hear, O Israel, the Lord our God is one.'[248] So throughout Schoenberg's life there may be detected a continuing endorsement of the expressive power of music to convey an experience of the divine that can only be hinted at in words.

The positive potentiality of such music is, however, in some ways more evident in his two most famous pupils, Alban Berg and Anton Webern. Despite the severity of their subject matter, Berg's two operas in this style, *Wozzeck* and *Lulu*, are both richly lyrical and expressionist, with hints of tonality helping to maintain interest. A striking feature is the way in which *Wozzeck* fails to end on a conclusive chord, thereby perhaps warning that the tragic torments of the soldier could all too easily be repeated in new contexts. For a religious dimension, however, it is to Webern, an Austrian Catholic, that we must turn. Schoenberg had stressed his debt to the earlier tradition.[249] Webern took a similar position.[250] Sadly, a tragic accident brought his life abruptly to a premature close just after the end of the

[246] Act 1, scene 2. The form of speech used is known as *Sprechstimme*, a kind of sing-song declamation that Schoenberg had already used in *Pierrot Lunaire* to suggest alienation. A form of approximate pitch notation in which the performer 'speaks' or half-sings notated pitches, it was once more accurately known as *Sprechgesang*.

[247] Schoenberg wrote texts of 15 psalms of his own composition, but had only finished setting one to music by the time of his death in 1951. That hauntingly ends suspended in the air with the words: 'and yet I pray'. *A Survivor from Warsaw* dates from 1947.

[248] The *Shema* (Deut. 6.4–9) is set in full.

[249] There is a fine passage in *The Theory of Harmony* which insists that true originality can only build on the past: 'it is the natural growth of the tree of life' (401).

[250] Stressed in his 1933 lectures *The Path to the New Music* and elsewhere: Shawn, *Arnold Schoenberg's Journey*, 50–1; K. Bailey, *The Life of Webern* (Cambridge: Cambridge University Press, 1998), 194.

Second World War. Although the corpus of his works is not large, they do illustrate well two conspicuous features of the atonal approach: first, that without words it is difficult to give some sense of direction that will aid concentration and maintain interest while such music is being played; secondly, that alternative sources of interest in the immediate moment have therefore to be supplied. Although it is often claimed that Schoenberg was expressive in a way that Webern was not, this seems to me quite wrong, as though the latter was purely formalist in his approach.[251] Certainly, Webern's various settings for words written by his soul-mate, Hildegard Jone, display a mystical intensity that they both shared. A good example is his *Second Cantata* (op. 31), which Webern himself described as rather like a *missa brevis*.

While it is true that it was Webern's more strictly formalist approach that was to exercise the greater influence on the avant-garde music that was to become so fashionable after the Second World War, intense listening to his relatively short instrumental pieces can, I think, give us access to the same types of experience as Webern felt were foundational to his own faith.[252] Fortunately, some of his diaries survive which indicate an enthusiastic and essentially religious response to music, not least to that of Beethoven and Wagner. Extremely irritated by applause at Bayreuth, he observed of Wagner's *Parsifal*: 'one can only sink to one's knees, silent and dumb, and pray'. Again, of a performance of Beethoven's Ninth he remarked that 'it was the holiest hour of my life up to now'.[253] Such experiences strengthened his conviction that this is what he should seek to emulate in his own music. A good example from his own works might be the third of his *Five Pieces for Orchestra* (op. 10). Alternating solo instruments generate bell-like sounds that induce a great feeling of unearthly calm and stillness. Again, the break-up of the sound into small successive units in the first movement of his Symphony (op. 21) recalls the individual elements of his Alpine mountain walks that for

---

[251] The op. 20 Trio of 1926 was his first dodecaphonic work based on twelve-tone principles.

[252] Pierre Boulez and Karlheinz Stockhausen among those who have preferred Webern. Stockhausen has also exhibited a concern for spiritual issues, most notably in his seven-opera cycle *Licht* (1977–2002).

[253] Quoted in Bailey, *The Life of Webern*, 18–19, 33.

him spoke so powerfully of God in nature, in particular the intricacy of rock crystals and the variety of mountain flowers.[254]

Along with Schoenberg the other composer to have had a decisive impact on twentieth-century music is Igor Stravinsky (1882–1971). Born to a wealthy, educated and musical, if somewhat unloving, family in St Petersburg,[255] he initially studied under Rimsky-Korsakov, absorbing his strongly nationalist and atheistic values. Moving to Paris in 1910, he worked there with Diaghilev and the Ballets Russes. Whereas his first major work, *The Firebird*, was fairly conventional, *The Rite of Spring* (1913) evoked vociferous protests from its audience. Now widely regarded as the most important and influential musical work of the twentieth century,[256] it gains its power from extensive use of dissonance, and through confounding rhythmic expectations. One commentator speaks of the dissonant elements 'firing... off at one another like so many particles in an atomic accelerator'.[257] Intriguingly, Stravinsky himself identified it as one of the three key works of the twentieth century, along with two others by Schoenberg.[258] But so affected was Stravinsky by the initial audience's reaction that he only consented once more in his life to watch a staged performance, insisting that it worked better in any case as a concert piece.[259] That is not entirely true, as there is a fine match between the story of a pagan spring rite of human sacrifice and the various points at which dissonance strikes or the rhythms speed up, are in flux, or slow down.[260] Stravinsky identified a pantheistic element to the tale. Although he would undoubtedly have rejected any such comparison,

[254] The first example is atonal but not a twelve-tone composition; the latter both. For the effect of the Alps on him, see ibid. 110.

[255] He speaks of being closest to his nurse: Stravinsky and Craft, *Memories and Commentaries*, 9. Although baptized and given a religious education, his parents were not churchgoers: 5, 16–17.

[256] It was voted the century's most influential piece of music by readers of the *BBC Music Magazine* (Dec 1999).

[257] S. Walsh, *The Music of Stravinsky* (Oxford: Clarendon Press, 1988), 44. The novelty lay in the fact that the dissonance, rather than being given a delayed resolution, was left quite unresolved.

[258] *Pierrot Lunaire* and *Gurrelieder*: Stravinsky and Craft, *Memories and Commentaries*, 256.

[259] Ibid. 92.

[260] Stressed in P. Hill, *Stravinsky: The Rite of Spring* (Cambridge: Cambridge University Press, 2000), 14, 39, 52, 72–3. The musical ending comes as an anticlimax unless the dancer is seen collapsing on stage: 88–9. For Stravinsky's own ballet-orientated description, see 93–5.

the engagement of his contemporary Alexander Scriabin at the time with similar religious concerns does come to mind.[261]

The strength of objections to the piece derived from the score's apparent lack of order and coherence. There is much irony in this, as a repeated theme of Stravinsky's later reflections on music was just such a concern. In 1940 he gave a series of lectures at Harvard on *The Poetics of Music*, in which revolution is contrasted with true development and ordered progress.[262] Within that framework Wagner and the late Verdi are taken to task for imposing only a superficial order.[263] For Stravinsky dissonance is not itself the issue. It only appears out of step with tradition because all too often critics adopt too short a time-span for their perspective, in effect only from the seventeenth century onwards.[264] Music continues to seek some kind of repose but this need only be through the resolution of dissonance when expectations are narrowly confined to one particular kind of conceptual structure. The lectures adopt a Neo-Platonic view, with the One emerging through the music out of the many.[265] That viewpoint is used in the lectures' concluding sentence to point to a single 'Supreme Being' as the source of such order. So it is perhaps not surprising that when, after the death of Schoenberg in 1951, Stravinsky himself adopted the twelve-note technique it was a sense of order that he sought to invoke. It is from this period that many of his religious works date.

His *Mass* anticipates that trend, at least in its structural simplicity.[266] Here, despite his Orthodox faith, he adopted the usual Latin text, but not because he wanted to emulate particular composers of the past.

---

[261] For Stravinsky, see ibid. 93. *Le Poème Divine* of Scriabin (now sometimes transliterated as Skryabin) came out in the same year (1913). Its musical ideas were heavily influenced by Theosophy, a movement that also affected a number of artists, among them Mondrian.

[262] Even the *Rite of Spring* is portrayed as a true development and emphatically not as a revolution: I. Stravinsky, *Poetics of Music* (Cambridge, Mass.: Harvard University Press, 1942), 9–10.

[263] Ibid. 43, 60–2. He also speaks of Wagner's 'adulterated religiosity' (60).

[264] Ibid. 34–9. He is thinking of the diatonic system of major and minor keys.

[265] e.g. ibid. 69. For the stress on order, see 23, 65, 76. That also explains his stress on creativity as discovery and not simply inspiration: 50–5.

[266] The result is what has been called 'very cold music': A. Whittall, *Musical Composition in the Twentieth Century* (Oxford: Oxford University Press, 1999), 130. However, if the Creed suggests moral earnestness on the part of the congregation, the Sanctus does at least convey joy.

Mozart's masses especially drew his fire.[267] Rather it was because in theory he held to the belief that sacred music should be performed in church, whereas his own native Orthodoxy (to which he had by this time returned) refused to allow the use of instruments, which Stravinsky regarded as essential to the work. His late religious compositions, such as *Canticum Sacrum, Threni* and *Abraham and Isaac*, imply that he wanted to associate religious music with a particular style, and an austere one at that.[268] Repeatedly throughout his life he made the claim that music should not be treated as expressive.[269] It had its own formal language, and that was enough.

But much of his music belies those claims. That can be seen especially in his middle period (from 1920 to 1950), when he adopted a style that became known as Neoclassicism. Here elements in the works of earlier composers are adapted to produce somewhat dislocated and usually ironic arrangements or else fresh compositions that recall but also subvert the listener's memories of conventions from the past. So, for example, the 'Dumbarton Oaks' Concerto, while largely an original work, contains allusions to two of Bach's Brandenburg Concertos, while the ballet *Pulcinella* borrows extensively from music then thought to be by Pergolesi. Again, *The Rake's Progress* could be seen in some ways as a modern version of Mozart's *Don Giovanni*. The issue of repentance, however, has moved from the opera's end to being a repeated feature of the rake's life, so suggesting our own more anxious and uncertain age.[270]

Stravinsky was a complicated character. Thanks to the conductor Robert Craft, who in effect became his adopted son, there is much that is positive on record that helps to enhance Stravinsky's reputation. Others, however, have detected a profoundly flawed and self-centred individual.[271] In consequence it remains a moot point

[267] 'These rococo-operatic sweets of sin': quoted in Walsh, *The Music of Stravinsky*, 193.

[268] *Canticum Sacrum* less so than the other two, perhaps partly because it is not a consistently twelve-tone composition.

[269] See e.g. Stravinsky and Craft, *Memories and Commentaries*, 270.

[270] Not that either opera reaches a happy resolution. Don Giovanni refuses to repent, while in *The Rake's Progress* Tom sees too late the folly of his ways and dies of grief.

[271] The central theme in C. M. Joseph, *Stravinsky Inside Out* (New Haven, Conn.: Yale University Press, 2001). Described as 'fraught with frailties' (the concluding judgement of the book, 270), he is portrayed as obsessed with his personal reputation. He also perpetuated in relations with his children the same sort of problems as he himself had experienced growing up: 6, 30, 65–6, 72.

whether we should interpret his conversion back to Orthodoxy in 1925 as purely religious or in part motivated by the strains of his then adultery (the acceptance of which he seems to have forced upon his wife).[272] What cannot be disputed is the profoundly Christian character of the type of music he produced during this period, even where its surface theme is not explicitly so. An obvious case in point is *Oedipus Rex* and *Persephone*, which have been described as 'The Christian *Rites of Spring*'.[273] Certainly, the classical legends are well adapted to bring out notions of atonement, while the music is given a liturgical and ritual character that helps to underline the eternal rather than merely transitory significance of the events in question.[274] In a similar way his *Symphony of Psalms* is rather more than just a setting of three of the Latin Vulgate's psalms. They take us from desolation (Psalm 39) through release (Psalm 40) to transcendence (Psalm 150), where exuberant praise alternates with radiant calm.

Symphony in C, like the *Symphony of Psalms*, was dedicated to God. But to my mind it is not in its surprisingly confident voice that God is to be found but rather in his much earlier *Symphonies of Wind Instruments*.[275] That piece is dedicated to the memory of Debussy. Although it shows no sign of that particular composer's influence, its dedication perhaps explains why it has a solemn ritual character like that of a procession.[276] Throughout the great diversity of Stravinsky's various styles, ritual was in fact a recurring theme. Ritual need not of itself be religious, but it does implicitly

---

[272] On the adultery (from 1921) and his subsequent marriage in 1940, see ibid. 73–4, 85, 180.

[273] Walsh, *The Music of Stravinsky*, 134.

[274] Aided in the case of *Oedipus Rex*, Stravinsky believed, by his decision to have Cocteau's French version of *Oedipus* translated into Latin by the theologian Jean Daniélou: Stravinsky and Craft, *Memories and Commentaries*, 159–60, 164. Atonement is introduced into both works by making the sacrifice voluntary (through Gide's adaptation in the case of Persephone): Walsh, *The Music of Stravinsky*, 142, 154.

[275] 'Surprisingly confident' because *Symphony in C* was written at a time (1939) when his wife and daughter died, and he himself was ill.

[276] Stravinsky claimed that among the previous generation of composers his greatest debt lay with Debussy (d. 1918): Whittall, *Musical Composition*, 117. Although Debussy never abandoned tonality, he weakened it in favour of impressionist sketches. For a discussion of impressionist music, including its religious applications, see M. Fleury, *L'Impressionisme et la musique* (Paris: Fayard, 1996), esp. 339–471.

raise the question of God through its concern to find an appropriate place for the individual in his or her world. What I suggest Stravinsky's ritualistic music does, whether the theme is pagan or Christian, vocal or instrumental, is to reaffirm a religious placement for human beings, despite the threatening disorder that was such a prominent feature of twentieth-century history. Dissonance and ritual are thus not enemies but the composer's way of opening up his listeners' lives to God.

Stravinsky and Schoenberg thus both illustrate how the extraordinary changes that have taken place to classical music over the course of the twentieth century can nonetheless be seen, like religious belief itself, as part of a creative and developing tradition. So far from their music being inimical to Christians, it can help them to come to terms with the way in which religious belief also changes and develops both at a personal level and corporately. Although in a moment our attention will turn to a composer who consistently stressed the timelessness of God, that can only ever be one side of what it is to experience the divine through our world. No less important is the ability of God to help us to come to terms with such change.

Humour and the Timeless in Poulenc and Messiaen

One way to conclude this chapter might have been to offer some reflections on the state of contemporary classical music. Against such a course is the difficulty of making solidly based judgements about composers who are still in mid-careers. So what I have chosen to do instead is end with someone now dead who is almost universally regarded as the twentieth century's greatest religious composer, Olivier Messiaen (1908–1992). Partly by way of transition and partly for contrast I have chosen to preface my discussion with a few brief remarks on his fellow Frenchman and contemporary, Francis Poulenc (1899–1963). Although from his late thirties onwards a committed Roman Catholic, Poulenc was otherwise quite different in character and approach. It will also help illustrate how remarkably varied are the ways in which music can raise the question of God.

Poulenc's earliest influences came from Eric Satie but Stravinsky was soon to join him. His ballet *Les Biches* was commissioned by Diaghilev and could be read as an adaptation of Stravinsky's *Rite of Spring* to a more domestic (and modern) French setting.[277]

---

[277] So W. Mellers, *Francis Poulenc* (Oxford: Oxford University Press, 1993), 16.

Certainly, Stravinsky admired the result and continued to speak
well of Poulenc's music in much later years.[278] Although Poulenc
produced quite a number of works for the stage, his real *métier* was
as a songwriter. The songs, like the stage works, often have a
distinctly sardonic edge. So, for instance, in his *Le Bestiaire* cycle
in several cases the music runs counter to conventional estimates of
the animals in question. In 'La Sauterelle' the grasshopper is given
slow, elegant music rather than the energetic hopping which might
have been anticipated. 'Le Dauphin' has a melancholic air, presumably to remind us that the lives of dolphins are not just a matter
of play but can also have their tragic aspect. Sometimes Poulenc
carries further parodies that were already implicit in the words, as in
the later 'Berceuse', where a babysitter rocks the cradle, while
father is out at mass and mother at the cabaret.[279]

Although he fathered an illegitimate child, Poulenc was in fact
homosexual, and some of his lovers were to have a marked impact on
his compositions.[280] Some have detected strong connections between
his sexuality and his spirituality (he returned to the Catholic faith in
1936).[281] While there could be an element of truth in this, more
interesting to my mind is the way in which sitting as it were on the
then margins of society leads to what might be called an inverted or
tragicomic view of the world. The kind of impact this has on some of
his songs has already been noted. More pertinent here is the added
depth it gives to some of his religious compositions.

By common consent the two most impressive of these (indeed, of his
music more generally) are his opera *Dialogues of the Carmelites* (1957) and
his *Gloria* (1959), though the Flute Sonata must come a close third.
According to some surveys, by the end of the twentieth century the
Gloria was apparently the second most frequently performed French
piece of classical music anywhere in the world.[282] Traces of Stravinsky's

---

[278] Ibid. 23, 179 (in the latter passage Stravinsky is shown to be still an admirer of
Poulenc's music in 1946). Stravinsky's influence on Poulenc is apparently most marked
just after the First World War, as can be seen in Poulenc's sonata for two clarinets (1918).

[279] *Le Bestiaire* set poems by the painter Raoul Dufy. 'Berceuse' is from
another song cycle, which utilizes words from the writings of the poet Max
Jacob.

[280] He had five main affairs over the course of his life (including his post-conversion
period): R. D. E. Burton, *Francis Poulenc* (London: Absolute Press, 2002), 14.

[281] 'A possible synthesis of sexuality and spirituality': ibid. 16, 43–60.

[282] B. Ivry, *Francis Poulenc* (London: Phaidon, 1996), 208. Ravel's *Boléro* was the most
popular. Even so the results are somewhat surprising. What, for instance, of Fauré's
Requiem?

influence are still present.[283] It is marvellously exuberant, but it also has its comic aspects. Poulenc spoke of being inspired by frescoes of angels sticking out their tongues and by some monks playing football.[284] Unfortunately, he did not go on to tell us precisely what he meant. At times the music sounds like a primitive fiesta. Further into the piece it might even make one think of a rustic clog dance. Perhaps the point is that religious celebration should not always be associated with solemnity and formality. Apparent incongruities such as those acts of angels and monks might after all give us better access to the sort of innocent joy that is to be found through the divine.

The *Dialogues of the Carmelites* had its origins in a German story translated into French by Georges Bernanos and modified in the process.[285] In particular a new focus is introduced, in substitutionary atonement, not in this case in respect of Christ himself but rather through one Christian suffering vicariously on behalf of another.[286] Poulenc's enthusiasm for such a theme may have been in part generated by his own personal conviction that his most recent lover's early and unexpected death[287] had in fact allowed him to live longer. Certainly, one of the great dramatic moments of modern opera occurs when Blanche (the central figure) observes the death in agony and in doubt of the First Prioress, the very woman whose own conventual name she had taken.[288] In effect she bears Blanche's own doubts and fears on her behalf. Such mystical substitution is a theology which modern individualism finds not merely surprising but also shocking. However, it is by no means the only unexpected slant given to the plot and accompanying music. Indeed, it is precisely its paradoxical features that make this opera so fascinating and help to explain its undoubted power and popularity. So, for example, despite the fact that it is a story about nuns, there is still an ensemble equivalent in the texture of its sound to a love

---

[283] Mellers, *Francis Poulenc*, 148.

[284] Ibid. 147.

[285] Gertrude von le Fort had produced a short novel based on a true historical incident that had taken place during the French Revolution, when some nuns had been martyred. Bernanos (famous for his *Diary of a Country Priest*) had adapted the novel as a play.

[286] Burton, *Francis Poulenc*, 95–6.

[287] A travelling salesman, Lucien Roubert, who died unexpectedly of pleurisy: Ivry, *Francis Poulenc*, 170, 178–9.

[288] Act I, scene 4. The young, childlike Constance also plays an important role in Blanche's eventual salvation.

duet, as brother and sister movingly sing together.[289] Again, the opera ends with a military march that turns into a *Salve Regina*. Recurring thuds are heard from the percussion as each of the nuns is executed in turn.

This repeated pattern of the unexpected and sardonic in his compositions helps Poulenc to suggest that things may not always be quite as they seem. In effect, the opera suggests that love can flourish in ways other than the obvious, while revolutionary ideals may after all need religion as counterpoise and balance. His music is thus intended as deliberately subversive. By opening closed minds it allows us to find the action of God in the unexpected, elegance in a grasshopper and an instrument of salvation in cries of dereliction: 'Que suis-je à cette heure, moi misérable, pour m'inquiéter de Lui! Qu'il s'inquiète donc d'abord de moi!'[290]

In comparison with Poulenc, Messaien led a simple and uncomplicated life. Throughout he remained a devout Catholic and indeed for most of it was organist of the same Parisian church, La Trinité. When to this is added the fact that almost all his music is religious, it is very easy to reach the conclusion that his music will inevitably reflect a somewhat narrow, introspective mind. But his genius was quite otherwise. In composing his own sacred works, Stravinsky had sought to return such compositions to performance in church. Messaien took a quite different view. Instead, he sought to open up people to the possibility of experiencing God through music in the concert hall or listening at home. More accurately, as he preferred to express it, music allows God to draw near. In his view 'music like poetry brings us to God, through image and symbol and in their obvious deficiency in falling short of the full Truth'.[291] This concern to bring God into the concert hall is perhaps why, with regard to the work that made his name at the end of the Second World War, *Trois petites liturgies de la Présence divine*, objections came from the devout no

---

[289] In Act II, with the usual tenor and soprano.

[290] Hysteria and terror are how the music portrays Blanche's still unresolved response to the Prioress' wild arioso, railing (like Christ on the cross) against God: 'Wretch that I am, why trouble myself at this hour with Him! Let him first trouble himself with me!' (my translation).

[291] My free translation of St Francis' words when near to death in Messaien's opera *Saint François d'Assise*: 'musique et poésie m'ont conduit vers Toi: par image, par symbole, et par défaut de Vérité'.

less than from secularists.[292] In pursuance of that wider aim, he adopted a distinctive style. Although he helped mediate Schoenberg to others, his more obvious sympathies were with Stravinsky or, perhaps more accurately, Stravinsky as modified through the impressionism of Debussy.[293] Added to this was his continuing interest in bird sounds and in early or exotic musical forms, including eastern, Hindu music.[294]

The aim was to create colours in particular moments rather than follow through the traditional sonata or symphonic structure. 'Colours' does seem exactly the right word to use, as Messiaen had a powerful synaesthetic sense, whereby particular chords and modes came to be associated with corresponding colours.[295] This can be seen at work in what he called the 'modes of limited transposition', which he based on the twelve semitones of the octave and which he associated with particular colours.[296] For those of us who do not encounter visual stimuli in sounds it is perhaps easier to think by analogy. So, for example, in the fifteenth section of his famous piano piece *Vingt regards sur l'Enfant-Jésus* he mixes the colours of what he called mode 2 with the key of F major to conjure up the warmth and intimacy of the mystical love between Jesus and St Teresa of Lisieux.

Another, more easily comprehensible way of focusing on the immediate moment is non-retrogradable rhythms. Under ancient Hindu influence Messiaen created palindromes of perfect symmetry such that there could be no sense of retracing one's steps, even if one tried to do so, and so no sense of time.[297] Temporal direction is now firmly subordinated to this gift of conveying the vertical, a transcendence that offers access to a different type of timeless reality. Nowhere is this perhaps more evident than in his *Quatuor pour la fin du temps*, written while he was a prisoner of war at Görlitz.

[292] As one commentator puts it, 'it sets out . . . to transfer something . . . of the Church's liturgy to the concert-hall, an operation which is discomfiting to the non-believer as well as to the conservative Catholic': R. S. Johnson, *Messiaen* (London: Dent, 1975), 11–12.

[293] So Johnson, ibid. 182–5.

[294] A. Perier, *Messiaen* (Paris: Éditions du Seuil, 1979), 14–15.

[295] For some examples, see Johnson, *Messiaen*, 19–20.

[296] Explanations and examples of this and another key element in Messiaen's technique, non-retrogradable rhythms (described in the next paragraph), are provided in J. M. Wu's 'Mystical Symbols of Faith', in S. Bruhn (ed.), *Messiaen's Language of Mystical Love* (New York: Garland, 1998), 85–120, esp. 86–104.

[297] 'Going back' was simply going forward once more.

Taking his cue from the angel's proclamation in Rev. 10.6 that 'there will be no more time', at various points in the composition just such a sense of timeless reality is conveyed.[298] If birdsong is introduced to conjure a longing for freedom, repetition and non-retrogradable rhythms are used in the opening movement to suggest the divine timelessness that he sees as undergirding the eventual assumption of humanity through Christ into that same timelessness.[299]

Although Messiaen read widely in theology, it was Aquinas to whom he most often turned. What he believed he found there was a sense of a graded reality whereby different empirical levels point beyond themselves, and so eventually to ultimate reality. So, for example, on the question of love, he establishes a hierarchy of love that moves from the sort found in *Don Giovanni* to the *Tristan* variety to maternal love, with divine love then at its apex.[300] As some of his remarks on his *Des canyons aux étoiles* make clear, he has no doubt that all of creation points beyond itself to God.[301] That is why the apparently 'secular' *Turangalîla Symphony* is not really an exception to the generally religious character of his writing.[302] Stravinsky was especially severe on that particular composition.[303] For him it was too light-hearted. Indeed, it is a common complaint against Messiaen that there is little of the crucifixion in his works. His nearest approach is perhaps in his treatment of St Francis'

---

[298] While the Greek allows this interpretation and it is adopted in the Authorized Version, most modern translations (e.g. RSV, NEB) are probably correct in supposing that the real meaning is that 'there will be no more delay'.

[299] The 15-note melody for the cello is non-retrogradable, the 17-note for the piano simply endlessly repeated. The final movement praises 'the immortality of Jesus', by which Messiaen understands Christ's humanity. For birds as symbols of freedom, see A. Pople, *Messiaen: Quatuor pour la fin du temps* (Cambridge: Cambridge University Press, 1998), 40–1, 44.

[300] Wu, 'Mystical Symbols', 75.

[301] 'In moving from the canyons to the stars and higher to the resurrected in Paradise, to glorify God in all his creation, that is then pre-eminently a religious work: of praise and of contemplation': my translation of Messaien's words in C. Massip (ed.), *Portrait(s) d'Olivier Messiaen* (Paris: Bibliothèque nationale de France, 1996), 43.

[302] For Messiaen it is 'a hymn to joy' in which the earthly patterns and reflects the heavenly: ibid. 39.

[303] Quoted in A. Whittall, *Exploring Twentieth-Century Music* (Cambridge: Cambridge University Press, 2003), 65. Stravinsky's hostility to Messiaen was all the more surprising given the fact that Stravinsky saw himself (like Schoenberg did) as being 'under Divine Authority': ibid. 57.

stigmata in his opera *Saint François d'Assise*. Even there, though, his most enthusiastic writing is reserved for the 'Canticle of Brother Sun' and St Francis preaching to the birds.[304] For some Christians that might be enough to rule his music out of court. But it is surely important to acknowledge that experience of the divine will inevitably be multifaceted, with some composers better at inducting us into one aspect rather than another.

To say that much in Messiaen's support is scarcely to exempt him from criticism. Certainly, sometimes it is hard not to convict him of being too clever by half. His attempt to convey the doctrine of the Trinity in his *Méditations sur le mystère de la Sainte Trinité* is not something that can be heard, only followed in a commentary. While some of the leitmotifs are clear, his attempt to produce a note-for-note correspondence with the individual letters of a selected passage of Aquinas produces all sorts of compromises that make the 'plot' hard to follow even for the intense and musically well-educated listener.[305] Again, in his transcriptions of birdsong much effort is required to recognize even familiar breeds.[306] Perhaps, as with Bach, it is more appropriate sometimes to speak of an offering intended only for God's ears.[307] But that is scarcely true generally. Messiaen in effect offers us an extension of the incarnation in which West and East, sound and colour, human invention and the music of nature, visible and invisible, all combine to draw creation and its Creator closer together.[308] In all of this believer and non-believer alike can scarcely avoid hearing the glories of nature or a timeless presence. God is, as it were, brought alongside, but whether something further happens remains of course entirely with the individual wills and dispositions of those who are listening.

That is equally true of the rest of the music discussed in this chapter. It is not that God is forced upon anyone. Rather, it is a matter of favourable conditions being set under which experience

[304] The 'Canticle,' is set in scene 2; for the preaching to the birds, see scene 6.

[305] He uses a French translation, but modifies it considerably in order to produce the desired result. For further details, see A. Shenton, 'Speaking with the Tongues of Men and Angels', in Bruhn (ed.), *Messiaen's Language*, 225–45, esp. 235.

[306] There are changes in speed, intervals and register. For some words in his defence, see Johnson, *Messiaen*, 117.

[307] Or perhaps the angels as well: Shenton's suggestion, 'Speaking', 240–1.

[308] The analogy with the two natures of Christ as divine and human is suggested by Fr Pascal Ide: 'Olivier Messiaen théologien?', in Massip (ed.), *Portrait(s) d'Olivier Messiaen*, 45.

of the divine does at least become a realistic possibility. What status should be accorded to the traditional arguments for God's existence is too large an issue to open here. So let me merely state baldly my own view, that none is valid, in the sense of offering decisive proof. What they do is open up the individual to certain possibilities. The music I have been discussing, I suggest, functions no differently. But it does possess this added advantage: that it speaks to the whole person, engaging the body, imagination and emotion no less than the intellect. That is one reason why God can be found by music in such a wide variety of forms: in intelligible order and in the sublime, in suffering that expects resurrection and suffering that does not, in hesitant exploration and in the confident assertion of faith, in humour and in solemnity, and in the timeless and the temporal. There is of course some appearance of conflict, but, as I have sought to stress throughout, aspectival conflict does not necessarily entail ultimate contradiction.[309]

I turn now to consider some popular forms of music, wrongly seen by some as essentially antithetical to the very possibility of mediating religious experience.

---

[309] That is, experience only ever reveals God partially, aspects of the divine, as it were. So it remains the task of the intellect to bring them into some kind of compatible resolution.

6

Pop Music

No doubt for many readers to go further down the road of 'secular' experience from classical music to contemporary popular music is already a stage too far. Their first thought may be to skip this chapter and move on immediately to the next as more naturally congenial. Since that chapter also addresses allegedly 'secular' music, such a decision would probably not produce quite the results they desire. But in any case I hope that readers will be patient, as I try to face head on some of the objections against taking pop music seriously in a theological context.

It is often claimed that pop music must of necessity lie at the opposite extreme from true religious experience since the superficiality of music and lyrics alike deprives it of all depth. Gospel music and similar attempts to introduce a religious dimension, it is said, can only at most sustain already existing beliefs, not help in any way to initiate them. Indeed, it might even be claimed that as a medium pop music is wrongly placed here in a group of chapters devoted to the auditory, since so much of the effect of pop is a matter not of the aural at all but of the visual. The success of a band can so often depend on physical looks, clothes, the use of readily identifiable symbols, and so on.

The superficiality of pop music is of course a long-standing complaint. For Theodor Adorno it was the new substitute for religion, in deadening the masses to wider and deeper questions about society.[1] If that was a critique from the left, the right has not been slow in identifying rock in particular as a corrupter of the morals of youth. An inherent sensuality in its rhythms is seen as appealing to baser and more primitive instincts. These are important criticisms. However, even if truth were entirely on their side, that of itself would not be a decisive argument for ignoring pop music, as is overwhelmingly the

---

[1] Views first adumbrated by Adorno in the 1930s, and available in his *Introduction to the Sociology of Music* (New York: Seabury Press, 1976), chs 1–2.

case currently among theologians and indeed among academics more generally. Often it is the only form of non-visual culture to penetrate the modern home. As Bruce Springsteen has remarked: 'If you grow up in a home where the concept of art is like twenty minutes in school everyday that you *hate*, the lift of rock is just incredible. . . . Rock and roll reached down into all those homes where there was no music or books or anything. . . . That's what happened in my house.'[2] So, if religion is to survive, it needs to take this form of expression with maximum seriousness. What I therefore want to do in the pages that follow is first consider the aesthetics of pop music in general before focusing on how specific artists might facilitate religious experience. In that latter part of the chapter I shall deliberately spread the net very widely to include not just 'light' popular music but also the various types to which Christians have sometimes taken most exception, among them hard rock and rap.

The Aesthetics of Pop

In conceding the numerous differences between popular and classical music, it is also important not to exaggerate them. If nowadays a classical performance is heard in hushed silence, it is as well to note that until at least the nineteenth century such contrasts would have been far less marked. Audiences often actively participated, with responses appreciative or otherwise, or else only half listened while engaged in other activities. Thus the 'sacralized' contemplation that now greets the modern classical concert is a relatively new phenomenon. What has been called the 'distracted reception' that is held to be characteristic of modern pop was once nearer to how all music was once received, although 'distracted' is perhaps not quite the right word.[3] It is not that the music is being ignored but that it is received along with other sensory input such as the listener's own participation and the perceived responses of

---

[2] Quoted in D. Marsh, *Born to Run: The Bruce Springsteen Story* (New York: Dell, 1981), 219–20.

[3] The phrase 'distracted reception' comes from an influential essay: W. Benjamin, 'The Work of Art in the Age of Mechanical Reproduction', in his *Illuminations* (London: Fontana, 1973), 243. The approach to classical works is described as 'sacralised' in S. Frith, *Performing Rites: Evaluating Popular Music* (Oxford: Oxford University Press, 1996), 29.

the audience in general.[4] Again, commercialization has always been an element in the production of music. So, although the modern world has witnessed an intensification of this process, this can hardly all be blamed on pop. Even Beethoven modified initial versions of particular works in order to make them more marketable.[5] In any case, however exploitative a particular artist may intend to be, he or she must still cherish other aims and values that correspond with the listeners' wishes, if they are to succeed financially.

That said, the present contrast with classical music needs to be faced, and its significance assessed.[6] Although the difference between contemplative engagement and a more active involvement is most marked in stage performances, this is also, as often as not, carried over into the recording studio and the resultant CD. Listeners to popular music sing the words or drum their fingers along to the beat (or whatever) in a much more demonstrative way than would usually be the case with someone listening to a classical disc. That contrast has often been taken to indicate the primacy of performance for pop music. Certainly, some groups have valued the opportunities given by live performance for creative improvisation. In the 1960s The Grateful Dead's live performances of previously released material were often long and unpredictable, and some contemporary bands continue that tradition of improvisation.[7] But in an age of increasing appreciation of technological refinement many now feel themselves pulled in a quite different direction. It is common for artists to model their live performances on earlier recordings made in the studio, or even to mime words or mix live and recorded elements in the music in order to achieve a better effect.[8] Equally, the point for the listener in attending

---

[4] This input is likely to have a major influence, especially on the impressionable young.

[5] His Op. 130 String Quartet (with its Grosse Fuge) and Hammerklavier Sonata: T. Gracyk, *Rhythm and Noise: An Aesthetics of Rock* (London: I. B. Tauris, 1996), 199.

[6] None of what follows is intended to suggest a purity in classical audiences that pop lacks. 'Contemplation' can be mixed with the cult of particular conductors, and so on.

[7] Although in the case of The Grateful Dead this was often drug-induced, it was seen as aiding the musical goal of greater freedom. The Sheffield band Gomez provide a contemporary example of extensive use of improvisation.

[8] For how such modelling of live performance on prior recordings worked out in practice for Elvis Presley, see Gracyk, *Rhythm and Noise*, 13–14. Even the apparent chaos of what The Sex Pistols produced was evidently carefully contrived first in the studio: ibid. 41–2.

a concert is sometimes not primarily to hear the singer or band perform at their best but rather to mix with others who share their own high evaluation of the recorded version. A further complication is the way in which for many the primary means of reception has become much more private and personal, through the Walkman and more recently the MP3 player. Favourite singers and bands now accompany individuals into all sorts of contexts from which they might once have been excluded, thus effectively producing what some have called 'the soundtrack of peoples' lives'.[9]

Any evaluation that simply parallels methods of assessment in classical music is thus wrongly directed. So used are musicologists to scrutinizing the score of a classical work as their primary standard of measurement that it is easy to suppose that this is also how pop music should be assessed. The inevitable result is that it is judged hopelessly naïve and simplistic by comparison.[10] But increasingly those who study the aesthetics of pop music are urging that the focus should be quite different: not on the structure of the music but on the totality of its reception by the listener.[11]

This also relates directly to the issue of the oft-repeated claim that pop music, especially rock, is inherently sensualist. Allan Bloom, the American cultural critic, for example, devotes an entire chapter of his influential work *The Closing of the American Mind* to attacking rock. He describes its beat as 'a nonstop, commercially packaged masturbational fantasy'.[12] The problem with such a critique is that it lacks care. Although more heavily accentuated, the

---

[9] The phrase is used by Simon le Bon. This issue is pursued in more detail in M. Bull, *Sounding Out the City: Personal Stereos and the Management of Everyday Life* (Oxford: Berg, 2000); T. DeNora, *Music in Everyday Life: Soundtrack, Self and Embodiment in Everyday Life* (Cambridge: Cambridge University Press, 2000).

[10] And not just musicologists. The philosopher Nelson Goodman defines music by its score, with the same inevitable result: *Languages of Art* (Indianapolis: Hackett, 1976), 112–13. Again, for similar reasons Anthony Storr concludes that pop music is 'trivial' and 'monotonous' and likely only to appeal to the 'unsophisticated': *Music and the Mind* (London: HarperCollins, 1993), 63, 76, 179.

[11] For a musicologist who takes the listener seriously, and finds much musical analysis problematic as a result, see N. Cook, *Music, Imagination and Culture* (Oxford: Clarendon Press, 1990), e.g. 223.

[12] A. Bloom, *The Closing of the American Mind* (New York: Simon and Schuster, 1987), 75.

beat of pop music actually uses a metre common to classical music as well.[13] This is probably no accident, because the way in which musical rhythms have developed has clearly something to do with the rhythms of the body, not least that of the heartbeat. While it is true that beat becomes more prominent in pop, to suggest that it necessarily thereby conjures up images of sex would be as absurd as making the same claim for the beat of trains on a railway track. There too was once the same pronounced rhythm, at least before the era of continuous track.[14] Even where sex is the theme of the lyrics, caution is still necessary. In general, human beings scarcely like listening to sad songs because it makes them sad. Instead, what is valued is the cathartic effect or else the generation of feelings of empathy for those in situations described by the song. Presumably, a similar range of possibilities also exists for songs about sex. If they actually helped generate sexual arousal, it is surely more likely that they would be avoided, not least because arousal in the absence of fulfilment is hardly likely to be a pleasing condition. Much more plausible, therefore, is the view that what is liked is the endorsement of certain attitudes. So it is the social history of certain types of singing that is relevant here, not the musical forms as such.[15]

Popular music adopts many guises, and so it would be misleading to talk of a single audience.[16] Love ballads and folk music are not only quite different from rock, heavy metal or rap but also there is huge variation within each genre. In heavy metal and rock words are usually much less easy to identify. This is not just a function of noise or volume. Rap is usually played just as loud, but part of the achievement of the rapper is seen to be in the creation of an urban verbal rhyming patois of challenge and exchange, and so the words

---

[13] Rock in particular, like much classical music, is usually in 'common' or 4/4 time. The difference is that, whereas in classical music this usually takes the form *one* two *three* four with a weaker emphasis on *three* than on *one*, rock democratizes the process and so it becomes much more obvious what is going on. Within pop more generally one obvious exception to such a pattern is the standard reggae beat of one *two* three *Four*, with a strong emphasis on *two* and *four*.

[14] In Chuck Berry's 'Johnny Be Good' Johnny learns how to play his guitar in time to the passing pulse of freight trains.

[15] A view endorsed by both Frith and Gracyk: e.g. Frith, *Performing Rites*, 123.

[16] Some are even prepared to speak of 'a mass audience' as really 'a fiction', since, though 'numerically dense', it is 'highly diversified': so I. Chambers, *Popular Culture: The Metropolitan Experience* (London: Routledge, 1986), 202.

must be heard. By contrast, in rock the words have become merely one element in a totality, and not necessarily the most important at that. Examples are legion. So one illustration will suffice here. In Led Zeppelin's 'Houses of the Holy' imitation of a specific drum sound appears to have been the primary aim, with the lyrics only added subsequently.[17] So in assessing the experience one has frequently to look elsewhere than to the words. The simplicity of beat, melody and vocals can all be compensated by the timbre of the overall sound. Indeed, it has been suggested that one reason why relatively simple forms of beat, melody and vocals can bear frequent replaying is precisely because timbre is much harder to retain in the memory, just as loudness is in part explained by certain timbres only becoming recognizable at higher volumes.[18]

Where the words are audible, it surely goes almost without saying that they do not simply function on their own. The music helps to create their meaning, and so that is why it must be wrong to attempt any overall assessment that excludes this wider frame. Indeed, at a more basic level it is important to realize that the words may sometimes be functioning as more like an additional instrument than with intrinsic significance in their own right. A good example here is the early work of R.E.M. The singer Michael Stipe's lyrics have been described as 'the audio equivalent of doctor's handwriting on a prescription'.[19] Although fans suspected a secret code, Stipe eventually admitted in 1994: 'You know there aren't words, *per se*, to a lot of the early stuff. I can't even remember them.'[20] But of course elsewhere meaning is important, with precise enunciation integral to that meaning. To state the obvious, the Beatles' line 'She loves you' means something quite different, depending on whether the stress as sung is on 'She', 'loves' or 'you'.[21] Again, Bob Dylan has received much positive appreciation for his poetry, but it would be wrong to

[17] For details, see Gracyk, *Rhythm and Noise*, 65. Gracyk also applies the point to the group's most famous song, 'Stairway to Heaven'. As I indicate later, I totally disagree.

[18] This point is helpfully developed by Gracyk, ibid. 57–61. For volume and amplifiers also affecting timbre, see 112, 120.

[19] D. Buckley, *R.E.M. Fiction: An Alternative Biography* (London: Virgin, 2002), 90. He is referring to early albums such as *Murmur* (1983) and *Reckoning* (1984).

[20] Quoted ibid. 91.

[21] That is, 'She' rather than someone else, 'loves' rather than 'likes' or 'hates', and 'you' rather than someone else.

suppose that nothing significant is added by the tone and quirkiness with which it is delivered. Even if he was exaggerating, John Lennon was on to something important when he observed that 'you don't have to hear what Bob Dylan is saying, you just have to hear the way he says it'.[22]

As another example, consider the ironic tone in Dolly Parton's voice, perhaps the key to explaining why she could become a gay icon.[23] If in her case the tone was deliberate, it is a moot point how often it is the listener and not the performer who is to blame when vocals are read differently from intended. An obvious case in point is Bruce Springsteen's 'Born in the USA'. Originally intended as a reflection on Vietnam veterans returning to the country without hope of employment, in the 1984 election its rousing chorus was successfully deflected by Republicans into something quite different, a celebration of American national pride.[24] Springsteen is someone to whom I shall return later, as is Bob Dylan, who provides a more recent example. Originally intended as an general anti-war anthem that indicted as much the USA nuclear programme as the country's opponents, his 'Masters of War' has more recently been redeployed as an endorsement of the entirely externally directed, so-called 'war on terror' against Osama Bin Laden and others.[25]

But, it may be said, however interesting all this is, it is an irrelevance to my concerns in this book since religion only ever enters into pop music at the margins. Certainly, very little is written on the subject. But this is not to say that performers and listeners have not themselves engaged with the issue. Both sometimes talk of being taken out of themselves, and while this is not usually in a religious direction it could be. Mick Jagger has described such experience when performing as 'the transcendental moment' when in jazz parlance 'one is gone'.[26] So, although many have felt that a choice between religion and pop was forced on them, not all have gone in the direction of retreat like Little Richard or Cat Stevens.[27]

---

[22] J. Wenner, *Lennon Remembers* (San Francisco: Straight Arrow Books, 1971), 188.

[23] Apparently submissive lyrics are undermined by her tone of voice.

[24] For other examples, see Frith, *Performing Rites*, 165–6.

[25] On the album *The Freewheelin' Bob Dylan* (1962).

[26] See D. Ehrlich, *Inside the Music: Conversations with Contemporary Musicians about Spirituality* (Boston: Shambhala, 1997), 56–66, esp. 60–1.

[27] Little Richard abandoned singing rock and roll for the ordained ministry; Cat Stevens' conversion marked the end of a conventional singing career.

U2 continue as a highly successful band. Again, although now ordained and acting as a minister in Memphis, Al Green continues to insist that his love songs function no less effectively than his explicitly religious lyrics in offering a medium of access to God.[28] The popularity of Green's falsetto voice draws attention to another intriguing element about pop music, the extent to which the higher vocal range is associated with intimacy and thus possibly also with spiritual experience.[29] Yet even where the break seems final, it has not always proved so. Cat Stevens, for instance, has recently returned to singing, admittedly under strict conditions deemed compatible with his deeply held Muslim faith.[30] Equally, his pre- and post-conversion lives are not as abruptly contrasted as they might initially seem. Several of his earlier songs in fact explored the possibility of faith.[31]

It would be a mistake in any case to confine the possibility of such experience to scenarios where the performer is of explicit faith. Songwriters reflect the uncertainties of the age, and so there is much more exploration going on than might initially have been expected. U2 and Bob Dylan have both explored charismatic Christianity but with significantly different results. Again, ventures have been made into other religions. George Harrison achieved a major success in making the inherent spirituality of Hindu music more accessible to western ears, particularly through his support for the music of Ravi Shankar.[32] If despite its references to Hare Krishna, Harrison's hit 'My Sweet Lord' still had an essentially western feel, the 2002 concert celebrating Harrison's life and work included a fine sitar composition of his own, 'The Inner

---

[28] Green speaks of 'all one music, all one message of love': ibid. 172–9, esp. 174. The way in which U2 almost split up over the issue is discussed below.

[29] Bing Crosby and Elvis Presley are two other obvious examples; for further discussion, see Frith, *Performing Rites*, 194–6. The Bee Gees have consistently sung falsetto, as in their soundtrack for the film *Saturday Night Fever*.

[30] As in the album from Yusuf Islam (his new name) and Friends, *Night of Remembrance* (2004), a charity concert celebrating twenty years of the Islamia School.

[31] As in the track 'Jesus' (where Buddha also gets a mention) on the album *Buddha and the Chocolate Box* (1971).

[32] They first met in 1966. As well as attempting to learn to play the sitar, Harrison also became heavily involved in the Hare Krishna movement: B. Harry, *George Harrison Encyclopedia* (London: Virgin, 2003), esp. 261–2, 281–2, 298–303, 319–22, 338–40. Harrison also introduced and edited Shankar's autobiography, *Raga Mala* (Guildford: Rain, 1997). For Shankar's own presentation of the religious dimension to his music, particularly valuable is the DVD *Ravi Shankar in Portrait* (2002).

Light'. Harrison had also gone on pilgrimage to Varanasi just before his death.[33] The reaction of Harrison's fellow-Beatle John Lennon to such an endorsement of religion was to write his song 'God Part II', in which God is listed among the things he no longer believes in. U2 in due course produced a counter-version.[34]

More recently U2's lead singer Bono joined Mick Jagger of the Rolling Stones in a song that explicitly thanks Christ for bringing 'joy in everything'.[35] Nor was that the first time that such themes appeared in Jagger's work. In an early Stones album, *Exile on Main Street*, one song movingly pleads for greater intimacy with Christ: 'You don't want to walk and talk about Jesus, | You just want to see his face'.[36] Jagger had in fact sung as a child in a church choir, and the first song specially written for the Stones was actually an adaptation of a traditional gospel song, 'The Last Time'.[37] None of this is to suggest that Jagger is really a secret believer, only that contrasts are not as clear as are commonly supposed.

Again, much of the lyrical output of Rick Wakeman has toyed with mythologies of various sorts.[38] Nonetheless, his on-line biography currently ends by quoting the prayer of a Confederate soldier whom he describes as a 'kindred spirit': 'I asked for power that I might have the praise of men. I was given weakness that I might feel the need of God.'[39] Such sentiments do not entail that he should now be firmly pigeonholed in one particular position, any more than Steven Morrissey's 'I Have Forgiven Jesus'[40] should force us to place that singer wholly on the other side. In Morrissey's case there is frequently deliberate ambiguity in his lyrics (and not

---

[33] 'My Sweet Lord' was the top-selling single in Britain during 1971: Harry, *George Harrison Encyclopedia* 276. 'The Inner Light' is recorded on *Concert for George* (2002).

[34] 'God Part II', on the *Rattle and Hum* album (1998). Lennon's original version had appeared in his *John Lennon/Plastic Ono Band* album (1970). To complicate matters, Kylie Minogue produced a third version that followed U2's track in rhythm and Lennon's in its lyrics.

[35] 'Joy', on Jagger's solo album *Goddess in the Doorway* (2001). Another track even speaks of how 'God gave me everything'.

[36] 'Just Want to See His Face', on *Exile on Main Street* (1972).

[37] D. Loewestein and P. Dodd (eds), *According to the Rolling Stones* (London: Weidenfeld and Nicolson, 2003), 6, 89.

[38] As in albums such as *Journey to the Centre of the Earth* (1974), *Myths and Legends of King Arthur* (1975) and *Zodiac* (1988).

[39] 'RWCC > Rick Wakeman Biography', at <www.rwcc.com/biogra.asp>.

[40] Available on the albums *You are the Quarry* (2004) and *I Have Forgiven Jesus* (2005).

just about his sexuality) that means that his Catholic upbringing
might still have the last word.[41] But whether so or not, the important point to note is that lyrics can often be just as much about
exploration as about commitment in any particular direction.

Clearly also, sometimes it may only be the melody as such that
attracts the singer and not the song's content. To take a quite
different example, at a time when the group was deep into drugs
and sado-masochistic sex, Velvet Underground covered a number
about Jesus that includes the line 'Help me in my weakness'.[42] It is
unlikely that the words were intended seriously. Nonetheless, the
lyrics are delivered straight, and so could be experienced in this way
by a listener. More problematic might be thought to be a song like
Primal Scream's 'Higher than the Sun'.[43] Here the 'religious' lyrics
and accompanying music were almost certainly intended to encourage a drug-induced state rather than anything to do with religion.
Even so, someone in ignorance of this fact might still find in the
meditative music an opening towards God. Authorial intention can
hardly be the final arbitrator. My point is thus not that religious
belief lurks everywhere, but that music can open up such possibilities for the listener, even where any such idea was very far from
the mind of the artists concerned. Reverting to The Rolling Stones
as an example, while 'Sympathy for the Devil' might well elicit one
type of reaction from an audience, there are plenty of other songs
from them that hint at alternative possibilities and opportunities,
whatever the actual beliefs of the group. In the following sections,
therefore, it makes sense to take a representative range of material
rather than narrowly confine our attention to those who might be
labelled orthodox or conventional Christians.

I now turn to consideration of specific examples, which for
convenience's sake I have gathered together under two main head-
ings, 'In the Mainstream' and 'On the Margins'. Such a division,
readers should note, is somewhat arbitrary. The sort of music treated

---

[41] The sexual ambiguity is to the forefront in M. Simpson, *Saint Morrissey*
(London: SAF Publishing, 2004). A forthcoming book on the singer by Gavin
Hopps, *Morrissey: The Pageant of His Bleeding Heart* (London: Continuum),
includes a chapter on 'Morrissey and God'.

[42] 'Jesus', on the album *The Velvet Underground* (1969). 'Covering' is the
technical term for performance of music originally written for others.

[43] The final track on their album *Screamadelica* (1992). The first track, 'Movin'
On Up', raises similar issues.

under the latter (heavy rock and rap) is still listened to by millions of devoted followers. It is simply that to most religious believers—wrongly in my view—it seems even further removed from any possibility of transmitting a sense of the divine.

In the Mainstream

In the final section of this chapter I want to examine more closely those variants that are usually judged most antithetical to religion (heavy rock/metal and rap) to see whether they do indeed foreclose all possibility of religious experience. Here, however, I focus on the sort of popular music that is found most easily accessible by the population at large. Religious critiques have been directed in some circles even against the Beatles.[44] So even more universal pop has had to face religious objections, but in my view those problems are largely the creation of the critics' over-suspicious minds. Nevertheless, it is important to take seriously the objection that such music is necessarily ephemeral and so unlikely to elicit anything of significance for religion. I begin therefore by saying something about the apparent triviality of so many of the songs of major names in pop before focusing more narrowly on two individuals and two groups (all very successful) that have in fact taken the Christian faith seriously.

The lyrics of the Beatles as a group are often contrasted negatively with the greater depth that they then achieved as individual songwriters. However, if the progression of the phenomenal success of their hits across the late sixties is analysed carefully, what one discovers is that the group itself demonstrated considerable development. In their earlier phase there were marked contrasts to the Stones: the focus was on the positive side of relationships, there was virtually no social comment, and poetic devices such as metaphor were sparse.[45]

---

[44] For such attacks, often far-fetched, see J. Barnard, *Pop Goes the Gospel* (Welwyn: Evangelical Press, 1983); E. Holmberg, *Hell's Bells: The Dangers of Rock and Roll* (Gainsville, Fla.: Reel 2 Real Ministries, 1994). Hidden, devilish meanings are alleged, for example.

[45] The Lennon–McCartney partnership offered 55% positive relationships to the Stones' 18%; 15% social comment to the Stones' 55%; and 30% poetic device to the Stones' 60%: so J. Fitzgerald, 'Lennon–McCartney and the Early British Invasion, 1964–6', in I. Inglis (ed.), *The Beatles, Popular Music and Society* (Basingstoke: Macmillan, 2000), 53–85, esp. 58.

Emotional relationships in which personal pronouns predominate, however, gradually gave place to more reflective themes.[46] Such use of personal pronouns helped their audiences to engage. So the simpler words and themes should not by any means be discounted. The songs could be used as means of personal self-exploration, as the young sang along to them. As a couple of commentators have observed, the frequent use of the second-person pronoun without the introduction of people's names 'creates both a sense of specific immediacy and of general applicability'.[47]

The strange alchemy between the brooding, cynical John Lennon and the ebullient, optimistic Paul McCartney also ensured a degree of tension in how the words were conveyed that encouraged rather more than simple reception without any further engagement. So, for example, in 'She Loves You' (1963) Lennon's downbeat approach to speech inflections contrasts nicely with McCartney's harmonies. Again, in 'She's Leaving Home' their contrasting vocal styles are used to enhance the difference between two contrasting estimates of what departure from home might mean, the one a gentle lament, the other a cynical virtual monotone.[48] While in 'Help' (1965), with its opening in B minor, Lennon is clearly in the lead, McCartney's 'Yesterday' of the same year strikes a quite different mood, with the introduction of a string quartet in the background. Of those songs that reached the top of the hit parade it is perhaps 'Eleanor Rigby' and 'Let It Be' that are, religiously, the most interesting. Although the latter is actually a reflection on the death of his mother Mary, McCartney's use of gospel rhythms generated much hostility from Lennon. By its positioning on the album, Lennon deliberately sought to undermine the song's seriousness and attempt at spiritual uplift.[49] It was also McCartney who played the major role in 'Eleanor Rigby'. The indifference of the priest Father MacKenzie

[46] For a computer analysis of the extent of the change between 1962–5 and 1966–70, see C. Cook and N. Mercer, 'From Me to You: Austerity to Profligacy in the Language of the Beatles', in Inglis (ed.), *The Beatles*, 86–104.

[47] Ibid. 92.

[48] 'She's Leaving Home' is on the album *Sgt. Pepper's Lonely Hearts Club Band* (1967).

[49] On the album *Let It Be* (1970), Lennon placed the title track between sounds of a young boy pleading 'Now we'd like to do "Hark the Angels Come"' and a ribald ditty about a Liverpool prostitute. For the argument between the two, see I. MacDonald, *The Beatles at No. 1* (London: Pimlico, 2003), 90–2.

and the fact that his sermon will not be heard were intended not as an attack on religion as such but rather as a sad reflection on a more general loss of communal values. So it is not just songs of uplift that work religiously in this area. The haunting string octet in the background of 'Eleanor Rigby' intensifies the sense of something lost, of what might have been and so of what could possibly be recaptured.

Madonna has had a hit in the British charts every year since 1984.[50] For much of that time she has had a controversial relationship with Christianity. So she would seem a good case to take as our other general example. The product of a devout Catholic home, her public persona is not, as many think, a deliberate insult to the Virgin Mary but her actual baptismal name.[51] It was her gay dance teacher, Christopher Flynn, who encouraged her early rebellion (at 15). This revolt was to become most evident in the videos that have accompanied some of her albums, most notably *Like a Virgin* (1984), *Like a Prayer* (1989) and *In Bed with Madonna* (1991).[52] If it was their sexually explicit character that raised most questions, *Like a Prayer* also has burning crosses and a black Jesus. Both her children, however, have been baptized (the second in Dornoch Cathedral in the north of Scotland) and she herself described her second marriage ceremony nearby (in 2000) as 'truly a magical religious experience'.[53]

Although none of this appears to mark a return to Christianity, she has shown increasing interest in spiritual issues, particularly under the influence of Rabbi Philip Berg and his Kabbalah movement. The result in her 2003 album *American Life* was not only the rejection of materialism as able to offer any ultimate satisfaction but also a song which declares, 'I'm not religious … But I feel such love | Makes me want to pray'. There is even a positive reference to Christ himself. One song asks, 'Jesus Christ will you look at me | Don't know who

[50] Her collection of her greatest hits to date, *Immaculate Collection* (1990), had sold 22 million copies worldwide.

[51] She was born into a large Catholic family in 1958 and baptized Madonna Louise (Ciccone).

[52] The last was in fact a documentary based around her 1990 world tour. The video *Like a Prayer* is analysed in T. Beaudoin, *Virtual Faith: The Irreverent Spiritual Quest of Generation X* (San Francisco: Jossey-Bass, 1998), 74–5, 90–2.

[53] Quoted in V. Chow, *Madonna* (London: Kandour, 2004), 133. For Rabbi Berg, see 141–2.

I'm supposed to be'.[54] However, the song concludes a long way from Christianity: 'But in the process I forgot | That I am just as good as you'. Nonetheless, the reference does show that the issue is not entirely resolved for her, as indeed is confirmed by a reference to her childhood prayers in a subsequent track.[55] The temptation is to detect closure rather than a mind pulling in two directions at once. So, for example, Christian critics saw only sex outside of marriage in 'Papa Don't Preach' and not the decision to keep the resultant child.[56] Contradictory and confused ramblings should, therefore, not be discounted. The very fact of issues being expressed raises the possibility of hearers being moved further by the music in one particular direction rather than another. Hesitant openness may work no less effectively than firm affirmation, and perhaps more so for those naturally suspicious of religion.

Dylan and Springsteen

Christian commentators have reacted with hostility not only to non-Christian song but also against some leading figures who have professed the Christian faith. In the case of the two singers and two groups I am now about to discuss the danger has been that they would be pressurized into conformity rather than allowed their own distinctive voice. Fortunately, their different theological biases can help alert us to precisely that problem. Certainly, in the case of the two singers it is hardly likely that Bob Dylan's conversion to conservative evangelical Christianity would evoke the same resonances as Bruce Springsteen's return to the Catholicism of his youth. Although Springsteen's writing is scarcely on the same level as that of Dylan, who has even been nominated for the Nobel Prize for Literature, it does make sense to consider them together.[57] Dylan

---

[54] The first quotation is from 'Nothing Fails', the second from 'X-Static Process'. The reference to Christ could possibly be an expletive, but her delivery suggests otherwise.

[55] 'Mother and Father'.

[56] 'Papa Don't Preach' appears on *True Blue* (1986).

[57] The nomination was made in 1996, and supported by, among others, Gordon Ball (an American literature scholar), Andrew Motion (Poet Laureate) and Christopher Ricks (a former Cambridge professor, appointed Professor of Poetry at Oxford in 2004).

horrified conventional lovers of folk music with his introduction of an electric guitar into his act at the Newport Folk Festival in 1965.[58] Springsteen has never used anything else.' Both share a style that might be characterized as folk rock. A further element of commonality is that during the long period of Dylan's decline in popularity and originality Springsteen was often spoken of as the new Dylan.[59]

Dylan is a Jew by parentage and also by early upbringing, and this no doubt explains the appearance of biblical allusions in his lyrics long before his conversion.[60] The strong protest element in some of these explains in part his popularity in the sixties, but the natural power of his poetry and music should not be discounted.[61] Although there were signs of a growing religious interest prior to his conversion in 1978, many of his fans took that conversion as a betrayal.[62] It led to an intensive three-month course at the Vineyard Fellowship, where he was encouraged to read the book of Revelation as pointing to the end-times in our own day. Russia and Iran, for example, were identified as Gog and Magog.[63] That produced some harsh, judgemental lyrics that further contributed to the decline in his popularity.[64] However, some non-believers did try to enter imaginatively into his new world, and in retrospect

[58] For what happened at Newport, see N. Williamson, *The Rough Guide to Bob Dylan* (London: Rough Guides, 2004), 54.

[59] In their 1981 tours Dylan followed hard on the heels of Springsteen and usually to unfavourable comparisons: C. Heylin, *Bob Dylan: Behind the Shades: Take Two* (London: Penguin, 2001), 540–2. Already in 1975 Springsteen was outselling Dylan by three to one. Springsteen, though, did support Dylan during his lean period: ibid. 624.

[60] He was born Robert Allen Zimmerman in 1941 and in 1954 he duly celebrated his bar mitzvah.

[61] Powerful protest songs include 'A Hard Rain's A-Gonna Fall' (Cuban missile crisis), 'With God on Our Side (militarism) and 'The Times They Are A-Changin,' (civil rights).

[62] The album *John Wesley Harding* (1967) seems in some ways to anticipate his future direction. For the story of how a silver cross thrown onto the stage by an admirer led subsequently to an experience of the presence of Christ in his hotel room, see Heylin, *Bob Dylan*, 491.

[63] Rev. 20.8. For the Vineyard Fellowship and the teachings on the immediate future espoused by one of its leading members, Hal Lindsey, see ibid. 492–500, 517–18.

[64] *Saved* (1980), the second album after his conversion, was less accommodating than the first (*Slow Train Coming*, 1979), perhaps because of the hostility he had encountered (in part self-induced, since in the early days he made no concessions to the non-believing members of his audience).

Shot of Love (1981) in particular is now often viewed as a great album.[65] One track, 'Every Grain of Sand', has met with virtually universal acclaim. Nonetheless, despite that praise, after the flop of *Saved* in 1979 almost 18 years were to elapse before any of his albums were once more to make the top twenty. Many were rightly dismissed, though *Oh Mercy* (1989) seems in a rather different category. With the highly successful *Time Out of Mind* (1997), however, what was new was not, as is sometimes claimed, the suppression of religion but rather its outworking in less explicit forms. Gone is the arrogant self-certainty, and in its place has come a more humble fellow-seeker. One lyric, 'Tryin' to Get to Heaven', says it all.

In seeking to determine why Dylan succeeds in speaking to so many one could of course point to the range of experience to which he alludes, from the intimately personal to the major social issues of the day. But to succeed more is surely required than this. There are his gifts as a poet, seen perhaps most notably in 'Visions of Joanna', described by the present Poet Laureate, Andrew Motion, as 'the best song lyric ever written'.[66] There is also his juxtaposition of unusual images, and of unexpected, provocative rhymes such as end/again or silence/violence.[67] His voice too can add to the effect with pregnant pauses that give added meaning to the words that follow,[68] or else jerky delivery in conflict with words of calm to suggest tension between longing and reality.[69] Not least is the way in which all this is set to music, with the short solo instrumentals sometimes the most powerful element in the composition—for

[65] The atheist Christopher Ricks is insistent on 'the ways in which art is invaluable in giving us sympathetic access to systems of belief that are not our own': *Dylan's Visions of Sin* (London: Viking, 2003), 377–9, esp. 377.

[66] Quoted in M. J. Gilmour, *Tangled Up in the Bible: Bob Dylan and Scripture* (New York: Continuum, 2004), 6. For the words to 'Visions of Joanna', see, B. Dylan, *Lyrics 1962–2001* (New York: Simon and Schuster, 2004), 193–4.

[67] For some helpful comments, see Ricks, *Dylan's Visions*, 30–48, 290. As an example of images juxtaposed, note the combination of the smell of burning wood and the sweet scent of magnolia blossom in 'Blind Willie McTell,' Dylan, *Lyrics*, 478.

[68] An effective use of pauses is, 'Series of Dreams' on *Oh Mercy*. Note too the deliberate gasping for breath in 'Ring Them Bells' (same album). For a profound analysis of this album, see P. Williams, *Bob Dylan: Performing Artist*, vol. 3, *1986–1990 and Beyond* (London: Omnibus, 2004), 171–211.

[69] As in 'Watching the River Flow' and 'Time Passes Slowly' (both from *New Morning*, 1970).

example, the use of the saxophone to conclude 'Where Teardrops Fall' or the piano invocation with which 'Ring Them Bells' begins.[70] Perhaps most powerful of all is Dylan's use of the harmonica. In 'Blowin' in the Wind' this wind instrument is itself allowed to give the answer, while its very frailty is used with haunting effect to underline the message of 'Every Grain of Sand', with its moving recognition of the universal human need to stretch out in longing beyond our own personal resources.[71]

Some of the examples I have given have religious themes, some not. Controversially, Pope John Paul II chose 'Knockin' on Heaven's Door' for the World Eucharistic Congress.[72] Personally, I prefer Dylan's own later self-correction, 'Tryin' to Get to Heaven', with its less self-assertive tone.[73] Certainly some of Dylan's earlier lyrics had a rather worrying arrogance about them both towards God and his fellow human beings.[74] He may even have thought of himself as having had some sort of special divine commission that made him immune to ordinary critique.[75] Where he draws us with him is when words and music combine to suggest a longing for something more than anything around us could possibly provide. In 'Every Grain of Sand' he does this by setting restless human uncertainty against the quiet divine care he sees reflected in the lapping motions of the sea on the shore's numerous grains of sand. In 'Where Teardrops Fall' his method is to draw us first into what looks like an ordinary love story only to find it transformed into a relationship with God.

Eight years younger than Dylan, Springsteen's background is also quite different.[76] Working class rather than middle class, his home was also a Catholic one. His earliest experiences of religion, however,

---

[70] Both on *Oh Mercy*.

[71] From *Shot of Love*: Dylan, *Lyrics*, 451.

[72] At Bologna in 1997. The controversy was not about the choice of songs but the alleged payment of $350,000: Heylin, *Bob Dylan*, 704–5; Williamson, *Rough Guide*, 186

[73] To compare and contrast the words of these two songs, see Dylan, *Lyrics*, 313, 564. The former are quite trivial, the latter profound.

[74] Even the normally sympathetic Ricks finds one verse of 'Watered-Down Love' impossible to defend, and rightly dropped: *Dylan's Visions*, 469. For nastiness towards an ex-lover (Joan Baez), see 'Ballad in Plain D': Dylan, *Lyrics*, 129–30.

[75] In 'Highway 61 Revisited' (ibid. 178) he actually identifies himself with Isaac (61 was the number of his local highway and his own father was called Abraham). Elsewhere, he is like Christ 'betrayed by a kiss'. For further details, see Gilmour, *Tangled up in the Bible*, 35–6.

[76] He was born in 1949, Dylan in 1941.

were decidedly negative. He tells of how 'a nun even stuffed me in a garbage can under her desk because, she said, that's where I belonged'.[77] His education was also fairly minimal. He himself has said that it was rock and roll that came nearest to both an education and a religion in his earlier life: 'it's like [Elvis] came along and whispered a dream, and then we all dreamed it somehow'.[78] As well as exploring more personal experience, like Dylan he has also focused on social issues, though these tend to be of a more domestic kind.[79] In particular, his gravel-like voice can echo the frustrations of unemployed working-class men (as in 'Born in the USA') or poor Mexican immigrants (as in 'The Line' or 'Balboa Park').[80] Still his most popular song, 'Born in the USA' is actually about a Vietnam veteran returning home only to find himself bereft of any work. Its rousing chorus, however, makes it understandable why, as already noted, for so many it became instead a kind of substitute American anthem. Springsteen was in the end reconciled to the result.[81] In any case, in albums such as *Darkness on the Edge of Town* (1978) and *Nebraska* (1982) he had already fought hard to provide an effective blue-collar voice, one that would counter the predominantly negative media images of this sector of society at this time.[82]

In the collection he has produced of the words to his songs, he himself is quite candid about the way in which religious belief gradually returned. Identifying the theme of an early song as 'the search for redemption' he observes: 'over the next twenty years I'd work this one like only a good Catholic boy could'.[83] It was a river that ran much deeper than that somewhat flippant remark implies. He speaks of a continuing, far from easy search for transcendence.[84]

[77] Both this and the following quotation are in C. Sandford, *Springsteen Point Blank* (London: TimeWarner, 1999), 22.

[78] For music as education, note his song 'No Surrender': 'We learned more from a three minute record, baby, than we ever learned in school': B. Springsteen, *Bruce Springsteen Songs* (London: Virgin, 2003 edn), 176.

[79] Early on he decided that rock 'was capable of conveying serious ideas . . . and that . . . people . . . were looking for something': E. Alterman, *The Promise of Bruce Springsteen* (Boston: Little, Brown and Co., 2001 edn), 19.

[80] 'Phil Spector melted down and mixed with gravel' is one description of his voice: ibid. 101. For lyrics to these three, see Springsteen, *Bruce Springsteen Songs*, 169, 284, 286.

[81] Ibid. 164–5.

[82] For some examples of this problem, see Alterman, *Promise*, 135–8.

[83] Springsteen, *Bruce Springsteen Songs*, 35. He is commenting on 'Incident on 57th Street'.

[84] Ibid. 68.

His lyrics wrestle with the recognition that such an encounter only becomes possible through risk, and in particular the risk of commitment to other human beings. So on his album *The River* (1980) he asks in one song:

> You're so afraid of being somebody's fool
> Not walkin' tough, baby, not walkin' cool
> You walk cool but darlin' can you walk the line
> And face the ties that bind.

In another he expresses the desire: 'And I wish God would send me a word, I send me something I'm afraid to lose'.[85] In *Tunnel of Love* (1987) the theme song compares the experience of being in love to entering the dark uncertainty of a fairground tunnel, while the title track of the subsequent album (*Human Touch*, 1992) declares: 'You can't shut off the risk and the pain, I Without losin' the love that remains I We're all riders on this train'.[86] But the experience is not simply a human one, for through that risk comes awareness of the divine love that makes it all possible. So of husband and wife he writes:

> At their bedside he brushed the hair
> From his wife's face as the moon
> Shone on her skin so white
> Filling their room in the beauty of God's fallen light.[87]

Again, commitment to one's children evokes a similar deeper dimension to the experience:

> Well now on a summer night in a dusky room
> Comes a little piece of the Lord's undying light
> Crying like he swallowed the fiery moon.[88]

With *The Rising*, his 2002 album, there also came recognition of how self-sacrifice opens up new possibilities. If the repeated 'Up the stairs, into the fire' moved many of his listeners to tears as they recalled the heroic ascent of the firemen during the September 11th disaster, they were also urged to use what had happened to widen their own commitments: 'May your faith give us faith I May your hope give us hope I May your love give us love'.[89] Springsteen does not hesitate to

---

[85] From 'The Ties that Bind' and 'Drive All Night': ibid. 103, 130.
[86] Ibid. 203, 221.
[87] From 'Cautious Man' on *Tunnel of Love*: ibid. 199.
[88] From 'Living Proof' on *Lucky Town* (1992): ibid. 252.   [89] Ibid. 310.

speak of the song as containing 'the religious image of ascension'. So it is perhaps therefore not all that surprising that he chose to 'bookend' 'Into the Fire' with the album's title track, which he describes as a 'secular stations of the cross' that passes beyond to 'the opening sky'.[90] Its catchy chorus, 'Come on up for the rising', is thus about much more than merely transcending human difficulties. Implicitly, it can also be seen to be about Christ's own resurrection and the possibilities for new life that this offers to us.

Although his hostility to the Roman Catholic Church has undoubtedly softened, none of this should be taken to mark a return to orthodox Catholicism.[91] Yet, as the internationally acclaimed sociologist Andrew Greeley has observed, from *Tunnel of Love* onwards he has in effect become a Catholic 'liturgist' of considerable importance: he attempts to correlate 'the self-communication of God in secular life with the overarching symbols/narratives of his/our tradition'.[92] In all of this Springsteen has adopted a variety of different musical styles. He speaks, for example, of adopting a deliberately more 'raw' approach with *The River* album of 1980, and certainly it includes hard rock as well as country and blues.[93] There are also borrowings from the likes of Chuck Berry, the Byrds, and Eagles, but, as the title track indicates, he is also capable of combining a Hank Williams chorus with something utterly new, with the bursts of piano and harp that give this particular track its power.[94] Of course there will always be those who resist being exposed by his music to new dimensions in their experience. Perversely, the title track on *Tunnel of Love* has even been interpreted as simply a metaphor for the vagina, but the music suggests otherwise, as heavy beat and swelling guitar open up into a chorus in which the singer's now straining voice insists on going beyond darkness into the brightness of a new day. If Dylan indicates what can be achieved through a very public endorsement of the specifics of one version of Christianity, Springsteen illustrates how

[90] By 'secular' I do not think he means 'non-religious' but rather human experience in the ordinary world that is analogous to, but still different from, Christ's own stations.

[91] Although his failed first marriage was according to Catholic rites, his second was in fact Unitarian: Sandford, *Springsteen Point Blank*, 320: cf. also 346–7.

[92] Quoted from the journal *America* in Alterman, *Promise*, 186–7.

[93] Springsteen, *Bruce Springsteen Songs*, 97.

[94] For the borrowings, see Sandford, *Springsteen Point Blank*, 180–1; for the vagina reference, ibid. 282.

commitment to a much vaguer faith can nonetheless also allow millions the possibility of seeing their own experience and world differently in the light of a God at work within it.[95]

Both Dylan and Springsteen are Americans. The nearest European example of a similar type of music is perhaps Van Morrison. Born in 1945 in Protestant east Belfast, in the late seventies he returned to a faith that has also been influenced by Scientology. There are some intriguing examples of the difference a religious perspective can make on albums such as *Beautiful Vision* (1982), *A Sense of Wonder* (1984) and *Avalon Sunset* (1989). The obvious complaint that might be made against such music is its overconfident tone. An album such as *Avalon Sunset*, for example, has none of the grit or hard realism that one finds in Dylan and Springsteen. Instead, God is everywhere, from great landscapes to paintings and architecture.[96] *A Sense of Wonder*, however, offers a more balanced perspective. It is, he suggests, a vision not easily won. But once won, it can make for joy even in the most adverse of circumstances.[97] Yet something is still missing. The words remain more effective than the music. The truth seems to be that Morrison is much better at creating a sense of peace or wonder than he is at working through struggle.

Pop Bands: U2 and Nick Cave and The Bad Seeds

In turning now to bands rather than individuals, I want to consider one such from Ireland and the other from Australia. One theory of how U2 got its name is from the U2 crisis that erupted as the lead singer of this group was being born. In 1960 a plane of this type was shot down over the Soviet Union, and this was to generate a major crisis in Russian–American relations.[98] Alternatively, the appeal may more straightforwardly have lain in its verbal simplicity and in the inclusive character of the pun, 'you too' hinting at the band's

[95] *Tunnel of Love* sold over 3 million copies.

[96] All the tracks are positive. Landscape: 'These are the Days'; paintings and architecture: 'When Will I Ever Learn to Live in God'.

[97] As in 'If Only You Knew' and 'Let the Slave'.

[98] The pilot, Gary Powers, was paraded before the world media. The Cuban missile crisis came two years later, caused in part by information gathered by means of the same type of plane. For U2's choice of name, see E. Dunphy, *Unforgettable Fire* (New York: Warner, 1988), 5, 98.

desire to work closely with its audience.[99] Their lead singer, Paul Hewson, or Bono as he is now better known, was brought up in a religious home, as was guitarist The Edge (Dave Evans), the other major contributor to the band's lyrics and compositions.[100] All the members of the band attended the same non-denominational school in the suburbs of Dublin, and it was there that an early version of the band was first formed.[101] Disenchantment with religion (and quarrels with parents) coincided with the launching of a singing and performance career.[102] It looked, therefore, as though that aspect of their lives was now firmly in the past, when a chance encounter in a local coffee house led them to attend a small charismatic church known as the Shalom group.[103] Although one member of the band remained firmly agnostic, and at one time it looked as though they would break up on account of such religious divisions, in the end they stayed together.[104] Religion has continued to be a significant, if changing, influence on the nature of their repertoire.

A more recent example of a singer similarly embedded in charismatic Christianity is the English pop star Daniel Bedingfield.[105] There the relationship seems an uncomplicated one. With U2, however, the pressures from Shalom were found to be too great.[106] To the chagrin of some of their followers, it is now a more inclusive form of belief

---

[99] The book about them most popular with fans is W. Flanagan, *U2: At the End of the World* (London: Bantam, 1995). Significantly, Flanagan was also chosen to write the introduction to *U2: The Complete Songs* (London: Wise Publications, 1999).

[100] Hewson's father was a Roman Catholic, his mother (who died when he was 14) Church of Ireland. Evans' father was Welsh and an elder in the Presbyterian Church.

[101] Mount Temple, a comprehensive school.

[102] For some incidents, including punk and 'mooning', see Dunphy, *Unforgettable Fire*, 63–9, 77, 116.

[103] Partly under the influence of another group known as the Virgin Prunes: for the story, see ibid. 132–4.

[104] Adam Clayton (the agnostic) felt excluded. Larry Mullen and The Edge both surmised that their Christian belief called them elsewhere, and almost left. See ibid. 174–5, 202–5.

[105] Seen in his 2004 album *Second First Impressions*, where the album's vote of thanks begins: 'The Author of all Creativity, my Father God; Champion of the Underdog, Yeshua, the Christ; the Catalyst and Comforter, the Spirit of Holiness'. 'Holiness' is also one of the tracks.

[106] For its fundamentalist extremes, see N. McCormick, *I Was Bono's Doppelgänger* (London: Penguin, 2004), 125–6, 138.

that is espoused.[107] Perhaps as a result the imagery is also richer. No longer content simply to quote scripture, biblical metaphors are developed in interesting ways.[108] Indicative too of that change is what Bono recently chose as a gift for an unbelieving friend: instead of a Gospel or Bible, it was Tolstoy's *The Kingdom of God is Within You*.[109] Musically, that change of attitude is best expressed in the 1987 track 'I Still Haven't Found What I'm Looking For'.[110] The spring and bounce in the background acoustic guitar and bongos, however, ensure that the message still remains an essentially optimistic one. Indeed, in their early days it was the character of the music on its own rather than the match of music and words that especially caught people's attention. This was thanks mainly to the contribution of The Edge, who already in his early twenties was creating an unusual sonic world of echoes, drones and bright, shiny, ringing effects.[111]

Like Dylan and Springsteen they use their music to comment on social issues.[112] Not surprisingly, given their Irish background, 'Sunday Bloody Sunday' is one of their most effective songs, not only for content but also for the way in which a high, jolting rhythm from The Edge combines with a strutting, martial melody below from Larry Mullen.[113] But many other concerns of the day are also addressed, such as the track that concludes *The Joshua Tree*, 'Mothers of the Disappeared'. Here the drone is accentuated by the treatment of the piano as more percussive than melodic keyboard, and so, as the words require, 'In the wind we hear their laughter | In the rain we see their tears. | Hear their heartbeat, we hear their heartbeat'.

---

[107] For an evangelical defence of such changes, as in part due to irony, see S. Stockman, *Walk On: The Spiritual Journey of U2* (Lake Mary, Fla.: Relevant Books, 2001).

[108] Two pertinent examples are 'Until the End of the World' (from *Achtung Baby*, 1991) and 'The First Time' (from *Zooropa*, 1993). The first takes the perspective of Judas, the second tells a parable about someone running away from God.

[109] McCormick, *I was Bono's Doppelgänger*, 296. It was a 1996 gift to McCormick, who has been a friend of Bono's since schooldays.

[110] From the album *The Joshua Tree*.

[111] Bono has jokingly described the style as 'Zen Presbyterian'.

[112] Apart from those examples listed another is their music for the film *Philadelphia* (1993), a story of prejudice against a lawyer with AIDS. A more extensive contribution to a film score is *Music from The Million Dollar Hotel* (2000), of which the best number is perhaps 'Falling at Your Feet'.

[113] From the *War* album (1982). There is a powerful performance on the *Rattle and Hum* 1988 DVD, where Bono uses the deaths at Enniskillen earlier that same day to plead for peace.

Religion sometimes makes its appearance within those protest songs, as in these lines from 'Sunday Bloody Sunday:' 'The real battle is just begun | To claim the victory Jesus won'.[114] But more commonly it is given separate treatment. In earlier days the lyrics might be based on scripture, and that was no doubt one reason why Bono was asked to write the introduction to one recent edition of the Psalms.[115] An incidental result was quite a number of songs that centred on praise.[116] But disillusionment with institutional religion has led to a greater focus on experience. As Bono has put it: 'I'm not into religion. I am completely anti-religious. Religion is a term for a collection, a denomination. I am interested in personal experience of God.'[117] The resultant style of writing is to determine the mood first, then the music, and only finally deliver the words in a sort of stream of consciousness.[118] 'Where the Streets Have No Name' had its origins in a visit to Ethiopia and the experience of that country's natural beauty as contrasted with so much waste in the developed world.[119] At one level it can be heard as evocative of that contrast, especially in the long rising scale that introduces the description of the mountain towns of Ethiopia. Intriguingly, however, in live performance the song has moved far beyond this point into what is clearly an expression of religious experience. This is perhaps most obvious in a recorded performance from Boston where Bono, bathed in light, links the song with the words of Psalm 116: 'What can I give back to God? . . . I'll lift high the cup of salvation' (vv. 12–13).[120] In effect, the imagery is being used to describe heaven, as a swelling organ-like keyboard, Edge's ringing guitar sound, a pulsing rhythm section and Bono's urgent vocals all combine to force a sacramental moment, with the image of those mountains now linking two different worlds.

---

[114] *U2: The Complete Songs*, 91.

[115] '40', the last track on the *War* album, is based on Psalm 40. For Bono's introduction to the Psalms, see *The Canongate Pocket Book of the Psalms* (Edinburgh: Canongate, 1999); also available in the collection of such introductions, *Revelations* (Edinburgh: Canongate, 2005), 135–40.

[116] As in the 'Gloria' that opens their *October* album of 1981.

[117] Quoted in McCormick, *I was Bono's Doppelgänger*, 114.

[118] Dunphy, *Unforgettable Fire*, 208, 306.

[119] For this element in the background to the song (from the album *The Joshua Tree*), see M. Chatterton, *U2: The Ultimate Encyclopedia* (London: Fire Fly, 2004 edn), 251.

[120] Available as a DVD: *Elevation Tour: Live from Boston* (2001). The translation of the psalm is by Eugene Peterson.

Not that the group always succeeds in matching music and words. 'Yahweh', a song on their most recent album, is a case in point.[121] It is concerned to express the desire for a personal divine remaking, but in my view it is better read than heard. Although there are some nice touches, such as the use of a mandolin on the words 'the sun is coming up' and the ascending guitar riff that reflects the upwardness implied in the lyrics, it fails to connect in its conclusion. Rather than providing an accompanying musical image, in response to the plea 'Take this heart | And make it break', the music is simply aborted abruptly.[122] With the gentle romantic melody for 'Grace', however, words and music are perfectly aligned:

> Grace, it's the name for a girl
> It's also a thought that changed the world ...
> Grace she carries a world on her hips ...
> No twirls or skips between her fingertips ...
> Grace makes beauty out of ugly things.[123]

Set alongside 'I Still Haven't Found What I'm Looking For', the two songs perhaps best encapsulate the group's overall religious message: experience of a caring divine presence combined with restless (but not hopeless) dissatisfaction at human corruptions of that basic insight.

The other group I have chosen is Nick Cave and The Bad Seeds. Here, as their name suggests, the focus is on the lead singer, much more so than is the case with U2. Nor is this by any means the only difference. For much of his career Cave has had a depressing, not to say jaundiced, view on the world that has only lightened in more recent times. As such his style was, initially at least, representative of what became known as Goth rock, a mixture of rock and punk, though as the years advanced a variety of new musical styles were added. The musical range is one factor that contributes to making his songs such attractive listening but almost equally appealing is the quality of the lyrics. While their imagery, even when overwhelmingly negative, can rouse the imagination of all kinds of listeners, for a Christian there is the added attraction of the repeated use of biblical imagery and allusion. Not that this has always betokened belief.

---

[121] The relevant album is *How to Dismantle an Atomic Bomb* (2004).

[122] Perhaps the aborting is meant to represent the heart breaking, but if so it is not the first thought that comes to mind on listening to the piece.

[123] From the 2000 album *All that You Can't Leave Behind*.

Cave was born in Australia in 1957 to a schoolteacher father and a librarian mother.[124] They were practising Anglicans and Cave's earliest public performance was in association with the church. It was a loving family where reading was encouraged, and Cave got to know well the King James or Authorized Version of the Bible. Intriguingly, he mentions St John of the Cross and Johnny Cash as the two major influences on his earliest singing and writing styles.[125] At art college in Melbourne, however, rebellion set in.[126] He heard that his father had died in a road accident while he was under arrest for drunkenness. His habit of heroin addiction seems to have begun at this point and was to last until 1989, while his home base moved between London, Berlin and São Paulo. In some ways the addiction may have helped his creativity, and so even now he does not wish to disown that past.[127] It was a creativity that was to express itself in film appearances and scores, as well as in a recent ballet production.[128] It also led to a rather strange novel, *And the Ass Saw the Angel*, which tells an odd tale of a fundamentalist community in the rural heartlands of the United States, where William Faulkner, James Joyce and Gabriel Garcia Márquez can be seen to be among the pertinent influences.[129]

But it is the music that is our concern here. After the breakup of his earlier group, The Birthday Party, Cave's first album with The Bad Seeds was *From Her to Eternity* in 1984. The clanging, almost industrial howl is in marked contrast to *Tender Prey* (1988), where Cave uses the lower register of his baritone voice to good effect in ballads that

[124] He was born at Warracknabeal, a small town about 300 kilometres from Melbourne. His father taught English.

[125] In the audio biography *Maximum Nick Cave* (Chrome Dreams, 2005). Factual information (unless otherwise noted) has been derived from here or from the web site <www.nick-cave.com>.

[126] Caulfield Institute of Technology, now part of Monash University.

[127] 'I was a junkie for 20 years. I'm not going to deny all that. That would be to trust the whole reborn thing, whether it's religious or cleaning up': quoted at <www.contactmusic.com>.

[128] Films include Wim Wenders' *Wings of Desire* (1987) and Tom DiCillo's *Johnny Suede* (1991). The Sydney Dance Company took his *Underland* (2005) on a tour of a number of countries (including England) in 2005: further details at <www.bad.seed.org>.

[129] *And the Ass Saw the Angel* (London, Penguin, 1989). Although there is a clear plot, I failed to detect any obvious 'message', if there was one.

explore what is still for him a dark world.[130] The album opens and closes with what has become one of his best-known songs, 'The Mercy Seat'. It tells of an innocent man going to the electric chair. To me the second version is the more powerful, as it builds more gradually to a crescendo in its repeated refrain about 'An eye for an eye | And a truth for a truth'. Cave has said that what maintained his interest in religion during his dark period was the Old Testament God, that 'maniacal, punitive god who dealt out to long suffering humanity punishments that had me drop-jawed in disbelief at the very depths of their vengefulness. The Old Testament spoke to that part of me that railed and spat at the world.'[131] In this song it is implied that it is such a malevolent god who had instigated the act in the first place. That might suggest a tirade against religion, but the violent death in the electric chair is movingly juxtaposed (without resolution) against Jesus' peaceful life as a carpenter.[132] So the ageing Johnny Cash was perhaps right when in recording his own moving version he spoke of forms of religion that dehumanized people in encouraging endorsement of such punishments.[133] While in the album's second song, 'Up Jumped the Devil and Staked his Claim', the Devil does precisely that, as the title of 'New Morning' promises, that song does at least envisage the possibility of a fresh start.[134]

The 1997 album *The Boatman's Call*, however, is the first to make love songs central, though still with more than a touch of sadness. The piano has now also firmly replaced percussion as the main instrument. The track 'Far From Me' alludes to the end of his relationship with his former girlfriend, P. J. Harvey.[135] Some have seen in the trauma involved the source of his return to church attendance, but Cave has vehemently denied this. He himself puts it thus:

[130] On *From Her to Eternity* there is extensive use of drums and percussion, with the keyboard in a very subordinate, largely staccato role. Only 'In the Ghetto' and 'The Moon is in the Gutter' anticipate his ballad style of the future, though even here the mood remains a gloomy one.

[131] *Maximum Nick Cave*, 1st track.

[132] As well as on the album cover, the lyrics are also available in N. Cave, *The Complete Lyrics 1978–2001* (London: Penguin, 2001), 135–8. For the juxtaposition, see the first two long stanzas on 136.

[133] On the album *American III: Solitary Man* (2002).

[134] There is also a song about John the Baptist, although he is never named ('Mercy').

[135] He has since married (Susie Bick).

One of the things that I guess excites me about belief in God is the notion it's so unbelievable, irrational and sometimes absurd. So to put your hand up and say 'I believe in God' seems a difficult thing to do, particularly considering the way things are going in the world. But that's also why it is so exciting. It is about imagination and mystery. And that for me is what art is about as well. So they are very much tied together.[136]

However, as the album's opening words make clear, he has still not come the whole way. 'I don't believe in an interventionist God', he sings, while in a poem written at about the same time he comments: 'God is gone ... I found the eternal woman | The fire that leapt from Solomon's pages'.[137]

So it is to *No More Shall We Part* (2001) that we must turn for a clearer reflection of Cave's new position. The more positive tone is reflected not only in greater use of the warmer sounds that piano and strings can bring but also in a consistently higher voice register.[138] If the guitar and piano arrangement for the opening 'As I Sat by her Side' is perhaps unnecessarily simple, 'The Sorrowful Wife' and 'We Came Along this Road' are quite beautiful piano compositions, while 'Gate to the Garden' offers a fine use of guitar arpeggio to accompany the theme of finding God in human love. Despite its 'gospel' chorus 'How have I offended thee?', 'Oh my Lord' is primarily an attack on his critics. But it does end with the deeper thought that our sorrows can sometimes be the answer to our prayers. The oscillations in his attitude to religion find a new focus in 'God in the House', a quite brilliant parody of small-town conformity and preoccupations, where the people have even 'bred all our kittens white so you can see them in the night'. So religion is also a timid affair: 'If we all hold hands and very quietly shout | God is in the house'.

One reason for surveying the changing themes that make up Cave's songs is to give a wider context to the important lecture that he delivered at the South Bank in 1999 on 'The Secret Life of the Love Song'.[139] There he describes how 'the actualising of God through the medium of the Love Song remains my prime

[136] Quotation and further details at <www.contactmusic.com>.

[137] Cave, *Complete Lyrics*, 290. Together with other poems eventually not used on that album, it is listed under '*The Boatman's Call*'.

[138] Here one might compare opera and the way in which the conventional practice is to use a tenor voice for the hero and a bass for the villain.

[139] The lecture opens Cave, *Complete Lyrics*, 2–19. The quotations following are from 6, 7, 10–11.

motivation as an artist. I found that language became a poultice to the wounds incurred by the death of my father.' If that seems an odd comment in view of the depressing nature of his earlier writing, it is important to note that for him love is inseparable from pain: 'Though the Love Song comes in many guises—songs of exaltation and praise, songs of rage and despair, erotic songs, songs of abandonment and loss—they all address God, for it is the haunted premise of longing that the true Love Song inhabits ... it is the cry of one chained to the earth and craving flight, a flight into inspiration and imagination and divinity.' So divine love is found in the ambiguous and often twisted character of human love, where exploitation and abuse often lurk not far beneath the surface. Indeed, much the same applies when the object of such love is God himself. Using as his example Psalm 137 with its terrible concluding verses, he observes: 'What I found time and time again in the Bible, especially in the Old Testament, was that verses of rapture, of ecstasy and love could hold within them apparently opposite sentiments—hate, revenge, bloody-mindedness etc.—these sentiments were not mutually exclusive. This idea has left an enduring impression on my song-writing.'

That complexity is why Cave's way of allowing us to share in his experience of the divine is, it seems to me, not so much through single songs as through an album as a whole or perhaps even selectively listening to his entire corpus.[140] Only that way can we feel completely the conflicting pressures that force an opening into that wider perspective. So, significantly, in collections of his songs he has deliberately represented those contrasts. Again, his most recent release is of two albums in a single sleeve, one definitely more raucous and negative than the other.[141] If the gentler of the two opens with a piece of dark humour, in the next number the gurgling sound of the recorders that speaks of a love that is 'breathless without you' is much more typical of what follows.[142] The other album in general offers a more jaded view, as well as a return to the weightier reliance on percussion that had characterized his

[140] e.g. through such as the CD *The Best of Nick Cave and The Bad Seeds* (1998) or the DVD *God is in the House* (2001).

[141] *Abattoir Blues/The Lyre of Orpheus* (2004).

[142] *The Lyre of Orpheus* opens with a parody of the legend of how Orpheus discovered the music of the lyre.

earlier music. Even so, the opening heavy rock anthem, 'Get Ready for Love! Praise Him!', contains the quintessential lines:

> I searched the seven seas and I've looked under the carpet
> And browsed through the brochures that governed the skies
> Then I was just hanging around, doing nothing and looked up to see
> His face burned in the retina of your eyes.

So in striving to open listeners to the possibility of religious experience, Cave does not ignore the more negative aspects of human existence. Rather, he uses such exposure to take his listeners to a significant point beyond, where these can be experienced anew but now with an explicitly religious dimension.

On the Margins

In this section I want to investigate a rather different sort of pop music, the type that often seems to my fellow-Christians at the furthest possible remove from religion. So, as I indicated earlier, by 'on the margins' I mean the perceived margins of belief, not an indicator of the extent of such music's popularity. Indeed, millions have bought and continue to buy hard rock, heavy metal and rap. The promiscuity, profanity, violence and devil-may-care attitude that often goes with such genres is often thought sufficient to condemn any serious assessment out of hand. The violence of some of Cave's imagery and the occasional swearword in his lyrics may help remind us that the issues are not quite that simple. While not discounting the need for purely negative judgements on some bands' work, what I want to suggest is that human nature is usually much more complex than any simple either–or allows. A wrestling with the possibility of religious experience is in fact to be found in some surprising quarters. The fact that this is usually outside the context of orthodox Christianity does not by any means entail that God has absented himself from the lives of such individuals. As I have emphasized elsewhere, there is a generosity in God that is wider than many a theologian's narrow curtailing of divine activity.[143] I shall conclude the chapter with rap and some forms of soul but I want to begin with hard rock and heavy metal.

---

[143] A point I stressed in the introductory chapter to this work's predecessor: *God and Enchantment of Place* (Oxford: Oxford University Press, 2004), 6–8, 22.

Hard Rock and Heavy Metal

Given how important a role the loudness of the music exercises in these genres, clearly the invention of the electric guitar was a decisive moment in what led to their emergence. It is therefore not without irony that that instrument's earliest exponents had quite different aims from their heavy rock successors. The ordinary, acoustic guitar probably came to America, like the banjo, via African slaves. Whereas the decisive shape of its later direction was provided by someone often identified as black though in fact of mixed race (Jimi Hendrix), in its earlier forms the electric guitar was employed by both white and black musicians but with quite different aims from those of Hendrix.[144] Charlie Christian in the 1930s, Les Paul in the Forties and Chet Atkins in the fifties all sought greater purity of sound than the instrument had originally offered. Conflicting resonance that was caused by the top of the guitar and a string both vibrating at the same time was solved by the invention of the solid-body guitar, while the extraneous hum produced by the electric signal was countered by doubling the coils in the pick-up system.[145] Atkins further developed the instrument's range with his finger-picking style, but the aim remained a real purity of sound.[146]

It was in Chicago that Muddy Waters and Chuck Berry first began to experiment with distortion and the still wider range provided by fret technique.[147] Race was an important element in the instrument's earlier history. Despite his talents, the black Charlie Christian was usually only allowed to play in Benny Goodman's sextet and almost never in his big band.[148] Both Waters and Berry were managed by whites in a patronizing way that inevitably increased tensions.[149] If Berry struck white Americans as exuberant

[144] Ethnically, Hendrix (1942–1970) was a mixture of black, white and Cherokee.

[145] S. Waksman, *Instruments of Desire: The Electric Guitar and the Shaping of Musical Experience* (Cambridge, Mass.: Harvard University Press, 1999), 39, 42, 51.

[146] The index finger picks out the melody, the thumb, usually with a pick, the bass accompaniment, thus giving a richer sound: ibid. 88.

[147] Distortion results when amplifiers are at maximum volume. Fretting the slide device on the strings allows access to the notes between the frets: ibid. 120, 138.

[148] Ibid. 30.

[149] Ibid. 133–6. The relevant record company (Chess Records) was run by two Jewish immigrants, Leonard and Phil Chess.

adolescence, Muddy Waters came closer to the fantasized black threat that has so plagued racial relations in the United States. It is from this time on that the guitar was played standing, with the musician 'putting out' or asserting himself, as in the ghetto.[150] That was important for what came later, as the instrument now became an extension of the body and an integral element in its expression. Assertiveness, aggression and sensuality could all be given clearer form. While gentler emotions could also be indicated, on the whole these were conveyed more by the voice or music rather than by the instrument as such. Distortion also introduced a destabilizing element that allowed a 'prophetic' factor to be part of the resultant noise, in the sense that the norms implicit in the underlying tune or words were implicitly now made subject to challenge.[151] This was carried a stage further in the deliberate use of feedback, sometimes restrained, as in its application by Eric Clapton, and sometimes with ferocious abandon, as with Jimi Hendrix.[152] The extent to which such developments were viewed in racial terms can be seen in Norman Mailer's notorious essay, 'The White Negro'.[153]

That challenge was displayed with particular finesse in Jimi Hendrix's performance of 'The Star-Spangled Banner' at the Woodstock festival of 1969. The performance provided what is 'probably the most complex and powerful work of American art to deal with the Vietnam war and its corrupting, distorting effect on successive generations of the American psyche'.[154] Whether that was Hendrix's own view is a moot point.[155] In any case, such a political evaluation should not blind us to the purely musical qualities of the performance.

[150] Ibid. 129–30. Waksman suggests that within such a setting rap music was a natural trajectory from such black exploitation of the aggressive potential of the new sound.

[151] Cf. J. Attali, *Noise: The Political Economy of Music* (Minneapolis: University of Minnesota Press, 1985), 5, 19.

[152] For Clapton's use within a relatively traditional blues style, cf. his 1965 album *John Mayall's Bluesbreakers*.

[153] In N. Mailer, *Advertisements for Myself* (London: André Deutsch, 1961), 277–328, esp. 281ff.

[154] C. S. Murray, *Crosstown Traffic: Jimi Hendrix and Post-War Pop* (London: Faber and Faber, 2001 edn), 32; cf. 68. The 'overkill' performance took place before a crowd wallowing in a sea of mud and struggling with the effects of tear gas. Little wonder that a version was later used in the Vietnam film *Apocalypse Now*. The performance is recorded on the video/DVD *Jimi Hendrix* (1973/2000), track 15.

[155] Hendrix was himself a former serviceman who only left the service because of an injury sustained during a parachute jump. Interviews suggest strong patriotism and compassion for rising casualties competing against one another.

Here was a musician who could employ the instrument to its full capacity like no other. It is as well to bear that in mind when considering his treatment of his guitar as a phallus. At the 1967 Monterey Festival he simulated sexual intercourse with his guitar rammed against the amplifiers.[156] While Hendrix was promiscuous, it would be a mistake to reduce such actions simply to an early version of what later became known as 'cock rock', music that draws attention to the genital area by thrusting hips and groin-positioned guitars.[157] He seems in fact to have been quite a shy and courteous individual, and such a performance was, he insisted, his way of drawing an audience towards a proper appreciation of the music in its own right.[158] That may sound implausible. But even songs that appear to be about nothing more than superficial relations with women could on his view draw us, through the music, into a deeper dimension of reality.[159]

That claim is particularly important in understanding his attitude to religion. His flamboyant dress style may in part have been a reaction to the fact that he had been expelled from church at the age of eight for being improperly attired.[160] Certainly, that experience resulted in his rejection of all institutional religion. Nonetheless, as some frustratingly brief comments make clear, he did believe that music like his own could provide an alternative form of access to the divine. Whether influence from Voodoo may have played a part is still a matter of contention.[161] What is evident is that he did detect in his music the ability to perform a number of characteristically religious functions. For a start music makes us more open, more receptive: 'We try to make our music so loose and hard-hitting so it hits your soul hard enough to make it open. ... Our

---

[156] For the visual impact, see the opening scenes of the video/DVD *Jimi Hendrix*.

[157] The term, now widely used in popular music criticism, derives from S. Frith and A. McRobbie's article 'Rock and Sexuality', in S. Frith and A. Godwin (ed.), *On Record: Rock, Pop, and the Written Word* (London: Routledge, 1990), 371–89.

[158] So Murray, *Crosstown Traffic*, 88–92; Waksman, *Instruments of Desire*, 205.

[159] See his explanatory liner note to *Band of Gypsies* (1970), quoted in Murray, *Crosstown Traffic*, 200.

[160] He was wearing 'tennis shoes' with a suit. In telling the story, he ends by remarking, 'once you carry God inside yourself, ... you're part of Him, and he's part of you': T. Brown (ed.), *Jimi Hendrix Talking* (New York: Omnibus, 2003), 87.

[161] References to Voodoo are usually read as mere metaphor, but Murray speculates that there may be something more: *Crosstown Traffic*, 139–40.

music is shock therapy . . . The soul must rule, not money or drugs. You should rule yourself, and give God a chance.'[162] Again, else-where he observes: 'I can explain everything better through music. You hypnotise people to where they go right back to their natural state which is pure positive . . . And when you get people at their weakest point, you can preach into the subconscious what we want to say.'[163] If the second extract sounds somewhat manip-ulative, his intentions are good: to purge the heart of evil and violent emotions.[164] Music, he suggests, is 'more spiritual than anything now. . . . the art of words means nothing, you know. So therefore you have to rely on a more earthier substance.'[165] Indeed so convinced was he of such a spiritual role for music that he spoke on a number of occasions about 'the electric church'. By that it is clear that he meant rather more than simply opening up our subconscious. There was also the potential for gaining a different perception on reality that would include experience of the divine.

Of his song 'Purple Haze' he once remarked that his intention was to make reality and fantasy clash, because 'you have to use fantasy in order to show different sides of reality'.[166] How this impinges on experience of God is perhaps best illustrated from 'Voodoo Chile'. The uncanny words use everything from science fiction to William Blake to establish a sense of strangeness or otherness, and this is also reflected in the music. A great range of blues styles is pursued, perhaps to suggest the exhaustion of possibilities. The piece then ends in such a free form that the listener is plunged either into a feeling of the complete collapse of everything or else into some vague sense of supernatural otherness. Hendrix had already hinted at the second possibility in his lyrics, where he laid claim to be our mystic guide from elsewhere.[167]

Only a year after Hendrix's own early death from a drug overdose another influential pop star also interested in unconventional religion was to suffer a similar fate.[168] So before turning to heavy metal I want

[162] Quoted ibid. 201.
[163] Quoted in Waksman, *Instruments of Desire*, 170.
[164] For the cathartic view, see Brown (ed.), *Jimi Hendrix Talking*, 46.
[165] Ibid. 99.
[166] Ibid. 62.
[167] He speaks of the moon turning red when he was born. 'Voodoo Chile' is on the *Electric Ladyland* album (1968).
[168] Jim Morrison was a year younger when he died at 27 in 1971.

to look first at the work of Jim Morrison and The Doors. Morrison's short life was much more marked by sexual excess, alcoholism and drugs than was the case with Hendrix.[169] That is powerfully brought out in Oliver Stone's 1991 film *The Doors*, where despite the title the story-line is almost exclusively focused on Morrison and his gradual disintegration, with his early death the inevitable result. Nonetheless, Stone is concerned to emphasize (along with many others) that there was also an important spiritual dimension to Morrison's life. So the film opens with some lines from his poetry: 'Let me tell you about heartache and the loss of God | Wandering, wandering in hopeless night'. And it ends in a similar way: 'Death makes angels of us all | And gives us wings | where we had shoulders | smooth as ravens' claws. | No more money, no more fancy dress | This other Kingdom seems by far the best'.[170] Much too is made of Morrison's belief that he had inherited some shamanistic powers from an Indian whose death in a road accident he had witnessed as a child.[171]

Although there is an element of false romanticism in the way Morrison has been treated since his death, not least in the treatment of his grave at Père-Lachaise cemetery in Paris, which has become a major pilgrimage site, it cannot, I think, be denied that that licence goes with, and indeed in some sense is part of, a real spiritual quest. Arthur Rimbaud was one of Morrison's favourite poets, and his life exhibited a similar pattern.[172] On his deathbed Rimbaud was received back into the Roman Catholic Church of his youth. It was not for that reason alone, however, that the Catholic convert Paul Claudel promoted his poetry.[173] It was because Rimbaud pushed the

---

[169] In 1970 he was even arrested and sentenced to prison for 'lewd conduct' on stage that included simulated masturbation, drunkenness and indecent exposure.

[170] The latter is almost the concluding lines of 'An American Prayer': D. Sugerman (ed.), *The Doors Complete Lyrics* (London: Abacus, 2001 edn), 208; the former, again near the end of the relevant song, comes from 'To Come of Age', ibid. 194. Both poems appear on the posthumous 1978 album *An American Prayer*.

[171] The road crash is alluded to in 'Awake, Ghost Song', ibid. 189.

[172] Rimbaud (1854–1891) wrote all his poetry between the ages of 15 and 20 or possibly 25. He had a tempestuous love affair with another, older poet, Paul Verlaine. Creativity, Rimbaud believed, came through experimentation with self-induced states of delirium. Leonardo DiCaprio offers a rather lacklustre portrait of him in the 1995 film *Total Eclipse*.

[173] Claudel wrote a controversial introduction to the 1912 *L'œuvre complète* (Paris: Mercure).

language of experience in unfamiliar Symbolist directions that helped give the spiritual side of life a new credibility in late nineteenth-century France. In a similar way Morrison's choice of name for his group had little to do with Aldous Huxley's mescaline experiences.[174] The real debt was to William Blake: 'When the doors of perception are cleansed, things will appear as they truly are, infinite.' As Morrison himself was to put it later, 'There are things known and there are things unknown, and in between are the doors.'[175]

Of all their hits 'Break On Through (to the Other Side)' is perhaps the one where that message is most explicit. Organ, guitar and cymbal combine with Morrison's smooth baritone voice to urge the listener to go through the doors: 'The gate is straight | Deep and wide | Break on through to the other side.' At the same time there is a roughness and sensuality about the presentation that suggests that this will only come through the unravelling of ordinary assumptions: 'un long dérèglement de tous les sens', as Rimbaud expressed it.[176] Ironically in view of that aim, it has a more sexual feel than 'Light My Fire', where the musical form provided by another member of the band (Robbie Krieger) seems to act almost as a pastiche of Morrison lust-fired lyrics. More commonly, however, it is Morrison himself who calls into question any exclusively sexual reading of his words. So, for example, an Oedipal scenario may conclude 'The End', but as such it is part of a failed quest: 'Ride the snake/to the lake'.[177]

'Unknown Soldier' is a moving tribute to those who lost their lives in the Vietnam War, a tribute that has been renewed recently in a violin concerto specially written for Nigel Kennedy around this and other key Doors songs, Jaz Coleman's *Doors Concerto*.[178] The transformation of their music into classical form may seem perverse, but the process in reverse was not unknown to The Doors themselves.[179]

---

[174] Reflected in Huxley's book *Doors of Perception* (London: Chatto and Windus, 1954).

[175] Sugerman (ed.), *Doors Complete Lyrics*, 4, 10.

[176] One of several unacknowledged allusions to Rimbaud in Stone's film, according to W. Fowlie, *Rimbaud and Jim Morrison* (London: Souvenir, 1995), 4.

[177] Sugerman (ed.), *Doors Complete Lyrics*, 35–7, esp. 35. Later the lyrics include a reference to the murder of the singer's father and intercourse with his mother.

[178] J. Coleman, *Doors Concerto* (Decca, 2000), played by the Prague Symphony Orchestra with Kennedy as violin soloist.

[179] There is a Doors adaptation of Albinoni's familiar Adagio on the 1985 video *The Doors Dance on Fire*.

In Coleman's concerto each of the nine movements has a spiritual theme. 'Love Street', for example, is used to express reconciliation between living and dead, while some tracks pursue wider issues, such as reincarnation in 'Hello, I Love You'. The opening track, 'Riders on the Storm', has been so transformed by the use of a Vietnamese pentatonic scale that it perhaps is no longer easily recognized by the typical Doors fan. Even so the choice of this number for the introduction seems to me exactly right for what claims to be a spiritual work. Morrison may sing 'Into this world we are thrown | Like a dog without a bone', but of course the point is that the bone can perhaps be found. Indeed, the optimistic character of Morrison's accompanying music with its lively organ beat set against, and eventually overcoming, the lashing rain and pounding waves surely suggests as much. Unfortunately, it was not to be so for Morrison, though he did pray: 'O great creator of being, grant us one more hour to perform our art and perfect our lives.'[180] Towards the end of his life he was toying with Buddhism, but he also wrote: 'Now I'm a lonely Man | Let me back into the Garden ... Give me songs to sing | and emerald dreams to dream.'[181] The tragedy was that it was an unrealized longing, whereas at least for Hendrix one gains the impression of something received and enjoyed.

In the same year as Morrison's death there also emerged what is widely regarded as by far the best album to come from the British band Led Zeppelin. It was the group's fourth, initially untitled but now commonly called *The Four Symbols* album after the insignia used on the cover to identify its four members. Led Zeppelin is often credited with giving the decisive impetus to what became known as heavy metal.[182] Certainly their lifestyle and some of their lyrics and presentations on stage lend credibility to that claim, though even their best-known number in this genre, 'Whole Lotta Love', seems quite mild compared with what was to follow.[183] In any case, as one female musicologist has argued at length, there was more than one way of reading that stage act other than crude 'cock rock'. For women the

[180] Part of 'An American Prayer'.

[181] This comes from his final poem, 'Paris Journal', which he left with his wife at his death: J. Morrison, *The American Night* (London: Penguin, 1991), 200–1. For some short Buddhist poems, see 188–9.

[182] e.g. Waksman, *Instruments of Desire*, 238.

[183] On the album *Led Zeppelin II* (1969). A groaning guitar glissando is matched with a jungle rhythm, as Plant sings 'I'm gonna give you every inch of my love'.

'girlish whine' of Robert Plant, the lead singer, allowed them to hear their own voice as sometimes part of what was being said. It was a perception aided by the looseness of the grammar, which left it sometimes ambiguous who the true subject was; so the man no less than the woman was 'emotionally vulnerable and available'.[184] Even the crotch position for Jimmy Page's guitar could be read not as phallic but as the musician's mistress being tenderly caressed.[185]

Whether persuasive as a defence or not, more relevant here is another dimension to their compositions. The most popular track on the 1971 album was to become 'Stairway to Heaven'. Although one of their songs does assume something like orthodox Christianity,[186] that is clearly not so in this case. A subsequent video performance of a related, earlier song ('Dazed and Confused') has Page climbing up a mountain in pursuit of a hooded hermit who then, unveiled, turns out to be the guitarist himself.[187] From this one might conclude that 'Stairway to Heaven' is also about self-exploration and discovery. But that does not seem quite right, since the musical structure is of a gradually increasing crescendo where volume alone indicates the revelation of something greater than oneself. Strings and recorders provide a fanfare opening, with the electric guitar joining them at the end of the second verse on the words, 'Oh, and it makes me wonder'. The long-delayed drums follow at the end of the fourth verse as 'the forests ... echo with laughter'. Then, after a guitar solo in response to the discovery that the 'stairway lies on the whispering wind', the pace quickens still further towards the track's final explosive climax.

Fanfares like the song's introduction have of course a long history of association with religious revelation, but this of itself need not necessarily entail something divine in this case.[188] Presumably, the

[184] S. Fast, *In the Houses of the Holy: Led Zeppelin and the Power of Rock Music* (Oxford: Oxford University Press, 2001), 159–201, esp. 189, 194, 198.

[185] Ibid. 186. Waksman agrees. Countering Murray's talk of 'gang rape', he notes the way in which the break in the middle section of the throbbing riff calls into question any unassailable male potency: *Instruments of Desire*, 249–50.

[186] 'In My Time of Dying', on a subsequent album, *Physical Graffiti* (1975). It is a moving adaptation of a Blind Willie Johnson 1927 number mediated through Bob Dylan: C. Welch, *Led Zeppelin: Dazed and Confused* (London: Carlton, 1998), 88. Although Page had been a choirboy, no member of the band maintained an explicit faith into adulthood.

[187] On the 1976 video *The Song Remains the Same*. 'Dazed and Confused' first appeared on *Led Zeppelin I* in 1969.

[188] Fast lists a number of classical and biblical examples: *In the Houses of the Holy*, 49–50. Think, for instance, of the sounding of the trumpet when the Ten Commandments are given to the people of Israel: Exod. 19.16; 20.18.

precise character of the music's impact will depend in part on participants' prior assumptions about what might be feasible. Nonetheless, it is fascinating to observe how many fans have interpreted the number in essentially religious terms, while at the same time insisting that the music ensures that it is an experience of the body no less than of the mind.[189] The song has thus become for many a participatory narrative ritual. Perhaps a comparison with Page's architectural interests is relevant here. Later in life he subsequently acquired the London home of William Burges (Tower House). Like all Burges' creations, among them Cardiff Castle and Cork Cathedral, there is an element of mystery and ritual in its elaborate patterning.[190]

Indeed, some of Page's actions with his bow and theramin in live performances have been compared to the priest's sprinkling of the faithful with holy water at a traditional mass.[191] That may sound implausible, unless the nature of a theramin is properly understood. In the late 1960s it was a piece of high-tech equipment used to produce a sound at varying pitch according to the distance of the performer's body from the instrument. The need to use arm and hand to trigger the sound is not dissimilar to a formal priestly sign of blessing.[192] It is true that the lady of the song is trying to buy a stairway to heaven. But her wrong approach only adds to the tension in the music as the audience is pulled over a quite different threshold.[193]

Page did indeed devote much energy to exploring the writings and actions of the early twentieth-century occultist Aleister Crowley, but the precise nature of his interest should not be distorted.[194] Rather than any intrinsic fascination with evil as such, it was more a

---

[189] Fans speak of 'otherworldly music' and 'the closest thing to hymns that we have': quoted in Fast, *In the Houses of the Holy*, 51.

[190] Page agreed to open an exhibition on Burges' work in Cork during the year in which it was cultural capital of Europe: see *Conserving the Dream* (Cork: Cork Public Museum, 2005), 2.

[191] Fast, *In the Houses of the Holy*, 38. Page sometimes used a bow rather than fingers or pick for his guitar.

[192] Illustrated perhaps most clearly on the lengthy version of 'Dazed and Confused' on the video *The Song Remains the Same*.

[193] For the song as 'liminal' in the anthropologist Victor Turner's sense, see Fast, *In the Houses of the Holy*, 54–5.

[194] Page's interest in Crowley (1875–1947) even extended as far as buying his former house on Loch Ness. For further details of the relationship, see A. Fyfe, *When the Levee Breaks: The Making of Led Zeppelin IV* (London: Unanimous, 2003), 101–5.

matter of readiness to experiment with unconventional means of accessing other dimensions of reality. So it is really fully consistent with the band's initial interest in J. R. R. Tolkien's myths and then their increasing fascination with eastern mysticism. That interest in Tolkien is reflected in another number on the same album, in a folk song about border wars, 'The Battle of Evermore'.[195] In a subsequent recording Indian musical influences were added when the British-born singer Najma Akhtar was asked to join Page and Plant in a fresh performance.[196] 'Kashmir', the title of the band's other great song of mystery, might also suggest Indian influence, but in fact the lyrics were written during a holiday in Africa while Plant was crossing the Moroccan desert.[197] Apparently, the idea for the drumbeat came first, with its suggestion of a solemn and rather arduous procession or pilgrimage. Arabic elements are evident in the music and these, combined with the slow, insistent rhythm, help to create a sense of otherness, as does the way in which Plant collapses into incoherence before what is revealed: 'not a word could I relate ... oh, oh.'[198] 'Kashmir' is by no means just another hippy song. In the course of its projected journey the attempt is being made to initiate listeners into something very much more. It would be a serious mistake to confine such experiences to more familiar genres. Indeed, the erotic use of semitone movement from dissonance to consonance in Plant's singing technique may well hark back to earlier forms of church singing.[199]

Led Zeppelin disbanded in 1980. Unfortunately for religion it was the sexual side of the band's music that had much the greater impact. In heavier versions of rock an almost exclusive preoccupation with sex and violence became the norm, and references to any kind of spirituality are therefore rare. Although the popularity of a band like the Australian group AC/DC could be interpreted charitably as just allowing young men to come to terms with their

---

[195] In 'Ramble On' (on the album *Led Zeppelin II*) Plant actually assumes the identity of Gimli the dwarf.

[196] On the 1994 album *No Quarter: Jimmy Page and Robert Plant Unledded*. For further details, see Fyfe, *When the Levee Breaks*, 121–3.

[197] Welch, *Led Zeppelin*, 89–91.

[198] For the Arabic elements, note the riff in the second section and the mellotron melody and Plant's vocal melisma in the third: Fast, *In the Houses of the Holy*, 97–8.

[199] So Fast, who contrasts the more ornate Old Roman melodies that were superseded by Gregorian chant: ibid. 43–4.

hormones,[200] American troops going into battle to the sound of Slayer or college students enjoying the destructive fantasies of Insane Clown Posse or Marilyn Manson are more worrying.[201] Even so, ethical issues are sometimes faced, and in some quite unexpected ways. So, for example, although Glam Rock bands were often as macho in their lyrics as other forms of heavy metal, the cross-dressing did help open debate on gay and bisexual issues.[202] Nirvana, the hugely popular grunge band of the early 1990s, likewise sometimes adopted a simplified version of the same behaviour on stage.[203] In their case a sympathetic motivation is clear both from the writings of the lead singer, Kurt Cobain, in general and from his concern in particular for his sister Kimberly, who was a lesbian.[204]

Cobain had undergone a brief evangelical conversion when he was seventeen. In his subsequent short adult life he consistently expressed hostility towards organized religion.[205] Yet he continued to use the word 'sacred' in a positive sense.[206] So, although his only song to refer to Christianity does a somersault with the words of an old gospel number, one should perhaps read this less as an attack on

[200] For an autobiography that revolves round admiration for this band and provides some useful insights into the thinking of heavy metal fans, see S. Hunter, *Hell Bent for Leather* (London: Harper, 2005).

[201] Slayer was apparently the favourite listening of young American troops during the second war with Iraq. Manson's autobiography itemizes the extremes to which he has gone, but provides little explanation of the reason, apart from a perverted grandfather and an unloving father: M. Manson, *The Long Hard Road Out of Hell* (London: Plexus, 1998). For a more objective assessment, cf. the video *Marilyn Manson: Demystifying the Devil* (2000).

[202] David Bowie, Marc Bolan of T. Rex and the New York Dolls are examples from the seventies; all discussed in B. Hoskyns, *Glam!* (London: Faber and Faber, 1998). Poison would be a 1980s example. The film *Velvet Goldmine* (1998) depicts the often still quite secret and tentative exploration of the earlier period. Wayne Studer itemizes the changing nature of gay lyrics over the two decades: *Rock on the Wild Side* (San Francisco: Leyland, 1994).

[203] Dressing in padded bras and skirts. 'Grunge' might be described as hard rock combined with punk.

[204] C. R. Cross, *Heavier than Heaven* (London: Sceptre, 2001), 229–30. For two sustained attacks on sexism, see K. Cobain, *Journals* (London: Penguin, 2002), 177–9, 276.

[205] Cross, *Heavier than Heaven*, 59–60. He became a Baptist for three months in 1984 under the influence of his friend Jesse Reed. For religion as oppressive, see Cobain, *Journals*, e.g. 140.

[206] For 'sacred' used positively, see ibid. 99, 121.

all religion as such and more as an expression of 'self-hate ... so great that even the all-welcoming Jesus Christ rejects him'.[207] A couple of decades earlier, MC5 of 'Kick Out the Jams' fame also turned their back on religion apart from one number, 'Sister Anne', which is a tribute to a Salvation Army sister. Here the tribute is wholly positive, if somewhat muddled by her turning at one point into a Catholic nun.[208] Granted, these two examples are very small openings, but they do remind us of the unpredictability of human nature and of the potential for divine grace to operate in unexpected ways.

Patti Smith is best known for her album *Horses* (1975) and for her poetry in general. The daughter of a Jehovah's Witness mother and an atheist father, she was a white child in a rough, black quarter of Philadelphia, which goes some way towards explaining her brittle rebelliousness.[209] Harsh rituals in a factory job are reflected in one of her songs, 'Piss Factory'.[210] Moving to New York, she became a long-standing friend of the gay photographer Robert Mapplethorpe, and canvassed hard for the right of women to express their sexual desires as bluntly as men. She even toyed in the crudest terms with the idea of being the mistress of Jesus or of the Holy Spirit.[211] However, in 1976 she met Fred 'Sonic' Smith of MC5 and they were eventually to marry (in 1980), but not before Patti had produced an album that reflected her change of heart on the question of religion. Whereas *Horses* had opened with the words, 'Jesus died for somebody else's sins but not mine', now on *Easter* (1978) she prayed to the accompaniment of the twenty-third Psalm, 'Oh, God, I'm waitin' for you; waitin' to open your ninety-eight wounds ... Lead me, oh lead me.'[212] After the release of that album she retired from rock and became a mother in Detroit until the death of her husband from alcoholism. Thereafter she returned to singing once more. A clear

[207] So J. Hector, *Nirvana: The Complete Guide to their Music* (London: Omnibus, 2004), 55. Cobain committed suicide in 1994, aged 27. The song in question is 'Jesus Doesn't Want Me for a Sunbeam' (from the album *Unplugged in New York*).

[208] Although 'after Sunday school Mass she goes to see her man', the band at the conclusion of the song leave us in no doubt about her identity, as they transmogrify themselves into a typical Salvation Army sound.

[209] V. Bockvis, *Patti Smith* (London: Fourth Estate, 1998), 9–10.

[210] For the incident, see ibid. 23–4. 'Piss Factory'/'Hey Joe' was her band's very first single (1974).

[211] Ibid. 18–20, 125–6.

[212] On the track 'Privilege (Set Me Free)'.

religious dimension to her music has been retained. 'Trespasses', for example, has some beautiful imagery of a son confessing to his mother and her aiding his moves towards repentance and eventual forgiveness.[213]

Of course, such a change of heart is by no means unique in the world of rock. Alice Cooper is an example from Glam Rock. But his case is less interesting, for a number of reasons. The contrast with his past life is much less marked. His new lyrics are less likely to engage his former audience, presenting as they do the implicit threat of a hell at which he once mocked.[214] Finally, there is little attempt to convey through the music the attractiveness of his new lifestyle. Patti Smith makes much more of an effort to match the music to the variety of sentiments in her poetry, and thus has more success in conveying the range of encounters that a believer might have with God. So 'Ghost Dance', for example, fully evokes the sounds of an American Indian dance, even if its recurring chorus, 'We shall live again, we shall live', is modified in a Christian direction: 'Here we are, Father, Lord, Holy Ghost, | Bread of your bread, ghost of your host'. Similarly, 'Privilege' (about prayer) uses a slow introduction on electric organ and drums to suggest an insistent longing that gradually quickens into the cry 'Set me free', only to slow down twice more for a solemn recitation of the twenty-third psalm. If 'Easter' is more solemn than one might have expected, with only gradual lightening with high notes and accompanying bells, that is because the words are insistent about the cost of the resurrection as well as its potential for joy: 'I am the sword, the wound, the stain | Scorned transfigured child of Cain'.[215] On her most recent album 'Trespasses' is perhaps the most successful number. Beauty of words is perfectly matched with a music of regret that is nicely underlined by Smith modifying her normally rasping voice to a gentler timbre.[216]

That contrast between Cooper and Smith is by no means unique. Indeed, as with some of the examples given above, music written by

---

[213] On the 2004 album *Trampin'*. The language is in fact sufficiently ambiguous for it also to be a song about Christ bearing our sins and Mary as the mother who urges him on.

[214] As reflected in his 1994 album *The Last Temptation*. Contrast 'Go to Hell' on the 1976 album *Alice Cooper Goes to Hell*. More interesting is his scathing critique of contemporary America on the track 'Lost in America'.

[215] All three preceding examples come from *Easter* (1978).

[216] A new album *Twelve* has just appeared.

the uncertain searcher may well succeed better in conveying that otherness which is so intrinsic to divinity. A good case in point is the work of Jeff Buckley. We are fortunate to have some wonderful performances from this extraordinarily talented guitarist and singer who also died young.[217] His album *Grace* (1994) has no less than four tracks with explicitly religious titles. Although they are not quite as they seem, there is no shortage of admirers who have drawn religious inspiration from the music.[218] The extraordinary range of his voice enables listeners to share not only his rage and despair but also a longing for something better and possibly transcendent.[219] Yet Buckley was always insistent that he himself was entirely without such belief.[220] In such circumstances it is important not to let human subjective intention be the final arbitrator. Despite the religious allusions in 'Hallelujah' it was for Buckley simply a song about the failure of human love, but precisely because the music pulls in a rather different direction from the concluding words, the possibility of a different reading and thus of a different resultant experience is always there.[221] Indeed, the extent and seriousness of his engagement with the music of the major Sufi musician and composer Nusrat Fateh Ali Khan makes one wonder whether there were hidden aspects to his own longings or experience that he was not as yet prepared to reveal to a wider public. The mystical aspect of such influence can be seen in some of Buckley's own compositions. He even paid Nusrat the not inconsiderable tribute of learning Urdu pronunciation to sing one of his finer songs.[222] Irrespective of Buckley's own views, however, the important thing is that the music should have the final say, not the performer's own expressed intentions.

[217] At the age of 30 in 1997, drowning while swimming in a tributary of the Mississippi River.

[218] The title track is actually about the acceptance of death, while 'Eternal Life' advocates the rejection of such a hope: 'a prison for the walking dead'. 'Hallelujah' and 'Corpus Christi Carol' are more as one might expect.

[219] A range of four octaves according to *Guitar Player* 28.3 (Mar. 1994), 120.

[220] Ehrlich, *Inside the Music*, 149–59, esp. 157–8.

[221] The song is actually a cover from an original version by Leonard Cohen, whose more recent work has intriguingly moved in a more religious direction. He now seeks to combine aspects of Judaism and Zen Buddhism: ibid. 190–201. His 2001 album *Ten New Songs* has several songs about faith. For an analysis of his spiritual development, see D. Boucher, *Dylan and Cohen: Poets of Rock and Roll* (London: Continuum, 2004), esp. 219–31.

[222] 'Yeh Jo Halka Halka Saroor Hai' (about the intoxication of love as a religious experience), on *Live at Sin-é* (1993/2003).

A similar judgement must of course also apply in reverse, when music is, for instance, produced with an explicitly Christian aim, but fails to offer anything distinctive. A case in point is those groups that have been eager to wear the label 'Christian Rock Band' or 'Contemporary Christian Rock'.[223] It is to their credit that they have often done so in the teeth of opposition from family and the local church.[224] Even so, the value of such material has quite often to be questioned, despite sales in the millions. The lyrics of one of the earliest, Stryper, seldom stray far from a literal copying of scripture and so offer little by way of imaginative engagement.[225] If that charge cannot be laid against a more recent success, Creed, the accompanying music still seems to do little for the lyrics. Words and music as it were stand apart, and so it is almost as though two distinct experiences are on offer. Sometimes the hard rock is introduced immediately; sometimes with a little delay; and only very occasionally with quiet throughout.[226] The advantage of the quieter introduction is that the lyrics can then be heard clearly, but the type of music varies little in relation to what is being said. So word and music achieve quite different effects. But perhaps this is unfair. For what presumably such groups do is allow their audiences to enjoy the beat of powerful rock while at the same time remaining fully confident that their emotions are not being surreptitiously pulled in a direction contrary to their belief commitments. That conceded, it still remains the case that music is acting here as a conservator of belief rather than initiating the audience into new experiences of the divine.

---

[223] For a general survey, see M. Joseph, *Faith, God and Rock'n'Roll* (London: Sanctuary, 2003). Apart from the two groups mentioned later in the text, Jars of Clay, Pedro the Lion and POD ('Payable On Death) are also major players. POD is the most consistently heavy metal, with even an instrumental like 'Celestial' (on *Satellite*, 2001) only light or ethereal by comparison.

[224] For a brief counterattack, see ibid. 243–6.

[225] One album, *Soldiers Under Command* (1985), even has Isa. 53.5 on the front cover. 'Stryper' stands for 'salvation through redemption yielding peace, encouragement and righteousness'. For a surprisingly sympathetic view of them, and of POD, see Hunter, *Hell Bent for Leather*, 221–6.

[226] Examples of the first type are 'What If' and 'My Sacrifice'; of the second, 'With Arms Wide Open' and 'Don't Stop Dancing'; of the third, 'One Last Breath'. These songs are on either *Human Clay* (1999) or *Weathered* (2001).

Rap (and Soul)

If such Christian bands are rare in rock, they are even rarer in rap.
Rap may be defined as 'a form of rhymed storytelling accompanied
by highly rhythmic, electronically based music'.[227] As such it
can trace its roots to Jamaica and even earlier to African *griots*
(priest-poets).[228] Its more immediate antecedents, however, are
such things as graffiti on subway trains and break-dancing, both
attempts in the ghetto to find forms of expression that allowed
young blacks to have their own distinctive identity unfettered by
the imposed cultural values of wider America.[229] The first rap
record is commonly dated to the Sugarhill Gang's 'Rappers'
Delight' (1979)[230] Much of that early wave was focused on the
South Bronx, the most deprived area of urban New York.[231] Then
in the late 1980s a more aggressive and sexist form emerged on the
West Coast, often called gangster rap and this time associated with
another, equally socially deprived area, Compton in Los Angeles.
The lyrics of groups such as NWA ('Niggers With Attitude') and 2
Live Crew led to national campaigns that eventually resulted in
Parental Advisory stickers on most albums of this genre.[232]
Although the Beastie Boys were an early (and rare) example of
white youths engaging in rap, it is important to note that volumes
of sales indicate that the bulk of purchases for all rap is probably
among middle-class white youths, revelling in the rebellious character of the lyrics and indulging in the fantasy of participation in
such a gang culture. Any initial implausibility in this claim can be

---

[227] The definition given in T. Rose, *Black Noise: Rap Music and Black Culture in
Contemporary America* (Hanover, NH: Wesleyan University Press, 1994), 2.

[228] So A. Ogg with D. Upshal, *The Hip Hop Years: A History of Rap* (London:
Channel 4 Books, 1999), 13, 39. In the former case, the arrival of Kool Herc in New
York in 1967 is regarded as significant.

[229] Rose, *Black Noise*, 34–51. The importance of subway trains lay in the fact that
they allowed the graffiti artist to speak beyond the immediate borders of their 'hood'
(neighbourhood): 43.

[230] For the lyrics, see A. Ogg, *Rap Lyrics* (London: Omnibus, 2002), 6–10.

[231] In large part caused by the city's decision to break up communities to make
way for a new expressway: Rose, *Black Noise*, 30–3.

[232] For what happened in the early 1990s, see Ogg with Upshal, *The Hip Hop
Years*, 137–47. Both groups had pornographic lyrics. NWA added attacks on the
police, including 'Cop Killer', performed by Body Count, a hard rock offshoot band
that was formed by some members of NWA.

quickly countered by recalling the popularity of white gangster
films, or indeed an earlier generation's enjoyment of cowboys
massacring Red Indians. With Kid Rock and Eminem (both stem-
ming from another urban wasteland, the city of Detroit), white
versions were to become much more conspicuous. Eminem has
now already sold more than fifty million albums.[233]

In trying to evaluate the phenomenon it is important to avoid
any automatic imposition of middle-class assumptions and values.
Sociological studies of the ghettos have drawn attention to how
difficult it is to maintain 'decent' values in those deprived areas.
There is in fact an alternative 'code of the streets' to which even
those from 'good' families must to some degree conform if they are
to survive.[234] Aggressive assertiveness involving both language and
action is, for example, essential, as are certain styles of dress.[235]
Living behind such cover makes it easier to resist permanent harm
to oneself. Blanket condemnation by Christian ministers in fact
belies the complexities of the situation.[236] Nor do more general
American values help. The ubiquity in the media of material success
as a measure of self-worth means that drug-dealing becomes an
obvious, if insidious, temptation as a way out of the ghetto.[237] So it
is hardly surprising if the lyrics frequently identify wider corruptions in society, including biased actions on the part of the police.

So far as the music itself is concerned, its simple, repetitive form
might seem to deprive it of any merit. But it is important to note
that it reflects an African appreciation of rhythm over harmony, of
recurrence against resolution.[238] It is thus especially suited to making assertive comments, and as such the music is really very much
secondary to the words. It is here that evaluation must be focused,
in the dexterity of the repartee. Both the singer Elton John and the
poet and Nobel laureate Seamus Heaney have recognized as
much.[239] Its dark humour and subversion have been seen by

---

[233] N. Hasted, *The Dark Story of Eminem* (London: Omnibus, 2003), 213.

[234] The argument of E. Anderson, *Code of the Street* (New York: Norton,
1999). For switching between 'decent' and 'street', see e.g. 35–6, 93–6.

[235] Ibid. 67–76.

[236] Rose concludes by criticizing the approach of Calvin Butts, minister of
Abyssinian Baptist Church in Harlem: *Black Noise*, 183–5.

[237] Anderson, *Code of the Street*, 117–18.

[238] So Rose, *Black Noise*, 65–74.

[239] Commenting on the work of Eminem: Hasted, *The Dark Story of
Eminem*, 137, 196.

many as incompatible with Christianity: 'Christian hip-hop is like, like one big ... contradiction. Hip hop is supposed to be rebellious. It's supposed to be fightin' against the system. ... ain't supposed to be praising some white Jesus and supporting the quo'.[240] Certainly, religion has often exacerbated rather than helped problems in the ghettos. Stress on a guiding and controlling divine will has entailed a readiness among the young to accept the inevitability of pregnancy and even of death on the streets.[241] But there could be another side, and so it is worth examining how religion is in fact represented in this genre.

In marked contrast to the rest of the pop industry, one surprising feature of rap is the almost ubiquitous reference to God at the beginning of shout-outs that conclude albums or on lists of thanks on CD sleeves. All three of the current major figures—Jay-Z on the east coast, Tupac Shakur on the west and Eminem among whites—have expressed belief in God.[242] However, this has not gone with any significant discussion of the topic in their singing. If in the case of Eminem such belief may contribute to the great care he has shown in trying to discourage the young from adopting the lifestyle he portrays, with Tupac Shakur the sadness is that the fantasy eventually became a reality in his own life and contributed to his early death.[243]

This is not, however, to say that there are no major figures who have attempted to face the subject of religion. Early on in the rise of the genre Run-D.M.C. had a series of major hits in which, like P. M. Dawn, more positive attitudes were advocated.[244] Their lead singer eventually left to become a minister, though sadly his preaching continues to perpetuate the gospel of material success

[240] Put in the mouth of one of the characters in a tragic novel about two hip-hop artists, this one (Hannibal) in fact the product of a very authoritarian Christian home: H. Ptah, *A Hip-Hop Story* (New York: Pocket Books, 2002), 277.

[241] Anderson, *Code of the Street*, 135–8, 147. The average age for becoming a grandmother in the ghettoes is 37: ibid. 214.

[242] To express his debt to God for inspiration, Jay-Z has taken to referring to himself as God-MC or Jaz-hovah: *Maximum Jay-Z* (2002). On his first album, *Infinite* (1996), Eminem spoke of finding Christianity, and in interviews he has also mentioned praying: Hasted, *The Dark Story of Eminem*, 55–6. Ironically Tupac Shakur has become more influential rather than less after his death.

[243] For Eminem's care, ibid. 133–4. The film documentary *Tupac Shakur/Thug Angel: The Life of an Outlaw* (2002) presents a penetrating analysis of his dissolution. The poems he wrote at 19 (several religious) emphasize the contrast: T. Shakur, *The Rose that Grew from Concrete* (New York: Pocket Books, 1997), esp. pp. xi, 9, 33.

[244] See *The Best of P. M. Dawn* (2000); *Run-D.M.C. Greatest Hits* (2003).

that besmears rap lyrics in general.[245] To my mind, therefore, more interesting is the work of Arrested Development. In a song like 'Tennessee' we are offered a sort of open dialogue with God, with the state a symbol for a return to a more intimate relationship.[246]

Another positive influence was Krs-One. Increasingly his lyrics were to move in a more explicitly religious direction, and one recent release is wholly of this kind.[247] Unfortunately, he now sounds rather too much like a lecturing parent. A rap where the singer gets alongside listeners, as in his guest appearance on Public Enemy's *He Got Game* (1998), is thus of more interest.[248] Public Enemy also have a religious contribution of their own on the same disc. Both set the harshness of the rap lyrics against a more lyrical portrayal of religion: the heavy beat of rap in Krs-One's 'Unstoppable' is countered by a repeated high, bell-like sound; in Public Enemy's 'What You Need is Jesus' by a string orchestra and female chorus singing the refrain 'Jesus'. As such the long-standing contrast between the music of the Church and of the bar (gospel versus jazz or blues in an earlier version) is simply perpetuated, and so how religious belief might contribute to easing life on the streets is not clearly indicated. That is, the two forms of life are set in tension rather than integrated or reconciled.

More recent contributors have had to come to terms with the way in which hip-hop has developed into gangster rap, with much tougher scenarios and language. Performers feel that in order to be heard at all, they are now left with no alternative but to set themselves within similar contexts even where their message is intended to be rather different. One can see the result in an act like Q-Tip where, despite the explicit avowal of Islam, the language is still wholly that of the streets.[249] A rather brave attempt to tell a personal

---

[245] There is an interview in Ehrlich, *Inside the Music*, 202–13. P. M. Dawn seems the more impressive figure: ibid. 222–7.

[246] On the album *3 Years, 5 Months, and 2 Days in the Life of . . .* (1992).

[247] *Spiritually Minded* (2002). One might contrast this with an earlier album such as *Return of the Boom Bap* (1993).

[248] For interviews with both Krs-One and Public Enemy, see D. Goldstein (ed.), *Rappers Rappin* (Chessington, Surrey: Castle Communications, n.d.), 81–108.

[249] See *Amplified* (1999). As well as a dedication to Allah, each track is described as 'produced for the Ummah' (the Muslim community). Although a minority phenomenon in the United States, tensions are inevitably more acute in France, where most performers are Muslim: C. Béthune, *Pour une esthétique du rap* (Paris: Klincksieck, 2004), esp. 122–4.

story of redemption comes from Petey Pablo in *Diary of a Sinner: 1st Entry* (2001). The title is taken up in the introduction and again in the concluding tracks.[250] The intervening numbers, however, simply assume violence and sexual promiscuity, and indeed given their anthem-like character are perhaps more likely to be what appeals to purchasers of the album. More intriguing, therefore, is a recent, highly acclaimed CD, *The College Dropout* (2004), from a new figure to the scene, Kanye West. Although the usual dilemmas of life on the street are faced in street language, the basic beat of rap is enhanced musically in various kinds of ways and so when a gospel number is introduced it does not seem wholly out of place.[251] More satisfying, however, is the track 'Jesus Walks', where God is no longer set apart but the possibility of Jesus' engagement with such street dilemmas is presented in a lively and engaging way. Rather than the earlier examples of complete contrast, West raps against a bass chorus that provides a sounding beat ('bum-bum') lighter than the usual percussion, while the women singing 'Jesus walks' sing at a lower pitch and are thus brought nearer to the rest of the music. Integration of religion and street life is thus presented as a real possibility.[252]

Some attempts are now being made to introduce hip-hop into the local churches.[253] However, the difficulty remains for the Church in how to combat compartmentalism, with hip-hop inevitably so sanitized for worship that experience of God is seen as confined to a limited sphere that is not 'the real world out there'. These dilemmas are of course not new for black America. Soul originally was the attempt by blues singers to appropriate what was best in gospel music. If John Coltrane represents the best attempt to appropriate jazz for the churches, and Al Green a later example of someone trying to do the same for soul, the process continues into more recent times.[254] As the

[250] Tracks 14–17. The final track is a remix. Only 17 is in quite a different format from the rest of the album, with an orchestral background suggesting the peace that religion can give.

[251] Although not listed, the gospel track immediately precedes 'Spaceship' on the album. Clearly, the one is intended to help interpret the other.

[252] His 2005 DVD *College Dropout* includes several different ways of presenting the song and the background to them that well illustrates some of the dilemmas of how to bridge the gap between church and street.

[253] As in the work of Curtis Blow at the African Methodist Episcopal Church in Harlem.

[254] John Coltrane's best-known contribution is 'Love Supreme'; for the religious side of Al Green's singing, the film documentary *Gospel According to Al Green* (2003) is very enlightening.

tension between faith and music in black America is an issue to which I shall return in the next chapter, I want to end here with two rather different examples, set wholly outside the context of worship.

In the 1980s Prince produced a highly successful series of sexually explicit soul-like albums that he then attempted to continue into the nineties under his strange new symbolic name.[255] In 2000, however, he became a Jehovah's Witness convert. Declaring that 'cursing was cool when nobody would do it', his 2001 album *The Rainbow Children* was entirely devoted to the theme of religion.[256] However, it was a rather lacklustre effort, and, perhaps surprisingly, his occasional religious songs from the earlier period were on the whole much better. 'The Cross' from 1996, for example, offers a fine build-up of hope through a quiet, haunting, acoustic guitar gradually building into a metal crescendo in which, amazingly, the original sound can still be heard in the background.[257] In his most recent album dance, sexuality and religion all combine as he sings, 'this is just another one of God's gifts: musicology'.[258]

Lenny Kravitz is also someone of mixed race who has mixed sex and religion in his output, in part in imitation of Prince, though more recently his influences have widened to include Hendrix, Led Zeppelin, the Beatles and Stevie Wonder.[259] Particularly impressive is *Circus* (1995). Religious experience is presented as a natural part of the ordinary world, and no less than four tracks raise the question of God in a variety of styles. Heavy rock is used in 'Beyond the 7th Sky' to unite two lovers and God, with the solo music part adding an element of mystery. 'God is Love' is a more reflective piece that uses quiet electronic sounds to reinforce its message: 'if you are ready, He is always ready for you ... He gave us His Son ... gave us everything'. With 'In My Life Today' Kravitz gives a more soulful inflection to his voice, with its verbal content underlined

---

[255] An unpronounceable symbol which led to him being referred to as 'the artist formerly known as Prince'. For the convolutions of his career, see L. Jones, *Purple Reign* (Secaurus, NJ: Birch Lane, 1998).

[256] Quotation on *Maximum Prince* (2004).

[257] On the album *Sign of the Times*. For a similar judgement from a non-believer, see Jones, *Purple Reign*, 226.

[258] On the opening track of *Musicology* (2004), an album that deliberately draws on earlier black artists such as Stevie Wonder, George Clinton and James Brown.

[259] He is the son of an African-American mother and a Jewish father.

by an accompanying guitar and repeated refrain, 'You are the force and the strength'. Least successful is 'The Resurrection'; the lyrics are poor and the orchestral accompaniment seems only mildly affirmative.[260] Elsewhere Kravitz sometimes gives apparently secular songs a sudden religious twist.[261] So openness to religious experience is certainly a significant element in his work.

Too often have Christians imposed predetermined criteria on how music ought to induce religious experience. What I have sought to indicate in this chapter is how varied such possibilities are even in an area that to many has seemed a religious desert. God is present everywhere seeking a response. So it is quite wrong to suppose that only explicit belief will meet with an answering echo. Where lyrics and music work effectively together, a great variety of new possibilities can emerge, well beyond any controls from the composers or singers involved. At the same time those without explicit Christian belief also deserve some credit, in insisting upon wider horizons in terms of which, for example, love songs can be seen as pointing beyond themselves, or rock music allowed to conjure up transcendence. That is why it seems to me so unfortunate that the relatively few theological investigations of such music as there are fall so quickly into the trap of judging the artists by the strength of their antecedent Christian convictions or lifestyles, and not by the power of their music in its own right to provide significant openings for the out-workings of God's purposes. The major Christian reference book in the area, for example, examines from among what has been surveyed here only Dylan, U2 and those groups prepared to label themselves 'Christian' rock bands.[262] Fortunately, grace works much more widely than this.

It is that issue of the range of divine grace operating through music that I want to address more explicitly in the next chapter. While consideration of hymns and liturgical music is deferred until this volume's sequel, it is important to face here the extent to which the

---

[260] Phrases like 'The resurrection is here to stay' unfortunately sound pedestrian rather than inspiring.

[261] For examples, note what happens on tracks 12–14 of his *Greatest Hits* (2000) album.

[262] M. A. Powell, *Encyclopaedia of Contemporary Christian Music* (Peabody, Mass.: Hendrikson, 2002). This is not to decry such entries as are provided, for example, on Dylan: 277–86.

secularization of music is the Church's own fault.[263] Prince and Kravitz may seem a long way from what one might hear in church, but all black music can be seen as ultimately having its origins in the church. If the historical lines are less clear with 'white' music, not dissimilar issues are in fact raised, as we shall see.

---

[263] *God and Mystery in Words: Experience through Metaphor and Drama* (Oxford: Oxford University Press, 2008), chs 3 and 6.

7
Blues, Musicals and Opera

The combination of topics roughly indicated by the title of this chapter may seem somewhat arbitrary, but my intention here is rather more than just to gather up what has been left over from the discussion in the two previous chapters. Hymns and liturgical music have been deliberately excluded, and will therefore be dealt with in this volume's sequel.[1] What the surviving elements share in common is forms of song that may at one level, like pop music, be described as purely 'secular' but which, unlike pop music, to varying degrees and for different reasons could also be said (sometimes at least) to aspire to the sacred. That is to say, rather more seems to be going on than when pop tunes are adapted to religious themes. To illustrate how this is so, in the first section I explore how blues, jazz and soul in fact originated out of spirituals and in part as a legitimate protest against the failure of the more religious genre to deal adequately with life and all its problems. But, so far from this resulting in total secularization, a continuing engagement with religious experience can be detected. Much the same can be said of the nearest equivalents of blues, jazz and soul in the white community, the topic of the next section. If country music and musicals often seem much less earthed than the sort of lyrics that are generated from within the black community, revolt against pure romanticism is by no means uncommon, and in this spiritual themes can make their presence felt, once more in ways that seem to protest against religion too narrowly conceived. Finally, for some aficionados of opera it has become an alternative to religion, not least in the way it opens up the viewer and listener to a world of mystery or magic. Whether there is any essential conflict between opera and religion is the topic of the last section. There I shall argue, as in the two previous sections, that the themes of such music rightly

---

[1] *God and Mystery in Words: Experience through Metaphor and Drama* (Oxford: Oxford University Press, 2008), chs 3 and 6.

widen the range of religious experience beyond the church door. Indeed, without such a contribution Christianity would be seriously impoverished, given that its worship fights shy of so many of the dilemmas of ordinary life.[2]

Spirituals and the Devil's Blues

Here I want to examine the way in which the tradition of song has developed within the black American community. Its roots lie in the spirituals of slavery. It is from them that there emerged not only gospel music, their most obvious successor in time, but also what are often portrayed as their 'secular' rivals, blues, jazz and soul. In marked contrast to the hymn, spirituals were heavily social and political in content. Indeed, some have even claimed that this pre-empted the religious dimension, with biblical imagery really coded language for the real heart of the message, which lay quite elsewhere. That contention I would want to challenge. But there is little doubt that by those standards gospel music (the spirituals' nearest equivalent religious successor), with its more conventional religious sentiments, must be seen as marking a decline, with the real brunt of social reflection borne by what was deliberately set over against the Church in musical forms such as blues and jazz. Even so, these newer forms did not abandon the religious quest. Instead, that quest moved elsewhere, outside the immediate context of worship. How that enlarged the range of areas of human experience through which God might be mediated, and so inhibited still further retreat on the part of religion to a narrow range of concerns, will be a recurring theme.

Spirituals, Gospel and their Social World

Evidence for some overlap in conception between the type of song discussed here and more conventional hymns emerges from the high regard in which the hymn-writer Isaac Watts was held by nineteenth-century black Americans.[3] At the same time, that

---

[2] Amply illustrated in the discussion of hymns in *God and Mystery in Words*, ch. 3.

[3] e.g. the hymnbook *Freedom's Lyre* had more pieces by Watts than by any other writer: J. M. Spencer, *Protest and Praise: Sacred Music of Black Religion* (Minneapolis: Fortress, 1990), 48. They were known affectionately as 'Doctor Watts' songs': P. Oliver, M. Harrison and W. Bolcom, *The New Grove Gospel, Blues and Jazz* (London: Macmillan, 1986 edn), 7.

something profoundly different was occurring is well indicated by the way in which, in typical African-American fashion, the gospel singer Aretha Franklin (b. 1942) transforms a hymn like John Newton's 'Amazing Grace'. In a famous performance the original two verses are expanded to a full ten minutes thanks to the employment of elaborate musical ornaments, interjections and exchanges with the audience.[4] Such treatment was meted out not just to Newton but to numerous songs for which she is famous. Nor was she by any means alone in this. Marion Williams and Mahalia Jackson took similar liberties. Particularly conspicuous in the former is a feature still known as 'Doctor Watts style' from its treatment of those earlier hymns. The original melody is given a 'surge' as each syllable is drawn out over several improvised, inflected notes.[5] Mahalia Jackson equally sets her own agenda of time and pitch. Where trills may occur is quite unpredictable. She even takes breaths in the middle of words. All of this makes her accompanist (Mildred Falls) an unsung hero.[6] If a direct comparison is wanted with more conventional treatment of hymns, her performance of Charlotte Elliot's 'Just As I Am' provides a good example. There is so much elaboration that the melody is surely in part sustained by the listener's own memories. Yet such practices work quite brilliantly, not least in drawing attention to the significance of the words.[7] What the style indicates is a real freedom in communication that is essentially creativity in the immediate moment, and interactive with words and audience alike. But it is not just purely human interaction. As Jackson observes: 'Sometimes you feel like you're so far from God, and *then* you know those deep songs have special meaning. They bring back communication between yourself and God.'[8]

Although 'Amazing Grace' was written by Newton long after his conversion, it was still at a stage when he seems to have seen

---

[4] Her *Amazing Grace* album came out in the year of Mahalia Jackson's death (1972). For a more detailed description, see C. Small, *Music of the Common Tongue* (London: Calder, 1994), 105.

[5] Ibid. 108–9.

[6] For a collection of some of her finest performances (between 1947 and 1954), see *Mahalia Jackson: Queen of Gospel* (1993). Her 'Lord's Prayer' on that disc has a trill at 'daily' for understandable reasons, but why on 'be' (no. 9)? 'Just As I Am' is track 17.

[7] Most obvious in her treatment of 'thy blood was shed for me'.

[8] Quoted in J. Schwerin, *Got To Tell It: Mahalia Jackson Queen of Gospel* (New York: Oxford University Press, 1992), 27.

nothing wrong in principle with slavery.[9] It took William Wilber-force to persuade him otherwise. So there is an unfortunate irony in black women singing such a song when they themselves had been subject to oppression by the white majority in the United States. Jackson, for instance, as the granddaughter of slaves and herself born in a poor southern shack, had come to regard mistreatment by the police as routine.[10] So it is not surprising that 'I Been 'Buked and I Been Scorned' was one of her favourite spirituals.[11] Nonetheless, most of her gospel songs have more of a personal than political dimension. It is this that secured the popularity of her singing with whites, and thus also in due course her own wealth.[12] The more personal side was possibly in any case more important to Jackson, though she did participate in the civil rights movement.[13] Certainly, it is often asserted that such 'gospel music' (whose emergence is often equated with the end of the American Civil War and the rise of fundamentalism) has precisely that more personal character, as compared with the earlier spirituals.[14] To assess possible differences, we need therefore to go back to the beginning and understand the nature and origin of spirituals.

It is now increasingly acknowledged that the Africans who arrived in America as slaves did not in fact allow their lives and identities to be written *de novo* by the dominant white culture and its religion. Instead, they came with a distinctively African approach to religious belief, and much of this survived through its eventual absorption into their own version of Christianity. Indeed, until the Great Awakening in the mid-eighteenth century there may have been no sustained attempts at conversion.[15] The key feature of that

[9] The hymn was written in 1772, and Newton's conversion to the abolitionist cause probably did not take place till the mid-1780s: S. Turner, *Amazing Grace* (Oxford: Lion Hudson, 2002), 111, 124–7.

[10] Schwerin, *Got To Tell It*, 13–19, 21–2.

[11] She was requested to perform it by both Martin Luther King and Robert Kennedy: ibid. 131–2, 157.

[12] Helped by the white disc jockey Studs Terkel: ibid. 63.

[13] At her death in 1972 she was contemplating becoming a conventional preacher with her own temple, a project to which John D. Rockefeller Jr had contributed money: ibid. 173–5.

[14] Personal regeneration was seen as a prerequisite for any further social advance: Oliver *et al.* (eds), *The New Grove*, 189.

[15] So Small, *Music of the Common Tongue*, 82; cf. A. C. Jones, *Wade in the Water: The Wisdom of the Spirituals* (Maryknoll, NY: Orbis, 1993), 68. The Great Awakening began in the 1740s, with a second wave in 1800–35.

earlier religion was its thorough integration into every aspect of life, with music as a constant reinforcement for communal beliefs.[16] Because so much of it functioned as an accompaniment to work, rhythm was more important than harmony, the conventional organizing principle in European music. Two different rhythms might proceed in counterpoint with one another and be held together only by a common beat.[17] If that was one contrast with western music, another was improvisation, a willingness to respond to new circumstances as they arose. Or perhaps one should say that the contrast is with western music as it now is, since much more improvisation seems to have been accepted in the past in classical music than is the case now.[18] Perhaps the nearest parallel in contemporary classical music is with aleatoric composition, where some decisions are left to the performer, for instance about when to change a particular note (as in some of the music of Hans Werner Henze and John Cage).

As things stand, this is less obvious with spirituals than it probably would once have been. Our present expectations are largely derived from the late-nineteenth century attempt by the Fisk Jubilee Singers to preserve and popularize spirituals within the wider culture of the time.[19] In trying to achieve these aims, in all probability they gave the spirituals a more white 'feel' than was originally the case. Certainly, the close connection with song and dance in the traditional ring-shout suggests a high degree of informality. Singers either moved in a circle to the music or else swayed back and forth while joined in such a circle.[20] Greater

---

[16] Stressed on the very first page of T. L. Reed, *The Holy Profane: Religion in Black Popular Music* (Lexington, Ky: University Press of Kentucky, 2003), 1. Cf. Small, *Music of the Common Tongue*, 20.

[17] Even when downbeats do not always coincide, the common beat can still be recognized, producing in Africans what has been called an innate 'metronome sense': ibid. 25.

[18] Small contrasts Mozart's and Beethoven's attitude to the cadenza, with the development only specified in great detail in Beethoven's music. Small also draws attention to the liberties given to singers by Monteverdi in his original opera scores: ibid. 282, 286.

[19] Between 1871 and 1878, to raise money for the new black university at Nashville: ibid. 96. The extensive performance specifications are readily apparent in a modern collection such as M. Hogan (ed.), *The Oxford Book of Spirituals* (Oxford: Oxford University Press, 2002).

[20] For some more detailed descriptions, see Spencer, *Protest and Praise*, 142–8.

formality perhaps only came through experience of white hymn-singing at the open tent meetings during major evangelistic crusades. Even then the extent to which bodily movement continued to remain an implicit demand of the music can be seen in twentieth-century objections from preachers to the physical gestures that accompanied Jackson's songs.[21] It is almost as though movement in itself was taken to imply freedom and liberation. Another reason for suspecting more informal approaches is the early popularity of the banjo (probably itself an import from Africa). Even when the banjo was succeeded by the guitar, the finger-picking style of playing continued to be known among country musicians as 'nigger-picking'.[22] Likewise, although major attempts were made to suppress drums, that too suggests a more African style of response.[23] Nor is there any reason to think that the modern interactive style of African-American preaching only dates from a later age. Under slavery it would have been even more important for all to feel caught up in a similar perception of things.

It is at this point that we can perhaps see most clearly how such music would help effect an essentially social perception of God. As noted in Chapter 2, African religion saw the divine presence immanent everywhere, even if this was largely mediated through spirits, particularly spirits of ancestors.[24] One way therefore to read all those references in the spirituals to the great Old Testament heroes of the past, such as Moses and Daniel, is to see them invoked to be present with the community now as they face similar dilemmas.[25] It is, as it were, the reverse of a long tradition of European piety. The latter had asked worshippers to envisage themselves present during the life of Christ, at his birth and crucifixion most obviously.[26] Here, however, rather than congregations being urged

[21] Schwerin, *Got To Tell It*, 61, 78.
[22] Small, *Music of the Common Tongue*, 158. For a black gospel example of the technique, see the Blind Willie Johnson CD *Dark was the Night* (1995), with recordings originally from the 1920s.
[23] For their treatment by the Yoruba as a sacred instrument, and their forced suppression in America, see Spencer, *Protest and Praise*, 136–42; cf. Jones, *Wade in the Water*, 84.
[24] Jones suggests that in the spirituals 'God' is treated like the high God of African religion and 'Jesus' and 'Lord' more like one of those mediators: ibid. 79–80.
[25] So Small, *Music of the Common Tongue*, 84. The use of the present tense adds to that sense, as in 'Go Down, Moses'.
[26] For examples of this different sort of approach as applied to the Nativity, see my *Tradition and Imagination* (Oxford: Oxford University Press, 1999), 60–105.

to think themselves back in time in order to participate vicariously in those events, individuals from the past are now brought alongside the community to give shape and identity to their present experience.[27]

Because of the apparently otherworldly character of so many of the songs, many black American writers now very much stress the hidden code that lay beneath all those references to the imagery of heaven. Gatherings of the community could appear to the white slave-owners to be singing about one set of concerns, whereas their message was in reality quite different. So, for example, 'Canaan' could be about escape to freedom in the north of the country rather than crossing over to heaven.[28] Indeed, some commentators go so far in this direction as to claim that that was all that was really going on. So, although the language was borrowed from Christianity, the slaves' commitments really lay quite elsewhere.[29] I find this quite implausible. To see why, one need only recall how relatively few slaves ever escaped. If such hopes were really the main burden of their song, it must have aggravated discontent rather than done anything to relieve it. Rather, it is surely precisely because the lyrics could be read on two levels at once that the songs gained their extraordinary power. In effect, the songs declared that nothing was going to defeat the community in seeking release from their oppression. Of course, they would struggle to escape if they could, but, failing that, the masters would still not finally defeat them. Either way the slaves were sure of a better land where their value and rights would be finally secured. So God was experienced as working on both levels at one and the same time.

By contrast later 'gospel' songs do have a much more personal, individualistic dimension.[30] This may be due in part to the fact that the community was now much less united. The growth in gospel

<hr />

[27] With the best earlier parallel perhaps being invocation of the saints.

[28] Confirmed by the former slave Frederick Douglass: Jones, *Wade in the Water*, 43–4. 'Wade in the Water' could also be used as a reminder of how to put pursuers off the scent: ibid. 50. Likewise, the use of 'train' to refer to the underground railroad is well known: Spencer, *Protest and Praise*, 20.

[29] Jones' conviction that the young could not possibly be preoccupied with heaven (*Wade in the Water*, 55) fails to take seriously how many would die young under the conditions of slavery. It also leads him to postulate implausible hidden meanings that lack any historical support: cf. e.g. 46, 66.

[30] For various statistical analyses of content, see Spencer, *Protest and Praise*, 202–4.

songs corresponded to a time when there was great variety in the response among blacks to their new-found 'freedoms'. Some tried to work within the system towards their own advancement. In the South the perils of disunity were not fully appreciated until the hard-won rights were once more lost.[31] Such disunity and disenchantment had a marked impact on religious belief. It is estimated that by 1945 half the population of black America was lost to the Church.[32] It was only really with the civil rights movement that a greater sense of unity once more returned, with the churches once more playing a key role.

However, if not political in the strong sense of the term, it is not true that gospel music was without a social dimension. Black churches continued to have a much tighter sense of communal identity than their white equivalents. Indeed, as southerners at the beginning of the twentieth century fled north seeking employment, their primary social support was often the churches, and intimate small places at that, sometimes shopfronts with room for only thirty or fewer.[33] Not infrequently these churches were variations on Pentecostalism, which had its roots in the Azusa Street Revival of 1906, and now has over 400 million members worldwide. One of the great tragedies of that movement is that it was begun among blacks, in particular William J. Seymour, the son of a former slave, but eventually divided on racial grounds.[34] Yet, the style of worship, whether white or black, is equally grounded in black forms of worship and music. The strongly physical character of the music and interchanges with the preacher, for example, have clear precedents in the earlier black communities. To focus on informality as the key feature would, however, be a mistake. As many commentators observe, the success of such exchanges is

[31] In 1883 the Supreme Court reversed the Civil Rights Act of 1875. By 1900 (the year commonly used for marking the definitive emergence of gospel music) disenfranchisement was complete.

[32] Reed, *The Holy Profane*, 86.

[33] In 1928 Chicago this was true of 86% of all Holiness/Pentecostal churches: ibid. 69. For a more secular version, in the rent party, see Small, *Music of the Common Tongue*, 207–8.

[34] In 1914 white ministers withdrew from the interracial Church of God in Christ to form the Assemblies of God. It is only very recently that the historical display at the latter's headquarters in Springfield, Missouri has been altered to acknowledge this fact.

heavily dependent on practice and learned skills. The real heart of such practices lies in the mutual reinforcement that is taking place.[35] While that could of course be described as all that is occurring, certainly this is not how matters are experienced. Rather, it is the presence of the Spirit working in and through the congregation to unite them. Even so, many blacks felt that something was missing: a lack of realism in the churches' approach to their particular social world. It was partly for this reason that alternative forms of music began to emerge.

The Devil in Blues and Jazz

Social issues were certainly sometimes addressed in gospel, but the ethic was so absolute that it did mean that many found it necessary to seek refuge elsewhere, and this was one reason for the growth of the blues as an alternative musical culture among blacks. Although sometimes characterized as the music of the drinking house and of the brothel, matters turn out to be not that simple, despite the way in which many preachers at the time rejected blues music as of the devil himself. What a number of more recent commentators have noted is certain key features that actually indicate a continuing engagement of the blues with religion, almost despite itself. Certainly, God is frequently addressed.[36] The imagery of religion too is borrowed, even if sometimes used to make a contrary point. If 'holy roll' is an example of a Pentecostal term transferred to sexual intercourse, the great mass of such redeployed imagery is used positively.[37] Finally, many singers seem in fact to have moved back and forth between the two genres.[38]

Particularly intriguing are the three films recently produced by Martin Scorsese that examine this tension. If the one directed by Charles Burnett tends simply to juxtapose gospel and blues and the

---

[35] Stressed in Spencer, who identifies the rationale in a successful move from 'I' to 'we': *Protest and Praise*, 189–91.

[36] Spencer rightly insists that interjections which mention the divine name should be taken seriously as indicating a plea for divine help: ibid. 111–12.

[37] For 'holy roll', see Reed, *The Holy Profane*, 53. For more positive imagery, such as Noah's dove and Daniel in the lion's den, see 42–50; cf. Spencer, *Protest and Praise*, 107–31.

[38] e.g. Blind Lemon Jefferson remained a strict sabbatarian, while Robert Wilkins became an ordained minister: Spencer, *Protest and Praise*, 124, 128.

resultant uncertainties in the director's own childhood, that by Wim Wenders offers more by way of explanation and challenge.[39] The lives of three key performers are explored: Blind Willie Johnson, who never sang anything but religious lyrics despite his commitment to the blues idiom; Skip James, who had a gap of thirty years as a Baptist minister before returning to performance in the 1960s; and J. B. Lenoir, who moved indifferently from 'sacred' to 'secular' throughout his career.[40] The final film examines the key role played by the Jewish Chicago firm of Chess Records in bringing blues to a wider audience, all through the eyes of the modern rap artist Chuck D (of Public Enemy). While there is a strong social element throughout, almost no reference to religion occurs until the concluding song, in which a Muddy Waters hit is adapted for rap lyrics that are clearly spiritual and Christian in content.[41]

So one way of reading the blues is to see it as a plea for recognition of a more complex social reality. Just as modern rap addresses the issue of drugs as a presence that cannot be ignored despite the churches pretending otherwise, so blues sought to find God within problems of gambling, alcoholism and imperfect sexual relationships.[42] Indeed, if we pursue the last-mentioned a little further, it is often the hypocrisy of church members that is attacked, with similar problems identified within their own walls. Thus the church deacon seems to have become a particular object of ridicule, with him seen as using his power to seduce female members of the congregation.[43] Given the nature of the themes, perhaps there was no easy way in which these could be addressed in the songs of the Church, without undermining the essentially upbeat character of divine praise.

Yet the irony is that blues, despite its name, is also itself upbeat, with the music often suggesting a more positive outcome than the

[39] All are available on DVD (2003): Charles Burnett, *Warming by the Devil's Fire*; Wim Wenders, *The Soul of Man*; Marc Levin, *Godfathers and Sons*.

[40] Recognition of Wenders' international reputation as a film director and of his willingness to consider religious themes has earned him an honorary doctorate in theology from the University of Fribourg in Switzerland.

[41] Waters' LP *Electric Mud* is used to illustrate the way in which blues could transmute into new genres, as is the influence of one of his songs in giving the Rolling Stones their name.

[42] For a detailed version of the argument that the blues are really secular spirituals, see J. Cone, *The Spirituals and the Blues* (New York: Seabury Press, 1972).

[43] For deacon caricatures in the 1940s and 1950s, see Reed, *The Holy Profane*, 78–81.

surface meaning of the words. How this is achieved is intriguing. Classic blues usually has three lines to each stanza, with each line consisting of four bars, two for the words and two for the accompanying instrument's reply. That is not, however, where the interest lies, as the underlying harmonic structure is simple and predictable. Rather, the general tone is set instead by the rhythm, the melody and unexpected inflections in voice or instrument. So, for instance, rather than following strictly the classical major or minor scales, flattening of notes occurs, and there is a generally freer approach to pitch, with, for example, the voice sliding down at the end of a note, vibrato, falsetto yells and numerous other devices. All are calculated to create a particular mood that is usually more optimistic than not.[44] Perhaps that is not enough of itself to bring songs in this style within the possibility of church worship. Certainly, many fail to display the kind of overlap with religion I am considering here.[45] Even so, the fact that such overlap can and does occur is surely sufficient to demand acknowledgement of the two types of experience as both legitimate, as both capable of conveying God's presence in the community's midst. So the problem is not so much the exclusion of blues singing from the local church as that local church's failure to admit that such songs might after all have something to do with God.

There was a similar problem over attitudes to jazz, as it began to develop in the very early years of the twentieth century independently of church tradition. The likely origins of the term in sexual slang already hint at the extent of the potential divorce.[46] Yet, despite the common roots of jazz and blues, jazz was to develop in a quite different direction. By the 1930s it was already considered highbrow, primarily instrumental and capable of crossover between the races, whereas blues remained mainly vocal, lowbrow and overwhelmingly black.[47] An element of rebellion, however, remained as part of the attraction of jazz. So those artists who sought to bring the medium and religion back together once

---

[44] For a more detailed discussion, see Small, *Music of the Common Tongue*, 198–204.

[45] More serious themes seem to have been commoner in earlier music. Contrast the CD collection *The Encyclopedia of Early Blues Classics* (2001) and the three-CD collection *Blues Blues Blues* (1997).

[46] It appears to be related to jissom/jism: so Small, *Music of the Common Tongue*, 324–5.

[47] The contrasts are Reed's in *The Holy Profane*, 27.

more faced an uphill task. 'Respectability' was not quite what was wanted, though in itself that said more about problems in the nature of the Church than anything inherent in the medium as such. Outside jazz circles, Duke Ellington's attempts to bridge the gap are probably most widely known. Those who have been privileged to participate in a performance of his *Sacred Concerts* in the context of an actual liturgical performance will be well aware of the power of such music.[48] They were written originally as occasional pieces (hence their alternative name, *Sacred Pieces*). Integrating the most appropriate of these into a eucharistic celebration helped not only to give them greater coherence but also an enhanced expressiveness. Nonetheless, for many they were seen as marking a decline from the excitement of Ellington's earlier years. Then the degree of improvisation had been much stronger, with the detailed arrangement of specific pieces often left to key instrumentalists. So, for instance, his trumpet concerto is actually called *Concerto for Cootie* precisely because the actual performance of the piece was built around decisions by the trumpeter himself, Cootie Williams. By contrast, *Sacred Pieces* has been labelled 'a victory for "classical" respectability'.[49]

Among jazz enthusiasts the finest integration of jazz and faith is commonly acknowledged to be found in the religious works of John Coltrane, pre-eminently in *A Love Supreme* of 1964.[50] Here there is a degree of spontaneity and improvisation that Ellington is widely felt to lack. Coltrane had led a troubled life that included drug addiction, and this piece was planned as his offering to the God who had preserved him through all life's traumas. Although sometimes interpreted as referring to Christ, despite his Christian upbringing there seems little doubt that a more general reference was intended, one that saw a universal God operative everywhere.[51] His first wife had

[48] Performed first with mixed results at Westminster Abbey and St Paul's, it was only with the work of Canon Bill Hall and the Stan Tracey Orchestra at Durham Cathedral (in 1990 and 1993) that an appropriate eucharistic context was found: available on CD, *Duke: The Durham Connection*.

[49] Small, *Music of the Common Tongue*, 336.

[50] Currently available on several discs. He produced one further major religious album, his *Meditations* of 1966.

[51] This is to take issue with David Ford's interpretation in *Self and Salvation* (Cambridge: Cambridge University Press, 1999), 280–1. For a more detailed critique, see my 'The Glory of God Revealed in Art and Music: Learning from Pagans', in M. Chapman (ed.), *Celebrating Creation* (London: Darton, Longman and Todd, 2004), 43–56, esp. 53–5.

converted to Islam, and he himself repeatedly declared that he thought all religions embodied essentially the same message, that of love.[52] Significantly, in the poem that he wrote to accompany the piece, there is not one mention of Jesus Christ, though plenty of God and his care. Both his parents were children of ministers, and so it is quite likely that the title comes from an influential tract with a similar title by the Scottish minister Henry Drummond, who had insisted on the priority of love over the specifics of faith.[53]

It is also such universalism that emerges from the music itself. Coltrane widened the scope of jazz by blending elements of African ritual with Indian and Arabian influences.[54] In the opening section, 'Acknowledgement', an eastern gong leads into a tenor saxophone fanfare that itself yields to the other instruments in the quartet before Coltrane himself takes up the main four-note figure that is this section's primary tune. At first it appears as a simple bass riff. Later it is heard in the saxophone part and then repeated at different pitches, incorporated into longer melodic phases, and so forth. If that sounds boring, it is anything but, as it is subjected to numerous modulations, with frequent changes of key that produce an unsettling but challenging effect. The eventual utterance of the title words that correspond to the four-note figure is in effect unnecessary because through that very variation Coltrane has already informed us that 'God is everywhere—in every register, in every key'.[55] Indeed, in its only publicly performed version, at Antibes, the words were omitted. In view of the criticism noted earlier against the more formal character of Ellington's religious music, it is interesting to note that increased improvisation also meant that the piece as a whole in that version extended from 33 minutes to 48.

The absence of the words in this particular case could of course be used to argue against the view that there is anything inherently religious in such music after all. It might be said that it is only Coltrane's intentions that made it so. Certainly, there is nothing in the music of itself that compels such a reading. Yet, in the vocal version the words play such an insignificant role that this consideration can hardly be the

---

[52] For the background to the album, see A. Kahn, *A Love Supreme* (London: Granta Books, 2002). For his first wife's views, see 46, for his own, e.g. p. xx.

[53] H. Drummond, *Love: The Supreme Gift* (1891).

[54] V. Wilmer, *As Serious as Your Life: John Coltrane and Beyond* (London: Serpent's Tail, 1992 edn), 32, 36.

[55] Kahn, *A Love Supreme*, 102, quoting Lewis Porter.

final arbiter. Perhaps a more adequate answer can be given by comparing Coltrane's performance with the work of someone with whom he had once collaborated intimately, the famous Miles Davis. There is almost as much improvisation in the latter's influential *A Kind of Blue* (1959), but the mood is scarcely the same. As one recent analyst of this work observes, whereas Davis' music suggests 'drifting through the haze of a summer's day' or 'a perfect after-midnight record', Coltrane, as well as offering 'spiritual ecstasy', is 'dark and full of tumult', suggesting a searching unrest.[56] In other words, both open wider possibilities, but only Coltrane is able to offer, though not compel, access to something beyond ourselves.

Soul, Reggae and Sexuality

Attempts at integration were also evident in soul, a development of the fifties and sixties that is sometimes described as a reintegration of gospel and blues. Admittedly, it began in what seemed to be a straight purloining of the sacred for a secular role. Ray Charles' hit, 'I Got a Woman', was set to the music of a gospel song, 'My Jesus is All the World to Me'. But the fact that similar melodies could be used indifferently for both secular and sacred themes might be taken to indicate an overcoming of the earlier absolute antitheses between blues and gospel.[57] While few of James Brown's songs are explicitly religious and some major on sex, most endorse identification with the poor and marginalized and support communal values, as in 'Say it Loud—I'm Black and I'm Proud' and 'Get on the Good Foot'.[58] Al Green, another well-known figure in this genre, eventually decided to major on religious themes, reflected in his decision to pursue ordained ministry.[59] Even so, he did not wholly abandon his earlier commitment to the love song, as on his view that form could also draw listeners closer to God. More puzzling was Marvin Gaye, who despite his death as long ago as

[56] R. Cook, *It's About That Time: Miles Davis On and Off Record* (London: Atlantic, 2005), 118, 200. In terms of the openness of Davis' composition, he speaks of 'an elusive . . . possibility' where 'the solos could go anywhere' (113–14).

[57] e.g. by M. Haralambos, *Right On! From Blues to Soul in Black America* (London: Eddison, 1974), esp. 155.

[58] For a helpful survey, see the DVD *James Brown: Soul Survivor* (2003).

[59] His work at his own Full Gospel Tabernacle Church in Memphis and elsewhere is explored in the 2003 DVD *Gospel According to Al Green*.

1984, perhaps remains the most intriguing figure in the field. If 'Sexual Healing' is his best-known number, his religious songs, such as 'God is Love', are scarcely less familiar.[60] His was a troubled and tragic life that culminated in his own murder by a father to whom, ironically, he had once dedicated one of his songs on the theme of 'Joy'. Such details need not concern us here. What is fascinating is the continuing popularity of his music, and in particular the way in which virtually indistinguishable formats are used to deliver indifferently secular and religious themes.[61]

For some that is enough to denude songs with religious content of any serious worth. But such a judgement would, I believe, be very wide of the mark, and for a number of reasons. First, while it is sometimes helpful to emphasize the distinctiveness of religious experience, at other times this can be counterproductive. It may seem so remote as to offer no obvious or easily comprehensible point of access. In using the same sort of music religion can be seen to inhabit the ordinary and everyday, and so not be kept at bay as an apparently impossibly distant prospect. Of course, the danger is that it will come to assume some inappropriate aspects from that to which it is being compared. This is no doubt one reason why hymns to marching tunes, such as 'Onward, Christian Soldiers', have largely ceased to be sung in church.[62] But the positive side of such comparisons (which organizations such as the Salvation Army rightly exploits) is the sense of community solidarity and personal self-respect that the imagery helps to cultivate, not least among the downtrodden poor, towards whom their mission is primarily directed. The embrace of God is no less concerned with such values.

But, secondly, as well as anchoring religion in ordinary life, the appeal to analogous experience can also help to give depth to what is seen as a related but distinct encounter. The fact that in soul the implicit comparison is commonly with sexual intimacy can scarcely be seen as in itself a legitimate objection, since that kind of

---

[60] For some insight into the man and his music, see the double DVD *Marvin Gaye: Searching Soul* (2002).

[61] With both usually occurring on the same album. For attempts at separation, note *The Sexual Healer* (mainly that) and *What's Going On* (mostly religious).

[62] The title of Arthur Sullivan's rousing tune, *St Gertrude*, may be thought to indicate a different intention, but was merely a compliment to the Gertrude in whose house he stayed when the tune was composed: J. R. Watson, *An Annotated Anthology of Hymns* (Oxford: Oxford University Press, 2002), 319.

comparison runs deep within most religious traditions, including of course Christian mysticism, not to speak of the Bible itself.[63] What is often thought to give credibility to such objections is the promiscuous lifestyle of so many whose music legitimates such comparisons. As most are black, and the issue ranges over a wide spectrum of different genres, it seems best to face the issue head on. Take, for instance, reggae, and its most famous exponent, Bob Marley. Coming to international fame in 1973, his brief life was tragically cut short by cancer in 1981.[64] The song that brought him to a wider audience, 'I Shot the Sheriff', reflects the violent gang warfare of his native Jamaica, though in fact there is little of such imagery in his lyrics as a whole.[65] Instead, he has been described as a combination of 'the fire of political rebellion, the fire of spiritual belief and the fire of sensual love'.[66] That can easily be detected in the album which *Time* magazine declared in 2000 the album of the century, *Exodus* (1977).[67] The majority of the songs integrate religion into their theme, with even the most sensual, 'Turn your Lights Down Low', containing a reference to God.[68] Certainly, there can be no doubt about the sincerity of Marley's religious convictions. He attended church each week, and was well accustomed to spirit possession. When his body was laid out in state in Jamaica on his death, it held a guitar in one hand and a Bible in the other.[69] That such commitment took the form of Rastafarianism is

---

[63] Not least through the long-standing tradition of allegorical interpretation of the Song of Songs, which influenced, among so many others, Origen, Bernard of Clairvaux and John of the Cross.

[64] He was only 36. He died of a cancer that had begun as a melanoma in the toe.

[65] The original version had 'I shot the cop'. As such it would have anticipated future rap lyrics: J. Collingwood, *Bob Marley: His Musical Legacy* (London: Cassell, 2005), 92.

[66] Ibid. 44.

[67] 'One Love' on the same album was declared song of the century by the same issue of *Time*.

[68] 'Let Jah moon come shining in | into our life again' ('Jah' is the Rastafarian way of referring to God). Absent, however, is his favourite spiritual image of the train. For an example with Peter Tosh, another member of his group, the Wailers, using it in an opposed sense, see the CD *Bob Marley and the Wailers: The Very Best of the Early Years 1968–74* (1991), tracks 8 and 9. Not that religion is absent from Tosh's work. A creative example, integrating Handel, modern technology and reggae, is 'The Creation' on the album *Bush Doctor* (1978).

[69] R. Marley, *My Life with Bob Marley* (London: Pan, 2004), 163, 172; Collingwood, *Bob Marley*, 115.

well known.[70] To outsiders the key role assigned in Rastafarianism to the Emperor Haile Selassie of Ethiopia seems puzzling and strange, but what such connections offer is a strong assertion of black self-worth.[71] The result is that the social implications of religion are also strongly reflected in many of his songs.

However, that did go with a promiscuous lifestyle that produced in his short life eleven children by eight different mothers.[72] His wife documents a repeated pattern of casual affairs.[73] Both were from broken homes, and she herself met Marley and fell in love with him on the rebound from another affair that had resulted in pregnancy at eighteen.[74] How far such behaviour generally among the black community can be traced back to their shameful treatment under slavery is an open question.[75] Certainly, the pattern of men being separated from their womenfolk and required to direct their energies elsewhere was firmly established at that time. Although nominally the ideal usually remains the conventional one, in practice alternative behaviour meets with such wide acceptance that it is necessary to face a real scenario in which deep religious conviction and engagement run easily alongside promiscuity.

The phenomenon continues into the present. As already indicated in the previous chapter, rap artists are often found singing anthems in celebration of promiscuity while at the same time including in their album 'shout-outs' (or acknowledgements) what seem sincere thanks to God or Jesus Christ.[76] While some could be declared perfunctory, that is hardly true of the great majority. This is not the place to arbitrate the moral issues. My concern here is simply to insist on the genuine character of such religion, and thus also of the manner of its expression in music.

---

[70] A three-disc *Rastafari Box Set* is available from Trojan (2000). All the songs are from the 1970s and '80s, and so provide an excellent overall impression of how in general the religion was being expressed during Marley's adulthood.

[71] Marley's 'Selassie is the Chapel' dates from 1968 (the emperor had visited Jamaica two years previously). For the influence of black Coptic art, see Collingwood, *Bob Marley*, 68–9.

[72] Ibid. 136.

[73] Marley, *My Life*, e.g. 88, 97, 101, 104, 110, 161.

[74] Ibid. 13, 24.

[75] see Collingwood, *Bob Marley*, 12–13.

[76] Four-letter-word celebrations of promiscuity go along with thanks to God in the CDs of the likes of Akinyele ('first and foremost'), Ant Banks ('first of all'),

Many white Christians have abandoned a great raft of prohibitions that have been largely retained among the black Rastafarian community, among them the doctrine of hell and opposition to abortion, contraception, homosexuality and the eating of pork.[77] So the accusation of inconsistency or hypocrisy should not be lightly made; nor should the phenomenon prevent us from learning from the forms religious expression and experience has taken among such groups.

None of this is to deny the importance of moral considerations, but it is to suggest that something vital will be lost if the absolute contrast between gospel and blues still insisted upon by so many continues to be maintained. Those singers and performers of blues, jazz and reggae who have sought to bring a more complex world within the orbit of the divine are on to something important that contrasts markedly with the virtual absence of social and political issues from most white forms of worship and religious song.

White Parallels in Country Music and Musicals

Despite the title of this section it is not really possible to point to anything like a comparable debate in the nearest equivalent intermediate ground between classical and pop among white musicians, in country music and musicals. Nonetheless, there are a few parallels that can be drawn. These will be interesting to pursue, not least because these two traditions are often credited with black origins, at least in part. American folk music is said to be a combination of the style of English ballads and Negro spirituals, while musicals are apparently a combination of the operetta tradition and black minstrelsy.[78] Although in general both are far removed from the themes

Kotton Mouth ('Da Good Lord'), Lil Wayne and Ludacris. More specific thanks include the following: Clay D ('Thanks to God for all things made possible . . . Also, thanks to Reverend and Mrs C. Wood and Trinity M. B. Church'); D J Quick ('God for letting me live long enough'); Devin ('I'd like to start by thanking God for all he's blessed me with—the gifts of life and love'); Hype Boys ('We'd like to praise God for steering us in tha right direction and keeping us together through tha hardships'); Fredro Starr ('Thank you, Lord, Jesus Christ'); 10 Degrees Below ('All praise is due to the Creator').

[77] Marley, *My Life*, 39, 80.

[78] For the former point, see Small, *Music of the Common Tongue*, 154–60; for the latter, 144–52, 255.

of either explicit religious commitment or religious experience, there are some significant exceptions. So it is worth pursuing the issue to explore what sort of parallels might be drawn. If we take country music first, it is interesting to observe more readiness to include religious themes in recent years. So, for example, chart-topping numbers have included titles such as the following: George Strait's 'I Found Jesus on the Jailhouse Floor' and 'Love Without End, Amen'; Carrie Underwood's 'Jesus, Take the Wheel'; Brad Paisley's 'When I Get Where I'm Going'; Tim McGraw's 'Live Like You Were Dying'; and Garth Brooks' touching and much-praised 'Unanswered Prayers'. In effecting such changed attitudes, the rise in American evangelicalism and the religious right have undoubtedly played their part. But relevant too is country music's most famous twentieth-century exponent, the baritone Johnny Cash (1932–2003). So we may take Cash as representative of the genre.

Although born into poverty during the Depression years, Cash's troubles really came with success rather than failure, including a period of severe drug addiction.[79] His first marriage also failed, though it would be true to say that it had been in trouble for some considerable time. June Carter had in fact been the real love of his life long before they eventually married.[80] Throughout, however, he remained faithful to the Pentecostal type of religion to which he had converted at the age of twelve.[81] This was eventually to include participation in some Billy Graham Crusades, a novel about St Paul and various evangelistic films.[82] Although sometimes claimed as a poet,[83] few of his lyrics in my view merit that description. In particular, most of those about God are

[79] For Cash's Depression farmstead, see S. Miller, *Johnny Cash: The Life of an American Icon* (London: Omnibus, 2003), 7–12; for his drug addiction, 85, 99, 125, 135, 273; for associated vandalism, 99, 127.

[80] For his failed marriage, see ibid. 43, 77, 107, 113, 145. There is also a good film that explores the complexities in the relationship: *Walk the Line* (2005).

[81] Miller, *Johnny Cash*, 27.

[82] For cash and Billy Graham, see ibid. 195, 200; his novel about St Paul is *Man in White* (London: Harper and Row, 1986); his best-known film is *The Gospel Road* (1973).

[83] The claim in the Introduction to D. Cusic (ed.), *Johnny Cash: The Songs* (Edinburgh: Mainstream, 2005): 'certainly a poet' (9). Of roughly 300 pages of lyrics, 50 are in the 'God' section. For an especially bad example, note Jesus as 'The Greatest Cowboy of Them All' (92).

surprisingly trite and commonplace, and that despite the intimacy of encounters with the divine that he himself has recorded.[84]

Although there are technical elements that explain the popularity of his singing, much should be credited to his lyrics, where he engages with social issues. He himself described his restless, agitated rhythms as owing something to the Morse code of his military service years.[85] The frequent change of key at the start of each new verse also adds to the sense of an urgent demand for attention. While some of the more social songs might be classed as conservative, as in his commitment to marital fidelity and national pride, others are radical, not least in his sympathetic attitude towards prisoners and Native American culture.[86] Cash performed a number of times in American prisons, particularly Folsom and San Quentin, but it is above all his empathy for the individual driven to crime by poverty or who loses touch with his wife while in prison that has most immediate impact.[87]

For the most part such themes are treated apart from religious belief. That is a pity as, where integration occurs, he is often at his very best. 'All of God's Children Ain't Free' is a good example, as is the treatment of Jesus as a vagrant in 'Jesus was a Carpenter'. Another intriguing instance is the thanks he expresses to God in 'Abner Brown' for the positive influence on his own life of the local drunk and his story-telling.[88] Most familiar of all is his own personal anthem, 'Man in Black'.[89] Cash in various songs declares sympathy for the struggles of modern youth. He even suggests that song gives an outlet that was once provided by the churches.[90] It is therefore all the more surprising that he appears to have thought that prayer and worship require the exclusion of more contentious issues. His last album to win some major awards did at least make a valiant

[84] Treated more extensively in his autobiography, but for brief allusions to a few of these, see Miller, *Johnny Cash*, 28–31, 161–2, 230.

[85] For the Morse code comment, see ibid. 63.

[86] To fidelity, 'I Walk the Line' (Cusic, *Johnny Cash*, 291); to national pride, 'Ragged Old Flag' (ibid. 188–9); for his attitude to American Indians, note the album *Bitter Tears—Ballads of the American Indian* (1964).

[87] Two examples of the latter are 'Dear Mrs' (Cusic, *Johnny Cash*, 162–3) and 'This Side of the Law' (ibid. 169).

[88] For lyrics, ibid. 70, 84–5, 210–11.

[89] For lyrics, ibid. 351. Here there is an ironic change of mood. Jesus is introduced initially as someone who brings unqualified good, only for this to be subverted later, as allusion is made to the ambiguities of war.

[90] Ibid. 353 ('What is Truth?'); Miller, *Johnny Cash*, 195.

effort to get beyond the narrowly conventional. 'Meet Me in Heaven' reflects on the still traumatic death of his brother in childhood, while 'Spiritual' focuses on human loneliness and vulnerability in the face of death.[91] But in the trilogy of albums intended to sum up his life's work God is once again put in a separate category, while his very last album reduces religion to little more than mere sentimentality.[92] Perhaps in the end established conventions were just too strong for him to run counter to them. That may well explain why in his last days he retreated from public worship to his own private chapel.[93]

Musicals might seem at first sight to present even more of a problem. Their origins in minstrelsy were, after all, specifically devised to make black songs acceptable to white audiences. The face-paint on the white performers' faces ensured that whatever was said was treated as belonging to an artificial, innocuous and non-threatening world. The musicals of Rodgers and Hammerstein, Lerner and Loewe, Cole Porter and so on seem all too easily to fit into a similar pattern. Their optimism conforms too closely to the individualistic utopias of the American dream, where underlying social problems are simply ignored. God is not allowed in, partly no doubt because of the absence of religious belief among so many of the collaborators but also, more significantly perhaps, because religion was viewed as potentially too divisive.[94]

The latter justification has had a long history. Most recently, it was evident in the 2002 revival of *Godspell*. In that production by Scott Schwartz, the son of the original composer, the resurrection ending of his father, Stephen, was deliberately omitted. The reason given was that otherwise some of the audience would feel excluded from full

---

[91] Both on *Unchained* (1996). The former (Cusic, *Johnny Cash*) is for once quite poetic. His brother is not mentioned by name, but these were the words placed on his tombstone.

[92] The trilogy, *Love, God* and *Murder*, was released in 2000. *Life*, released posthumously in 2004, includes as its religious content only 'I Talk to Jesus Every Day' and 'Lead Me Gently Home', both devoid of personal or social critique.

[93] For that retreat, see Miller, *Johnny Cash*, 351.

[94] All were brought up in agnostic households. Rodgers moved to explicit atheism, even refusing his children any form of religious instruction. For further details, see I. Bradley, *You've Got to Have a Dream: The Message of the Musical* (London: SCM Press, 2004), 72.

participation in what was taking place on stage.[95] That seems to me a small-minded response. Our imagination and thus our experience will never be enlarged unless there is some exposure to what we do not endorse and may even regard with suspicion. So in my view the original show's ending was far more effective than the later production's rather anodyne 'We Can Build a Beautiful City'. In the earlier version the disciples had carried Jesus' body to the accompaniment of 'Long Live God', and then a final reprise had taken up once more the musical's theme song, 'Prepare Ye the Way of the Lord'. If this much can be said in defence of the more explicitly Christian content of the original version of *Godspell*, the same point also applies in the opposite direction in respect of *Jesus Christ Superstar*.

In that musical Christians are not only invited to see Jesus from the perspective of Judas but also to hear the institution of the Eucharist in a radically new way. Self-indulgent conversation on the part of the disciples is interrupted by Jesus' comment: 'For all you care about, this wine could be my blood | For all you care this bread could be my body'. Most powerful of all is the musical's most popular song, 'I Don't Know How to Love Him'. At one level it merely continues the western tradition of falsely equating Mary Magdalene with the loose woman who was the penitent sinner.[96] More importantly, that very fallibility allows anyone to enter into her questioning and so explore Jesus' significance for themselves. The music captures perfectly the inevitable oscillations that will occur in any such process.

Andrew Lloyd Webber, the composer of *Jesus Christ Superstar*, stems from a church home, and may well be more religious than his public statements suggest.[97] Although not the librettist, in his case, unlike most composers of musicals, the music is usually composed first, and so sets the tone.[98] Certainly, another of his compositions, *Cats*, has more Christian content than did T. S. Eliot's original poems, and that despite the fact these were written long after Eliot's

---

[95] So the programme notes for the version I saw in Newcastle the following year. Schwartz senior's collaborator, John-Michael Tebelak, had seriously contemplated ordination.

[96] For the origins and development of that tradition, see my *Discipleship and Imagination* (Oxford: Oxford University Press, 2000), 31–61.

[97] His father was a church organist, some of whose compositions are once more available on disc, e.g. *Sacred Music of William Lloyd Webber* (1999).

[98] Tim Rice was his collaborator on *Jesus Christ Superstar*, Richard Stilgoe and Trevor Nunn on *Cats*, Jim Steinman on *Whistle Down the Wind*.

conversion to Christianity. In order to give unity to the poems a cat-like heaven is introduced, and with it an opening prologue in which organ chords praise 'the mystical divinity of unashamed felinity'. The intention is not, I think, to mock but to provide a sort of cat-like parallel that emphasizes both the otherness of divinity ('mystical') and its connection with its worshippers (the human equivalent is being in the divine image). The same intensification of the religious dimension turns out to be true of *Whistle Down the Wind*, when comparison is made with the original version of this story of how country children came to mistake a criminal for Jesus.

On the other hand, the early Lloyd Webber–Rice *Joseph and the Amazing Technicolor Dreamcoat* stands, despite its subject matter, at a much greater distance from religious belief than might have been anticipated. Indeed, God is entirely absent, despite the biblical topic. The present Archbishop of Canterbury has taken particular exception to its theme song, 'Any Dream Will Do', and rightly so.[99] Not that this makes the musical any less worthy of our attention, since it reminds those of us who are Christians that the Joseph story can be read in more than one way. Even the biblical version scarcely always merits our unqualified endorsement.[100] Moral and spiritual perceptions will never grow unless we are exposed to different ways of reading the biblical stories, and much the same applies to musicals, as different emphases are generated by new directors and producers.

Schwartz junior's treatment of his father's *Godspell* has already been mentioned as one such example. Both the 1973 and 2000 film versions of *Jesus Christ Superstar* moved in the opposite direction from the original stage performance. The themes now became more explicitly religious rather than less. In the 1973 version, the sombre landscapes demanded a more reflective mood, despite the incongruity of the hippie bus. Even the resurrection is hinted at in the way the film ends, with the now empty cross set against a rising sun that has already coloured the sky a brilliant red. The 2000 version achieves its effects by quite different methods. Set against a backdrop of threatening

---

[99] In his 2002 Richard Dimbleby Lecture, available at <www.archbishopof canterbury.org/sermons_speeches/2002/021219.html>.

[100] Joseph's treatment of his brothers, though understandable, seems unnecessarily vindictive (Genesis 42–45), though some might plead that such conduct should be read in the light of his final act of forgiveness.

urban violence, Christ dies in an explosion of light. The film this time ends in a reprise of the theme song, our only vision a series of glowing lamp bulbs forming the shape of a cross.[101] By contrast, the history of *The Sound of Music* is more like *Godspell*. The film version lowered the religious content. In effect, Julie Andrews ousted the stage version's larger role for the Abbess and her convent.

In noting this, what I am struggling towards is rejection of any idea that ability to generate religious experience through such a medium be assessed in proportion to explicit religious content. Quite a few individuals I have known have linked specific songs from more secular musicals with their own more religious aspirations. 'You'll Never Walk Alone' from *Carousel* may not mention God, but it can suggest the perseverance through adversity that faith requires: 'Walk on through the wind, | Walk on through the rain, | Though your dreams be tossed and blown'. Indeed, the local doctor in introducing this final song speaks of the need for 'faith' as well as 'courage'.[102] Similarly, 'Somewhere Over the Rainbow' from the *Wizard of Oz* engages us with the possibility of realizing an ideal world that could for some suggest its sacramentalizing. That would then be nicely encapsulated in the imagery of the film itself. God gives back to the world the colour that it at present lacks.[103] Even that most apparently frivolous of songwriters, Cole Porter, may, if one perseveres, be found to have another dimension to his writing. As the director of a recent film about him puts it, there is in his lyrics 'a confusion and questioning about what love is about' and 'that is why his songs have lasted so long'.[104] So there is no need to focus narrowly on the most explicitly religious musicals, such as the marvellous evocation of Jewish communal identity in *Fiddler on the Roof* or on the dramatic

---

[101] The 1973 version was filmed on location in Israel; the 2000 film is of a new stage version.

[102] Note also the song's use in the aftermath of the Hillsborough football disaster.

[103] In the film Dorothy and her dog run away from her drab native Kansas (presented in black and white) to a world of glorious technicolour, only to return once more to Kansas to see it in a new and positive light. For the sacramental aspect, see H. Carpenter, *Dennis Potter: A Biography* (London: Faber and Faber, 1998), 348.

[104] Irwin Winkler on the DVD *De-Lovely* (2005). As Kevin Kline (who plays Porter) observes, this may have resulted in part from the fact that he was 'a gay man, the great love of whose life was a woman'.

evocation of conversion and forgiveness in *Les Misérables*, excellent though both are.[105] Something can even be gained from that most apparently perverse of productions, *Jerry Springer—The Opera*. Of course, the endless stream of four-letter words and obscenity are difficult to take, not least when much of the music is rather fine.[106] Yet, while no doubt true that the opera as a whole was in part gratuitously intended to shock, it was rather sad the way in which Christian hostility focused on the mockery of Christ and Mary in its second part and totally ignored the equally devastating treatment of ordinary humanity in its first part.[107] A society that enjoys television programmes that treat participants as freaks is unlikely to make much sense of the notion of the sacred. The two scriptwriters' primary motive was comic. So there is some reluctance on their part to admit to a more serious intention, but one of them does speak of the aim being 'compassion on some level'.[108] Even Jerry Springer himself, however, expressed reservations about lines such as these: 'Nothing is wrong, nothing is right, | Everything that lives is holy'. In the end, issues are posed rather than resolved. The blasphemy lies mostly in the devil's words (ironically, played by a practising Christian), while God is given one of the show's finest songs: 'It so ain't easy being me | Millions of voices making all the wrong choices, | Then turning round and blaming me'. The show stands at a huge distance from the dream world of the typical musical, but that can hardly make it fundamentally anti-religious.[109] When he saw the London performance for the first time, even Springer was left anxious at the end whether he had been redeemed

---

[105] So far only a concert performance of *Les Misérables* (1995 at the Albert Hall) is available more widely on video or DVD. The religious theme is surprisingly prominent, even from the very opening number. To date there have been nine adaptations of Hugo's novel to the screen, varying greatly both in religious content and in the extent of divergence from Hugo's text (updated to Holocaust France, for example, in Lelouch's 1995 version).

[106] Winner of numerous awards, it is now available on DVD (2005).

[107] Act I (first performed at the 2002 Edinburgh Festival) is based on the Chicago TV programme *The Jerry Springer Show*, which has participants confess publicly for the first time to their partners' various sexual faults. Act II has Springer dreaming of himself in purgatory and being asked to act on behalf of the devil in arraigning Christ.

[108] Stewart Lee. Richard Thomas (who was also responsible for the music) is more reluctant.

[109] In Act I one of the characters does sing 'I want to dream again', while at the end Springer offers dreams as his bribe for escaping hell.

or damned. So, hopefully, some of the audience too might reflect more deeply in their laughter at life's 'losers'.[110]

That said, it looks as though we are back with the issue that has dominated so much of this chapter, the difficulty of integrating religious worship and sensitivity to social issues. Black worship once held the two in creative tension, but throughout the twentieth century it looked as though they were being pulled apart. If the light music of white popular culture has on the whole been far more escapist, it would be a mistake to suggest that such themes are absent except at the extremes, such as in *Jerry Springer*. While Leonard Bernstein's *West Side Story* owes most to Shakespeare's *Romeo and Juliet*, it does at least face the issue of New York's gang culture. Again, *Carousel*, though thoroughly typical of the genre in so many ways, nonetheless does deal directly with some social issues: in this case, failures of communication in human relationships, the man taking to crime to support the child he has fathered, the woman finding she can only express her love for him once he is dead.[111] One hesitates, therefore, to ascribe the popularity of songs from musicals at funerals entirely to escapism.[112] It may also indicate dreaming about a more integrated world, and the Church's singular failure to provide such a vision in terms that are readily comprehensible to the great mass of the population.

Although opera could, like musicals, be accused of similar forms of escapism, on the whole its advocates have been concerned to identify more profound aims. Sometimes, these have overlapped with those of religion. As in their origins sacred oratorio and secular opera were not always sharply distinguished, and religious themes have been taken up once more in more recent times, it is worth asking whether opera too might offer the possibility of religious experience.

Religious Dimensions to Opera

Most discussions of the origins of opera identify two sources. One (which is usually given lesser prominence) is the precedent in sung

---

[110] 'Bring On the Losers' is one of the songs in Act I.

[111] That the film is so moving is all the more remarkable, given its rather crass initial context: the man allowed back to earth for one day to redeem himself.

[112] For such choices at funerals, see Bradley, *You've Got to Have a Dream*, 8; for the dream theme more generally, ibid. *passim*.

plays performed in churches, of which the best known is perhaps the thirteenth-century *Ludus Danielis* from Beauvais. Much more stress, however, is usually laid on the work of the Camerata, a group of intellectuals working in Florence from about 1570 onwards who included as theoreticians Giovanni Bardi and Vicenzo Galilei and as composers Giulio Caccini, Emilio de'Cavalieri and Jacopo Peri. What worried the group was the way in which contemporary musical singing practice obscured the words. Instead of elaborate polyphony, what was needed, they argued, was a return to the standards of the ancient Greek stage, where music was used to augment and enhance the sense of the words. Since no actual examples of such music were known, only theoretical discussions, re-creating such a world was, inevitably, a somewhat academic exercise. However, the writings of the group do reveal the key role assigned to moral and religious concerns. Galilei, for example, was a strong advocate of the harmony of the spheres, while Cavalieri seems to have moved indifferently between composing what we would now call opera and what we now call oratorio.[113]

These two genres, it should be noted, at least initially were defined by where they were performed rather than necessarily by content. So classical allegories might find their way into churches and not just biblical themes or the lives of the saints, while explicitly religious stories were also found performed in theatres. Thus in the following century Marc-Antoine Charpentier's only complete public opera, *David et Jonathas* (1687), was in fact deliberately sacred in its theme.[114] It had been commissioned by the Jesuits. So it is perhaps not altogether surprising that some other examples of sacred opera by Jesuit priests also survive.[115] One at least displays a largeness of vision that acknowledges God at work not just within Christianity but also in the ancient world and among different races and nations. Of course, that crossing of genres no longer pertains,

[113] Galilei was the astronomer's father. Cavalieri's *Rappresentatione di anima e di corpo* of 1600 might more suitably be classified as an oratorio.

[114] Discussion and analysis in C. Cessac, *Marc-Antoine Charpentier* (Portland, Ore.: Amadeus Press, 1995), 183–96.

[115] Two examples are available on a CD, *The Jesuit Operas* (1999). The shorter (Zipoli's of 1755) was intended for the mission field in Bolivia; Kapsberger's of 1622 is the one referred to in the next sentence. It is firmly homophonic, with figured bass.

but it is worth bearing this more complex history in mind, as I now consider some of the material still in the current repertoire.

Admittedly, for many these days opera is no more than a form of entertainment, involving largely absurd plots, but tolerable nonetheless for the beautiful music that so often goes with them. For others, however, and these tend to be the most committed, an almost religious devotion is noticeable, most notably perhaps in relation to Wagner's works but also more widely. The sort of language to which I am alluding is familiar: 'Opera is a mystery... like the rites of initiation in a pagan religion.... Opera... is a form of almost religious aspiration, reaching for the sky from which music first poured down like Apollo's sunlight.'[116] It is tempting to put such comments down to the ramblings of a fanatic, especially where opera is presented at times as offering an alternative to religion and then with equal zeal proposed as undermining all religion.[117] But what such comments do undoubtedly reveal is the continuing religious resonances that some feel still inhabit the genre. So it is worth examining what might, if anything, legitimate such attitudes, before considering whether a more specifically Christian response is possible.

One element surely of relevance is the extent to which the medium really does provide another way of viewing our own more mundane, everyday reality. Certainly, the ordinary dilemmas of human existence are granted heightened significance. While this happens also with drama or song on their own, the combination is more insistent in opera's impact, in ways that draw upon the different principles of acting involved. Perhaps the contrast can be put in this way. All human life includes an element of concealment (we tend to protect ourselves against easy, total disclosure). Conventional stage acting usually reflects this, with the plot as a result only slowly revealing underlying emotional intensities. That is to say, the stage actor, in order to preserve verisimilitude in his reflection of human behaviour, must necessarily retain an element of restraint in portraying their adopted personage. Only gradually is the total character revealed. In the case of opera singers, however,

---

[116] From the first and final pages of P. Conrad, *A Song of Love and Death: The Meaning of Opera* (London: Chatto and Windus, 1987), 11, 360.

[117] In common with quite a number of other enthusiasts, Conrad cannot seem to decide finally between the two options. For opera as an attack on religion, see ibid. 13, 78, 183.

such caution is thrown to the winds. They have little choice but to become almost immediately wholly embodied representations. The music and singing in effect compel such more insistent disclosure. So the dilemmas and emotions of the person in question quickly emerge in their starkest intensity. In addition, the type of singing expected means that all the resources of the singers' bodies must be put into expressing what it is they represent. In more than any other type of singing, it is the whole body of the opera singer that is deployed. That is what necessitates their large physique, even if this at times sits very oddly with the alleged beauty of some heroines.[118] All this, of course, at one level makes the acting more obviously artificial. But in another sense it can actually make it all more real, precisely because nothing is now held back as to what is at stake.

Not that this applies to all operas. Sometimes, the composer's aim is purely comic in intent. Sometimes too either composer or producer will provide a contemporary context. Although popular in modern presentations, in my view such an approach generally weakens the opera's impact. A different world drawn from the past or from mythology more naturally chimes with this exaltation of the mundane as a mirror to our own world. That is no doubt why an alternative strategy is sometimes attempted where the original intended setting was in fact modern (or at least contemporary with the composer). Various stage devices are employed to lift the work beyond any suggestion of a purely conventional setting. A good example of this is Zeffirelli's 1982 version of Verdi's *La Traviata*. Nineteenth-century Paris in effect becomes the setting for a re-enactment of Christ's Passion. To set the mood the film begins with a view of Notre-Dame. It ends by underlining the Lenten nature of the carnival beneath her bedroom window as she dies: Lent of course heralds Christ's own passion.[119]

Admittedly, a new or more august perspective does not necessarily of itself entail religious insight or the possibility of spiritual experience. My point is simply that the very forms of opera nudge spectators in that direction, without of course compelling any such change of view. Love, alienation, sacrifice or any other of opera's

---

[118] Maria Callas tried to solve the problem by dieting, with disastrous results for her voice.

[119] There are numerous other nudges in this direction, e.g. the appearance of Alfredo's virginal sister adapted to suggest the Virgin Mary.

major themes are removed from the merely localized and exalted to the sphere of the eternal. How much that is a function of the nature of the genre, how much part of composers' intentions, is a moot point. It would be implausible to suggest that the latter is true in every instance. However, composers might well find themselves pulled in such directions almost despite themselves. Certainly, a case can be made out for suggesting that the nature of this presumed spiritual world which casts light on our own has corresponded remarkably closely to wider metaphysical assumptions of the time.[120] So at the dawn of opera in a composer like Monteverdi there is a closeness between the two worlds that not only reflects the Neo-Platonic graded hierarchies of the time but also common assumptions about the natural tonality of speech.[121] That is why the apotheosis at the end of Monteverdi's *Orfeo* (1607) can seem entirely natural.[122]

In composers like Lully and Mozart that approach then yields to the Cartesian notion of two quite distinct spheres, with the relationship between the two worlds now quite inexplicable. The point is that, although the supernatural is still quite common and harmonies between the two worlds are asserted, the move from recitative to aria now goes with the placing of the voice on the purely human side of the divide.[123] Finally, from that wholly transcendent perspective the spiritual eventually transmogrifies into what is merely a deeper aspect of ourselves: in Kantian terms, asserting a noumenal value to our lives that is not easily reducible to purely empirical realities. Here the uncanny madness in Donizetti's *Lucia di Lammermoor* and the menacing landscape in Weber's *Der Freischütz* is seen as presenting the kinds of issue that are then given an underlying rationale in the operas of Wagner.[124]

---

[120] An argument pursued with impressive detail in G. Tomlinson, *Metaphysical Song: An Essay on Opera* (Princeton: Princeton University Press, 1999).

[121] Renaissance attachment to Neo-Platonism, as in the writings of Marsilio Ficino, is well known. Tomlinson also notes various contemporary treatises in which the singing voice is assigned to the heavenly side of the divide, so making the appearance of the supernatural on the opera stage entirely fitting: ibid. 16–24.

[122] For a fine exposition of the Platonic spirituality behind the opera, see the account by stage director Gilbert Deflo on *L'Orfeo* (BBC/Opus Arte, 2002).

[123] Tomlinson, *Metaphysical Song*, 40–7. In his view Mozart is more of a transitional figure than Lully: 62–3.

[124] Ibid. 94, 105.

It is one thing to accept the basic plausibility of such a developmental analysis; quite another to be bound by it in its entirety. No doubt our wider social context exercises a profound and lasting influence on our conceptual thinking in ways of which we may be scarcely aware. Even so, it would be depressing indeed if ever we were forced to concede the impossibility of stepping beyond the confines that are now set before us. No room would then be left for God or indeed for any further changes in metaphysics. Opera would only reflect where most are, rather than where they might be. That is why it is important to remain open to the possibility of re-enchantment.[125]

One obvious way of doing so is to resist any dogmas concerning the primacy of authorial intention. Wagner is an obvious case in point. A century or so ago it was fashionable in England to treat his final opera, *Parsifal*, as his conversion tribute-piece to Christianity. Nietzsche's condemnation of the opera could then be wheeled out in support of just such a contention.[126] This will not do. Although Wagner remained interested in religious questions throughout his life, his position at the point of death was perhaps nearer to Buddhism than it was to Christianity.[127] But, even were he proved to have been totally without religious conviction, this would still not require his listeners to opt for a similar secular reading.[128]

At the very least Wagner saw this particular opera as pre-eminently his own personal experiment in religious drama. Indeed, he described the opera as a *Bühnenweihfestspiel*. Although some have sought to

[125] Tomlinson wonders whether we have moved to a final stage, 'Ghosts in the machine', in which metaphysics is no longer possible: ibid. 127–56, esp. 156.

[126] Notoriously, in Nietzsche's *The Case Against Wagner* Bizet's *Carmen* is held up as the new model of a Dionysian exuberance uncontaminated by Apollonian moderation: *Basic Writings of Nietzsche*, ed. W. Kaufmann (New York: Modern Library, 1992), 601–48.

[127] That the basic message of *Parsifal* is a Buddhist one with a Christian overlay is advocated in P. Bassett, *Wagner's Parsifal: The Journey of a Soul* (Kent Town, South Australia: Wakefield Press, 2000), esp. 76–7. One recent German biography speaks of only a superficial connection 'with Schopenhauer and Christianity', and fails to mention Buddhism: J. Köhler, *Richard Wagner: The Last of the Titans* (New Haven, Conn.: Yale University Press, 2004), 601. That is surely a mistake. His wife's diaries indicate a continuing preoccupation with Buddhism even a few months before his death; e.g. the entry for 27 Sept. 1882.

[128] Perhaps because he finds in *Parsifal* Wagner's 'crowning achievement', Bryan Magee is insistent not only that Wagner had no Christian intentions but that it should not be interpreted in this way: *Wagner and Philosophy* (London: Penguin, 2001). But authorial intention is one thing, the effect of the drama quite another.

reduce the significance of this fact by translating the term as 'festival work to consecrate a stage', Wagner's own comments in his essay *Religion and Art* suggest rather more, and so the conventional translation as 'sacred festival drama' should in my view stand.[129] So this would seem to open up the possibility that it might be experienced as such. His father-in-law, the Abbé Franz Liszt, certainly took just such a view.[130] The forgiveness of Kundry and her 'baptism' can therefore for the Christian be seen as suggesting a more than purely human transformation, while the intersecting musical themes do hint at a larger reconciliation.[131] The fact that *Parsifal* is now less frequently performed than many of Wagner's other operas may possibly speak volumes about the breadth of Wagner's sympathies and the narrowness of those of his followers. While not endorsing Christianity, he entered sympathetically within its conceptual framework in a way that his modern admirers consistently fail to do.[132]

Nor need such possibilities be confined to the opera that lies nearest to Christian concerns. The *Ring*, with its destruction of Valhalla and its gods, can present a real challenge to certain ways of viewing God that is in the end confirmatory of faith. In much the same way, to draw a visual analogy, Francis Bacon's Crucifixions might encourage new ways of looking at the significance of Christ's passion, despite Bacon's atheism. Precisely because of Bacon's stress on the pointlessness of such suffering, the believer is drawn at one and the same time to perceive more deeply both the costliness and essential arbitrariness of human suffering and the possible relevance of Christ in engagement with that apparent meaninglessness.[133] Similarly, by the conclusion of *Götterdämmerung*, the final work in the cycle, the petulant Wotan is rightly seen to have had his day,

---

[129] For the former view, see M. Ashman, 'A Very Human Epic', in N. John (ed.), *Parsifal* (London: John Calder, 1986), 7. But for Wagner's own position, see W. A. Ellis (ed.), *Religion and Art* (Lincoln, Nebr.: University of Nebraska Press, 1994), 211–52.

[130] As in his comment quoted in Bassett, *Wagner's Parsifal*, 78.

[131] The leitmotifs or mottos deliberately lack the clarity of those of his early operas, so that themes can be subtly interwoven with one another, as can be seen, for example, with that belonging to the Grail.

[132] For a typical example of the modern view, see Ashman, 'A Very Human Epic', 7–14. Moving Amfortas' wound from the side to the groin is among the ideas canvassed (9).

[133] For my own approach to that subject, see 'The Problem of Pain', in R. Morgan (ed.), *The Religion of the Incarnation* (Bristol: Bristol Classical Press, 1989), 46–59, esp. 56–7.

and the ring corrupted by the lust for power and self-assertiveness is now rightly returned to its owners. But as the redemption theme recurs for the last time and peace at last reigns with the final D flat major chord, it is a judgement not just against pagan gods and heroes but also against all attempts, including biblical and Christian, to make God in our own image.

An interesting intermediate case is *Tristan und Isolde*. While it glorifies a love that denies marriage vows, it does so in a way that does not follow modern society in showing them scant respect. Instead, the redemption of the lovers is seen as lying in a mutual commitment to death, with the audience not even told whether their love has ever actually been physically consummated.[134] Indeed, to do so under these conditions would be to challenge its sacred, absolute character. That is why the focus of the music is so obsessively on inner states rather than external actions.[135] Wagner is trying to characterize the possessiveness of an erotic desire that refuses to be domesticated into the love and friendship that supposedly condition Christian marriage.[136] So the listener is challenged more to an alternative religious outlook than to the total denial of religion as such. Although more radical, it is thus not unlike Graham Greene's questioning of Catholic dogma on adultery and suicide in his more serious novels.[137]

So the kind of challenge which *Tristan* presents is quite different from that offered by Mozart's *Don Giovanni* and which so fascinated Kierkegaard.[138] On his view a Christian reading should not focus on the Commendatore's demand at the end that Don Giovanni

---

[134] R. Scruton, *Death-Devoted Heart: Sex and the Sacred in Wagner's Tristan and Isolde* (Oxford: Oxford University Press, 2004), 131–2.

[135] For the way in which its all-embracing chromaticism produces a desperate yearning for the return of the diatonic, see R. Taylor, *Richard Wagner: His Life, Art and Thought* (New York: Taplinger, 1979), 139–40.

[136] The contrast is explored at length by Scruton. The most obvious difference is that, whereas the latter aims at the good of the other, the former wants the whole you just as you are (see e.g. *Death-Devoted Heart*, 153). Michael Tanner sets the opera against Bach's *St Matthew Passion* as the two great religious works of our culture. *Wagner* (Princeton: Princeton University Press, 1996), ch. 11.

[137] Though strictly speaking Greene gave the title 'novel' only to his serious work, the rest being described as 'entertainments'. For a good analysis of Greene on holy sinners, see R. Sharrock, *Saints, Sinners and Comedians: The Novels of Graham Greene* (Notre Dame, Ind.: University of Notre Dame Press, 1984).

[138] S. Kierkegaard, *Either/Or Part I* (Princeton: Princeton University Press, 1987), 45–135.

renounce his past. Rather, it should find in the music a worthy celebration of the aesthetic, of the fervour and passion that Christianity has so often denied in its history but which rightly belongs to faith itself.[139] This is to offer a more complicated diagnosis of how music and plot interact in the construction of the opera, and rightly so. Consider a quite different opera of Mozart, one on which Kierkegaard did not comment, *The Magic Flute.* It is hard to believe that this came from the hand of the same composer. Yet its underlying serious Masonic intentions can scarcely be denied.[140] Mozart himself was a Mason. Masonic symbolism is taken up in the music itself. It is even possible that some details in the plot are intended to allude to contemporary treatment of Masons.[141] Yet of itself, as with Kierkegaard's example, that scarcely prevents a religious response or experience of a quite different kind. Even modern Masons are more likely to be moved by the purged spiritual love between Tamino and Pamina, to which the simpler innocence of Papagena and Papageno provides such an effective foil.

So it is not just confirmations of a Christian view of the world such as Puccini's *Suor Angelica* that can deepen experience of the divine.[142] What is from a different religious perspective, or even an apparently utterly opposed one, may be no less effective. Something that takes us to the brink in quite a different direction may end up by shocking us into a renewed perception of the true worth of its alternative, and so open us to just such an experience of God. One such case might be Richard Strauss' *Salome.* The libretto comes almost unchanged from Oscar Wilde's play, but with an orchestral backing that greatly intensifies the sense of a wild sexual

---

[139] Kierkegaard attaches particular blame to the verbal, mystical tradition of the later Middle Ages: ibid. 70–4, 86–90.

[140] For a brief account of the evidence, see P. Branscombe, *Die Zauberflöte* (Cambridge: Cambridge University Press, 1991), 35–44, 137–8.

[141] The overture is often taken to provide the first clue, with its key of E flat, which has three flats (the Masonic favoured number) and three opening chords. The Queen of the Night, best known for her difficult coloratura aria 'Die hölle Rache', is sometimes taken to allude to the hostile empress Maria Theresa.

[142] Although too saccharine for modern taste, this story of a nun forgiven by Mary for bearing an illegitimate child has a beautiful opening and quite a number of fine tunes.

obsession that knows no bounds.[143] Musically, the Baptist is allowed no adequate response. Yet, precisely because the senses are left reeling from Salome's lack of restraint, the final result is likely to be anything but endorsement.

Equally, Verdi is surely at his best, not when pulling the strings of conventional religion as in *Nabucco*, but rather in an opera like *Don Carlos*, where despite the *deus ex machina* of its ending the struggles are so much more real.[144] The tormented love of Carlos for his father Philip's wife and, under his friend Rodrigo's instigation, his growing eagerness to act on behalf of his people is nicely set against the terrifying ruthlessness of the Grand Inquisitor and Philip's cynical compliance with his wishes. Musically, the contrast seems initially quite simple: the gloomy bass of Philip against the gentle tenor sound of Carlos, or the idealistic heroine in Elizabeth's soprano moderated by the volatile mezzo of her maid, Eboli. But development of the plot is often at its most effective when such voices do not behave as one might expect: Carlos for instance when drawing his sword on his father, Rodrigo when attacking Philip's 'horrible, dreadful peace'.[145] If all this suggests an anti-religious plot, the reality is more complex. The final appearance of the saintly Charles V, who now takes his grandson under his care, is presumably meant to imply heavenly endorsement for Carlos' growth in stature.[146] So in the midst of so much misuse of religion a religious reading is after all legitimated. In a similar way the possibility for more negative estimates lie just beneath the surface of apparently more favourable operas such as *Nabucco* or *Aida*. Thus the former has been described as 'the fanaticism of the Old Testament set to music', while the latter's reference to 'triumph with the help of

---

[143] Singers of the title role are caught in a double bind. Their physique is seldom suited to the famous Dance of the Seven Veils, yet without such a physique they are unlikely to be up to competing with the volume from the orchestra, especially in brass and woodwind.

[144] Despite its most famous chorus ('Va, pensiero, sull' alli dorate') evoking Psalm 137, the plot is curiously indifferent to any attempt at biblical verisimilitude. The Babylonians, for example, are frequently called Assyrians.

[145] The latter duet, at the end of Act II, is among the most disturbing and powerful moments in the whole opera.

[146] Here I disagree with the virtually unanimous judgement that this change to Schiller's play was 'ludicrous': e.g. F. Toye, *Verdi: His Life and Works* (London: Victor Gollancz, 1962), 385. What this ignores is the common estimate in European Catholicism of Charles V as a saint.

divine providence', so far from being an endorsement, may actually be intended as a subtle critique.[147] It is thus the openness of plots and the interpretative music that goes with them, not clearly fixed horizons, which generate possibilities. That is no doubt why even in modern 'operas' or opera-oratorios designed for church or church-related contexts, such as Benjamin Britten's *Church Parables*, or more recently John Adams' *El Niño* and Kari Tikka's *Luther*, it was a wise decision not to stack the cards too heavily in favour of the essential rightness of one particular religious perspective.[148] Thus in *El Niño* we are offered what is essentially a Latin American nativity but one in which numerous different perspectives on Mary are allowed to play off against each other.[149] Similarly, although in Tikka's opera Luther's hymns are used as commentary, the character portrayed in the music as a whole attracts us precisely because we are allowed to see him warts and all.[150] Ironically in that particular opera in some ways it is the music that allows us the fewer liberties. Key signature plays a large part in guiding our emotions. B flat minor, for example, is used for death and E minor and major for what is life-affirming. Ideally, both music and words should be less than predictable, if they are to work their maximum effect in challenging us to perceive reality in new ways.

Sadly, it remains true that Christians are on the whole still too ready to find in critique a denial of faith rather than a challenge to fresh thinking. Not that this fault is unique to them. The philosopher Sir Bernard Williams drew from Janáček's *The Makropulos Case* the conclusion that no value could ever attach to limitless life after death, including the Christian conception of such a life.[151] The irony is that Janáček's purpose had been quite otherwise. The opera is really about the appropriateness of limits to life of the kind

[147] For the comment on *Nabucco*, see ibid. 232. For *Aida* as an attack on German imperialism, see B. Meier, *Verdi* (London: Haus, 2000), 106.

[148] Both are available on DVD: that of *El Niño* was released in 2000, *Luther* in 2004. The *Luther* DVD is set in the magnificent modern Temppeliaukio Church in Helsinki. *El Niño*'s première was actually in a Parisian theatre near Notre-Dame, to which Adams saw himself as consciously relating.

[149] Adams seeks to counteract the male bias of the Gospels with the writing of female Hispanic poets.

[150] His fights with the devil, his hostility to the peasants' rebellion, and so on.

[151] 'The Makropulos Case: Reflections on the Tedium of Immortality', in B. Williams, *Problems of the Self* (Cambridge: Cambridge University Press, 1973), 92–100.

we have in the here and now, and so is in no sense anti-religious. Indeed, the heroine twice recites the Lord's Prayer, the second time as the opera ends with her dying. Apart from the opera's lyrical opening, the music is sparse and dissonant until the opera's close, which again would seem to support such a conclusion. So lack of imaginative openness can be a fault in great intellectuals, no less than in more ordinary beings.[152]

How much any of the above reflections applies to the typical contemporary opera audience is an intriguing question. So quick does applause ring out once the curtain falls, or continuity become interrupted with congratulatory applause for familiar arias or choruses, that one suspects that for many it is now the music alone which is being allowed to work its impact. But the situation with regards to music in church is not necessarily otherwise. There are few insistent demands that congregations should always be provided with the words of anthems. Even with hymns it is interesting how few are now known by heart. It is almost as though the totality of the experience is no longer a concern. To my mind that is a sad and severe limitation. But it does at least help explain why so often the task for opera these days is seen largely in terms of evoking a world of magic rather than mystery. The degree of enchantment now possible is superficial rather than deep. Yet in *Moses und Aron*, one of the great operas of the twentieth century, Schoenberg surely got it exactly right. As with hymn and anthem, so with opera there is the potential to do so much more: to hint at or suggest an alternative world that might invade our own.[153]

Opera in some ways best illustrates the overall theme of this part of the book, of music being at one and the same time ethereal and material. As I suggested in this part's introduction, the combination is in fact characteristic of all music, but some variants point more in one direction than in the other. Listening to a classical symphony, an audience may become so absorbed in the sound of the music that they are left unaware of the physical efforts being put in by the musicians themselves. By contrast, in heavy rock, the physical gyrations of the performers may be what most attracts the audience rather than the music itself. With opera, however, the paradox can

---

[152] I say this as someone privileged to have had Williams as supervisor for my Cambridge philosophy doctorate.

[153] For further comments on Schoenberg's opera *Moses und Aron*, see 282–3.

be at its most intense, as when some beautiful love duet with sensitive and delicate colouring is performed by two heavyweights whose sheer bulk seems destined to pull our thoughts in a quite different direction. Yet in the end the imagination seems to win through, and find no difficulty in allowing the ethereal the final say. In eucharistic performance there are not dissimilar problems, if in reverse. The props, wafer and wine, are light and insubstantial. But Christianity's claim is that they mediate something heavy, no less than the weight of divine glory, in the incarnate Christ once more present to his people. How to think of that bodily presence is the topic of the brief concluding part of this book.

Part III

The Eucharistic Body

III

The Eucharistic Body

IN the previous part of this book I was concerned with the way in which music can help communicate the divine. As such, music is seldom, if ever, a purely mental experience. Indeed, it is not uncommon for every aspect of our bodily identity to be involved. Yet, despite such potential, the tendency remains within Christianity to view music as merely a useful adjunct to words. What really matters, it is affirmed, are the sentences of scripture and their use in liturgy and in song. Chapter 5 with its discussion of instrumental music sought to challenge that view, as I indicated how everything from experiences of awe to rival attitudes to suffering might be expressed through instrumental music working on its own. More pertinent to what follows might be Karlheinz Stockhausen's 1974 work *Inori*. During the 1960s Stockhausen had spent a significant amount of time in Japan, and it was from Japan that this commission came. *Inori* is the Japanese for prayer, and in the work a large orchestra that includes some Japanese 'instruments' (such as prayer bowls) accompanies two soloists who mime various prayer gestures in strict time to the music of the orchestra. Lasting over an hour, the music is based on a simple chromatic melody in a manner that has been compared to the *cantus firmus* of medieval chant. What is fascinating is what wide commendation the piece has received, not just on musical grounds but also because of the way in which audiences have found themselves caught up into similar attitudes of reverence and prayer.[1] As such it provides a powerful reminder not only of the power of instrumental music but also of how bodily gestures

---

[1] For a musical evaluation, see M. Kurtz, *Stockhausen* (London: Faber and Faber, 1992); for theological, A. Nocent, 'Gestures, Symbols and Words in Present-Day Western Liturgy', in L. Macdonald and D. Power (eds), *Symbol and Art in Worship* (Edinburgh: T. & T. Clark, 1980), 19–27, esp. 19–20.

when working in unison with music can sometimes speak no less powerfully than words.

It also offers a salutary reprimand to all those Christians who refuse to step beyond a definition of their faith as exclusively a religion of the word. What that ignores is the realities of how human beings communicate, the way in which, as the first part of this book suggested, body is no less integral to who we are than the words that express our minds. Indeed, in choosing the visual symbols of bread and wine to represent his own presence, Christ himself can be claimed to have endorsed just such a view. That is one reason why in the first of the two chapters that follow I seek to set understanding of Christ's eucharistic body in a more firmly material context. But there is also a deeper reason: that this is how in any case Christianity through most of its long history has regarded matters. It is only really in the modern world that understanding of Christ's presence has moved primarily towards conceiving of it in terms of a presence within the gathered community or else as some sort of rarefied personal presence, essentially no different from the ubiquity of divinity. Transubstantiation is, admittedly, by any reckoning an implausible use of Aristotelian metaphysics. It did, however, have the merit that it thereby preserved some sense of it being important that we relate to Christ as having had and continuing to have a bodily identity like our own. Luther and Calvin may have rejected the particular philosophical analysis proposed but not, it should be noted, the underlying concern behind such metaphysics, to guarantee the believer's continuing engagement with Christ's humanity.

But how might liturgy help worshippers towards some sense of that material presence? There is, I think, no simple answer. The final chapter provides a few pointers, at the same time indicating the need for a further volume. For too long liturgical study has been treated as the Cinderella of theological study, concerned, as it were, with prettifying the agenda but not with the heart of what theology is about. As that chapter indicates, part of the fault lies, I believe, with liturgists themselves. The task of liturgy needs desperately to be set in a much wider context that takes seriously not just the history of liturgy or even current theological concerns more generally but the whole range of ways in which human beings experience their environment and through that environment God himself.

In that task, the long discussion of music that has preceded this part of the book may perhaps suggest some ways forward. Despite superficial appearances to the contrary, music is not essentially ethereal. Without the material, for most of us the reality is lost. Even with a genius like Beethoven who could only hear his own complicated late scores in his head, such hearing was parasitic on what had once been a fuller experience. Moreover, even he seems to have left conductors some latitude of freedom in interpretation, so important did he see active creative involvement by the lead players in what was being performed. The score on its own was simply not enough. In a similar way, then, it would be absolute folly to think that all that was required to produce a satisfactory experience of Christ's presence in the eucharist was mere repetition of the words of institution.

Technically, of course, that is what the western Church finally decided, but it did so to its own hurt. Formal 'validity' is scarcely the same thing as a lively sense of personal relationship with Christ. For that to be achieved, it is important that there be appropriate equivalents to the active physical involvement of performers in the deliverance of a composer's piece. What that will entail is detailed attention to the characteristics of Christ's 'music', not just the facts of his life but also the sort of person he was, the type of language he used, and so on. The result will therefore be engagement with a wide range of pointers that can renew the individual's sense that this particular piece is Christ's very own. So apart from the bread and wine other symbolic actions and their verbal equivalents in metaphor become equally pertinent, just as in conveying a well-loved composer to an audience the conductor will usually draw attention to familiar features rather than attempt to hide them. Some indicators are offered in the chapter that concludes this book, but the issue is so important that a separate volume will also follow.[2] In the meantime, I turn to consider how the ethereal eucharistic body must also be seen in essentially bodily or 'material' terms: salvation concerns the health of the body no less than that of the soul.

[2] *God and Mystery in Words: Experience through Metaphor and Drama* (Oxford: Oxford University Press, 2008).

8

Healing and Presence

ONE of the earliest descriptions of the eucharist is of it as 'the
medicine of immortality'.[1] What was meant is that through Christ
can come life eternal for humanity in general. Although the term
used is 'immortality', because of the connection with the material
elements in the eucharist clearly the thought must have been not
simply of immortality of the soul but also, as with Christ himself, of
resurrection of the body, or in other words the survival of the
whole person. In this connection talk of medicine is no idle
metaphor. Not only is it supposed that the eucharist can bring
healing to body no less than soul, such language also reflects the
intimate relation and interdependence which the ancient world saw
as existing between body and soul and which modern medicine is
only now slowly recovering. For reasons that I shall note shortly,
the Bible has little to say on the subject of connections between
religion and medicine. In this, however, it was quite untypical in the
ancient world, where the interactions were deep and long-lasting.
The healing touch of the divine came as much to the body as to the
soul. That perception is worth examining in its own right but also
as an introduction to the whole question of how the eucharist
should be understood. In modern discussions it is not uncommon
to find embarrassment expressed at the readiness with which earlier
ages endorsed strongly physical imagery. Rather than following that
path, I want to explore reasons why it might be important, in the
search for salvation for the whole person, to recover the involvement of body no less than soul. But first I shall preface that discussion with some consideration of the powerful connections made
between religion and medicine in the ancient world. What this will

---

[1] Ignatius, *Ephesians* 20.2, from no later than 117, the date of Ignatius' martyrdom: 'the medicine of immortality and the remedy against death that enables us to
live in Jesus Christ for evermore' (my translation).

illustrate is that, despite its lack of often basic knowledge of the body, the ancient world exhibited a more integrated conception of health than usually pertains in the modern.

Medicine in Antiquity

Although as a caring profession, medicine continues to attract a larger proportion of religious believers than in the population at large, even for doctors it has often now become largely a matter of administering the appropriate technology, small or large. So the net result is that medicine, as in so many other areas of life, has become largely secularized. Yet for much of history this was not so. Those earlier connections with religion are often seen as functioning essentially as a default mechanism, with religion as a last resort when all else had failed. But that is to make past attitudes altogether too simple. There was of course an element of this, but also considerably more interaction than is commonly now appreciated. In fact what I want to suggest is that even now this interaction might offer some reinforcing pointers towards the more holistic assumptions about health that are slowly beginning to emerge in the modern world. In this, biblical perceptions can make an important contribution. But the scriptures almost wholly ignore the practice of medicine. So I begin instead in the wider ancient world, where religion and medical practice were heavily intertwined.

In the Classical World

For Christians snakes inevitably have heavily negative overtones thanks to the role of the creature in the story of the Fall. Even the Bible, however, is found admitting that its movements can at times be impressive: 'Three things there are which are too wonderful for me, four which I do not understand: the way of a vulture in the sky, the way of a serpent on the rock, the way of a ship out at sea, and the way of man with a girl' (Prov. 30.18). It is to the wider ancient world, though, that we must turn for a generally more favourable estimate. In the Mesopotamian *Epic of Gilgamesh*, dating from at least 2000 BC, Gilgamesh seeks the tree of eternal life, only to have it robbed from him at the last moment by a serpent, who thus acquires immortality instead of humanity.[2] It is not hard to see why the snake might be thought to have acquired just such a power. It has the ability to cast off and renew its own skin. It can thus, as it were, start life afresh. It was precisely in virtue of this capacity that the snake came to function as the principal symbol of medicine at work in the ancient world. In that role it became the perennial companion of the Greek god of health, Asclepius, or Aesculapius as he was known in the Latin-speaking world.[3] Temples dedicated in his honour existed throughout the classical world, including Rome itself. Perhaps the most famous was at Epidaurus, not far from Corinth.[4] Each would have had a statue of the god with a dog at its feet and carrying a staff, with a serpent wound round about it.

Although doctors were generally known as Asclepiads (the tribe, as it were, associated with Asclepius),[5] it would be misleading to suggest that they always saw themselves as working under the god or his temple's supervision. Certainly, there is evidence to suggest that some may have worked closely with temples and perhaps even on occasion within the temple precincts, but in general the pattern of interaction seems to have been somewhat more indirect.[6] Depending perhaps in part on how positively the patient viewed the medical profession, the role of the temple was basically one of supplementary consultation that could either precede or follow action by a doctor in a quite different context. To the modern mind inevitably it must seem a strange form of consultation, involving as it did incubation, or sleeping overnight in just such a temple. But the expectation was that during the night the god would address the patient's condition through a dream, and that dream would recommend some appropriate course of action, whether medical in the narrow sense or otherwise. So sometimes the recommendation was

---

[2] *The Epic of Gilgamesh*, tr. N. K. Sandars (Harmondsworth: Penguin, 1960), 6, 113–14.

[3] Although this is the explanation most commonly given, its role as a house pet (where the snake could function in a mild and beneficial role) is held to be more significant by the Edelsteins, editors of the definitive edition of texts on Asclepius: E. J. Edelstein and L. Edelstein, *Asclepius: Collection and Interpretation of the Testimonies* (Baltimore: Johns Hopkins University Press, 1998), ii, 228; but contrast e.g. i, 366.

[4] It was actually about five miles outside of the town: ibid. i, 195.

[5] Ibid. i, 104–7.

[6] The shrine at Cos, with which Hippocrates was associated, provides better evidence for interaction than does Epidaurus: R. Jackson, *Doctors and Diseases in the Roman Empire* (London: British Museum, 1988), 151–2; cf. 154.

for a potion or surgery, while at other times it was for rest or more exercise.[7] Occasionally, though, it seems to have been the case that it was the temple's dogs or snakes who took over, and the patient would find in the morning that sores had been licked clean by one or other animal.

To comprehend the last of these treatments, it is important to recall that at least some breeds of snakes can be domesticated just like dogs, and that this is indeed what happened in the ancient world.[8] Scepticism may be the initial reaction to such a prominent role for dreams. If so, this needs to be set against numerous testimonies from the ancient world that speak of cures being effected in this way. Some have been recovered from commemorative pillars raised at particular shrines.[9] If priestly manipulation could be posited as an explanation in those instances, the same cause cannot be assigned to the witness of individual writers. Indeed, even sceptical historians are now on the whole inclined to a more positive assessment of the temples' claims.[10] To see why it is necessary to recall that people in the ancient world did go in very large numbers to such shrines. So it is highly unlikely that the shrines could for long have got away with a complete fabrication of the truth. There were special dormitories for overnight incubation, known as *abata* or *adyta*, a word normally reserved for only the most holy part of temples.[11] Here the sick could easily compare notes with one another on the effect of the recommended treatment.

This is not to say that there was never any trickery. The writer Lucian of Samosata, for instance, records a famous case in the second century AD. An obscure Paphlagonian town on the Black Sea coast succeeded briefly in becoming an object of pilgrimage because a certain Alexander claimed that Asclepius had incarnated

[7] For the range of exercise recommended, including the composition of mimes and songs to moderate 'the motions of the passions' (as noted by Galen), see Edelstein and Edelstein, *Asclepius*, i, 209.

[8] The particular species involved was *Elaphe longissima*, 'a harmless yellow species now native to south-east Europe': Jackson, *Doctors and Diseases*, 142.

[9] For example, at Epidaurus: Jackson, 145–50.

[10] True of both the Edelsteins and Jackson: Edelstein and Edelstein, *Asclepius*, ii, 142–58, esp. 147, 168; Jackson, *Doctors and Diseases*, 152. For a more negative view from a doctor and historian, who insists on seeing the temple only as last resort, see G. Majno, *The Healing Hand: Man and Wound in the Ancient World* (Cambridge, Mass.: Harvard University Press, 1991 edn), 201–5.

[11] Edelstein and Edelstein, *Asclepius*, ii, 191.

himself for the moment in his 14-foot-long pet snake, Glycon. The creature was apparently capable of performing some quite impressive tricks.[12] Against such stories, however, must be set the comments of the famous orator Aristides, who wrote favourably and at length of his experience over several years of frequent visitations to such shrines because of recurring ill-health.[13] Also to be taken into account is the witness of the two most famous doctors of the classical world: Hippocrates from the fifth century BC, who seems to have had some sort of association with the shrine of Asclepius on his native island of Cos; and Galen from the second century AD, who also endorsed Asclepius' cult, though in his case he interpreted it as a manifestation of the one monotheistic God in whom he believed (though not himself a Christian). Galen was the principal doctor to the emperor Marcus Aurelius. Significantly, it is to a dream in which Asclepius appeared that he assigns his refusal to follow the emperor as he embarks on fresh military campaigns on the German frontier, as also his cure from an earlier abscess.[14]

In trying to comprehend the popularity of such dream methods, a number of factors may be highlighted. Pertinent certainly is the fact that medicine was still in its infancy. So when the practitioner succeeded, more often than not it was without quite understanding why. Modern tests on the remedies advocated can sometimes throw up surprisingly positive results for ancient medicine, but in the main consulting a doctor remained a highly risky business.[15] Dreams could at least give a potential patient the necessary psychological strength to face illness, while, if it was really a new lifestyle that was required, the pressure to change might now be experienced as overwhelming.[16] No doubt individuals came with various expectations that were then clarified or otherwise. Indeed, we know that on occasion even advice

---

[12] In evoking ancient attitudes, made very effective use of in R. L. Fox, *Pagans and Christians* (London: Penguin, 1986), 241–50.

[13] Usefully summarized in Jackson, *Doctors and Diseases*, 152–7.

[14] Edelstein and Edelstein, *Asclepius*, i, 263; Jackson, *Doctors and Diseases*, 184.

[15] Majno gives a number of examples where modern experiments have confirmed ancient practice, e.g. in the use of verdigris and myrrh against bacteria, even though the former may simply have been chosen for its 'healthy' colour (green) and the latter because of its pleasant smell: *The Hesling Hand*, 112–15, 217.

[16] The Edelsteins stress the way in which such dreams built upon patients' existing experience, and so confirmed what in a sense they might already know: *Asclepius*, ii, 164–5.

on one's occupation was on offer, as when a boxer was given some professional tips on improving his technique.[17] This is perhaps less surprising than it may initially seem. Athletic games were in fact held at Epidaurus after the major four-yearly Isthmian games, while at Ephesus there were even medical contests, though the precise details are unknown.[18]

Medicine in the Christian Tradition

Just as Rome eventually succumbed to the power of Asclepius, so too did Egypt, and in a context where religion again operated alongside medicine.[19] The culture that eventually produced the Christian religion, however, was much more ambiguous in its attitudes to medicine. That is one reason why I began this discussion with the classical world, as its more integrated approach was eventually also to become Christianity's own. In trying to comprehend possible reasons for the difference, relevant to note is how, as the centuries advance, references to doctors in Mesopotamia (positive or otherwise) actually decline. Religion seems in effect to take over the whole role, with the only form of alternative consultation now available, at least if Herodotus is to be believed, being advice from passers-by.[20]

This is perhaps the context against which Old Testament attitudes should be set. If the only consultation on offer was through a pagan god, one can quite see why medicine would therefore be regarded with some suspicion. At all events, that might help explain why King Asa of Judah is condemned because 'even in his disease he did not seek the Lord, but sought help from physicians' (2 Chron. 16.12). The fact that his name is connected etymologically to words for healing, however, may possibly indicate a much deeper involvement in such temple practices.[21] Admittedly, more

---

[17] Ibid. i, 162.

[18] For the former, see Jackson, *Doctors and Diseases*, 144; for the latter, Edelstein and Edelstein, *Asclepius*, ii, 212. Both towns had renowned temples to Asclepius.

[19] According to Livy worship of Asclepius was introduced to Rome (on an island in the Tiber) after a plague had afflicted the city in 292 BC. In Egypt under the Ptolemies the native healing god Imhotep came to be identified with Asclepius. Both cultures also accepted the work of doctors, even if sometimes with reluctance, as in the case of Cato: Jackson, *Doctors and Diseases*, 10.

[20] Majno, *The Healing Hand*, 40; Herodotus, *Histories* 1. 197.

[21] 'Asa' may be short for Asa-El and so like Rapha-El mean 'God heals'.

positive references to doctors can be found in Ecclesiastes and Tobit,[22] but that can scarcely be said to mark a major shift towards more positive attitudes. Again, Luke may be described as 'a physician', but even his Gospel fails to record the involvement of a single doctor in Jesus' story.[23] One possible explanation could of course be that Jesus mostly engaged with classes of individuals that would have been unlikely to be able to afford the services of doctors.[24] But I suspect that something more fundamental is at stake, and that is that even by New Testament times the issue of causation had still not been satisfactorily resolved.[25] If the belief persisted that illness is a function of sin, then inevitably it would be spiritual rather than purely medical answers that would be sought.[26] By contrast, elsewhere in the ancient world purely physical explanations were much more readily accepted. If these were still far from modern in approach (such as appeal to the influence of winds or the wrong balance of 'humours'), they were at least heading in the right direction.[27]

When Christianity advanced into the pagan world, it was therefore faced with a major dilemma. On the one hand, the cult of Asclepius was undoubtedly flourishing, and as such it did present a real and viable alternative to Christianity. Yet on the other, as we have just noted, medicine receives no significant endorsement from scripture.

---

[22] Ecclus. 38.12–15. The story of Tobit is more complicated since, though Raphael eventually takes the place of doctors, it is the use of remedies of the time that he advocates; here I follow the analysis of O. Temkin, *Hippocrates in a World of Pagans and Christians* (Baltimore: Johns Hopkins University press, 1991), 92.

[23] The reference to Luke as doctor is Col. 4.14. It is hazardous to draw any implications from this. It may simply be a way of distinguishing this Luke from someone else of the same name. Better perhaps as a positive reference to doctors is Luke 5.31.

[24] Temkin's suggestion: *Hippocrates*, 104.

[25] For an account of why the New Testament is really much more ambiguous on this issue than it is often taken to be, see my *Discipleship and Imagination* (Oxford: Oxford University Press, 2000), 213–14.

[26] The historical conditioning of biblical language, unfortunately, continues to be circumvented by those who seek both to apply modern medical description to the biblical cases and still claim ultimate causation in demons: e.g. J. Wilkinson's widely used *The Bible and Healing: A Medical and Theological Commentary* (Grand Rapids: Eerdmans, 1998), 71–3. Even that author, however, on occasion retreats before the obvious meaning of the text: e.g. on 1 Cor. 11.29–30: 191–2.

[27] If the Greek theory of humours is better known, Majno observes that an appeal to winds as an explanation occurs right across cultures—in China, India and Greece: *The Healing Hand*, 310.

On the contrary, references are frequent in the Old Testament to disease as divine punishment and in the Gospels to the role of demons. So what was the Church to say on the subject? One extreme response, represented by ascetics, was to insist that Christians should rely wholly on God for their health, with any other option taken to express a real lack of commitment and trust in him.[28] That, for instance, was the view adopted by the fourth-century Egyptian hermit Macarius: 'You must never bring fleshly afflictions before mundane physicians, as if Christ, in whom you believe, were unable to cure you.'[29] A similar position was taken by the Syrian Simeon Stylites, who lived for 37 years at the top of a narrow pillar sixty feet above the ground. Indeed, a carving survives from the sixth century of Simeon high up on that pillar, warding off a snake that is trying to weave its way upwards towards him.[30] There seems little doubt that it is not just the serpent of Genesis that is seen as assailing him but also the snake of Asclepius and his doctors.

Fortunately, that never became the dominant view. So not only was the medicine expounded by its pagan advocates taken seriously, it was also incorporated into Christian self-understanding. The writings of Galen became the standard medical textbook throughout the Middle Ages. Indeed, the sign for a doctor became Asclepius' caduceus, his wand with the snake climbing up it. In that process, Galen's piety undoubtedly helped, for he saw each part of the workings of the body that he investigated witnessing to the providence of God, and said so in the texts that the western world inherited.[31] Such more positive attitudes also made possible the first founding of hospitals in anything like the modern sense. Although the Roman army did have special recovery units known as *valetudinaria*, it seems that it is to Basil of Caesarea in the fourth century that we owe the first such institution for the general public.[32] Monastic orders were particularly good at

[28] Temkin, *Hippocrates*, 149–70.

[29] For the quotation in full, see ibid. 157.

[30] For incidents from the life of Simeon, see ibid. 168; for the carving, 146.

[31] Majno entitles the relevant chapter 'Galen—and into the Night', and notes how Galen's providential theories could lead him radically astray: *The Healing Hand*, 395–422, esp. 397–8, 409. Even so, his achievements both as an experimenter and as a discoverer should not be underrated, for example in establishing the brain and not the heart as the centre of mental activity (contra Aristotle), or the key role of the arteries: cf. Majno, *The Healing Hand*, 396–7, 407–8.

[32] Military hospitals were a regular part of the Roman army and significant institutions; the evidence for civilian hospitals is meagre, and suggestive of only a

such work for their own members, and also in preserving and advancing knowledge in this area.[33] Even so, perhaps because of anxieties about the personal payments involved, such work was eventually forbidden to the clergy, and so any necessary connection between religion and medicine was gradually lost.[34]

It may be thought impossible now to reverse this trend towards secularism, so great that even in countries where hospitals continue to be owned by churches their actual practice is often indistinguishable from their secular counterparts.[35] But I wonder whether this is really a necessary consequence. With appropriate qualifications, Africa might suggest an alternative model. If 'witch-doctor' and modern doctor were once seen as diametrically opposed, now it is not uncommon to find the local shaman referring clients to the professional medic. More intriguing, perhaps, the reverse also occurs, not least where some form of psychological illness is involved.[36] That shaman is also sometimes the leader of one of the newer Christian sects that have sprung up all over Africa. So parallels may perhaps be drawn with the longer-standing practice within the Ethiopian church. There it is the role of certain clerics to letter and paint certain rolls that are then used to help combat illness.[37] Often depicted with mysterious eyes, they hang by the patient's bedside not only to ward off evil spirits but also to evoke a changed attitude in the

very minimum care for the poor, which is why Basil is normally given the credit: Majno, *The Healing Hand*, 381–93; Jackson, *Doctors and Diseases*, 65, 133–6; Temkin, *Hippocrates*, 162–4.

[33] Less good, though, at founding such institutions for others. The earliest English hospital (St Peter's, York) did not appear till 936 (refounded under the Augustinian rule in 1135): S. Rubin, *Medieval English Medicine* (New York: Barnes and Noble, 1974), 184–8. Bernard of Clairvaux apparently continued the ascetic line on doctors: ibid. 176.

[34] These prohibitions were introduced in the twelfth and thirteenth centuries: ibid. 193.

[35] 'Often', but of course not always. Chaplains and medical professionals can sometimes be found working in close cooperation, and not always only in church hospitals.

[36] The precedent set by Dr Henri Collomb and his psychiatric hospital in Dakar is quoted in V. Lanternari's article on the subject in *The Encyclopedia of Religion* (New York: Macmillan, 1987), 9, 305–12.

[37] These clerics are known as *dabtara*, and are regarded as continuing to act in the traditions of the biblical Magi. The scrolls are usually made the same height as the patient concerned. For further details, see J. Mercier, *Art that Heals: The Image as Medicine in Ethiopia* (New York: Prestel, 1997), esp. 40–59.

patient.[38] A recent touring exhibition of such work made comparisons with the role that painting can sometimes play in helping schizophrenics to overcome their condition; the painting can both express a situation and be an agent towards seeing it in a new way.[39] Such remarks draw us a little closer to modern western society. But there is no need to confine such interconnections to illnesses of a purely mental kind, for, as is becoming increasingly apparent, many apparently physical ailments have as part of their causation a heavy diet of mental or spiritual factors. Indeed, as older illnesses find their resolution, stress and lifestyle seem to play a much larger role in generating their nearest modern equivalents.[40] While not discounting the contribution of alternative medicine, there would seem no need to raise that particular issue here in order to see the point.[41] Resort to Asclepius is beyond meaningful recall, but the more holistic approach implied is surely of continuing relevance. Spirituality, psychology and physical health were all alike addressed.[42] Since music was one recommended approach at the shrines, modern medical use to reduce stress may not be quite so original as is sometimes supposed.[43] Unfortunately, apart from the hospice movement, Christian writing on health still seems overwhelmingly preoccupied with ethical issues.[44]

[38] For illustrations of the use of eyes, see ibid. 56, 88–93, 96–8.

[39] In a separate article in Mercier, *Art that Heals*, by H. Maldiney, 'Plastic Meaning and Psychosis: Anthropological Meaning and Therapeutic Effects of the Works of the Mentally Ill', ibid. 22–31.

[40] Apart from lack of exercise and improper diet, stress is known to be a major cause of high blood pressure. This also pertains in many other apparently purely physical conditions.

[41] It is interesting to observe, though, that while in the West such alternative medicines are often presented as 'eastern', the East itself initially reacted against them, only to incorporate them once more in the late twentieth century. By 1980 37% of doctors in Japan were prescribing herbal or acupuncture treatments, while resort to religious healers has also increased: M. Picone, 'The Ghost in the Machine: Religious Healing and Representation of the Body in Japan', in M. Feher (ed.), *Fragments for a History of the Human Body* (New York: Zone, 1989), ii, 467–89.

[42] Apart from the examples already quoted, purity of thought was also encouraged, as well as solutions to recurring migraines: Edelstein and Edelstein, *Asclepius*, i, 164; Jackson, *Doctors and Diseases*, 161.

[43] One such modern medical example is Lee Bartel's three-CD set: *Solitudes: Music for Your Health* (1998).

[44] For the key role of Dame Cecily Saunders in that movement, see C. Saunders (ed.), *St Christopher's in Celebration: Twenty-One Years at Britain's First Modern Hospice* (London: Hodder and Stoughton, 1988).

It is in offering a more integrated perspective to health in general that the Bible can still, I would suggest, make its appropriate contribution. In English translations of the New Testament the connection between health and salvation[45] is only occasionally brought to the forefront of our horizons. For the original Greek readers this was much more immediately apparent, not least because the root from which the English words 'salvation' and 'saviour' are ultimately derived is also used in the sense of 'to heal' or 'make whole'. Although not the most commonly used word under such circumstances,[46] its presence indicates that a cure is not just a matter of 'safety' from threat but also of deliverance to a new quality of existence. It is that quality of existence that makes it appropriate to call such lives 'graced', to which, inevitably, clinical medicine can only make a partial contribution.[47]

When considering the story of Moses raising up a bronze serpent on a standard (Num. 21.4–9), most biblical commentators these days suggest that what was presupposed was probably a piece of sympathetic magic: trying to ward off snake bites by, as it were, yet more snakes being introduced into the equation. Yet conceivably it could also be a sign of a cult not unlike that of Asclepius, for certainly centuries later in Israel's history under King Hezekiah the worship of the snake had to be prohibited (2 Kgs 18.4).[48] Whatever the explanation, far more interesting is how the story is eventually applied in the New Testament. For there we find the Christ of St John's Gospel declaring that 'as Moses lifted up the serpent in the wilderness, so must the Son of man be lifted up, that whoever believes in him may have eternal life' (3.15). In effect, Christ has himself become the serpent, with these verses anticipating not just the cross but also what happened thereafter, the sloughing off of the old skin of mortality and Christ the new man now permanently available to us all for our transformation and redemption. So, by a nice reversal of Eden, it does after all become possible for the Christian without disloyalty to appropriate and

---

[45] As in the paralytic also having his sins forgiven (Mark 2.1–12), or in such juxtapositions as the healing of a blind man and the uncovering of the disciples' blindness (Mark 8.13–26).

[46] The comparative figures are given in Wilkinson, *The Bible and Healing*, 77.

[47] Here Wilkinson is right: ibid. 20–30.

[48] Baal's consort, Astarte, was sometimes depicted with a serpent, while the nearest equivalent to Asclepius was the god Eshmun.

learn from all those pagan dreams of Asclepius: perfect health in the image of a snake, body and soul as one. This extended discussion of medicine and religion may seem to have taken us far from the eucharistic body, the topic with which I began this section, but I believe this not to be so. What it has demonstrated is how to the ancient mind generally health and salvation were a matter of concern for body and soul alike. Even Plato was no exception, as his interest in the educative value of the gymnasium and of dance can be used to illustrate.[49] So unless the eucharistic body addressed the question of salvation for body no less than soul, it would have seemed to the ancient mind to have addressed only half the issues. I shall now seek to explain why in my opinion we should take a similar view.

Eucharistic Presence

Obviously eucharistic theology could easily turn into a book in its own right. So it is possible to address only a select range of questions here. In assessing attitudes in the early Church recent scholarship has admitted much wider variety in both theology and practice than would have been conceded in the past.[50] Even universal use of bread and wine cannot be taken for granted. Instances of the use of salt, fish, oil and cheese can all be quoted. Use of bread and water was also quite common, and not just among those already regarded as 'unorthodox'.[51] Although some suggest that such practices were inspired by reservations about the association of meat and wine with pagan sacrifice, this seems to me unlikely.[52] The difficulties created by meat and by wine were in fact of a quite

---

[49] For Plato on dance, see *Laws*, bks 2 and 7, and my discussion in Chapter 2. As the *Symposium* indicates, although Plato thinks the highest order of existence dispenses with the body, even he believes this is not achievable unless the body first reflects the right kind of soul.

[50] It was partly to counter the absence of uniformity in eucharistic verbal formulae that Dom Gregory Dix developed his theory of a uniform fourfold pattern of action: *The Shape of the Liturgy* (London: SPCK, 1937), 208–14.

[51] For cheese, see A. McGowan, *Ascetic Eucharists* (Oxford: Clarendon Press, 1999), 95–107; for oil and salt, 115–25; for fish, 127–40; for bread and water, 143–250. Justin Martyr and some of Cyprian's fellow-bishops may possibly be included among the last contingent: 151–5, 204.

[52] A recurring theme in McGowan: e.g. ibid. 60–7, 270–4.

different order. If desired, wine could easily be dissociated from libations in a way that was not true for meat and sacrifice, since meat was commonly sold as the leftovers from sacrificial ritual whereas libations only took place in the home at the meal itself. In any case, in the ancient world total escape from sacrificial ritual was an impossibility. Even bread was to some degree tainted, since the harvest would have been subject at an earlier stage to cereal offerings and so on. Much more likely as a cause is ascetic suspicion of the body as a source of corruption, with meat and wine seen as representing a decline from a primitive ideal. It is not just the Bible that assumes a vegetarian existence in the beginning before the Flood. The Pythagoreans and Plato adopted a similar position.[53]

It is possible that there may even be some residual signs of such attitudes within the New Testament itself. So, for instance, the weak brethren mentioned by Paul may perhaps have adopted just such a stance. Even the phrase 'breaking of bread' in Acts could possibly recall a reluctance to use wine, though of course, if so, it would not reflect Luke's own position.[54] He himself is quite clear about the nature of the eucharistic celebration, as are the other Evangelists and Paul himself. Not that there is complete unanimity. Thanks to the absence of an institution narrative in John, he has sometimes been interpreted as anti-eucharistic.[55] This is emphatically not my view. Indeed, in Chapter 3 I argued that John represents a move within the early Church to a more explicit identification of the wine with Christ's blood as a way of indicating that the eucharist involved a sharing in his divinity no less than in his humanity. Hitherto, for Jews blood had been seen as a unique prerogative belonging to God alone.[56]

It is, however, that image as applied to Christ's humanity that I wish to pursue further here. My suggestion will be that, however different their theologies are in other respects, the major branches

---

[53] Gen. 9.1–5; Plato, *Politicus* 271d–272b. Although the dominant position among Pythagoreans, other views appear also to have been held: M. Detienne, 'La Cuisine de Pythagore', *Archives de Sociologie des Religions* 29 (1970), 141–62.

[54] For the weak brethren, see 1 Cor. 8.7–10; Rom. 14.1–3, 20–1. For 'breaking of bread', see Acts 2.42, 46; 20.7, 11; 27.35. H. Lietzmann makes much of the latter in his *Mass and Lord's Supper* (Leiden: Brill, 1979).

[55] Most notably by Bultmann.

[56] e.g. Gen. 9.4. See also the relevant section of Chapter 3 ('Wine and the Divine Life') 165–71.

of the Christian church did in the past share a common emphasis on access to Christ's humanity as a way of mediating that divinity. The question of Christ's continuing bodily identity was thus integral to approaches otherwise as different as those of Aquinas, Luther and Calvin. As such there is a marked contrast with much modern Christian writing and thinking, where it is the divine presence that is stressed and the body relegated either entirely to the past or else treated as 'mere metaphor'. My discussion proceeds by three stages. First I consider the kind of relationship presupposed between Christ's humanity and our own. Then I examine what sense can be made of such a localized humanity, before returning one last time to the image of health and the eucharist as medicine for the body no less than for the mind.

Incorporation into Christ's Humanity

In pursuing such a relationship the Fourth Gospel makes wide use of the imagery of incorporation, mediated particularly through the metaphor of the vine and its branches.[57] Paul instead focuses on the body and its parts, with two slightly different metaphors appearing, one in his earlier and one in his later writings.[58] Corporatist language is also strong in the Old Testament. Rather than interacting entirely with particular individuals, God is portrayed as relating to the people as a whole, and this is reflected in his most common titles as 'God of Abraham, Isaac and Jacob' or else as 'God of Israel'. While such an understanding could bring blessings and promise for all, it also led to conceptions of punishment that would be quite unacceptable in the modern world. An entire family is punished for the sin of one of its members, and even unborn generations are held accountable for what happened in the past, as the familiar language of the Ten Commandments makes clear: 'visiting the sins of the fathers upon the children unto the third and fourth generation of them that hate me' (Exod. 20.5).[59] Although

---

[57] John 15.1–17.

[58] In Paul's earlier writings, Christ is identified with the whole body: 1 Cor. 12.12–27; Rom. 12.4–5. In later or Pseudo-Paul, Christ is equated with the head: Col. 1.28; Eph. 1.23. For a brief analysis of Paul's various uses of 'body of Christ', see D. E. H. Whiteley, *The Theology of St Paul* (Oxford: Blackwell, 1970), 190–9.

[59] For the punishment of an entire family, see the story of Achan in Joshua 7. The verse from Exodus is quoted from the Holy Communion service in the *Book of Common Prayer* (1662). The AV has 'iniquity'.

there are protests within the Hebrew Bible against such ideas, most notably in Ezekiel (e.g. ch. 18), it is not improbable that part of Jesus' own self-understanding was based on related ideas. While it is possible that 'Son of Man' on Jesus' lips is simply a periphrasis for 'this man', more likely its origins lie in the Danielic Son of Man, who embodies the entire people.[60] If so, there would be a natural continuity in the kind of incorporationist language subsequently adopted by Paul.

Many today are deeply suspicious of such imagery. Certainly, as a means of assigning praise or blame it is woefully inadequate. What it does acknowledge, however, is that even in our own highly individualistic age we are much more than mere independent self-creations. Hidden or only partially acknowledged influences from the surrounding society, family and friends play as large a part in making me the sort of person I am as any consciously made decisions of mine. Taking that reality seriously could form an important element in a contemporary rationale for infant baptism.[61] In part what the parents are acknowledging is that whether the child ever comes to conscious faith or not is heavily dependent on a whole chain of influences stretching back into childhood and now put under the grace of God in this ceremony.[62]

The difference between the modern world and the past is not so much the nature of such influences as the kind of attitude with which they are regarded. The modern tendency is to try to shake free of any such conditioning, so far as possible; the ancient was often to glory in it. It is now extremely hard for modern individuals to envisage societies where their members' primary consciousness was of themselves as parts of a greater whole, but there is no doubt that this has often been the situation in the long history of humanity, perhaps predominantly so. Apart from ancient Israel, it is

---

[60] Dan. 7.13–14. Impressively argued in C. F. D. Moule's *The Origin of Christology* (Cambridge: Cambridge University Press, 1977), despite an earlier complaint of mine that Moule tried to push his argument too far: see my *The Divine Trinity* (London: Duckworth, 1985), 105–9.

[61] Such an approach is adopted in a recent Doctrine Commission report of the Church of England: *We Believe in the Holy Spirit* (London: Church House, 1991), 78–81.

[62] A perspective also endorsed by Calvin: *Institutes of the Christian Religion*, ed. J. T. McNeill (Philadelphia: Westminster Press, 1960), 4.1.4 (ii, 1016); 4.16.20 (ii, 1243).

possible to explore examples not only from the ancient world more generally but also from the medieval, and even in more recent times among people such as the Inuit or in Japan before the Second World War.[63] Among the Eskimo peoples this is even enshrined linguistically: it is possible to speak of Eskimo-here or Eskimo-not-here, but not otherwise to differentiate between persons.[64] That is, in contrast to most other languages, Inuit allows no distinction between the second and third person; one can speak only of 'Eskimoness' here (that is, I) or over there (you or her).

Currently there is a surprising lack of interest in the subject and so a dearth of suitable material to which to refer. This is unfortunate, as without some conception of this notion it seems to me impossible to make sense of the great contrast that now exists between contemporary understandings of the eucharist and the view that has dominated most of the Church's history. Indeed, as I mentioned in the introduction to this part and at the beginning of this chapter, it seems to me no exaggeration to claim that Aquinas, Luther and Calvin all share more in common on this matter with each other than they do with the great majority of Christians in the contemporary world. I do not mean by this the claim that the modern Church has simply relapsed into some form of Zwinglianism, with remembrance of Christ's past actions seen as principally what is taking place.[65] On the contrary, there is often a lively sense of Christ being active in and through the service. Where the difference lies is rather in thinking that that activity is solely a matter of Christ's divinity, his ability to be present everywhere, and not something unique and extraordinary because intimately bound up with the continuing existence of his full humanity and thus also of his body. Indeed, so far as his present humanity is envisaged as relevant at all, this tends to be thought of in terms of the people present in church being bonded together as part of a single community as 'Christ's body', another feature prominent in Zwingli's theology.[66]

[63] For some historical examples and analysis, see my 'Trinitarian Personhood and Individuality', in R. J. Feenstra and C. Plantinga (eds), *Trinity, Incarnation and Atonement* (Notre Dame, Ind.: University of Notre Dame Press, 1989), 48–78.

[64] R. Harré, *Personal Being* (Oxford: Blackwell, 1983), 85–9.

[65] For expositions of Zwinglianism, especially with regard to the controversy with Luther, see J. Rilliet, *Zwingli: Third Man of the Reformation* (London: Lutterworth, 1964), 213–67; W. P. Stephens, *The Theology of Huldrych Zwingli* (Oxford: Clarendon Press, 1986), 218–59.

[66] Most commentators devote so much attention to Zwingli's argument about bread and wine as 'signs' that this feature is virtually ignored. But note passages

'Body' is of course in all these uses being stretched in its meaning. To state the obvious, whatever Christ's present body is like, it cannot be literally material, as though with sufficient progress in science we might one day be able to reach where it now is. Its nature has somehow to be reconciled with the fact that heaven, God's dwelling place, is a non-material reality and indeed omnipresent, just as God is. It is both everywhere and nowhere, if one may express it thus. Yet none of this should be taken to indicate the abandonment of any notion of some degree of equivalence to material reality. Christianity claims that it is the totality of Christ's human identity that survived death, not just its more mental or spiritual aspects. Scientific analogies are of limited use. So, for example, one might speak of a parallel universe, but the difficulty is that on the scientific conception such universes do not interact, whereas it is essential to Christianity that heaven and earth do somehow relate to one another. So, however strained the analogies, it remains vital to talk of a 'body' in that other world, and not just retreat from such a conception as so much of the contemporary Church appears to do.

This is not to say that Christ's humanity is ignored entirely, but the tendency is to think of a present divinity that brings with it the history of a past humanity that was once alive on this earth rather than of a human body that continues into our own present day. That this is in fact the situation is suggested by the way in which Ascension Day is now treated as a sort of minor appendix to Easter rather than its culmination, in the permanent exaltation of humanity into the life of God.[67] For most of Christian history the Ascension was seen as mattering not simply because Christ could then be treated as forerunner of our own future destiny, but more importantly because only through incorporation into that humanity was it thought that our own salvation was possible. Through mingling with what was incorruptible our own corruption would eventually be transformed

such as the following: 'Those ... who take part ... show themselves to be members of the whole church who believe in Christ who was offered for us. Hence it is also called "union" or "communion" by Paul': G. R. Potter (ed.), *Huldrych Zwingli* (London: Edward Arnold, 1978), 99.

[67] With occasional exceptions: e.g. D. Farrow, *Ascension and Ecclesia* (Grand Rapids: Eerdmans, 1999); G. S. Dawson, *Jesus Ascended* (London: T&T Clark, 2004).

also into incorruptibility. The divine nature in C[hrist]
incorruptible and so through association with that renders his body
could achieve a similar status. our own too

Such claims brought with them their own di_tive set of
problems. The most obvious was how to achieve a appropriate
intimacy with Christ's body. If this is a truly human b it must
also, like ours, be of finite dimensions and so unlike div_ry be in
one place rather than another, and that place is heaven, not ere on
earth. Intriguingly, Aquinas, Luther and Calvin all accepte that
premise.[68] Where they differed was in the nature of the miracle
required to overcome the problem. In outline, Aquinas has the
miracle of transubstantiation, whereby Christ's body and blood
draw close to replace the substance of bread and wine, leaving
only their accidents; Luther instead has the two realities side by
side, the divinity miraculously granting to the humanity the ability
to be present everywhere, like itself; finally, Calvin has the believer's spirit caught up to heaven to unite with Christ's humanity
there.

Much modern Catholic theology has preferred terms such as
'transsignification'.[69] But, however inadequate Aquinas' use of Aristotelian metaphysics is judged to be, it is surely worth investigating
what Aquinas was attempting to achieve through his defence of such
terminology. This is important, not least because, as we shall find, it
draws him closer to Luther and Calvin than might otherwise be
appreciated. Aquinas' thought needs to be set in the context of earlier
disputes where less literal readings had been rejected, first in the ninth
century in Paschasius Radbertus' dispute with his fellow-monk
Ratramnus (from the same abbey of Corbie), and then again in the
following century with Lanfranc's response to the challenge of
Berengar of Tours. Paschasius expressed well what more literal readings were trying to achieve: 'While Christ is in the Father because of
the nature of their shared divinity, we, on the other hand, are in Christ

---

[68] As of course did Zwingli.

[69] E. Schillebeeckx, *The Eucharist* (London: Sheed and Ward, 1977 edn), 107-21;
M. Gesteira Garza, *La eucaristia, misterio de comunión* (Madrid: Ediciones Cristiandad,
1983), 524ff. For an interesting modification in the direction of deeming the bread
and wine to be the body and blood of Christ, see M. Dummett, 'The Intelligibility of
Eucharistic Doctrine', in W. J. Abraham and S. W. Holtzer (eds), *The Rationality of
Religious Belief* (Oxford: Clarendon Press, 1987), 231-61.

The Eucharistic Body

because of hi... ly nativity, and he again believed to be present in us through th...ery of the sacraments.'[70] Aquinas sought to defend that basic...eption but in a way that excluded crude physical consumpt...

Certa..., he conceded the necessity of a miracle, since every finite l...lized presence in moving from place to place 'must pass th...ugh all the intermediate places, and there is no question of th...n the present case'.[71] At the same time he notes that though soul is the form of the body it cannot be that it takes the place of bread and wine, since it is of a quite different kind of reality (non-physical); so Christ's divinity and soul can only be there in the eucharistic elements 'by natural concomitance'.[72] But this must apply equally to Christ's quantitative dimensions—his size and appearance—since the whole of Christ is supposed to be present in each piece of wafer however small, in each sip of wine. The result is that 'Christ's body in this sacrament is in no way localized'; there is no way in which it can be measured, subdivided and so on.[73] In effect, 'it is always in heaven in its proper appearance and it is on many other altars under its sacramental appearance'.[74]

These are huge qualifications that suggest to me at least that what matters for Aquinas is the presence of the human Christ in or along-side each particle of consecrated matter. Earlier Church decisions at the Fourth Lateran Council in 1215 had forced him to adopt the language of 'in' but his use of the terminology of 'concomitance' and 'association' imply that given a free hand he might well have been equally happy with talk of two worlds meeting. At least that is the direction in which we are pulled by one particular analogy he offers for how Christ can be said to be present in each part of a broken host: 'when a mirror is unbroken, there is only one image, but when the mirror is broken, you have a separate image in each of its parts'.[75] Adapting the analogy, we may think of the relation between the heavenly world and our own as like the numerous points of contact

---

[70] *Patrologia Latina* 139, 383c (my translation). For a helpful discussion of Paschasius' views, see G. Macy, *The Theologies of the Eucharist in the Early Scholastic Period* (Oxford: Oxford University Press, 1984), 44–72.

[71] *Summa Theologiae*, Blackfriars tr., lviii (London: Eyre and Spottiswoode, 1965), 3a.75.3 (p. 63).

[72] Ibid. 3a.76.1 (p. 95).   [73] Ibid. 3a.76.5 (p. 109).

[74] Ibid. 3a.76.11 (p. 111).   [75] Ibid. 3a.76.3 (p. 103).

between the many parts of the broken mirror and the single original of the image which they are reflecting. Perhaps at this juncture one might draw on a popular children's classic, *The Lion, the Witch and the Wardrobe* by C. S. Lewis, to help clarify issues. In the novel contact with the supernatural world of Narnia is established by passage through a magic wardrobe. The temporal and spatial coordinates of neither Narnia nor our own world are affected as the children cross back and forth over into the other world. When the children return to this world, they are enriched by their adventures but with no sense of time having elapsed on earth in the interim. There is intersection, but without crude physical or material change.

Intriguingly Luther, without referring us back to Aquinas, appeals to exactly that same image of the broken mirror. The mirror 'broken into a thousand pieces' still retains 'the very same face . . . whole and entire in every piece of the mirror'.[76] Where he differs from Aquinas is in insisting that the very meaning of heaven entails that Christ is already close: 'Christ's body is everywhere because it is at the right hand of God which is everywhere, although we do not know how that occurs'.[77] Although this thought is sometimes expressed in the dry phraseology of 'consubstantiation', that distorts the very personal categories which Luther favours. For him, an analogy with the incarnation is entirely appropriate. To those who object to the idea that 'the single body of Christ is present in a hundred thousand places, wherever bread is broken, and that the massive limbs should there be so concealed that no one sees and feels them', he responds that 'equally well . . . it is not reasonable that God should descend from heaven and enter into the womb; that he who nourishes, sustains and encompasses all the world should allow himself to be nourished and encompassed by the Virgin'.[78] Indeed, in considering the various participants in the Nativity, Luther does not hesitate to declare that Christ wishes 'to be just as close to us bodily as he was to them' and 'so, when we eat Christ's flesh physically and spiritually, the

---

[76] From *Confession Concerning Christ's Supper* (1528): *Martin Luther's Basic Theological Writings*, ed. T. F. Lull (Minneapolis: Fortress, 1989), 395.

[77] Ibid. 383.

[78] From *The Sacrament of the Body and the Blood of Christ—Against the Fanatics* (1526): ibid. 317.

food is so powerful that it transforms us into itself, and out of fleshly, sinful mortal men makes spiritual, holy, living men'.[79]

Some of this, though, is sleight of hand. The difference from the incarnation lies precisely in the fact that the incarnate body was not ubiquitous. Being fully human meant that Jesus was shaped by one particular culture and set of circumstances rather than another. So if he continues to be human in his post-mortem state, he must retain at least some of those particularities of what it is to be human. Otherwise, his humanity simply merges into his divinity. That is why deriving the significance of 'right hand of God' from the meaning of divinity in general seems to me to approach matters the wrong way round. In its biblical context the phrase surely speaks of status, power and authority rather than of any multi-locational capacity. Indeed, the way in which the imagery is employed has Jesus move in one particular direction rather than another (i.e. upwards) in order to secure that position.[80]

It is considerations such as these that made Calvin search for an alternative solution. Like Aquinas and Luther he did so in a way that left unchallenged the Church's basic assumption that any relation to Christ's divinity must be mediated through access to his continuing humanity. 'By bidding us eat,' he writes, 'Christ indicates that his body becomes one substance with us', and so that is why communion, when devoutly taken, can overcome the fear of death.[81] Indeed, there is so much mystical language of union in Calvin (much of which appears to draw on St Bernard of Clairvaux) that one of his fellow Reformers, Bullinger, even accused him of being a 'papist', and modern readings of his views as essentially Catholic are by no means uncommon.[82] Certainly, as the years advanced, Calvin's views seem to have become less Protestant.[83] He remained firmly wedded

---

[79] Two quotations used by Paul Althaus in his discussion of Luther's eucharistic theology in his *The Theology of Martin Luther* (Philadelphia: Fortress, 1966), 375–403, esp. 394, 401–2.

[80] Mark 16.19; Acts 2.33; Heb. 10.12; 1 Pet 3.22.

[81] see Quoted in B. A. Gerrish, *Grace and Gratitude: The Eucharistic Theology of John Calvin* (Edinburgh: T&T Clark 1993), 128. For further relevant quotations and commentary, see 83.

[82] For Bernard's influence, see ibid. 72, 99; for Catholic readings, 2–9.

[83] In response to Lutheran challenges, he was even prepared to speak of feeding on the actual 'substance' of Christ's flesh: Ibid. 178–9.

however, to Zwingli's insistent claim that Christ's ascended body must be that of a limited human being and so could be nowhere else than in heaven. The result was that he posited a series of miracles that are in some ways no less remarkable than transubstantiation: that believers are caught up by the Spirit into heaven to feed on their Saviour there.[84]

As already noted, contemporary theology, more often than not, fights shy of any such emphasis on the human side of Christ's presence. For some, such questions are simply a diversion when set against the more important issue of the creation of Christ's ecclesial body within the community of faith.[85] Even where the Ascension is still treated as important, its potential impact is lessened by insistence that the ascended Christ must be mediated either through the historical Jesus or else through a future full eschatological realization of his presence with us.[86] So one way or another a present distance between Christ and the believer is maintained, which is the very thing Aquinas, Luther and Calvin were all concerned to avoid. Some suggest that modern understandings of space and time can help solve the conceptual problem.[87] Although that might prove helpful in generating analogies (for example, in terms of my earlier mention of parallel universes touching), I would be reluctant to go too far down that route, as, whatever heaven is, it is not something accessible to the world of science. Rather, the two beliefs must continue to be held in creative tension. Heaven, God's world, is a non-material reality. Christ has nonetheless entered into that reality, with his body no less than his soul sharing the full presence of God. What the actual equivalent in heaven of his former material body might be, however, remains beyond any adequate human imagining, as Paul had already noticed at the beginnings of Christianity.[88]

---

[84] Calvin himself explicitly speaks of 'many miracles' being involved: *Institutes*, 4.17.24 (ii, 1390).

[85] True even for Gerrish, Calvin's own expositor on this subject: *Grace and Gratitude*, 189–90.

[86] For the former, see Dawson, *Jesus Ascended*, 50–2; for the latter, Farrow, *Ascension and Ecclesia*, 3, 220–1, 267–73.

[87] e.g. T. F. Torrance, *Space, Time and Resurrection* (Grand Rapids: Eerdmans, 1976), 123–32.

[88] 1 Cor. 15.35ff. Perhaps it is here that Bishop Berkeley's ingenious account of perception in this world might find its legitimate place. In heaven God ordains non-material images, equivalent to what physical perception creates in this world.

Localized Presence of a Transformed Humanity

One recent study of sixteenth-century French Calvinism has postulated that the real contrast between Calvinism and Catholicism lies
quite elsewhere, on the question of power.[89] Even here, however,
I would want to suggest that more was shared in common than is
often the case with the modern Church. The author contrasts what
he sees as two quite different conceptions of how Christ relates to
the sacrament. On the Catholic side, there is a wholly immanent
Christ who is at the disposal of the wider society as much as by the
Church. As illustration he notes how by this time Corpus Christi
festivities had fallen into the charge of local municipalities and away
from the Church itself, while the monarchy exploited its characteristic ritual in order to attach to itself a similar semi-divine status.[90]
Although Calvin sought to play down any politically revolutionary
implications in his own theology, the contrast could scarcely be more
marked. For Calvin the Church was a holy gathering set apart from
the rest of society, with Christ only acting with sovereign power on
those who had been given the gift of faith.[91] Transubstantiation is
wrong because it 'abases' Christ, putting him entirely at the mercy of
scandalous priests and even mice, which were conceded the opportunity of eating him.[92] Catholics in the meantime objected that, if
Christ is kept in heaven, this calls into question whether there is any
real possibility of participation at all.[93]

   Certainly, these are more than mere superficial differences,
reflecting as they do divergent understandings of what powers
Christ has delegated to his Church, how the objectivity of the
sacraments is best defended, and so on. What cannot be conceded,
however, is any notion that on the one hand Calvin wants action
from a distance while on the other Catholicism seeks to place Christ
as close as possible on the very tongue of the individual. As we have
seen, Calvin constantly sought to break down the distance. Equally,
whatever the theory, in its actual practice through most of its

----

[89] C. Elwood, *The Body Broken: The Calvinist Doctrine of the Eucharist and the
Symbolization of Power in Sixteenth-Century France* (New York: Oxford University
Press, 1999).

[90] Ibid. 12–26, esp. 20, 25.

[91] Calvin's emphasis meant that others felt safe in moving to a 'higher' doctrine
of the eucharist. See, for example, Farel's change of view: ibid. 91–2.

[92] For the former, see ibid. 64; for the latter (as expressed by Viret), 93.

[93] Ibid. (quoting Benoist), 124.

history Catholicism also needed to assert Christ acting from a distance. Although Christ's presence on the altar was affirmed, because of infrequent communion only occasionally could that presence be mediated directly to the body of the believer.

So, just as Calvin's use of the analogy of the sun and its rays needs to be set against his employment of the language of intimacy and incorporation, equally on the Catholic side the relative infrequency of communion in the Middle Ages meant that believers were in effect expected to be acted upon from a distance, from altar to pew, as it were, without any physical act intervening.[94] In an attempt to render such practice consonant with more traditional theology it was sometimes asserted that the priest consumed the host on the community's behalf. But this was in effect to concede that what matters is not so much any actual eating as the impact of the human Christ on the believer. Indeed, unless we are to suppose that the Church has deprived believers of their sustenance through most of its history, it looks as though Catholic and Protestant alike must say that actual consumption is of less moment than securing an intimate relationship between Christ's humanity and our own.

This is a conclusion that modern Catholic and Protestant theology alike might well want to resist, not least as both have moved throughout the course of the twentieth century both in theory and in practice to more frequent communion. I would not wish to contest the essential rightness of that move. Equally, however, I fail to see why practices such as adoration of the sacrament should not be seen as complementary rather than necessarily antithetical. The later Middle Ages is commonly cited to illustrate how badly things can go wrong, with the elevation of the host clearly replacing reception as the eucharist's focal point. It is a practice that gained momentum from the beginning of the thirteenth century onwards.[95] In a recent impressive study the author speaks of the generation of an entire symbolic system from it, all arising out of the central paradox of an act of apparent cannibalism.[96] Certainly, other studies

---

[94] For Calvin's use of the analogy of the sun and its rays, see *Institutes*, 4.17.12 (ii, 1373).

[95] The first occurrence is usually dated to Paris just after the death of Bishop Eudes de Sully in 1208. For a more complex history, see M. Rubin, *Corpus Christi: The Eucharist in Late Medieval Culture* (Cambridge: Cambridge University Press, 1991), 56–63.

[96] Ibid., esp. 5, 359–60.

support her conception of a society firmly focused on the body. Indeed, it has been suggested that during this period the soul takes on so many properties of the body that in effect it has itself become a sort of body.[97] Not only did purgatory demand it, so did the heavenly vision of the saints.[98] Again, liturgical and non-liturgical activities associated with the popes of the time witness to a similar focus that created considerable tensions over how their bodies should be viewed. While for some it was their mortality that should be stressed, others thought that their office as 'Vicar of Christ' carried with it the possibility of a different sort of body.[99] So various devices were tried to secure longevity or even immortality, among them alchemy.[100] It is possible that that search may even explain the legend of Pope Joan: the pope's body would after all be perpetuated through heirs, just as with other monarchs.[101]

But, while it is true that stories about the host were generated that presuppose a depressing literalism that contrasts markedly with Aquinas' refined position, it nonetheless seems to me odd to describe the power of such symbolism as ultimately lying in a fascinated attraction and repulsion that the cannibalist image evoked.[102] After all, the actual consumption of the host was invisible to the congregation except when they themselves participated once a year. What was visible was the host itself as a sign of a presence at one and the same time divine and human. It was thus the sense of an active localized presence that I would suggest was central, perhaps much like the way that in the previous millennium there had been an obsession with

[97] C. W. Bynum, *The Resurrection of the Body* (New York: Columbia University Press, 1995), 155.

[98] For fires of purgatory, see e.g. ibid. 281; for the heavenly vision, 266–7 (in Aquinas), 283–91 (The debate between John XXII and Benedict XII).

[99] For an examination of the contrasting approaches, see A. Paravicini-Bagliani, *The Pope's Body* (Chicago: University of Chicago Press, 2000). The earlier approach had been to use ritual to contrast the office and the man (28, 54). One example of the change was the usurpation of the title 'Vicar of Christ' from the eleventh century onwards (58–9).

[100] Popes began to take an interest in medical matters (ibid. pp. xiv–xv, 179–93). Alexander III wrote to the legendary Prester John for advice (199). Clement V even took to drinking gold (227–9).

[101] Paravicini-Bagliani's suggestion: ibid. 232–4; cf. p. xvi.

[102] Rubin comments that Aquinas' conception of 'Christ's physical presence' realized 'only in an invisible spiritual, and non-materialist way, was not easily teachable, nor did it purport to be so': *Corpus Christi*, 25. For examples of extreme literalism, see 108–29, esp. 116.

relics of the saints that continued into the new era. Indeed, in the first millennium the host had often itself been spoken of as a relic.[103] Mention of relics makes one recall some of the absurdities into which the Church has sometimes fallen. But *abusus non tollit usum*: illegitimate applications do not entail that all such practice is inappropriate. If the service of Benediction has dangers in suggesting that it is priests who really dispense and have authority over Christ's power, simple prayer and adoration of the sacrament during exposition can help build faith in a Saviour who can transform and shape the individual believer's life.[104] Indeed, it is on this aspect that recent papal support for the return of some elements in former practice has focused.[105] There has also been a welcome retreat from the Council of Trent's insistence that the eucharistic body be identified with the body immolated on the cross.[106] Here the Counter-Reformation shared with the Reformation a rather narrow concentration on what Christ had done on the cross. It was the offering made in death itself that was seen as constituting the point of propitiation and reconciliation, and with that went great emphasis on the suffering endured.

Within Catholicism that had the further unfortunate consequence that individuals then came to believe that in adding to Christ's treasury of merit they themselves were called not merely to suffering as a means to a good end (clearly a good thing, if the only option available) but also to think of suffering, whether self-imposed or otherwise, as in itself necessarily redemptive for others. Some of the unfortunate consequences of such attitudes have already been

[103] The Council of Chelsea of 816 makes the link explicit when it recommends that at the consecration of a new church a host should be deposited 'along with the other relics' *(cum aliis reliquiis)*: A. W. Haddam and W. Stubbs (eds), *Councils and Ecclesiastical Documents Relating to Great Britain and Northern Ireland* (Oxford, 1872), iii, 580.

[104] Apart from the elaborate ritual of the priest using a monstrance to bless the people, the actual form of the traditional Benediction service is distinctly odd. Prayers are most commonly addressed to Mary rather than Christ (incorporated originally from confraternity devotions to Mary).

[105] For two examples of support from John Paul II, see B. J. Groeschel and James Monti, *In the Presence of Our Lord: The History, Theology, and Psychology of Eucharistic Devotion* (Huntington, Ind.: Our Sunday Visitor, 1997), 147, 171.

[106] For Trent and a critique, see D. N. Power, *The Sacrifice We Offer: The Tridentine Dogma and its Reinterpretation* (Edinburgh: T. & T. Clark, 1987), esp. 75–6. The narrower focus was already being attacked as early as the nineteenth century in the work of Matthias Scheeben: A. Nichols, *The Holy Eucharist* (Dublin: Veritas, 1991), 95–6.

noted in Chapter 4. Two more recent examples from modern France will suffice here. Charles de Foucault, founder of the Little Brothers of Jesus, sought to live simply and humbly among the Arab tribesmen of the Sahara desert. That was noble and laudable. Less sensible was the deliberate imposition of uncomfortable accommodation and unappetizing food.[107] Again, the French composer Francis Poulenc came to believe that a friend dying of tuberculosis had actually suffered as a substitute for himself, and so allowed him a longer life.[108]

What such ideas ignore is the existence of the human Christ before and after Calvary. It was the totality of his life that Jesus offered to his Father and not just his death, while the ascended Christ surely has the ability to take the individual beyond that fact of death and into a deeper relationship with himself. Even as the sacrifice on Calvary is recalled, something matters more than simply the present Christ's identity with that particular past moment in his life, however important it was. There is the question of how every feature of Christ's life might affect his followers, including his resurrection and ascension. Equally, although surprisingly little is written about this aspect, the Christ that is encountered in the eucharist must surely have a humanity that continues to change and develop, because only that way can it continue to have an appropriate impact on our world. Little could be achieved even by a perfect humanity if it had ossified as human beings were two thousand years ago. Not least, there needs to be growth in comprehension about what it might be like to be a practising Christian in any of the succeeding centuries. Such knowledge is presumably mediated to Christ through his divinity, but this does not mean that it is simply a function of that divinity. To know something as a human being and to know it as divine are not at all the same thing. Not only are human beings' options firmly circumscribed, temptation is for them, unlike for God, a daily reality. But what these options are varies with social conditions. So knowing what options are possible and what is a real temptation mean detailed awareness of specific settings and their potential implications. To take an

---

[107] The deliberate imposition is much stressed in Fergus Fleming's study of de Foucault and another French figure of the desert, Henri Laperrine: *The Sword and the Cross* (London: Faber and Faber, 2004), e.g. 152, 205.

[108] For the key role of Lucien Roubert's illness in the generation of Poulenc's opera *Dialogues of the Carmelites*, see R. D. E. Burton, *Francis Poulenc* (Bath: Absolute Press, 2002), 95–101. See also my discussion of Poulenc in Chapter 5.

example at random, in the past many a woman must have embarked on marriage with real fear that she would soon meet her death in pregnancy, whereas in the modern western world this is no longer so. Again, temptation through abuse of wealth has become a trap for most of us in the western world, whereas in Jesus' own day even the moderately well-to-do were quite rare.

Body Healed and Saved

So to return finally to the issue of health and salvation, Christ's humanity is envisaged as coming close in order to create Christ-like beings in their own distinctive context, one where body and soul point in the same direction in this life and become a fully integrated whole in the next. Earlier (in Chapter 4) I discussed some of the motives that led to extreme asceticism in the Middle Ages, including attempts to live off the consecrated host. There, I suggested that one motive might have been the public power it gave, as in the case of Catherine of Siena. Not all known instances were of this kind. An intriguing case from seventeenth-century Venice is that of Maria Janis, whose desire was to keep the matter entirely secret. The detailed reports of the Inquisition survive. What they reveal is a peasant girl too poor to become a nun but determined nonetheless along with her parish priest to pursue a life of total sanctity and dedication to Christ.[109] Her asceticism had nothing to do with hatred of body and everything to do with bodily identification with, and incorporation into, Christ. Indeed, secret eating of food other than the host was indulged in, as a way of maintaining bodily health.[110]

Not that we should go to the other extreme and suppose that a physically healthy body is really the aim; rather, it is that, if there is pain or disease in body or soul, these can be reorientated towards the good. All this may seem a long way from our earlier discussion of bodies as beautiful, sexual and ugly, but it is not. Those represent three distinct ways of seeing ourselves, those around us, and

[109] Her story is finely told in F. Tomizza, *Heavenly Supper: The Story of Maria Janis* (Chicago: University of Chicago Press, 1991). The secret was kept for five years before prying neighbours reported the matter to the Inquisition.
[110] Tomizza offers a sympathetic interpretation: it was seen as a necessary relapse in order for her to recover strength to continue with her resolve: ibid. 173–4.

Christ himself. The temptation is to see such conceptions as having
nothing particularly to do with salvation since the focus is on body
and not mind or soul. In reality, as we have seen, they are in fact
three key ways of integrating body and mind. It is through envisaging Christ under such categories that we also progress in envisaging
ourselves. So I return one last time to the bodies considered in
Chapters 1 and 4.

So far from only ever providing false aspirations, the beautiful
body can sometimes truly offer a genuine reflection of divine
grace, especially where that beauty is experienced as sheer gift.
While containment and radical independence may speak of divine
aseity, such aspects are unlikely in and of themselves to produce
engagement. So it is when such beauty is presented in the form of
openness and even vulnerability that it is most likely to succeed
in drawing us closer to the divine, and so also, through grace,
help towards our transformation. Hence artistic representations of
Christ do need to be taken seriously, and recognition given to the
fact that sometimes a beautiful but vulnerable Buddha might speak
better of God than some of the powerful, muscular Christs towards
which the Church as patron has so often inclined. Again, it is quite
wrong to think of the sexual body's only role as the principal way
towards sexual relations, fulfilling or otherwise. It can also act as a
powerful metaphor that draws us into new ways of relating to our
surroundings, as well as to other people. Hinduism and Christian
Baroque art have much to teach us here. Sensuousness is only an
enemy when it falls into selfishness. So, instead of succumbing to
modern reductionism, the Church needs to insist that there is a
better way, one that has been embraced for most of human history.
That way is where the sensuous body is acknowledged and valued
without necessarily immediately being seen as either requiring
immediate seduction (the modern view) or its rejection and nega-
tion (so often the Christian response in the past). Finally, because
of the empathy it arouses, the ugly body can give us a deep affective
life that enables our emotions and hearts to play as large a role in our
religious life as our intellects. As we have seen, it can even allow
moral beauty to shine through the most haggard face or body when
complete integration of body and soul is present.

So I end this chapter by reaffirming the connection between
eucharistic theology and the various discussions of body that have
preceded it. It is precisely because body is so integral to who and

what we are that the Christian eucharist rightly focuses on the body of a particular human being who was both God and man. That is why it is so important to get the liturgical celebration of that fact right. The short coda that follows offers some brief reflections on this issue.

9

The Liturgical Imperative

God and Enchantment of Place, the first volume in this series, began with a chapter that argued for a broader definition of sacrament that potentially at least might include all of life, and, so far as my own focus was concerned, especially its cultural aspects. This volume now ends with the eucharist itself. The progression has been deliberate, because I have been rebelling throughout against views of religious experience that strongly oppose the sacred and secular, revealed and natural religion. Of course the story of Christ and the rite he instituted contain numerous unique features that can only be justified, if at all, by appeal to biblical revelation. But this does not mean that it therefore stands wholly apart from a wider sense of how people might experience God.

Certainly, a key element in revealed religion is the challenge it offers to the wider world. Too often, however, in their eagerness to endorse that challenge, theologians give scant recognition to the way in which God has already established patterns in the world he created on which Christian revelation builds. Grace operates everywhere, if only our minds and hearts can be generous enough to allow our eyes to perceive it.

That is why I have sought to place the eucharistic body in the much wider context of how body in general might mediate the divine. It is not just the symbolism associated with bread and wine that will affect the sort of experience we have at the altar rail and in the service as a whole, but also the additional assumptions we bring along in respect of our own understanding of body and of Christ's body in particular.

It matters, for instance, whether Christ is envisaged as still crucified or now resurrected and so beyond the worst: whether his body is seen as still bearing its wounds and its pains or somehow transcending these in a glorified body. Particularly in the western tradition of Christianity there has been a long tradition of presupposing the former: that in the offering of the mass Christ's sacrifice is renewed, with him still essentially identified with it but painlessly. Or at any rate that is the official view. Too often the ordinary believer has thought of Christ continuing in pain, whereas what is important is the believer's identification with what was achieved once and for all upon the cross, a unique self-offering, not any permanence in suffering.[1] That is why images of both suffering and glorification need to be held in creative tension as the communicant advances towards the altar, both the sense of what Christ has once done and where he is now and can lead us also. The modern practice in both Catholic and Protestant liturgies of widening the range of reference in the consecration prayer beyond what once occurred is therefore warmly to be welcomed.

But it is also important to appreciate that such changes in perception are unlikely to be effected by tinkering with the words alone. In recent years there has been a commendable move among some liturgists away from a narrow focus on the history of rites and the words used. Adopting the name 'liturgical theology', it has sought to examine what kind of theology is implicit in the enacted liturgy as a whole, what is being expressed in the conjunction of words and corresponding symbols.[2] That is a most welcome widening of horizons. Certainly, it can be salutary to compare and contrast evaluations based on language alone and those that range more widely. Take the three Anglican liturgies of 1549, 1552 and 1662. Traditional estimates of their degree of catholicity or otherwise are usually wholly based on the words that have been adopted, most obviously perhaps in the three different formulae adopted for the words of administration. But a full picture only really emerges once due attention is given to accompanying rubrics that specify the manner of performance.[3] 1549 and 1552 are discovered to be even further apart than comparison of the words of the two services might suggest. Again, while on the surface 1662 looks remarkably similar to 1552, the rubrics, or small print as it were, give a quite

---

[1] For a modern attempt to preserve the pain as a permanent 'moment' in God's life, see H. U. von Balthasar, *The Glory of the Lord* (Edinburgh: T. & T. Clark, 1989), vii, 533–4.

[2] For a helpful introduction, see S. Burns, *Worship in Context* (London: Epworth, 2006), 3–24, 127–212.

[3] For an excellent discussion of such issues, see B. Nichols, *Liturgical Hermeneutics* (Frankfurt am Main: Peter Lang, 1996), 53–86, esp. 77–80 for rubrics on presence in 1549 and 1552.

different meaning. As one noted Protestant liturgist observes, 'in wording (and thus in explicit doctrine) the service stands where it stood in 1552. And yet the "feel" of it is subtly changed. ... The consecration is a priestly event. The consecrated elements have a special character independent of reception.'[4] Much of that can be put down to the accompanying rubrics, about how the liturgy should be performed, in other words the bodily actions now seen as essential.

In the work of current practitioners of liturgical theology there is much that is valuable and important.[5] Don Saliers is perhaps the least frightened of the language of experience. As he observes, 'the liturgy is not a static system or structure to which we bring our life experience; rather, it is a crucible for meanings that, if entered into with our whole humanity, makes experience possible: deeper gratitude, deeper awe, a greater capacity for suffering, hope, and compassion'.[6] However, there is still a tendency among the group as a whole to follow the historical approach of earlier liturgical scholarship and look to the past for appropriate models. That seems to me a bad principle, and not because there is nothing to learn from the past. As readers of my earlier volume and indeed of this one also will be very aware, I think the past often provides the best critique of the present. Nonetheless, it is unfortunate if this is assumed to be always the case. It is not just meanings of words that change but equally the symbolic resonances of bodily actions, and so what meant one thing in an earlier generation might convey something quite different to the average worshipper in our own day.

That is why liturgical performance cannot just stand alone, but needs always to be explored against a wider backdrop. For better or for worse (for worse in my view), liturgists have rarely engaged in such explorations. As liturgy is a dramatic act, comparison with

---

[4] C. Buchanan, *What did Cranmer Think he was Doing?* (Bramcote, Nottingham: Grove Books, 1992 edn), 31.

[5] James White died in 2004. The other major Protestant figure, apart from Don Saliers, is Gordon Lathrop, who has produced a trilogy: *Holy Things* (1993), *Holy People* (1999) and *Holy Ground* (2003), all published by Fortress Press.

[6] D. E. Saliers, 'Symbol in Liturgy, Liturgy as Symbol: The Domestication of Liturgical Experience', in L. J. Madden (ed.), *The Awakening Church: 25 Years of Liturgical Renewal* (Collegeville, Minn.: Liturgical Press, 1992), 75; cf. also his support for similar ideas in Joseph Gelineau more generally, 70.

secular drama seems not only inevitable but right and proper. As an exercise in the verbal dexterities of language, the use of metaphor elsewhere also needs to be explored, as well as appropriate frames within which to assess the success or otherwise of the sermon. Is the right analogue a didactic lecture, a political diatribe, an exercise in rhetoric, or what? In some ways the particular answer is less important than the acknowledgement of the appropriateness of the search for such wider contexts.

The reason why is because with that acknowledgement will come recognition of the fact that revealed theology does not stand alone. It was set by God within a particular world of which he is also the creator. In my earlier pair of volumes, *Tradition and Imagination* and *Discipleship and Imagination*, I urged that rather than allowing itself to be conditioned by society and pretending otherwise, the Church needs to become more consciously self-aware of the dialogue upon which it is engaged, sometimes rightly responding to the pressures that lead it to read its texts in fresh ways, and sometimes rightly not responding. So, similarly here, there is a need to enter creatively into dialogue with a world in which some symbols and metaphors from the past continue to work and others no longer exercise their power. That certainly does not mean that the current or 'secular' must always win. Sometimes the effort should rightly be made to resist present pressures and assumptions. The ugly and the wasted, for example, have a value with which our present society finds it very hard to engage. But at other times perseverance will turn out to be simply perverse. The next volume will provide no shortage of examples where I believe this to be the case. Since the wider world is also a sphere of divine action, it would be folly to ignore consideration of how divine presence has been mediated both in the present and the past through more 'secular' forms, and the possibility of their adaptation and use in liturgical contexts in the here and now.

That is why in the next and final volume in this series, *God and Mystery in Words: Experience through Metaphor and Drama*, I intend to set liturgy in the wider context of ordinary staged drama. There is a wealth of reflection on which the Church might draw, not least from the twentieth century itself. Nor will it do to suppose such thoughts applicable only to the more obviously staged elements in the celebration of the eucharist. Equally pertinent is how the Bible is read and preached. As with liturgical study, here too a change of focus is observable among some biblical scholars in recent years.

They too are now willing to use the language of performance as an interpretative category.[7] The historical origins of the text are not necessarily how it is received today, or even how it ought to be received in application to contemporary Christian living. Were such observations to be used as an excuse for avoiding disturbing historical questions, as is indeed all too often the case, that would seem to me deeply regrettable. Equally, care will be needed to avoid all the emphasis moving towards reception, as though all that matters is the congregation's response. Decisions of director and actors are also integral to an audience's reaction in the theatre, and so any adequate pursuit of the analogy will need to give no less attention to formative factors. Too much deference to the text as written, for example, often continues to work against easy intelligibility for readings in church. Not only are introductions still resisted but even the supplying of details that are not immediately deducible from the chosen extract on its own.[8] Again, the reluctance of modern preachers to see themselves as necessarily called to something rather more than simple presentation means that the long tradition of Christian rhetoric is now almost wholly ignored (wrongly in my view).[9] In short, both reading and preaching involve an element of acting, and that requires serious consideration.

So too does the type of language used. Contemporary liturgists have demonstrated a commendable desire to extend the range of material available. The liturgical year is now greatly enhanced by a great wealth of material recommended for use. There has also been a great explosion in hymn-writing. What is lacking, however, is any sustained reflection on what might be achieved thereby. Metaphor is really the verbal equivalent in words of symbol in action. Fundamental to religious belief is the conviction that, however much the divine has put of itself into the creation, it remains of a fundamentally different order. So, in trying to relate to God, metaphor and symbol are inescapable. That should mean that the poet is seen as the theologian's and liturgist's natural ally. But poets are in fact seldom treated

[7] e.g. F. Young, *The Art of Performance: Towards a Theology of Holy Scripture* (London: Darton, Longman and Todd, 1990); S. C. Barton, 'New Testament Interpretation as Performance', *Scottish Journal of Theology* 52 (1999), 179–208.

[8] e.g. the nature of the relationship between the various characters mentioned in some particular story, or the difference between 'Judah' and 'Israel'.

[9] Here I have the support of Augustine, *De doctrina Christiana*, 2.40.60–2.42.63.

as such. So not only does their religious role go largely unacknowledged but also there is little attempt to draw on their insights, to see how biblical metaphors might be renovated and renewed. Even with hymn-writers it is rare to find old metaphors used in fresh or startling ways, far less the creation of new and challenging ones.

I cannot pretend to have all the answers. All I can do in the volume that follows is illustrate how helpful it might be to seek that broader context for the Church's words. God can be experienced through a secular poet's metaphors and through the drama of the modern stage, no less than in church. Theologians often write as though the integrity of biblical revelation and the Church's witness is inevitably compromised through acknowledgement of such links. The truth seems to me quite otherwise. The more separate and isolated the Bible and liturgy are kept, the more likely it is that the decline of religion will be accelerated, and its contribution marginalized to only a small element in human life. Fortunately, God has not been as foolish as his declared representatives here on earth. In his generosity he makes himself available to human beings in every possible context, simply in virtue of the fact that he is creator of it all.

That is why I end by appealing for more dialogue with ordinary human experience, not less. The Church has the greatest possible gift to offer the world in the God who became human for our sake and adopted a bodily identity that continues into his present existence. So it rightly has things to say about and through the body, things perhaps as elementary as teaching the value of correct posture in walking.[10] But it cannot successfully offer the full dimensions of such insights on the body to the world without heeding where the world now is. The divine speaks in that world but not necessarily in the language and bodily expression that long centuries of custom have made familiar to the Church. So the Church must always be an *ecclesia semper reformanda*, eager to hear how that eternal message might be best expressed in the more transient forms of our own culture. That is why painters have constantly sought to re-envisage even the Last Supper. Poussin is one of the few artists deliberately to have sought a reconstruction.[11] More commonly, the artist's details have drawn

---

[10] An observation in P. H. Pfatteicher, *Liturgical Spirituality* (Valley Forge, Pa.: Trinity Press International, 1997), 110–11; cf. 9.

[11] For 100 examples, including both Poussin (166) and Dali (200), see J. Hasting (designer), *Last Supper* (London: Phaidon, 2000).

that event into the viewers' own world, whether he be, for instance, Jacob Jordaens in the seventeenth century or Salvador Dali in the twentieth.[12] Only within such a focus will the grace that the divine has accorded the human body truly then become, as my subtitle indicates it should be, 'a sacrament in ordinary': God experienced in the everyday but always greater than any particular experience or conception of him.

---

[12] For an illustration of Jordaens' *Last Supper* and commentary, see Plate 2.

INDEX